BMW Owners Workshop Manual

Peter G Strasman

Models covered
BMW 320, 320i, 320i SE; 1990 cc 6-cyl
BMW 323i; 2316 cc
BMW 325i, 325i SE, 325i Sport; 2494 cc

Covers major mechanical features of Convertible models
Does not cover 325i X or revised range introduced September 1987

(815 - 4P2)

ABCDE
FGHIJ
KLMN

Haynes Publishing Group
Sparkford Nr Yeovil
Somerset BA22 7JJ England

Haynes Publications, Inc
861 Lawrence Drive
Newbury Park
California 91320 USA

Acknowledgements

Thanks are due to the Champion Sparking Plug Company Limited who supplied the illustrations showing the spark plug conditions. Duckhams Oils provided lubrication data. Thanks are also due to Sykes-Pickavant who provided many of the workshop tools, and all those at Sparkford who assisted in the production of this manual.

A book in the **Haynes Owners Workshop Manual Series**

Printed by J. H. Haynes & Co. Ltd, Sparkford, Nr Yeovil, Somerset BA22 7JJ, England

ISBN 1 85010 447 6

British Library Cataloguing in Publication Data

Strasman, Peter G., *1923–*

BMW 320, 320i, 323i & 325i owners workshop manual

1. Cars. Maintenance & repair – Amateurs' manuals

I. Title II. Series

629.28'722

ISBN 1-85010-447-6

Contents

BMW 320 (Series 1)

BMW 323i (Series 2)

About this manual

Its aim

The aim of this manual is to help you get the best value from your vehicle. It can do so in several ways. It can help you decide what work must be done (even should you choose to get it done by a garage), provide information on routine maintenance and servicing, and give a logical course of action and diagnosis when random faults occur. However, it is hoped that you will use the manual by tackling the work yourself. On simpler jobs it may even be quicker than booking the car into a garage and going there twice, to leave and collect it. Perhaps most important, a lot of money can be saved by avoiding the costs a garage must charge to cover its labour and overheads.

The manual has drawings and descriptions to show the function of the various components so that their layout can be understood. Then the tasks are described and photographed in a step-by-step sequence so that even a novice can do the work.

Its arrangement

The manual is divided into thirteen Chapters, each covering a logical sub-division of the vehicle. The Chapters are each divided into Sections, numbered with single figures, eg 5; and the Sections into paragraphs (or sub-sections), with decimal numbers following on from the Section they are in, eg 5.1, 5.2, 5.3 etc.

It is freely illustrated, especially in those parts where there is a detailed sequence of operations to be carried out. There are two forms of illustration: figures and photographs. The figures are numbered in sequence with decimal numbers, according to their position in the Chapter – eg Fig. 6.4 is the fourth drawing/illustration in Chapter 6. Photographs carry the same number (either individually or in related groups) as the Section or sub-section to which they relate.

Some figures throughout the manual show components fitted to left-hand drive cars.

There is an alphabetical index at the back of the manual as well as a contents list at the front. Each Chapter is also preceded by its own individual contents list.

References to the 'left' or 'right' of the vehicle are in the sense of a person in the driver's seat facing forwards.

Unless otherwise stated, nuts and bolts are removed by turning anti-clockwise, and tightened by turning clockwise.

Vehicle manufacturers continually make changes to specifications and recommendations, and these, when notified, are incorporated into our manuals at the earliest opportunity.

Whilst every care is taken to ensure that the information in this manual is correct, no liability can be accepted by the authors or publishers for loss, damage or injury caused by any errors in, or omissions from, the information given.

Introduction to the BMW

The BMW models covered by this manual are soundly constructed and mechanical components are engineered to fine limits. A buyer contemplating the purchase of one of these cars will be reassured by the knowledge that they are absolutely conventional in design and should cause no problems in overhaul or repair.

The cars are available in two or four-door Saloon versions, with manual or automatic transmissions. The manual gearboxes have four or five speeds, the five-speed boxes being available as Overdrive or Sport (close ratio) units. Automatic transmissions have three or four speeds.

Throughout the manual early E21 models are referred to as Series 1, while the later E30 models are termed Series 2.

General dimensions, weights and capacities

For information applicable to later models, see Supplement at end of manual

Series 1

Dimensions

Length	4355.0 mm (171.5 in)
Width	1610.0 mm (63.4 in)
Height (unladen)	1380 mm (54.3 in)
Wheelbase	2563 mm (100.9 in)
Ground clearance (laden)	145.0 mm (5.7 in)
Front track	1387.0 mm (54.6 in)
Rear track:	
320 models	1396.0 mm (55.0 in)
323i models	1401.0 mm (55.2 in)

Weights

Kerb weight (all fluids, no occupants):	
320 models:	
Manual	1090 kg (2403 lb)
Automatic	1100 kg (2425 lb)
323i models:	
Manual	1110 kg (2447 lb)
Automatic	1120 kg (2470 lb)
Trailer load (maximum):	
Unbraked	500 kg (1102 lb)
Braked	1200 kg (2646 lb)
Roof rack load (maximum)	75 kg (165 lb)

Capacities

Engine:	
With filter change	4.25 litre (7.48 Imp pts)
Without filter change	4.00 litre (7.04 Imp pts)
Manual gearbox:	
Getrag 240 five-speed	1.0 litre (1.76 Imp pts)
Getrag 242 four-speed	1.0 litre (1.76 Imp pts)
Getrag 245 Overdrive and Sport	1.5 litre (2.64 Imp pts)
ZF S 5-16 five-speed	1.0 litre (1.76 Imp pts)
Automatic transmission:	
Fluid change:	
ZF3	2.0 litre (3.5 Imp pts)
ZF4	3.0 litre (5.3 Imp pts)
Refill from dry	7.5 litre (13.2 Imp pts)
Final drive	0.95 litre (1.7 Imp pts)
Power-assisted steering	1.2 litre (2.1 Imp pts)
Fuel tank:	
Series 1	58.0 litre (12.8 Imp gal)
Series 2	55.0 litre (12.1 Imp gal)
Cooling system:	
Without air conditioner	10.5 litre (18.5 Imp pts)
With air conditioner	11.0 litre (19.4 Imp pts)

Series 2

Dimensions

Length	4325.0 mm (170.3 in)
Width	1645.0 mm (64.8 in)
Height (unladen)	1380.0 mm (54.3 in)
Wheelbase	2570.0 mm (101.2 in)
Ground clearance (laden)	123.0 mm (4.8 in)
Front track	1407.0 mm (55.4 in)
Rear track	1415.0 mm (55.7 in)

Weights

	Two-door	Four-door
Kerb weight (all fluids, no occupants):		
320i models:		
Manual	1060 kg (2337 lb)	1085 kg (2392 lb)
Automatic	1080 kg (2381 lb)	1105 kg (2436 lb)
323i models:		
Manual	1090 kg (2403 lb)	1115 kg (2458 lb)
Automatic	1110 kg (2447 lb)	1135 kg (2502 lb)
Trailer load (maximum):		
Unbraked	500 kg (1102 lb)	
Braked	1200 kg (2646 lb)	
Roof rack load (maximum)	75 kg (165 lb)	

Capacities

See the capacities for Series 1 models

Jacking and Towing

Jacking

The jack supplied with the car tool kit should only be used for roadside wheel changing (photo). If repair or overhaul operations are to be carried out then use a trolley, hydraulic bottle or screw type jack located in one of the following positions.

Under the sill jacking points
Under the sill seam, directly adjacent to the jacking points
Under the front crossmember (use a wooden block)
Under the final drive/differential (use a wooden block)

When removing a roadwheel, chock the opposite wheel and release the roadwheel nuts or bolts. Raise the car and remove the nuts or bolts and the wheel. Wait until the car is again on the ground before fully tightening the nuts or bolts.

Detailed instructions are not given in this manual before each operation as to the best method of obtaining access to the underside of the car, but it is preferable to have the car over an inspection pit, raised on a hoist or on ramps. Failing this, use one of the jacks specified earlier in this Section and **always** supplement it with axle stands.

Towing

The front or rear towing eyes may be used when towing, or being towed provided a resilient (nylon) type of tow rope is used (photos).

When towing cars with automatic transmission, restrict the towing distance to between 25 and 30 miles (40 and 50 km) unless the propeller shaft is removed or an extra 1.0 litre (1.8 pints) of transmission fluid is added. Restrict the towing speed to 30 mph (50 kph). Reduce the fluid level to normal on completion of the tow.

Rear towing eye

Tool kit jack

Front towing eye

Buying spare parts and vehicle identification numbers

Buying spare parts

Spare parts are available from many sources, for example: BMW garages, other garages and accessory shops, and motor factors. Our advice regarding spare parts is as follows:

Officially appointed BMW garages – This is the best source of parts which are peculiar to your car and are otherwise not generally available (eg: complete cylinder heads, internal gearbox components, badges, interior trim etc). It is also the only place at which you should buy parts if your car is still under warranty; non-BMW components may invalidate the warranty. To be sure of obtaining the correct parts it will always be necessary to give the storeman your car's engine and chassis number, and if possible, to take the old part along for positive identification. Remember that many parts are available on a factory exchange scheme – any parts returned should always be clean! It obviously makes good sense to go to the specialists on your car for this type of part for they are best equipped to supply you.

Other garages and accessory shops – These are often very good places to buy material and components needed for the maintenance of your car (eg; oil filters, spark plugs, bulbs, fan belts, oils and grease, touch-up paint, filler paste etc). They also sell general accessories, usually have convenient opening hours, charge lower prices and can often be found not far from home.

Motor factors – Good factors will stock all of the more important components which wear out relatively quickly (eg; clutch components, pistons, valves, exhaust systems, brake cylinder/pipes/hoses/seals/shoes and pads etc). Motor factors will often provide new or reconditioned components on a part exchange basis – this can save a considerable amount of money.

Vehicle identification numbers

Modifications are a continuing and unpublicised process in vehicle manufacture quite apart from major model changes. Spare parts manuals and lists are compiled upon a numerical basis, the individual vehicle number being essential to correct identification of the component required.

The vehicle identification plate is located within the engine compartment (photo). On earlier models it is to be found on the right-hand wing valance and on later models on the body front cross rail.

The number is also stamped into the wing valance top surface (photo).

The engine number is stamped into a machined face just below the ignition distributor mounting (photo).

Vehicle identification number

Vehicle identification plate

Engine number

General repair procedures

Whenever servicing, repair or overhaul work is carried out on the car or its components, it is necessary to observe the following procedures and instructions. This will assist in carrying out the operation efficiently and to a professional standard of workmanship.

Joint mating faces and gaskets

Where a gasket is used between the mating faces of two components, ensure that it is renewed on reassembly, and fit it dry unless otherwise stated in the repair procedure. Make sure that the mating faces are clean and dry with all traces of old gasket removed. When cleaning a joint face, use a tool which is not likely to score or damage the face, and remove any burrs or nicks with an oilstone or fine file.

Make sure that tapped holes are cleaned, and keep them free of jointing compound if this is being used unless specifically instructed otherwise.

Ensure that all orifices, channels or pipes are clear and blow through them, preferably using compressed air.

Oil seals

Whenever an oil seal is removed from its working location, either individually or as part of an assembly, it should be renewed.

The very fine sealing lip of the seal is easily damaged and will not seal if the surface it contacts is not completely clean and free from scratches, nicks or grooves. If the original sealing surface of the component cannot be restored, the component should be renewed.

Protect the lips of the seal from any surface which may damage them in the course of fitting. Use tape or a conical sleeve where possible. Lubricate the seal lips with oil before fitting and, on dual lipped seals, fill the space between the lips with grease.

Unless otherwise stated, oil seals must be fitted with their sealing lips toward the lubricant to be sealed.

Use a tubular drift or block of wood of the appropriate size to install the seal and, if the seal housing is shouldered, drive the seal down to the shoulder. If the seal housing is unshouldered, the seal should be fitted with its face flush with the housing top face.

Screw threads and fastenings

Always ensure that a blind tapped hole is completely free from oil, grease, water or other fluid before installing the bolt or stud. Failure to do this could cause the housing to crack due to the hydraulic action of the bolt or stud as it is screwed in.

When tightening a castellated nut to accept a split pin, tighten the nut to the specified torque, where applicable, and then tighten further to the next split pin hole. Never slacken the nut to align a split pin hole unless stated in the repair procedure.

When checking or retightening a nut or bolt to a specified torque setting, slacken the nut or bolt by a quarter of a turn, and then retighten to the specified setting.

Locknuts, locktabs and washers

Any fastening which will rotate against a component or housing in the course of tightening should always have a washer between it and the relevant component or housing.

Spring or split washers should always be renewed when they are used to lock a critical component such as a big-end bearing retaining nut or bolt.

Locktabs which are folded over to retain a nut or bolt should always be renewed.

Self-locking nuts can be reused in non-critical areas, providing resistance can be felt when the locking portion passes over the bolt or stud thread.

Split pins must always be replaced with new ones of the correct size for the hole.

Special tools

Some repair procedures in this manual entail the use of special tools such as a press, two or three-legged pullers, spring compressors etc. Wherever possible, suitable readily available alternatives to the manufacturer's special tools are described, and are shown in use. In some instances, where no alternative is possible, it has been necessary to resort to the use of a manufacturer's tool and this has been done for reasons of safety as well as the efficient completion of the repair operation. Unless you are highly skilled and have a thorough understanding of the procedure described, never attempt to bypass the use of any special tool when the procedure described specifies its use. Not only is there a very great risk of personal injury, but expensive damage could be caused to the components involved.

Tools and working facilities

Introduction

A selection of good tools is a fundamental requirement for anyone contemplating the maintenance and repair of a motor vehicle. For the owner who does not possess any, their purchase will prove a considerable expense, offsetting some of the savings made by doing-it-yourself. However, provided that the tools purchased are of good quality, they will last for many years and prove an extremely worthwhile investment.

To help the average owner to decide which tools are needed to carry out the various tasks detailed in this manual, we have compiled three lists of tools under the following headings: *Maintenance and minor repair, Repair and overhaul,* and *Special.* The newcomer to practical mechanics should start off with the *Maintenance and minor repair* tool kit and confine himself to the simpler jobs around the vehicle. Then, as his confidence and experience grow, he can undertake more difficult tasks, buying extra tools as, and when, they are needed. In this way, a *Maintenance and minor repair* tool kit can be built-up into a *Repair and overhaul* tool kit over a considerable period of time without any major cash outlays. The experienced do-it-yourselfer will have a tool kit good enough for most repair and overhaul procedures and will add tools from the *Special* category when he feels the expense is justified by the amount of use to which these tools will be put.

It is obviously not possible to cover the subject of tools fully here. For those who wish to learn more about tools and their use there is a book entitled *How to Choose and Use Car Tools* available from the publishers of this manual.

Maintenance and minor repair tool kit

The tools given in this list should be considered as a minimum requirement if routine maintenance, servicing and minor repair operations are to be undertaken. We recommend the purchase of combination spanners (ring one end, open-ended the other); although more expensive than open-ended ones, they do give the advantages of both types of spanner.

Combination spanners - 10, 11, 12, 13, 14 & 17 mm
Adjustable spanner - 9 inch
Gearbox/rear axle drain plug key
Spark plug spanner (with rubber insert)
Spark plug gap adjustment tool
Set of feeler gauges
Brake bleed nipple spanner
Screwdriver - 4 in long x ¼ in dia (flat blade)
Screwdriver - 4 in long x ¼ in dia (cross blade)
Combination pliers - 6 inch
Hacksaw (junior)
Tyre pump
Tyre pressure gauge
Oil can
Fine emery cloth (1 sheet)
Wire brush (small)
Funnel (medium size)

Repair and overhaul tool kit

These tools are virtually essential for anyone undertaking any major repairs to a motor vehicle, and are additional to those given in the *Maintenance and minor repair* list. Included in this list is a comprehensive set of sockets. Although these are expensive they will be found invaluable as they are so versatile - particularly if various drives are included in the set. We recommend the ½ in square-drive type, as this can be used with most proprietary torque wrenches. If you cannot afford a socket set, even bought piecemeal, then inexpensive tubular box spanners are a useful alternative.

The tools in this list will occasionally need to be supplemented by tools from the *Special* list.

Sockets (or box spanners) to cover range in previous list
Reversible ratchet drive (for use with sockets)
Extension piece, 10 inch (for use with sockets)
Universal joint (for use with sockets)
Torque wrench (for use with sockets)
'Mole' wrench - 8 inch
Ball pein hammer
Soft-faced hammer, plastic or rubber
Screwdriver - 6 in long x $\frac{5}{16}$ in dia (flat blade)
Screwdriver - 2 in long x $\frac{5}{16}$ in square (flat blade)
Screwdriver - 1½ in long x ¼ in dia (cross blade)
Screwdriver - 3 in long x ⅛ in dia (electricians)
Pliers - electricians side cutters
Pliers - needle nosed
Pliers - circlip (internal and external)
Cold chisel - ½ inch
Scriber
Scraper
Centre punch
Pin punch
Hacksaw
Valve grinding tool
Steel rule/straight-edge
Allen keys
Set of 'Torx' keys (later models)
Selection of files
Wire brush (large)
Axle-stands

Special tools

The tools in this list are those which are not used regularly, are expensive to buy, or which need to be used in accordance with their manufacturers' instructions. Unless relatively difficult mechanical jobs are undertaken frequently, it will not be economic to buy many of these tools. Where this is the case, you could consider clubbing together with friends (or joining a motorists' club) to make a joint purchase, or borrowing the tools against a deposit from a local garage or tool hire specialist.

The following list contains only those tools and instruments freely available to the public, and not those special tools produced by the vehicle manufacturer specifically for its dealer network. You will find occasional references to these manufacturers' special tools in the text of this manual. Generally, an alternative method of doing the job without the vehicle manufacturers' special tool is given. However, sometimes, there is no alternative to using them. Where this is the case and the relevant tool cannot be bought or borrowed, you will have to entrust the work to a franchised garage.

Valve spring compressor
Piston ring compressor
Balljoint separator
Universal hub/bearing puller
Impact screwdriver
Micrometer and/or vernier gauge
Dial gauge
Stroboscopic timing light
Dwell angle meter/tachometer (mechanical breaker type distributor)
Universal electrical multi-meter
Cylinder compression gauge
Lifting tackle
Trolley jack
Light with extension lead

Buying tools

For practically all tools, a tool factor is the best source since he will have a very comprehensive range compared with the average garage or accessory shop. Having said that, accessory shops often offer excellent quality tools at discount prices, so it pays to shop around.

Remember, you don't have to buy the most expensive items on the shelf, but it is always advisable to steer clear of the very cheap tools. There are plenty of good tools around at reasonable prices, so ask the proprietor or manager of the shop for advice before making a purchase.

Care and maintenance of tools

Having purchased a reasonable tool kit, it is necessary to keep the tools in a clean serviceable condition. After use, always wipe off any dirt, grease and metal particles using a clean, dry cloth, before putting the tools away. Never leave them lying around after they have been used. A simple tool rack on the garage or workshop wall, for items such as screwdrivers and pliers is a good idea. Store all normal wrenches and sockets in a metal box. Any measuring instruments, gauges, meters, etc, must be carefully stored where they cannot be damaged or become rusty.

Take a little care when tools are used. Hammer heads inevitably become marked and screwdrivers lose the keen edge on their blades from time to time. A little timely attention with emery cloth, a file or grindstone will soon restore items like this to a good serviceable finish.

Working facilities

Not to be forgotten when discussing tools, is the workshop itself. If anything more than routine maintenance is to be carried out, some form of suitable working area becomes essential.

It is appreciated that many an owner mechanic is forced by circumstances to remove an engine or similar item, without the benefit of a garage or workshop. Having done this, any repairs should always be done under the cover of a roof.

Wherever possible, any dismantling should be done on a clean, flat workbench or table at a suitable working height.

Any workbench needs a vice: one with a jaw opening of 4 in (100 mm) is suitable for most jobs. As mentioned previously, some clean dry storage space is also required for tools, as well as for lubricants, cleaning fluids, touch-up paints and so on, which become necessary.

Another item which may be required, and which has a much more general usage, is an electric drill with a chuck capacity of at least 5/16 in (8 mm). This, together with a good range of twist drills, is virtually essential for fitting accessories such as mirrors and reversing lights.

Last, but not least, always keep a supply of old newspapers and clean, lint-free rags available, and try to keep any working area as clean as possible.

Spanner jaw gap comparison table

Jaw gap (in)	Spanner size
0.250	1/4 in AF
0.276	7 mm
0.313	5/16 in AF
0.315	8 mm
0.344	11/32 in AF; 1/8 in Whitworth
0.354	9 mm
0.375	3/8 in AF
0.394	10 mm
0.433	11 mm
0.438	7/16 in AF
0.445	3/16 in Whitworth; 1/4 in BSF
0.472	12 mm
0.500	1/2 in AF
0.512	13 mm
0.525	1/4 in Whitworth; 5/16 in BSF
0.551	14 mm
0.563	9/16 in AF
0.591	15 mm
0.600	5/16 in Whitworth; 3/8 in BSF
0.625	5/8 in AF
0.630	16 mm
0.669	17 mm
0.686	11/16 in AF
0.709	18 mm
0.710	3/8 in Whitworth; 7/16 in BSF
0.748	19 mm
0.750	3/4 in AF
0.813	13/16 in AF
0.820	7/16 in Whitworth; 1/2 in BSF
0.866	22 mm
0.875	7/8 in AF
0.920	1/2 in Whitworth; 9/16 in BSF
0.938	15/16 in AF
0.945	24 mm
1.000	1 in AF
1.010	9/16 in Whitworth; 5/8 in BSF
1.024	26 mm
1.063	1 1/16 in AF; 27 mm
1.100	5/8 in Whitworth; 11/16 in BSF
1.125	1 1/8 in AF
1.181	30 mm
1.200	11/16 in Whitworth; 3/4 in BSF
1.250	1 1/4 in AF
1.260	32 mm
1.300	3/4 in Whitworth; 7/8 in BSF
1.313	1 5/16 in AF
1.390	13/16 in Whitworth; 15/16 in BSF
1.417	36 mm
1.438	1 7/16 in AF
1.480	7/8 in Whitworth; 1 in BSF
1.500	1 1/2 in AF
1.575	40 mm; 15/16 in Whitworth
1.614	41 mm
1.625	1 5/8 in AF
1.670	1 in Whitworth; 1 1/8 in BSF
1.688	1 11/16 in AF
1.811	46 mm
1.813	1 13/16 in AF
1.860	1 1/8 in Whitworth; 1 1/4 in BSF
1.875	1 7/8 in AF
1.969	50 mm
2.000	2 in AF
2.050	1 1/4 in Whitworth; 1 3/8 in BSF
2.165	55 mm
2.362	60 mm

Safety first!

Professional motor mechanics are trained in safe working procedures. However enthusiastic you may be about getting on with the job in hand, do take the time to ensure that your safety is not put at risk. A moment's lack of attention can result in an accident, as can failure to observe certain elementary precautions.

There will always be new ways of having accidents, and the following points do not pretend to be a comprehensive list of all dangers; they are intended rather to make you aware of the risks and to encourage a safety-conscious approach to all work you carry out on your vehicle.

Essential DOs and DON'Ts

DON'T rely on a single jack when working underneath the vehicle. Always use reliable additional means of support, such as axle stands, securely placed under a part of the vehicle that you know will not give way.
DON'T attempt to loosen or tighten high-torque nuts (e.g. wheel hub nuts) while the vehicle is on a jack; it may be pulled off.
DON'T start the engine without first ascertaining that the transmission is in neutral (or 'Park' where applicable) and the parking brake applied.
DON'T suddenly remove the filler cap from a hot cooling system – cover it with a cloth and release the pressure gradually first, or you may get scalded by escaping coolant.
DON'T attempt to drain oil until you are sure it has cooled sufficiently to avoid scalding you.
DON'T grasp any part of the engine, exhaust or catalytic converter without first ascertaining that it is sufficiently cool to avoid burning you.
DON'T allow brake fluid or antifreeze to contact vehicle paintwork.
DON'T syphon toxic liquids such as fuel, brake fluid or antifreeze by mouth, or allow them to remain on your skin.
DON'T inhale dust – it may be injurious to health (see *Asbestos* below).
DON'T allow any spilt oil or grease to remain on the floor – wipe it up straight away, before someone slips on it.
DON'T use ill-fitting spanners or other tools which may slip and cause injury.
DON'T attempt to lift a heavy component which may be beyond your capability – get assistance.
DON'T rush to finish a job, or take unverified short cuts.
DON'T allow children or animals in or around an unattended vehicle.
DO wear eye protection when using power tools such as drill, sander, bench grinder etc, and when working under the vehicle.
DO use a barrier cream on your hands prior to undertaking dirty jobs – it will protect your skin from infection as well as making the dirt easier to remove afterwards; but make sure your hands aren't left slippery. Note that long-term contact with used engine oil can be a health hazard.
DO keep loose clothing (cuffs, tie etc) and long hair well out of the way of moving mechanical parts.
DO remove rings, wristwatch etc, before working on the vehicle – especially the electrical system.
DO ensure that any lifting tackle used has a safe working load rating adequate for the job.
DO keep your work area tidy – it is only too easy to fall over articles left lying around.
DO get someone to check periodically that all is well, when working alone on the vehicle.
DO carry out work in a logical sequence and check that everything is correctly assembled and tightened afterwards.
DO remember that your vehicle's safety affects that of yourself and others. If in doubt on any point, get specialist advice.
IF, in spite of following these precautions, you are unfortunate enough to injure yourself, seek medical attention as soon as possible.

Asbestos

Certain friction, insulating, sealing, and other products – such as brake linings, brake bands, clutch linings, torque converters, gaskets, etc – contain asbestos. *Extreme care must be taken to avoid inhalation of dust from such products since it is hazardous to health.* If in doubt, assume that they *do* contain asbestos.

Fire

Remember at all times that petrol (gasoline) is highly flammable. Never smoke, or have any kind of naked flame around, when working on the vehicle. But the risk does not end there – a spark caused by an electrical short-circuit, by two metal surfaces contacting each other, by careless use of tools, or even by static electricity built up in your body under certain conditions, can ignite petrol vapour, which in a confined space is highly explosive.

Always disconnect the battery earth (ground) terminal before working on any part of the fuel or electrical system, and never risk spilling fuel on to a hot engine or exhaust.

It is recommended that a fire extinguisher of a type suitable for fuel and electrical fires is kept handy in the garage or workplace at all times. Never try to extinguish a fuel or electrical fire with water.

Fumes

Certain fumes are highly toxic and can quickly cause unconsciousness and even death if inhaled to any extent. Petrol (gasoline) vapour comes into this category, as do the vapours from certain solvents such as trichloroethylene. Any draining or pouring of such volatile fluids should be done in a well ventilated area.

When using cleaning fluids and solvents, read the instructions carefully. Never use materials from unmarked containers – they may give off poisonous vapours.

Never run the engine of a motor vehicle in an enclosed space such as a garage. Exhaust fumes contain carbon monoxide which is extremely poisonous; if you need to run the engine, always do so in the open air or at least have the rear of the vehicle outside the workplace.

If you are fortunate enough to have the use of an inspection pit, never drain or pour petrol, and never run the engine, while the vehicle is standing over it; the fumes, being heavier than air, will concentrate in the pit with possibly lethal results.

The battery

Never cause a spark, or allow a naked light, near the vehicle's battery. It will normally be giving off a certain amount of hydrogen gas, which is highly explosive.

Always disconnect the battery earth (ground) terminal before working on the fuel or electrical systems.

If possible, loosen the filler plugs or cover when charging the battery from an external source. Do not charge at an excessive rate or the battery may burst.

Take care when topping up and when carrying the battery. The acid electrolyte, even when diluted, is very corrosive and should not be allowed to contact the eyes or skin.

If you ever need to prepare electrolyte yourself, always add the acid slowly to the water, and never the other way round. Protect against splashes by wearing rubber gloves and goggles.

When jump starting a car using a booster battery, for negative earth (ground) vehicles, connect the jump leads in the following sequence: First connect one jump lead between the positive (+) terminals of the two batteries. Then connect the other jump lead first to the negative (–) terminal of the booster battery, and then to a good earthing (ground) point on the vehicle to be started, at least 18 in (45 cm) from the battery if possible. Ensure that hands and jump leads are clear of any moving parts, and that the two vehicles do not touch. Disconnect the leads in the reverse order.

Mains electricity

When using an electric power tool, inspection light etc, which works from the mains, always ensure that the appliance is correctly connected to its plug and that, where necessary, it is properly earthed (grounded). Do not use such appliances in damp conditions and, again, beware of creating a spark or applying excessive heat in the vicinity of fuel or fuel vapour.

Ignition HT voltage

A severe electric shock can result from touching certain parts of the ignition system, such as the HT leads, when the engine is running or being cranked, particularly if components are damp or the insulation is defective. Where an electronic ignition system is fitted, the HT voltage is much higher and could prove fatal.

Routine maintenance

Maintenance is essential for ensuring safety, and desirable for the purpose of getting the best in terms of performance and economy from the vehicle. Over the years the need for periodic lubrication – oiling, greasing and so on – has been drastically reduced, if not totally eliminated. This has unfortunately tended to lead some owners to think that because no such action is required the items either no longer exist or will last for ever. This is a serious delusion. It follows therefore that the largest initial element of maintenance is visual examination. This may lead to repairs or renewals.

The following service intervals are given for both mileage and time. For low mileage cars it is preferable to use the time intervals.

On models with a service indicator (Chapter 10, Section 33), the indicated maintenance intervals will vary according to driving style and conditions.

Every 250 miles (400 km) or weekly – whichever comes first

Check the engine oil level. Top up if necessary (photo)
Check the coolant level. Top up if necessary (photo)
Check the clutch hydraulic fluid level. Top up if necessary (photo)
Check the tyre pressures
Check the brake hydraulic fluid level. Top up if necessary (photo)
Check the battery electrolyte level (if necessary). Top up as required (photo)
Check the washer fluid level. Top up if necessary (photo)
Check the operation of all lamps, washers and other systems

After first 1200 miles (2000 km) – new vehicles

Change the engine oil and filter – Chapter 1
Check all hoses for leaks
Check the torque of the manifold nuts – Chapter 3
Check the ignition timing – Chapter 4
Change the gearbox oil (manual) – Chapter 6
Check the fluid level in the automatic transmission – Chapter 6
Change the final drive oil – Chapter 8
Check the brake hydraulic system for leaks
Check the power steering fluid level (if applicable) – Chapter 11
Check front wheel alignment – Chapter 11
Check the valve clearances. Adjust if necessary – Chapter 1

Every 10 000 miles (15 000 km) or annually – whichever comes first

This service interval is recommended by the vehicle manufacturer, but for the home mechanic, where no labour charges are incurred, experience has proved that a service interval of half that recommended will greatly contribute to improved performance and longer life.

Where this proposal is accepted, clean and regap the spark plugs and check the condition of the contact points and the dwell angle (on cars fitted with mechanical breaker type ignition) at the half-yearly service. Renew after a full year (or the specified mileage) has elapsed.

Change the engine oil and filter (photo) – Chapter 1
Check the valve clearances. Adjust if necessary – Chapter 1
Check the drivebelt condition and tension. Renew/retension as necessary – Chapter 2
Renew the air cleaner element – Chapter 3
Check the carburettor/fuel injection settings. Adjust if necessary – Chapter 3
Check the exhaust system for security and corrosion – Chapter 3
Renew the spark plugs – Chapter 4
Renew the mechanical contact breaker points (if fitted) – Chapter 4
Check the transmission oil level (manual and automatic) – Chapter 6
Check the driveshaft and steering gear gaiters for splits, and the joints for wear. Renew where necessary – Chapter 7
Inspect the tyres for wear and damage
Change the roadwheels from front to rear to even out tyre wear. **Do not** change from side to side
Check the final drive oil level – Chapter 8
Check the brake pads/linings for wear. Renew as necessary – Chapter 9
Adjust the rear brakes (manual adjusters) – Chapter 9
Check the headlamp beam alignment
Inspect the wiper blades. Renew if necessary – Chapter 10
Check the power steering fluid level (if applicable) – Chapter 11
Check the steering and suspension for worn bushes and joints. Renew as necessary – Chapter 11
Check the front wheel alignment – Chapter 11
Lubricate all controls, linkages, locks and hinges

Annually, regardless of mileage

Renew brake fluid – Chapter 9

Every 20 000 miles (30 000 km) or two years – whichever comes first

In addition to, or instead of, the 10 000 mile/annual service

Renew the coolant – Chapter 2
Clean the fuel filters – Chapter 3
Renew the clutch fluid – Chapter 5
Change the oil in the manual gearbox (photos) – Chapter 6
Change the fluid and filter in the automatic transmission – Chapter 6
Check the hub bearings for wear. Renew/adjust as necessary – Chapter 7
Change the oil in the final drive (photos) – Chapter 8
Check the brake hoses and pipelines for leaks and security. Renew as necessary – Chapter 9
Inspect handbrake shoe linings (models with rear disc brakes) – Chapter 9
Check the condition of the seat belts. Renew as necessary – Chapter 12

Every 40 000 miles (60 000 km) or every four years – whichever comes first

In addition to, or instead of, the 20 000 mile/2 year service

Renew the timing belt – Chapter 1
Renew the fuel filters – Chapter 3
Renew the brake servo filter – Chapter 9
Renew the power steering filter (if fitted) – Chapter 11

Additional items which should be attended to when necessary

Cleaning

Examination of components requires that they be cleaned. The same applies to the body of the car, inside and out, in order that deterioration due to rust or unknown damage may be detected. Certain parts of the body frame, if rusted badly, can result in the vehicle being declared unsafe and it will not pass a test for roadworthiness.

Adding engine oil

Adding coolant to the expansion tank

Clutch fluid reservoir (Series 1)

Brake fluid reservoir

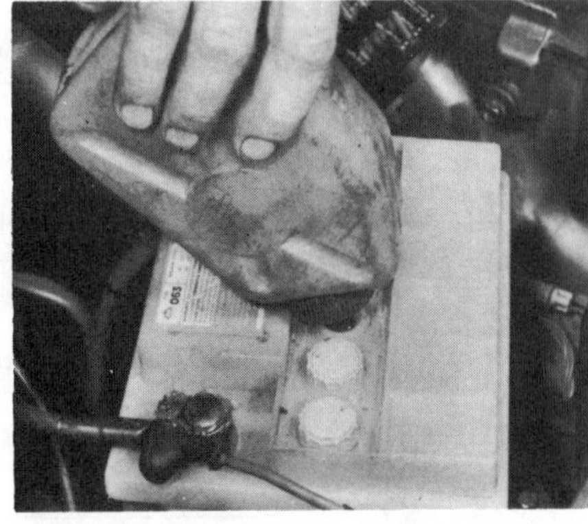
Topping-up the battery electrolyte

Topping-up the washer fluid (typical)

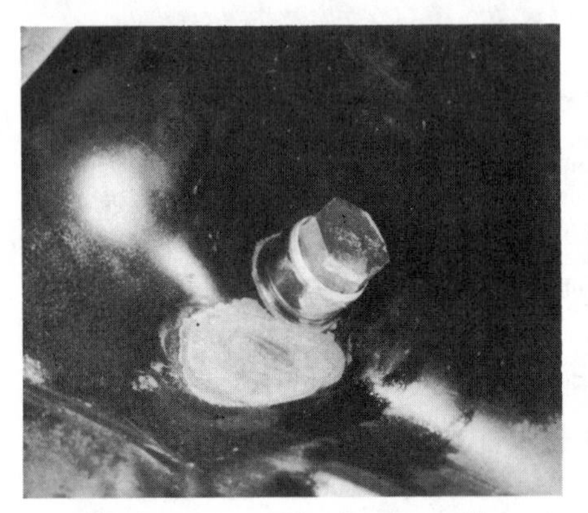
Engine sump drain plug (typical)

Manual gearbox drain plug (typical)

Filling the manual gearbox (typical)

Rear axle drain plug (typical)

Rear axle filler plug (typical)

Engine compartment – Series 1, 320

1 Wiper arm
2 Clutch fluid reservoir
3 Front suspension strut turret
4 Coolant expansion tank
5 Brake servo vacuum hose
6 Washer fluid reservoir
7 Carburettor
8 Engine oil dipstick
9 Fusebox
10 Battery
11 Thermostat housing and diagnostic plug
12 Radiator
13 Oil filler cap
14 Brake vacuum servo (booster)
15 Brake master cylinder reservoir

Engine compartment – Series 2, 320i

1 *Wiper arm*
2 *Front suspension strut turret*
3 *Clutch fluid reservoir*
4 *Brake vacuum servo (booster)*
5 *Brake master cylinder reservoir*
6 *Fusebox*
7 *Washer fluid reservoir*
8 *Oil filler cap*
9 *Radiator*
10 *Throttle vacuum control*
11 *Airflow meter*
12 *Battery*

Front end, viewed from underneath – Series 2, 320i

1 *Brake hydraulic pipes*
2 *Gearbox mounting*
3 *Gearbox drain plug*
4 *Suspension track control arm*
5 *Steering shaft flexible coupling*
6 *Exhaust pipe*
7 *Anti-roll bar*
8 *Brake caliper*
9 *Tie-rod*
10 *Steering rack*
11 *Oil filter*
12 *Engine sump pan*
13 *Crossmember*
14 *Fan*
15 *Radiator*
16 *Radiator drain plug*

Rear end, viewed from underneath – typical

1 *Exhaust silencer*
2 *Fuel filler pipe*
3 *Shock absorber*
4 *Driveshaft*
5 *Final drive/differential*
6 *Suspension track control arm*
7 *Fuel pump/filter*
8 *Fuel tanks*

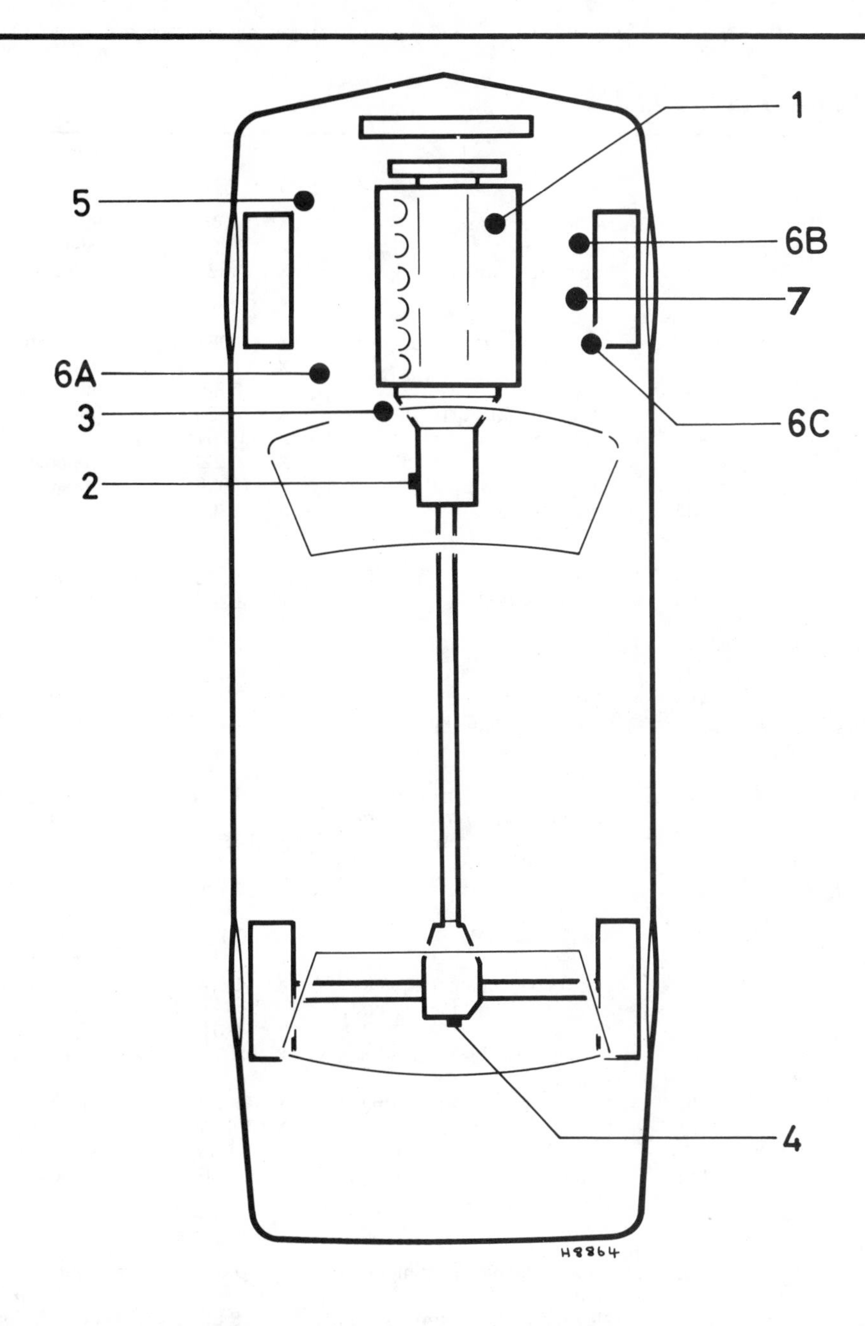

Recommended lubricants and fluids

Component or system	Lubricant type/specification	Duckhams recommendation
Engine (1)	Multigrade engine oil to API-SE or -SF	Duckhams QXR or Hypergrade
Manual gearbox (2)	Gear oil, viscosity SAE 80, to API GL-4	Duckhams Hypoid 80
Automatic transmission (3)	Dexron II type ATF	Duckhams D-Matic
Final drive (4)	BMW approved hypoid gear oil, viscosity SAE 90	Duckhams D12001
Power steering (5)	Dexron II type ATF	Duckhams D-Matic
Brake and clutch hydraulic systems (6)	Hydraulic fluid to SAE J 1703 or DOT 4	Duckhams Universal Brake and Clutch Fluid
Cooling system (7)	BMW approved antifreeze	Duckhams Universal Antifreeze and Summer Coolant

Conversion factors

Length (distance)					
Inches (in)	X 25.4	= Millimetres (mm)	X 0.0394	= Inches (in)
Feet (ft)	X 0.305	= Metres (m)	X 3.281	= Feet (ft)
Miles	X 1.609	= Kilometres (km)	X 0.621	= Miles
Volume (capacity)				
Cubic inches (cu in; in³)	X 16.387	= Cubic centimetres (cc; cm³)	X 0.061	= Cubic inches (cu in; in³)
Imperial pints (Imp pt)	X 0.568	= Litres (l)	X 1.76	= Imperial pints (Imp pt)
Imperial quarts (Imp qt)	X 1.137	= Litres (l)	X 0.88	= Imperial quarts (Imp qt)
Imperial quarts (Imp qt)	X 1.201	= US quarts (US qt)	X 0.833	= Imperial quarts (Imp qt)
US quarts (US qt)	X 0.946	= Litres (l)	X 1.057	= US quarts (US qt)
Imperial gallons (Imp gal)	X 4.546	= Litres (l)	X 0.22	= Imperial gallons (Imp gal)
Imperial gallons (Imp gal)	X 1.201	= US gallons (US gal)	X 0.833	= Imperial gallons (Imp gal)
US gallons (US gal)	X 3.785	= Litres (l)	X 0.264	= US gallons (US gal)
Mass (weight)				
Ounces (oz)	X 28.35	= Grams (g)	X 0.035	= Ounces (oz)
Pounds (lb)	X 0.454	= Kilograms (kg)	X 2.205	= Pounds (lb)
Force				
Ounces-force (ozf; oz)	X 0.278	= Newtons (N)	X 3.6	= Ounces-force (ozf; oz)
Pounds-force (lbf; lb)	X 4.448	= Newtons (N)	X 0.225	= Pounds-force (lbf; lb)
Newtons (N)	X 0.1	= Kilograms-force (kgf; kg)	X 9.81	= Newtons (N)
Pressure				
Pounds-force per square inch (psi; lbf/in²; lb/in²)	X 0.070	= Kilograms-force per square centimetre (kgf/cm²; kg/cm²)	X 14.223	= Pounds-force per square inch (psi; lbf/in²; lb/in²)
Pounds-force per square inch (psi; lbf/in²; lb/in²)	X 0.068	= Atmospheres (atm)	X 14.696	= Pounds-force per square inch (psi; lbf/in²; lb/in²)
Pounds-force per square inch (psi; lbf/in²; lb/in²)	X 0.069	= Bars	X 14.5	= Pounds-force per square inch (psi; lbf/in²; lb/in²)
Pounds-force per square inch (psi; lbf/in²; lb/in²)	X 6.895	= Kilopascals (kPa)	X 0.145	= Pounds-force per square inch (psi; lbf/in²; lb/in²)
Kilopascals (kPa)	X 0.01	= Kilograms-force per square centimetre (kgf/cm²; kg/cm²)	X 98.1	= Kilopascals (kPa)
Millibar (mbar)	X 100	= Pascals (Pa)	X 0.01	= Millibar (mbar)
Millibar (mbar)	X 0.0145	= Pounds-force per square inch (psi; lbf/in², lb/in²)	X 68.947	= Millibar (mbar)
Millibar (mbar)	X 0.75	= Millimetres of mercury (mmHg)	X 1.333	= Millibar (mbar)
Millibar (mbar)	X 1.40	= Inches of water (inH$_2$O)	X 0.714	= Millibar (mbar)
Millimetres of mercury (mmHg)	X 1.868	= Inches of water (inH$_2$O)	X 0.535	= Millimetres of mercury (mmHg)
Inches of water (inH$_2$O)	X 27.68	= Pounds-force per square inch (psi, lbf/in², lb/in²)	X 0.036	= Inches of water (inH$_2$O)
Torque (moment of force)				
Pounds-force inches (lbf in; lb in)	X 1.152	= Kilograms-force centimetre (kgf cm; kg cm)	X 0.868	= Pounds-force inches (lbf in; lb in)
Pounds-force inches (lbf in; lb in)	X 0.113	= Newton metres (Nm)	X 8.85	= Pounds-force inches (lbf in; lb in)
Pounds-force inches (lbf in; lb in)	X 0.083	= Pounds-force feet (lbf ft; lb ft)	X 12	= Pounds-force inches (lbf in; lb in)
Pounds-force feet (lbf ft; lb ft)	X 0.138	= Kilograms-force metres (kgf m; kg m)	X 7.233	= Pounds-force feet (lbf ft; lb ft)
Pounds-force feet (lbf ft; lb ft)	X 1.356	= Newton metres (Nm)	X 0.738	= Pounds-force feet (lbf ft; lb ft)
Newton metres (Nm)	X 0.102	= Kilograms-force metres (kgf m; kg m)	X 9.804	= Newton metres (Nm)
Power				
Horsepower (hp)	X 745.7	= Watts (W)	X 0.0013	= Horsepower (hp)
Velocity (speed)				
Miles per hour (miles/hr; mph)	X 1.609	= Kilometres per hour (km/hr; kph)	X 0.621	= Miles per hour (miles/hr; mph)
Fuel consumption*				
Miles per gallon, Imperial (mpg)	X 0.354	= Kilometres per litre (km/l)	X 2.825	= Miles per gallon, Imperial (mpg)
Miles per gallon, US (mpg)	X 0.425	= Kilometres per litre (km/l)	X 2.352	= Miles per gallon, US (mpg)

Temperature

Degrees Fahrenheit = (°C x 1.8) + 32

Degrees Celsius (Degrees Centigrade; °C) = (°F - 32) x 0.56

**It is common practice to convert from miles per gallon (mpg) to litres/100 kilometres (l/100km), where mpg (Imperial) x l/100 km = 282 and mpg (US) x l/100 km = 235*

Fault diagnosis

Introduction

The vehicle owner who does his or her own maintenance according to the recommended schedules should not have to use this section of the manual very often. Modern component reliability is such that, provided those items subject to wear or deterioration are inspected or renewed at the specified intervals, sudden failure is comparatively rare. Faults do not usually just happen as a result of sudden failure, but develop over a period of time. Major mechanical failures in particular are usually preceded by characteristic symptoms over hundreds or even thousands of miles. Those components which do occasionally fail without warning are often small and easily carried in the vehicle.

With any fault finding, the first step is to decide where to begin investigations. Sometimes this is obvious, but on other occasions a little detective work will be necessary. The owner who makes half a dozen haphazard adjustments or replacements may be successful in curing a fault (or its symptoms), but he will be none the wiser if the fault recurs and he may well have spent more time and money than was necessary. A calm and logical approach will be found to be more satisfactory in the long run. Always take into account any warning signs or abnormalities that may have been noticed in the period preceding the fault – power loss, high or low gauge readings, unusual noises or smells, etc – and remember that failure of components such as fuses or spark plugs may only be pointers to some underlying fault.

The pages which follow here are intended to help in cases of failure to start or breakdown on the road. There is also a Fault Diagnosis Section at the end of each Chapter which should be consulted if the preliminary checks prove unfruitful. Whatever the fault, certain basic principles apply. These are as follows:

Verify the fault. This is simply a matter of being sure that you know what the symptoms are before starting work. This is particularly important if you are investigating a fault for someone else who may not have described it very accurately.

Don't overlook the obvious. For example, if the vehicle won't start, is there petrol in the tank? (Don't take anyone else's word on this particular point, and don't trust the fuel gauge either!) If an electrical fault is indicated, look for loose or broken wires before digging out the test gear.

Cure the disease, not the symptom. Substituting a flat battery with a fully charged one will get you off the hard shoulder, but if the underlying cause is not attended to, the new battery will go the same way. Similarly, changing oil-fouled spark plugs for a new set will get you moving again, but remember that the reason for the fouling (if it wasn't simply an incorrect grade of plug) will have to be established and corrected.

Don't take anything for granted. Particularly, don't forget that a 'new' component may itself be defective (especially if it's been rattling round in the boot for months), and don't leave components out of a fault diagnosis sequence just because they are new or recently fitted. When you do finally diagnose a difficult fault, you'll probably realise that all the evidence was there from the start.

Electrical faults

Electrical faults can be more puzzling than straightforward mechanical failures, but they are no less susceptible to logical analysis if the basic principles of operation are understood. Vehicle electrical wiring exists in extremely unfavourable conditions – heat, vibration and chemical attack – and the first things to look for are loose or corroded connections and broken or chafed wires, especially where the wires pass through holes in the bodywork or are subject to vibration.

All metal-bodied vehicles in current production have one pole of the battery 'earthed', ie connected to the vehicle bodywork, and in nearly all modern vehicles it is the negative (–) terminal. The various electrical components – motors, bulb holders etc – are also connected to earth, either by means of a lead or directly by their mountings. Electric current flows through the component and then back to the battery via the bodywork. If the component mounting is loose or corroded, or if a good path back to the battery is not available, the circuit will be incomplete and malfunction will result. The engine and/or gearbox are also earthed by means of flexible metal straps to the body or subframe; if these straps are loose or missing, starter motor, generator and ignition trouble may result.

Assuming the earth return to be satisfactory, electrical faults will be due either to component malfunction or to defects in the current supply. Individual components are dealt with in Chapter 10. If supply wires are broken or cracked internally this results in an open-circuit, and the easiest way to check for this is to bypass the suspect wire temporarily with a length of wire having a crocodile clip or suitable connector at each end. Alternatively, a 12V test lamp can be used to verify the presence of supply voltage at various points along the wire and the break can be thus isolated.

If a bare portion of a live wire touches the bodywork or other earthed metal part, the electricity will take the low-resistance path thus formed back to the battery: this is known as a short-circuit. Hopefully a short-circuit will blow a fuse, but otherwise it may cause burning of the insulation (and possibly further short-circuits) or even a fire. This is why it is inadvisable to bypass persistently blowing fuses with silver foil or wire.

Spares and tool kit

Most vehicles are supplied only with sufficient tools for wheel changing; the *Maintenance and minor repair* tool kit detailed in *Tools and working facilities,* with the addition of a hammer, is probably sufficient for those repairs that most motorists would consider attempting at the roadside. In addition a few items which can be fitted without too much trouble in the event of a breakdown should be carried. Experience and available space will modify the list below, but the following may save having to call on professional assistance:

Spark plugs, clean and correctly gapped
HT lead and plug cap – long enough to reach the plug furthest from the distributor
Distributor rotor, condenser and contact breaker points (if applicable)
Drivebelt(s) – emergency type may suffice
Spare fuses
Set of principal light bulbs
Tin of radiator sealer and hose bandage
Exhaust bandage
Roll of insulating tape
Length of soft iron wire
Length of electrical flex
Torch or inspection lamp (can double as test lamp)
Battery jump leads
Tow-rope
Ignition waterproofing aerosol
Litre of engine oil
Sealed can of hydraulic fluid
Emergency windscreen
Worm drive clips
Tube of filler paste

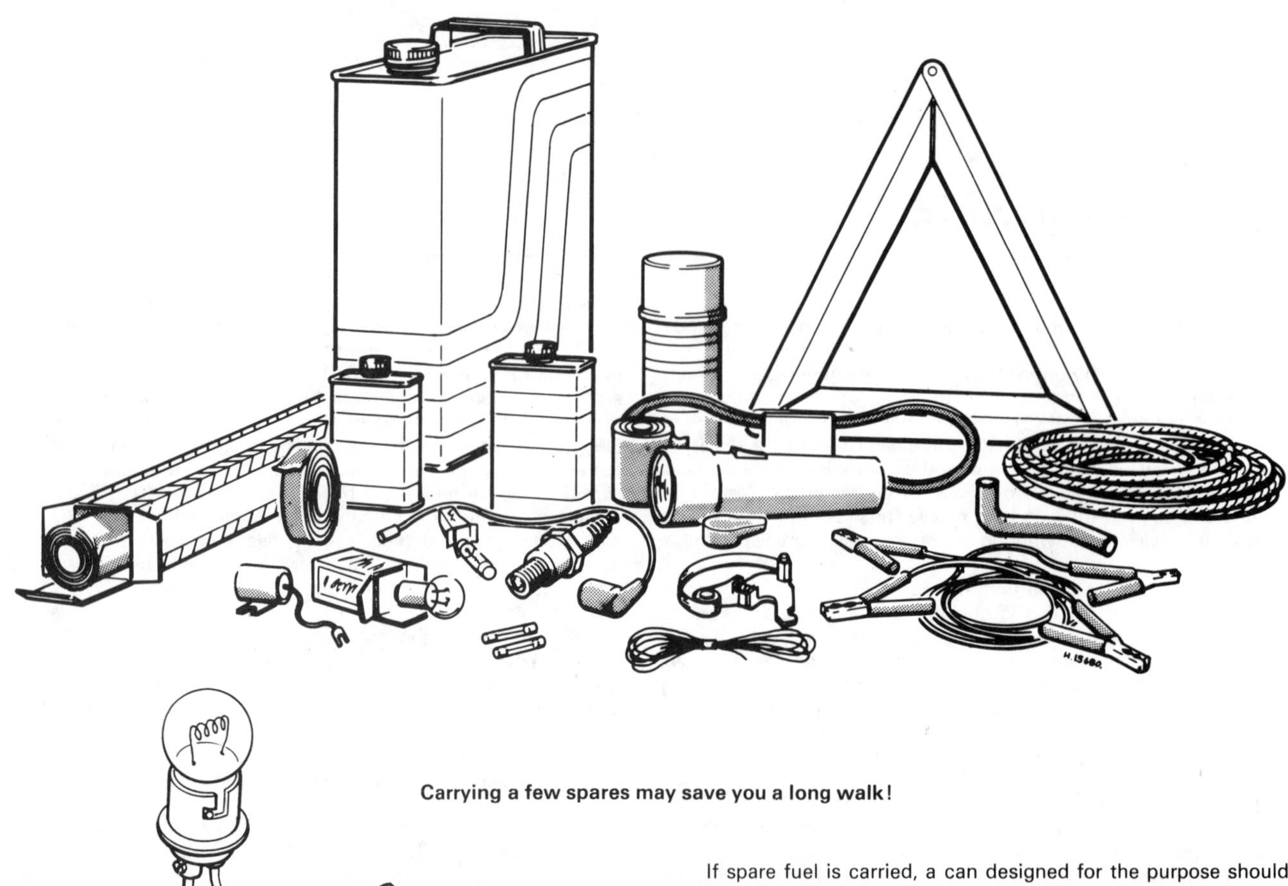

Carrying a few spares may save you a long walk!

A simple test lamp is useful for checking electrical faults

Crank engine and check for spark. Note use of insulated tool to hold plug lead. Use a spare plug, not one removed from engine (fire risk)

If spare fuel is carried, a can designed for the purpose should be used to minimise risks of leakage and collision damage. A first aid kit and a warning triangle, whilst not at present compulsory in the UK, are obviously sensible items to carry in addition to the above.

When touring abroad it may be advisable to carry additional spares which, even if you cannot fit them yourself, could save having to wait while parts are obtained. The items below may be worth considering:

Throttle cable
Cylinder head gasket
Alternator brushes
Tyre valve core

One of the motoring organisations will be able to advise on availability of fuel etc in foreign countries.

Engine will not start

Engine fails to turn when starter operated

Flat battery (recharge, use jump leads, or push start)
Battery terminals loose or corroded
Battery earth to body defective
Engine earth strap loose or broken
Starter motor (or solenoid) wiring loose or broken
Automatic transmission selector in wrong position, or inhibitor switch faulty
Ignition/starter switch faulty
Major mechanical failure (seizure)
Starter or solenoid internal fault (see Chapter 10)

Starter motor turns engine slowly

Partially discharged battery (recharge, use jump leads, or push start)
Battery terminals loose or corroded
Battery earth to body defective
Engine earth strap loose
Starter motor (or solenoid) wiring loose
Starter motor internal fault (see Chapter 10)

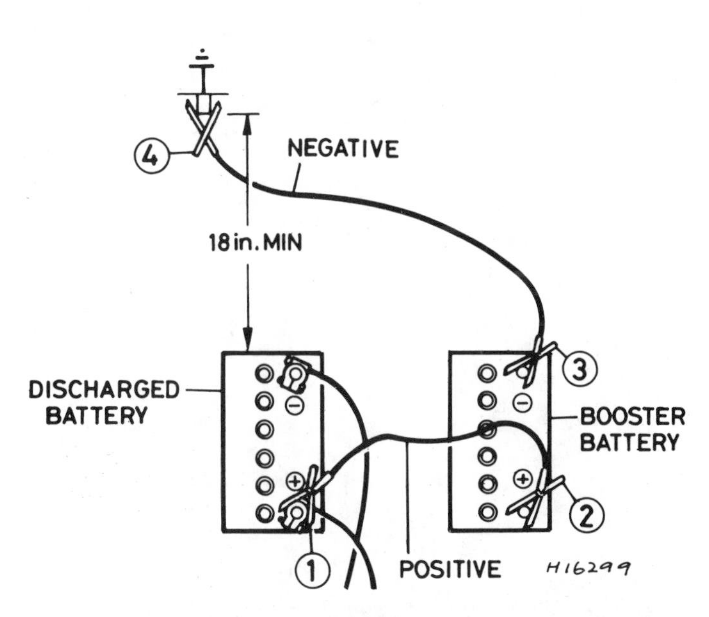

Jump start lead connections for negative earth – connect leads in order shown

Starter motor spins without turning engine
Flat battery
Starter motor pinion sticking on sleeve
Flywheel gear teeth damaged or worn
Starter motor mounting bolts loose

Engine turns normally but fails to start
Damp or dirty HT leads and distributor cap (crank engine and check for spark)
Dirty or incorrectly gapped distributor points (if applicable)
No fuel in tank (check for delivery)
Excessive choke (hot engine) or insufficient choke (cold engine)
Fouled or incorrectly gapped spark plugs (remove, clean and regap)
Other ignition system fault (see Chapter 4)
Other fuel system fault (see Chapter 3)
Poor compression (see Chapter 1)
Major mechanical failure (eg camshaft drive)

Engine fires but will not run
Insufficient choke (cold engine)
Air leaks at carburettor or inlet manifold
Fuel starvation (see Chapter 3)
Ballast resistor defective, or other ignition fault (see Chapter 4)

Engine cuts out and will not restart

Engine cuts out suddenly – ignition fault
Loose or disconnected LT wires
Wet HT leads or distributor cap (after traversing water splash)
Coil or condenser failure (check for spark)
Other ignition fault (see Chapter 4)

Engine misfires before cutting out – fuel fault
Fuel tank empty
Fuel pump defective or filter blocked (check for delivery)
Fuel tank filler vent blocked (suction will be evident on releasing cap)
Carburettor needle valve sticking
Carburettor jets blocked (fuel contaminated)
Other fuel system fault (see Chapter 3)

Engine cuts out – other causes
Serious overheating
Major mechanical failure (eg camshaft drive)

Engine overheats

Ignition (no-charge) warning light illuminated
Slack or broken drivebelt – retension or renew (Chapter 2)

Ignition warning light not illuminated
Coolant loss due to internal or external leakage (see Chapter 2)
Thermostat defective
Low oil level
Brakes binding
Radiator clogged externally or internally
Electric cooling fan not operating correctly (if applicable)
Engine waterways clogged
Ignition timing incorrect or automatic advance malfunctioning
Mixture too weak

Note: *Do not add cold water to an overheated engine or damage may result*

Low engine oil pressure

Gauge reads low or warning light illuminated with engine running
Oil level low or incorrect grade
Defective gauge or sender unit
Wire to sender unit earthed
Engine overheating
Oil filter clogged or bypass valve defective
Oil pressure relief valve defective
Oil pick-up strainer clogged
Oil pump worn or mountings loose
Worn main or big-end bearings

Note: *Low oil pressure in a high-mileage engine at tickover is not necessarily a cause for concern. Sudden pressure loss at speed is far more significant. In any event, check the gauge or warning light sender before condemning the engine.*

Engine noises

Pre-ignition (pinking) on acceleration
Incorrect grade of fuel
Ignition timing incorrect
Distributor faulty or worn
Worn or maladjusted carburettor
Excessive carbon build-up in engine

Whistling or wheezing noises
Leaking vacuum hose
Leaking carburettor or manifold gasket
Blowing head gasket

Tapping or rattling
Incorrect valve clearances
Worn valve gear
Worn timing belt
Broken piston ring (ticking noise)

Knocking or thumping
Unintentional mechanical contact (eg fan blades)
Worn drivebelt
Peripheral component fault (generator, water pump etc)
Worn big-end bearings (regular heavy knocking, perhaps less under load)
Worn main bearings (rumbling and knocking, perhaps worsening under load)
Piston slap (most noticeable when cold)

Chapter 1 Engine

For modifications, and information applicable to later models, see Supplement at end of manual

Contents

Specifications

General

Engine type	Six-cylinder in-line, ohc (overhead camshaft) with carburettor or fuel injection	
Designation (all capacities):		
Up to 1981	M60	
1981 on	M20	
Capacity	1990 cc (121.4 cu in) or 2316 cc (141.3 cu in)	
Data:	**1990 cc**	**2316 cc**
Bore	80.0 mm (3.15 in)	80.0 mm (3.15 in)
Stroke	66.0 mm (2.60 in)	76.8 mm (3.02 in)
Compression ratio:		
Series 1	9.2:1	9.5:1
Series 2	9.8:1	9.8:1
Power output:		
Series 1	90 kW (122.4 PS) at 6000 rpm	105 kW (142.8 PS) at 5800 rpm
Series 2	92 kW (125.1 PS) at 5800 rpm	102 kW (138.7 PS) at 5300 rpm (pre 1984) or 110 kW (150.0 PS) at 6000 rpm (1984 on)
Maximum torque:		
Series 1	160 Nm (118 lbf ft) at 4000 rpm	190 Nm (140 lbf ft) at 4600 rpm
Series 2	165 Nm (122 lbf ft) at 4500 rpm	205 Nm (151 lbf ft) at 4000 rpm
Compression pressure:		
Engine warm and in good condition, throttle fully open, starter cranking		
Minimum pressure	10.0 bar (142.2 lbf/in^2)	
Good above	11.0 bar (156.5 lbf/in^2)	

Cylinder block

Material	Cast iron
Number of cylinders	6
Bore size:	
Standard	80.010 to 80.020 mm (3.1500 to 3.1504 in)
First rebore	80.260 to 80.270 mm (3.1598 to 3.1602 in)
Second rebore	80.510 to 80.520 mm (3.1697 to 3.1701 in)
Maximum out-of-round	0.01 to 0.02 mm (0.0004 to 0.0008 in)
Maximum taper	0.01 mm (0.0004 in)
Maximum piston-to-bore clearance:	
M60	0.10 to 0.15 mm (0.0040 to 0.0060 in)
M20	0.01 to 0.15 mm (0.0004 to 0.0060 in)

Pistons and rings

Piston diameter:	
Standard	79.97 to 79.99 mm (3.1484 to 3.1492 in)
Oversizes	0.25 mm (0.01 in) and 0.50 mm (0.02 in)
Standard piston-to-bore clearance:	
M60	0.025 to 0.045 mm (0.0010 to 0.0018 in)
M20	0.01 to 0.04 mm (0.0004 to 0.0016 in)
Maximum piston weight difference	10.0g (0.35 oz)
Gudgeon pin bore	22.000 to 22.004 mm (0.86614 to 0.86630 in)
Gudgeon pin outside diameter	21.996 to 22.000 mm (0.86598 to 0.86614 in)
Gudgeon pin clearance in piston:	
Mahle type pistons	0.001 to 0.005 mm (0.00004 to 0.00020 in)
KS type pistons	0.002 to 0.006 mm (0.00008 to 0.00024 in)
Number of piston rings	Two compression, one oil control
Top compression ring:	
End gap	0.3 to 0.5 mm (0.012 to 0.020 in)
Groove clearance:	
Mahle piston	0.060 to 0.092 mm (0.0024 to 0.0036 in)
KS piston	0.050 to 0.082 mm (0.0020 to 0.0032 in)
Second compression ring:	
End gap	0.3 to 0.5 mm (0.012 to 0.020 in)
Groove clearance:	
Mahle piston	0.030 to 0.062 mm (0.0012 to 0.0024 in)
KS piston	0.040 to 0.072 mm (0.0016 to 0.0028 in)
Oil control ring:	
End gap	0.25 to 0.50 mm (0.0098 to 0.0197 in)
Groove clearance:	
Mahle piston	0.020 to 0.052 mm (0.0008 to 0.0020 in)
KS piston	0.030 to 0.062 mm (0.0012 to 0.0024 in)

Crankshaft

Number of main bearings	7
Bearing bore in crankcase:	
Red	65.000 to 65.010 mm (2.5591 to 2.5594 in)
Blue	65.010 to 65.019 mm (2.5594 to 2.5598 in)
Journal diameters:	
Standard:	
Red	59.980 to 59.990 mm (2.3614 to 2.3618 in)
Blue	59.971 to 59.980 mm (2.3611 to 2.3614 in)
First regrind:	
Red	59.730 to 59.740 mm (2.3516 to 2.3520 in)
Blue	59.721 to 59.730 mm (2.3512 to 2.3516 in)
Second regrind:	
Red	59.480 to 54.490 mm (2.3417 to 2.3421 in)
Blue	59.471 to 59.480 mm (2.3414 to 2.3417 in)
Main bearing shell thickness:	
Standard:	
Red	2.480 to 2.490 mm (0.0976 to 0.0980 in)
Blue	2.490 to 2.500 mm (0.0980 to 0.0984 in)
First undersize:	
Red	2.605 to 2.615 mm (0.1026 to 0.1030 in)
Blue	2.615 to 2.625 mm (0.1030 to 0.1033 in)
Second undersize:	
Red	2.730 to 2.740 mm (0.1075 to 0.1079 in)
Blue	2.740 to 2.750 mm (0.1709 to 0.1083 in)
Crankshaft running clearance:	
Red	0.030 to 0.070 mm (0.0012 to 0.0028 in)
Blue	0.030 to 0.068 mm (0.0012 to 0.0027 in)
Crankshaft endfloat	0.080 to 0.163 mm (0.0031 to 0.0064 in)
Crankpin diameters:	
Standard	44.975 to 44.991 mm (1.7707 to 1.7713 in)
First regrind	44.500 to 44.660 mm (1.7520 to 1.7583 in)

Flywheel

Minimum thickness	25.0 mm (0.98 in)

Connecting rods and big-end bearings

Small-end diameter	24.000 to 24.021 mm (0.9449 to 0.9457 in)
Big-end shell thickness:	
Glyco type:	
Standard	1.481 to 1.493 mm (0.0583 to 0.0588 in)
First undersize	1.606 to 1.618 mm (0.0632 to 0.0637 in)
KS type:	
Standard	1.484 to 1.494 mm (0.0584 to 0.0588 in)
First undersize	1.609 to 1.619 mm (0.0633 to 0.0637 in)
Connecting rod endfloat	0.021 to 0.067 mm (0.0008 to 0.0026 in)

Cylinder head

Material	Light alloy
Rocker shaft bore diameter	17.500 to 17.543 mm (0.6890 to 0.6907 in)
Rocker shaft running clearance	0.016 to 0.052 mm (0.0006 to 0.0020 in)
Valve guide bore in head	13.000 to 13.018 mm (0.5118 to 0.5125 in)
Oversizes	13.1, 13.2 and 13.3 mm (0.5157, 0.5197 and 0.5236 in)

Valves

Valve seat angle	45°
Valve seat width:	
Inlet	1.50 mm (0.059 in)
Exhaust	1.65 mm (0.065 in)
Valve length (inlet and exhaust)	102.3 to 102.7 mm (4.028 to 4.043 in)
Head diameter:	
Inlet	39.984 to 40.000 mm (1.5742 to 1.5748 in)
Exhaust	33.984 to 34.000 mm (1.3380 to 1.3386 in)
Stem diameter:	
Inlet	6.960 to 6.975 mm (0.2740 to 0.2746 in)
Exhaust	6.945 to 6.960 mm (0.2734 to 0.2740 in)
Minimum thickness of valve head edge (after grinding in)	1.2 mm (0.047 in)
Valve seat angle	44° 10′ to 44° 30′
Maximum clearance of valve stem in guide	0.1 mm (0.0039 in)
Valve spring free length	43.5 mm (1.1713 in)
Coil diameter	31.70 to 32.10 mm (1.248 to 1.264 in)
Valve clearances (engine cold)	0.25 mm (0.010 in)
Valve timing:	
0.5 mm (0.02 in) clearance between cam base circle and rocker arm contact face	
Inlet valve opens	11° BTDC
Inlet valve closes	47° ABDC
Exhaust valve opens	51° BBDC
Exhaust valve closes	7° ATDC

Camshaft

Number of bearings	7
Running clearance	0.059 to 0.100 mm (0.0023 to 0.0039 in)
Endfloat	0.2 mm (0.0079 in)
Cam lift	6.5009 to 6.6609 mm (0.2559 to 0.2622 in)

Timing belt

Type	Flexible
Number of teeth	111
Belt width	25.4 mm (1.0 in)

Intermediate shaft

Number of bearings	2

Oil pump and lubrication

Type	Gear-driven from extension of the distributor driveshaft
Clearance:	
Gear teeth to pump body	0.016 to 0.054 mm (0.0006 to 0.0021 in)
Gear endfloat (maximum)	0.11 mm (0.0043 in)
Gear backlash (maximum)	0.2436 mm (0.0096 in)
Oil pressure:	
At idle	0.5 to 2.0 bar (7.25 to 29.0 lbf/in^2)
At maximum speed	5.0 to 6.0 bar (72.5 to 87.0 lbf/in^2)
Oil capacity:	
With filter change	4.25 litre (7.48 Imp pts)
Without filter change	4.00 litre (7.04 Imp pts)
Oil type/specification	Multigrade engine oil to API-SE or -SF (Duckhams QXR or Hypergrade)
Oil pump relief valve spring free length	43.80 to 44.02 mm (1.724 to 1.733 in)
Crankcase oil pressure relief valve free length	68.0 mm (2.677 in)

Torque wrench settings

	Nm	lbf ft
Main bearing caps	65	48
Big-end caps:		
Stage 1	20	15
Stage 2	Tighten the bolts through 70°	
Front cover:		
M6 bolts	10	7
M8 bolts	22	16
Rear cover:		
M6 bolts	10	7
M8 bolts	22	16
Belt tensioner	22	16
Cylinder head bolts:		
Stage 1	35	26
Wait twenty minutes		
Stage 2	60	44
Run engine to operating temperature		
Stage 3	Tighten the bolts through 20 to 30°	
Rocker cover nuts	6	4
Oil drain plug	60	44
Sump pan bolts	10	7
Flywheel or driveplate bolts	100	74
Crankshaft damper pulley bolt	22	16
Crankshaft damper bolt	400	295
Camshaft sprocket bolt	60	44
Rocker adjuster bolt	10	7
Intermediate shaft sprocket bolt	40	30
Oil pump relief valve plug	28	21
Oil pump mounting bolts	22	16
Oil pump cover bolts	9	7
Pressure relief valve	40	30
Exhaust manifold nuts	22	16
Engine mounting bush bolts	50	37
Engine mounting bracket bolts	24	18
Bellhousing bolts	80	59

1 General description

The engine is of six-cylinder, in-line type, with an overhead camshaft driven by a toothed belt which has a tensioner.

The cylinder block is of cast iron while the cylinder head is of light alloy.

The crankshaft is of cast steel and runs in seven main bearings.

The connecting rods are of forged steel construction with light alloy pistons and chromium plated compression rings.

The valve clearances are adjustable by means of ecentric cams on the rocker arms.

The camshaft is supported in seven bearings machined directly in the cylinder head.

The lubrication system is of pressurised type with an oil pump located within the sump and driven from an extension on the distributor driveshaft. The oil filter is of full-flow disposable cartridge type.

Warning – vehicles equipped with air conditioning

Whenever overhaul of a major nature is being undertaken in the engine, components of the air conditioning system will obstruct the work. If such items of the system cannot be unbolted and moved aside sufficiently far within the limits of their flexible connecting pipes to avoid such obstruction, the system should be discharged by your dealer or a competent refrigeration engineer.

As the system must be completely evacuated before recharging, the necessary vacuum equipment to do this is only likely to be available at the specialists.

The refrigerant fluid is Freon 12 and, although harmless under normal conditions, contact with the eyes or skin must be avoided. If Freon comes into contact with a naked flame, then a poisonous gas will be created which is injurious to health.

2 Engine oil and filter

1 The engine oil level should be checked at the weekly maintenance inspection with the car standing on a level floor and the engine cold.

2 Withdraw the dipstick, wipe it clean on a non-fluffy rag and reinsert it so that the loop is towards the front of the car. Withdraw the dipstick for the second time and read off the oil level.

3 The level should be between the LOW and HIGH marks. If necessary, top up to the upper mark with oil of the specified type (see Recommended lubricants and fluids). Avoid overfilling.

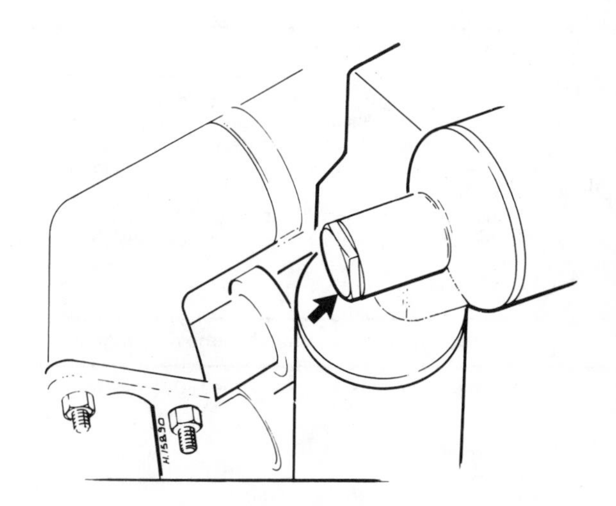

Fig. 1.1 Oil filter on cars fitted with air conditioning (Sec 2)

Unscrew the hollow bolt (arrowed) and remove the adaptor to gain access to the filter

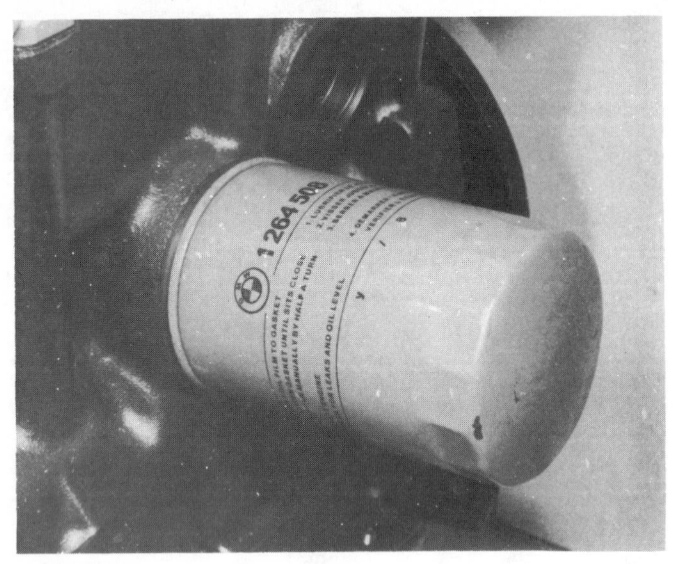

2.9 Oil filter

4 Engine oil is added through the filler hole in the rocker cover.
5 At the specified intervals (see Routine Maintenance), and with the engine hot, remove the oil filler cap and then unscrew the drain plug (17.0 mm) and catch the oil in a suitable container.
6 When all the oil has drained, refit the plug.
7 Unscrew the oil filter and discard it. An oil filter removal tool will almost certainly be required and, in cases where the filter is stuck tight, it may be necessary to drive a screwdriver right through the filter casing and use it as a lever to unscrew the filter.
8 To remove the filter on cars equipped with air conditioning, unscrew the adaptor hollow bolt (32.0 mm), remove the assembly and then unscrew the filter cartridge from the adaptor.
9 Smear the rubber sealing ring of the new filter with engine oil and screw it into position using hand pressure only (photo). On cars with air conditioning always renew the filter aluminium seal.
10 Refill the engine with a suitable quantity of the specified oil.
11 Start the engine and run it for a few minutes. It may take a few seconds for the oil pressure warning lamp to go out, this is normal and is due to the new filter having to fill with oil.
12 Switch off the engine and wait a few minutes for the oil to drain back into the sump and then check the oil level and top up, if necessary.

3 Crankcase ventilation system

1 A positive type system is installed whereby gases, which accumulate in the engine crankcase, are drawn out through a spring-loaded tube into the inlet manifold. The gases are then drawn into the engine combustion chambers, where they are burned during the normal combustion cycle.
2 Maintenance consists only of checking the hoses for tightness, and periodically removing them and cleaning out any residue which may have accumulated (photos).

4 Major operations possible without removing engine

1 The following operations may be carried out with the engine in position in the car

Valve clearance adjustment
Timing belt renewal
Cylinder head – removal and refitting
Sump pan – removal and refitting
Oil pump – removal and refitting
Piston/connecting rods – removal and refitting
Front end cover oil seal renewal
Camshaft oil seal renewal
Distributor driveshaft bearing renewal

3.2A Crankcase vent tube and spring

3.2B Upper end of crankcase vent tube. O-ring arrowed

3.2C Lower end of crankcase vent tube. Seal arrowed

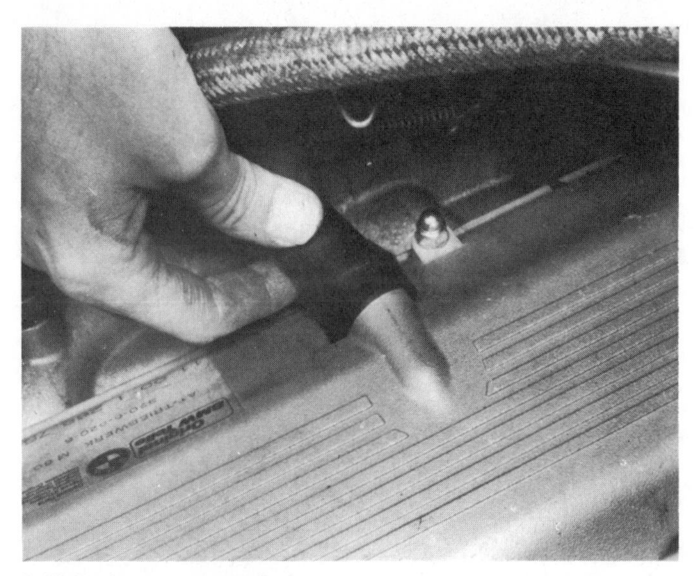

3.2D Rocker cover vent pipe

5 Valve clearances – adjustment

1 The valve clearances should be checked with the engine cold.
2 Remove the spark plugs.
3 On carburettor models, remove the air cleaner (Chapter 3).
4 Disconnect the hoses from the rocker cover.
5 Unscrew the rocker cover fixing nuts and take off the cover.
6 The camshaft may be turned using a $\frac{1}{2}$ in drive ratchet wrench inserted into the adaptor visible in the centre of the upper part of the timing belt cover, or by using the crankshaft pulley bolt.
7 Turn the camshaft until No 1 piston (timing belt end) is at TDC on its compression stroke. The compression can be felt being generated if a finger is placed over No 1 spark plug hole.
8 The valves being checked will be correctly positioned when the symmetrically opposite valves are rocking (one valve closing as the other one opens).
9 Adjust the valves in the following sequence, counting from the timing belt.

Valves to adjust	Valves rocking
Cylinder 1	*Cylinder 6*
Cylinder 5	*Cylinder 2*
Cylinder 3	*Cylinder 4*
Cylinder 6	*Cylinder 1*
Cylinder 2	*Cylinder 5*
Cylinder 4	*Cylinder 3*

10 The valve clearances on both inlet and exhaust valves are the same (see Specifications).
11 Check the valve clearances with a feeler blade of the specified thickness. If adjustment is required, release the locknut on the rocker arm and move the eccentric cam by inserting a cranked rod (2.5

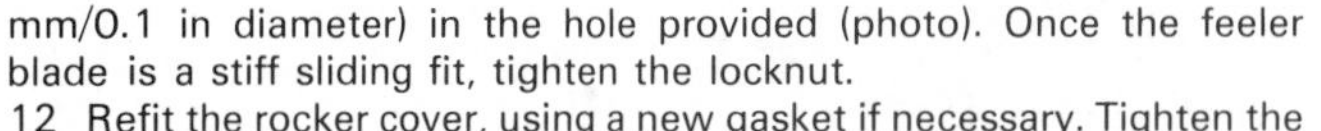

mm/0.1 in diameter) in the hole provided (photo). Once the feeler blade is a stiff sliding fit, tighten the locknut.
12 Refit the rocker cover, using a new gasket if necessary. Tighten the nuts in the order shown – Fig.1.2, but do not overtighten.
13 Refit the air cleaner on carburettor models (Chapter 3).

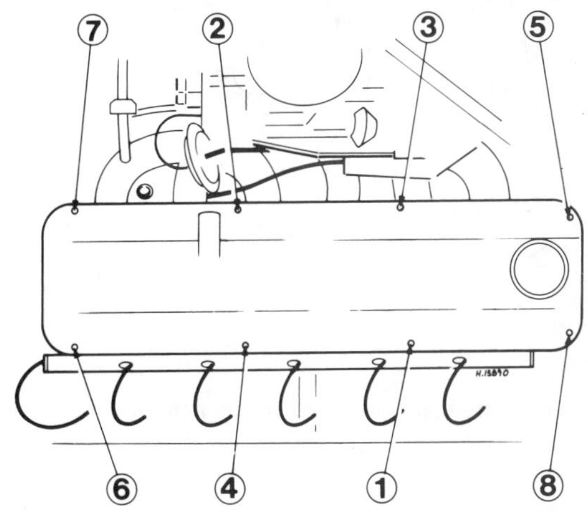

Fig. 1.2 Rocker cover nut tightening sequence (Sec 5)

6 Timing belt – renewal

Note: *It is important not to rotate the crankshaft or camshaft with the timing belt removed as the pistons may strike the valves*

1 The timing belt will require renewal if inspection shows it to be frayed or worn. It is recommended that it is renewed as a matter of routine if it has been in use for the specified mileage (see Routine Maintenance) as an insurance against costly engine damage.
2 Drain the cooling system (Chapter 2).
3 Disconnect the two large coolant hoses from the front end of the cylinder head.
4 Remove the HT lead support bracket from the lifting lug at the top of the timing belt cover.
5 Release the alternator mounting and adjuster link bolts. Push the alternator in towards the engine and slip the drivebelt from the pulley.
6 Unscrew the crankshaft vibration damper bolts. Prevent the damper from turning by applying a socket to the pulley hub centre bolt. Remove the damper/pulley.
7 Unbolt the alternator adjuster strap from the belt cover. Unbolt and remove the belt cover with the engine lifting lug (photo). Slip the TDC sensor from its clips.
8 Remove the spark plugs.
9 Turn the crankshaft by means of the $\frac{1}{2}$ in drive adaptor or crankshaft pulley hub bolt until No 1 piston (at timing belt end) is at TDC. In this position, the arrow on the camshaft sprocket and the mark on the crankshaft pulley hub will be aligned with their cylinder head and end cover marks.
10 If the belt is to be used again, mark its running direction.
11 Release the tensioner bolts, push the pulley to its fully retracted position (photo) and then take off the belt.

5.11 Adjusting a valve clearance

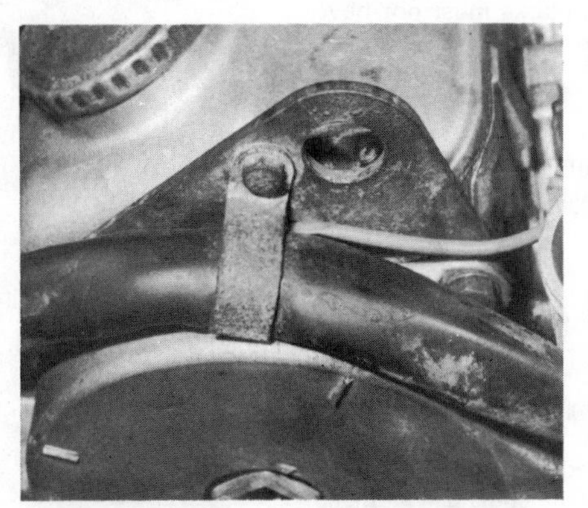

6.7 Timing belt cover with lifting lug and harness clip

6.11 Method of restraining belt tensioner spring

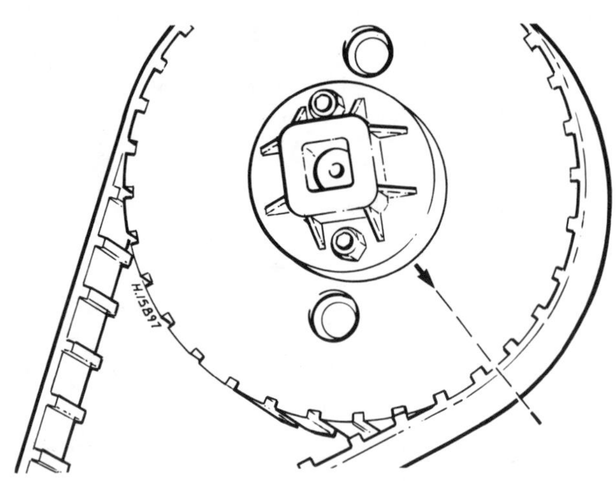

Fig. 1.3 Camshaft sprocket and cylinder head alignment marks (Sec 6)

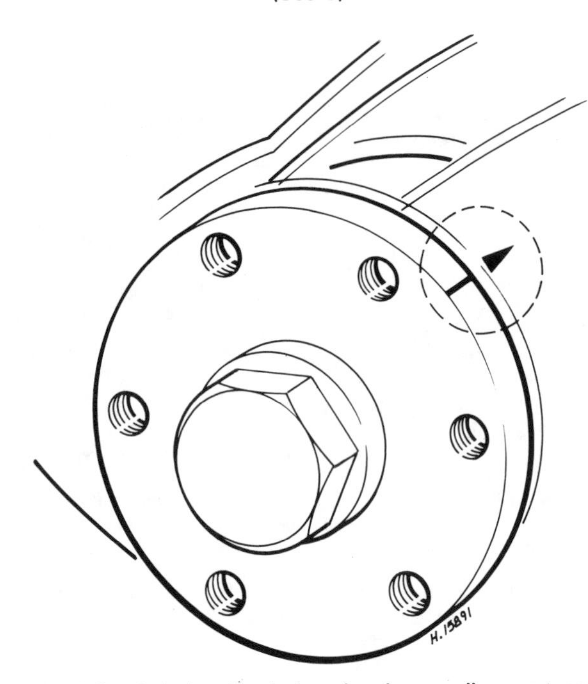

Fig. 1.4 Crankshaft pulley hub and end cover alignment marks (Sec 6)

12 **Do not** turn the crankshaft while the belt is removed.
13 Before fitting the belt, remove the distributor cap and check that the notch in the rim of the distributor body is in alignment with the one on the governor. The camshaft and crankshaft marks must not have moved.
14 Fit the belt, applying slight tension to the run of the belt which passes over the tensioner pulley (photos).
15 Release the belt tensioner.
16 Using the camshaft sprocket adaptor, turn the belt two turns against the direction of normal rotation. Lock up the tensioner bolts.
17 Check the alignment of the sprocket and hub marks with No 1 piston at TDC.
18 Fit the spark plugs and belt covers (photos).
19 Fit the crankshaft damper/pulley making sure that the positioning dowel locates correctly in its hole.
20 Push the TDC sensor into its belt cover clips and set it so that there is a clearance of between 0.2 and 2.0 mm (0.008 and 0.080 in) between the sensor and the crankshaft damper (photo).
21 Fit the drivebelt and tension it, as described in Chapter 2.
22 Reconnect the coolant hoses. Fill and bleed the cooling system, as described in Chapter 2.
23 Check the ignition timing (Chapter 4).

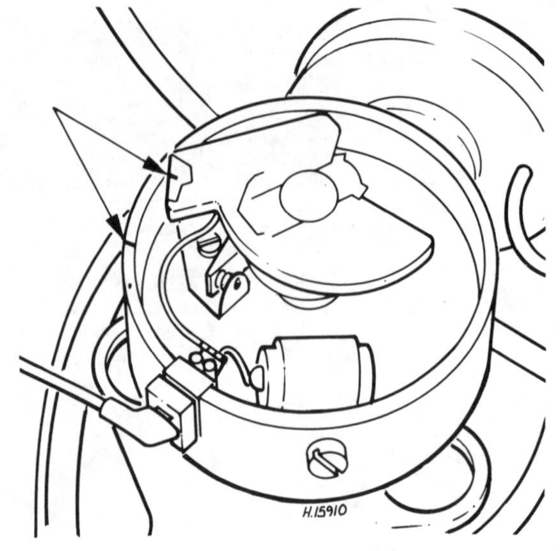

Fig. 1.5 Distributor body and governor alignment marks (Sec 6)

6.14A Fitting the timing belt

6.14B Timing belt fitted

6.18A Belt rear cover

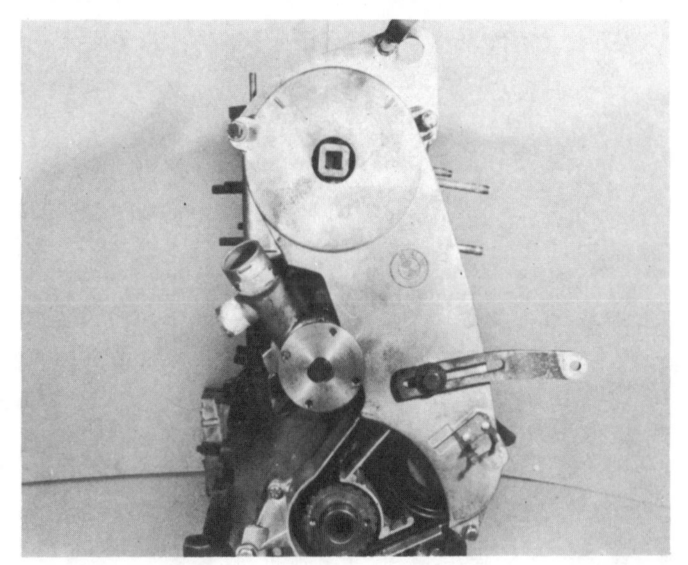
6.18C Belt cover fitted

6.18B Alternator belt adjuster link stud

6.20 TDC sensor in clip

7 Cylinder head – removal and refitting

1 Remove the air cleaner (Chapter 3).
2 Unscrew the fixing nuts and take off the rocker cover.
3 Disconnect the exhaust downpipe from the manifold and release the exhaust downpipe support bracket (photo).
4 Drain the cooling system, as described in Chapter 2.
5 Disconnect the negative lead from the battery.

Carburettor engines

6 Disconnect the cylinder head coolant hoses (photo), and the electrical leads from the coolant temperature switches.
7 Disconnect the fuel hoses from the base of the carburettor. Identify the hoses as to which is flow and return.
8 Disconnect the electrical leads from the fuel cut-off valve and automatic choke on the carburettor.
9 Disconnect the accelerator cable from the carburettor, the cruise control cable (if fitted) and the kickdown cable on cars with automatic transmission.
10 Disconnect the distributor vacuum hoses and the lead from the heat sensitive switch.
11 Disconnect the coolant hoses from the carburettor.
12 Disconnect the brake vacuum servo hose from the intake manifold.

7.3 Unscrewing exhaust downpipe flange bolt

7.6 Coolant hoses at thermostat housing

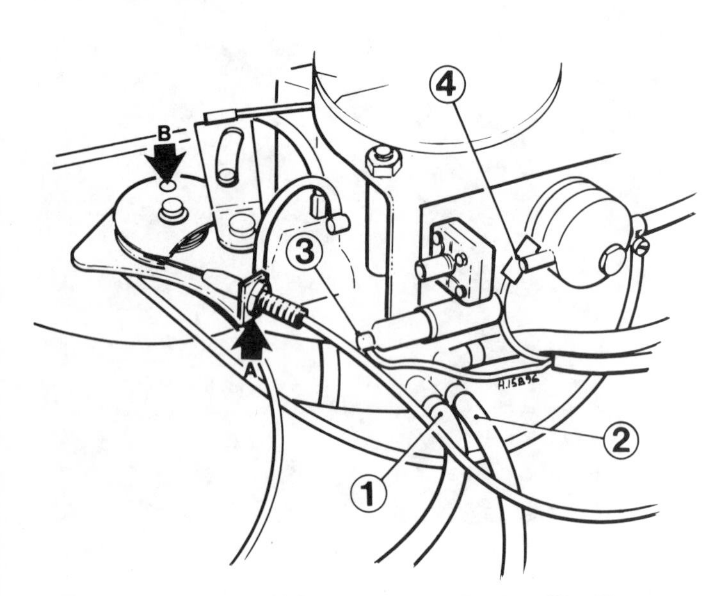

Fig. 1.6 Leads and hoses at the carburettor (Sec 7)

1 Fuel hose (return)
2 Fuel hose (supply)
3 Automatic choke lead
4 Fuel cut-off valve lead
A Cable locknut
B Cable nipple

13 Disconnect the coolant hose from the rear end of the cylinder head.
14 Pull the throttle cable out in a downward direction through the hole in the intake manifold.

Fuel injection engines (K-Jetronic)

15 Remove the air intake duct and airflow sensor.
16 Disconnect the accelerator cable.
17 Identify and then disconnect the six fuel injector pipes from the mixture regulator. Remove the pipe clip.
18 Disconnect the fuel line (7) and the clip (8) – Fig. 1.9.
19 Disconnect the hoses – Fig. 1.10 – also the vacuum hoses and the electrical plugs from the cold start valve and air slide. Disconnect the fuel injectors.
20 Disconnect the coolant hoses (1 and 2) and the brake vacuum servo hose – Fig. 1.11. Disconnect the diagnostic socket.
21 Disconnect the coolant hoses and electrical leads shown in Fig. 1.12 and also from the air valve holder on the intake manifold (photo).

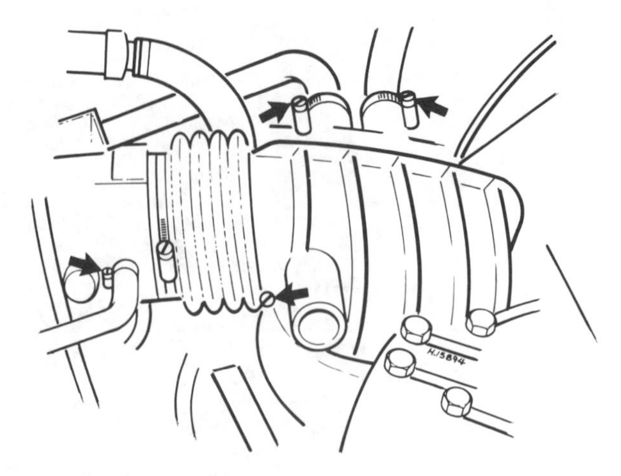

Fig. 1.7 Air intake duct securing screws (arrowed) – fuel injection models (Sec 7)

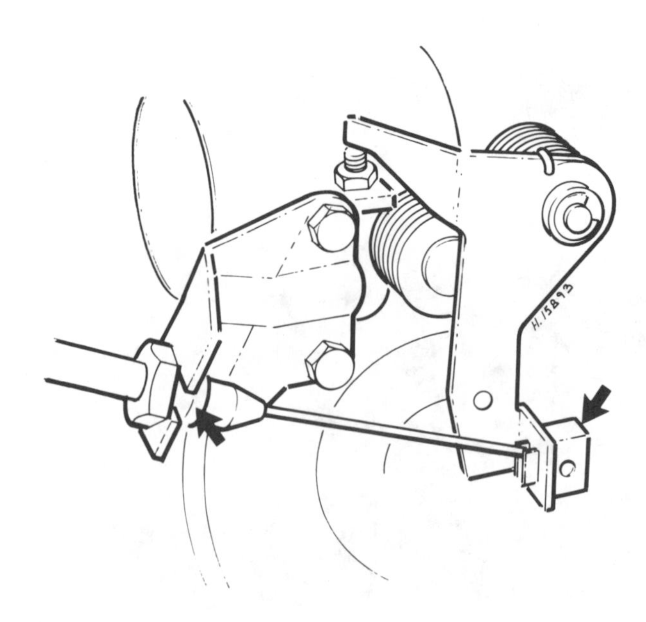

Fig. 1.8 Accelerator cable attachment points (arrowed) – fuel injection models (Sec 7)

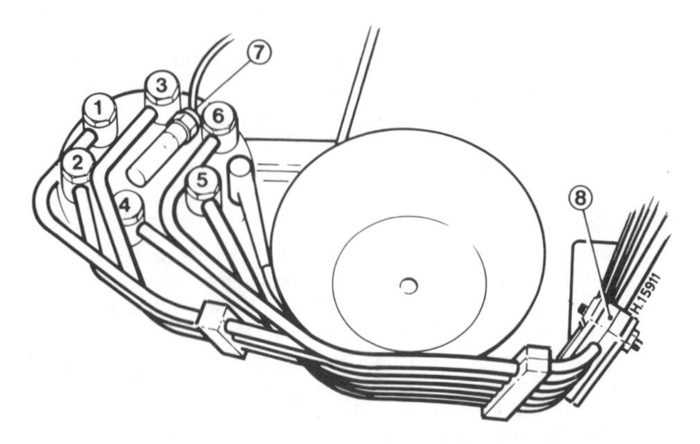

Fig. 1.9 Mixture regulator – fuel injection models (Sec 7)

1 Injector pipe
2 Injector pipe
3 Injector pipe
4 Injector pipe
5 Injector pipe
6 Injector pipe
7 Fuel supply pipe
8 Clip

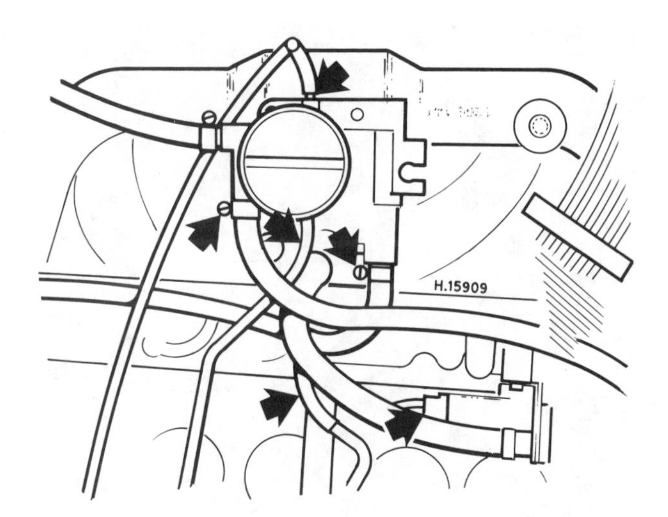

Fig. 1.10 Cold start valve and air slide connections – arrowed (Sec 7)

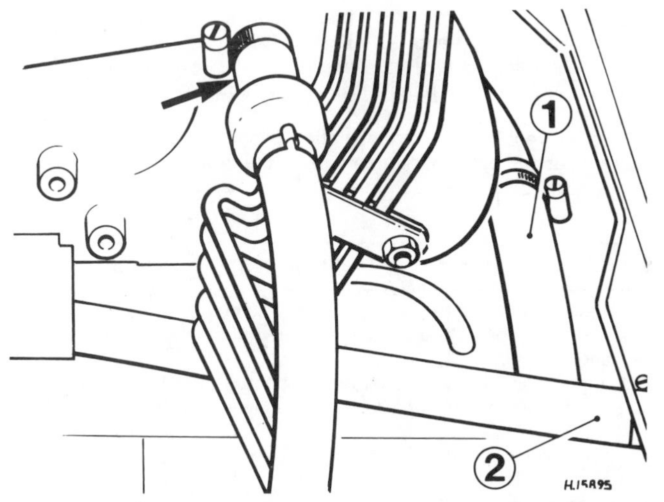

Fig. 1.11 Coolant hose connections (1 and 2) and the air collector vacuum hose – arrowed (Sec 7)

7.21 Air valve

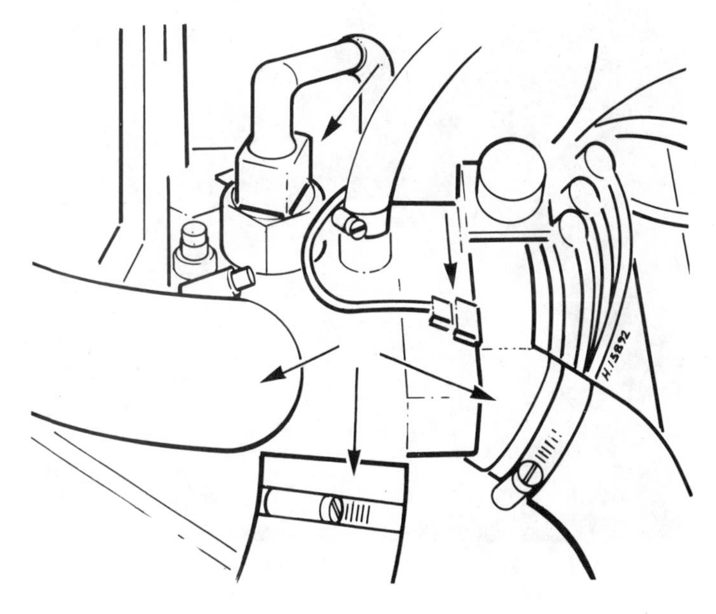

Fig. 1.12 Branch flange connections – arrowed (Sec 7)

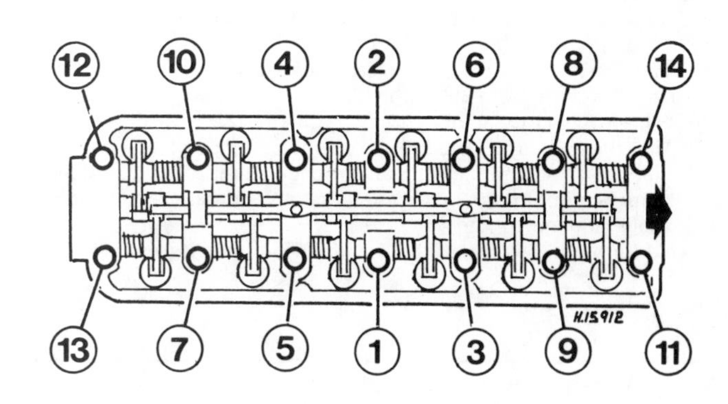

Fig. 1.13 Cylinder head bolt tightening sequence (Sec 7)

All engines

22 Disconnect the HT leads from the spark plugs. Remove the dipstick guide tube. Unclip the TDC sensor wire.

23 Take off the distributor cap and place it to one side of the engine compartment.

24 Remove the timing belt, as described in the preceding Section.

25 Unscrew the cylinder head bolts evenly and progressively in the reverse order to that shown in Fig. 1.13. Remove the cylinder head and gasket.

26 If the cylinder head is to be dismantled and reconditioned, refer to Section 18, otherwise remove all carbon and dirt from the cylinder head and block mating surfaces. Carbon should also be removed from the piston crowns and combustion recesses in the cylinder head.

27 Mop out any dirt or oil from the bolt holes in the cylinder block. Any oil left in these holes could cause the block to crack as the bolts are screwed in.

28 Clean the top surface of the block thoroughly and locate a new gasket in position. If the head has had the mating surface ground a thicker gasket **must** be used.

29 Lightly smear the cylinder head bolts with oil, lower the head into position and then screw in the bolts finger tight.

30 Tighten the bolts in the sequence shown in Fig. 1.13 through the first two stages given in the Specifications

31 Reconnection and tensioning of the timing belt is described in Section 6.

7.36 Torque tightening a head bolt by the angle method

8.5 Sump locating flange

32 Reconnection and refitting of the other components is a reversal of removal, but observe the following.

33 When refitting the ignition TDC sensor (only of use to service stations having the appropriate monitoring equipment), make sure that it is located in its clips so that there is a gap between the sensor and the crankshaft damper of between 0.2 and 2.0 mm (0.008 and 0.080 in).

34 Check and adjust the valve clearances, as described in Section 5. Adjust the accelerator cable (Chapter 3).

35 Fill and bleed the cooling system (Chapter 2).

36 After the engine has been run to operating temperature, tighten the cylinder head bolts through the angle specified for Stage 3, following the sequence in Fig. 1.13. Make up a cardboard template to indicate the angle required (photo).

37 No further tightening of the cylinder head bolts is required.

8 Sump pan – removal and refitting

1 Unbolt and remove the semi-circular cover plate from the lower part of the flywheel housing.

2 Drain the engine oil.

3 On Series 2 models, release the steering gear from the front crossmember (see Chapter 11), then disconnect the earth lead (1) and pull the lead from its clip (2) – Fig. 1.14.

4 Unscrew and remove the sump pan bolts, lower the pan until the oil pump and pressure relief valve can be removed, then lift away the pan.

5 Before refitting, clean the mating flanges thoroughly and use a new gasket and apply gasket cement to the front and end cover joints on the crankcase flange (photo).

9 Oil pump – removal and refitting

1 If the engine is in the car, remove the sump pan as described in the preceding Section. If the engine has been removed, unbolt the sump pan and remove it.

2 Unbolt and remove the oil pump (photo).

3 If required, the oil pressure relief valve can be unscrewed and removed.

4 If the original pump is being refitted, remove the filter screen retainer and clean the screen (photo).

5 Overhaul is described in Section 19.

6 The pump driveshaft engages in the distributor drivegear, make sure that the thrust washers are in position (photos). Before refitting the pump, fill it with engine oil to prime it (photo).

7 Tighten the pump bolts to the specified torque.

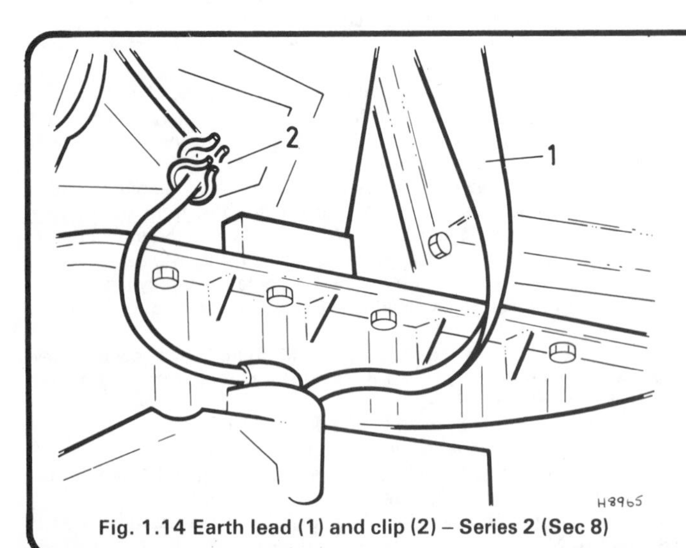

Fig. 1.14 Earth lead (1) and clip (2) – Series 2 (Sec 8)

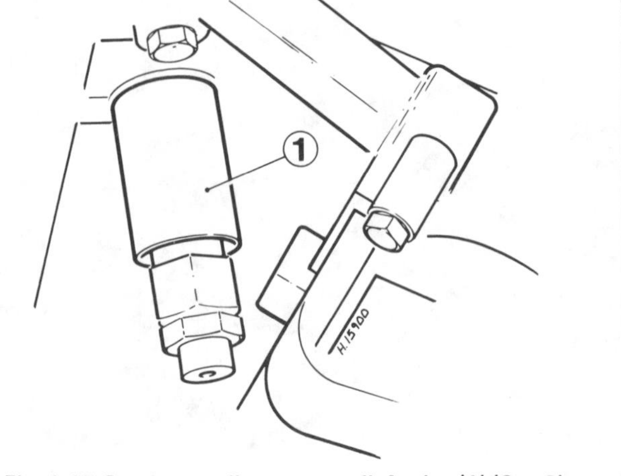

Fig. 1.15 Crankcase oil pressure relief valve (1) (Sec 9)

9.2 Removing the oil pump

9.6B Fitting the oil pump driveshaft

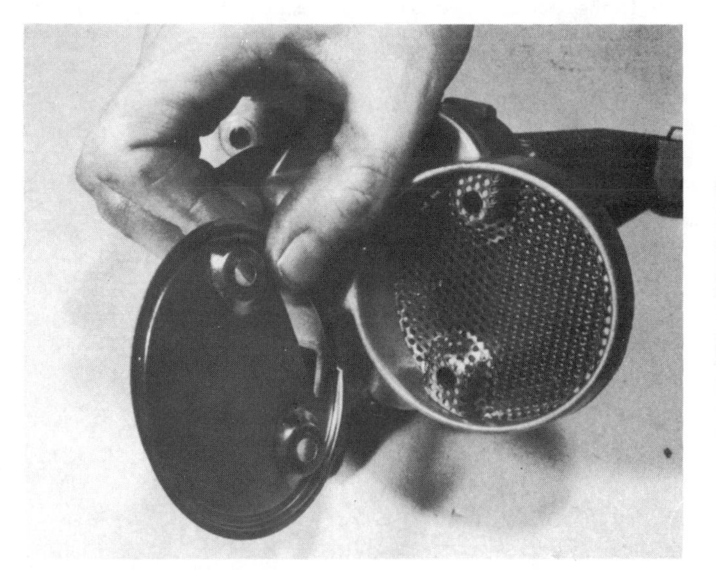
9.4 Oil pump pick-up filter

9.6C Priming the oil pump

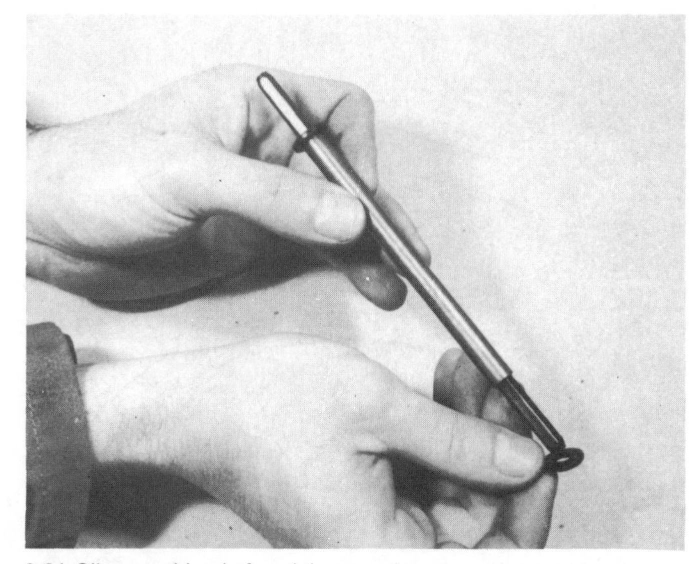
9.6A Oil pump driveshaft and thrustwashers

10 Piston/connecting rods – removal, dismantling, reassembly and refitting

1 Remove the cylinder head, as described in Section 7.
2 Remove the sump and oil pump (refer to Sections 8 and 9).
3 The connecting rods and their caps are engraved for match, but not numbered for sequence so mark and number them from the timing belt end of the engine.
4 Unbolt the big-end caps and remove them. Keep the bearing shells with their caps and rods if they are to be used again.
5 Push the piston/rod assembly up out of the bore.
6 The piston can be removed from the rod after extracting the circlips and pushing out the gudgeon pin (photos). If it is too tight to be removed by finger pressure, warm the piston in hot water.
7 Note the directional arrow on the piston crown which indicates the timing belt end of the engine when the piston is installed. Note also the relationship of the arrow to the rod big-end engraved markings, the latter being towards the oil filter side of the crankcase.
8 New pistons are supplied with matching gudgeon pins.
9 Piston sets should be of the same make and weight group.
10 If the purpose of removing the pistons was to fit new rings, proceed in the following way.

10.6A Gudgeon pin circlip

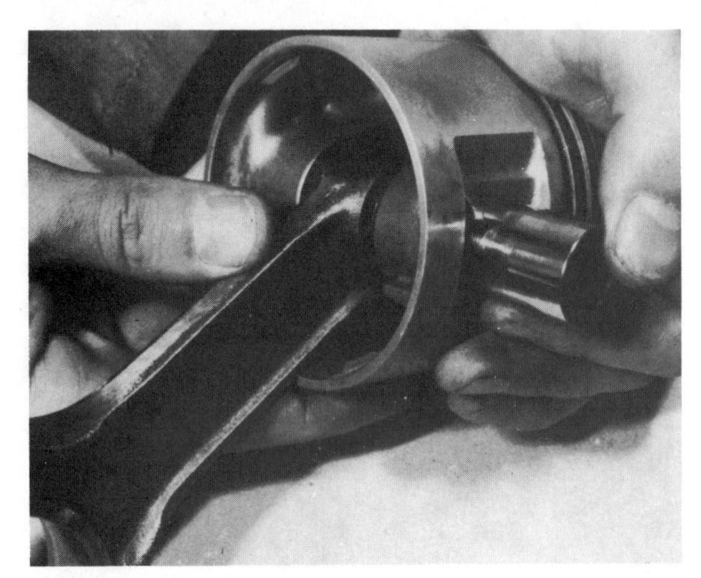

10.6B Removing the gudgeon pin

10.6C Piston/connecting rod components

11 Expand the rings with the fingers and remove them from the piston in an upward direction.
12 Clean the piston ring grooves free from carbon. A piece of broken piston ring is useful for this. Make sure that the groove oil return holes are clear.
13 The top compression ring of new ring sets should be stepped to avoid the ring contacting the wear ridge at the top of the bore. Most proprietary piston ring sets are supplied stepped.
14 Check each ring in its piston groove to see that it has the specified clearance.
15 Push each ring down the cylinder bore and check the end gap. This should be within the specified tolerance. The safest way to fit the new rings to the piston is to slide them down three old feeler blades, placed at equidistant points between the ring and the piston. Fit the oil control ring first. Some proprietary rings are of two rail and an expander type which should be fitted in accordance with the manufacturers' instructions.
16 When all the rings are fitted, stagger the end gaps at equidistant (120°) points to prevent gas blow-by.
17 When fitting new piston rings for use in the worn cylinder bores, the hard glaze in the bores should be removed using a glaze busting tool or by rubbing with fine glasspaper. Try and obtain a cross-hatched appearance. This roughening of the bores will help the new rings to bed in.
18 Oil the piston and rings liberally and fit a ring compressor (photo).
19 Fit the bearing shell into the rod recess and then insert the rod into its correct bore so that the compressor stands squarely on the top face of the cylinder block (photo).

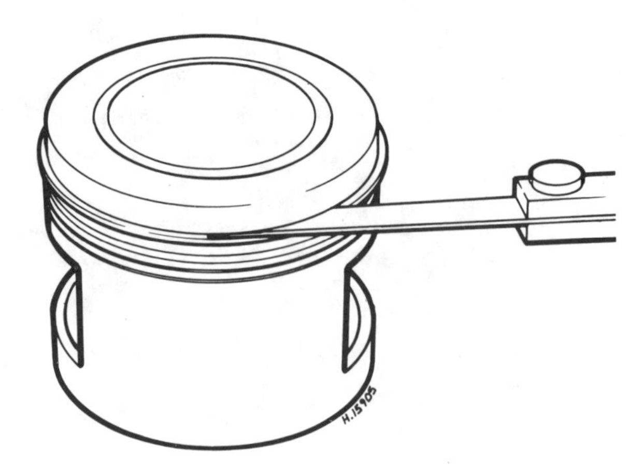

Fig. 1.16 Checking the piston ring-to-groove clearance (Sec 10)

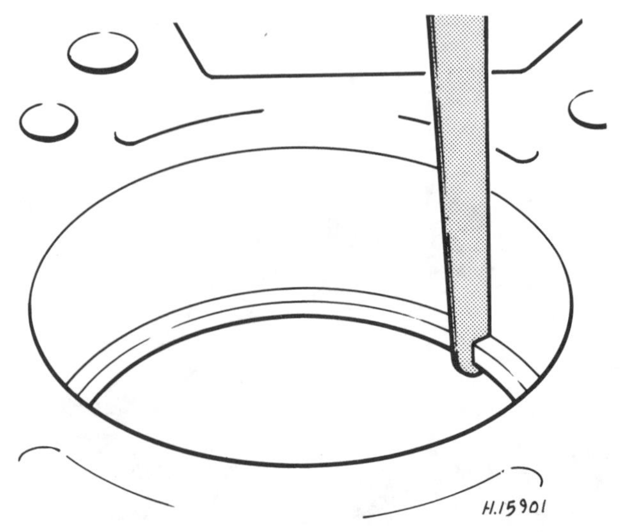

Fig. 1.17 Checking the piston ring end gap (Sec 10)

10.18 Fitting piston/rod into bore

10.19 Driving piston into cylinder bore

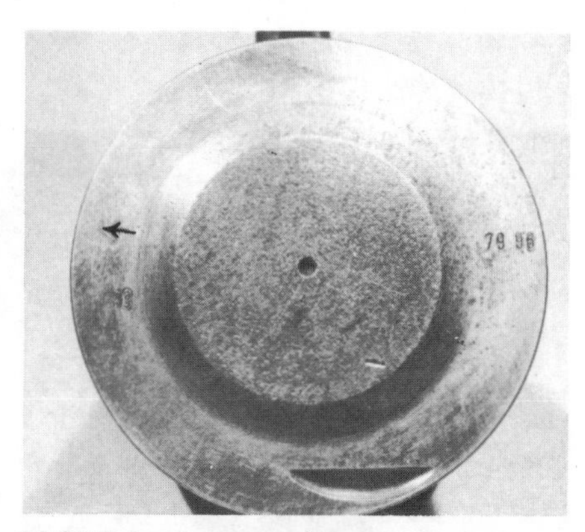
10.20 Piston crown markings

10.22A Fitting a big-end cap

10.22B Tightening a big-end cap bolt

11.5 Drawing off crankshaft damper hub

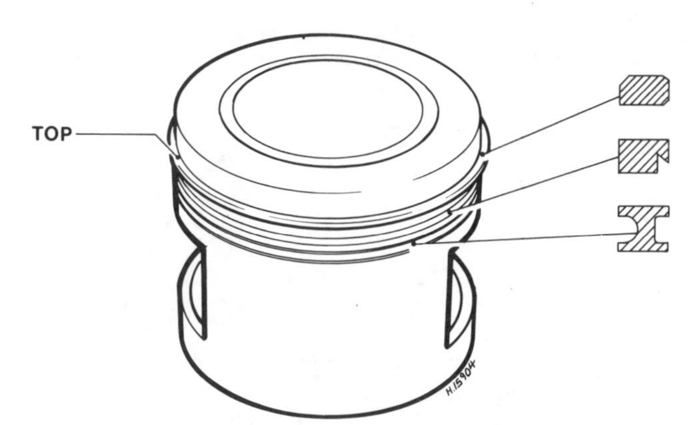

Fig. 1.18 Cross-sectional diagram of the original piston rings (Sec 10)

20 Check that the piston directional arrow is towards the timing belt (photo).
21 Place the wooden handle of a hammer on the centre of the piston crown and drive the piston downwards. The piston and rings will enter the bore and the compressor will be released. Oil the crankshaft crankpins.
22 Draw the rod down and connect it to the crankshaft. Fit the cap, complete with bearing shell, use new bolts and tighten to the specified torque (photos).
23 Fit the remaining piston/rods in a similar way.
24 Fit the sump pan and oil pump, and the cylinder head, all as described in earlier Sections.

11 Front end cover oil seals – renewal

1 Refer to Chapter 2 and remove the radiator.
2 Remove the alternator drivebelt.
3 Remove the crankshaft damper/pulley.
4 Unscrew the crankshaft damper hub bolt. To prevent the crankshaft rotating, bolt a length of flat steel bar to the damper hub bolt holes and use the bar as a lever against rotation.
5 Refit the bolt and screw it in two or three threads only. Use a puller to draw off the hub (photo).
6 Remove the timing belt, as described in Section 6.
7 Again using a puller, draw the belt sprocket from the crankshaft (photo).

11.7 Drawing off crankshaft sprocket

11.8A Intermediate shaft sprocket bolt

11.8B Intermediate shaft sprocket

11.10 Front end cover and oil seals

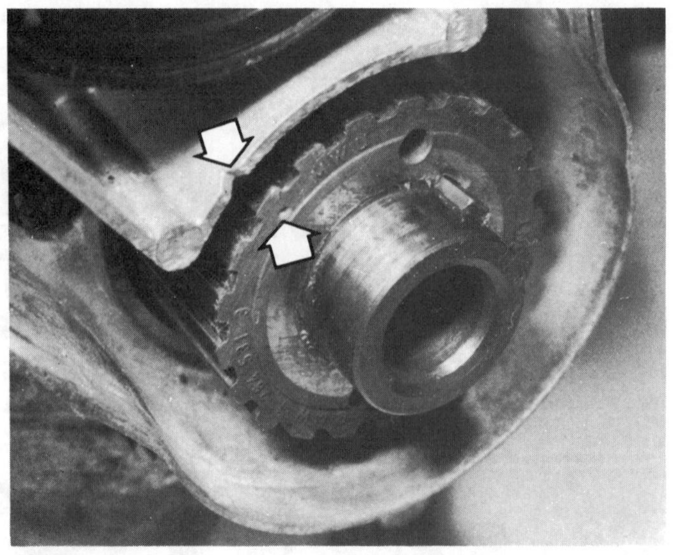

11.12 Crankshaft sprocket with tapped holes visible. Note timing marks – arrowed (No 1 piston at TDC)

8 Unscrew the intermediate shaft sprocket bolt (photo). Use a pin wrench to prevent the sprocket from turning. Remove the bolt, washer and sprocket (photo).

9 Unscrew the fixing bolts and take off the front end cover. Take care not to damage the sump pan gasket.

10 Remove the old oil seals and drive the new ones in until they are flush (photo). Fill the seal lips with grease.

11 Refitting is a reversal of removal, but note the following points.

12 When refitting the crankshaft sprocket note that the tapped holes must be visible (photo).

13 Tighten all bolts to the specified torque.

12 Camshaft oil seal – renewal

1 Refer to Section 6 and remove the timing belt.

2 Using an Allen key, unbolt and remove the adaptor on the camshaft sprocket. Unbolt the sprocket retaining plate.

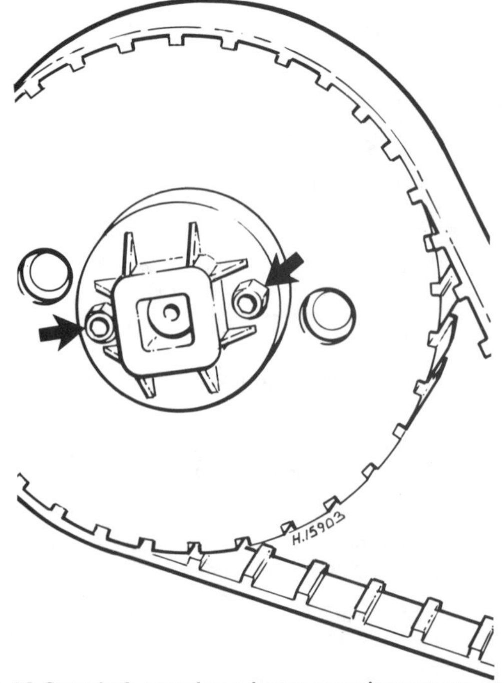

Fig. 1.19 Camshaft sprocket adaptor securing screws – arrowed (Sec 12)

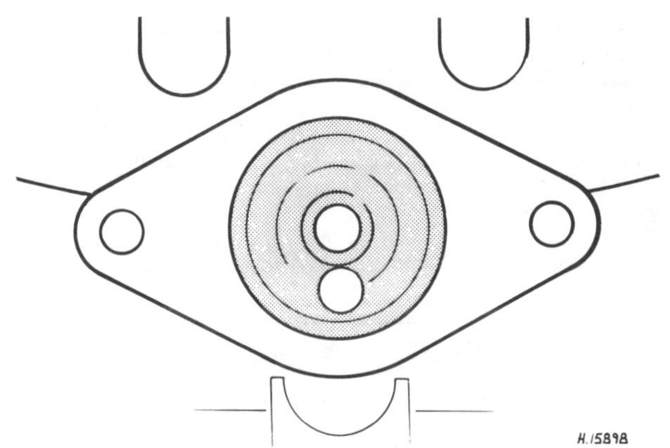

Fig. 1.20 Camshaft retainer (Sec 12)

3 Remove the camshaft sprocket.
4 Unbolt and remove the retainer and renew both the oil seal and the O-ring.
5 Fill the oil seal lips with grease and place a sleeve on the end of the camshaft so that the oil seal lips will not be damaged when the camshaft retainer is fitted.
6 Refit the components by reversing the removal operations. Refer to Section 6 for the timing belt refitting procedure.

13 Distributor driveshaft bearing – renewal

1 Refer to Chapter 4 and remove the distributor.
2 Remove the oil pump, as described in Section 9.
3 The needle roller type bearing can now be driven upwards and removed using a mandrel of suitable length and diameter.
4 Work grease into the bearing and drive it fully into its recess.
5 Refit the oil pump and the distributor.

14 Engine – method of removal

1 The engine is removed in an upward direction after first having withdrawn the gearbox or automatic transmission, as described in Chapter 6.

15 Engine – removal

1 With the transmission removed (Chapter 6), open the bonnet and support it in the open position. With the help of an assistant, remove the bonnet, as described in Chapter 12. Remove the air cleaner (Chapter 3). Drain the engine oil.
2 Drain the cooling system and remove the radiator and coolant expansion tank (Chapter 2)
3 Disconnect both battery leads.
4 On cars equipped with power steering, unbolt the pump and tie it to one side of the engine compartment. There is no need to disconnect the fluid hoses. On cars equipped with air conditioning, unbolt the compressor and tie it to one side of the engine compartment. **Do not** disconnect the refrigerant lines (see the warning in Section 1).

Carburettor engines

5 Disconnect the flexible hose from the fuel inlet hose pressure regulator and the fuel pump. Plug the hoses.
6 Disconnect the accelerator cable from the carburettor.
7 Disconnect the coolant and vacuum hoses.

Fuel injection engines

8 Remove the air intake duct.
9 Disconnect the fuel injector pipelines from the fuel distributor.
10 Disconnect the fuel flexible hoses from the fuel distributor.
11 Release the nuts and move the mixture regulator, with the air cleaner housing, upwards.
12 Disconnect the accelerator cable from the throttle valve housing, also the cruise control cable (where fitted).
13 Disconnect all the fuel system electrical plugs, identifying each for correct refitting.

All engines

14 Disconnect the coil leads and the electrical leads from all engine sensors. Pull the wiring harness plug from the fusebox (photo) and unclip the harness from the wing valance.
15 Remove the alternator, otherwise it will be obstructed by the battery mounting platform when the engine is removed.
16 Disconnect the plug from the TDC sensor.
17 Attach a hoist or other lifting gear to the engine lifting lugs which are located at the front and rear ends of the cylinder head. Just take the weight of the engine. Make sure that the lengths of the lifting chain or rope are unequal so that the engine will be inclined downward at the rear when lifted. Failure to observe this requirement will mean that the front of the engine will not clear the body top rail or the rear bulkhead.
18 Disconnect the earth strap and the left-hand engine mounting (photos).
19 Disconnect the right-hand engine mounting (photo).
20 Raise the engine and move it forward and out of the engine compartment (photo).
21 If the engine is to be renewed on an exchange basis, remember to remove all the parts from the old unit which are not supplied with the new one.

15.14 Main engine harness plug at fusebox

15.18A Engine-to-body earth strap

15.18B Left-hand engine mounting

15.19 Right-hand engine mounting

15.20 Removing engine

16 Engine – dismantling (general)

1 With the engine removed from the car, clean away external dirt using a water soluble solvent, or paraffin, and a stiff brush.
2 Ideally, the engine should be located on a bench, but if dismantling must be carried out on the floor, at least place a sheet of hardboard or plywood under it.
3 Gather together all the necessary tools, gaskets, gasket cement, grease, oil and a supply of clean rag. A torque wrench is essential.

17 Engine – complete dismantling

1 Commence dismantling by removing the ancillary items listed.

Distributor – Chapter 4
Carburettor or fuel injector air collector – Chapter 3
Fuel pump – Chapter 3
Manifolds – Chapter 3
Oil filter – Chapter 1
Clutch – Chapter 5

2 Remove the timing belt, as described in Section 6.

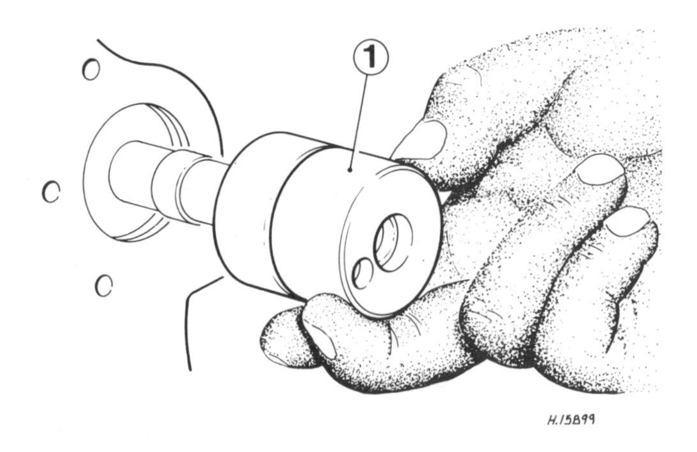

Fig. 1.21 Removing the intermediate shaft (1) (Sec 17)

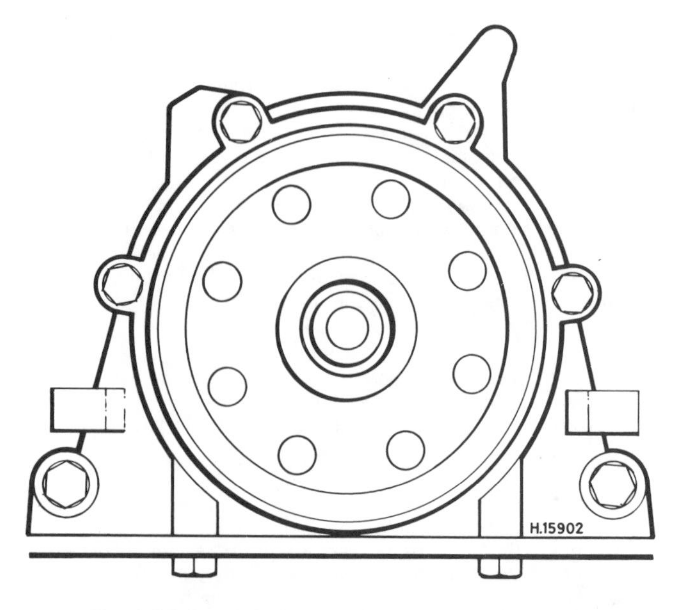

Fig. 1.22 Crankshaft rear oil seal retainer (Sec 17)

3 Remove the cylinder head, as described in Section 7.
4 Remove the sprockets and front end cover, as described in Section 11.
5 Unbolt and remove the intermediate shaft retaining plate and withdraw the shaft.
6 Jam the starter ring gear and unbolt and remove the flywheel (or driveplate – automatic transmission). New bolts must be used when refitting.
7 Remove the crankshaft rear oil seal retainer.
8 Take off the engine rear plate.
9 Move the engine onto its side and remove the sump pan.
10 Remove the oil pump and oil pressure relief valve.
11 Remove the piston/connecting rods, as described in Section 10.
12 Turn the cylinder block so that it is standing on its top face.
13 Unscrew the main bearing cap bolts and remove them.
14 Note that the main bearing caps are numbered one to seven from the timing belt end of the engine and then remove the caps. If the shells are to be used again (not recommended) tape them to their caps.
15 Lift the crankshaft from the crankcase, taking care that the crankcase bearing shells do not become mixed up if they are to be used again.

18 Cylinder head – dismantling and decarbonising

1 If the manifolds have not yet been removed, unbolt and remove them now.
2 Remove the rocker oil pipe (photo).
3 Release the cam adjuster nuts and set all valve clearances to maximum.
4 Remove the sealing plugs (photo).
5 Remove the retaining plate from the end of the rocker shafts and then extract the spring clips (photos).
6 The rocker shafts are now ready for withdrawal.
7 Turn the camshaft until the rocker arms on the exhaust side are no longer under pressure. Withdraw the rocket shaft.
8 Repeat on the inlet side.
9 The valves and their associated components should now be removed using a spring compressor.
10 Compress the first valve spring, extract the split collets. If the valve spring refuses to compress, do not apply excessive force but place a small block of wood under the valve head, remove the compressor and place a piece of tubing on the spring retainer and strike it a sharp blow to release the collets from the valve stem. Refit the compressor and resume operations – the collets should come out.
11 Gently release the compressor, take off the spring retaining cap, the valve spring and the spring seat. Remove the valve. Keep the valve with its associated components in numbered sequence so that they can be returned to their original positions. A small box with divisions is useful for this purpose.

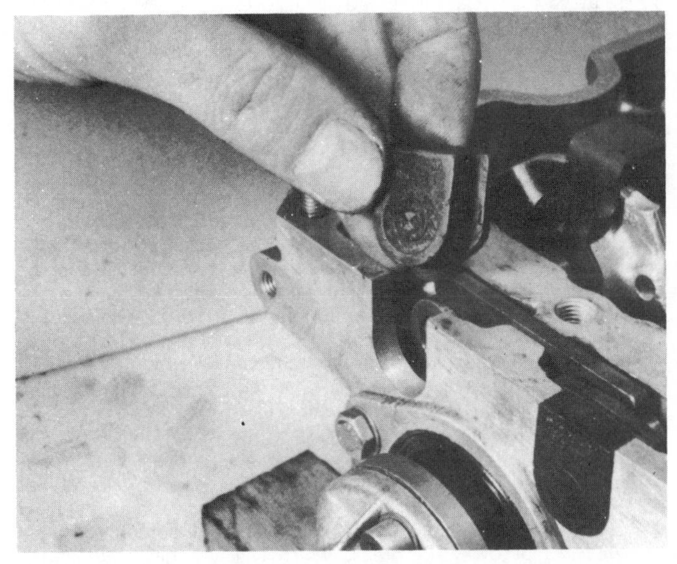
18.4 Rocker shaft sealing plugs

18.5A Removing rocker shaft retaining plate – note position of grooves (arrowed) in rocker shafts for location of plate

18.2 Rocker oil pipe

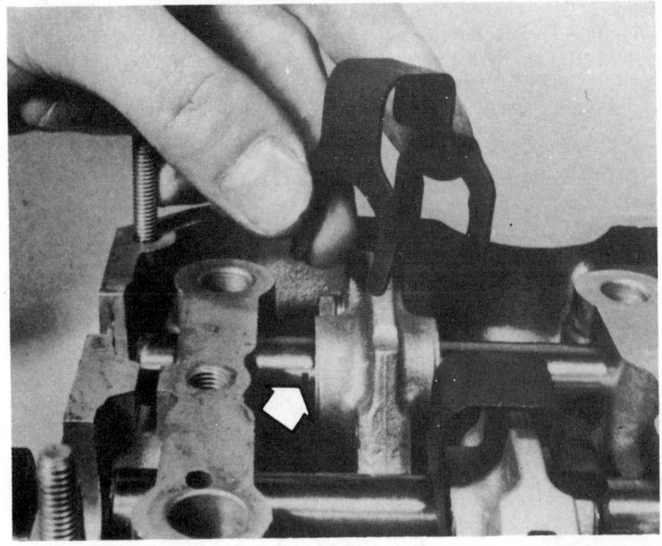
18.5B Removing rocker arm spring clip – note location groove in shaft (arrowed)

12 Remove the other valves in a similar way.
13 Bearing in mind that the cylinder head is of light alloy construction and is eaily damaged use a blunt scraper or rotary wire brush to clean all traces of carbon deposits from the combustion spaces and the ports. The valve head stems and valve guides should also be freed from any carbon deposits. Wash the combustion spaces and ports down with paraffin and scrape the cylinder head surface free of any foreign matter with the side of a steel rule, or a similar article.
14 If the engine is installed in the car, clean the pistons and the top of the cylinder bores. If the pistons are still in the block, then it is essential that great care is taken to ensure that no carbon gets into the cylinder bores as this could scratch the cylinder walls or cause damage to the piston and rings. To ensure this does not happen, first turn the crankshaft so that two of the pistons are at the top of their bores. Stuff rag into the other four bores or seal them off with paper and masking tape. The waterways should also be covered with small pieces of masking tape to prevent particles of carbon entering the cooling system and damaging the coolant pump.
15 Press a little grease into the gap between the cylinder walls and the two pistons which are to be worked on. With a blunt scraper carefully scrape away the carbon from the piston crown, taking great care not to scratch the aluminium. Also scrape away the carbon from the surrounding lip of the cylinder wall. When all carbon has been removed, scrape away the grease which will now be contaminated with carbon particles, taking care not to press any into the bores. To assist prevention of carbon build-up the piston crown can be polished with a metal polish. Remove the rags/masking tape and turn the crankshaft until two other pistons are at the top of the bore. Repeat the decarbonising process on these and the remaining pistons.

Valve grinding

16 Examine the head of the valves for pitting and burning, especially the heads of the exhaust valves. The valve seatings should be examined at the same time. If the pitting on the valve and seat is very slight, the marks can be removed by grinding the seats and valves together with coarse, and then fine, valve grinding paste.
17 Where bad pitting has occurred to the valve seats it will be necessary to recut them and fit new valves. This latter job should be entrusted to the local agent or engineering works. In practice it is very seldom that the seats are so badly worn. Normally it is the valve that is too badly worn for refitting, and the owner can easily purchase a new set of valves and match them to the seats by valve grinding.
18 Valve grinding is carried out as follows. Smear a trace of coarse carborundum paste on the seat face and apply a suction grinder tool to the valve head. With a semi-rotary motion, grind the valve head to its seat, lifting the valve occasionally to redistribute the grinding paste. When a dull matt even surface is produced on both the valve seat and the valve, wipe off the paste and repeat the process with fine carborundum paste, lifting and turning the valve to redistribute the paste as before. A light spring placed under the valve head will greatly ease this operation. When a smooth unbroken ring of light grey matt finish is produced, on both valve and valve seat faces, the grinding operation is complete. Carefully clean away every trace of grinding compound, take great care to leave none in the ports or in the valve guides. Clean the valves and valve seats with a paraffin soaked rag, then with a clean rag, and finally, if an air line is available, blow the valves, valve guides and valve ports clean.
19 Check that all valve springs are intact. If any one is broken, all should be renewed. Check the free height of the springs against new ones. If some springs are not within specifications, replace them all. Springs suffer from fatigue and it is a good idea to renew them even if they look serviceable.

Valve guides

20 Test the valves in their guides for side-to-side rock. If this is any more than almost imperceptible, new guides must be fitted. This is a job for your dealer as the guide and its fitting bore must be reamed and a special tool is required to locate the guide at its correct depth.

Cylinder head distortion

21 If there has been a history of leakage at the head gasket, the gasket face of the cylinder head can be checked for distortion by placing it on a sheet of plate glass or by using a straight-edge and feeler gauges. The head can be surface ground by an engine reconditioner to restore its flatness. **Note:** the original cylinder head thickness (125.0 to 125.2 mm/4.921 to 4.929 in) must not be reduced by more than 0.3 mm (0.012 in).

Camshaft

22 The camshaft can be withdrawn from the cylinder head after the adaptor, sprocket and retainer have been unbolted and removed.
23 Inspect the journals for wear or scoring. Unless they are in perfect condition, renew the shaft. The cam lobes should also be in top condition without any sign of scoring or erosion. If renovation is required it may be possible to have the shaft reprofiled. No provision is made for repair of the bearings in the cylinder head, they are machined directly into the head.

Rocker arms and shaft

24 Examine the rocker arms for loose, scored or worn pads. Where evident renew the arm(s).
25 The shafts should show no sign of scoring or wear, if they do, renew them. The shaft bearings are machined directly into the cylinder head.

Valve stem oil seals

26 Always renew these before reassembling the cylinder head. The seals can be pressed onto the valve guides using a piece of plastic tubing of suitable diameter (photo).

18.26 Valve stem oil seal (arrowed)

18.27 Inserting a valve

Reassembly

27 Commence reassembly by oiling the stem of the first valve and pushing it into its guide (photo).

28 Fit the spring seat, the valve spring (closer coils with paint mark towards the cylinder head) and the spring retainer (photos).

29 Fit the spring compressor, compress the spring until the split collets can be slipped into the valve stem cut-outs (photo).

30 Gently release the compressor, checking to see that the collets are not displaced.

31 Fit the remaining valves in a similar way and in their original sequence.

32 Lightly tap the end of each valve stem with a plastic or copper-faced hammer to settle the components.

33 Lubricate the camshaft bearings and insert the camshaft into the cylinder head (photo).

34 Fit the camshaft retainer, sprocket and adaptor (photo).

35 Fit the rocker shafts, passing them through the holes in the rocker arms as they are pushed into position (photo). Make sure that the large holes in the shafts are towards the valve guides and the grooves which accept the retaining plate are towards each other. Fit the retaining plate.

36 Fit the spring clips (photo).

37 If new rocker arms have been fitted, note the correct assembly of the cam adjuster. The setscrew has a flat on its head to lock against a cut-out on the rocker arm.

38 The manifolds can be bolted on now, using new gaskets, or left until the cylinder head is refitted.

39 If the thermostat housing was removed, bolt it on using new gaskets (photo).

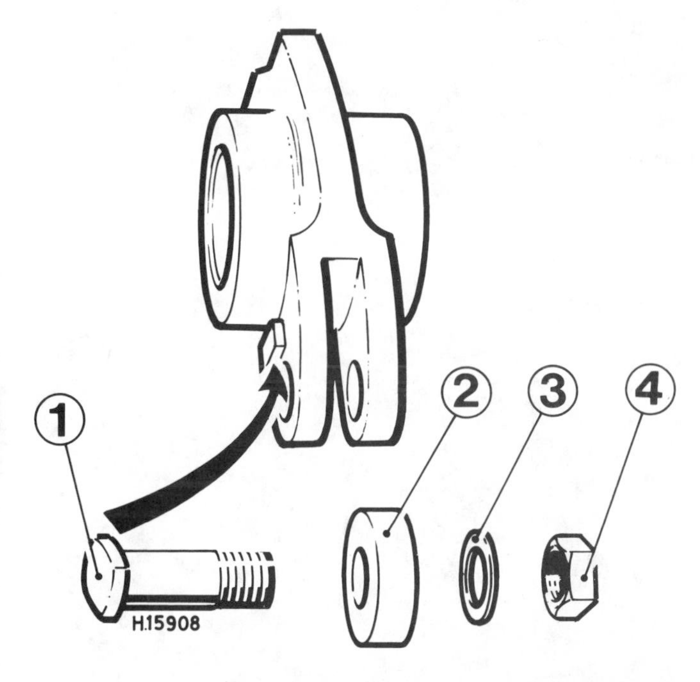

Fig. 1.23 Rocker arm components (Sec 18)

1 Setscrew (note flat on head)
2 Eccentric
3 Washer
4 Nut

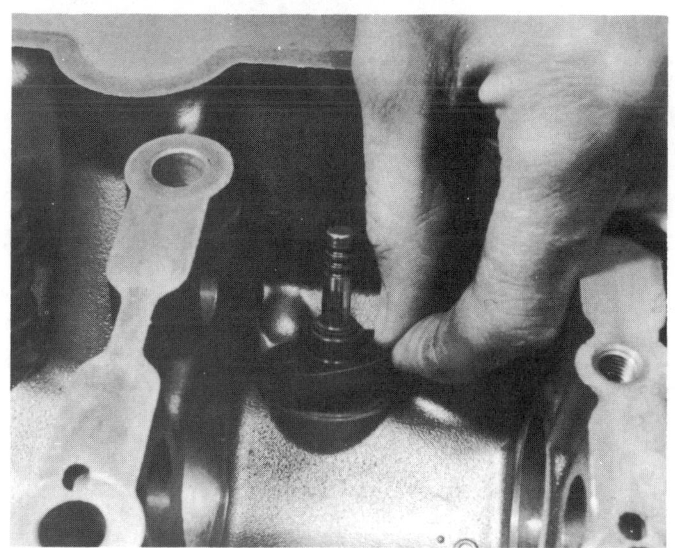

18.28A Spring seat

18.28B Valve spring

18.28C Valve spring retainer

18.29 Compressing a valve spring

18.33 Fitting the camshaft

18.34 Camshaft retainer

18.35 Fitting a rocker arm

18.36 Rocker arm clip fitted

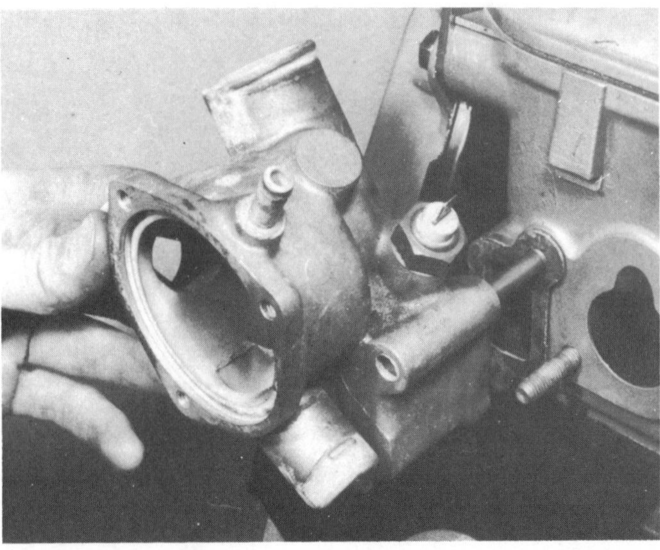
18.39 Thermostat housing

19 Examination and renovation

Cylinder block and crankcase

1 Examine the casting carefully for cracks, especially around the bolt holes and between cylinders.

2 The cylinder bores must be checked for taper, ovality (out-of-round), scoring and scratching. Start by examining the top of the cylinder bores. If they are at all worn, a ridge will be felt on the thrust side. This ridge marks the limit of piston ring travel. The owner will have a good indication of bore wear prior to dismantling by the quantity of oil consumed and the emission of blue smoke from the exhaust, especially when the engine is cold.

3 An internal micrometer or dial gauge can be used to check bore wear and taper against the Specifications, but this is a pointless operation if the engine is obviously in need of reboring due to excessive oil consumption.

4 Your engine reconditioner will be able to rebore the block for you and supply the correct oversize pistons to give the specified running clearance.

5 If the engine has reached the limit for reboring then cylinder liners can be fitted, but here again this is a job for your engine reconditioner.

6 To rectify minor bore wear it is possible to fit proprietary oil control rings, as described in Section 10. A good way to test the condition of the engine is to have it at normal operating temperature with the spark plugs removed. On cars with transistorized ignition, pull the plug from the control unit. Screw a compression tester (available from most motor accessory stores) into the first plug hole. Hold the accelerator fully depressed and crank the engine on the starter motor for several revolutions. Record the reading. Zero the tester and check the remaining cylinders in the same way. All six compression figures should be approximately equal and within the tolerance given in the Specifications. If they are all low, suspect piston ring or cylinder bore wear. If only one reading is down, suspect a valve not seating.

Crankshaft and bearings

7 Examine the surfaces of the crankpins and journals for signs of scoring or scratching and check for ovality or taper (photo). If the crankpin or journals are not within the dimensional tolerances given in the Specifications then the crankshaft will have to be reground.

8 Wear in a crankshaft can be detected while the engine is running. Big-end bearing and crankpin wear is indicated by distinct metallic knocking, particularly noticeable when the engine is pulling from low engine speeds. Low oil pressure will also occur.

9 Main bearing and journal wear is indicated by engine rumble increasing in severity as the engine speed increases. Low oil pressure will again be an associated condition.

10 Due to the fact that the crankshaft has a special surface treatment, grinding and the supply of matching shells should only be carried out by BMW. The service is carried out through their dealers.

11 Inspect the connecting rod big-end and main bearing shells for signs of general wear, scoring, pitting and scratching. The bearings should be matt grey in colour. If a copper colour is evident, then the bearings are badly worn and the surface material has worn away to expose the underlay. Renew the bearing shells as a complete set.

12 At time of major overhaul it is worthwhile renewing the bearing shells as a matter of routine even if they appear to be in reasonably good condition. Bearing shells can be identified by the marking on the back of the shell. Standard sized shells are usually marked STD or 0.00. Undersized shells are marked with the undersize, such as 0.25 mm.

13 Finally check the clutch pilot bearing in the rear end of the crankshaft. If it is worn it will have to be renewed. The bearing has associated components and a special tool will be required to extract them with the bearing. When the new bearing has been fitted, pack it with 1 gram (0.04 oz) of multi-purpose grease. When fitting the cover, make sure that it has the domed side facing out.

Connecting rods

14 Check the alignment of the connecting rods visually. If you suspect distortion, have them checked by your dealer or engine reconditioner on the special jig which he will have.

Pistons and piston rings

15 If the engine has been rebored then new oversize pistons with rings and gudgeon pins will be supplied.

16 Removal and fitting of piston rings is covered in Section 10.

Flywheel

17 Check the clutch mating surface of the flywheel. If it is deeply scored (due to failure to renew a worn driven plate) then it may be possible to have its surface ground provided the thickness of the flywheel is not reduced below the specified minimum.

18 If lots of tiny cracks are visible on the surface of the flywheel then this will be due to overheating caused by slipping of the clutch or by riding the clutch pedal.

19 With a pre-engaged type of starter motor it is rare to find the teeth of the flywheel ring gear damaged or worn, but if they are the ring gear will have to be renewed.

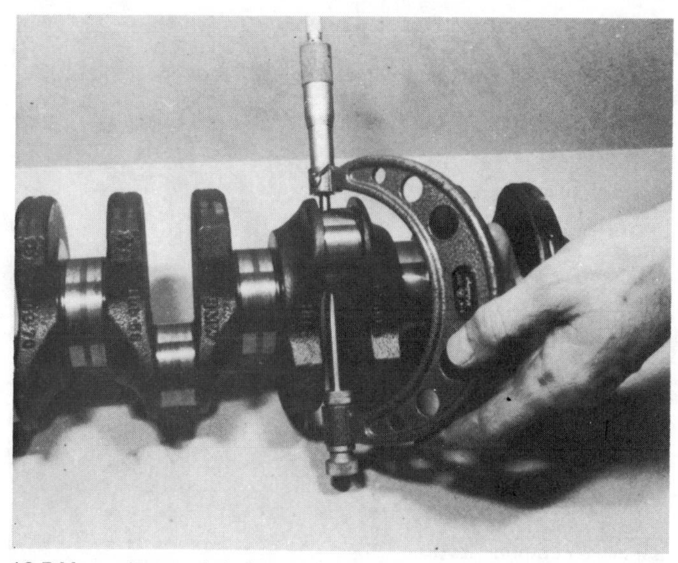

19.7 Measuring crankshaft wear

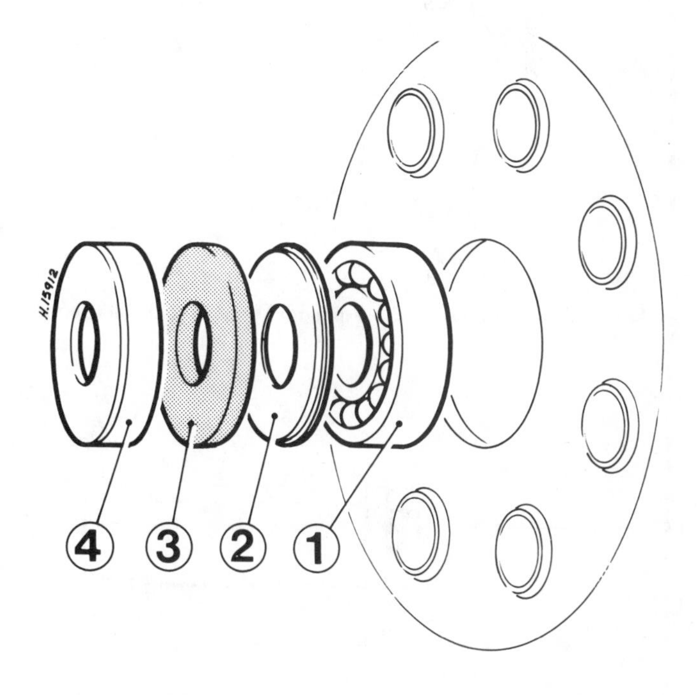

Fig. 1.24 Crankshaft clutch pilot bearing and associated components (Sec 19)

1 Bearing
2 Cover
3 Felt ring
4 Spacer

20 To remove the ring gear, drill a hole between the roots of two teeth, taking care not to damage the flywheel, and then split the ring with a sharp cold chisel.
21 The new ring gear must be heated to between 180 and 220°C (356 and 428°F) which is very hot, so if you do not have facilities for obtaining these temperatures, leave the job to your dealer or engine reconditioner. Tap the ring gear into position – chamfered side leading.

Driveplate (automatic transmission)

22 The driveplate is unusual in being separate from the starter ring gear which is an integral part of a lightweight flywheel. Renewal of the starter ring gear will necessitate renewing the flywheel.

Timing belt and tensioner

23 Examine the belt for cracking or fraying and tooth wear. If any of these conditions is evident or if the belt has been in service for near the renewal interval (see Routine Maintenance) it is recommended that it is renewed.
24 The tensioner should not be noisy or shaky when turned and have good spring action. Where these conditions are not met with, renew the tensioner complete.

Intermediate shaft

25 Inspect the condition of the shaft journals. If they are worn or scored, renew the shaft.
26 If the shaft gear teeth are worn or chipped, renew the shaft.
27 If there is excessive endfloat in the shaft, renewing the retainer plate may eliminate the problem. The shaft bearings are renewable and may be drawn out using a suitable distance piece, studding and nuts. When fitting the new bearings, make sure that the oil holes align correctly.

Oil pump and relief valve

28 Remove the pump cover and check the gears and housing for wear or scoring (photo).
29 Using feeler gauges check the following clearances.

Gear tooth to body (photo)
Gear backlash (photo)
Gear endfloat using a dial gauge or straight-edge across the top of the pump body (photo).

30 If any of the clearances are outside the specified tolerance, renew the worn components.
31 At major overhaul, remove the oil pressure relief valve which is mounted separately in the crankcase. Unscrew the valve, take off the outer sleeve, unscrew the plug and extract the spring and piston.
32 To remove the oil pressure relief valve which is located in the oil pump, depress the stop plate, extract the circlip and withdraw the stop plate, spring and piston (photo).
33 With both types of valve the length of the spring is important. If it is compressed below the specified free length, renew it; **never** attempt to stretch it.

Oil seals and gaskets

34 It is recommended that all gaskets and oil seals are renewed at major engine overhaul. Sockets are useful for removing or refitting oil seals. An arrow is moulded onto some of the seals to indicate the rotational direction of the component which it serves. Make sure that the seal is fitted the correct way round to comply with the arrow.

Cylinder head

35 This is covered in Section 18 during dismantling and decarbonising.

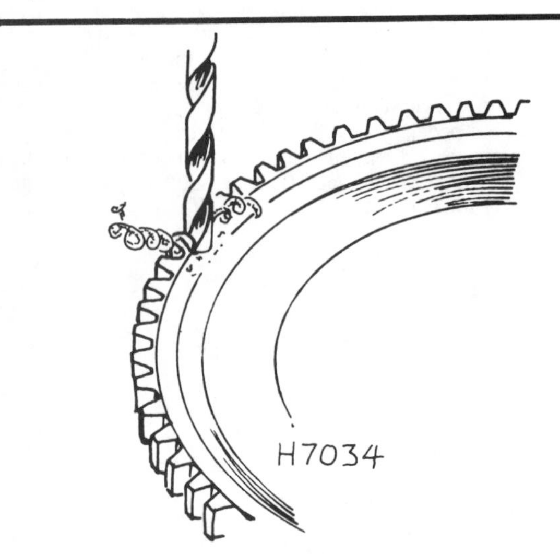

Fig. 1.25 Drilling the flywheel ring gear prior to removal (Sec 19)

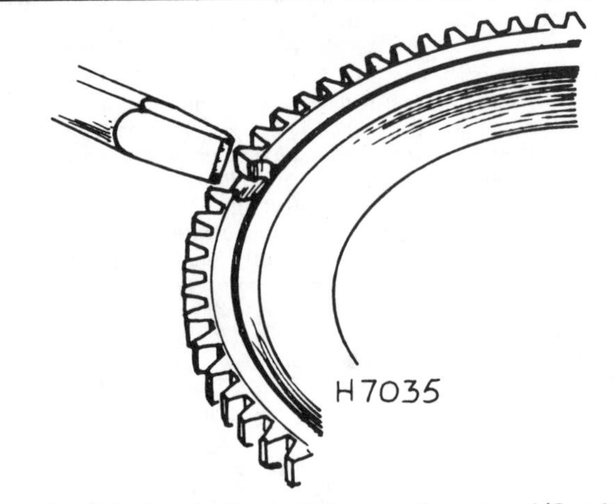

Fig. 1.26 Splitting the flywheel ring gear for removal (Sec 19)

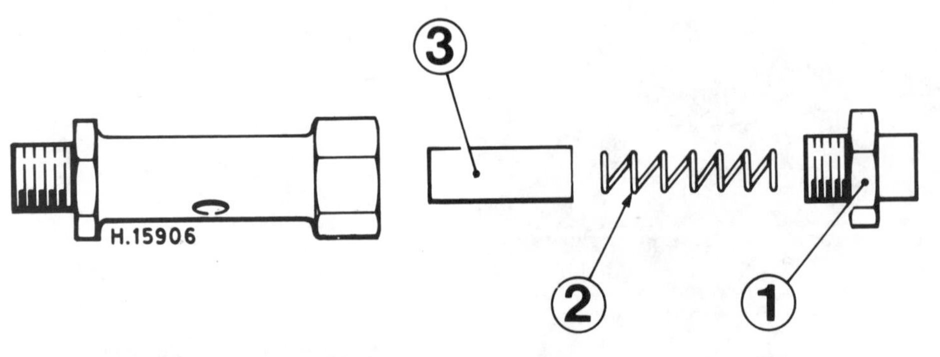

Fig. 1.27 Crankcase oil pressure relief valve components (Sec 19)

1 Plug *2 Spring* *3 Piston*

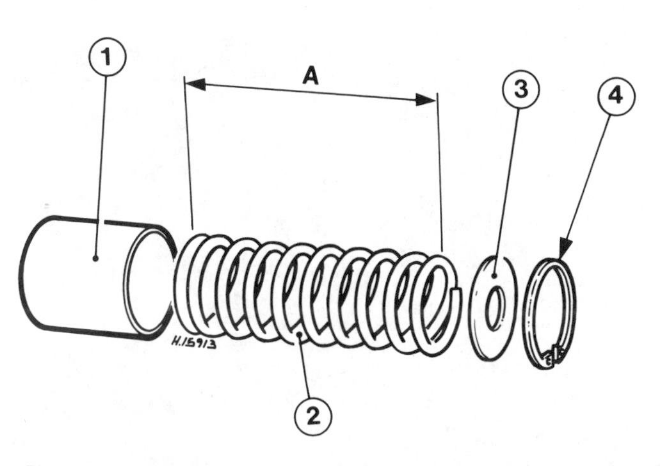

Fig. 1.28 Oil pump pressure relief valve components (Sec 19)

1 Piston
2 Spring
3 Stop plate
4 Circlip
A Spring free length

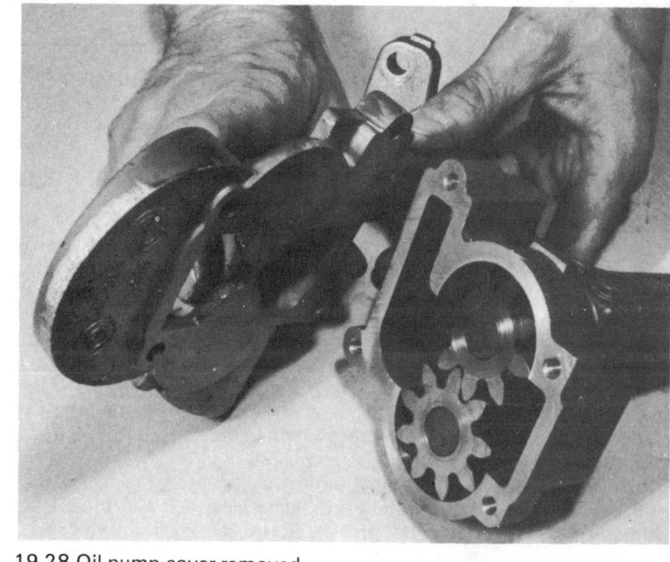
19.28 Oil pump cover removed

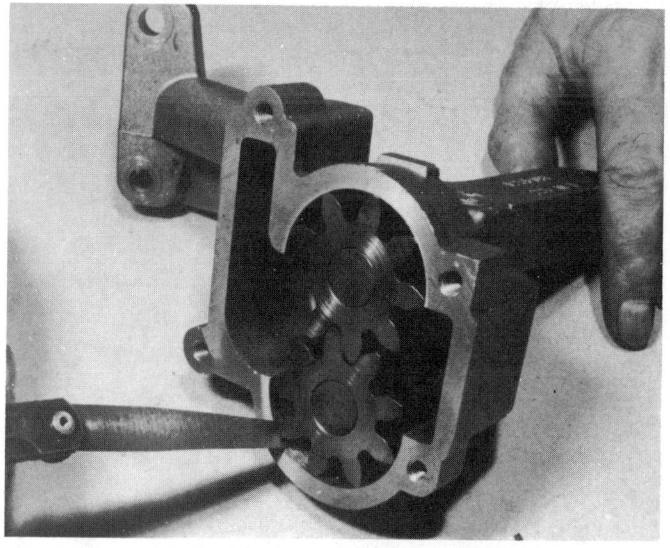
19.29A Measuring oil pump gear teeth-to-body clearance

19.29B Measuring oil pump gear backlash

19.29C Checking oil pump gear endfloat

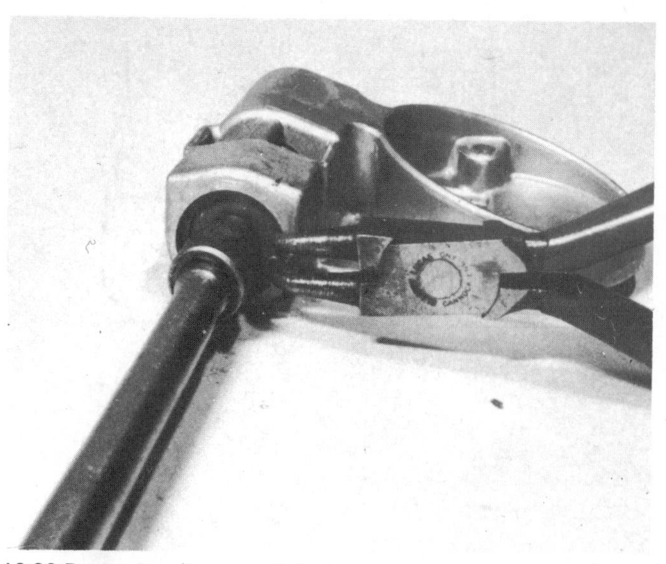
19.32 Depressing oil pump relief valve stop plate and extracting circlip

20 Engine – reassembly

1 During reassembly, observe absolute cleanliness and apply engine oil as each component is fitted. Tighten all fixing nuts and bolts to the specified torque.

2 Clean the crankcase recesses and locate the main bearing shells so that the oil holes are correctly aligned (photo). The shell which incorporates the thrust flanges is located in No 6 position, counting from the timing belt end of the engine.

3 Oil the shells and lower the crankshaft into position (photo).

4 Wipe out the bearing recesses in the main bearing caps and fit the shells (photo). Make sure that the notch in the shell will coincide with the one in its opposite half shell when the cap is fitted.

5 The main bearing caps are numbered 1 to 7 from the timing belt end of the engine. Fit them so that the shell notches coincide. Screw in the bolts and tighten to torque (photos).

6 Check the crankshaft endfloat using a dial gauge, or feeler blades inserted between a main bearing machined side face and the crank web (photo). Push the crankshaft fully in one direction and then the other in order to measure the complete endfloat. If excessive, then the problem will be with the shell bearing thrust flanges.

7 Fit the piston/connecting rods as described in Section 10. Turn the crankshaft to check that it turns smoothly.

8 Refit the oil pump (Section 9) and the pressure relief valve.

9 Fit the sump pan (Section 8).

10 Fit the engine rear plate.

11 Bolt on the crankshaft rear bearing retainer complete with new oil seal (photo). Use a new flange gasket.

12 Fit the flywheel or driveplate (automatic transmission) (photos). Use new bolts and apply thread locking fluid to them. Take care not to get any fluid under the bolt heads as it can give rise to noise at certain speeds. The flywheel has a locating dowel.

13 Fit the intermediate shaft and bolt on its retainer plate (photos).

14 Fit the front end cover using a new gasket (photo).

15 Fit the intermediate shaft sprocket, making sure that the dowel pin engages correctly.

16 Fit the belt sprocket to the crankshaft and then bolt on the damper hub. Turn the crankshaft until the mark on the hub is in alignment with the one on the front cover (No 1 piston at TDC).

17 If not already fitted, bolt on the camshaft sprocket, followed by the adaptor. Turn the camshaft until the arrow on the sprocket is aligned with the mark on the cylinder head (photo). This is important to prevent the valves impinging on the cylinder head when the cylinder head is fitted. This should now be done, as described in Section 7.

18 Refit and tension the timing belt, as described in Section 6.

19 Reconnect the ancillary components, including the mounting brackets if removed (photo).

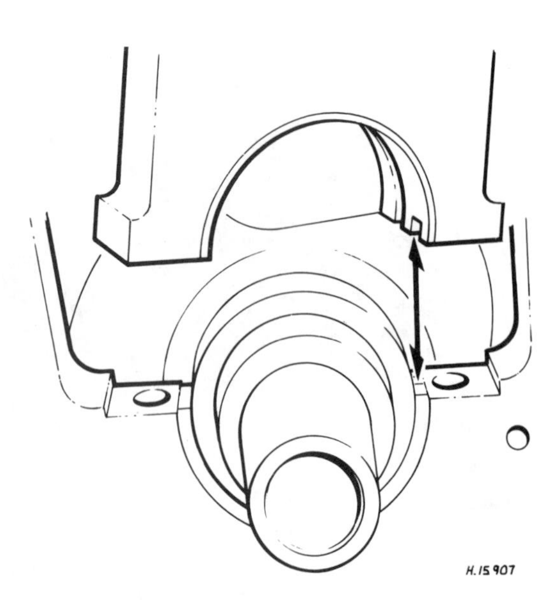

Fig. 1.29 Main bearing shell notch alignment (Sec 20)

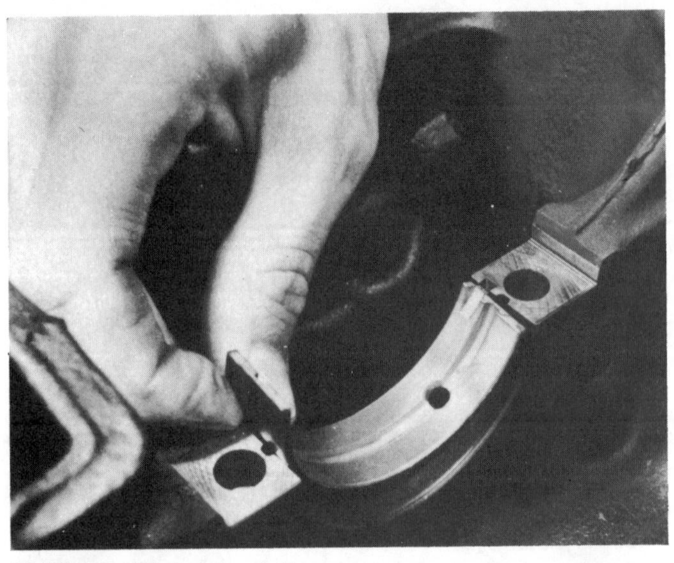

20.2 Fitting main bearing shell

20.3 Lowering crankshaft into position

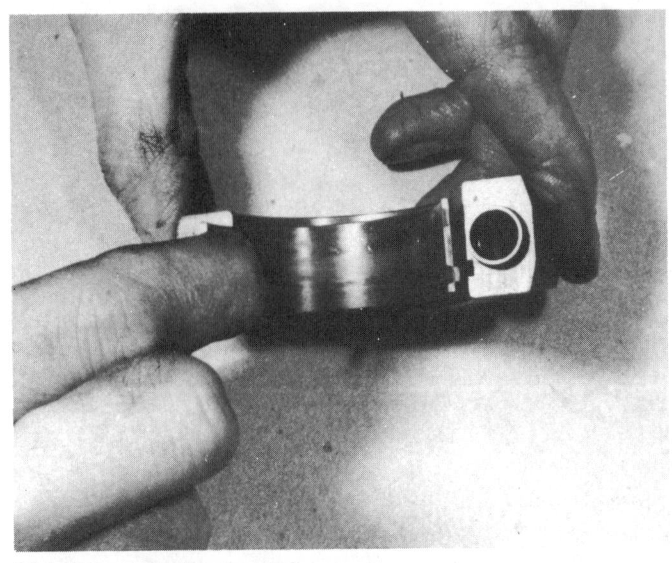

20.4 Fitting a cap bearing shell

20.5A Fitting a main bearing cap

20.5B Tightening main bearing cap bolt

20.6 Checking crankshaft endfloat

20.11 Crankshaft rear oil seal and bearing retainer

20.12A Flywheel mounting flange locating dowel (arrowed)

20.12B Fitting flywheel

20.12C Tightening flywheel bolt

20.13A Inserting intermediate shaft

20.13B Intermediate shaft retaining plate

20.14 Front end cover

20.17 Camshaft sprocket alignment marks (arrowed)

20.19 Engine mounting bracket

21 Engine – refitting

1 Connect lifting gear to the engine.
2 Lower it carefully into the engine compartment.
3 Connect the engine mountings and the earthing straps (photos).
4 Remove the lifting gear.
5 Reconnect the TDC sensor plug.
6 Reconnect the coil leads and electrical sensor leads, the starter leads and fusebox plug (photo).
7 Reconnect all coolant and vacuum hoses (photos).

Carburettor engines

8 Reconnect and adjust the accelerator cable (Chapter 3).
9 Reconnect the fuel hoses to the fuel pump and regulator (photos).

Fuel injection engines

10 Reconnect all the fuel system electrical plugs.
11 Reconnect the accelerator and cruise control cable (where fitted).
12 Refit the mixture regulator and air cleaner housing. Reconnect the exhaust downpipe.
13 Reconnect the hoses to the fuel distributor, also the fuel injector pipelines.
14 Refit the air intake duct.

All models

15 On cars equipped with air conditioning, reconnect the compressor and tension the drivebelt (Chapter 2).
16 Reconnect the steering pump on cars equipped with power-assisted steering.
17 Refit the radiator and expansion tank (photo).
18 Reconnect the coolant temperature switch leads (photo).
19 Fit the air cleaner (Chapter 3).
20 Fit the bonnet lid (Chapter 12).
21 Fit the gearbox or automatic transmission, as described in Chapter 6.
22 Fill the engine with oil.
23 Fill the cooling system (Chapter 2).
24 Reconnect the battery.

22 Initial start-up after major overhaul

1 Make sure the battery is fully charged and that all lubricants, coolant and fuel are replenished.
2 If the fuel system has been dismantled it will require several revolutions of the engine on the starter motor to pump the petrol up.
3 As soon as the engine fires and runs, keep it going at a fast tickover only (no faster), and bring it up to the normal working temperature.

21.3A Engine mounting connected

21.6A Oil pressure switch (arrowed) and cable routing

21.3B Earth strap at alternator mounting bracket

21.6B Sensor leads

21.6C Starter motor leads

21.7A Cylinder block hose connection

21.7B Hose connection at cylinder head rear adaptor

21.7C Intake manifold hose connection

21.9A Fuel pump

21.9B Fuel pressure regulator

21.17 Refitting the radiator

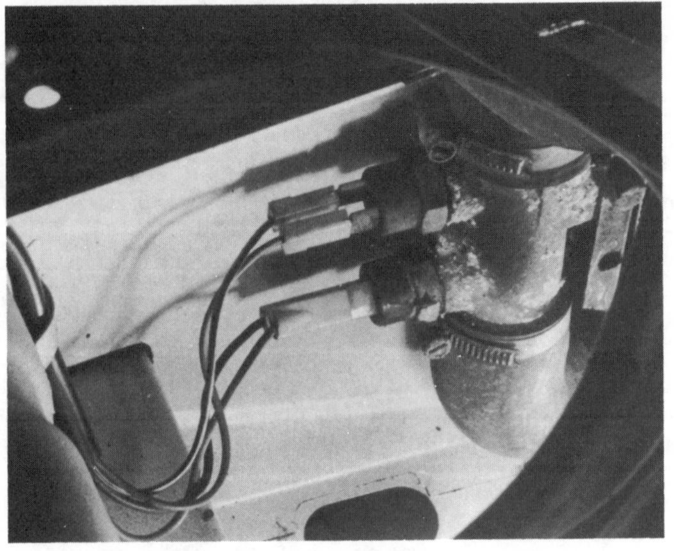

21.18 Coolant temperature switch leads

4 As the engine warms up there will be odd smells and some smoke from parts getting hot and burning off oil deposits. The signs to look for are leaks of water or oil which will be obvious if serious. Check also the exhaust pipe and manifold connections, as these do not always 'find' their exact gastight position until the warmth and vibration have acted on them, and it is almost certain that they will need tightening further. This should be done, of course, with the engine stopped.

5 When normal running temperature has been reached, adjust the engine idling speed, as described in Chapter 3 and the ignition settings (Chapter 4).

6 Stop the engine and wait a few minutes to see if any lubricant or coolant is dripping out when the engine is stationary.

7 Road test the car to check that the timing is correct and that the engine is giving the necessary smoothness and power. Do not race the engine – if new bearings and/or pistons have been fitted it should be treated as a new engine and run in at a reduced speed for the first 500 miles (800 km).

8 On cars built before September 1981, the cylinder head bolts should be tightened after the first 1200 miles (2000 km) as described in Section 7.

23 Fault diagnosis – engine

Symptom	Reason(s)
Engine fails to turn when starter control operated	
No current at starter motor	Flat or defective battery Loose battery leads Defective starter solenoid or switch or broken wiring Engine earth strap disconnected
Current at starter motor	Jammed starter motor drive pinion Defective starter motor
Engine turns but will not start	
No spark at spark plug	Ignition leads or distributor cap damp or wet Ignition leads to spark plugs loose Shorted or disconnected low tension leads Dirty, incorrectly set, or pitted contact breaker points (early models) Faulty condenser (early models) Defective ignition switch Ignition leads connected wrong way round Faulty coil (early models) Contact breaker point spring earthed or broken (early models)
No fuel at carburettor float chamber or at jets	No petrol in petrol tank Vapour lock in fuel line (in hot conditions or at high altitude) Blocked float chamber needle valve Fuel pump filter blocked Choked or blocked carburettor jets Faulty fuel pump
Engine stalls and will not restart	
Excess of petrol in cylinder or carburettor flooding	Too much choke allowing too rich a mixture or wet plugs Float damaged or leaking or needle not seating Float lever incorrectly adjusted
No spark at spark plug	Ignition failure – sudden Ignition failure – misfiring precedes total stoppage Ignition failure – in severe rain or after traversing water splash

Symptom	Reason(s)
No fuel at jets	No petrol in petrol tank Petrol tank breather choked Sudden obstruction in carburettor Water in fuel system
Engine misfires or idles unevenly	
Intermittent spark at spark plug	Ignition leads loose Battery leads loose on terminals Battery earth strap loose on body attachment point Engine earth lead loose Low tension leads on coil loose Low tension lead to distributor loose Dirty, or incorrectly set, or pitted contact breaker points (early models) Tracking across inside of distributor cover Ignition too retarded Faulty coil (early models) Slack timing belt
Fuel shortage at engine	Mixture too weak Air leak in carburettor Air leak at inlet manifold to cylinder head, or inlet manifold to carburettor
Lack of power and poor compression	
Mechanical wear	Burnt out valves Sticking or leaking valves Weak or broken valve springs Worn valve guides or stems Worn pistons and piston rings
Fuel/air mixture leaking from cylinder	Burnt out exhaust valves Sticking or leaking valves Worn valve guides and stems Weak or broken valve springs Blown cylinder head gasket (accompanied by increase in noise) Worn pistons and piston rings Worn or scored cylinder bores
Incorrect adjustments	Ignition timing wrongly set Contact breaker points incorrectly gapped (early models) Incorrectly set spark plugs Carburation too rich or too weak
Carburation and ignition faults	Dirty contact breaker points (early models) Fuel filter blocked Air cleaner blocked Distributor automatic advance and retard mechanisms not functioning correctly Faulty fuel pump giving top end fuel starvation
Excessive oil consumption	Excessively worn valve stems and valve guides Worn piston rings Worn pistons and cylinder bores Excessive piston ring gap allowing blow-by Piston oil return holes choked
Oil being lost due to leaks	Leaking oil filter gasket Leaking rocker cover gasket Leaking sump gasket Loose sump plug
Unusual noises from engine	
Excessive clearances due to mechanical wear	Worn valve gear (noisy tapping from rocker box) Worn big-end bearings (regular heavy knocking) Worn main bearings (rumbling and vibration) Worn crankshaft (knocking, rumbling and vibration)
Pinking on acceleration	Fuel octane rating too low Ignition timing over-advanced Carbon build-up in cylinder head Ignition timing incorrect Mixture too weak Overheating

Engine faults due to a malfunction in the fuel injection system are listed in Fault Diagnosis, Chapter 3

Chapter 2 Cooling, heating and air conditioning

For modifications, and information applicable to later models, see Supplement at end of manual

Contents

Specifications

General

System type	Front mounted radiator with expansion tank, belt-driven coolant pump and viscous fan
Expansion tank cap:	
Pressure relief valve opens	1.0 bar (14.2 lbf/in^2)
Vacuum valve opens	0.9 bar (12.8 lbf/in^2)
Thermostat opens	80°C (176°F)
Viscous fan:	
Type	Behr (to 1980) or Holset (1981 on)
Switch-on temperature (maximum speed)	72 to 80°C (162 to 176°F) – 2300 to 2500 rpm
Switch-off temperature (maximum speed)	65 to 70°C (149 to 158°F) – 800 rpm
Coolant capacity:	
Without air conditioner	10.5 litre (18.5 Imp pts)
With air conditioner	11.0 litre (19.4 Imp pts)
Antifreeze type	BMW approved antifreeze (Duckhams Universal Antifreeze and Summer Coolant)

Torque wrench settings

Torque wrench settings	Nm	lbf ft
Coolant pump mounting bolts	22	16
Drivebelt pulley bolts	9	7
Temperature sensor	26	19
Fluid cooler pipe unions (automatic transmission):		
At radiator	14	10
At transmission	40	30
Air conditioner:		
Compressor oil plug	16	12
Compressor mounting bolts:		
M8	23	17
M10	46	34
Pipe connections:		
$\frac{3}{4}$	38	28
$\frac{7}{8}$	40	30
$\frac{11}{16}$	46	34
Safety switch		
High pressure	24	18
Low pressure	17	13

1 General description

The cooling system is composed of a front-mounted radiator with a viscous coupling or electrically-driven fan, or both, a belt-driven coolant pump and a remotely-sited expansion tank (photo).

The system is of the semi-sealed or no-loss type in which any coolant displaced from the radiator due to expansion as the engine warms up is retained in the expansion tank and drawn back into the system when the engine cools.

A thermostat is fitted into the system to reduce coolant circulation during engine warm-up.

On cars with automatic transmission, a fluid cooler is incorporated in the right-hand radiator tank.

The heating system is based upon an engine coolant heated matrix inside the car with booster fan, all the necessary controls and heating and demisting ducts.

A fresh air ventilation system is used.

Air conditioning is a factory-fitted option available on certain models. When this is fitted, the additional electrically-operated fan is mounted on the evaporator ahead of the radiator.

2 Maintenance

1 With the semi-sealed system, no topping-up of the coolant should ever be needed. However, regularly check the coolant level in the expansion tank. If the addition of coolant is frequently required, inspect the system for a leak.

2 Keep the coolant pump drivebelt correctly tensioned (see Section 7) and regularly check the condition of all hoses and the security of their clips.

3 Every autumn, brush away the dirt and flies from the radiator fins. For a thorough job, use a jet from a cold water hose or air pressure from an air line applied to the rear face of the radiator. Access to the radiator front surface can be obtained after removal of the grilles (see Chapter 12).

3 Cooling system – draining, flushing and refilling

1 Drain the coolant when the engine is cold.

2 Remove the expansion tank cap and place the heater control lever to the maximum heat position.

3 Release the radiator bottom hose and allow the coolant to drain. A drain plug is fitted on Series 2 models (photo).

4 The drain plug on the cylinder block may also be removed, but this is rather inaccessible (photo).

5 If the system has been well maintained, there will be no evidence of rust or sediment and the hose can be reconnected, the drain plug(s) refitted and the system refilled immediately. However, if the system has been neglected, place a cold water hose in the expansion jar and flush the system until the water runs clear from the outlets.

6 If the radiator is particularly dirty or clogged, remove it and reverse flush it. Only if really necessary should a chemical cleaner be used and then strictly in accordance with the manufacturer's instructions.

7 When refilling, first release the screw which is located on the thermostat housing (photo). Pour antifreeze mixture (see Section 4) slowly into the expansion tank until coolant starts to run from the bleed screw hole. Tighten the screw.

8 Fit the expansion tank cap.

9 Run the engine at a fast idle until normal operating temperature is reached.

10 Switch off and top up the expansion tank to its mark using antifreeze mixture, not plain water.

3.3 Radiator drain plug (Series 2) – arrowed

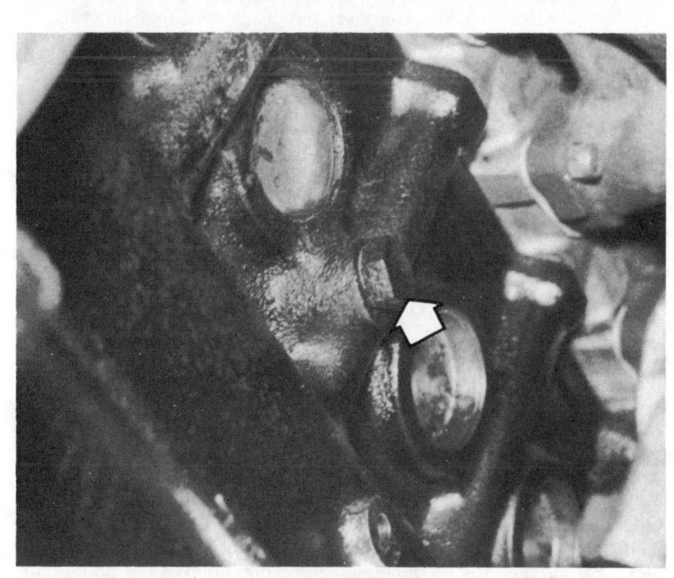

3.4 Cylinder block drain plug – arrowed

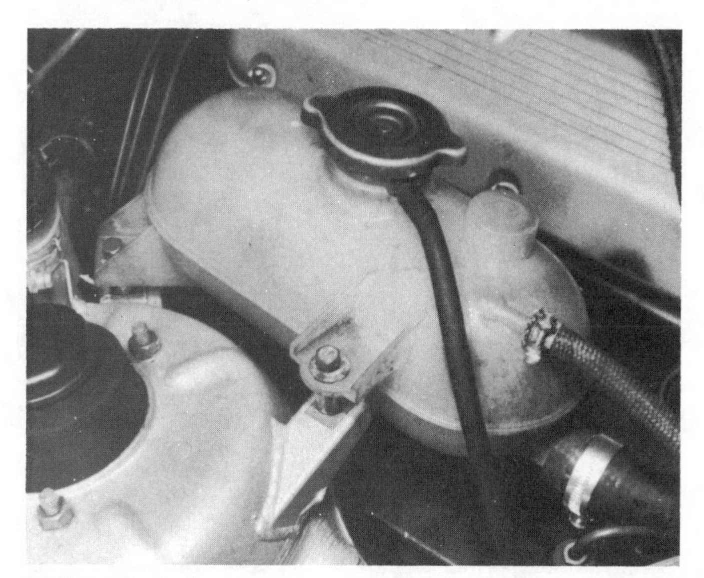

2.1 Expansion tank

3.7 Thermostat housing bleed screw

4 Coolant mixtures

1 **Never** fill the cooling system with plain water as apart from offering no protection against freezing, corrosion of the system will occur.
2 Use a good quality glycol-based antifreeze product in a minimum of $33\frac{1}{3}\%$ concentration with water to protect the engine against low temperatures and corrosion.
3 Renew the coolant at the intervals specified in Routine Maintenance.
4 Even in warm climates where antifreeze is not required, never use water alone but add a corrosion inhibitor.

5 Thermostat – removal, testing and refitting

1 Partially drain the cooling system.
2 Unbolt the thermostat housing cover, lift it off and withdraw the thermostat (photos).
3 If the thermostat is suspected of being faulty, suspend it in a pan of water and gradually heat the water. The thermostat valve should begin to open at the specified temperature.
4 Replace a faulty thermostat with one of similar temperature rating.
5 Refitting is a reversal of removal, but check the condition of the O-ring seal and renew if necessary.
6 Fill and bleed the cooling system (Section 3).

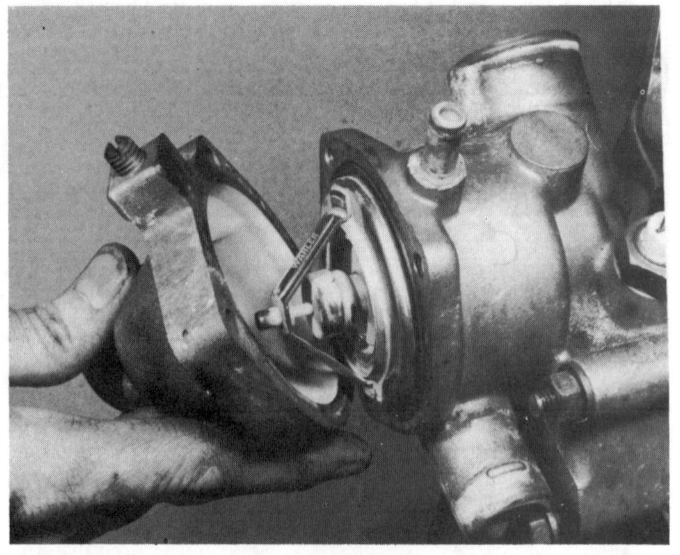
5.2A Removing the thermostat housing cover

6 Coolant temperature sensor – removal and refitting

1 If the temperature gauge does not operate, first check the wiring and connections from the sensor to the gauge. If this is in order, partially drain the cooling system and unscrew the sensor. The best test is by substitution of a new sensor.
2 Use a new sealing washer when screwing the sensor into the thermostat housing.
3 Top up the cooling system and bleed it (Section 3).
4 Access to the gauge is described in Chapter 10.

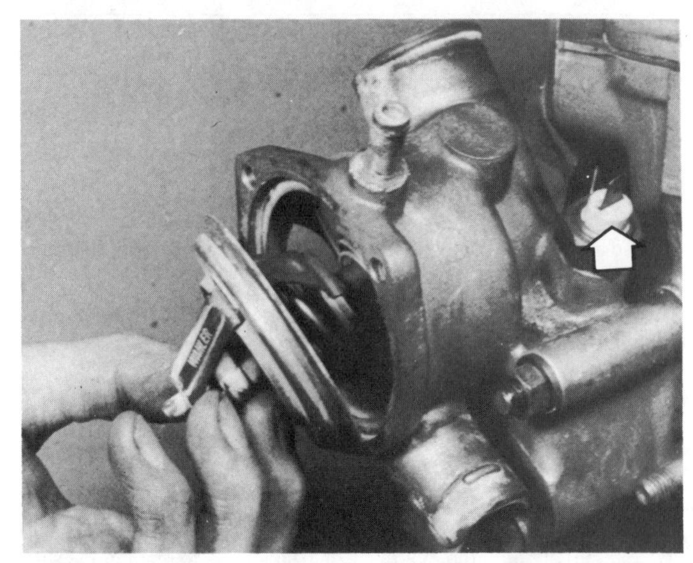
5.2B Removing the thermostat. Coolant temperature switch arrowed

7 Drivebelts – tensioning, removal and refitting

1 One, two or three belts may be fitted, depending upon the equipment fitted.
2 The tension of all belts should be maintained at between 5.0 and 10.0 mm (0.2 and 0.4 in) deflection at the mid-point of the longest run of the belt when depressed with moderate finger pressure (photo).
3 To adjust the tension, release the mounting bolts and adjuster link bolts and pull the alternator or power steering pump away from the engine or, in the case of an air conditioner compressor, push the compressor downwards. Tighten the bolts.
4 To remove a belt, release and push the driven unit as far as possible in order to release all the belt tension.
5 Slip the belt off the pulleys and remove it. Refit the new belt. If it is slightly too tight to slip over the pulley rim, **do not** lever it with a tool, but turn the crankshaft as the belt is pressed against the rim. It will then ride up and over the rim.
6 If an inner belt is to be renewed, an outer belt will first have to be removed to provide access.
7 Tension the belt as previously described and check the tension after the first few hundred miles running.

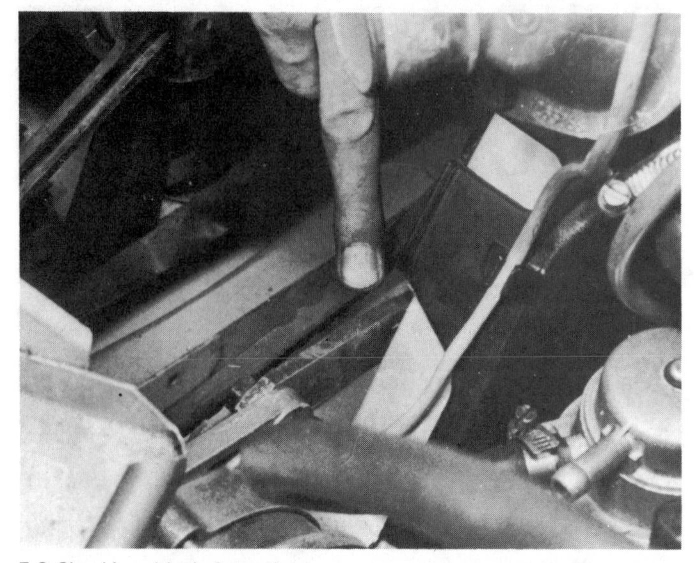
7.2 Checking drivebelt tension

8 Expansion tank – removal and refitting

1 Remove the tank cap and disconnect the lead from the coolant level sensor (where fitted).
2 Disconnect the hose from the tank (photo).
3 Unscrew the fixing screws and lift the tank from its mountings.
4 Clean out the tank thoroughly.
5 Refitting is a reversal of removal.
6 Refill the expansion tank with antifreeze mixture to the indicated level.

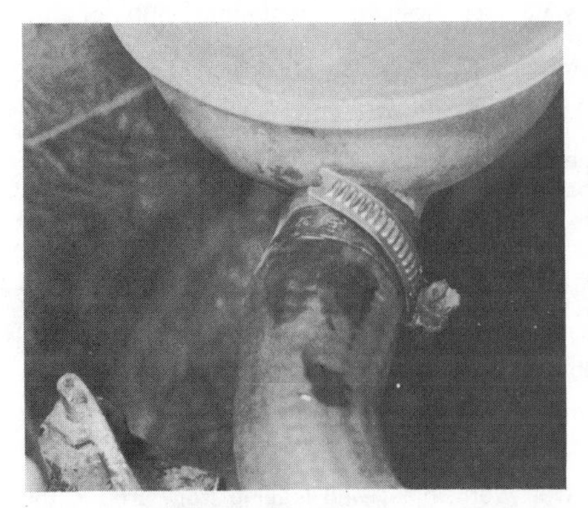

8.2 Expansion tank hose

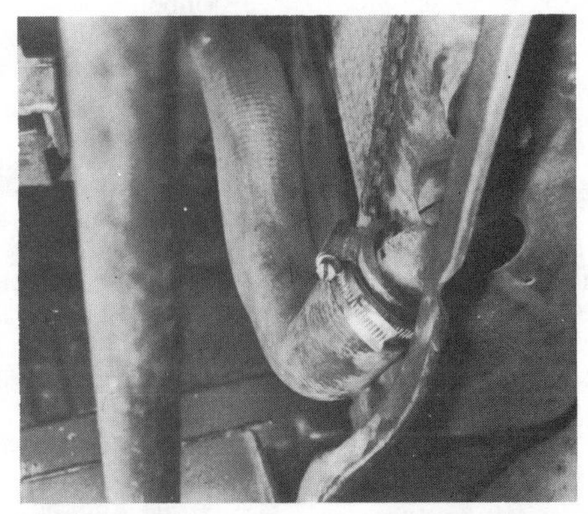

9.2 Radiator bottom hose

9.6A Releasing a radiator top mounting

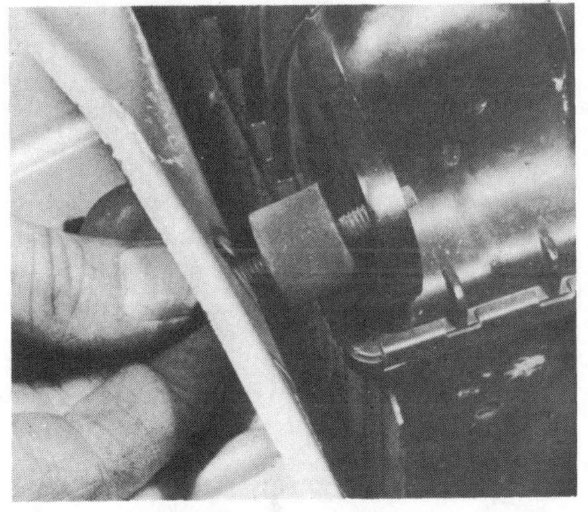

9.6B Radiator mounting cushion

9.6C Removing the radiator

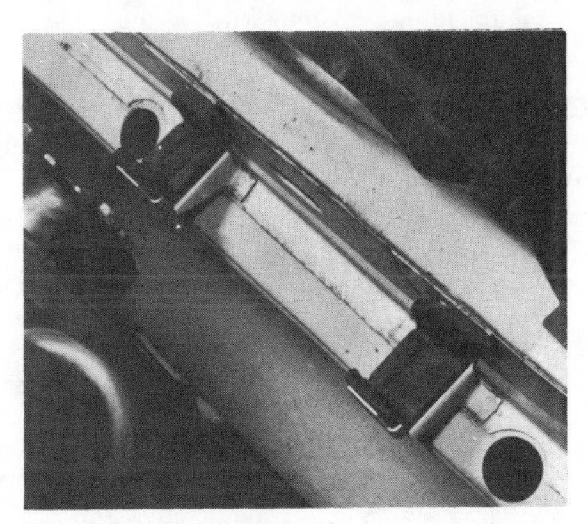

9.8 Radiator lower mountings

9 Radiator – removal and refitting

1 Drain the coolant, as described in Section 3.
2 Disconnect the coolant hoses from the radiator (photo), including the expansion tank hoses.
3 Where fitted, remove the fan cowl.
4 On cars fitted with automatic transmission, disconnect the fluid cooler lines from the radiator and cap their ends.
5 On cars equipped with an air conditioner, disconnect the electrical leads from the temperature switches which are located in the radiator.
6 Disconnect the radiator top mountings and lift the radiator from the engine compartment (photos).
7 If the radiator is clogged, try and clean it as described in Section 3. If it is leaking, have it repaired by a radiator repairer. Temporary repairs or home soldering seldom prove satisfactory.
8 Refitting is a reversal of removal, but first check that the base mounting insulators are in good condition (photo).
9 Fill and bleed the cooling system (Section 3).
10 Check the level of the automatic transmission fluid and top up.

10 Viscous coupling type fan

1 This is a fluid-filled sealed unit which adjusts the speed of rotation of the radiator cooling fan blades according to engine speed in much

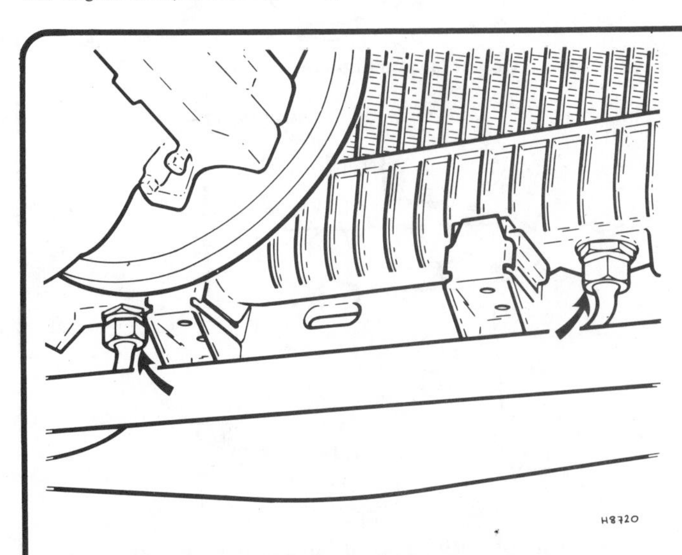

Fig. 2.1 Transmission fluid cooler lines at base of radiator – arrowed (Sec 9)

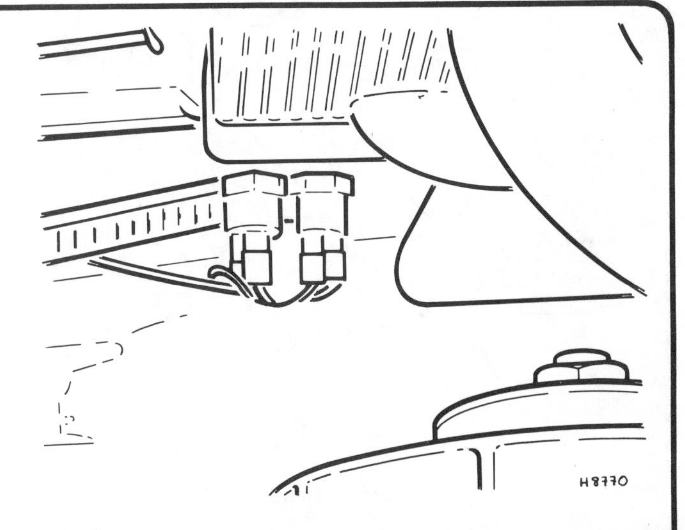

Fig. 2.2 Air conditioner temperature switches on radiator (Sec 9)

the same way as a torque converter operates in an automatic transmission.
2 Engagement of the fan may be temperature-controlled by the incorporation of a bimetal valve on certain models.
3 The coupling unit and the fan blades can be unbolted from the coolant pump hub without the need to disturb the drivebelt.
4 On earlier Behr type couplings, the fixing nut has a left-hand thread.
5 Due to the small working clearance, the rear-located fixing nut may require a cranked spanner to release it. The coolant pump pulley must be held against rotation by pinching the drivebelt runs together.
6 If the viscous coupling is obviously leaking fluid, renew the unit complete.

11 Auxiliary electrically-driven fan

1 This is fitted on certain models and also those with air conditioning, and it is mounted ahead of the radiator. The fan is controlled by a thermoswitch in the cooling system.
2 To remove the fan, first take out the radiator, as described in Section 9.
3 Remove the radiator grilles.
4 Release the condenser and take off the trim panel, then pull the condenser to the rear.
5 Disconnect the wiring plug and then unbolt and remove the fan with resistor.
6 Refitting is a reversal of removal.

12 Coolant pump – removal and refitting

1 Drain the cooling system (Section 3).
2 Remove the drivebelts and remove the fan and viscous coupling.
3 Unbolt the pulley/damper from the mounting hub on the crankshaft and remove it.
4 Disconnect the coolant hoses from the pump.
5 Unclip the TDC sensor and then remove the timing belt cover.
6 Use self-locking grips to restrain the belt tensioner spring and then unbolt and remove the coolant pump.
7 Clean away the old gasket.
8 While the pump is off, check that the plug for the main oil gallery is not leaking. If it is, drill a hole in the old one, remove the plug and any swarf, and drive a new one into position, first having applied thread locking fluid to its outer surface.
9 Refitting is a reversal of removal, use a new flange gasket.
10 Tension the drivebelt, fill and bleed the cooling system.

13 Coolant pump – overhaul

1 When a pump is well worn, noisy and leaking from around the bearing/shaft, it is recommended that a new pump is obtained.
2 For those preferring to overhaul the original pump, proceed in the following way.
3 Use an extractor to pull off the fan mounting hub.
4 Extract the circlip (1) – Fig. 2.3.
5 Press the shaft/bearing out of the pump body and impeller.
6 Obtain a repair kit which will contain a new shaft/bearing and seal.
7 Apply pressure to the bearing shoulders and press it into the pump body. Make sure that the longer part of the shaft is towards the impeller.
8 Support the end of the shaft and press on the impeller, but only far enough to provide a gap of between 0.4 and 0.8 mm (0.016 and 0.032 in) between the blades of the impeller and the pump body.
9 Again support the end of the shaft and press the fan mounting hub onto the shaft so that the shaft projects by between 4.1 and 4.4 mm (0.161 and 0.173 in).

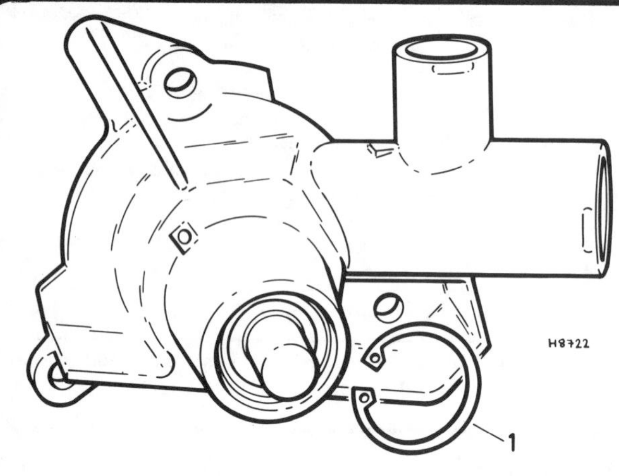

Fig. 2.3 Coolant pump bearing circlip (1) (Sec 13)

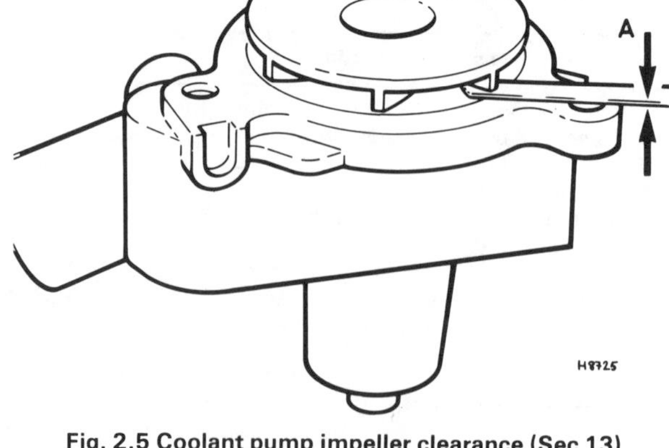
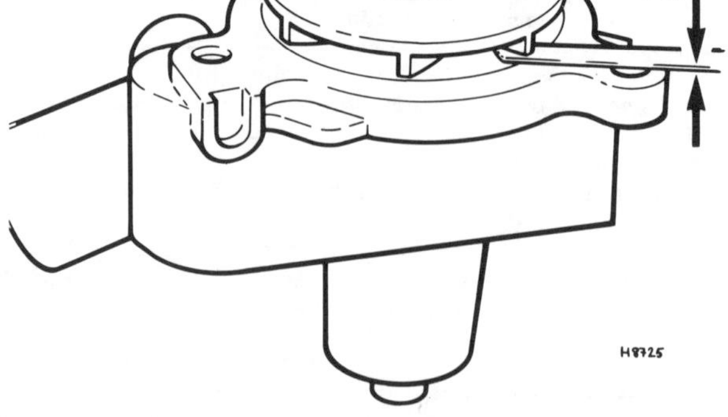

Fig. 2.5 Coolant pump impeller clearance (Sec 13)

A Impeller blades-to-body clearance

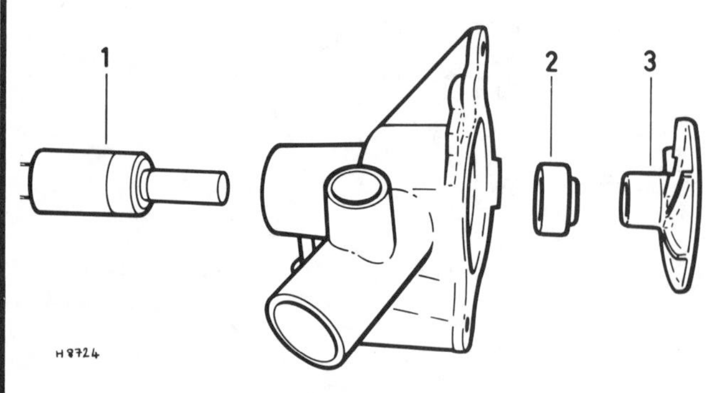

Fig. 2.4 Coolant pump components (Sec 13)

1 Bearing/shaft
2 Seal
3 Impeller

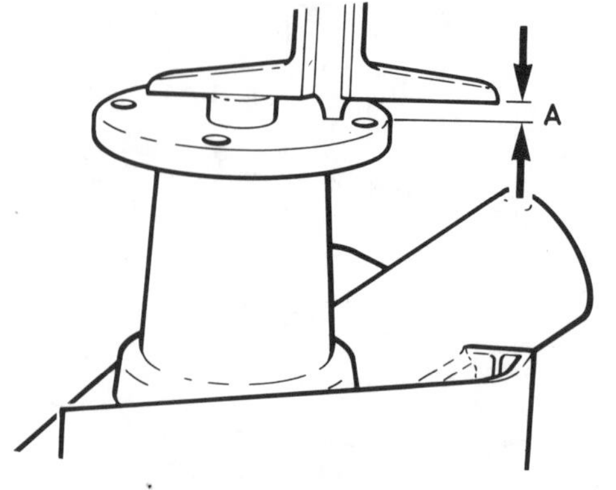

Fig. 2.6 Coolant pump hub position (Sec 13)

A Hub-to-shaft end distance

14 Heater controls (Series 1 models) – cable adjustment and renewal

Coolant valve control cable

1 Extract the screws and remove the facia panel under cover from the right-hand side.
2 Set the temperature control lever to COLD.

Sofica type

3 Detach the cable clip at the coolant valve on the heater casing and move the toothed sector until the marks on the sector and pinion are in alignment. Refit the cable clip.
4 To renew this cable, pull the knobs from the control levers.
5 Extract the retaining screws (1 to 4) – Fig. 2.8 – and remove the panel.
6 Detach the cable clip at the coolant valve and unhook the cable from the sector.
7 Detach the cable clip at the control lever end and remove the cable.
8 Refit by reversing the removal operations and then adjust as previously described.

Behr type

9 Release the cable clips on the coolant valve and press down the valve operating lever. Hold the lever in this position and reconnect the cable clips. On 1980 models fitted with this type of heater, push the lever in the direction of the arrow – Fig. 2.11 – before refitting the cable clip.

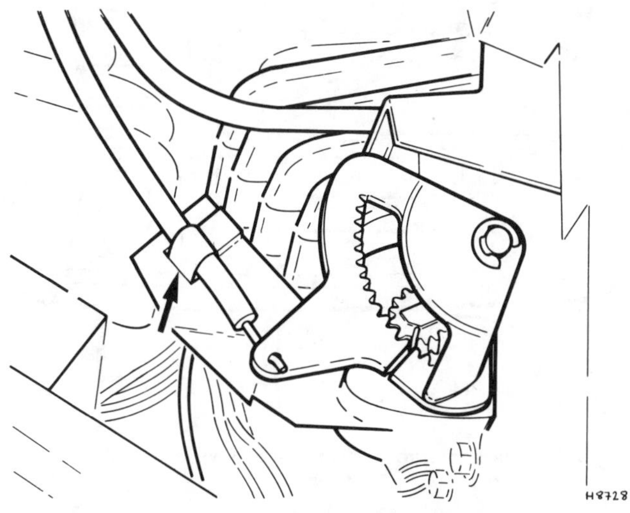

Fig. 2.7 Coolant valve sector and pinion alignment marks – Series 1 (Sec 14)

Cable clip arrowed

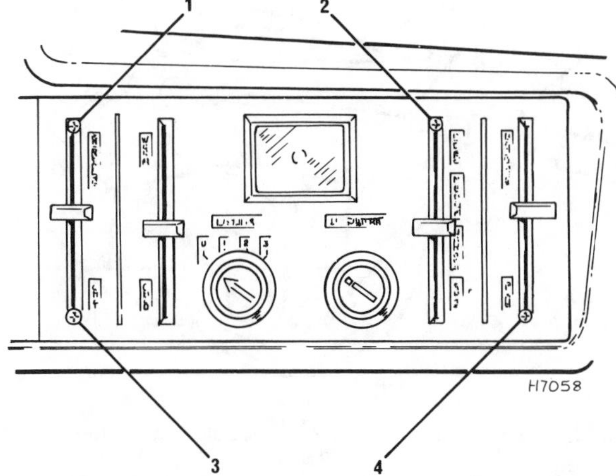

Fig. 2.8 Control panel fixing screws (1 to 4) – Series 1 (Sec 14)

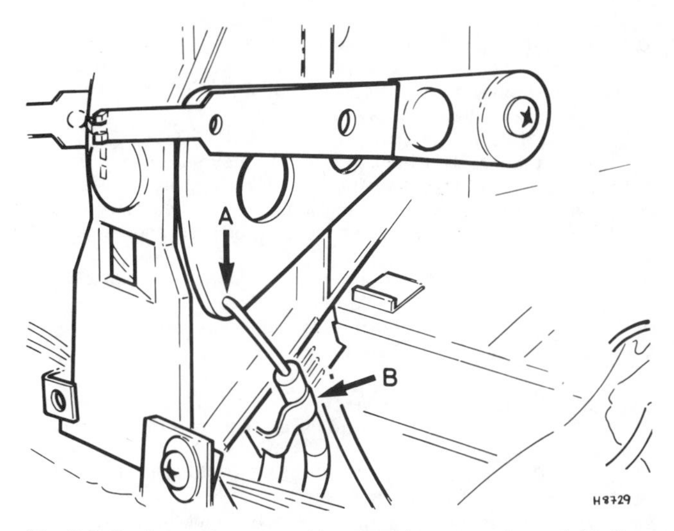

Fig. 2.9 Coolant valve control lever cable connection – A (Sofica type) – Series 1 (Sec 14)

B Cable clip

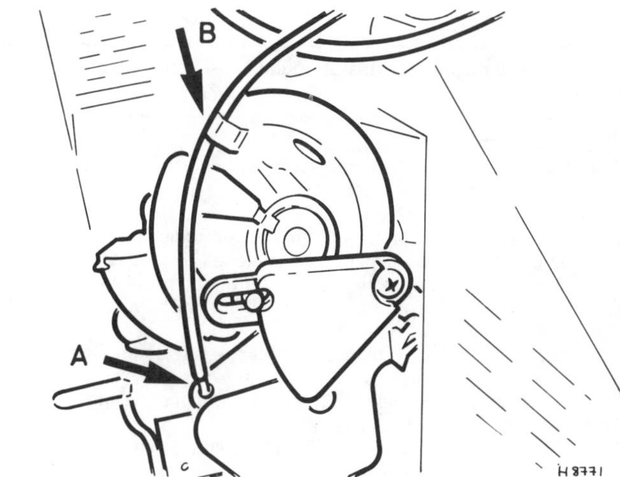

Fig. 2.10 Coolant valve control lever cable connection – A (Behr type) – Series 1 (Sec 14)

B Cable clip

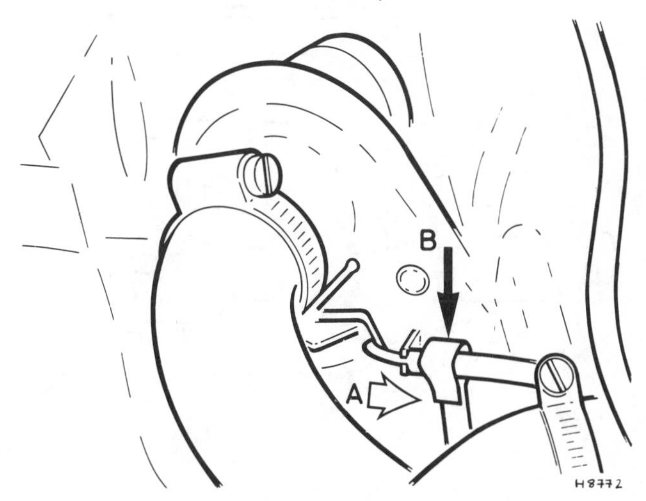

Fig. 2.11 Coolant valve cable reconnection (Behr type) – Series 1 (Sec 14)

Push the lever as far as possible (A) before refitting the cable clip (B)

Fresh air control cables

10 Remove the right-hand facia under cover.
11 Disconnect the glove compartment hinge pivots. Extract the screws and remove the trim from the side of the centre console.
12 Pull off the centre cover (snap fasteners).
13 Set both fresh air ventilation levers to CLOSED.
14 Release the cable positioning clips and move the cables until the air flaps are closed. Refit the clips without moving the cables.
15 To renew the cables, pull off the knobs from the control levers. On 1980 to 1982 models, unscrew the control nuts and remove the switch plate.
16 Extract the screws 1 to 4 and remove the panel – Fig. 2.8.
17 Disconnect the control cable from the lever.
18 Fit the cable by reversing the removal operations and adjust as previously described.

Demister flap control cable

19 Pull the knobs from the control levers. Remove the control lever panel escutcheon.
20 Move the control lever to the CLOSED position or, on 1980 to 1982 models, turn the knob to OFF.
21 Detach the cable clip and move the cable until the air distribution flaps are closed. Refit the clip. Check that the adjustment is correct by switching on the blower and feeling that no air is coming from the demister outlets.
22 Renewal of these cables can only be carried out after the heater has been removed, as described in Section 18.

15 Heater controls (Series 2 models) – cable adjustment and renewal

Footwell ventilation cable

1 Disconnect the battery and remove the facia panel under cover from the driver's side (Chapter 12).
2 Remove the centre console.
3 Remove the radio blanking panel or the radio (Chapter 10).
4 Remove the blanking panels or switches (Fig. 2.12).
5 Correct adjustment is assured, when the control lever and air flap are against their stops and the outer cable is flush with the stop (2) – Fig. 2.13.
6 If the cable is to be renewed, extract the screws and withdraw the heater control panel slightly.
7 Release the cable clamp (1) and disconnect the inner cable (2) from the lever (3) – Fig. 2.15.
8 Refer to Fig. 2.16 and prise off the clamp (1) disconnect the cable (1) from the lever (3).

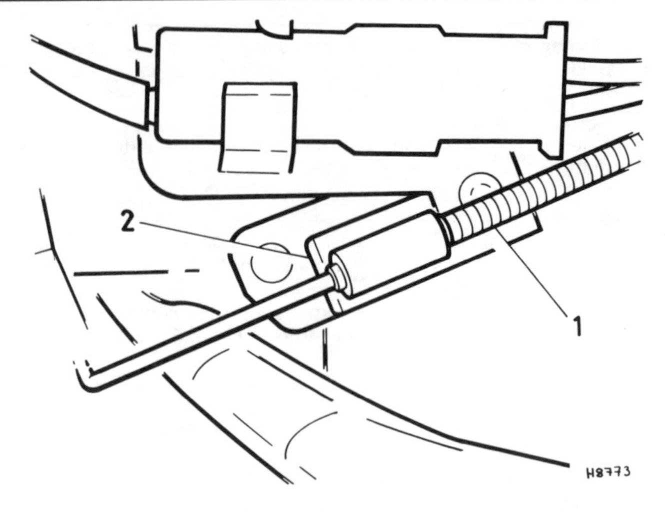

Fig. 2.13 Footwell vent cable setting – Series 2 (Sec 15)

1 Outer cable 2 Stop

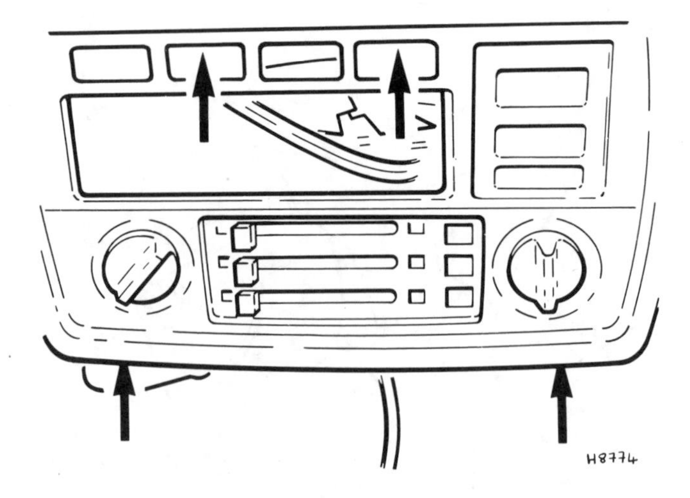

Fig. 2.14 Heater control panel fixing screws (arrowed) – Series 2 (Sec 15)

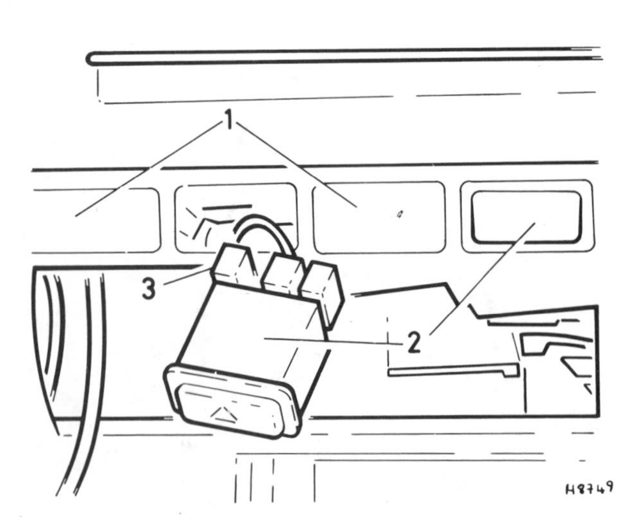

Fig. 2.12 Switch removed – Series 2 (Sec 15)

1 Blanking panels
2 Switches
3 Plug

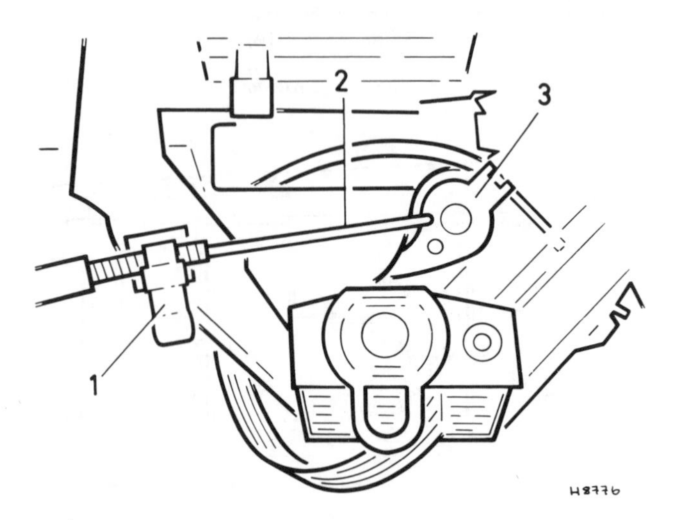

Fig. 2.15 Footwell flap control lever cable connection – Series 2 (Sec 15)

1 Cable clamp
2 Inner cable
3 Valve lever

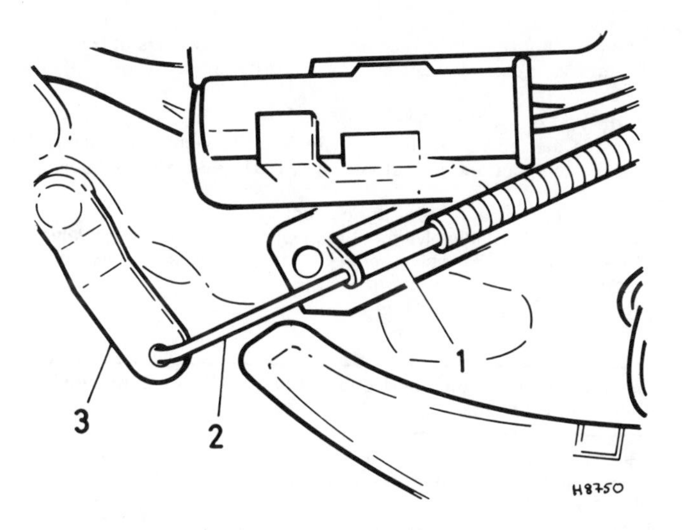

Fig. 2.16 Footwell flap cable connection – Series 2 (Sec 15)

1 Cable clamp
2 Inner cable
3 Valve lever

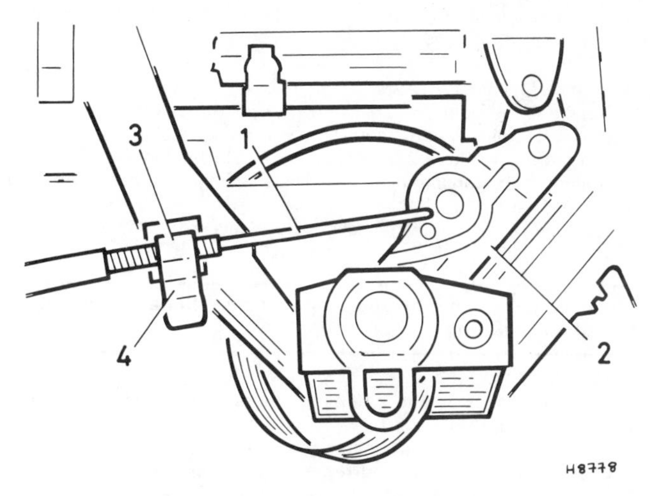

Fig. 2.18 Window demister control lever cable connection – Series 2 (Sec 15)

1 Inner cable
2 Flap arm
3 Adjuster sleeve
4 Cable clip

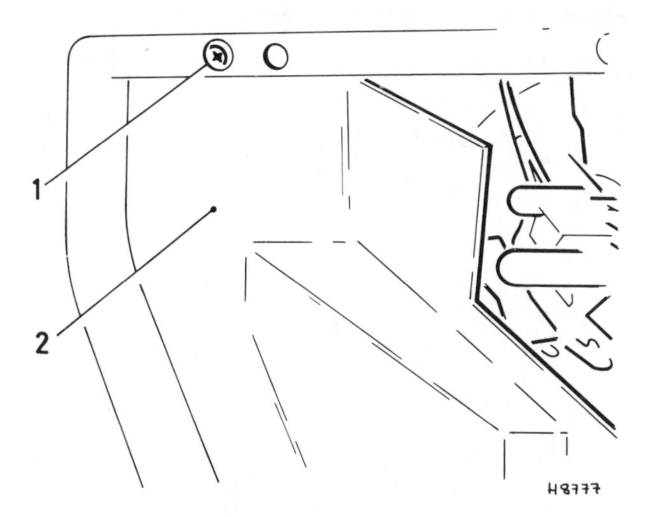

Fig. 2.17 Trim panel (2) and screw (1) – Series 2 (Secs 15, 17 and 21)

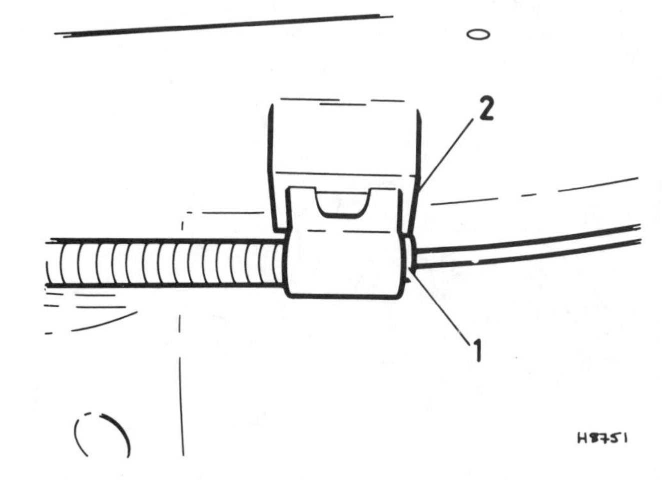

Fig. 2.19 Window demister cable sleeve (1) and stop (2) – Series 2 (Sec 15)

Front door window demister cable

9 Disconnect the battery and remove the facia panel under cover from the driver's side.
10 Remove the centre console.
11 Open the glove compartment lid and remove the check strap pins.
12 Remove the radio blanking plate, or the radio (Chapter 10).
13 Remove the blanking panels or switches from the centre control panel.
14 Extract the screws and withdraw the heater control panel slightly.
15 Extract the screw (1) and the trim panel (2) – Fig. 2.17.
16 Correct adjustment is evident if, with the sliding control and air flap against their stops, the sleeve is positioned so that it will enter its opening before being clamped. The sleeve at the opposite end of the cable must be flush with its stop – Fig. 2.19.
17 To renew the cable simply release the outer cable clamps and unhook the inner cable from the control levers.

Temperature flap valve cable

18 Carry out the operations described in paragraphs 9 to 15.
19 Adjustment is correct if, when the temperature selection wheel is set to the COLD or the WARM stop, the mixer valve flap is also in one of these positions. Adjust if necessary by turning the knurled nut (1) with the cable clamp (2) released – Fig. 2.20.

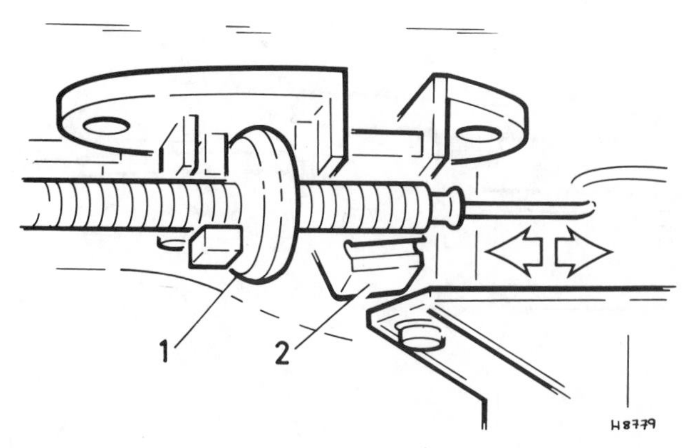

Fig. 2.20 Temperature flap valve cable adjustment – Series 2 (Sec 15)

Adjust the cable at either extreme of its travel (arrows) by releasing the clamp (2) and turning the adjuster (1)

20 To renew the cable, lift out the clamp (1) and disconnect the cable (2) from the lever (3) – Fig. 2.21.

Fresh air flap valve lever

21 Carry out the operations described in paragraphs 9 to 15.
22 The cable adjustment is correct when the cable sleeve (1) is flush with the stop (2) – Fig. 2.22 – also, with the sliding control and the air flap against their stops, the cable sleeve is so adjusted that it will drop into the opening. Fig. 2.18.
23 Disconnect the cable from clamps and levers to remove it.

16 Heater blower motor and coolant valve (Series 1 models) – removal and refitting

Blower motor

1 Working at the engine compartment rear bulkhead, extract the screws (arrowed) – Fig. 2.23.
2 Unbolt and remove the heater cover plate from the bulkhead.
3 Unscrew the two nuts and remove the water deflector plates.
4 Release the toggle clips and remove the upper section of the housing with the air intake cowls. Note that the flats on the cowls are at the bottom.

Sofica type

5 Release the motor securing toggle clip, lift the motor upwards and disconnect the electrical leads. The motor/fan unit should not be dismantled as the assembly is balanced during production.

Behr type

6 Press the housing upper sections out of the fasteners at the top and bottom very carefully. Lift out the motor/fan unit.

Coolant valve

7 Remove the facia panel under cover from the right-hand side.
8 Set the temperature control switch to HOT and drain the cooling system.
9 Disconnect the cable from the coolant valve.
10 Unscrew the coolant valve mounting bolts and withdraw the valve.
11 When refitting the valve, check that the seals are in good condition, otherwise renew them.
12 Refill and bleed the cooling system.

17 Heater blower motor and coolant valve (Series 2 models) – removal and refitting

Blower motor

1 The removal operations are very similar to those described in Section 16. If the blower switch must be removed, first take out the radio blanking plate or, if a radio is fitted, remove bolt (1) – Fig. 2.28 – open the glove compartment and extract the screw (1) and remove the panel (2) – Fig. 2.17.
2 Pull off the blower motor control knob and unscrew the switch locking nut.
3 Disconnect the switch wiring plug and remove the switch.

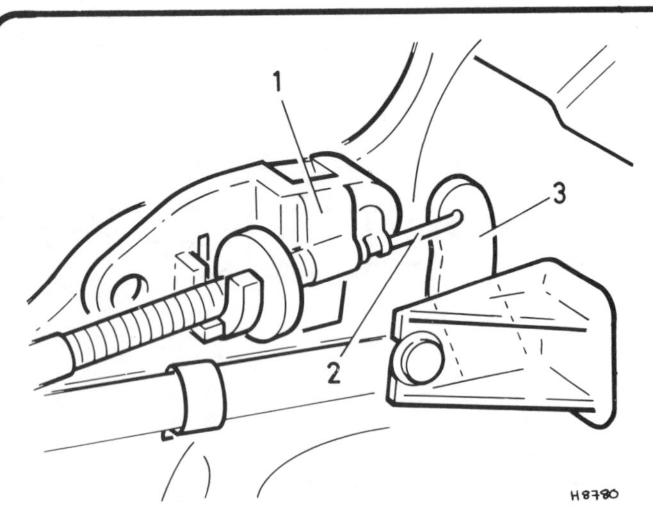

Fig. 2.21 Temperature flap valve cable clamp (1), inner cable (2) and lever (3) – Series 2 (Sec 15)

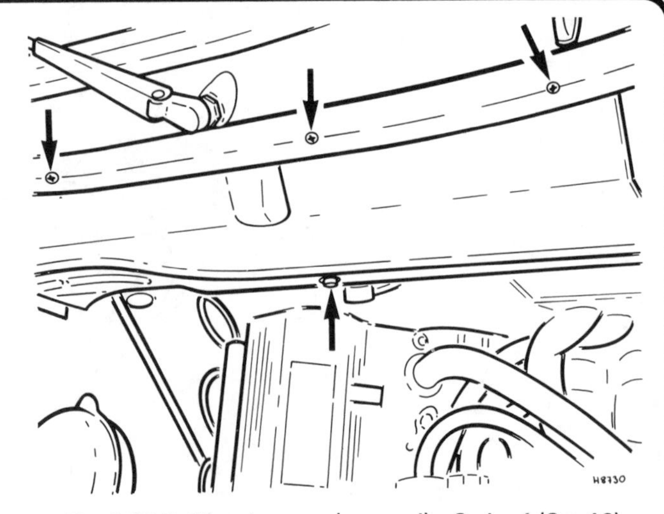

Fig. 2.23 Bulkhead screws (arrowed) – Series 1 (Sec 16)

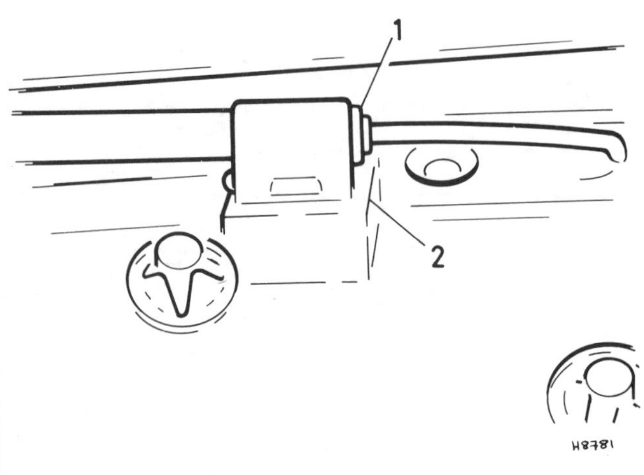

Fig. 2.22 Fresh air valve flap cable connection – Series 2 (Sec 15)

1 Cable sleeve *2 Stop*

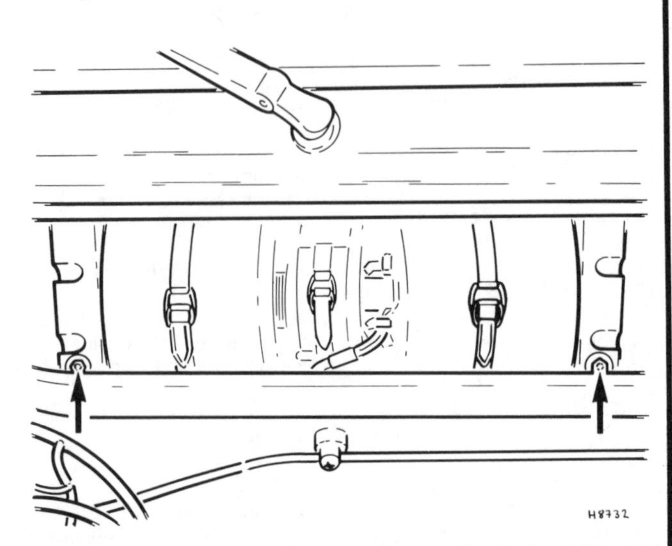

Fig. 2.24 Water deflector plate nuts (arrowed) – Series 1 (Sec 16)

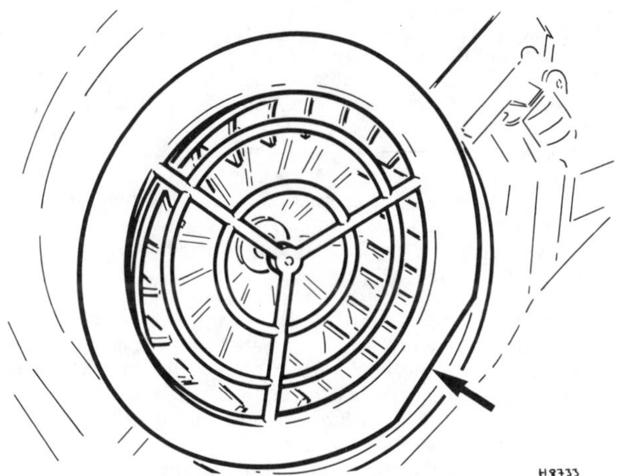

Fig. 2.25 Air intake cowl – Series 1 (Sec 16)

Flat (arrowed) must be at the bottom

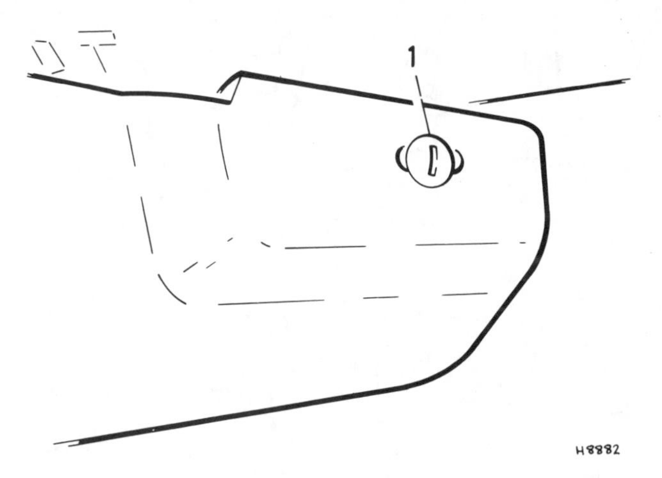

Fig. 2.28 Remove bolt (1) on cars with a radio fitted – Series 2 (Sec 17)

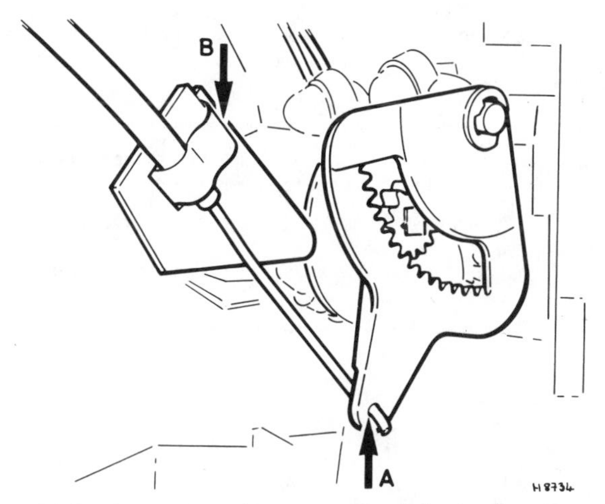

Fig. 2.26 Coolant valve cable connection (A) – Series 1 (Sec 16)

B Cable clip

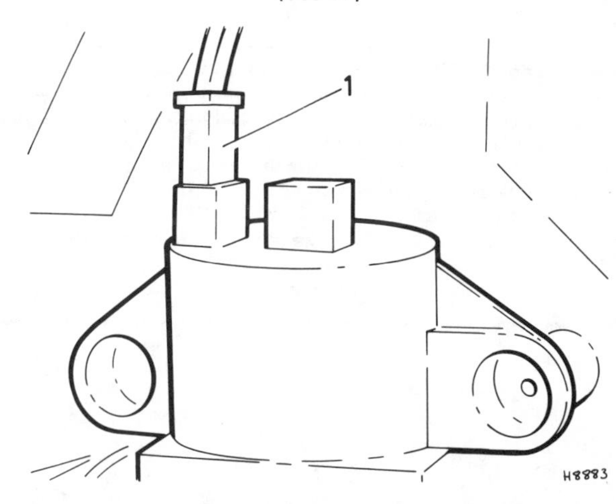

Fig. 2.29 Coolant valve electrical plug (1) – Series 2 (Sec 17)

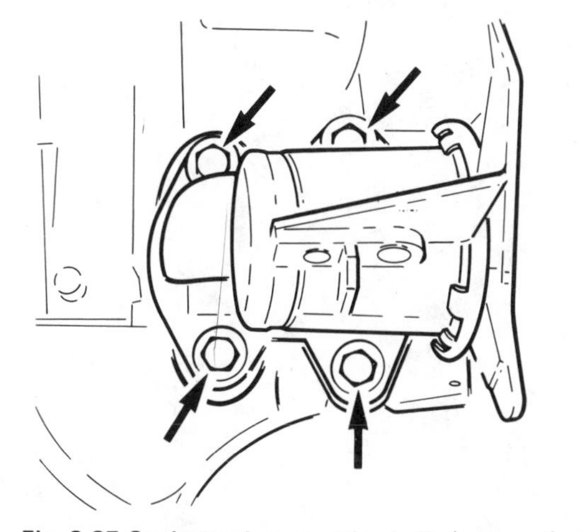

Fig. 2.27 Coolant valve mounting bolts (arrowed) – Series 1 (Sec 16)

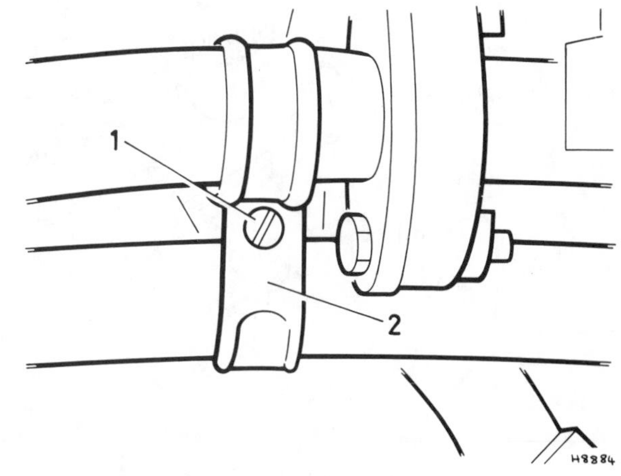

Fig. 2.30 Heater pipe bolt (1) and clamp (2) – Series 2 (Sec 17)

Coolant valve

4 Disconnect the battery negative lead.
5 Remove the facia panel under cover from the driver's side.
6 Extract the side fixing screws and lift away the centre console.
7 Set the heat control to MAXIMUM and drain the cooling system.
8 Disconnect the heater hoses from the pipe stubs on the engine compartment rear bulkhead.
9 Pull out the plug (1) – Fig. 2.29.
10 Remove the clamp (2) – Fig. 2.30.
11 Unscrew bolts (1 and 2) – Fig. 2.31 – and remove the coolant valve.
12 When refitting, renew the valve O-ring seals and bleed the cooling system.
13 The coolant valve, being electrically-operated, should be open when the current is off.

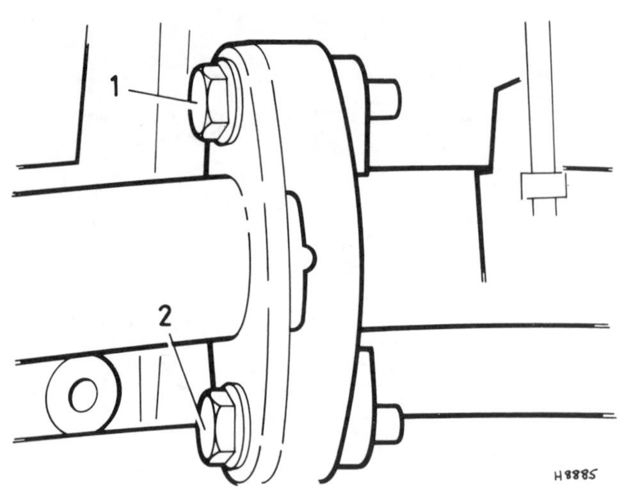

Fig. 2.31 Coolant valve flange bolts (1 and 2) – Series 2 (Sec 17)

18 Heater (Series 1 models) – removal and refitting

1 Remove the centre console, as described in Chapter 12. On cars with an air conditioner, remove the evaporator housing.
2 Disconnect the glove compartment hinge pivots. Extract the screws and remove the trim shown in Fig. 2.33.
3 Disconnect the battery negative lead.
4 Drain the cooling system with the temperature control lever set to HOT.
5 Pull off the knobs from the heater control levers.
6 Extract the screws and remove the heater control panel escutcheon. On 1980 to 1982 models remove the switch plate and instrument panel (Chapter 10).
7 Extract the screws and withdraw the control lever support frame.
8 Release the left and right-hand toggle clips and withdraw the heater cover.
9 Unbolt and remove the angled clamp.
10 Pull out the heater blower wiring plug.
11 Working at the engine compartment rear bulkhead, extract the screws (arrowed) in Fig. 2.23.
12 Unbolt the heater cover plate from the bulkhead.
13 Remove the water deflector plates (Fig. 2.24).
14 Disconnect the heater hoses at the bulkhead (photo).
15 Withdraw the heater into the car interior, turning it slightly as it is removed. Take care to protect the carpets against spillage of coolant.
16 The heater matrix may be removed after unclipping and separating the casing sections. Once this is done, release the toggle clips, lift off the upper section of the housing and outer air inlet cowls.
17 Unclip and remove the blower motor.
18 Detach the coolant valve from the heater matrix.
19 Pull off the foam rubber seal from the casing.
20 Release the spring clips and separate the halves of the heater casing.
21 Pull out the matrix.
22 If the matrix is clogged, try reverse flushing it or cleaning it as for the radiator (Section 3). If the matrix is leaking have it repaired by a radiator repairer.
23 The heater motor matrix resistor is now accessible for renewal if necessary.
24 Reassembly and refitting are reversals of the removal and dismantling operations, but note the following points.

Make sure, when connecting the electrical plugs, that the wire colours match

Check that the air distribution flap pivots are located positively in their holes

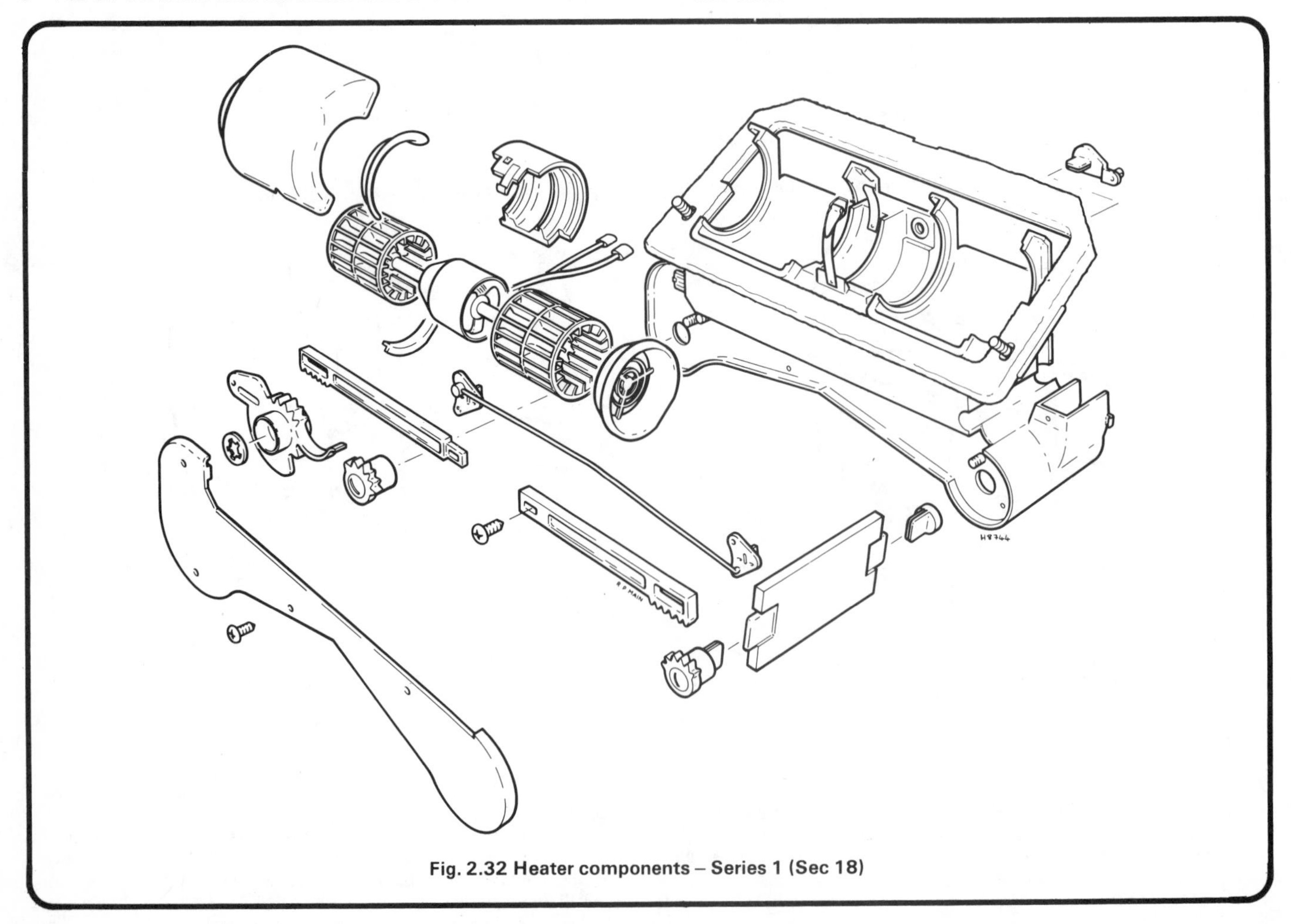

Fig. 2.32 Heater components – Series 1 (Sec 18)

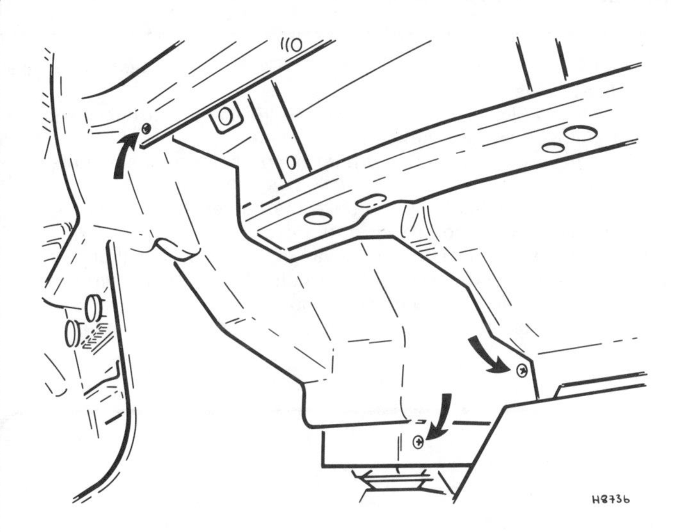

Fig. 2.33 Corner trim removal – Series 1 (Sec 18)

Securing screws arrowed

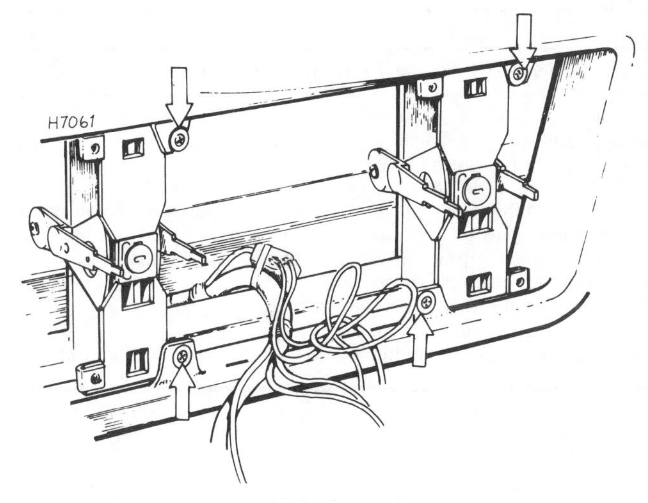

Fig. 2.34 Heater control lever support frame securing screws (arrowed) – Series 1 (Sec 18)

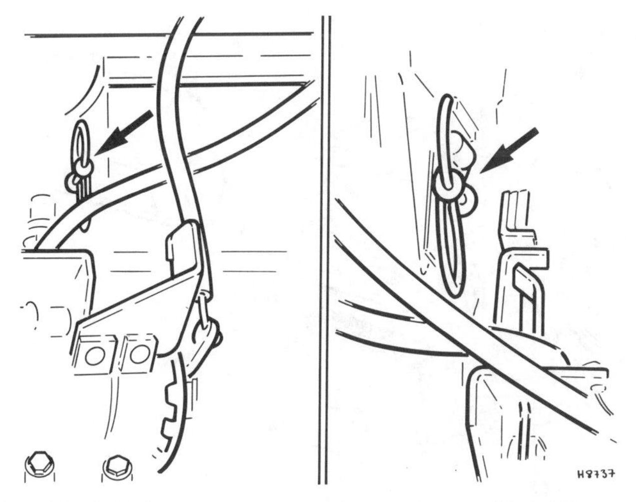

Fig. 2.35 Heater cover toggle clips – Series 1 (Sec 18)

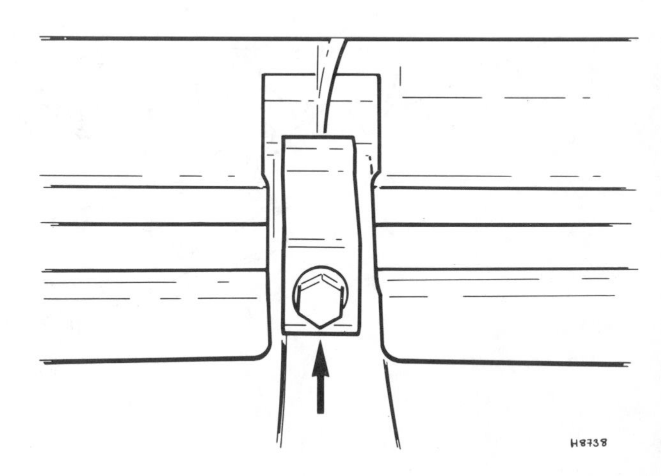

Fig. 2.36 Heater angled clamp securing bolt (arrowed) – Series 1 (Sec 18)

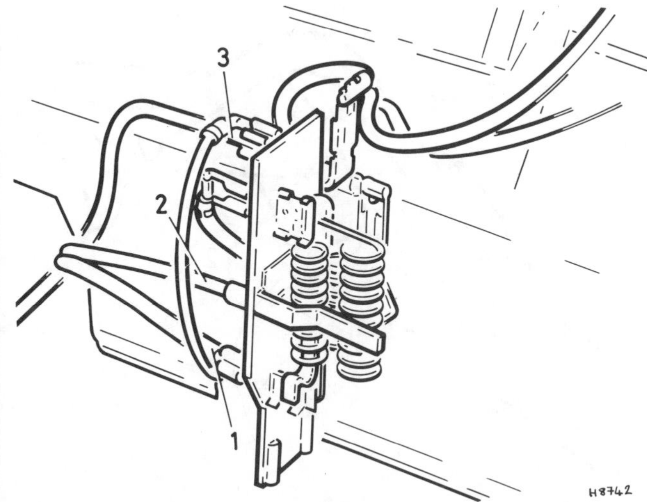

Fig. 2.37 Heater motor resistor – Series 1 (Sec 18)

1 Yellow
2 Green
3 Black

18.14 Heater hose connections at bulkhead – Series 1

19 Heater (Series 2 models) – removal and refitting

1 If the car is equipped with an air conditioner, have the system discharged by your dealer or a refrigeration engineer.
2 Disconnect the battery.
3 Remove the facia panels, as described in Chapter 12.
4 Working within the engine compartment, remove the cover plate from the upper part of the rear bulkhead.
5 Drain the cooling system and disconnect the heater hoses from the pipe stubs on the bulkhead.
6 Disconnect the heater blower motor wiring plug.
7 Disconnect the mounting bracket.
8 On cars with an air conditioner, disconnect the lines (1 and 2) and plug them immediately – Fig. 2.40. The system **must** have been discharged first.
9 Refer to Fig. 2.41 and remove the left-hand and right-hand rear duct connectors from the heater.
10 Remove the left-hand and right-hand heater mounting nuts (1) – Fig. 2.42.
11 Close the air flaps and remove the heater, taking care to avoid coolant spillage in the interior of the car.
12 Refitting is a reversal of removal, but make sure that all seals are in good condition. On cars with air conditioning, make sure that the condensate drain tubes are connected.
13 Fill and bleed the cooling system, have the refrigerant system recharged.

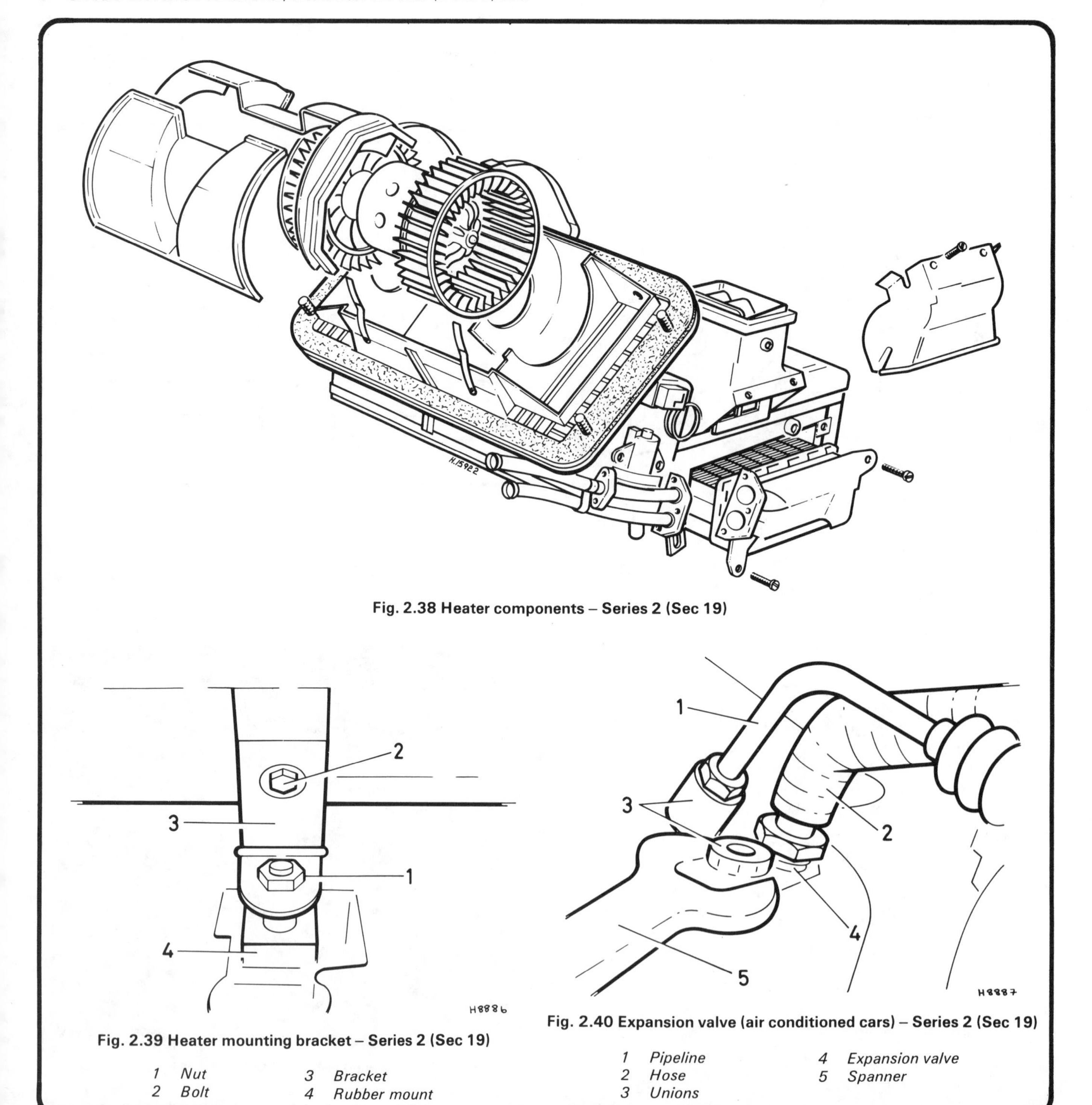

Fig. 2.38 Heater components – Series 2 (Sec 19)

Fig. 2.39 Heater mounting bracket – Series 2 (Sec 19)

1 Nut
2 Bolt
3 Bracket
4 Rubber mount

Fig. 2.40 Expansion valve (air conditioned cars) – Series 2 (Sec 19)

1 Pipeline
2 Hose
3 Unions
4 Expansion valve
5 Spanner

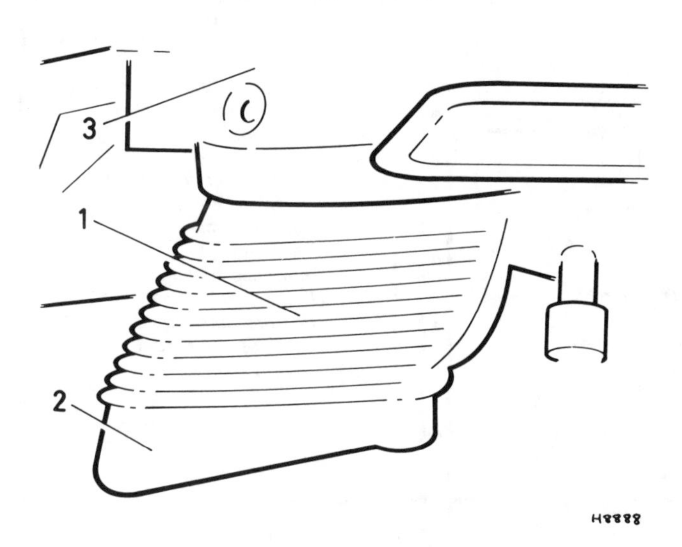

Fig. 2.41 Heater rear duct – Series 2 (Sec 19)

1 Connector
2 Duct
3 Heater casing

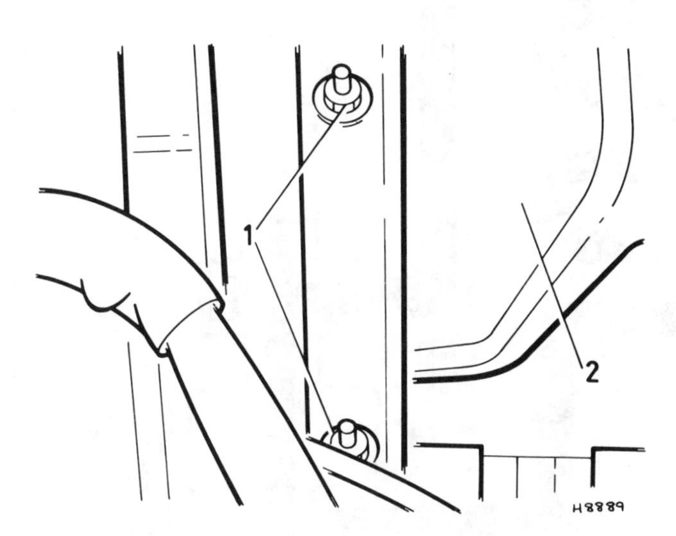

Fig. 2.42 Heater mounting nuts – Series 2 (Sec 19)

1 Nuts *2 Air flap*

20 Air conditioner – description and maintenance

1 Air conditioning can be specified as a factory-fitted option on later models. This is incorporated as a complete heating, ventilation and cooling unit.
2 The main components of the system include a belt-driven compressor, condenser and evaporator.
3 Regular maintenance includes keeping the compressor drivebelt correctly tensioned, as described in Section 7.
4 Always ensure that at least one air outlet grille is open when the air conditioner is switched on, otherwise the evaporator may ice up.
5 During the winter, always run the air conditioner for a few minutes once a month to keep the compressor shaft seals from becoming dry.

21 Air conditioner – removal and refitting of main components

1 Before any part of the system is disconnected or removed have it professionally discharged by your dealer or a refrigeration engineer. Refer to the warning in Chapter 1, Section 1.

Compressor

2 Discharge the system and disconnect the wiring plugs from the pulley magnetic coupling. Remove the air cleaner.
3 Disconnect the flexible hoses and disconnect the pipelines. Immediately seal the openings.
4 Release the mounting bolts, take off the drivebelt. Remove the mounting bolts, noting the position of spacers and washers.

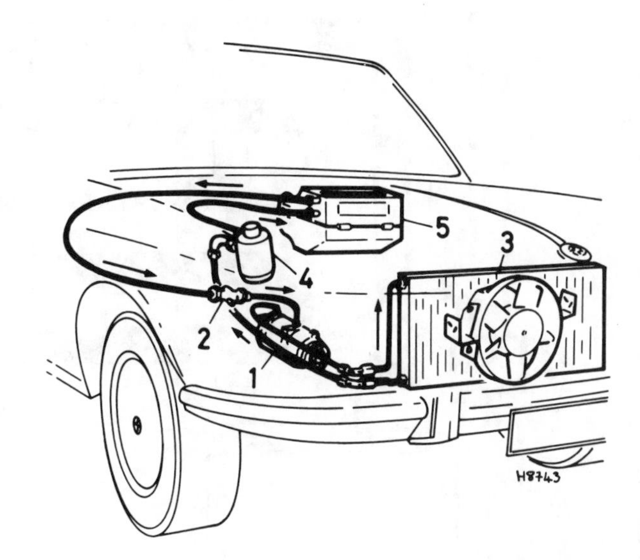

Fig. 2.43 Typical air conditioning system layout (Sec 20)

1 Compressor
2 Charge valve
3 Condenser
4 Receiver/drier
5 Evaporator

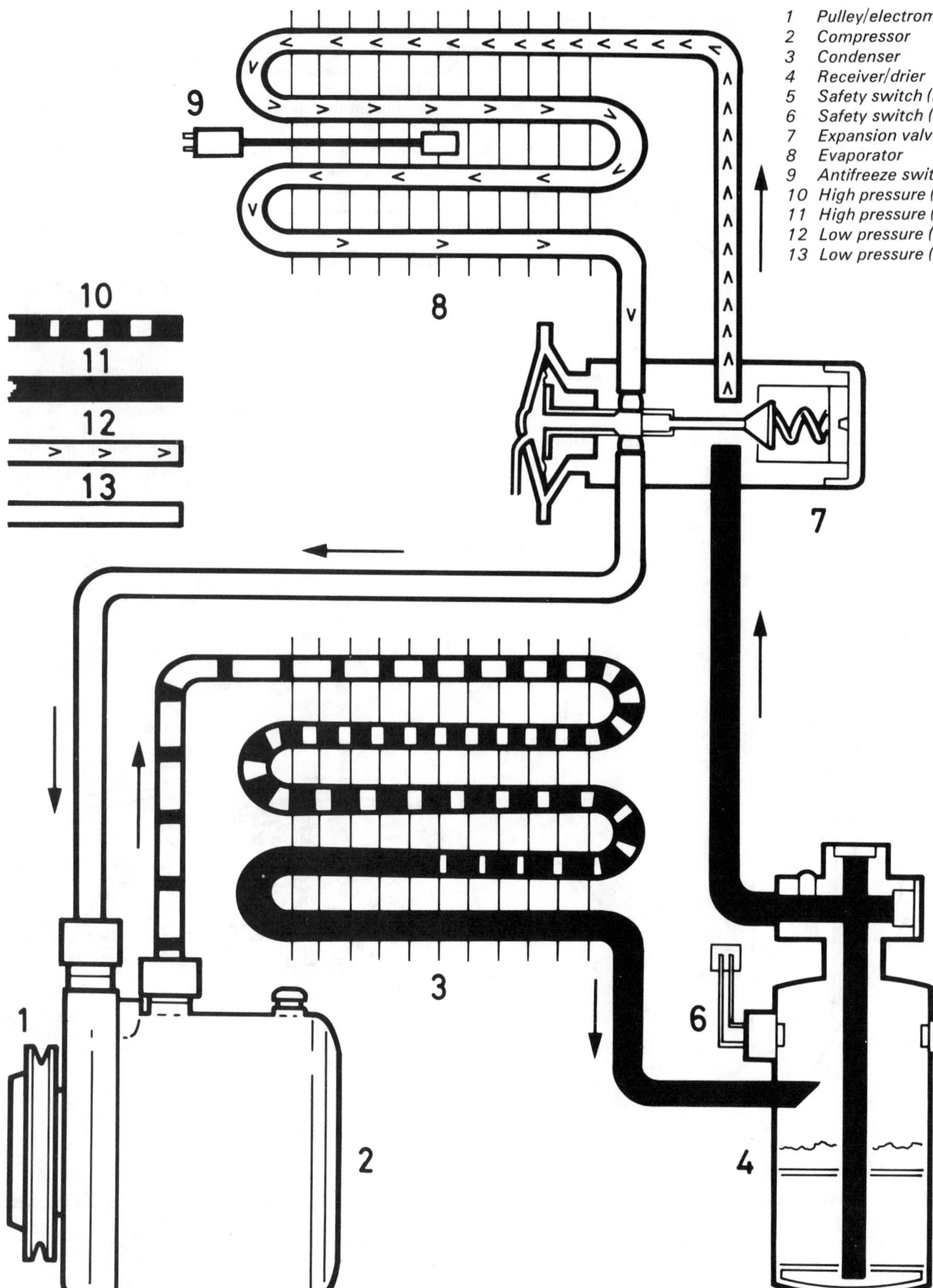

Fig. 2.44 Typical air conditioner refrigeration circuit (Sec 20)

1 *Pulley/electromagnetic clutch*
2 *Compressor*
3 *Condenser*
4 *Receiver/drier*
5 *Safety switch (low pressure)*
6 *Safety switch (high pressure)*
7 *Expansion valve*
8 *Evaporator*
9 *Antifreeze switch*
10 *High pressure (gas)*
11 *High pressure (liquid)*
12 *Low pressure (liquid)*
13 *Low pressure (gas)*

5 The stabiliser can be removed from the compressor by unscrewing the bolts and nut. The oil can be renewed by unscrewing the plug (1) – Fig. 2.45. Use the correct grade and quantity when refilling.

Expansion valve and evaporator

6 Disconnect the battery, remove the centre console and the facia panel under cover from the driver's side.
7 Open the glove compartment, unscrew the bolt (1) and remove the trim panel (2) – Fig. 2.17.
8 Extract the glove compartment check strap pins and then withdraw the glove compartment. Discharge the system.
9 Disconnect the pipelines now visible and cap the openings immediately. Grip the expansion valve when unscrewing the union nuts to prevent it from twisting.
10 Remove the expansion valve cover.
11 Withdraw the evaporator and disconnect the two remaining pipes from the expansion valve. Seal the openings immediately.
12 Remove the expansion valve.
13 To remove the evaporator completely, pull out the electrical plugs and unscrew the bolts.
14 Withdraw the temperature sensor, and switch located next to the evaporator.

Condenser

15 Remove the radiator, as described in Section 9.
16 Discharge the system.
17 Remove the right-hand radiator grille.
18 Disconnect the pipe unions at the condenser and seal the openings immediately.
19 Unscrew the mounting bolts and withdraw the condenser upwards.
20 Disconnect the electric fan wiring plug, and unbolt the fan from the condenser.

Drier

21 Discharge the system, remove the washer fluid reservoir.
22 Remove the bulkhead cover panel.
23 Disconnect the pipelines from the drier and seal the openings immediately.
24 Disconnect the plug from the safety switches.
25 Unbolt and remove the drier.

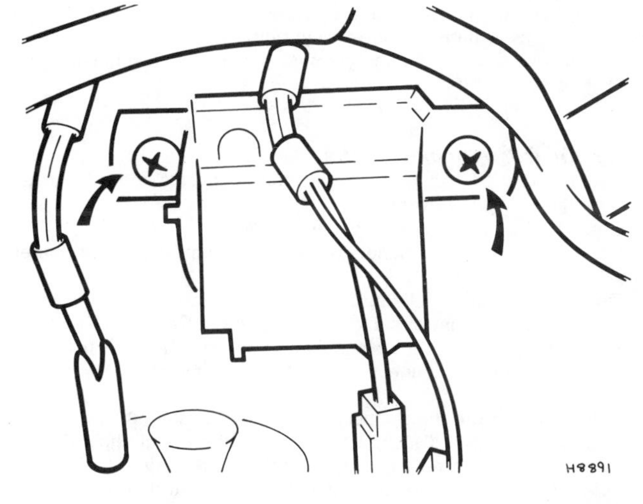

Fig. 2.46 Evaporator fixing bolts – arrowed (Sec 21)

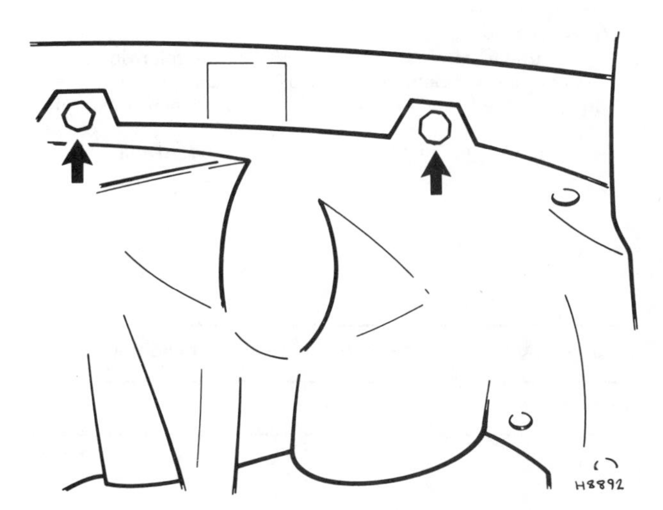

Fig. 2.47 Bulkhead cover panel securing bolts – arrowed (Sec 21)

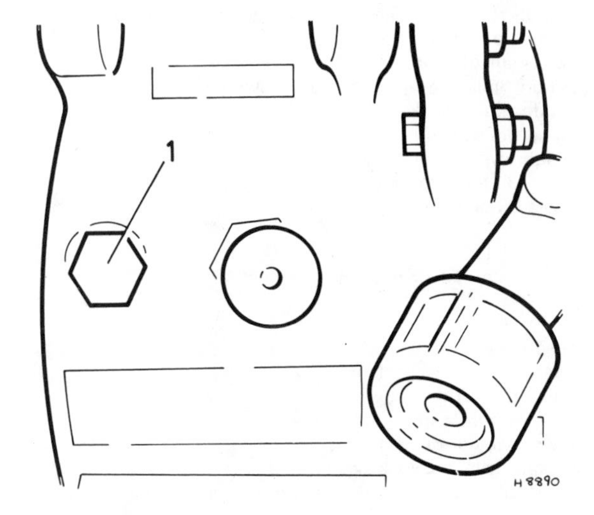

Fig. 2.45 Compressor oil plug (1) (Sec 21)

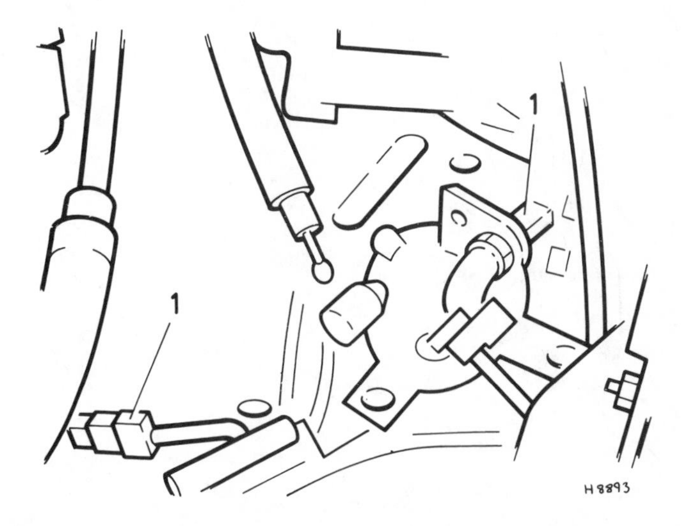

Fig. 2.48 Safety switches wiring plugs (1) (Sec 21)

Antifreeze switch

26 Disconnect the battery, remove the centre console and facia panel under cover from the driver's side.
27 Pull off the plugs from the evaporator.
28 Remove the expansion valve fixing bolts.
29 Carefully withdraw the temperature sensor and switch located next to the evaporator.

Motor for fresh air bypass flap

30 Disconnect the battery, remove the centre console and facia panel under cover from the driver's side.
31 Remove the radio blanking panel or radio.
32 Remove the blanking panels or switches from above the heater controls.
33 Extract the screws and withdraw the heater control panel slightly.
34 Disconnect the control cable, as described in Section 15.
35 Pull the plug from the air conditioner switch, the plug from the blower switch and disconnect the wire with the bulb holder – Fig. 2.49.
36 Pull the plug from the temperature control housing, the plug from the sliding control and disconnect the wire with the bulb holder from behind the heater control panel. Pull off the clock plug.
37 Disconnect the wiring plug and the flap control rod from the motor.
38 Unbolt and remove the motor with its mounting.

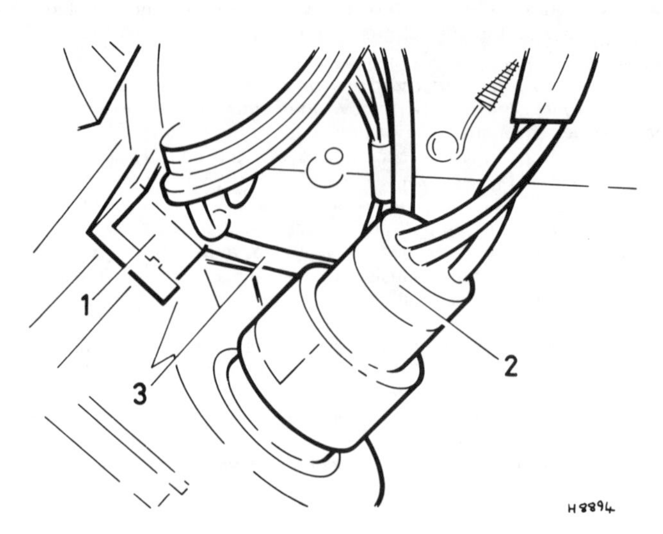

Fig. 2.49 Pull off the air conditioner switch plug (1), the blower switch plug (2) and the wire with the bulb holder (3) (Sec 21)

Refitting

39 This is a reversal of removal, but observe the following points.
40 Tighten nuts and bolts to the specified torque settings.
41 Straighten the fins of the evaporator and condenser when refitting these components.
42 Adjust the length of the air bypass flap rod so that the motor opens the flaps fully. Do this by turning the rod after first having disconnected it from the motor.
43 Check all pipeline seals and renew if necessary.
44 Have the system recharged professionally.

22 Fault diagnosis – cooling, heating and air conditioning

Symptom	Reason(s)
Overheating	Insufficient coolant in system Pump ineffective due to slack drivebelt Radiator blocked either internally or externally Kinked or collapsed hose causing coolant flow restriction Thermostat not working properly Engine out of tune Ignition timing retarded or auto advance malfunction Cylinder head gasket blown Engine not yet run-in Exhaust system partially blocked Engine oil level too low Brakes binding
Engine running too cool	Faulty, incorrect or missing thermostat
Loss of coolant	Loose hose clips Hoses perished or leaking Radiator leaking Filler/pressure cap defective Blown cylinder head gasket Cracked cylinder block or head Leak into transmission fluid (automatic transmission)
Heater gives insufficient output	Engine overcooled (see above) Heater matrix blocked Heater controls maladjusted or broken Heater control valve jammed or otherwise defective

Symptom	Reason(s)
Air conditioner	
Bubbles observed in sight glass of receiver drier	Leak in system Low refrigerant level
No cooling	No refrigerant
Expansion valve frosted over on evaporator	Faulty or clogged expansion valve Thermal bulb leaking
Insufficient cooling	Faulty expansion valve Air in refrigerant circuits Clogged condenser Receiver drier clogged Faulty compressor Compressor overfilled with oil

Chapter 3 Fuel system

For modifications, and information applicable to later models, see Supplement at end of manual

Contents

Specifications

General

Fuel tank capacity:	
Series 1	58.0 litre (12.8 Imp gal)
Series 2	55.0 litre (12.1 Imp gal)
Fuel octane requirement	4-star, 98 RON

Part A: Carburettor system

Fuel pump type ..... Mechanical, from intermediate shaft

Carburettor

Type	DVG Solex 4A1	
Code number	1 266 255	
Data:	**Stage 1**	**Stage 2**
Venturi	20.1 mm (0.79 in)	
Main jet	X97.5	
Needle		B5
Air correction jet	90	
Idle jet	42.5	
Idle air jet	110	
Additional air jet	100	
Additional fuel jet	57.5	
Code number	1 271 369.9	
Data:		
As code no 1 266 255 except for		
Idle air jet	115	
Additional air jet	80	
Additional fuel jet	52.5	
Code numbers	1 271 372.9 and 1 271 377.9	

Data:		
As code no 1 266 255 except for		
Idle air jet	125	
Additional air jet	130	
Additional fuel jet	70	
All code numbers:		
Float needle valve	2.5 mm (0.098 in)	
Idle speed	800 to 900 rpm	
CO content	0.5 to 1.5% at idle	

Torque wrench settings	**Nm**	**lbf ft**
Fuel pump to cylinder head	8	6
Carburettor mounting bolts	22	16
Manifold nuts:		
Inlet	30	22
Exhaust	22	16
Exhaust pipe-to-manifold nuts	65	48
Exhaust joint flange bolts	24	18
Exhaust support bracket nuts	24	18

Part B: Fuel injection system

Type	Bosch K-Jetronic or L-Jetronic
Data:	
Injector opening pressure:	
K-Jetronic	3.3 bar (47.8 lbf/in^2)
L-Jetronic	3.0 bar (43.5 lbf/in^2)
Idle speed:	
K-Jetronic	850 to 950 rpm
L-Jetronic	700 to 800 rpm
CO content	1.0 to 2.0% at idle

Torque wrench settings	**Nm**	**lbf ft**
Injector collar nut (K-Jetronic)	25	18
Temperature/time switch	30	22

1 General description

The fuel system may be of carburettor or fuel injection type, depending upon the model of car.

On carburettor models, the fuel pump is of mechanically-operated type from the intermediate shaft.

The fuel injection system is of Bosch Jetronic type (see also Section 22).

The fuel tanks are rear-mounted, and a temperature-controlled air cleaner is fitted.

PART A: CARBURETTOR SYSTEM

2 Air cleaner – element renewal

1 Prise back the toggle clips (photo) unscrew the centre nut and remove the lid.

2 Take out the element (photo) and wipe out the casing.

3 If the element is only slightly dirty, and has not been in use for its specified time (see Routine Maintenance) tap it on a hard surface or

2.1 Air cleaner toggle clip

2.2 Air cleaner element

apply compressed air from the inside to remove adhering dirt. Renew the element at the specified service interval.
4 Refit the lid.

3 Air cleaner – removal and refitting

1 Disconnect the cold air and hot air intake ducts from the air cleaner (photos).
2 Remove the nut from the centre of the air cleaner lid (photo).
3 Lift the air cleaner sufficiently high so that the connecting hoses can be identified and disconnected (photo).
4 Remove the air cleaner.
5 Refit by reversing the removal operations, make sure the sealing ring is in good condition (photo).

4 Air cleaner flap valve – adjustment

1 Remove the air cleaner, as described in the preceding Section.
2 Place the end of the air cleaner with the valve in a container of water at 15°C (59°F). After five minutes, the valve (1) should just close the air route (B) – Fig. 3.1.
3 At a water temperature below 8°C (46°F), the flap valve should

3.2 Unscrewing air cleaner cover nut

3.1A Air cleaner intake duct

3.3 Air cleaner hose connections

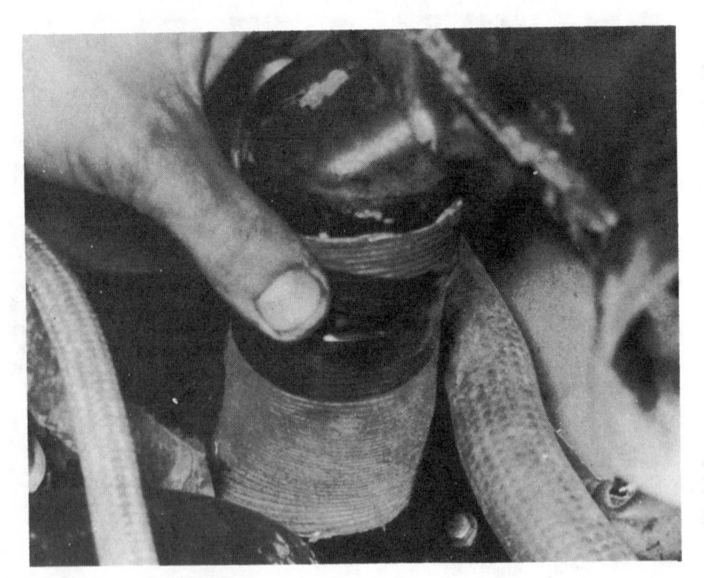

3.1B Hot air intake duct

3.5 Air cleaner sealing ring

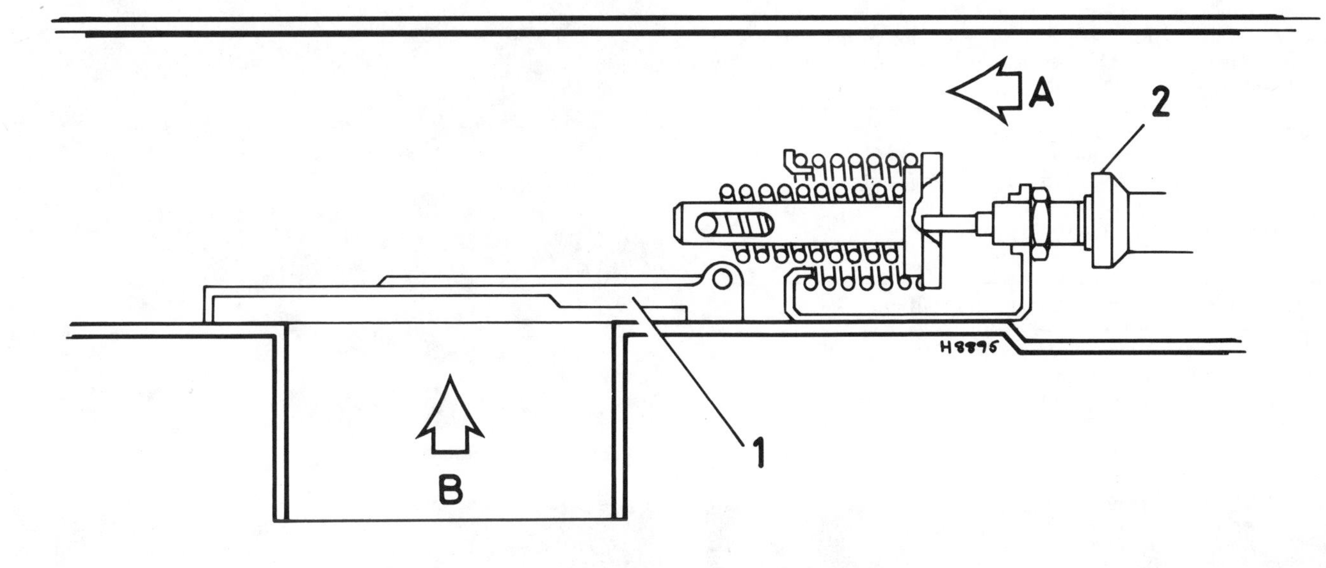

Fig. 3.1 Air cleaner temperature control (Sec 4)

A Cold air
B Warm air
1 Flap valve
2 Control unit

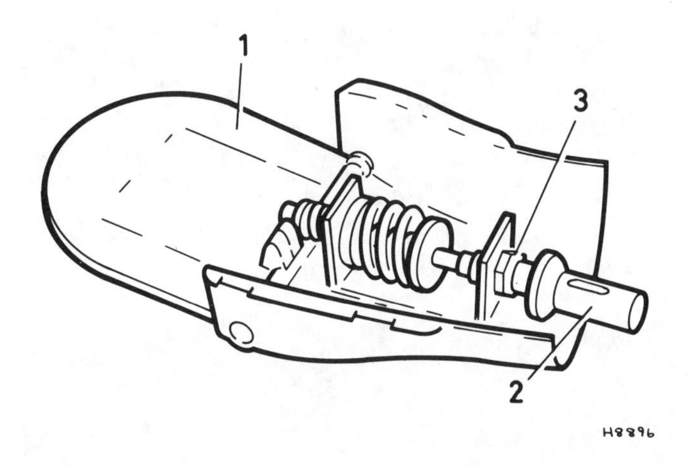

Fig. 3.2 Air cleaner temperature control unit (Sec 4)

1 Flap valve
2 Control element
3 Locknut

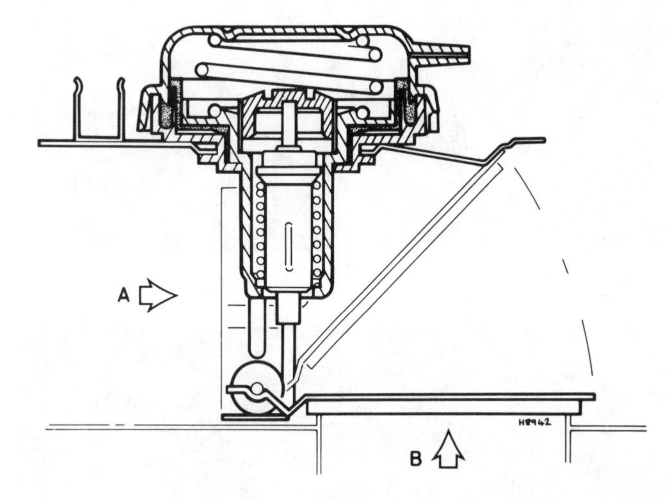

Fig. 3.3 Air cleaner vacuum control unit (Sec 4)

A Cold air
B Warm air

close the cold air route (A).

4 If adjustment is required, bend back the retaining lugs and remove the sensor/valve.

5 Release the nut (3) and adjust the element (2) – Fig. 3.2. Grease the valve flap pivots.

6 Some air cleaners have a vacuum connection. Cold air entry should be closed at an ambient temperature of between −18 and −20°C (0 and −4°F) and closed against warm air at between 3 and 5°C (37 and 41°F). If not, renew the vacuum capsule.

5 Fuel filters – cleaning

1 At the specified intervals, extract the screw from the centre of the fuel pump cover and lift up the cover.

2 Clean the filter screen and mop out any dirt from the pump. Refit the lid, making sure that the gasket is in good condition.

3 Also at the specified intervals, clean the fuel filter, which is part of the tank transmitter unit; removal of which is described in Section 7.

6 Fuel pump – testing, removal and refitting

1 If the fuel pump is suspected of being faulty, disconnect the inlet hose from the carburettor and place its open end in a container.
2 Have an assistant actuate the starter. Regular, well defined spurts of fuel should be seen to be ejected from the end of the pipe.
3 The fuel pump cannot be repaired, as it is a sealed unit, and any fault will mean a new pump.
4 Disconnect the two hoses from the pump, making sure to identify their fitted position first (photo).
5 Unbolt the pump from the crankcase.
6 Transfer the insulator block to the new pump and fit a new gasket to each side.
7 Refit by reversing the removal operation.

7 Fuel level transmitter – removal and refitting

1 Disconnect the battery negative lead and remove the rear seat cushion, as described in Chapter 12.
2 Remove the cover plate (photo).
3 Disconnect the fuel hoses and leads from the transmitter unit (photo).
4 By placing a large blade against the tabs, twist the transmitter

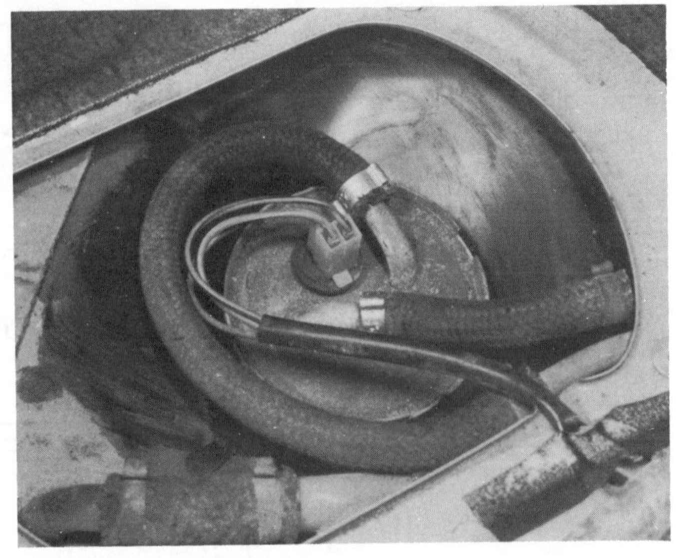

7.3 Fuel level transmitter

6.4 Fuel pump

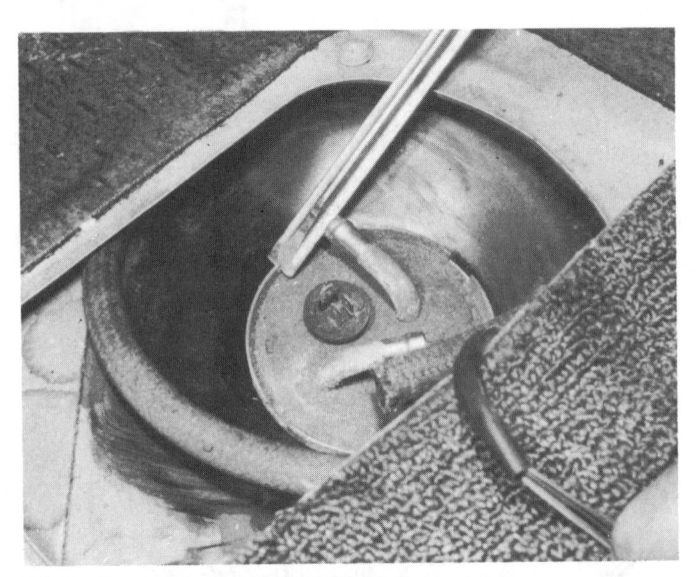

7.4 Unscrewing the fuel level transmitter

7.2 Removing fuel level transmitter cover plate screw

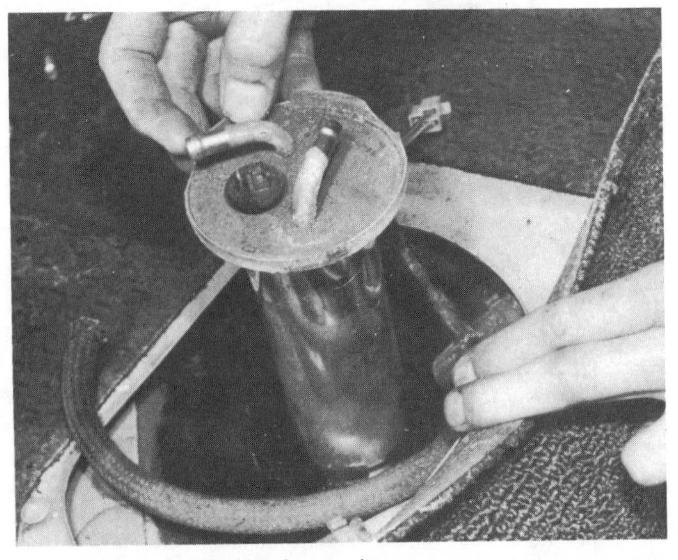

7.5 Withdrawing the fuel level transmitter

mounting plate to release it from the fuel tank (photo).
5 Withdraw the unit straight upwards (photo).
6 Clean the filter mesh (photo), check the condition of the sealing ring and refit the unit, in the reverse order to dismantling. If a new transmitter is being fitted, remove the retainer before installation.

8 Fuel tank – removal, repair and refitting

1 The fuel tank is in the form of two separate compartments connected by a hose.
2 Drain the fuel using the plug provided, or by syphoning.
3 Disconnect and remove the tank transmitter unit if the right-hand tank is being removed.
4 Disconnect the fuel filler pipe if the right-hand tank is being removed (photo). Remove the tank shields.
5 Unbolt and lower the tank until the breather and evaporation hoses can be disconnected.
6 A leaking fuel tank should be repaired by specialists – often radiator repairers will undertake this job. **On no account** attempt to weld or solder a fuel tank unless it has been steamed out for a generous period to remove all explosive vapour.
7 Refitting is a reversal of removal.

9 Carburettor – description

The carburettor is of 4-barrel, downdraught type with automatic choke (photos).

Features of the carburettor include a throttle damper, fuel shut-off solenoid valve and vacuum diaphragm unit.

The automatic choke is coolant-heated. At coolant temperatures above 17°C (63°F), a coolant temperature switch supplies current to an electric choke heater as well.

Tamperproof caps are fitted to detect and deter unqualified carburettor adjustments. This is particularly true in countries with strict emission control regulations – be sure you are not contravening any of these regulations when resetting the carburettor.

10 Carburettor – idling adjustment

1 Before carrying out this work, make sure that the ignition is correctly set and the valve clearances are as specified (Chapters 4 and 1).
2 Have the engine idling at the normal operating temperature. Turn the throttle speed screw (1) to obtain a speed of between 800 and 900 rpm – Fig. 3.4.

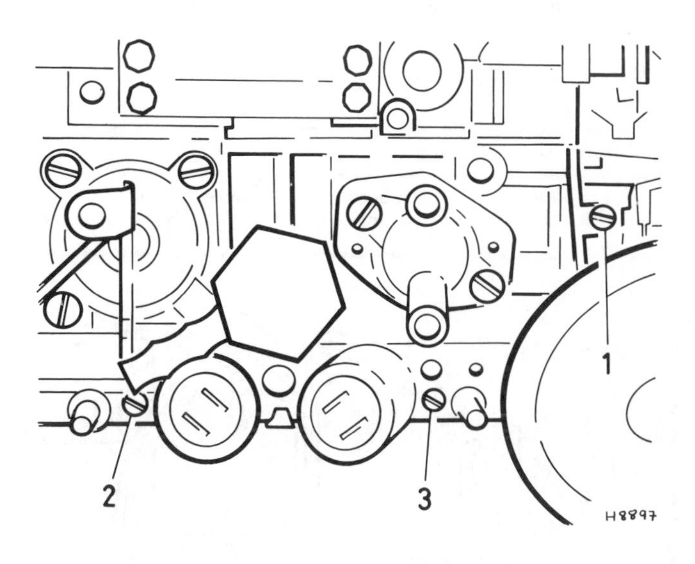

Fig. 3.4 Carburettor control screws (Sec 10)

1 Throttle speed screw
2 Idle mixture screw
3 Idle mixture screw

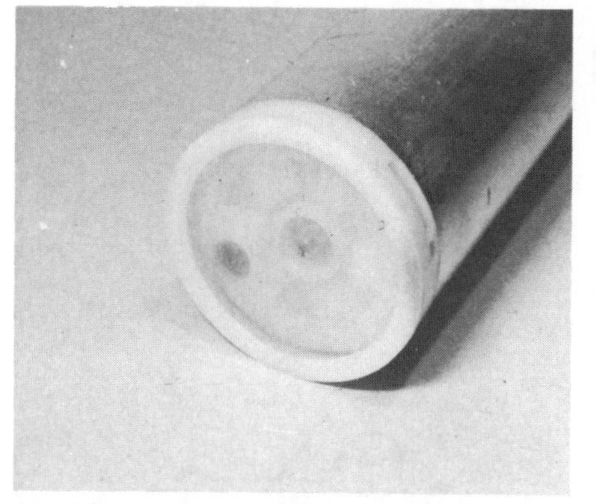

7.6 Filter mesh on fuel level transmitter

8.4 Fuel filler pipe

9.1A Carburettor from automatic choke side

9.1B Carburettor from throttle control side

9.1C Carburettor showing vacuum hose connections

9.1D Carburettor from fuel cut-off solenoid side

3 If the mixture setting requires adjustment, the most satisfactory way to adjust it is by connecting an exhaust gas analyser in accordance with the manufacturer's instructions. Remove the tamperproof caps.
4 Turn each of the mixture screws in sequence until the CO content of the exhaust gas is between 0.5 and 1.5% by volume.
5 Adjust the throttle speed screw again if necessary to bring the idle speed to the specified level.
6 If an exhaust gas analyser is not available, turn each mixture screw out in sequence until maximum idle speed is obtained and then turn each screw in until the idle speed just begins to fall. Readjust the throttle speed screw.
7 Fit new tamperproof caps.

11 Carburettor – cleaning

1 The need for complete carburettor overhaul seldom arises. When it does, the wear in internal components may indicate that a new or rebuilt unit would be a more economical alternative. The need for just a thorough clean will probably be all that is normally required.
2 Remove the air cleaner (Section 3).
3 Unscrew the four cover retaining nuts and eight screws, also the clip (1) – Fig. 3.5.
4 Disconnect the vacuum hose from the Stage 2 damper.
5 Lever off the carburettor cover with a screwdriver.
6 Remove the fuel inlet screw from the banjo union and clean the filter gauze.
7 Remove the retainer (1), float and needle valve with retaining spring (2) – Fig. 3.6.
8 Remove the idle jets (2) and idle air jets (1) – Fig. 3.7.
9 Blow air through the main jets (1) – Fig. 3.8.
10 Lift out the plunger (1) and spring (2) – Fig. 3.9.
11 Remove the keeper from the pivot (1) the lever (2) and jet needles (3) – Fig. 3.10. Blow through all jets and passages with air from a tyre pump. Mop out the float bowl.
12 Reassemble by reversing the dismantling procedure, use new gaskets as necessary.

Fig. 3.5 Carburettor cover retaining nuts and screws – arrowed (Sec 11)

1 Clip

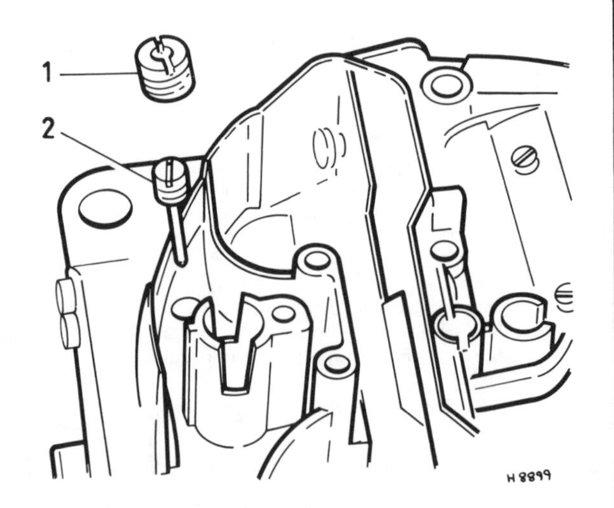

Fig. 3.7 Idle air jet (1) and idle jet (2) (Sec 11)

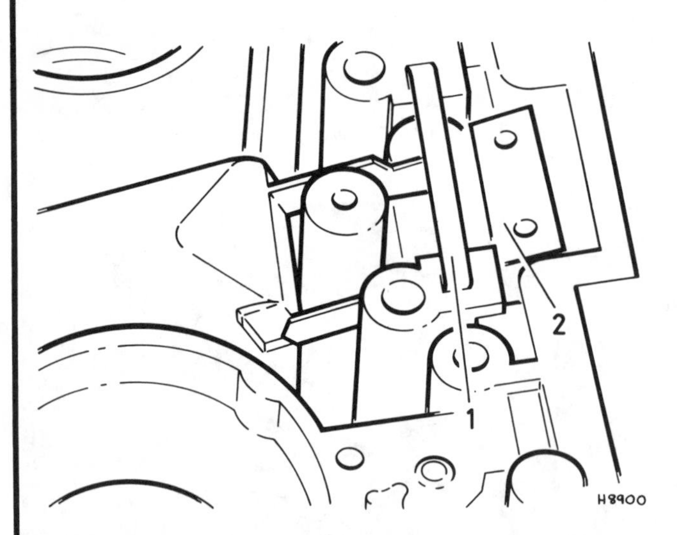

Fig. 3.6 Float retainer (1) and spring (2) (Sec 11)

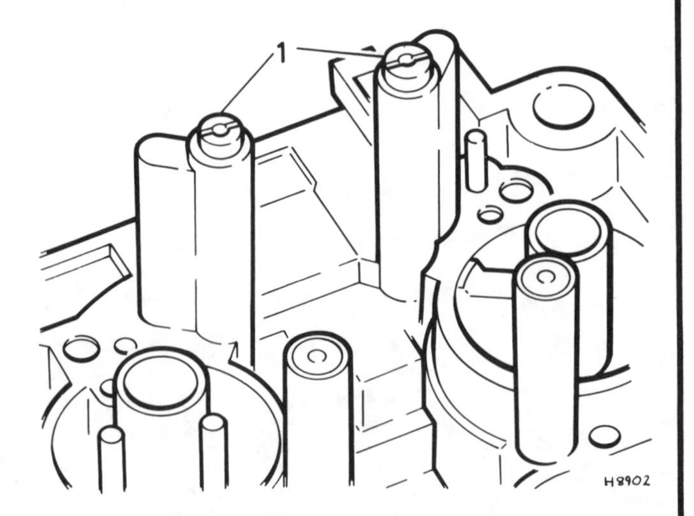

Fig. 3.8 Main jets (1) (Sec 11)

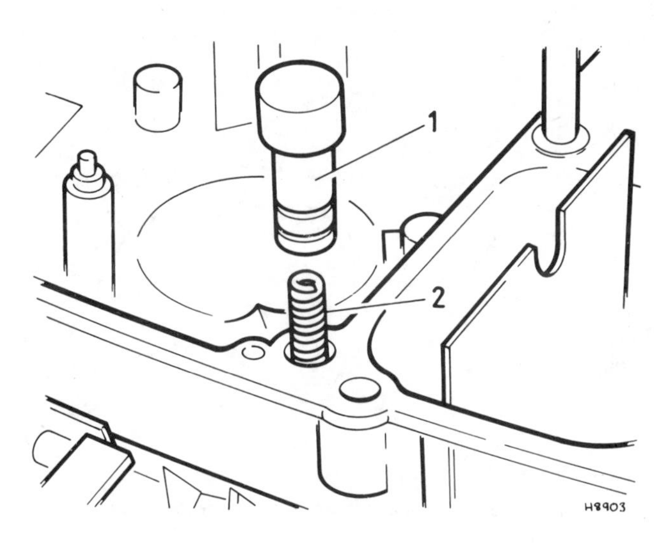

Fig. 3.9 Plunger (1) and spring (2) (Sec 11)

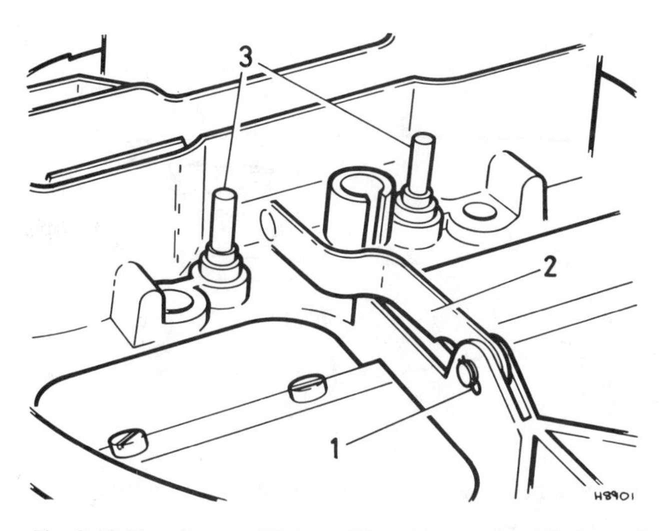

Fig. 3.10 Pivot keeper (1), lever (2) and jet needles (3) (Sec 11)

12 Automatic choke – adjustment

1 With the engine cold and the air cleaner removed, partially drain the cooling system and remove the choke housing cover with the coolant hoses attached.

2 Push the pull-down rod (2) against the intermediate lever (3) – Fig. 3.12.

3 Push lever (4) up to its stop. Check the choke valve plate gap (A) with a twist drill or gauge wire. This should be between 1.1 and 1.3 mm (0.043 and 0.051 in). Adjust if necessary by slackening the nut (5) and turning the electrical actuator (1).

4 Now switch on the ignition and wait 3 minutes. Press the rod (2) to the left against its stop. Move lever (4) against its stop – Fig. 3.12.

5 Using a 4.2 mm (0.165 in) diameter twist drill, check the choke valve plate gap (A). This should be 4.1 to 4.3 mm (0.161 to 0.169 in), otherwise alter screw (6).

13 Throttle butterfly actuator – adjustment

1 Check the gap (A) between the screw (1) and the throttle lever (2) – Fig. 3.13. It should be between 2.8 and 3.0 mm (0.110 and 0.118 in). Where necessary, release the locknut (3) and turn the screw (4).

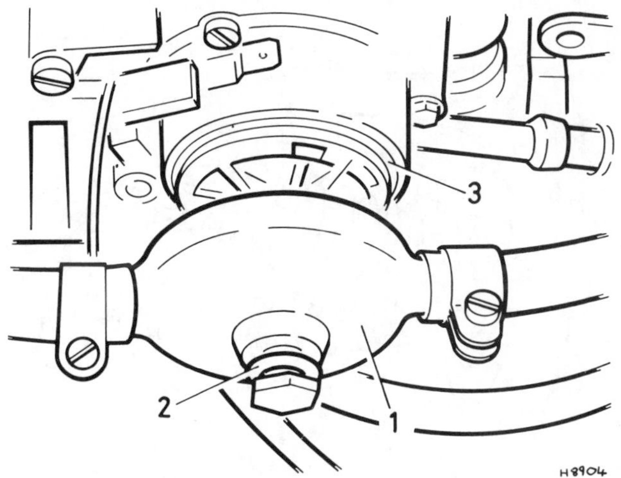

Fig. 3.11 Automatic choke housing (Sec 12)

1 Cover
2 Bolt
3 O-ring

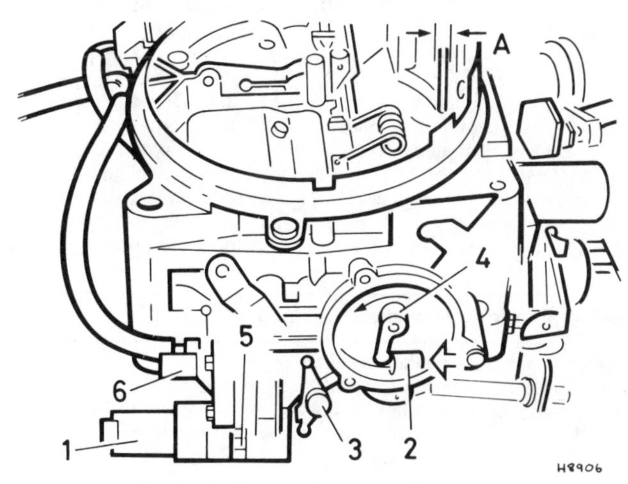

Fig. 3.12 Choke adjustment (Sec 12)

A Choke valve plate gap
1 Electrical actuator
2 Pull-down rod
3 Intermediate lever
4 Lever
5 Nut
6 Screw

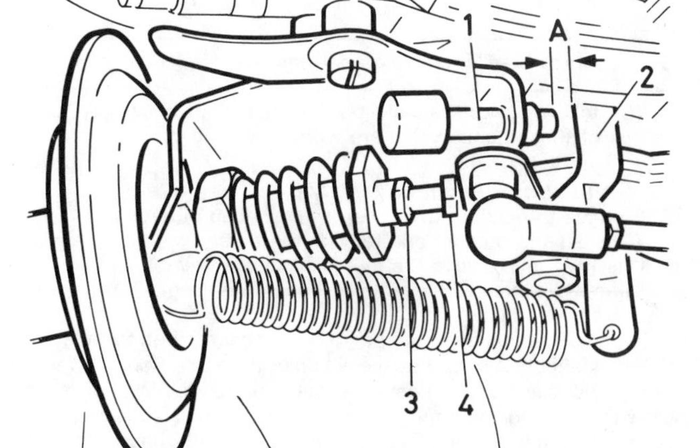

Fig. 3.13 Throttle butterfly actuator (Sec 13)

A Screw-to-throttle lever gap
1 Screw
2 Throttle lever
3 Locknut
4 Screw

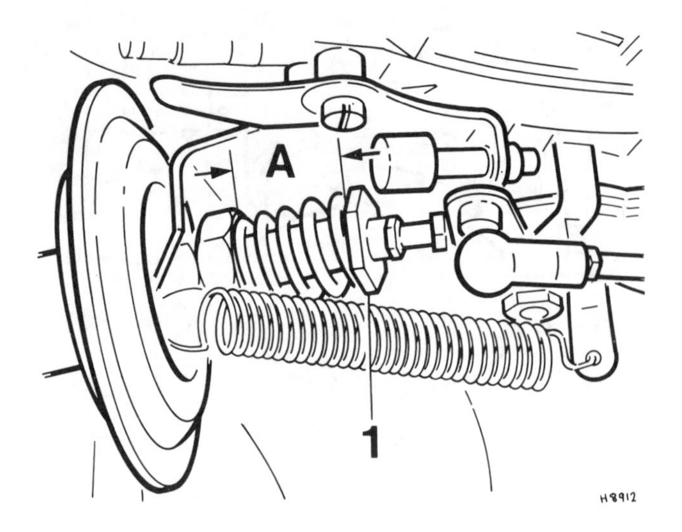

Fig. 3.14 Throttle actuator spring (Sec 13)

A Spring length *1 Nut*

2 Now check the spring length (A) – Fig. 3.14. This should be 23.0 mm (0.91 in) between the nuts, otherwise turn the nut (1).

3 A cause of hesitation when accelerating can be due to the guide roller not resting on the bearing surface when in the idling position. If necessary, loosen the stop screw of the throttle actuator until the idle stop screw is against its stop. Release the three gate fixing screws and move the gate to make the guide roller contact the bearing surface.

14 Carburettor – removal and refitting

1 Remove the air cleaner (Section 3).

2 Disconnect the coolant hoses from the automatic choke housing, making sure that the coolant is cool and not pressurised. Tie the open ends of the hoses up as high as possible to prevent loss of coolant.

3 Disconnect the fuel hose.

4 Disconnect the throttle linkage.

5 Disconnect the leads from the fuel shut-off solenoid valves and choke housing.

6 Identify and then disconnect the vacuum hoses.

7 Unscrew the carburettor mounting nuts and lift the carburettor from the intake manifold.

8 Refitting is a reversal of removal, use new gaskets and secure the return valve bracket under one of the mounting nuts.

15 Carburettor – dismantling and reassembly

1 The following work should be limited to that necessary for the renewal of those items which are worn or damaged.

Float and fuel inlet needle valve

2 Remove the carburettor cover, as described in Section 11.

3 Take out the retainer and remove the float.

4 Unscrew and remove the fuel inlet needle valve.

5 Refit by reversing the removal operations, engaging the spring from the float side.

6 To check the fuel level, fill the float chamber through the inlet hose until the fuel flow is cut off by the action of the valve. Carefully remove the top cover, and using a depth gauge, measure the level of the fuel below the float chamber rim (no gasket) at a point 18.0 mm (0.71 in) from the centre line of the float. The correct dimension is between 6.0 and 8.0 mm (0.24 and 0.32 in). If necessary, bend the float arms at the points arrowed in Fig. 3.16 and repeat the checking procedure.

Throttle block gasket

7 With the carburettor removed, extract the screws (1 and 2) – Fig. 3.17.

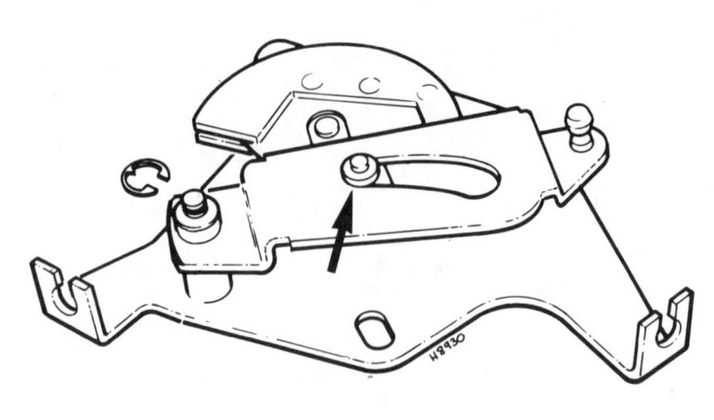

Fig. 3.15 Throttle actuator guide roller (Sec 13)

Arrow indicates guide roller-to-bearing surface contact

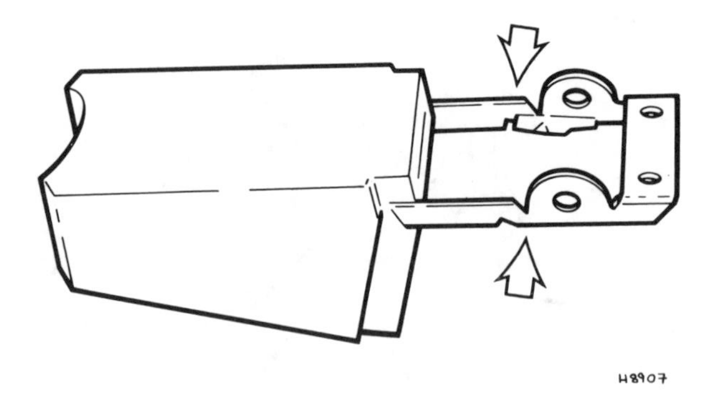

Fig. 3.16 Bend the float arms in the positions arrowed (Sec 15)

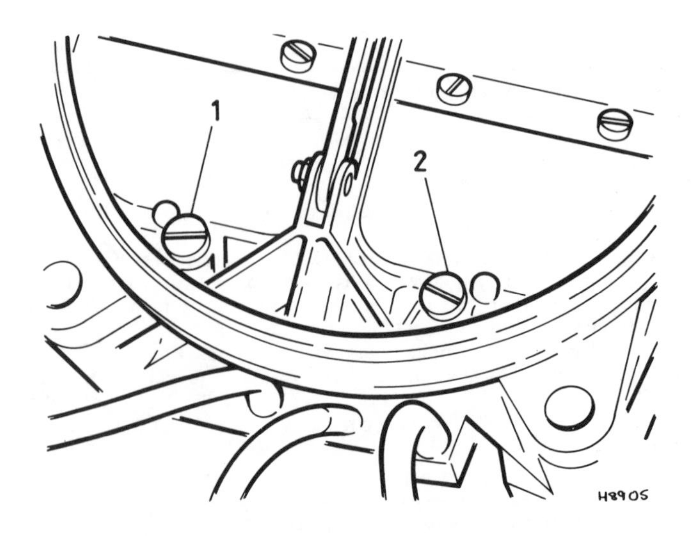

Fig. 3.17 Throttle block screws (1 and 2) (Sec 15)

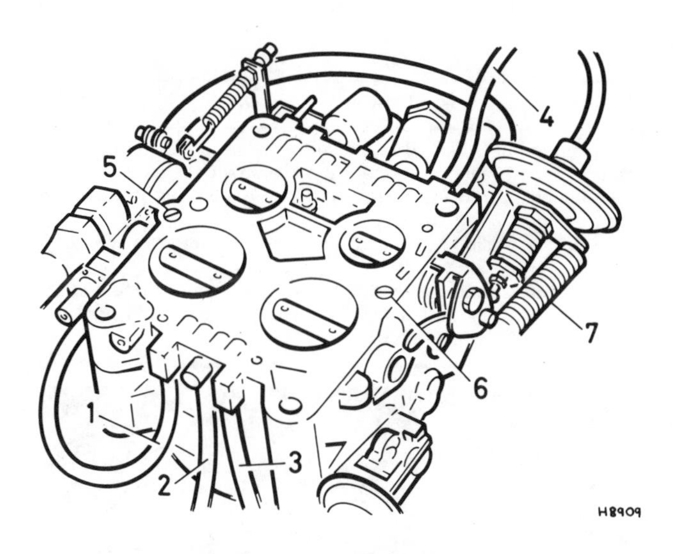

Fig. 3.18 Throttle block (Sec 15)

1 Vacuum hose
2 Vacuum hose
3 Vacuum hose
4 Vacuum hose
5 Screw
6 Screw
7 Spring

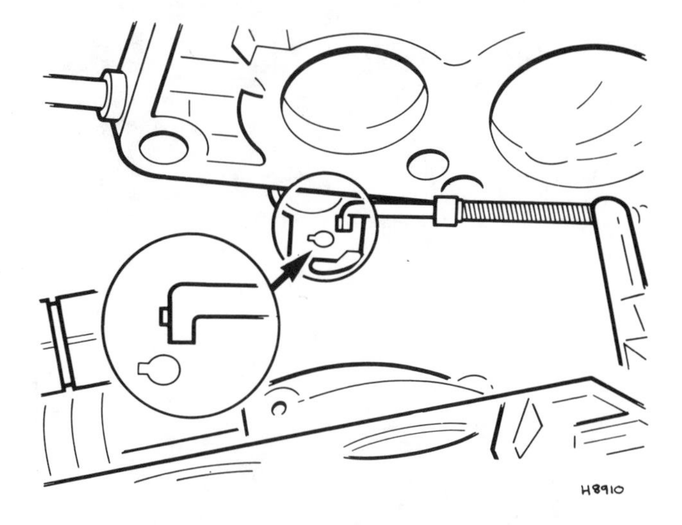

Fig. 3.19 Accelerator pump linkage (Sec 15)

8 Disconnect the vacuum hoses (1,2,3 and 4), remove screws (5 and 6) and unhook the spring (7) – Fig. 3.18.
9 Raise the throttle block and turn it through 180° to disconnect the accelerator pump linkage.
10 Refitting is a reversal of removal; always use a new gasket.

Idle cut-off (anti-diesel) valve

11 If the idle cut-off valve cannot be heard to click when the ignition is switched on, it is faulty and must be renewed. Take care not to damage the conical sealing face of the valve.

Choke heating element

12 Partially drain the coolant. Remove the bolt and pull the choke housing cover away.
13 Pull off the electrical lead, extract the three screws and remove the choke cover. A new cover is supplied complete with spira' element.
14 When refitting the choke cover, align the marks and ınake sure that the concave side of the intermediate plate is towards the heating spiral. Make sure that the actuating lever (2) enters the spring eye (3) when fitting the choke cover to the body – Fig. 3.22.

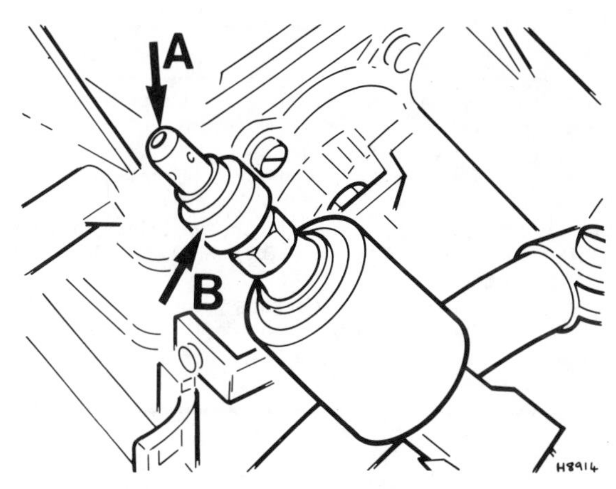

Fia. 3.20 Idle cut-off valve (Sec 15)

Check the condition of the conical sealing face (A) and the sealing ring (B)

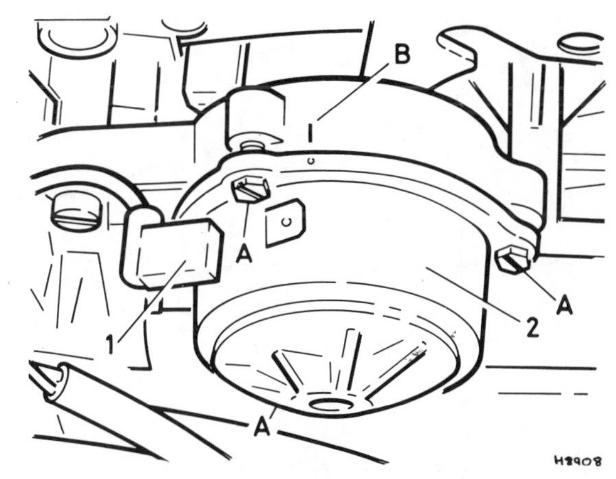

Fig. 3.21 Automatic choke (Sec 15)

A Screws
B Alignment marks
1 Heating element lead
2 Cover

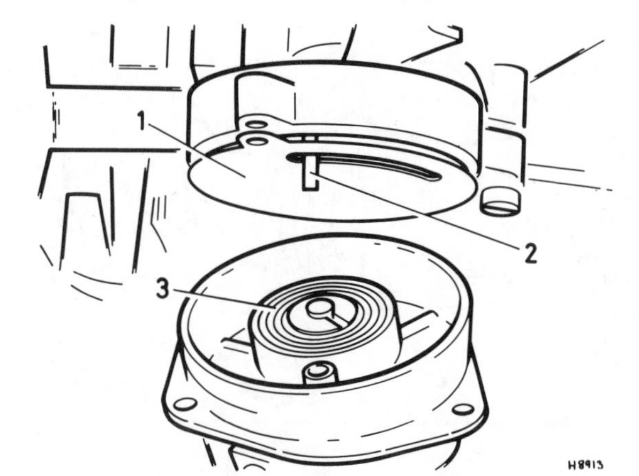

Fig. 3.22 Automatic choke components (Sec 15)

1 Intermediate plate
2 Actuating lever
3 Bi-metallic spring

General

15 All jets and air bleeds may be removed and blown through with air from a tyre pump and checked for correct size against specification. **Never** probe a jet with wire.
16 Obtain a repair kit which will contain all the necessary gaskets and other small items for use during reassembly.

16 Heat sensitive bypass starting system

1 A faulty unit will give rise to high CO content of the exhaust gas and the engine running on after switching off the ignition. Difficult idling will also occur when the engine is cold.

2 To check this system, first withdraw the assembly from the carburettor.

3 If the coolant is cold (20°C/68°F) there should be a gap (A) – Fig. 3.23 – of between 2.0 and 2.4 mm (0.079 and 0.095 in) between the plunger (1) and housing (2).

4 At normal operating temperatures the gap should be closed.

5 To adjust the bypass starting system cool the assembly to 20°C (68°F) and use the screw (3) to adjust the gap (A) to the dimension given in paragraph 3.

6 When refitting the unit, make sure that the slot faces upwards.

17 Throttle control torsion spring – renewal

1 Release the nut (1) and disconnect the cable (photo). On cars with automatic transmission, disconnect the kickdown cable.

2 Disconnect the rod (1) and unbolt and remove the throttle lever assembly – Fig. 3.24.

3 Prise off the E-clip (1), remove the wave washer (2) and lever (3) – Fig. 3.25.

4 Remove the second E-clip, disconnect the torsion spring and take off the wave washer and sector. Renew the bush and spring as necessary.

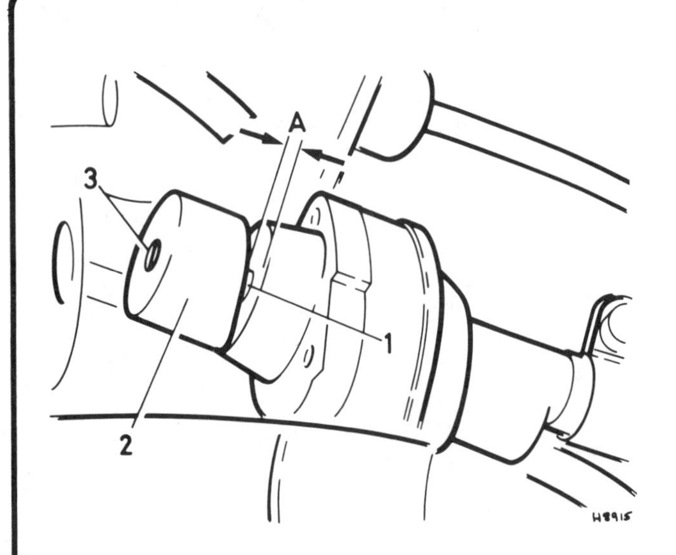

Fig. 3.23 Heat sensitive bypass (Sec 16)

A Gap
1 Plunger
2 Housing
3 Screw

17.1 Throttle cable locknut (1) and nipple (arrowed)

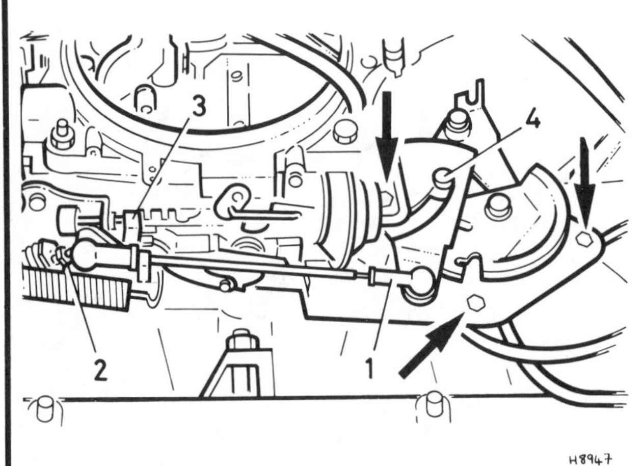

Fig. 3.24 Throttle connecting rod (Sec 17)

1 Rod
2 Positioner
3 Throttle lever
4 Guide roller
Arrows indicate securing bolts

Fig. 3.25 Throttle quadrant (Sec 17)

1 E-clip
2 Wave washer
3 Lever

18 Accelerator pedal – removal and refitting

Early models

1 The tread plate can be removed from the arm by prising up the bottom edge of the plate from the floor with a screwdriver and detaching the circlip from its upper pivot.
2 To remove the arm, first withdraw the facia under cover (Chapter 12). Disconnect the pedal return spring.
3 Slacken the accelerator cable until the cable can be unhooked from the pedal.
4 Release the clip – Fig. 3.26 – and remove the washer (1).
5 Push the accelerator pedal from its mounting.
6 Refitting is a reversal of removal. Adjust the cable as described in the next Section. Lubricate where necessary.

Some later models

7 The accelerator pedal has a balljointed rod connected to the pedal arm which operates a crankarm through the bulkhead (photo).
8 Removal and refitting is basically the same as that for early models.

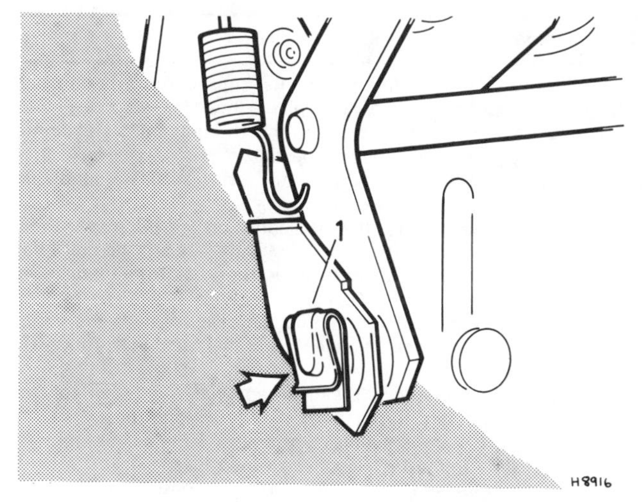

Fig. 3.26 Accelerator pedal pivot (Sec 18)

1 Washer *Remove clip (arrowed)*

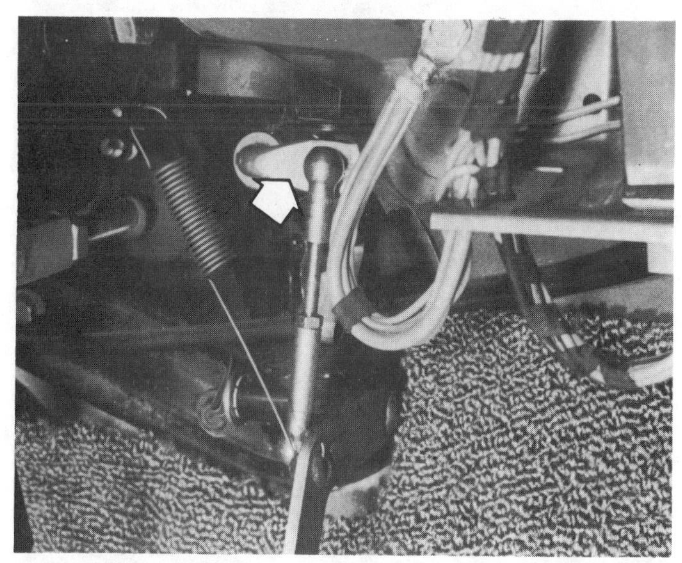

18.7 Accelerator pedal ball-jointed rod and crankarm (arrowed) – later models

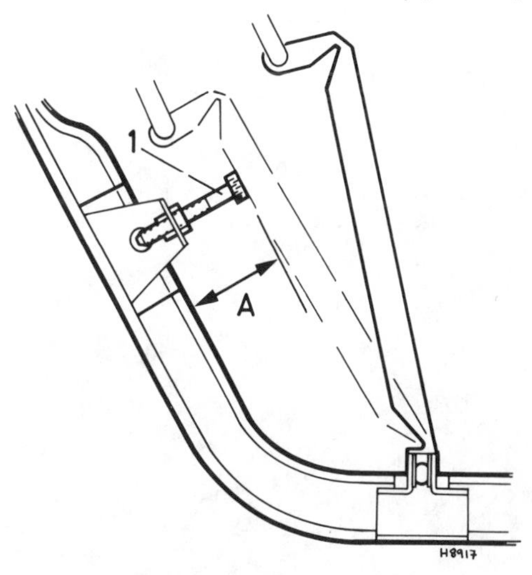

Fig. 3.27 Accelerator pedal position (Sec 19)

A Pedal depressed dimension *1 Pedal stop*

19 Accelerator cable – renewal and adjustment

1 Remove the air cleaner and the facia under cover.
2 Slacken the accelerator cable at the carburettor and unhook it from the pedal arm.
3 Release the cable bulkhead sleeve and disconnect the cable at the carburettor end both from the bracket and quandrant (see photo 17.1). Draw the cable through the bulkhead.
4 Refit the new cable by reversing the removal operations. Check that the pedal stop is so adjusted that when the pedal is fully depressed, dimension (A) is 47.0 mm (1.85 in) – Fig. 3.27. With the pedal released and the engine hot (choke out of action) adjust the cable end fittings to eliminate all slack. On models with automatic transmission, when the pedal is fully depressed it must depress the kickdown stop and the throttle butterfly arm must be against the stop (Chapter 6, Section 14).

20 Pressure regulator

1 This is installed in the fuel pressure line between the pump and carburettor, its purpose being to maintain a constant fuel pressure at the carburettor fuel inlet needle valve (photo).
2 A faulty unit cannot be dismantled, only renewed complete.

20.1 Fuel pressure regulator

21 Manifolds and exhaust system

1 The engine is of crossflow design, having the intake and exhaust manifolds on opposite sides of the cylinder head.
2 Always use new gaskets when fitting the manifolds and tighten the nuts to the specified torque (photos).
3 The intake manifold is coolant-heated and also has a connection for the brake servo vacuum hose.
4 The hot air collectors for the air cleaner on the exhaust manifold are subject to corrosion particularly around the area of the bolt heads (photo). A regular application of heat resisting paint may reduce this corrosion.
5 Before the intake manifold can be removed, remove the spring-loaded vent tube which runs between the crankcase and the underside of the manifold.
6 Before the exhaust manifold can be removed, the hot air collector plates must be unbolted to reach the manifold fixing nuts.
7 The exhaust system is simple to remove in sections as the joints are of flange type (photo). Disconnect the support bracket from the transmission (photo) and release the rubber mounting rings (photo). Use new sealing rings at the flanges and the manifold. The leading pipe at the manifold connects with the inboard pipe of the rear section.
8 Tighten all nuts and bolts to the specified torque.

21.4 Exhaust manifold hot air collector cover

21.2A Inlet manifold gasket

21.7A Typical exhaust pipe flange joints

21.2B Exhaust manifold section

21.7B Exhaust support

21.7C Exhaust mounting ring

PART B: FUEL INJECTION SYSTEM

22 General description

Two types of fuel injection system are fitted: the Series 1 models are equipped with the Bosch K-Jetronic system, and Series 2 models are fitted with the Bosch L-Jetronic system.

Bosch K-Jetronic

Fuel is drawn from the fuel tank by an electrically-operated pump, and is then fed, via a pressure reservoir and filter unit, to the fuel distributor unit. The fuel is then pumped direct to the fuel injectors which are located near the inlet valves, but mounted in four induction manifold branches. The system is of 'continuous acting' type, and the amount of fuel admitted to the injectors, by the fuel distributor, is governed by a pivoting baffle plate mounted in the air intake. Air drawn into the engine lifts the baffle plate, and this action moves a metering shuffle valve in the fuel distributor. The ratio of air to fuel is thus controlled to a fine degree. After the mixture is drawn into the engine cylinder, the normal four stroke combustion cycle takes place.

The fuel is maintained at a constant pressure by a pressure regulator, incorporated into the distributor unit, excess fuel being diverted through a return line to the fuel tank.

For cold starting, a solenoid valve injects fuel into the air intake for a period determined by the coolant temperature. In addition, a temperature sensitive (warm-up) regulator, working in conjunction with an additional air slide valve, is connected to the fuel distributor unit, and has the effect of increasing the amount of fuel injected by the injectors.

Later models are fitted with a throttle bypass valve in place of the additional air slide valve. On some versions this valve is coolant-heated.

A normal type throttle butterfly valve, mounted between the baffle plate and the engine cylinders, is connected to the accelerator pedal.

Bosch L-Jetronic

In fuel injection systems of Bosch L-Jetronic type the volume of air drawn in by the engine is measured.

Each cylinder has an independent injector.

An additional air slide valve bypasses the throttle butterfly stub pipe and controls the additional air volume required when the air is still cold. When the engine is warm, idle speed airflow control is by means of another bypass around the throttle butterfly.

Fuel supply and pressure is provided by an electric pump with line

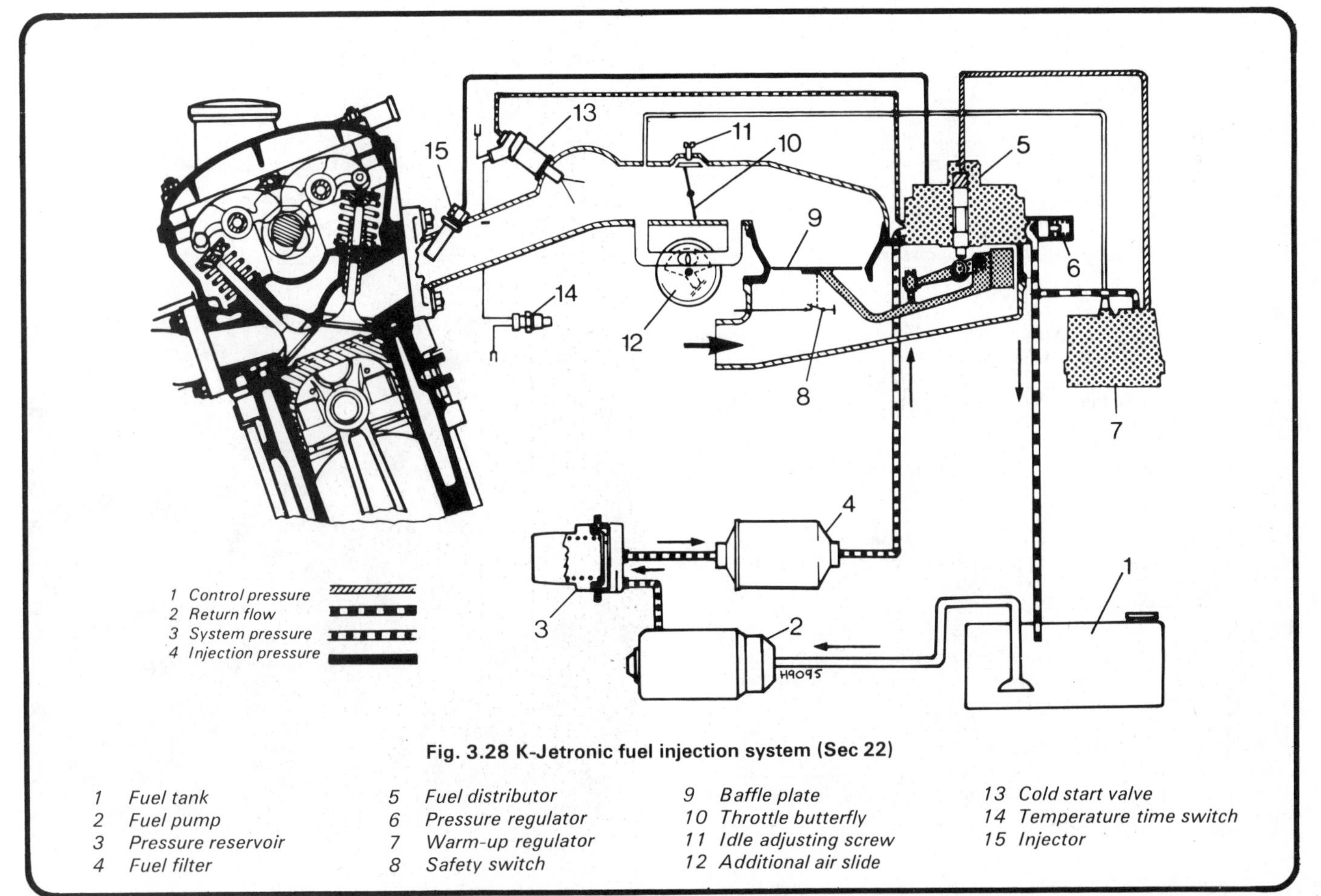

Fig. 3.28 K-Jetronic fuel injection system (Sec 22)

1 Fuel tank
2 Fuel pump
3 Pressure reservoir
4 Fuel filter
5 Fuel distributor
6 Pressure regulator
7 Warm-up regulator
8 Safety switch
9 Baffle plate
10 Throttle butterfly
11 Idle adjusting screw
12 Additional air slide
13 Cold start valve
14 Temperature time switch
15 Injector

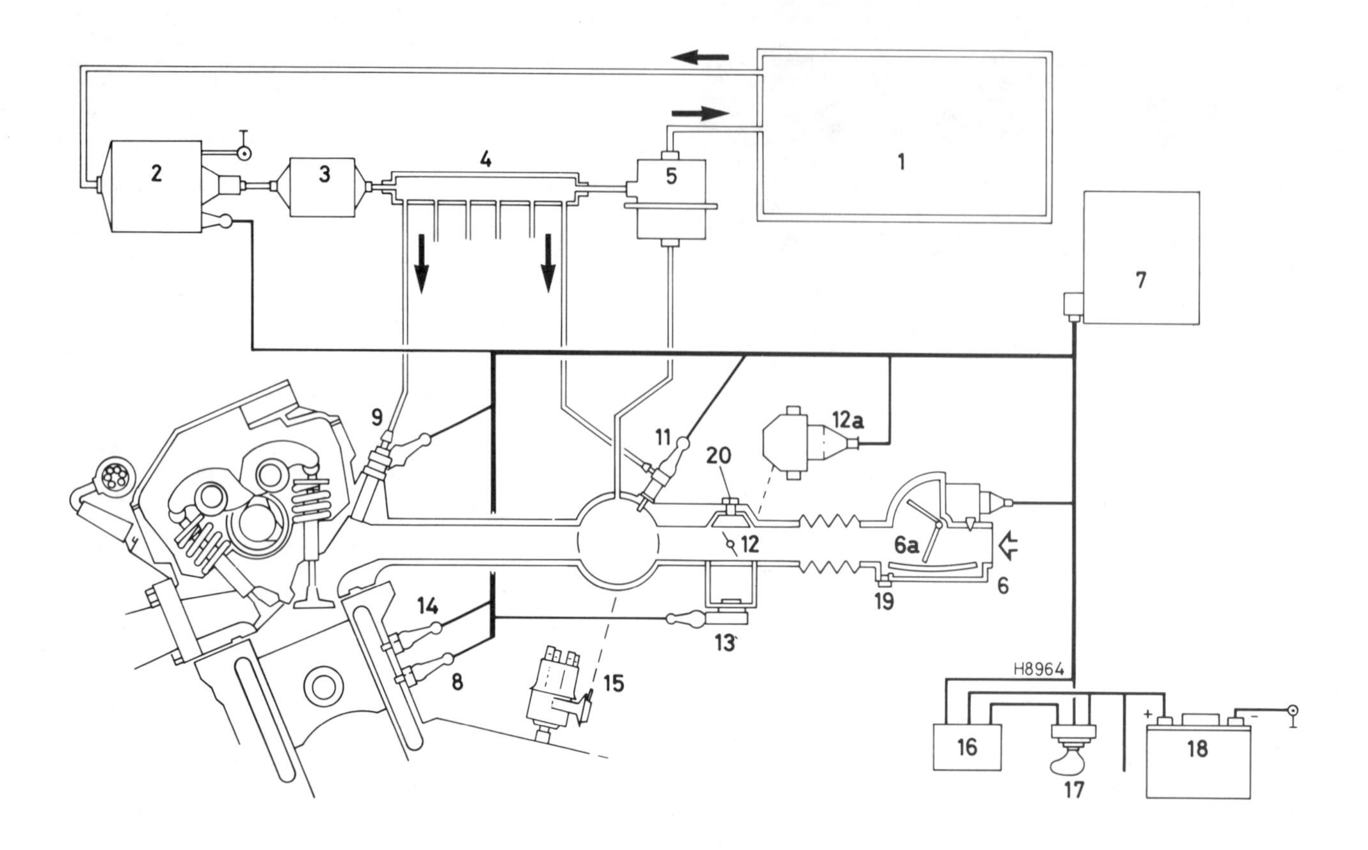

Fig. 3.29 L-Jetronic fuel injection system (Sec 22)

1 Fuel tank
2 Fuel pump
3 Fuel filter
4 Injection tube
5 Pressure regulator
6 Airflow sensor
6a Sensor plate
7 Control unit
8 Coolant temperature sensor
9 Injector
10 Intake pipe
11 Cold start valve
12 Throttle butterfly
12a Throttle switch
13 Throttle bypass valve (coolant-heated)
14 Temperature time switch
15 Distributor
16 Fuel pump relay
17 Ignition/starter switch
18 Battery
19 Mixture control screw
20 Idle speed control screw

filter and pressure regulator.

The volume of air drawn into the engine is measured by the air flow meter and this is converted into an electric impulse and transmitted to the control unit. A calculation is made to determine the quantity of fuel to be injected (based upon the engine running speed) into each cylinder.

Automatic cold start and warm-up devices, are incorporated in the system with corrections for idle speed and full load by contacts in the throttle butterfly switch. When the engine is on the overrun (throttle closed) fuel is shut off completely.

The electronic control unit processes information from the various engine sensors and sends an impulse to the electromagnetic fuel injectors to open them for a precisely defined period.

All types

Before making any adjustments to the fuel injection system be sure you are not contravening any emission control regulations.

23 Air cleaner – element renewal

1 Pull back the toggle clips and fold the air cleaner cover in the direction of the engine (photo).

2 Pull the element out from above.

3 Wipe the casing and fit the new element so that the word TOP is upward and the perforated plate is towards the mixture control unit.

23.1 Air cleaner element

24.1 Fuel filter – typical

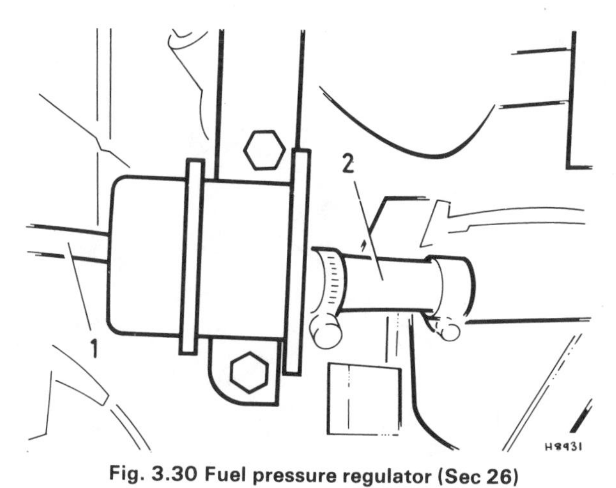

Fig. 3.30 Fuel pressure regulator (Sec 26)

1 Vacuum hose *2 Fuel hose*

24 Fuel filter – renewal

1 At the specified intervals, renew the filter by disconnecting the hoses (photo).
2 When refitting, make sure that the direction of fuel flow is correct.

25 Fuel pump – removal and refitting

1 Note the position of the connecting leads and disconnect them from the pump terminals (photo).
2 Unscrew the pump mounting nuts and clamp the flow and return hoses. Self-locking grips are useful for this.
3 Cut off the crimped type hose clip and disconnect the hose.
4 Remove the pump, complete with mounting.
5 The pump can be detached from the mounting.
6 Refitting is a reversal of removal, use new worm-type hose clips.
7 The pressure reservoir (if fitted) is mounted with the pump.
8 On some models, an auxiliary fuel pump is mounted in the fuel tank. It is removed and refitted with the fuel level transmitter (Section 7).

26 Fuel pressure regulator – removal and refitting

1 Pull off the vacuum hose (1) and fuel hose (2) – Fig. 3.30.
2 Unscrew the bolts and pull the pressure regulator out.
3 Refit by reversing the removal operations, but check the condition of the seal (1) – Fig. 3.32.

25.1 Fuel pump – L-Jetronic

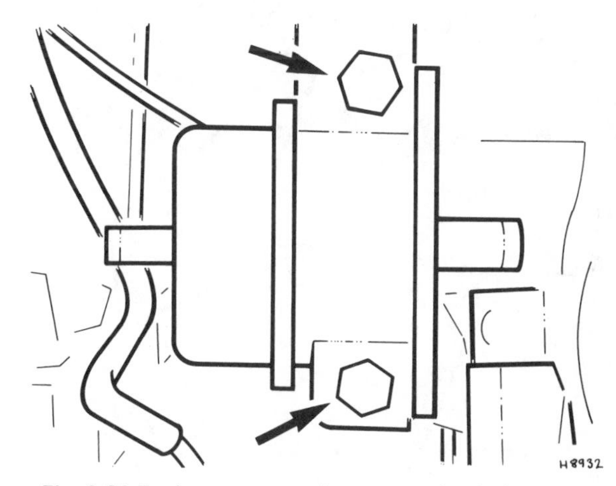

Fig. 3.31 Fuel pressure regulator mounting bolts – arrowed (Sec 26)

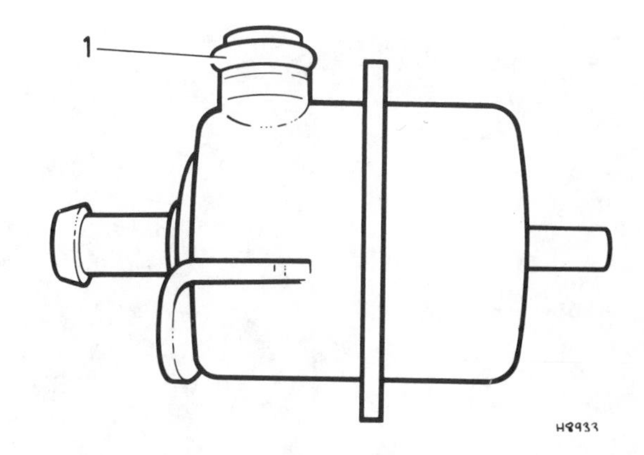

Fig. 3.32 Fuel pressure regulator seal (1) (Sec 26)

27 Fuel tank – removal and refitting

1 The operations are very similar to those described in Section 8, except that the tank connection is of rigid pipe type with union nuts.

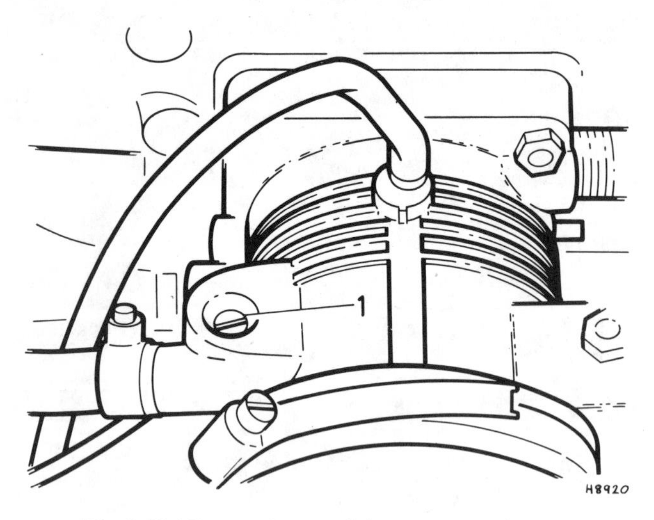

Fig. 3.33 Idle speed screw (1) – K-Jetronic (Sec 28)

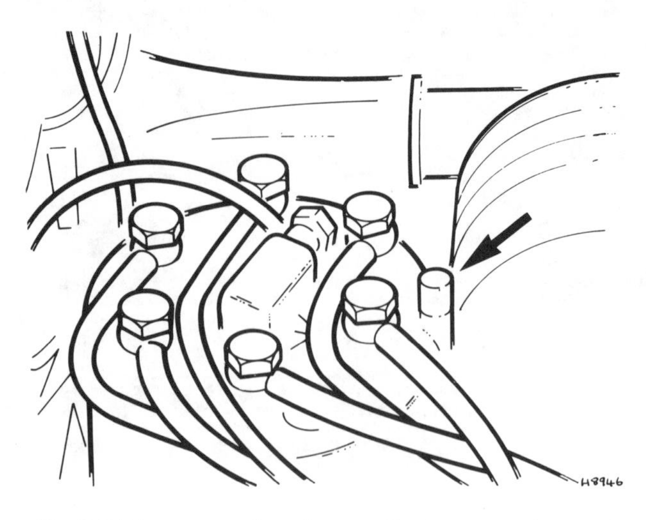

Fig. 3.35 Tamperproof cap (arrowed) – K-Jetronic (Sec 28)

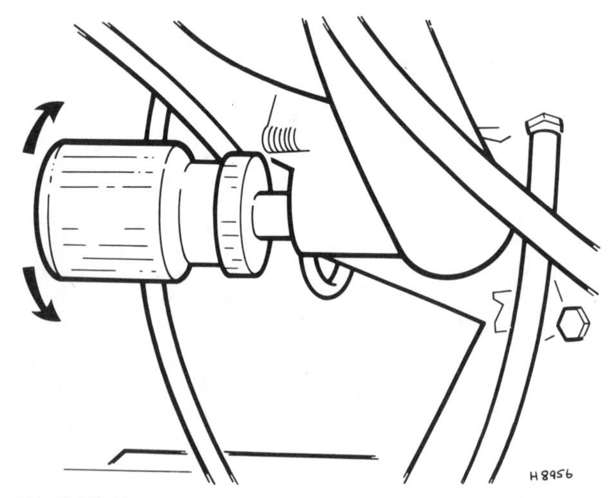

Fig. 3.34 Idle speed screw adjustment – L-Jetronic (Sec 28)
Screw is located in air bypass housing, on opposite side of manifold to throttle housing

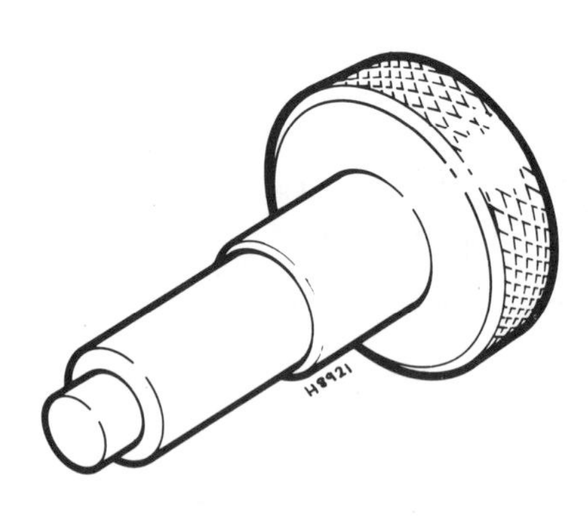

Fig. 3.36 BMW CO level adjustment tool No 13 1 100 (Sec 28)

28.4 Capped fuel mixture screw (arrowed) – L-Jetronic

28 Idle speed and mixture – adjustment

1 With the engine at normal operating temperature, turn the screw indicated – Fig. 3.33 or 3.34 – until the engine speed is as specified.
2 The mixture will not normally require adjustment; and in fact the screw is fitted with a tamperproof cap. If it must be adjusted special tools will be required. A tamperproof cap remover tool no 13 1 012 (K-Jetronic) or 13 1 011 (L-Jetronic), adjusting wrench 13 1 100 and CO measuring probes 13 0 020 for connection to an exhaust gas analyser.
3 Remove the plugs from the exhaust manifold and insert the probes connected to the exhaust gas analyser.
4 Remove the tamperproof cap (photo and Fig. 3.35) and then, with the engine idling at the normal operating temperature, use the special wrench to set the CO level to between 0.5 and 1.5%.
5 Fit a new tamperproof cap.

29 Fuel injection system – adjustment and checks

Throttle butterfly (K-Jetronic)

Adjustments for the L-Jetronic requires special gauges

1 The basic setting for the throttle butterfly should be carried out in the following way.

2 Remove the air intake hood and disconnect the accelerator cable.
3 Release the nut (1) and screw (2) until the stop (3) is free – Fig. 3.37. Now tighten the screw until the throttle butterfly just starts to lift. Tighten the screw through a further half a turn and tighten the locknut.
4 Adjust the accelerator cable, as described in Section 31.

Additional air slide (K-Jetronic)

5 Pull the plug (1) from the warm-up regulator – Fig. 3.38.
6 Disconnect both hoses from the additional air slide.
7 If the engine is cold, the air slide should be half open. Switch on the ignition and operate the starter. Check that current is present at the pin of the plug which is connected to the green/yellow wire.
8 Reconnect the plug and the two hoses, also the plug to the regulator. With the engine running, the air slide should close after five minutes. If it does not close even after tapping it, renew the air slide assembly.

Mixture regulator (K-Jetronic)

9 Detach the air intake duct (1) from the mixture regulator/throttle butterfly – Fig. 3.39.
10 Pull out the diode relay (D) and pump relay (P) – Fig. 3.40. Connect contact (87) from the pump relay base to B+; the fuel pump will run on.
11 With the pump running, raise the baffle plate using the hand or a magnet. Move the plate slowly up and over the range of movement. Lower the plate slowly and then pull up again immediately. Resistance should be immediately felt, without any free travel.
12 The baffle plate should be flush with the start of the tapered section of the air venturi or at most 0.5 mm (0.02 in) below.
13 Where necessary, adjust by detaching the mixture regulator from the intermediate housing and bend the shaped spring (2) – Fig. 3.41.
14 If the baffle plate is allowed to be too high, the engine will run on; if cold, poor starting will be the result.

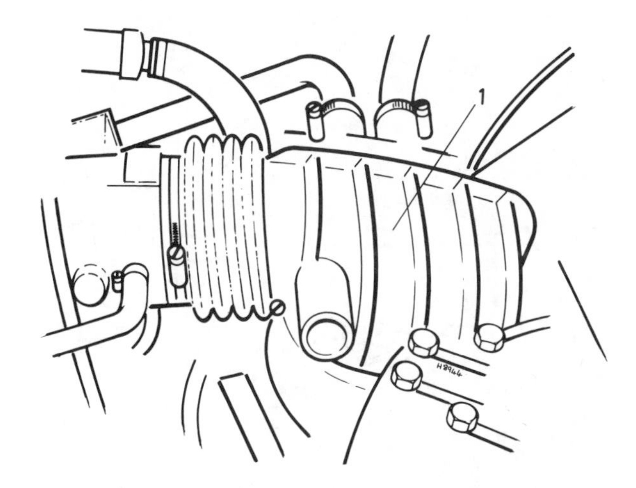

Fig. 3.39 Air intake duct (1) – K-Jetronic (Sec 29)

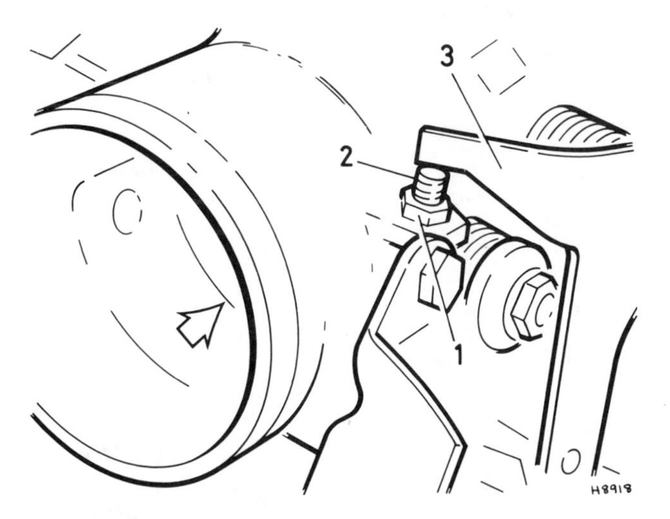

Fig. 3.37 Basic throttle butterfly setting – K-Jetronic (Sec 29)

1 Locknut
2 Screw
3 Stop
Throttle butterfly arrowed

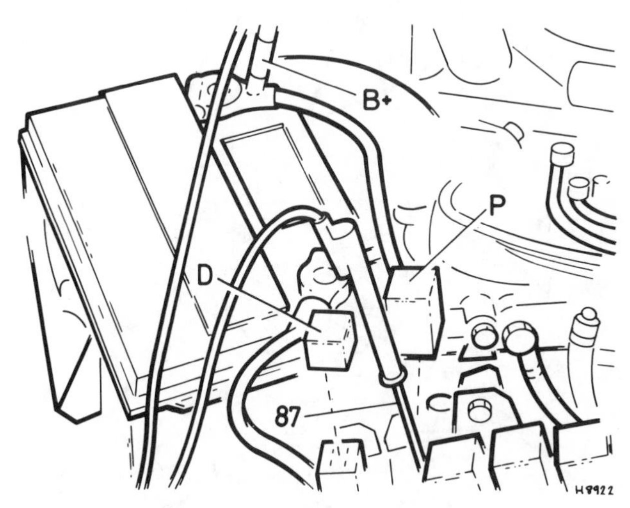

Fig. 3.40 Mixture regulator – K-Jetronic (Sec 29)

B+ Battery positive terminal
D Diode relay
P Pump relay
87 Probe to contact

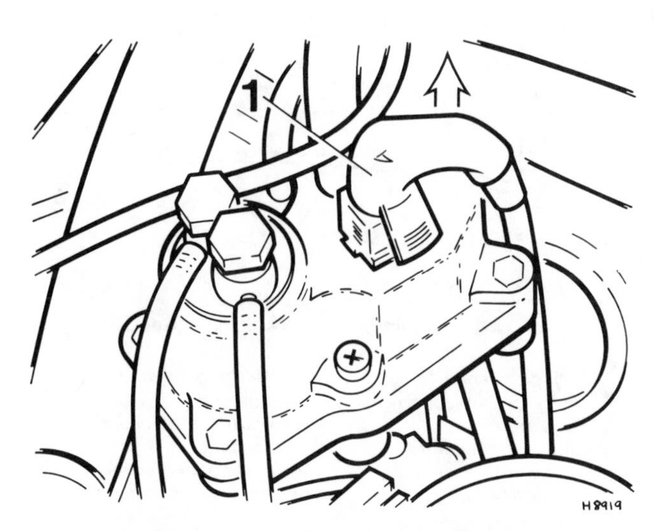

Fig. 3.38 Warm-up regulator – K-Jetronic (Sec 29)

Pull off the plug (1) in the direction arrowed

Cold start valve

15 Remove the valve with the fuel line attached (Fig. 3.48).
16 Connect bridging leads between the valve terminals and B+ and earth – Fig. 3.40.
17 Pull off the diode relay (D) and pump relay (P). Connect the contact (87) on the pump relay base with B+, the pump will operate and, by holding the start valve over a container, check that it sprays fuel. Pull off the start valve connections and dry the valve jet. No fuel must drip for a period of one minute.

Warm-up regulator (K-Jetronic)

18 Pull the plug (1) from the warm-up regulator – Fig. 3.38.

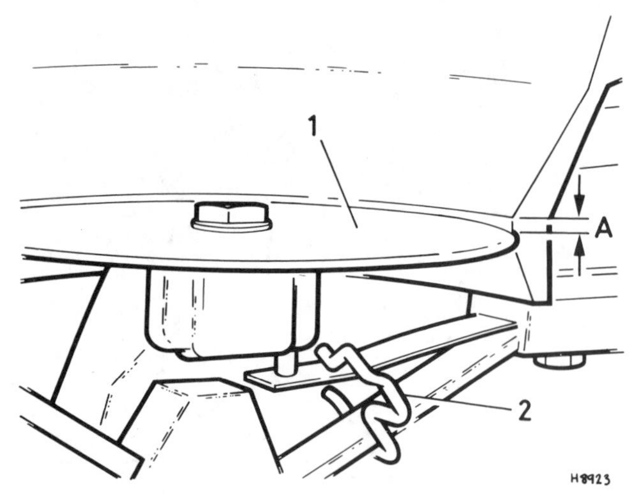

Fig. 3.41 Baffle plate (1) and shaped spring (2) – K-Jetronic (Sec 29)

A Maximum baffle plate depth

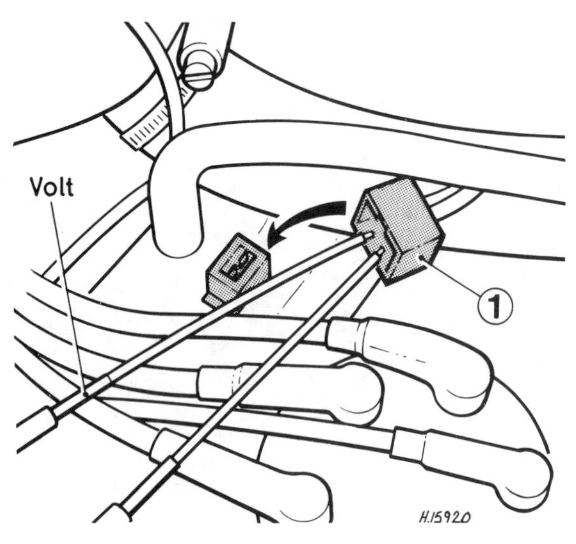

Fig. 3.42 Voltmeter connection to warm-up regulator plug (1) – K-Jetronic (Sec 29)

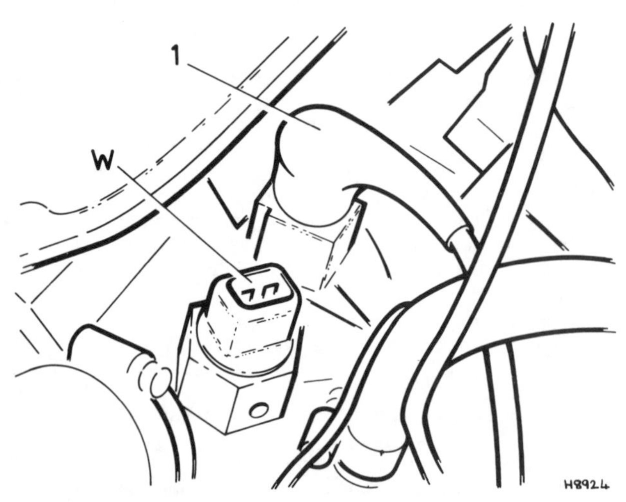

Fig. 3.43 Temperature time switch (Sec 29)

1 Plug W Switch terminal

19 Connect an ohmmeter to the regulator heater winding and check for open circuit.
20 Connect a voltmeter to the warm-up regulator plug (1) – Fig. 3.42. With the engine running, the minimum voltage should be 11.5V.

Temperature time switch

21 This switch controls the opening time of the cold start valve in relation to coolant temperature.
22 Disconnect the plug (1) and connect a test lamp to battery (+) and terminal W in the switch – Fig. 3.43. The lamp should be on at temperatures below 35°C (95°F) and out at higher temperatures.

30 Main components – removal and refitting

K-Jetronic

Mixture regulator

1 Remove the air intake duct.
2 Disconnect the connections from the fuel distributor.
3 Remove the fixing bolts and lift off the mixture regulator with fuel distributor.
4 Refitting is a reversal of removal, use new sealing washers and a gasket.

Fuel injectors

5 Disconnect the rocker cover breather hose and unscrew the injector pipe union nuts.
6 Unscrew the injectors and remove them. They may require levering out with two screwdrivers.
7 Refit in the reverse order to removal, but use new rubber rings smeared with petroleum jelly.

Throttle butterfly return springs

8 Disconnect the accelerator cable.

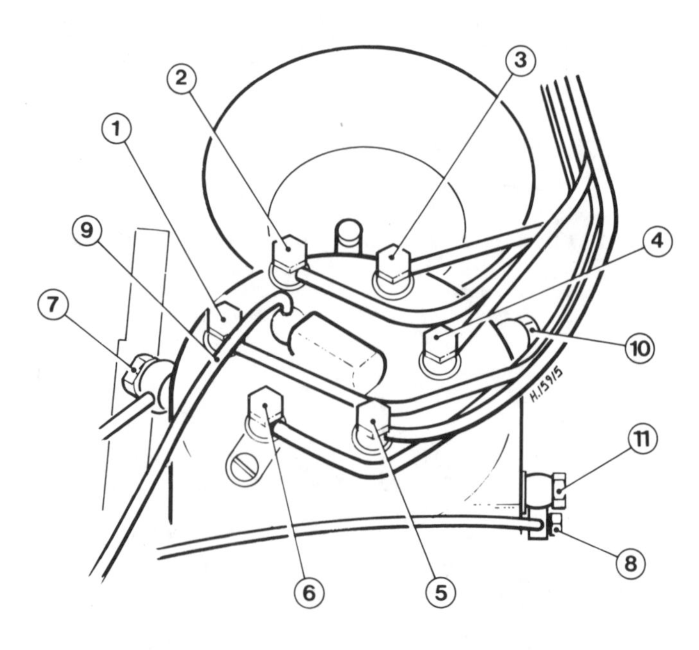

Fig. 3.44 Fuel distributor – K-Jetronic (Sec 30)

1 Injector connection
2 Injector connection
3 Injector connection
4 Injector connection
5 Injector connection
6 Injector connection
7 Cold start valve connection
8 Warm-up regulator connection
9 Warm-up regulator connection
10 Fuel filter connection
11 Return hose connection

9 Remove the E-clip (1), wave washer (2) and unhook the spring end (3) – Fig. 3.45.
10 Remove the lever (5) with the bush (4).
11 Unscrew the nut (7) and remove the linkage and springs.
12 Reassembly is a reversal of dismantling. Adjust the throttle butterfly on completion, as described in Section 29.

Warm-up regulator

13 Remove the fuel distributor cap, identify and disconnect the feed and return lines, and remove the vacuum hose and plug from the regulator.
14 Unscrew the bolts (1 and 2) – Fig. 3.46. and remove the warm-up regulator.
15 Refit by reversing the removal procedure.

Cold start valve

16 Disconnect the plug (1), the fuel line (2) and socket-headed bolts (3 and 4) – Fig. 3.47.
17 Remove the valve. Use a new O-ring seal when refitting.

Throttle housing

18 Remove the intake duct and then pull off the white and black vacuum hoses – Fig. 3.49. Disconnect the coolant hoses (3 and 4) and catch the coolant in a suitable container.
19 Unscrew the nut and disconnect the accelerator cable.

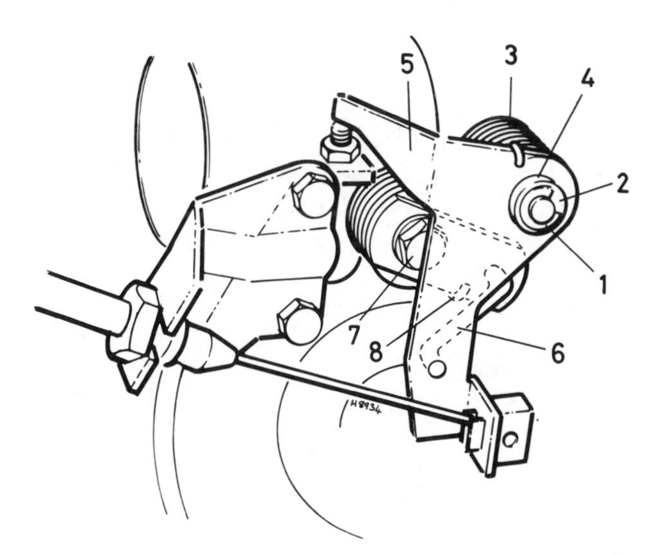

Fig. 3.45 Throttle butterfly connections – K-Jetronic (Sec 30)

1 E-clip
2 Wave washer
3 Spring
4 Bush
5 Lever
6 Linkage
7 Nut
8 Spring

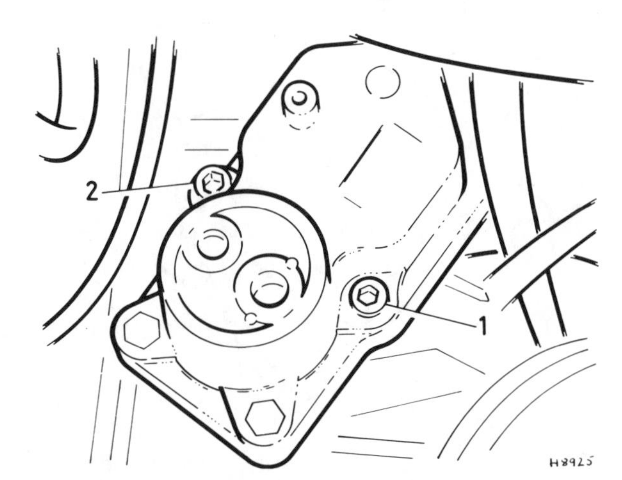

Fig. 3.46 Warm-up regulator fixing bolts (1 and 2) – K-Jetronic (Sec 30)

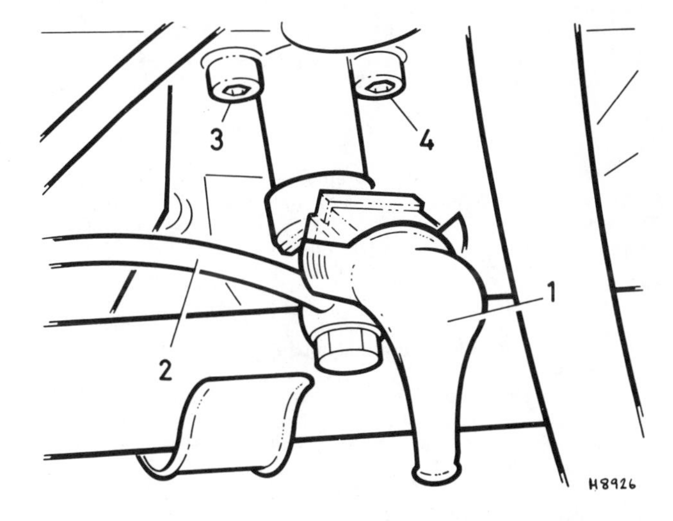

Fig. 3.47 Cold start valve – K-Jetronic (Sec 30)

1 Plug
2 Fuel line
3 Retaining bolt
4 Retaining bolt

Fig. 3.48 Removing the cold start valve – K-Jetronic (Secs 29 and 30)

O-ring arrowed

Fig. 3.49 Throttle housing – K-Jetronic (Sec 30)

1 Vacuum hose
2 Vacuum hose
3 Coolant hose
4 Coolant hose

20 Remove the fixing nuts and take off the throttle housing.

21 Refitting is a reversal of removal. Renew the gasket and adjust the accelerator cable, as described in Section 31. Bleed the cooling system on completion (Chapter 2).

Throttle bypass valve

22 Pull off the plug (1) and disconnect the air hoses (2 and 3) – Fig. 3.50.

23 Unscrew the fixing nuts and remove the throttle bypass valve.

24 On versions which have a coolant-heated type of valve, disconnect the hoses from connection (1) – Fig. 3.51 and the blocks (2). Bleed the cooling system on completion (Chapter 2).

L-Jetronic

25 Removal and refitting of the following components differs from the operations described for K-Jetronic models.

Throttle housing

26 Disconnect the cables (1, 2 or 3) as applicable – Fig. 3.52.

27 Pull off the vacuum hoses, the coolant hoses (1 and 2) – allowing the coolant to drain – and the air hoses (3 and 4) from the throttle housing (Fig. 3.53).

28 Remove the vacuum hoses (1 and 2), the air hose (3) and pull off the multi-pin plug (4) – Fig. 3.54.

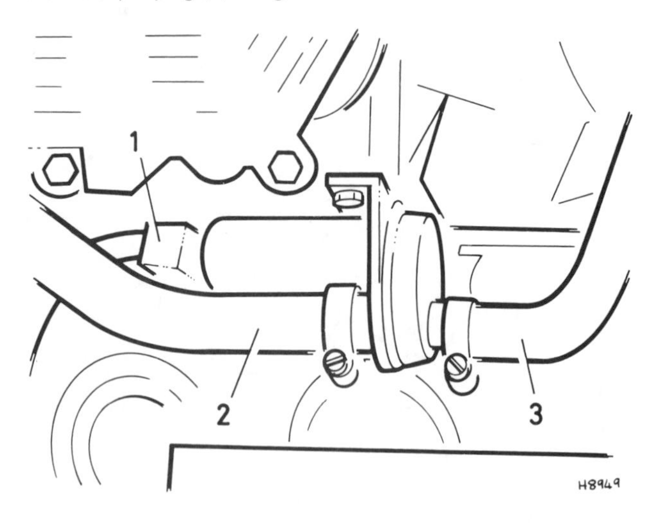

Fig. 3.50 Throttle bypass valve – K-Jetronic (Sec 30)

1 Plug
2 Air hose
3 Air hose

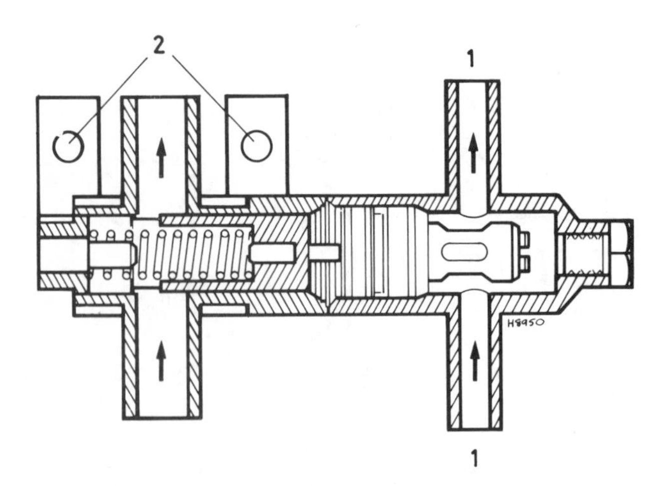

Fig. 3.51 Sectional view of the coolant-heated throttle bypass valve – K-Jetronic (Sec 30)

1 Coolant hose connections
2 Blocks

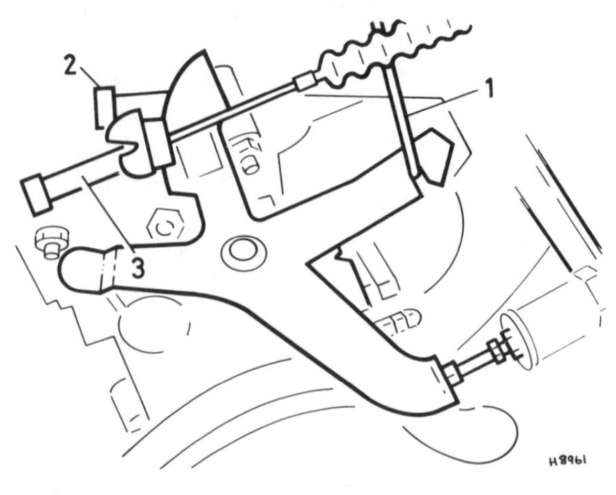

Fig. 3.52 Throttle housing cables – L-Jetronic (Sec 30)

1 Automatic transmission
2 Accelerator
3 Cruise control

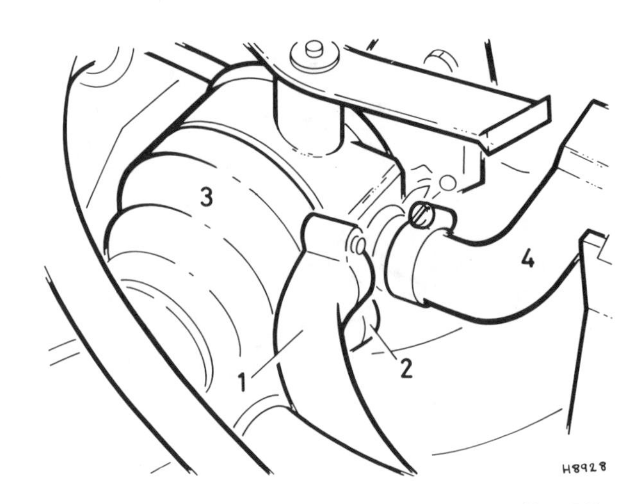

Fig. 3.53 Throttle housing hoses – L-Jetronic (Sec 30)

1 Coolant
2 Coolant
3 Air
4 Air

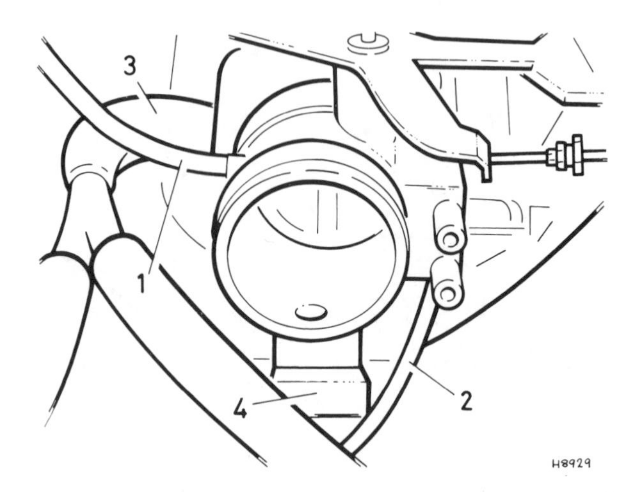

Fig. 3.54 Throttle housing connections – L-Jetronic (Sec 30)

1 Vacuum hose
2 Vacuum hose
3 Air hose
4 Plug

29 Remove the fixing nuts and take off the throttle housing. **Do not** separate the throttle switch from the housing, as a special gauge will be required to adjust it when refitting.
30 Refitting is a reversal of removal. Use a new gasket and bleed the cooling system (Chapter 2).

Throttle vacuum control

31 Pull off the hose (1), release the nut (2) and remove the vacuum control (3) – Fig. 3.55.
32 When refitting, adjust dimension (B) to between 32.8 and 33.2 mm (1.291 and 1.307 in) using screw (4).
33 Adjust dimension (A) to between 2.6 and 3.0 mm (0.102 and 0.118 in) using screw (2) – Fig. 3.56.

Control unit

34 Open the glove compartment and pull the pins from the retaining straps.
35 Remove the screws and place the glovebox cover to one side.
36 Depress the retainer (1) and pull out the multi-pin plug (2) – Fig. 3.57. Remove the control unit.

Air-flow sensor

37 Release the clamp and pull the duct from the airflow sensor.
38 Disconnect the multi-pin plug, unscrew the fixing nuts and withdraw the sensor.
39 Refitting is a reversal of removal. Renew the seal, if necessary.

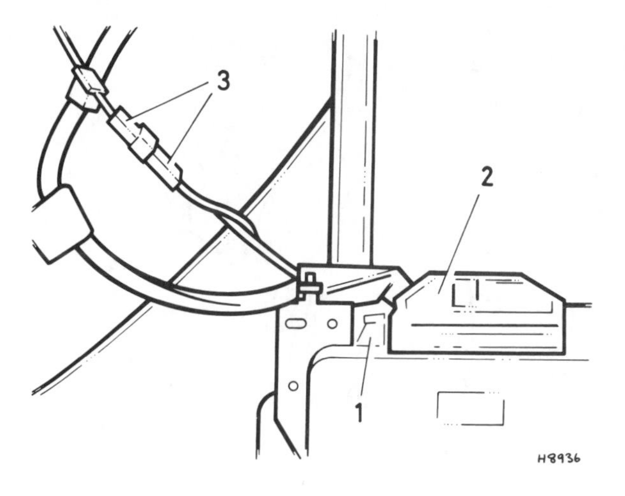

Fig. 3.57 Control unit – L-Jetronic (Sec 30)

1 Retainer
2 Plug
3 Spade connectors

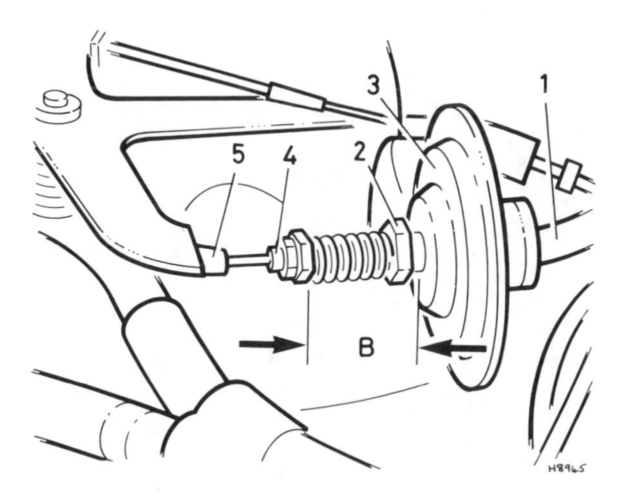

Fig. 3.55 Throttle vacuum control – L-Jetronic (Sec 30)

B Setting dimension
1 Hose
2 Nut
3 Vacuum control
4 Screw
5 Screw

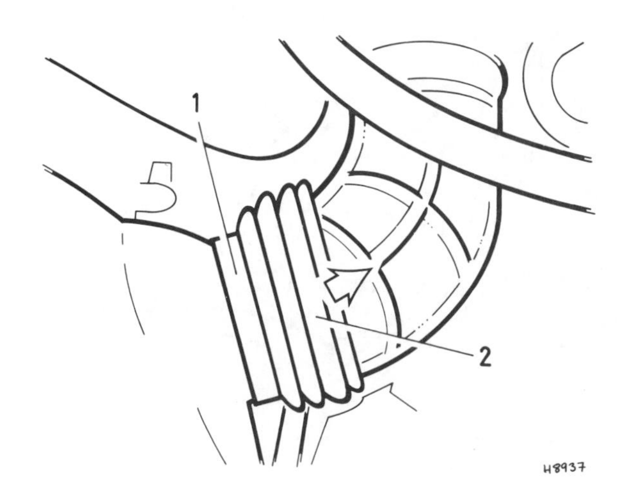

Fig. 3.58 Airflow sensor duct (2) – L-Jetronic (Sec 30)

1 Clamp
Disconnect the duct by pulling in the indicated direction (arrowed)

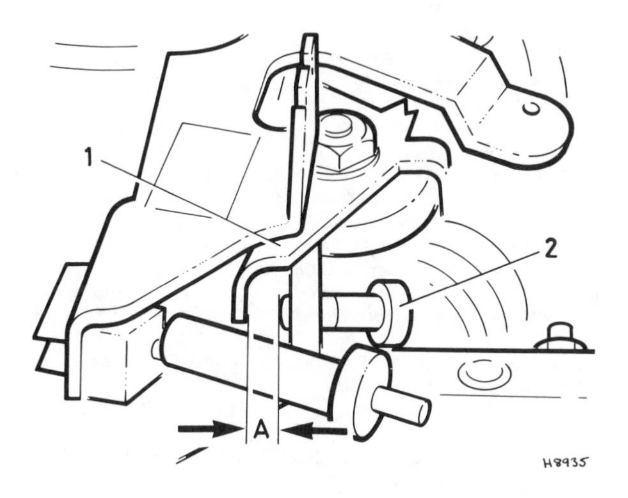

Fig. 3.56 Throttle vacuum control – L-Jetronic (Sec 30)

A Setting dimension
1 Control lever
2 Stop screw

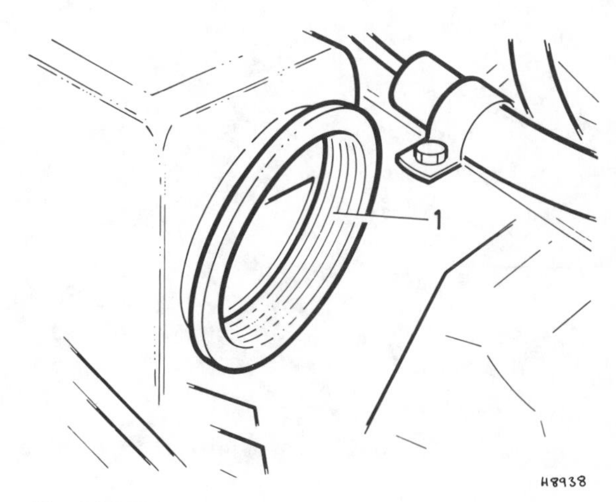

Fig. 3.59 Airflow sensor seal (1) – L-Jetronic (Sec 30)

Fig. 3.60 Temperature time switch – L-Jetronic (Sec 30)

1 Plug

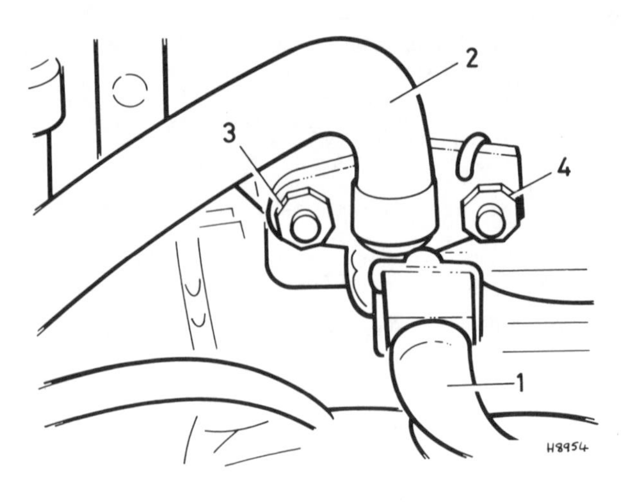

Fig. 3.62 Cold start valve – L-Jetronic (Sec 30)

1 Plug
2 Fuel line
3 Mounting bolt
4 Mounting bolt

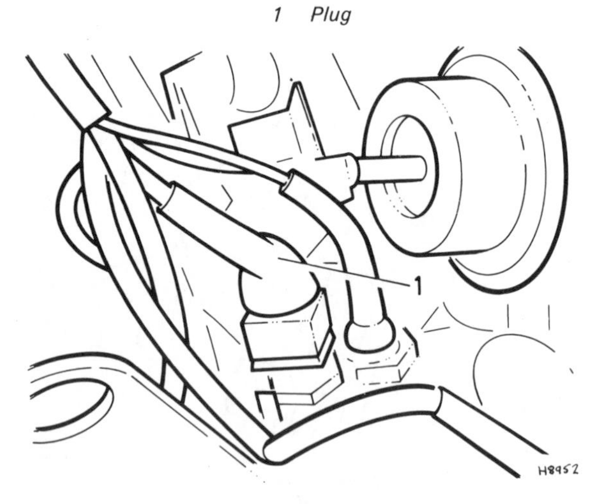

Fig. 3.61 Coolant temperature sensor – L-Jetronic (Sec 30)

1 Plug

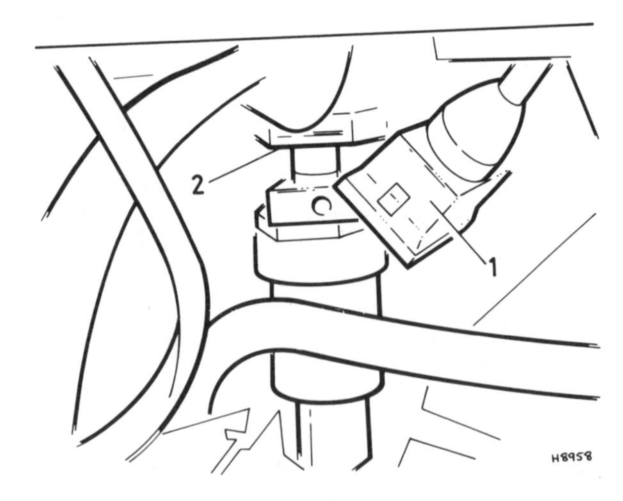

Fig. 3.63 Fuel injector plug (1) and circlip (2) – L-Jetronic (Sec 30)

30.50 Throttle control – L-Jetronic

1 Retainer
2 Washer
3 Linkage
4 Lever

Temperature time switch

40 Pull off the plug and unscrew and remove the switch.

41 Refit the switch using a new sealing washer.

Coolant temperature sensor

42 Pull off the plug and unscrew the sensor. Refit using a new sealing washer.

Cold start valve

43 Pull off the plug (1) and disconnect the fuel line (2) – Fig. 3.62.

44 Unscrew the mounting bolts (3 and 4) and withdraw the valve.

45 When refitting renew the seal.

Fuel injectors

46 Unscrew the four injection tube bolts and push the tube upwards until the fuel injectors have cleared the guide in the intake manifold.

47 Pull off the plug (1) and take out the circlip (2) – Fig. 3.63. Take off the fuel injector.

48 Refitting is a reversal of removal; use new O-ring seals.

Throttle shaft return springs

49 Disconnect the cables (kick-down – Chapter 6, cruise control – Chapter 10, accelerator – this Chapter).

50 Remove the retainer (1), washer (2) and disconnect the linkage (3) on the lever (4).

51 Raise the lever and turn it to relieve the spring tension. Remove the lever.

52 Remove the spring.

53 Disconnect the spring (1) and unscrew the nut (2) – Fig. 3.64.

54 Remove the washer (1) and lever (2) – Fig. 3.65.

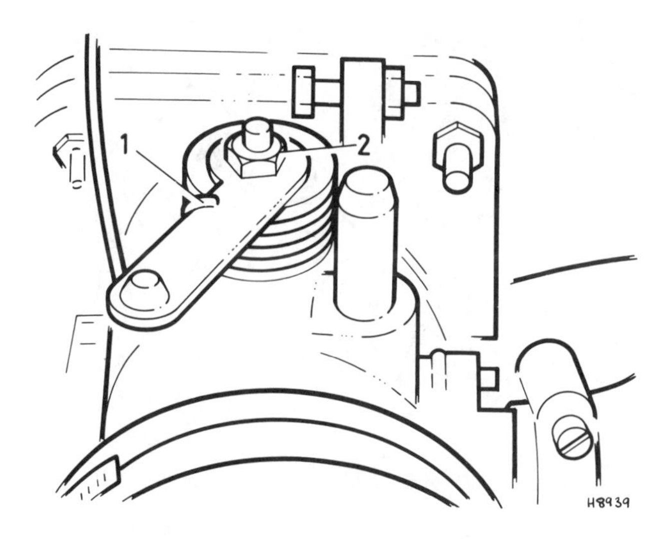

Fig. 3.64 Throttle shaft return spring (1) and nut (2) – L-Jetronic (Sec 30)

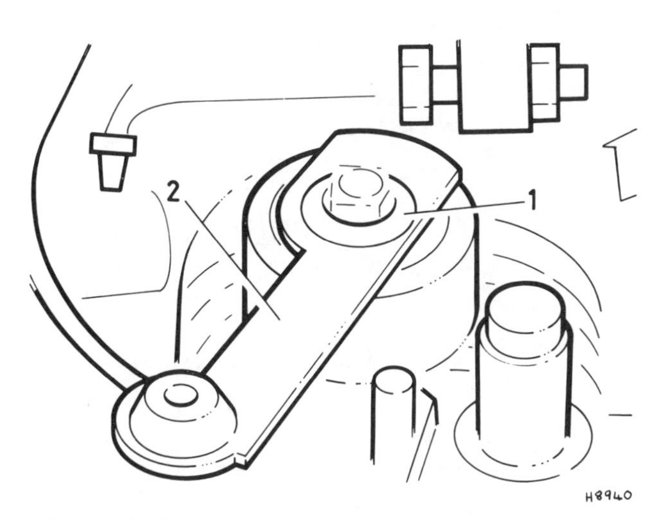

Fig. 3.65 Throttle shaft washer (1) and lever (2) – L-Jetronic (Sec 30)

55 Remove the sleeve (1) and spring (2) – Fig. 3.66 – also the wave washer.

56 Reassemble in the reverse order to dismantling and adjust in the following way. Pull off the tamperproof lock (1) and loosen the screw (2) until the lever (3) no longer rests on the screw – Fig. 3.67.

57 Place a finger on the lever and tighten the screw until the lever just begins to move. Turn the screw $\frac{1}{4}$ turn more and fit the tamperproof lock.

58 Adjust the kick-down cruise control and accelerator cables, as applicable, after reference to the appropriate Chapter.

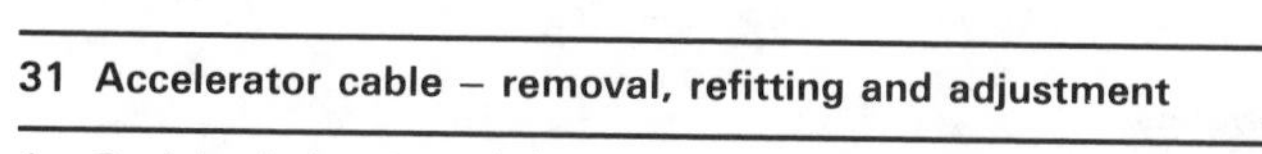

31 Accelerator cable – removal, refitting and adjustment

1 Push back the clamp (1) – Fig. 3.68 – and disconnect the cable (2) – pushing it out with the rubber pad.

2 Remove the nipple from the cable.

3 Remove the facia under cover and disconnect the cable from the accelerator pedal.

4 On models built up until the end of 1983, pull the cable out of the engine compartment rear bulkhead. On later models, compress the

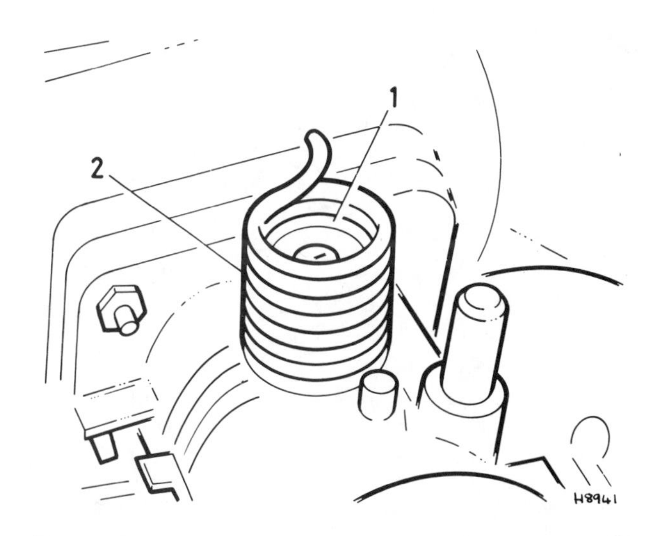

Fig. 3.66 Throttle shaft sleeve (1) and spring (2) – L-Jetronic (Sec 30)

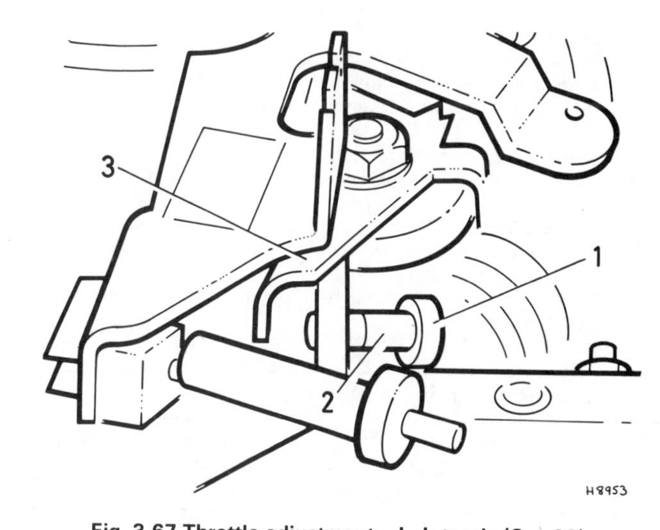

Fig. 3.67 Throttle adjustment – L-Jetronic (Sec 30)

1 Tamperproof lock
2 Screw
3 Lever

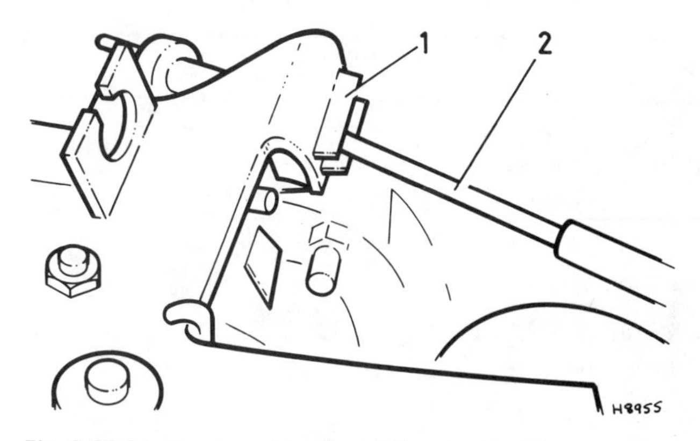

Fig. 3.68 Accelerator cable clamp (1) and cable (2) – L-Jetronic (Sec 31)

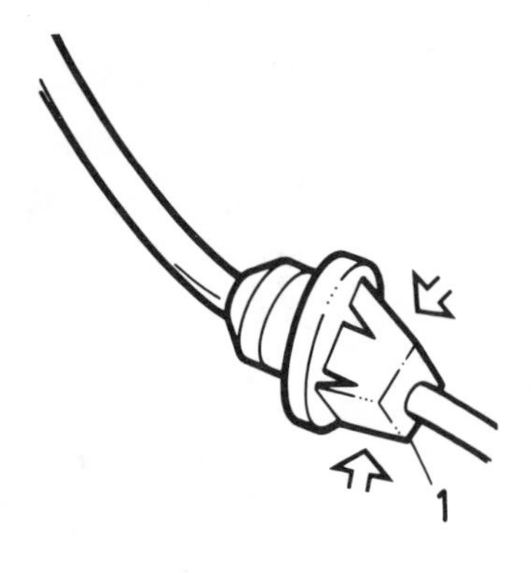

Fig. 3.69 Compress the cable locking claws (1) and pull the cable out of the bulkhead (Sec 31)

locking claws (1) first – Fig. 3.69.

5 Refit by reversing the removal operations and then adjust the cable as follows.

6 On models with K-Jetronic injection, set the basic throttle adjustment, as described in Section 29, paragraphs 1 to 3. Models with L-Jetronic injection should not need readjustment, but if this is necessary, the work should be entrusted to a BMW dealer, as special gauges are required.

7 Press the accelerator pedal against the stop (kick-down – automatic transmission) when the operating lever (1) – Fig. 3.70 – must be on the stop (2) with throttle wide open. If not, turn the screw (3) as necessary.

8 The slack at the nipple (2) should be between 0.2 and 0.3 mm (0.008 and 0.012 in) when the lever (1) is on the idle stop (3) – Fig. 3.71.

9 When the cable adjustment is complete, give the accelerator pedal a play of 0.5 mm (0.020 in) by screwing the stop on the floor down between 1 and 1½ turns.

10 Basic adjustment of the accelerator pedal is described in Section 19.

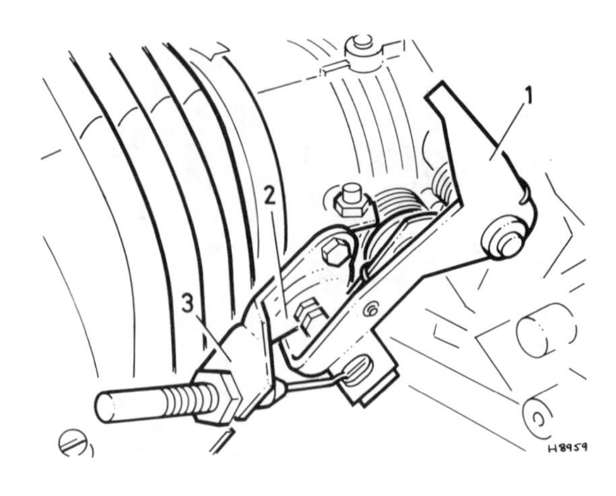

Fig. 3.70 Throttle in wide open position (Sec 31)

1 Operating lever
2 Stop
3 Screw

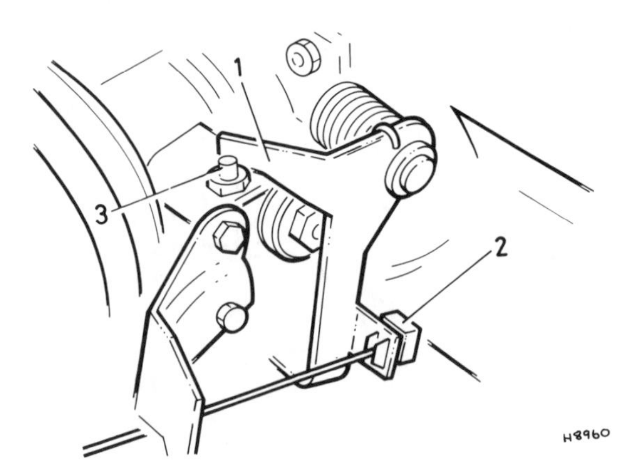

Fig. 3.71 Slack at throttle cable nipple (Sec 31)

1 Lever
2 Nipple
3 Idle stop

32 Manifolds and exhaust system

The exhaust manifolds and exhaust system are similar to those used in conjunction with carburettor engines, refer to Section 21.

33 Fault diagnosis – fuel system

Unsatisfactory engine performance and excessive fuel consumption are not necessarily the fault of the fuel system or carburettor. In fact they more commonly occur as a result of ignition and timing faults. Before acting on the following it is necessary to check the ignition system first. Even though a fault may lie in the fuel system it will be difficult to trace unless the ignition is correct. The faults below, therefore, assume that this has been attended to first (where appropriate).

Symptom	Reason(s)
Carburettor system	
Smell of petrol when engine is stopped	Leaking fuel lines or unions Leaking fuel tank
Smell of petrol when engine is idling	Leaking fuel line unions between pump and carburettor Overflow of fuel from float chamber due to wrong level setting, ineffective needle valve or punctured float
Excessive fuel consumption for reasons not covered by leaks or float chamber faults	Worn jets Over-rich setting Sticking mechanism Dirty air cleaner element Sticking air cleaner thermostatic mechanism Choke heater element burned out Defective temperature switch Broken Stage 2 valve plate torsion spring

Symptom	Reason(s)
Difficult starting, uneven running, lack of power, cutting out	One or more jets blocked or restricted Float chamber fuel level too low or needle valve sticking Fuel pump not delivering sufficient fuel Faulty solenoid fuel shut-off valve Induction leak
Difficult starting when cold	Weak mixture Incorrectly adjusted automatic choke
Starts when cold, but will not run	Choke butterfly setting incorrect Defective throttle butterfly positioner Heat sensitive bypass not working Pull-down diaphragm leaking Porous vacuum hoses
Difficult starting when hot	Automatic choke malfunction Accelerator pedal pumped before starting Vapour lock (especially in hot weather or at high altitude) Rich mixture
Engine does not respond properly to throttle	Blocked jet(s) Slack in accelerator cable Fuel tank vent blocked
Poor idling	Defective idle cut-off valve Idle jets blocked Leak on induction side Blocked heat sensitive bypass starting jets
Poor transition from idle to Stage 1	Accelerator pedal volume incorrect Blocked fuel passages Defective diaphragm Fuel level in carburettor too low
Poor transition from part load to full throttle	Leak at vacuum damper Passages blocked Broken torsion spring at Stage 2 butterfly
Engine runs on	Faulty idle cut-off valve

Fuel injection system

Symptom	Reason(s)
No cold start	Faulty pump or clogged filter Additional air valve not opening Start valve not opening Leak in fuel system Throttle valve plate not opening fully Defective temperature sensor Defective diode relay
Poor hot start	As for cold start then: Leaking injector Faulty heat/time switch
Poor idle	Baffle plate stop out of adjustment Vacuum system leaking Clogged fuel filter Incorrect mixture adjustment
Engine backfires	Weak mixture Fuel pressure fault Leaking starter valve
Engine runs on	Leaking fuel injector Stiff baffle plate or control plunger
Excessive fuel consumption	Low control pressure Start valve leaking Leak in system Rich mixture Faulty heat/time switch
Idle speed cannot be reduced	Incorrect control pressure Additional air valve not closing Baffle plate stop out of adjustment

Chapter 4 Ignition system

For modifications, and information applicable to later models, see Supplement at end of manual

Contents

Specifications

System type

320 models (to 1979)	Mechanical breaker distributor
All other models, including 320 (1980 on)	Breakerless distributor

Firing order

1-5-3-6-2-4 (No 1 at timing belt end)

Distributor (mechanical breaker)

Type	Bosch PFUD6
Contact points gap	0.35 mm (0.014 in)
Dwell angle	35 to 41°
Ignition timing:	
Static	10° BTDC
Dynamic (vacuum pipes disconnected)	22° BTDC at 1500 rpm

Distributor (breakerless)

Type	Bosch PGFUD 6
Air gap (star wheel reluctor)	0.35 to 0.70 mm (0.014 to 0.028 in)
Ignition timing (E21 only – for E20 see Supplement):	
Dynamic (vacuum pipe disconnected)	22° BTDC at 1500 rpm

Spark plugs

Champion	N9YC or equivalent
Electrode gap	0.6 to 0.7 mm (0.024 to 0.028 in)

Torque wrench settings

	Nm	lbf ft
Distributor clamp bolt	20	15
Spark plug	27	20

1 General description

The ignition system may be of mechanical contact breaker or breakerless (electronic) type, depending upon the model of car.

In order for the engine to run, an electrical spark must be produced at the spark plug to ignite the fuel/air mixture in the combustion chamber at exactly the right moment in relation to engine speed and load.

In the mechanical breaker system, low tension (LT) voltage is fed from the battery to the coil primary windings and then to the distributor contact breaker points. With the points closed, an elec-

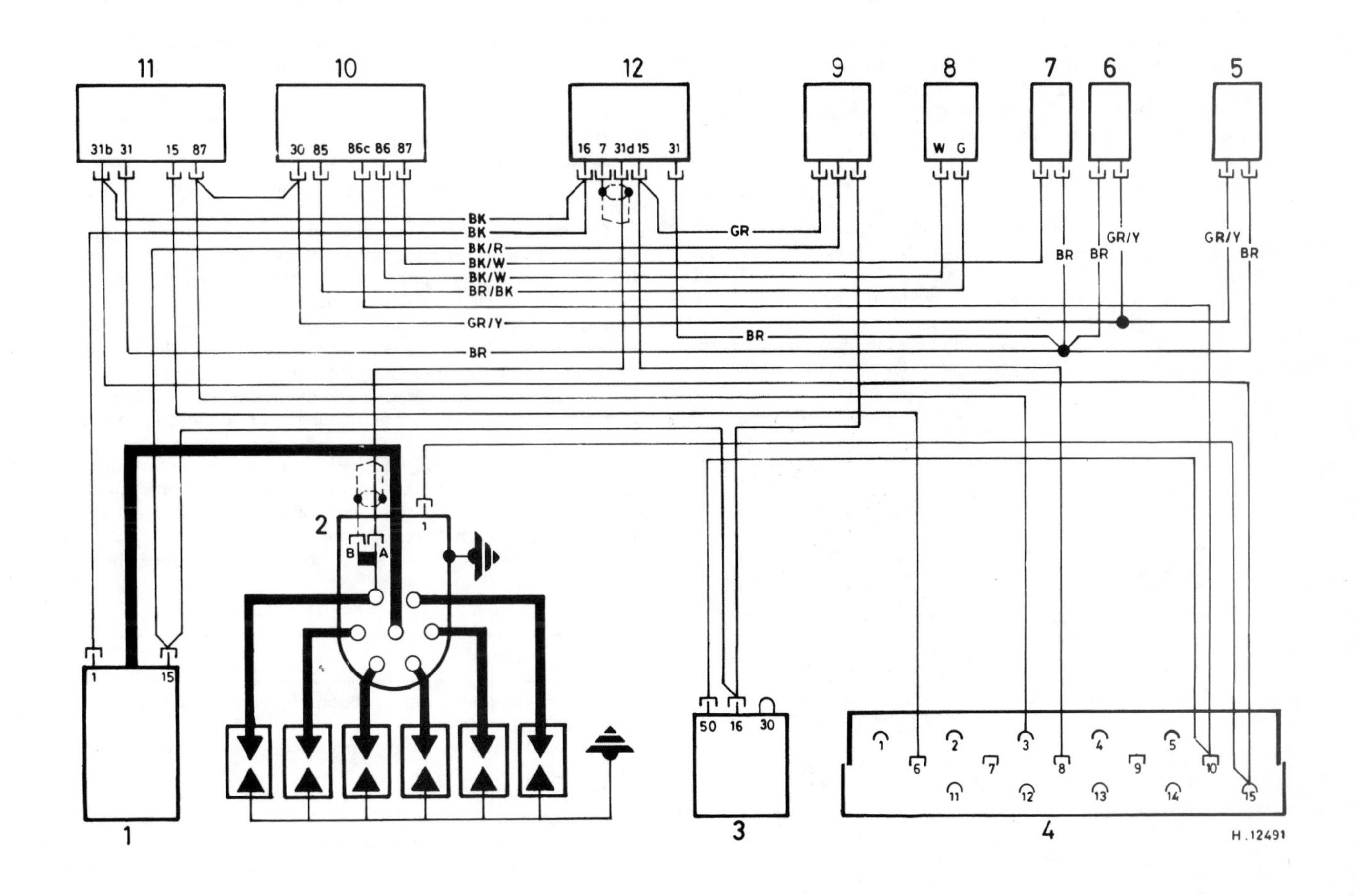

Fig. 4.1 Wiring diagram for the transistorised ignition and K-Jetronic fuel injection systems (Sec 1)

1 Coil
2 Distributor
3 Starter
4 Plug
5 Additional air slide
6 Warm-up regulator
7 Cold start valve
8 Thermo (heat-sensitive) time switch
9 Resistors
10 Diode relay
11 Fuel pump relay
12 Ignition control unit
BR Brown
GN Green
RT Red
SW Black

tromagnetic field is produced around the secondary high tension (HT) windings in the coil. When the points open, a high tension current is induced in the coil secondary windings which is fed through the distributor cap and rotor to each spark plug. The condenser (capacitor) in the distributor serves as a buffer for the surge of low tension current and also prevents excessive arcing across the contact breaker points.

In the electronic (breakerless) system, the secondary high tension (HT) circuit operates in an identical way to the conventional system, however the primary low tension (LT) circuit is operated electronically instead of by the contact breaker points. The distributor incorporates a star wheel with six arms which is attached to the shaft. As the plate rotates, the arms pass close to a sensor which contains a permanent magnet and coil, an impulse is created in the coil. The impulse switches off the transistor in the module which in turn causes a collapse of the voltage in the coil primary windings. HT current is thus induced in the coil secondary windings.

Both the mechanical breaker and electronic systems incorporate ignition advance mechanisms. Centrifugal advance is governed by weights attached to the distributor shaft which move outwards as the engine speed increases. The upper part of the shaft is rotated by the weights and so advances the ignition timing.

During part throttle operation, performance and fuel economy can be improved by advancing the ignition timing further than is done by the centrifugal weight mechanism. To do this, a vacuum capsule connected to the distributor baseplate advances the ignition timing when the carburettor throttle valve is only partly open.

Precautions

With an electronic ignition system it is very important to observe the following precautions.

Never attempt to switch the starter on if the distributor cap is off or the lead is disconnected from terminal 4 of the ignition coil.

Never disconnect the battery if the engine is running.

Never connect a test lamp to terminal 1 of the ignition coil.

Never connect the lead from terminal 1 of the ignition coil to earth or battery positive.

Never use terminal 1 of the ignition coil as a take off for an anti-theft system to prevent starting. Starter motor terminal 50 would be suitable.

2 Mechanical contact breaker – points servicing

1 At the specified service interval, depress the distributor cap screws and turn them through 90°. This will release the spring-loaded catches (photo). Take off the cap and place it to one side.
2 Pull off the rotor and remove the dust cover.
3 Open the points and examine the surfaces of the contact faces. If they are only slightly marked, apply two drops of oil to the felt pad at the top of the distributor shaft and smear the high points of the cam lobes with a trace of high melting-point grease. Refit the dust cover, rotor and cap.
4 Check the dwell angle and timing, as described later in this Chapter.
5 Where the points are found to be severely burned or eroded with a pip on one face and a crater on the other, the contact breaker must be renewed.
6 To do this, disconnect the breaker LT lead from the terminal on the distributor body. This is located by spring pressure.
7 Unscrew and remove the screw which holds the fixed contact arm to the baseplate. Lift out the breaker assembly.

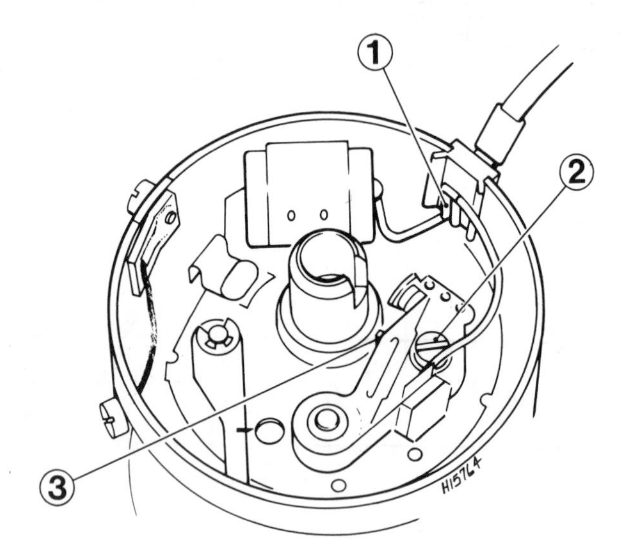

Fig. 4.2 Mechanical contact breaker distributor (Sec 2)

1 LT connection
2 Fixed contact screw
3 Contact arm rubbing block

2.1 Distributor cap. One retaining screw arrowed

8 Fit the new contact breaker, but leave the fixing screw finger tight.
9 Turn the crankshaft until the heel of the contact arm rubbing block is positioned on one of the cam lobe high points. Now adjust the points to the specified gap. Tighten the fixing screw.
10 Lubricate, as described in paragraph 3 and refit the dust cap, rotor and cap.
11 The dwell angle and ignition timing must now be checked and adjusted, as described in Sections 3 and 4.

3 Dwell angle – checking and adjustment

1 This operation applies only to cars with mechanical breaker ignition.
2 On modern engines, setting the contact breaker gap in the distributor using feeler gauges must be regarded as a basic adjustment only. For optimum engine performance, the dwell angle must be checked. The dwell angle is the number of degrees through which the distributor cam turns during the period between the instance of closure and opening of the contact breaker points. Checking the dwell angle not only gives a more accurate setting of the contact breaker gap but also evens out any variations in the gap which could be caused by wear in the distributor shaft or its bushes, or difference in height of any of the cam peaks.
3 The angle should be checked with a dwell meter connected in accordance with the maker's instructions. Refer to the Specifications for the correct dwell angle. If the dwell angle is too large, increase the points gap, if too small, reduce the points gap.
4 The dwell angle should always be adjusted **before** checking and adjusting the ignition timing.

4 Ignition timing

1 Have the engine at normal operating temperature. Disconnect the distributor vacuum pipes.
2 Connect a timing light (stroboscope) in accordance with the manufacturer's instructions.
3 Although a TDC sensor is fitted, this is of no use without the matching monitoring equipment. In order to check the timing, therefore, refer to the Specifications and observe the dynamic timing figure (degrees BTDC). An advance (BTDC) mark should be on the crankshaft vibration damper, if it is not, make a mark on the rim of the damper which is the specified number of degrees from the TDC (O) mark placed on the rim during production (photo). The BTDC (Z) mark must, of course, be made in the advance direction (clockwise) when the damper is viewed from the front. File a notch on the edge of the rim and paint it and the timing pointer white.

4.3 Timing marks on crankshaft vibration damper (set at TDC)

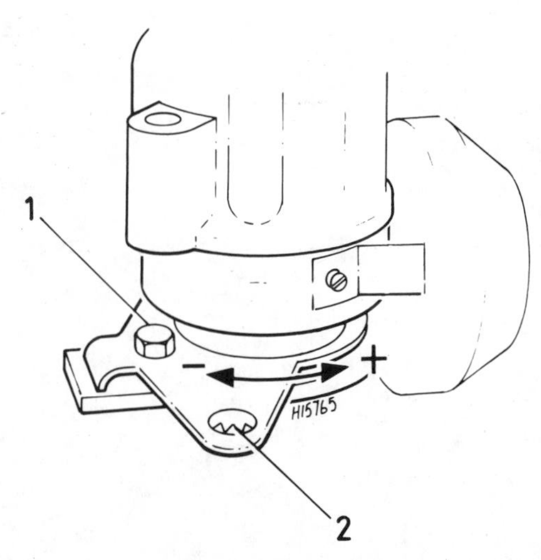

Fig. 4.3 Distributor clamp plate bolt (1) and levering teeth for advance/retard adjustment (2) (Sec 4)

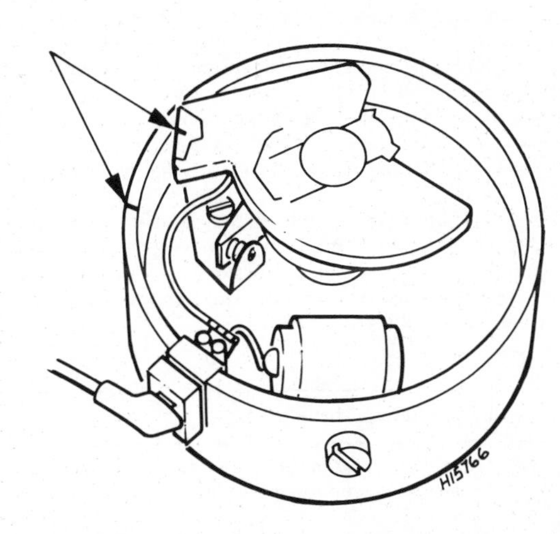

Fig. 4.4 Distributor-to-rotor alignment marks – arrowed (Sec 6)

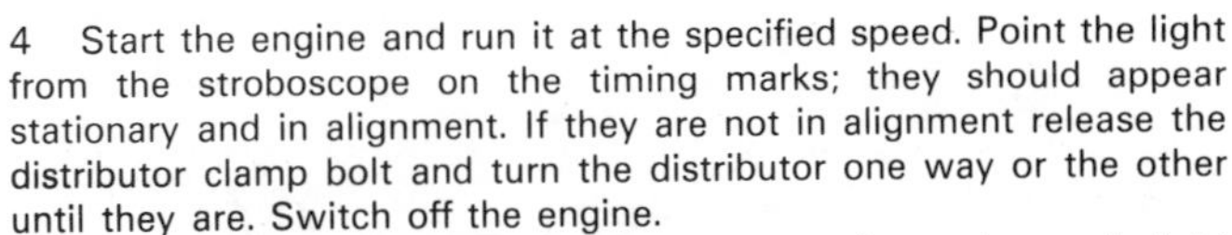

4 Start the engine and run it at the specified speed. Point the light from the stroboscope on the timing marks; they should appear stationary and in alignment. If they are not in alignment release the distributor clamp bolt and turn the distributor one way or the other until they are. Switch off the engine.

5 Tighten the distributor clamp bolt, remove the stroboscopic light and reconnect the vacuum pipes.

5 Breakerless distributor – servicing

1 Servicing is virtually eliminated except to keep the distributor cap clean and the system wiring securely connected.

2 Occasionally apply two drops of engine oil to the felt pad which is located in the recess at the top of the distributor shaft.

6 Distributor (mechanical breaker type) – removal and refitting

1 Remove the distributor cap, disconnect the low tension lead and the vacuum pipe.

2 Take off the rotor and dust cover, and then refit the rotor.

3 Turn the crankshaft until No 1 piston is at TDC. This is indicated when the mark on the rotor is adjacent to, and in alignment with, the one on the rim of the distributor body. Mark the relative position of the distributor body to the cylinder block.

4 Remove the distributor clamp plate bolt and withdraw the distributor.

5 Before refitting the distributor, make sure that No 1 piston is still at TDC.

6 Hold the distributor over its hole so that it is in its original relative position and align the rotor and rim marks. Now turn the rotor 25.0 mm (1.0 in) in a clockwise direction. Insert the distributor, as the gears mesh the rotor will turn and realign its mark with the one on the body rim.

7 Turn the distributor body until the points are just about to open then tighten the clamp plate bolt. Remove the rotor.

8 Reconnect the LT lead and vacuum pipe, fit the dust cover, rotor and cap.

9 Check and adjust the ignition timing, as described in Section 4.

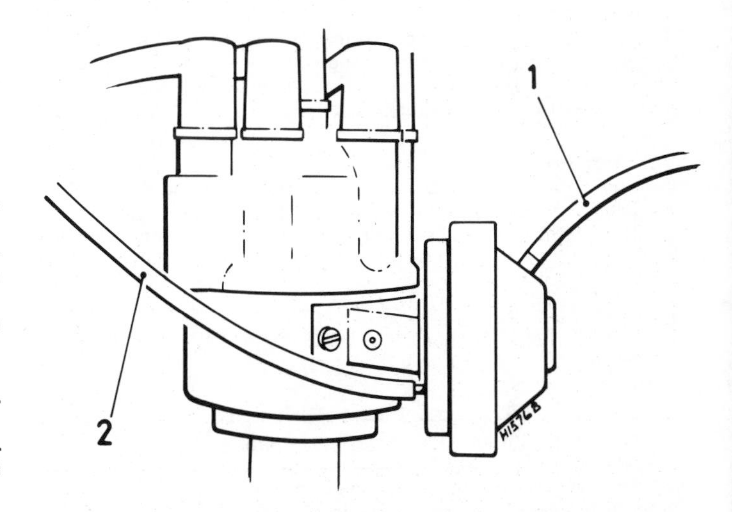

Fig. 4.5 Breakerless distributor vacuum pipes (1 and 2) (Sec 7)

7 Distributor (breakerless type) – removal and refitting

1 Pull off the plug and earth wire from the base of the distributor.

2 Remove the distributor cap, rotor and dust cap.

3 Disconnect the vacuum pipes. Up to March 1983 the black hose is for advance and white for retard. Do not mix them up.

4 After March 1983, the retard pipe incorporates an angled connector (photo).

7.4 Late model vacuum hoses (arrowed). The hose with the angled connector is the retard hose

5 Turn the crankshaft until No 1 piston is at TDC. This is indicated when the mark on the rotor is opposite the one on the rim of the distributor body.
6 Mark the relative position of the distributor body in relation to the cylinder block.
7 Unscrew the clamp plate bolt and withdraw the distributor (photo).
8 Before refitting the distributor, make sure that No 1 piston is still at TDC.
9 Hold the distributor over its hole so that it is in its original relative position to the engine and then align the rotor and rim marks. Now turn the rotor through 30° in a clockwise direction. Insert the distributor and, as the gears mesh, the rotor will turn and realign its mark with the one on the body rim.

7.7 Distributor clamp bolt (arrowed)

8 Distributor (mechanical breaker type) – overhaul

1 Overhaul of the distributor is limited by the availability of spares. A well worn unit should be renewed complete.

Condenser

2 This can be renewed without removing the distributor. A faulty condenser can be detected if the car is difficult to start or misfires, or if the points are severely eroded. The latter can also be caused by poor earth connections.
3 Take off the distributor cap, rotor and dust cover. Disconnect the condenser lead and extract the fixing screw.
4 In view of the relative low cost of the condenser it is not worth testing it, but rather substitute a new one.

Vacuum unit

5 Remove the distributor, take off the cap, rotor and dust cover.
6 Extract the circlip from the advance unit link arm pivot.
7 Extract the vacuum unit fixing screws, tilt the control unit and withdraw it. Refitting is a reversal of removal.

Drivegear

8 The distributor drivegear can be renewed if the securing pin is driven out.

9 Distributor (breakerless type) – overhaul

1 The overhaul operations should be limited to the following. A well worn distributor should be renewed complete.

Vacuum unit

2 With the distributor removed, extract the vacuum unit retaining screws.
3 Press the unit connecting link downwards to release the link from its pivot pin.

Pulse transmitter

4 Remove the cap, rotor and dust cover, then the vacuum unit.
5 Extract the circlip (1) and spring washer (2) – Fig. 4.8.
6 Using two screwdrivers inserted at opposite points, carefully prise up the star wheel.
7 Remove the thrust washer (1) then the three socket-headed screws from just inside the body rim, and finally the circlip (2) – Fig. 4.9.
8 From the outside of the body extract the screw (1) and remove the retaining plate (2) – Fig. 4.10.
9 Pull out the plug (3).
10 Extract the pulse transmitter fixing screws.
11 Reassembly is a reversal of dismantling but observe the following points.
12 Check the air gaps between the star wheel and the lugs on the pulse transmitter (Fig. 4.8). These should be as specified.
13 When locating the star wheel, make sure that it is pushed down squarely and that the cut-out in the distributor shaft is aligned with the plate lug, also check that the locating pin is correctly set.
14 When refitting the pulse transmitter, make sure that the terminal spades are towards the plug.

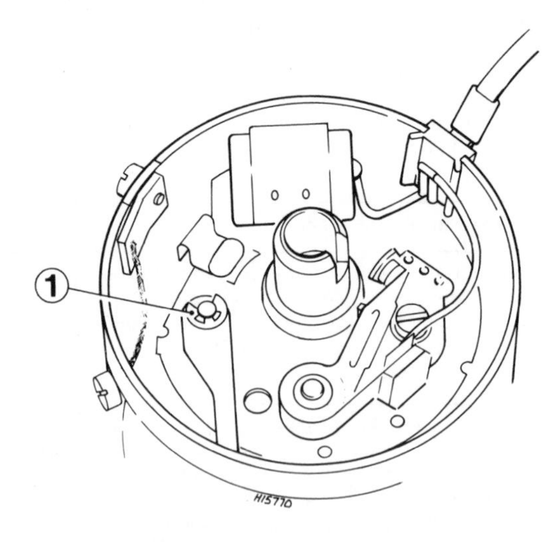

Fig. 4.6 Mechanical distributor vacuum advance unit link arm pivot circlip (1) (Sec 8)

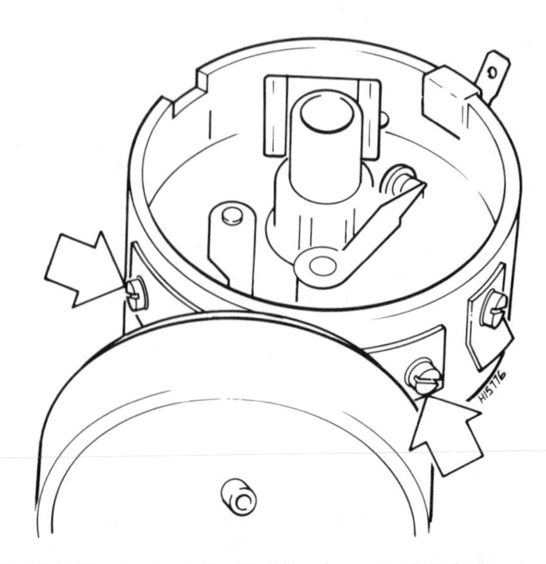

Fig. 4.7 Mechanical distributor vacuum unit fixing screws – arrowed (Sec 8)

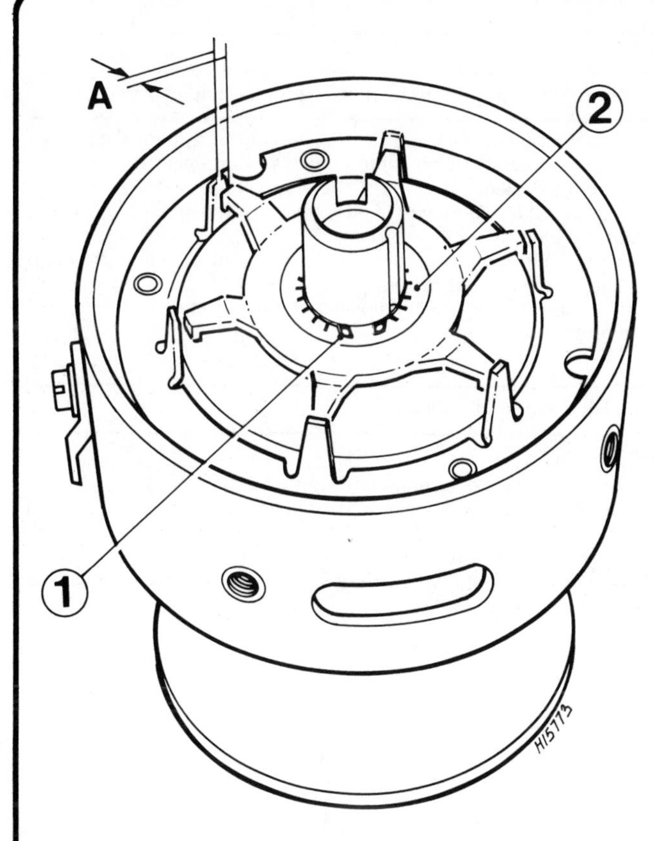

Fig. 4.8 Breakerless distributor (Sec 9)

1 Circlip
2 Spring washer
A Star wheel air gap

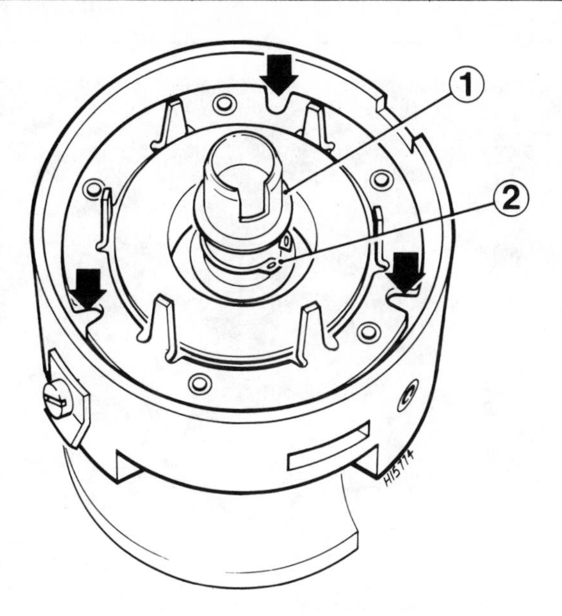

Fig. 4.9 Breakerless distributor (Sec 9)

1 Thrust washer
2 Circlip
Arrows indicate retaining screws

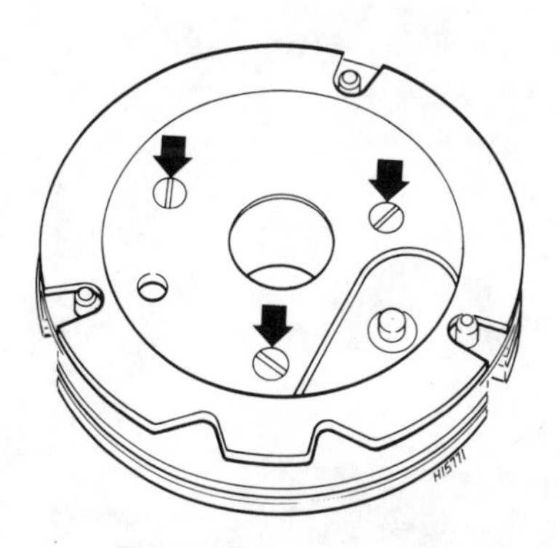

Fig. 4.11 Breakerless distributor (Sec 9)

Arrows indicate the pulse transmitter fixing screws

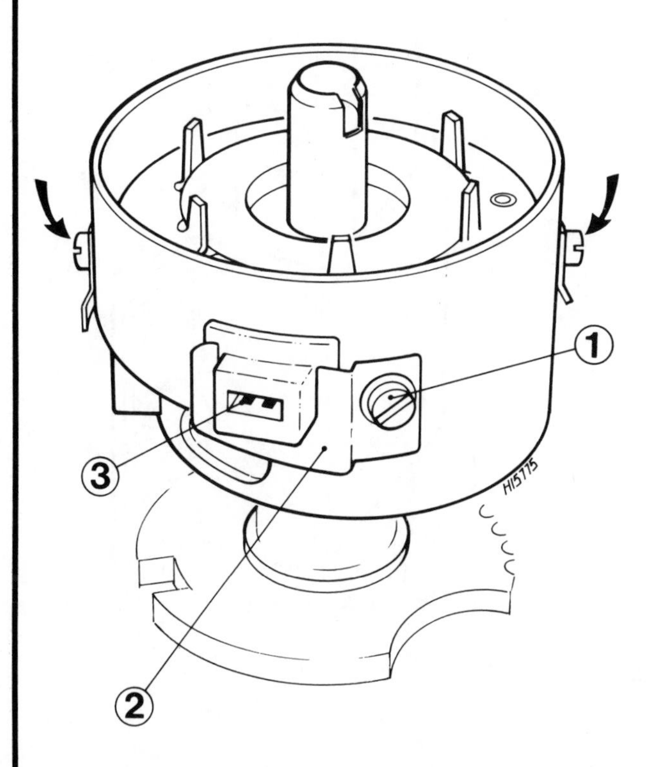

Fig. 4.10 Breakerless distributor (Sec 9)

1 Fixing screw
2 Retaining plate
3 Plug
Arrows indicate carrier plate screws

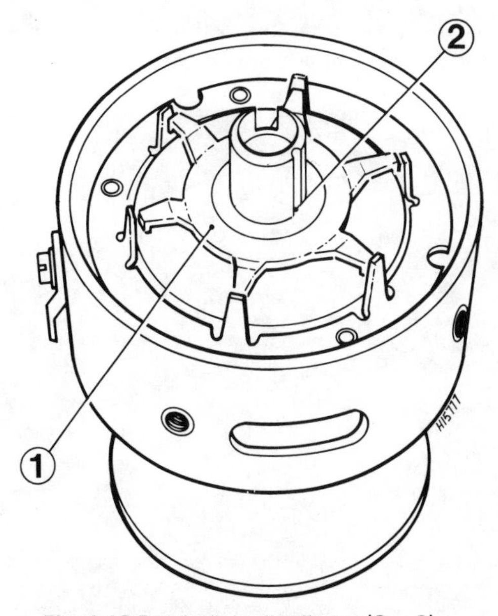

Fig. 4.12 Breakerless distributor (Sec 9)

1 Star wheel
2 Shaft cut-out

10.2 Electronic control unit and cover

11.1A Early type coil (mechanical breaker system)

11.1B Series 1 coil (electronic system)

10 Electronic system control unit – removal and refitting

1 On early models, simply pull out the plug and then remove the control unit screws. Lift the unit from the wing valance within the engine compartment.
2 On later models, remove the plug cover, lift the locking spring and pull out the plug (photo).
3 Unscrew the mounting bolts and lift the control unit away. From 1984 the unit is secured by nuts.
4 Refitting is a reversal of removal, but always renew a control unit with one of exactly similar type.

11 Ignition coil and resistor

Ignition coil

1 Removal is simply a matter of disconnecting the leads (having noted their correct locations) and unbolting the mounting clamp (photos).
2 **Never** renew a coil with one of a different type from the original. Coils for mechanical and breakerless systems are **not** interchangeable (photos).

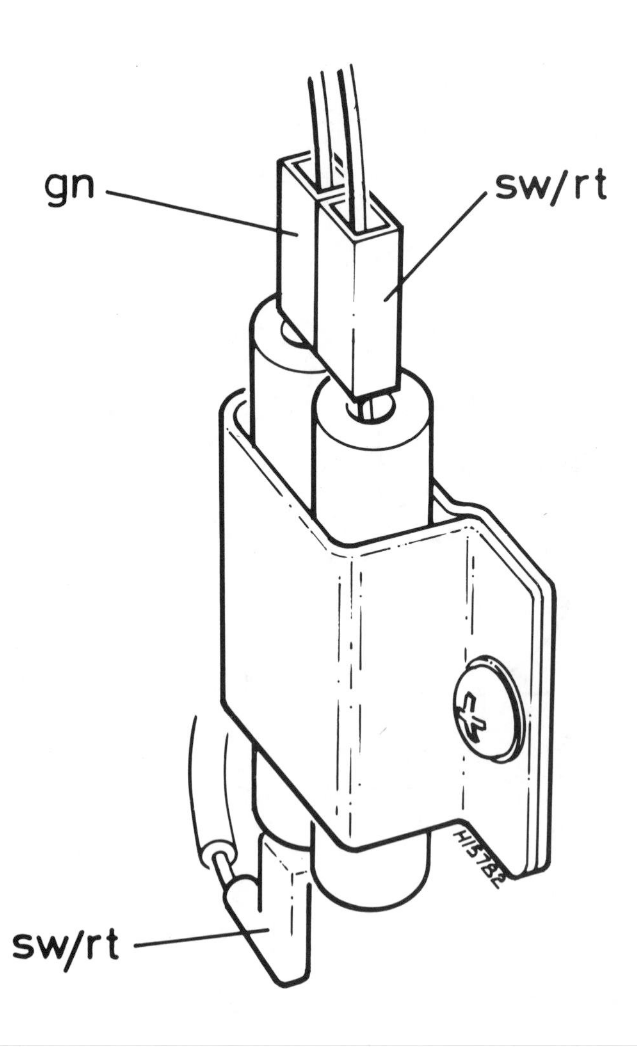

Fig. 4.13 Ignition coil resistor – mechanical distributor (Sec 11)

11.1C Series 2 coil (electronic system)

Ignition coil resistor

3 This is used in conjunction with mechanical breaker ignition systems.

4 To remove it, first lift out the battery, then disconnect the resistor leads (noting their correct locations) and extract the mounting plate screws.

12 Spark plugs and HT leads

1 Correctly functioning spark plugs are essential for efficient engine operation.

2 At the intervals specified in Routine Maintenance, the plugs should be removed, cleaned and regapped.

3 To remove the plugs, open the bonnet, and pull the HT leads from them. Grip the rubber end fitting, **not** the lead, otherwise the connection to the end fitting may fracture.

4 Brush out any accumulated dirt or grit from the spark plug recesses in the cylinder head, otherwise it may drop into the combustion chamber when the plug is removed.

5 Unscrew the spark plugs with a deep socket or a box spanner. Do not allow the tool to tilt, otherwise the ceramic insulator may be cracked or broken.

6 Examination of the spark plugs will give a good indication of the condition of the engine.

7 If the insulator nose of the spark plug is clean and white, with no deposits, this is indicative of a weak mixture, or too hot a plug (a hot plug transfers heat away from the electrode slowly, a cold plug transfers heat away quickly).

8 The plugs fitted as standard are specified at the beginning of this Chapter. If the top and insulator nose are covered with hard black-looking deposits, then this is indicative that the mixture is too rich. Should the plug be black and oily, then it is likely that the engine is fairly worn, as well as the mixture being too rich.

9 If the insulator nose is covered with light tan to greyish brown deposits, then the mixture is correct and it is likely that the engine is in good condition.

10 If there are any traces of long brown tapering stains on the outside of the white portion of the plug, then the plug will have to be renewed, as this shows that there is a faulty joint between the plug body and the insulator, and compression is being allowed to leak away.

11 Before cleaning a spark plug, wash it in petrol to remove oily deposits.

12 Although a wire brush can be used to clean the electrode end of the spark plug this method can cause metal conductance paths across the nose of the insulator and it is therefore to be preferred that an abrasive powder cleaning machine is used. Such machines are available quite cheaply from motor accessory stores or you may prefer to take the plugs to your dealer who will not only be able to clean them but also to check the sparking efficiency of each plug under compression.

13 The spark plug gap is of considerable importance, as, if it is too large or too small, the size of the spark and its efficiency will be seriously impaired. For the best results the spark plug gap should be set in accordance with the Specifications at the beginning of this Chapter.

14 To set it, measure the gap with a feeler gauge, and then bend open or close, the outer electrode until the correct gap is achieved. The centre electrode should never be bent as this may crack the insulation and cause plug failure if nothing worse.

15 Special spark plug electrode gap adjusting tools are available from most motor accessory stores.

16 Before refitting the spark plugs, wash each one thoroughly again using clean fuel in order to remove all traces of abrasive powder and then apply a smear of grease to the plug threads.

17 Screw each plug in by hand. This will ensure that there is no chance of cross threading.

18 Tighten to the specified torque. If a torque wrench is not available, just lightly tighten each plug. It is better to undertighten than strip the threads from the light alloy cylinder head.

19 When reconnecting the spark plug leads, make sure that they are refitted in their correct order 1-5-3-6-2-4. No 1 cylinder being at the timing belt end of the engine.

20 The spark plug leads require no routine attention other than being kept clean by wiping them regularly.

21 In order to minimise corrosion in the distributor cap lead sockets, smear the HT cable end fittings with a light coating of petroleum jelly.

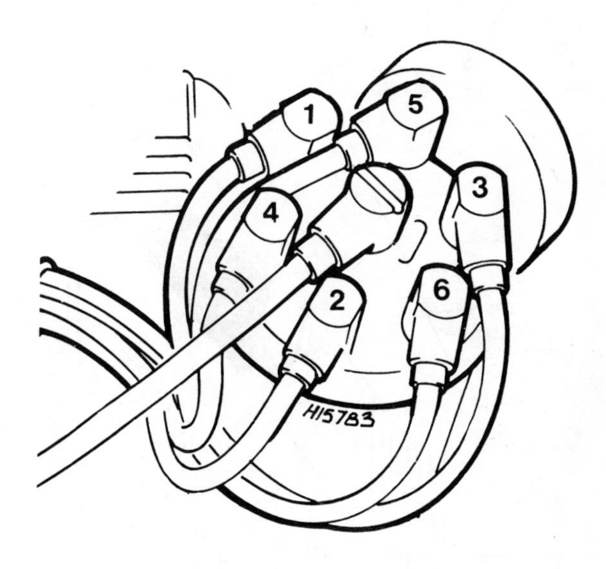

Fig. 4.14 HT lead connections at distributor cap (Sec 12)

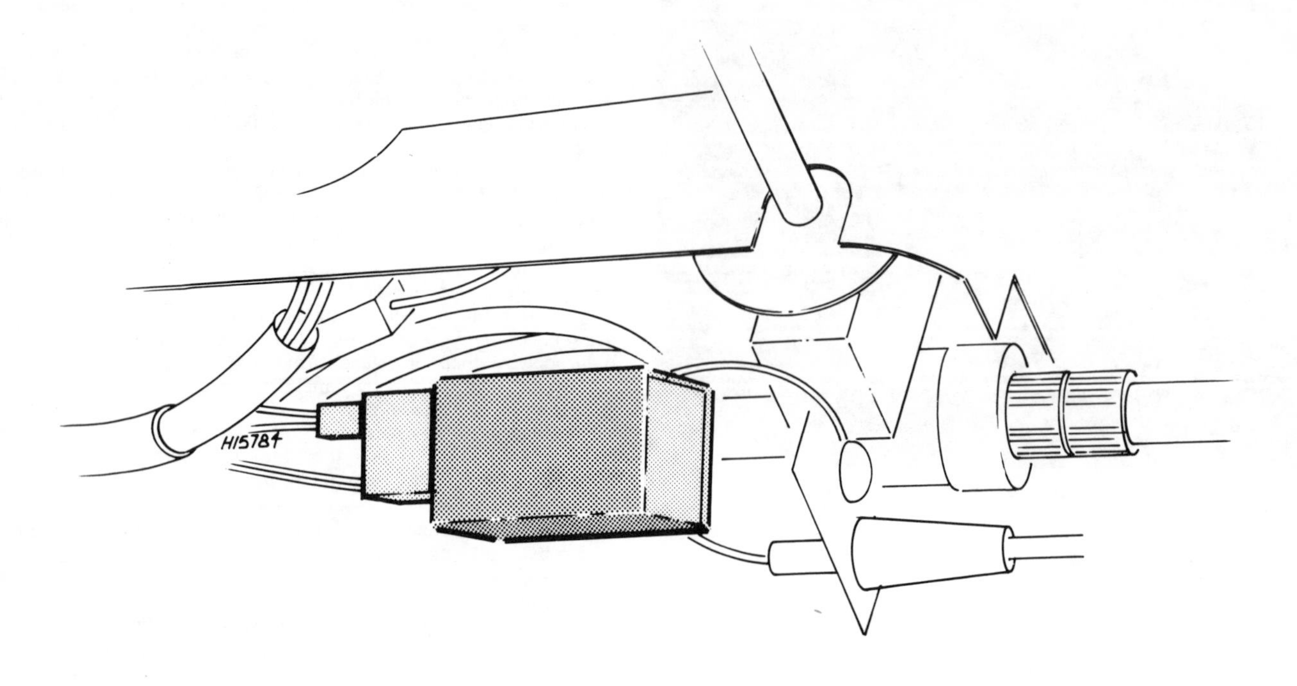

Fig. 4.15 Hazard warning flasher unit (Sec 13)

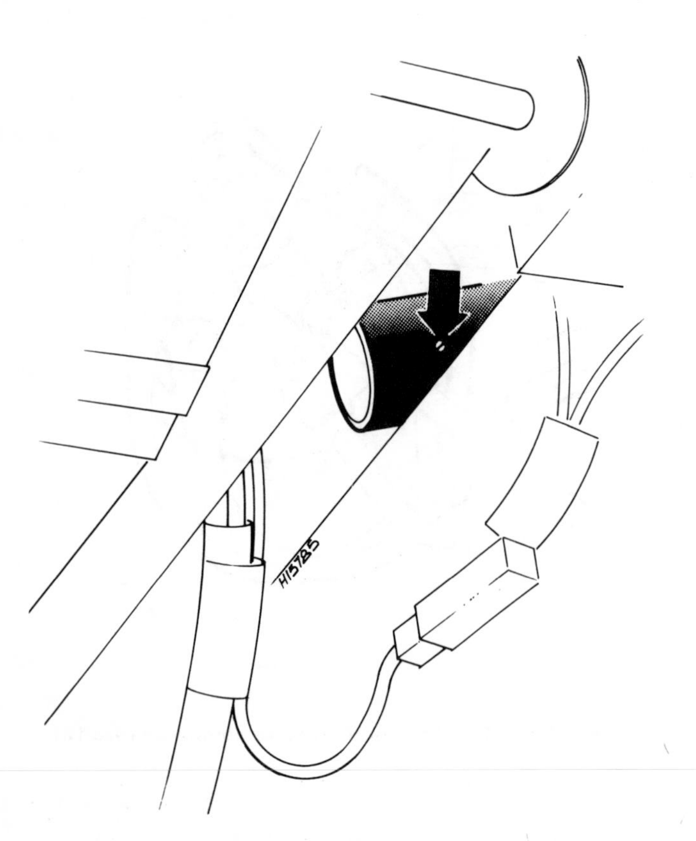

Fig. 4.16 Ignition switch grub screw – arrowed (Sec 13)

13 Ignition switch – removal and refitting

1 Disconnect the battery negative lead.
2 Remove the facia under cover from the driver's side.
3 Detach the hazard warning flasher unit from its mounting plate.
4 Release the wiring straps as necessary to obtain access to the rear of the ignition switch.
5 Extract the small grub screw and withdraw the ignition switch from the steering lock.
6 Disconnect the switch wiring plug.
7 Refitting is a reversal of removal, but make sure that the lock is set to the O position.

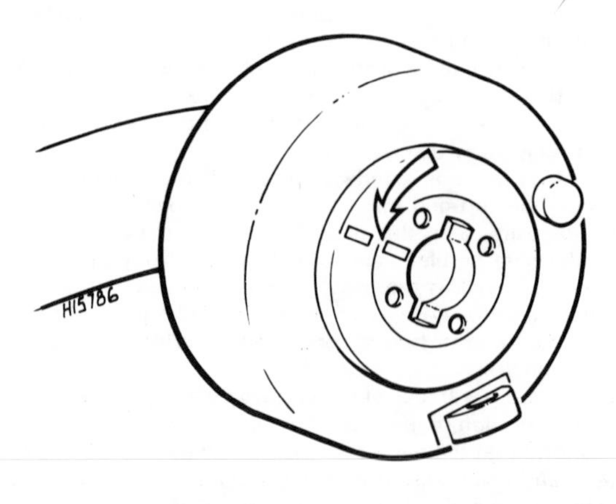

Fig. 4.17 Lock cylinder in O position – arrowed (Sec 13)

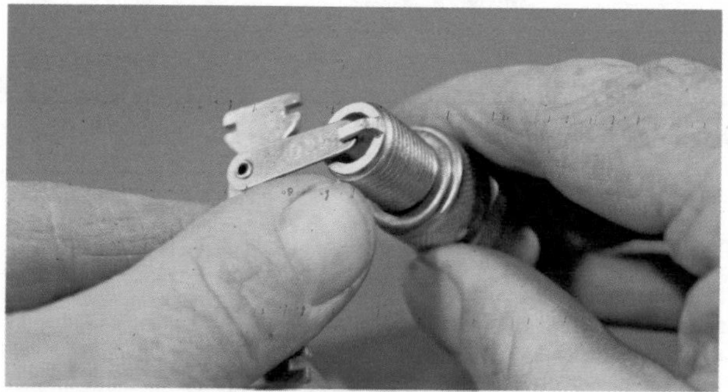

Measuring plug gap. A feeler gauge of the correct size (see ignition system specifications) should have a slight 'drag' when slid between the electrodes. Adjust gap if necessary

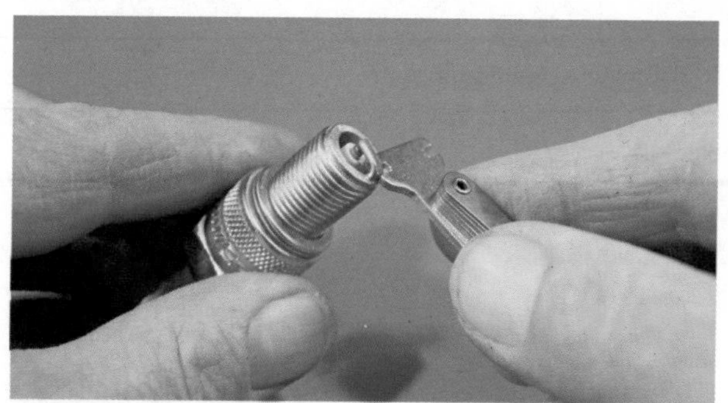

Adjusting plug gap. The plug gap is adjusted by bending the earth electrode inwards, or outwards, as necessary until the correct clearance is obtained. Note the use of the correct tool

Normal. Grey-brown deposits, lightly coated core nose. Gap increasing by around 0.001 in (0.025 mm) per 1000 miles (1600 km). Plugs ideally suited to engine, and engine in good condition

Carbon fouling. Dry, black, sooty deposits. Will cause weak spark and eventually misfire. Fault: over-rich fuel mixture. Check: carburettor mixture settings, float level and jet sizes; choke operation and cleanliness of air filter. Plugs can be re-used after cleaning

Oil fouling. Wet, oily deposits. Will cause weak spark and eventually misfire. Fault: worn bores/piston rings or valve guides; sometimes occurs (temporarily) during running-in period. Plugs can be re-used after thorough cleaning

Overheating. Electrodes have glazed appearance, core nose very white – few deposits. Fault: plug overheating. Check: plug value, ignition timing, fuel octane rating (too low) and fuel mixture (too weak). Discard plugs and cure fault immediately

Electrode damage. Electrodes burned away; core nose has burned, glazed appearance. Fault: pre-ignition. Check: as for 'Overheating' but may be more severe. Discard plugs and remedy fault before piston or valve damage occurs

Split core nose (may appear initially as a crack). Damage is self-evident, but cracks will only show after cleaning. Fault: pre-ignition or wrong gap-setting technique. Check: ignition timing, cooling system, fuel octane rating (too low) and fuel mixture (too weak). Discard plugs, rectify fault immediately

14 Fault diagnosis – ignition system

Symptom	Reason(s)
Mechanical breaker system	
Engine fails to start	Loose battery connections Discharged battery Oil on contact points Disconnected ignition leads Faulty condenser
Engine starts and runs, but misfires	Faulty spark plug Cracked distributor cap Cracked rotor arm Worn advance mechanism Incorrect spark plug gap Incorrect contact points gap Faulty condenser Faulty coil Incorrect timing Poor engine/transmission earth connections
Engine overheats, lacks power	Seized distributor weights Perforated vacuum pipe Incorrect ignition timing
Engine 'pinks'	Timing too advanced Advance mechanism stuck in advanced position Broken distributor weight spring Low octane fuel Upper cylinder oil used in fuel Excessive oil vapour from crankcase ventilation system or worn piston rings
Breakerless (electronic) system	
Starter turns, but engine will not start	Faulty or disconnected leads Faulty spark plug Air gap incorrect Fault in ignition coil Fault in pulse transmitter
Engine starts but runs erratically	Incorrect timing Fouled spark plug Incorrectly connected HT leads Crack in distributor cap or rotor Poor battery, engine and earth connections

Chapter 5 Clutch

Contents

Specifications

General

Type	Single dry plate, diaphragm spring with hydraulic actuation
Driven plate diameter	228.0 mm (8.98 in)
Release bearing type	Sealed ball

Hydraulic fluid type/specification

Hydraulic fluid to SAE J 1703 or DOT 4 (Duckhams Universal Brake and Clutch Fluid)

Torque wrench settings

	Nm	lbf ft
Pushrod locknut	6	4
Pushrod pivot nut	32	24
Pedal pivot nut	28	21
Master cylinder mounting bolts	24	18
Slave cylinder mounting bolts	26	19
Clutch cover bolts	24	18
Bellhousing-to-crankcase bolts:		
M8	26	19
M10	50	37
M12	80	59

1 General description

The clutch is of single dry plate and diaphragm spring type with hydraulic operation.

No maintenance is required except to occasionally check the fluid level in the clutch master cylinder reservoir.

No adjustment is required, the diaphragm fingers being constantly maintained in light contact with the release bearing.

2 Clutch master cylinder – removal, overhaul and refitting

Series 1 models

1 Working inside the car, disconnect the pushrod from the clutch pedal.
2 Release the pushrod locknut and unscrew and remove the pushrod.
3 Remove the hydraulic fluid from the master cylinder reservoir.
4 Working within the engine compartment, disconnect the hydraulic pipe from the master cylinder (photo).
5 Unbolt the master cylinder from the bulkhead and remove it.
6 Pull off the dust excluder, extract the circlip and withdraw the piston assembly.
7 Examine the surfaces of the piston and cylinder bore. If they are corroded or scored, renew the complete cylinder. If they are in good condition, discard the seals and obtain a repair kit which will contain all the renewable items. Clean all parts in hydraulic fluid or methylated spirit. Dip the piston in clean hydraulic fluid and insert it into the cylinder with the other components.
8 Fit the cylinder and set the pushrod length (A) – Fig. 5.4.
9 Bleed the clutch hydraulic system, as described in Section 9.

Series 2 models

10 Working under the bonnet, empty the hydraulic fluid from the master cylinder reservoir.
11 Disconnect the hydraulic pipe from the master cylinder where it emerges from the bulkhead.
12 Inside the car, remove the facia under cover on the driver's side for access to the pedals.

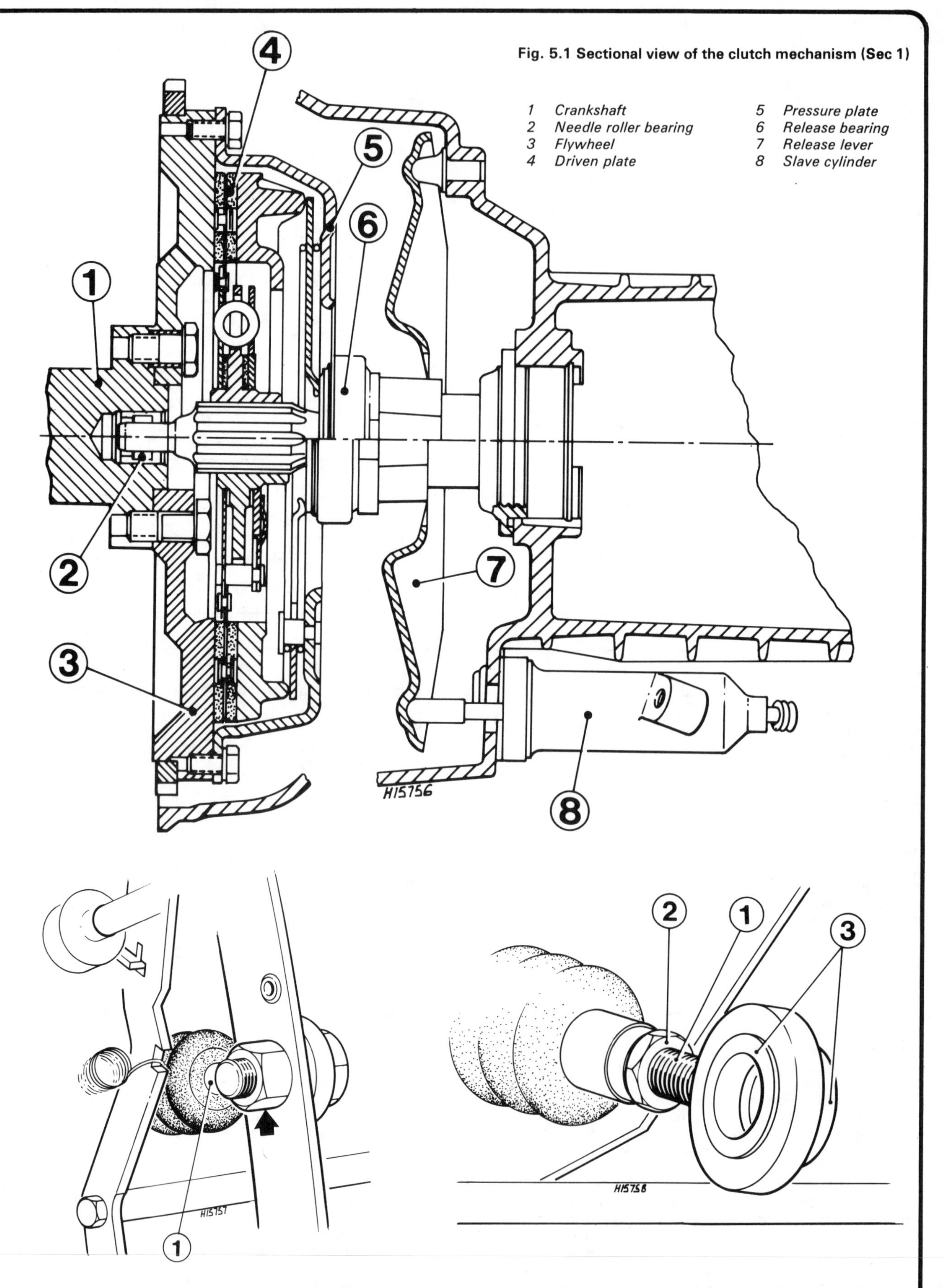

Fig. 5.1 Sectional view of the clutch mechanism (Sec 1)

Fig. 5.2 Clutch pushrod (1) pivot nut – arrowed (Sec 2)

Fig. 5.3 Pushrod (1), locknut (2) and eye (3) – Series 1 models (Sec 2)

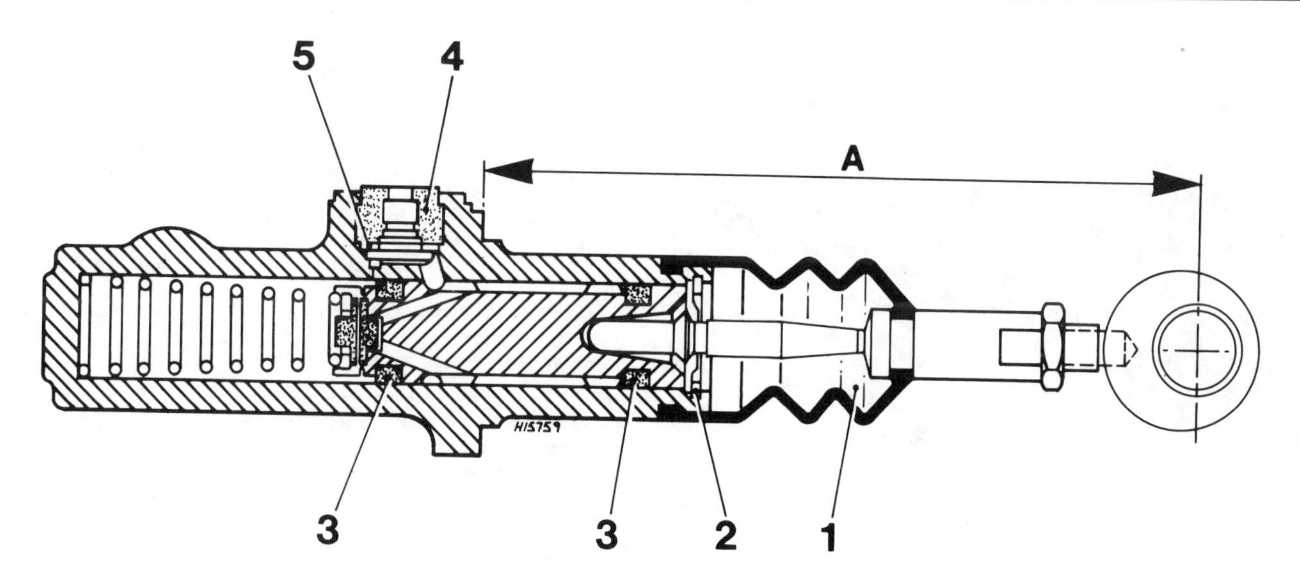

Fig. 5.4 Sectional view of the master cylinder – Series 1 models (Sec 2)

1 Dust excluder
2 Circlip
3 Seals
4 Plug
5 Washer
A = 139.5 to 140.5 mm (5.492 to 5.531 in)

2.4 Clutch master cylinder (RHD) – Series 1 models

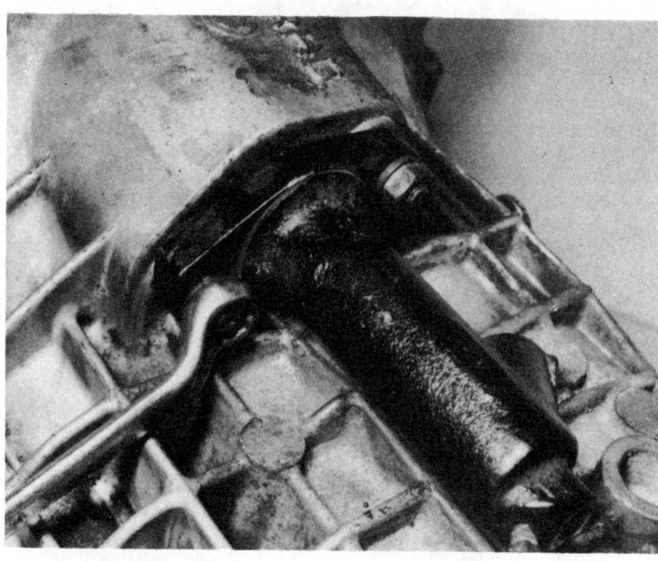

3.2 Unbolting the clutch slave cylinder

13 Remove the pushrod pivot nut and bolt from the pedal arm.
14 Prepare for hydraulic fluid spillage. Disconnect the fluid supply pipe from the master cylinder.
15 Remove the two securing bolts and withdraw the master cylinder from the pedal bracket.
16 Overhaul is as described in paragraphs 6 and 7.
17 Refitting is a reversal of removal, but note the following additional points:

(a) Adjust the eccentric at the pivot nut and bolt so that the pedal height and stroke are as shown in Fig. 13.16 (Chapter 13)
(b) Bleed the clutch hydraulic system on completion (Section 9)

3 Clutch slave cylinder – removal, overhaul and refitting

1 Remove the hydraulic fluid from the clutch master cylinder reservoir.
2 Due to the restricted space at the side of the clutch bellhousing, do not attempt to disconnect the hydraulic pipe from the slave cylinder, but unbolt the cylinder from the bellhousing (photo).

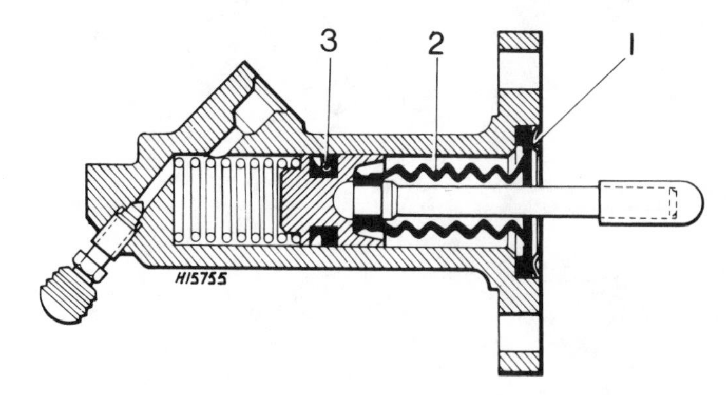

Fig. 5.5 Sectional view of the clutch slave cylinder (Sec 3)

1 Truarc ring
2 Dust excluder
3 Seal

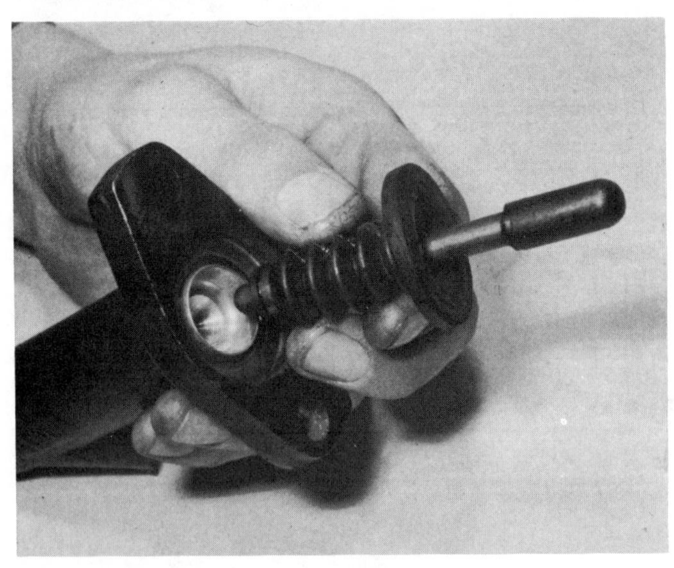

3.4A Removing the slave cylinder pushrod

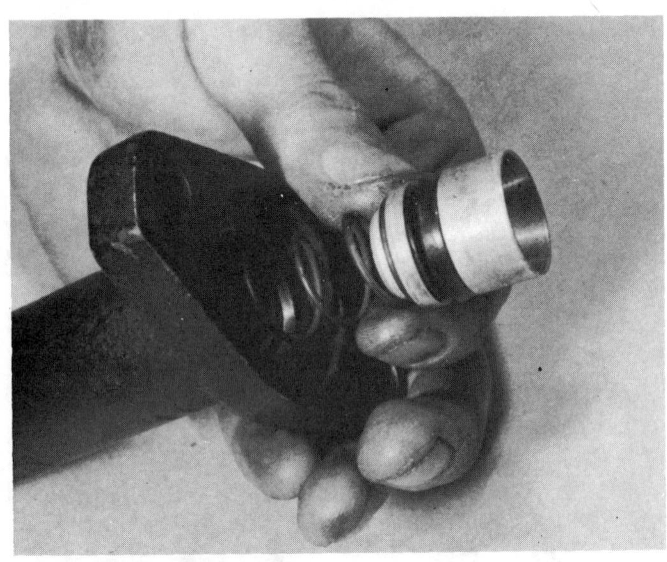

3.4B Removing the slave cylinder piston

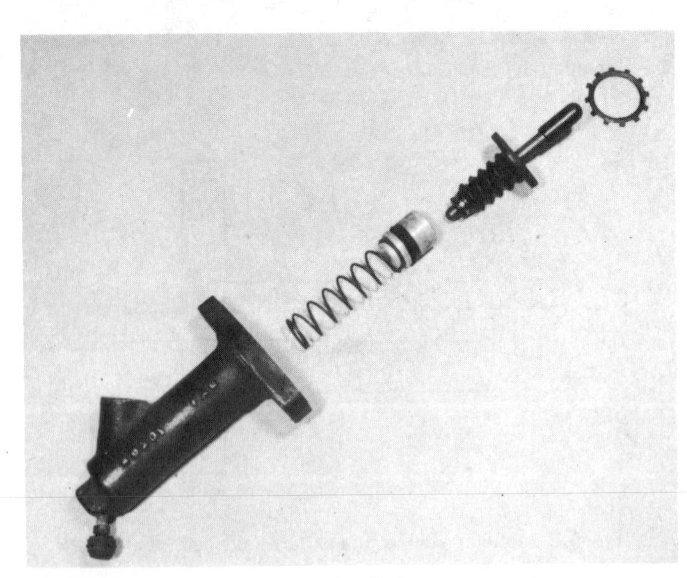

3.4C Exploded view of clutch slave cylinder components

3 Release the pipe run from its bracket and then withdraw the slave cylinder until it can be separated from the pipe.

4 Prise out the Truarc retaining ring and eject the piston assembly (photos).

5 Examine the surfaces of the piston and cylinder bore. If they are corroded or scored, renew the complete slave cylinder. If the components are in good condition, discard the seals and obtain a repair kit which contains all the renewable items.

6 Clean all the items in clean hydraulic fluid or methylated spirit – nothing else, and reassemble them.

7 Drive a new Truarc ring squarely into position to secure the internal components.

8 Connect the hydraulic pipe to the slave cylinder before bolting to the flywheel housing.

9 Bleed the system, as described in Section 9.

4 Clutch pedal – removal and refitting

Series 1 models

1 Extract the screws and remove the facia under cover from the driver's side.

2 Unhook the clutch pedal return spring.

3 Unscrew the pushrod pivot nut and disconnect the pushrod from the pedal arm.

4 Unscrew the nut from the pedal arm pivot bolt, withdraw the bolt and remove the pedal.

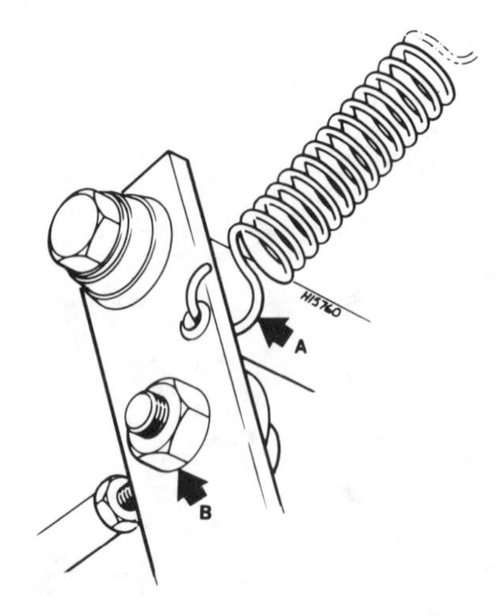

Fig. 5.6 Clutch pedal return spring (A) and pushrod pivot bolt nut (B) (Sec 4)

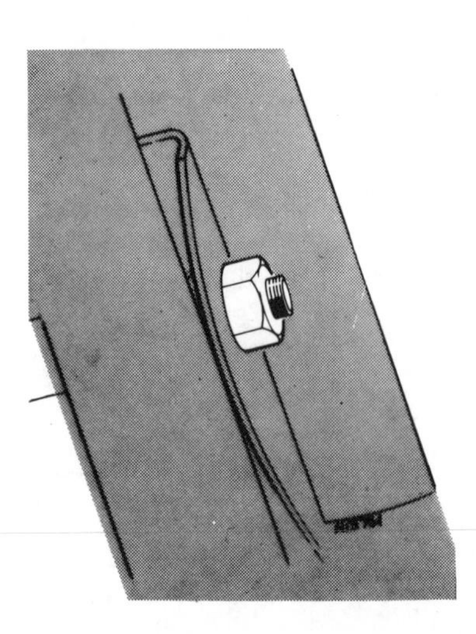

Fig. 5.7 Clutch pedal pivot bolt nut (Sec 4)

5 The bushes and spacer are renewable.
6 Apply grease to the pivots and reassemble by reversing the removal operations. Tighten both nuts to the specified torque.
7 Check that the distance between the bottom edge of the upper surface of the pedal pad and the floor (carpet peeled back) is as follows; if not, adjust the length of the pushrod.

LHD 251.0 to 259.0 mm (9.88 to 10.20 in)
RHD 259.0 to 267.0 mm (10.20 to 10.51 in)

Series 2 models

8 See Chapter 13, Section 10.

5 Clutch – removal

1 The need for renewal of the clutch will normally be apparent when the clutch is felt to slip.

2 The clutch is accessible only after removal of the gearbox, as described in Chapter 6.
3 Unscrew each of the clutch cover bolts a turn at a time in diagonally opposite sequence until the diaphragm spring pressure is relieved.
4 Lift the cover and driven plate from the flywheel.

6 Clutch – inspection

1 If the driven plate linings are worn down to the rivet heads, the plate should be renewed complete, **not** relined.
2 Check the pressure plate surface for scoring, and the diaphragm spring fingers for wear steps. After an extended mileage it is worthwhile renewing the pressure plate as routine to avoid further dismantling at a later date.
3 Inspect the surface of the flywheel. If this is scored or is covered in tiny cracks (caused by overheating) then it may be possible to have the flywheel refinished, provided the final thickness of the flywheel is not reduced below the specified minimum (see Chapter 1, Specifications), otherwise a new flywheel will have to be obtained.
4 Any oil contamination of the clutch components will indicate that either the crankshaft rear or gearbox front oil seal is at fault. This must be renewed before replacing the clutch. After an extended mileage it is worthwhile renewing both seals as routine to avoid dismantling at a later date.

7 Clutch release mechanism

1 Whenever the gearbox is removed to work on the clutch, take the opportunity to check the release components.
2 Release the spring (1), and withdraw the release lever (2) and bearing (3) – Fig. 5.8.
3 If the bearing is noisy when spun with the fingers, or if it has been in use for a good mileage, it is worthwhile renewing it.
4 Remove the bearing from the carrier and press the new one on so that it is positioned as shown – Fig. 5.9.
5 Apply molybdenum disulphide grease to the inner lubrication groove in the bearing carrier, to the bearing slides and to the pivot dimples of the release lever. Fit the pivot rubber cover.
6 Reassemble the components and reconnect the spring.

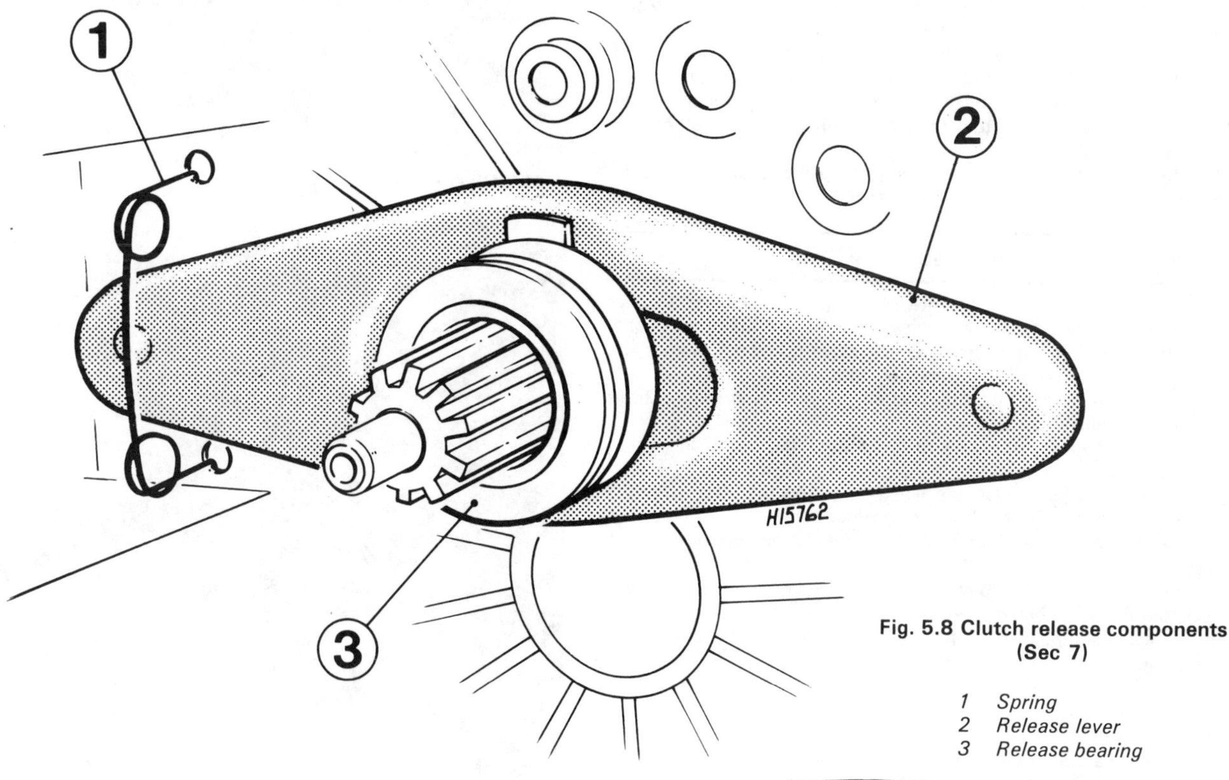

Fig. 5.8 Clutch release components (Sec 7)

1 Spring
2 Release lever
3 Release bearing

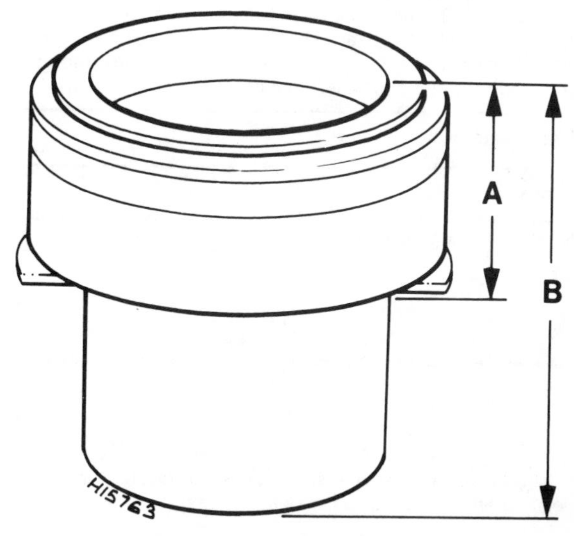

Fig. 5.9 Release bearing setting on holder (Sec 7)

A 30.25 mm (1.19 in) *B 52.10 mm (2.05 in)*

8 Clutch – refitting

1 With the flywheel and pressure plate surfaces absolutely clean, offer the driven plate to the flywheel so that its flatter surface is against the flywheel (photo).
2 Locate the clutch cover on its locating pins and screw in the cover bolts evenly, but only finger tight.
3 The driven plate must now be centralised so that, when the gearbox is offered up to the engine, the input shaft splines will pass smoothly through the hub of the driven plate. To do this, either use a clutch guide tool obtainable from motor accessory stores, an old input shaft or a rod bound with tape to match the diameter of the driven plate hub hole.
4 Slide the tool into the driven plate hub until its end engages in the pilot bearing in the rear end of the crankshaft. This will have the effect of centralising the driven plate (photo). Tighten the cover bolts to the specified torque and remove the tool.
5 Apply a trace of grease to the input shaft splines and offer the gearbox to the engine. It may be necessary to have an assistant turn the crankshaft slightly by applying a spanner to the damper bolt in order to align the splines so that the input shaft will pass through the hub of the driven plate.
6 Fit the bellhousing bolts, mounting, propeller shaft and clutch slave cylinder, all as described in Chapter 6.

8.1 Clutch cover and driven plate

8.4 Centralising the clutch driven plate

9 Hydraulic system – bleeding

1 The procedure with a pressure bleeding kit is similar to that described in Chapter 9 for the braking system, except that there is only one bleed screw – located on the clutch slave cylinder. Operate the clutch pedal a few times while bleeding the system.
2 Bleeding the clutch hydraulic system without a pressure kit is slightly more involved.
3 Fill the fluid reservoir – ensure it remains full during the entire bleeding procedure.
4 Attach a suitable hose to the bleed screw on the slave cylinder. The other end of the hose must be immersed in hydraulic fluid in a clean jar – this is to reduce the likelihood of air being drawn back into the system.
5 Pump the clutch pedal fully 10 times and keep it depressed. Have an assistant open the bleed screw and observe the fluid being ejected. If air bubbles still appear in the fluid, close the bleed screw and repeat the procedure.
6 When air bubbles no longer appear, close the bleed screw and top up the reservoir.
7 If air remains in the system after several attempts at bleeding (indicated by the clutch engagement point being towards the bottom of the pedal stroke), unbolt the slave cylinder. Press the slave cylinder pushrod into the cylinder as far as it will go and release it slowly, repeat this several times. This will drive any remaining air back into the fluid reservoir. Refit the slave cylinder on completion.

10 Fault diagnosis – clutch

Symptom	Reason(s)
Judder when taking up drive	Loose engine or gearbox mountings Badly worn friction linings or contaminated with oil Worn splines on gearbox input shaft or driven plate hub Worn input shaft needle bearing in flywheel
*Clutch spin (failure to disengage) so that gears cannot be meshed	Hydraulic system fault Incorrect release bearing to pressure plate clearance Rust on splines (may occur after vehicle standing idle for long periods) Damaged or misaligned pressure plate assembly
Clutch slip (increase in engine speed does not result in increase in vehicle road speed – particularly on gradients)	Incorrect release bearing to pressure plate finger clearance Friction linings worn out or oil contaminated
Noise evident on depressing clutch pedal	Dry, worn or damaged release bearing Incorrect pedal adjustment Weak or broken pedal return spring Excessive play between driven plate hub splines and input shaft splines

Symptom	Reason(s)
Noise evident as clutch pedal released	Distorted driven plate Broken or weak driven plate cushion coil springs Incorrect pedal adjustment Weak or broken clutch pedal return spring Distorted or worn input shaft Release bearing loose on retainer hub

* *This condition may also be due to the driven plate being rusted to the flywheel or pressure plate. It is possible to free it by applying the handbrake, engaging top gear, depressing the clutch pedal and operating the starter motor. If really badly corroded, then the engine will not turn over, but in the majority of cases the driven plate will free. Once the engine starts, rev it up and slip the clutch several times to clear the rust deposits.*

Chapter 6
Manual gearbox and automatic transmission

For modifications, and information applicable to later models, see Supplement at end of manual

Contents

Specifications

Part A: Manual gearbox

Type .... 4 or 5 forward speeds with synchromesh and reverse

Application

320 – Series 1 .... Getrag 242, 4-speed
320i – Series 1 and 2 .... Getrag 240, 5-speed
Getrag 245, 5-speed

323i:
Series 1 .... Getrag 240, 5-speed
Getrag 245, 5-speed
Series 1 and 2 .... Getrag 245, 5-speed Sport
Series 2 .... ZF S 5-16, 5-speed

Ratios

	240	242	245	245 Sport	ZF S 5-16
1st	3.72 : 1	3.76 : 1	3.68 : 1	3.76 : 1	3.72 : 1
2nd	2.02 : 1	2.04 : 1	2.00 : 1	2.32 : 1	2.04 : 1
3rd	1.32 : 1	1.32 : 1	1.33 : 1	1.61 : 1	1.34 : 1
4th	1.00 : 1	1.00 : 1	1.00 : 1	1.22 : 1	1.00 : 1
5th	0.81 : 1	–	0.81 : 1	1.00 : 1	0.82 : 1
Reverse	4.10 : 1	3.45 : 1	3.68 : 1	4.10 : 1	3.54 : 1

Lubrication

Lubricant type/specification .... Gear oil, viscosity SAE 80 to API-GL4 (Duckhams Hypoid 80)
Lubricant capacity:
240, 242 and ZF .... 1.0 litre (1.8 Imp pts)
245 and 245 Sport .... 1.5 litre (2.6 Imp pts)

Torque wrench settings	Nm	lbf ft
Gearbox-to-engine bolts:		
M8	26	19
M10	50	37
M12	80	59
Oil filler and drain plugs	60	44
Rear cover-to-rear casing bolts	10	7
Rear casing and main casing bolts	25	18
Clutch guide sleeve bolts	18	13
Reverse shaft to intermediate casing	49	36
Reverse gear shaft holder bolts	25	18
Output flange nut	100	74
Rear section locking plunger plug	40	30
Crossmember-to-body bolts	24	18
Crossmember-to-gearbox bolts	24	18
Layshaft nut (245 Sport)	60	44
Clamps to rear section (ZF S 5-16)	35	26
Selector lever bolt (ZF S 5-16)	45	33

Part B: Automatic transmission

Type ..... 3 or 4 forward speeds and reverse

Application

320 and 323i models up to 1982	ZF 3 HP-22 (3-speed)
320i and 323i models 1983 on	ZF 4 HP-22 (4-speed)

Ratios

1st	2.478 : 1
2nd	1.478 : 1
3rd	1.000 : 1
4th	0.730 : 1
Reverse	2.090 : 1

Fluid

Type	Dexron II type ATF (Duckhams D-Matic)
Fluid capacity (fluid change):	
ZF 3	2.0 litre (3.5 Imp pts)
ZF 4	3.0 litre (5.3 Imp pts)
Refill from dry	7.5 litre (13.2 Imp pts)

Torque wrench settings	Nm	lbf ft
Torque converter housing-to-engine bolts	80	59
Fluid pan bolts	8	6
Drain plug	16	12
Output flange nut	100	74
Torque converter-to-driveplate bolts	26	19
Crossmember to body	24	18
Selector arm nut	10	7
Flexible mounting to transmission	48	35

PART 1: MANUAL GEARBOX

1 General description

One of five different gearboxes may be fitted, depending upon model and year of production.

Both the four and five-speed gearboxes have synchromesh on all forward speeds. The five-speed units have synchromesh on reverse as well.

Gear change is by means of a floor-mounted remote control rod and lever.

2 Maintenance

1 At the intervals specified in Routine Maintenance, remove the oil level/filler plug from the side of the transmission using a 17.0 mm Allen key. If the oil is level with the bottom of the hole, then the level is correct. If oil is required, inject some into the hole until it just starts to run out. Refit the plug.

2 At the specified intervals remove the filler/level and drain plugs and drain the oil. The oil will drain more completely if it is hot, eg after a long run.

3 Once the oil has drained completely, refit the drain plug and fill the gearbox with the correct grade of oil until it just starts to dribble out of the filler/level plug hole. Screw in the plug.

3 Gearchange mechanism

Flexible gaiter

1 To renew the gaiter, unscrew the gear lever knob, on cars built up to 1980, or pull it off, on 1981 and later models.

2 Pull the gaiter up and off the gear lever.

Gear lever – removal and refitting

3 To remove the gear lever, first take off the knob and then engage reverse gear.

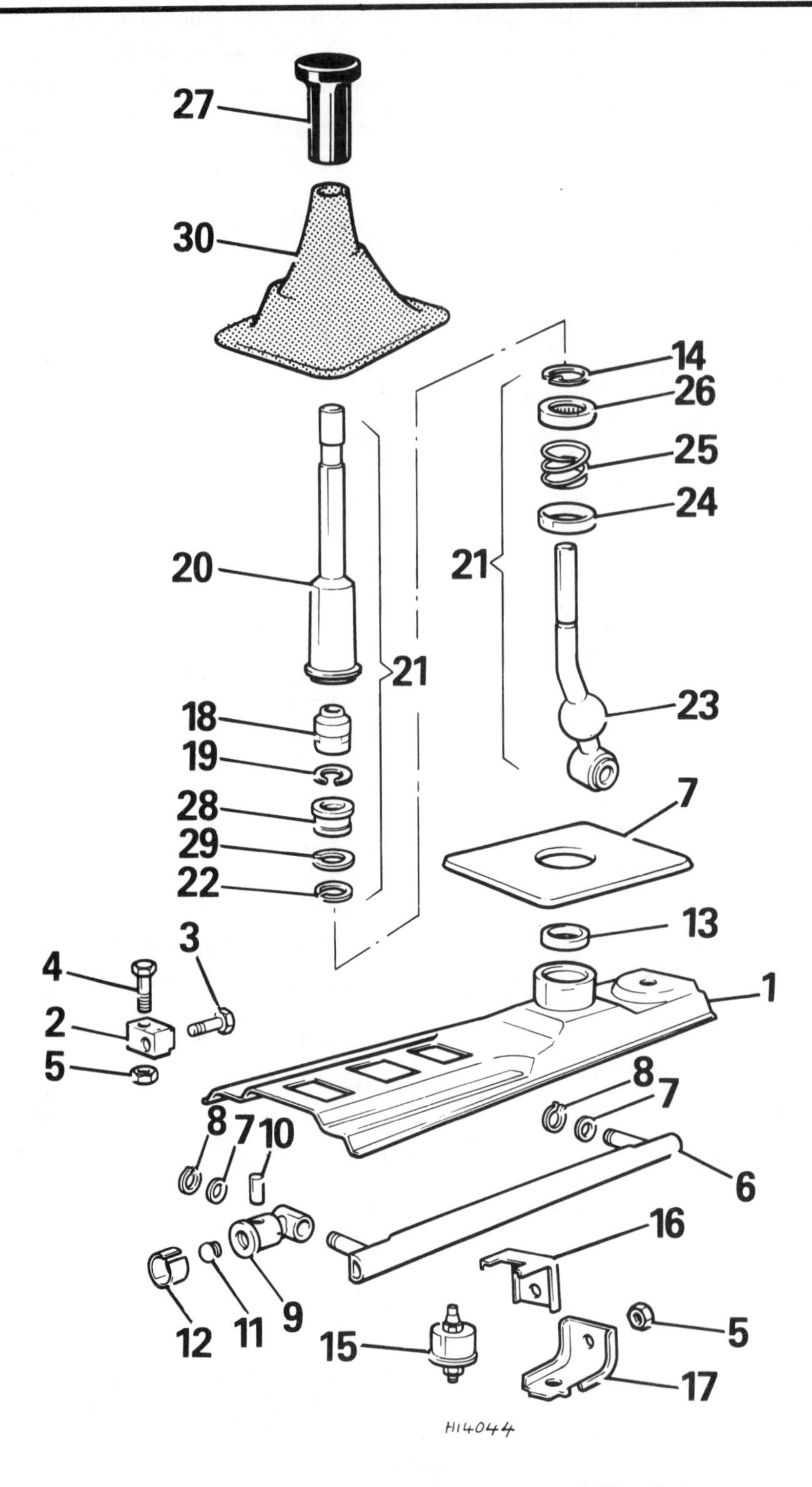

Fig. 6.1 Gearchange mechanism components (Sec 3)

1 Mounting console
2 Arm
3 Bolt
4 Bolt
5 Nut
6 Selector remote control rod
7 Spacer
8 Circlip
9 Joint
10 Pin
11 Lubrication pad
12 Spring sleeve
13 Bearing shell
14 Circlip
15 Flexible mounting
16 Bracket
17 Bracket
18 Cap
19 E-clip
20 Gear lever upper section
21 Gear lever components
22 Circlip
23 Gear lever lower section
24 Bearing shell
25 Coil spring
26 Spacer
27 Knob
28 Rubber ring
29 Washer
30 Gaiter

4 Working under the car, extract the circlip (1) and remove the washer (2) – Fig. 6.2.
5 Disengage the selector rod (3).
6 On versions which have a rear flexible mounting, unscrew the mounting bracket.
7 Pull the gaiter up the gear lever and extract the large circlip now exposed.
8 Withdraw the gear lever.
9 Refitting is a reversal of removal, but apply grease to the ball sockets.

Gear lever – dismantling and reassembly

10 Extract the circlip and separate the gear lever sections.
11 Pull the cap up the rod and then the remaining component parts, noting their fitted sequence.
12 Renew the ball sockets and rubber rings as necessary. Reassembly is a reversal of dismantling, but apply grease to the ball sockets.

Gearchange remote control rod joint – renewal

13 On cars with a four-speed gearbox, remove the two socket-headed gearchange lever mounting bracket bolts. These are very tight due to thread locking fluid having been applied. Always clean the threads and apply fresh fluid when refitting.
14 On cars with a five-speed gearbox, disconnect the propeller shaft from the transmission, as described in Chapter 7.

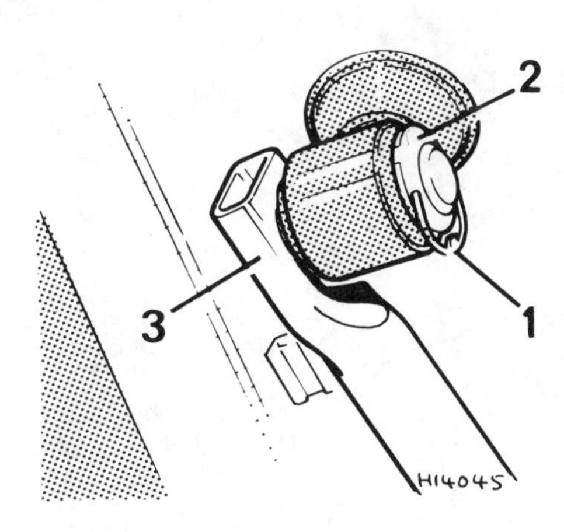

Fig. 6.2 Gearchange lever lower circlip (1), washer (2) and selector rod (3) (Secs 3 and 4)

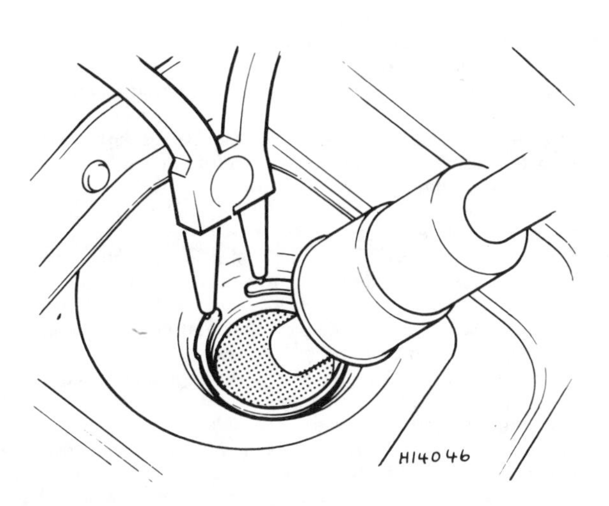

Fig. 6.3 Extracting gear lever circlip (Sec 3)

15 Engage reverse gear and remove the circlip and washer from the base of the gear lever under the car. Disconnect the remote rod.
16 Refer to Fig. 6.6 and push back the locking sleeve (1) and then tap out the pin (2).

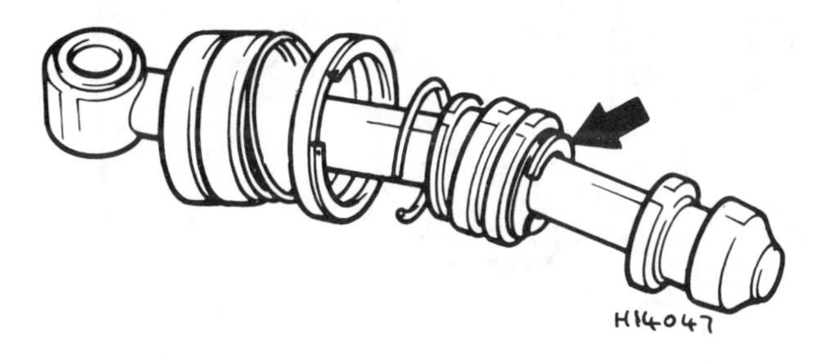

Fig. 6.4 Fitted sequence of gear lever components (Sec 3)

E-clip arrowed

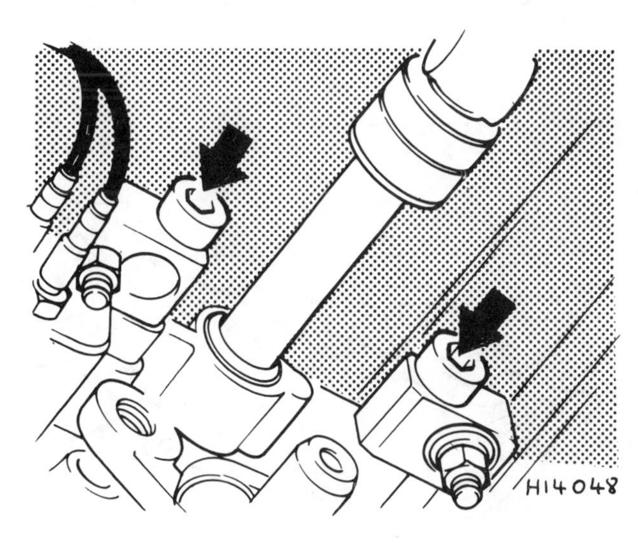

Fig. 6.5 Gearchange lever mounting bracket bolts (arrowed) – 4-speed gearbox (Sec 3)

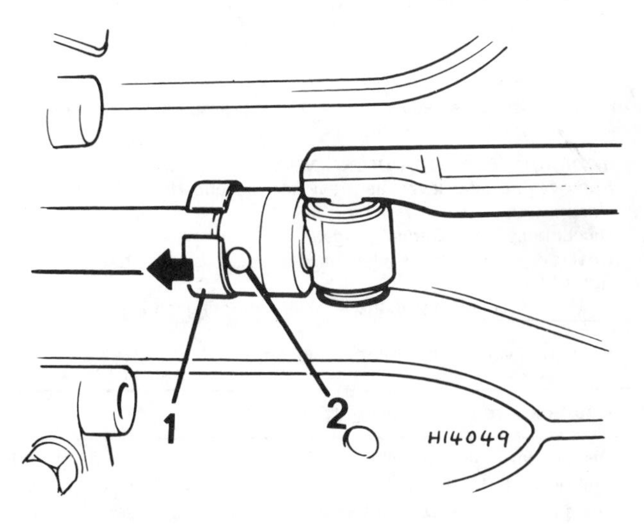

Fig. 6.6 Gear remote selector rod locking sleeve (1) and pin (2) (Sec 3)

Push back the sleeve in the direction of the arrow to remove the pin

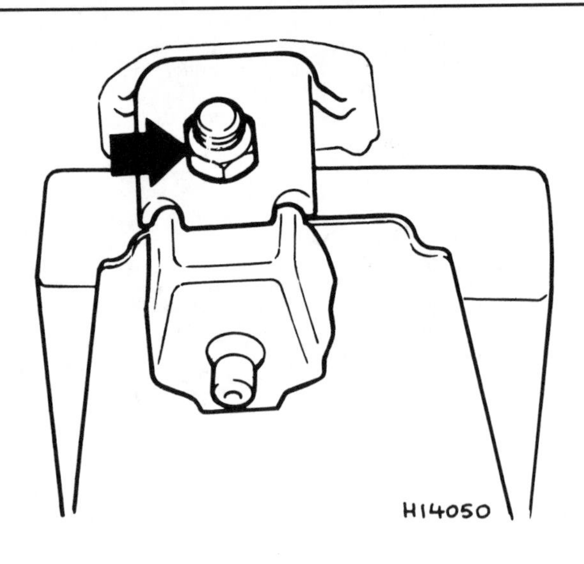

Fig. 6.7 Gear lever bracket retaining nut – arrowed (Sec 3)

4.6 Unscrewing speedometer drive lockbolt

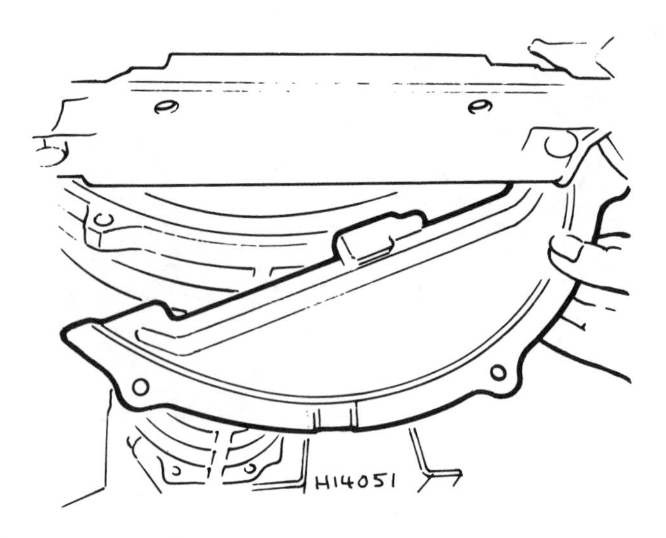

Fig. 6.8 Removing the flywheel cover plate (Sec 4)

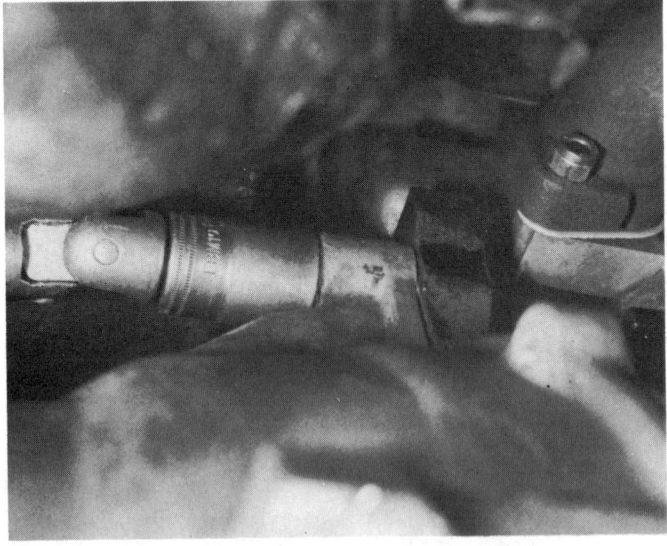

4.13 Unscrewing bellhousing-to-engine connecting bolt

17 Renew bushes as necessary and apply grease before reassembly, which is a reversal of dismantling.

Gearchange lever mounting bracket

18 Remove the gear lever, as previously described.
19 Unscrew the bracket retaining nut.
20 Disconnect the electrical plugs.
21 Unscrew the two socket-headed screws, as described in paragraph 13.
22 Check the condition of the flexible mounting pad and renew, if necessary.
23 Refit by reversing the removal operations.

4 Gearbox – removal and refitting

1 Disconnect the propeller shaft from the rear end of the transmission, as described in Chapter 7. Disconnect the battery.
2 Select reverse gear. Disconnect and remove the front section of the exhaust system.
3 Working under the car, remove the E-clip and take off the washer (Fig. 6.2).
4 Disconnect the remote control rod.
5 Remove the gearbox mounting bracket socket-headed screws, as described in Section 3, paragraph 13.
6 Unscrew the lockbolt (photo) and pull the speedometer drive cable from the gearbox.
7 Disconnect the electrical leads from the reverse lamp switch.
8 Unbolt the clutch slave cylinder and tie it to one side. There is no need to disconnect the hydraulic line.
9 From the front lower part of the flywheel bellhousing unbolt and remove the cover plate.
10 Support the gearbox on a jack and unbolt the mounting crossmember. Retain the shims which fit between the crossmember and the body.
11 Lower the gearbox until it rests on the front crossmember.
12 Unbolt the starter motor and pull it forward.
13 Unscrew and remove the bellhousing-to-engine connecting bolts (photo). Using a trolley jack, or with the help of an assistant, move the gearbox to the rear and downwards.
14 Refitting is a reversal of removal, but it is essential to centralise the clutch driven plate (Chapter 5) if the clutch has been disturbed. Screw in the bellhousing top bolts using a long extension before bolting up the rear crossmember, otherwise there is not enough room to reach the bolts.

5 Gearbox – overhaul (general)

1 If a gearbox is well worn and has been in service for a high mileage, consideration should be given to obtaining a new or exchange unit. This may well be more economical than the purchase of a large number of internal components.
2 Where perhaps only a synchromesh unit or bearing is worn then obviously overhaul will be a viable proposition.
3 Before overhauling a gearbox, clean away external dirt using a water soluble solvent, a steam cleaner or paraffin and a stiff brush.
4 Identify the gearbox by the type number moulded into the casing. Always use new oil seals and gaskets at reassembly.
5 A bearing puller, a two-legged extractor or a press will be needed for some operations, including dismantling of the mainshaft.
6 Certain adjustment shims will be required if new components are fitted and it may be possible to obtain a selection of various thicknesses in advance of overhaul on a sale or return basis.
7 Renew all circlips, roll pins, oil seals and gaskets as a matter of course.

6 Gearbox (Getrag 242, 4-speed) – overhaul

Dismantling into major assemblies

1 Unscrew the drain plug and drain the oil.
2 From within the bellhousing, detach the spring (1) and remove the clutch release arm (2) with the release bearing (3) – Fig. 6.9.
3 Unbolt and remove the guide sleeve. Retain the shims.
4 Extract the bearing circlip and remove the thrust washer.
5 The front bearing must now be removed, either by using a proper bearing puller or, if the bearing is to be renewed, by inserting two hooked rods between the balls and attaching them to a slide hammer.
6 Use a pair of pincers to pull out the cap (3) and then remove the spring (2) and selector rod plunger (1) – Fig. 6.11.
7 Unscrew and remove the lockbolt (1) – Fig. 6.12.
8 Drive down the dowel pins which locate the rear casing section to the main casing, then unscrew and remove the connecting bolts.
9 Withdraw the main housing, retaining any shims which are located

Fig. 6.9 Clutch release spring (1), release arm (2) and release bearing (3) – Getrag 242 (Sec 6)

Fig. 6.11 Selector rod plunger (1), spring (2) and cap (3) – Getrag 242 (Sec 6)

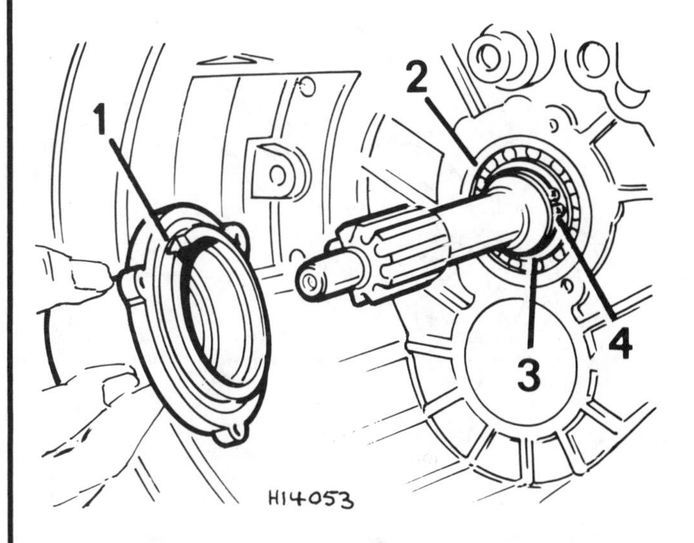

Fig. 6.10 Clutch guide sleeve (1), shim(s) (2), thrust washer (3) and bearing circlip (4) – Getrag 242 (Sec 6)

Fig. 6.12 Lockbolt (1) – Getrag 242 (Sec 6)

on the input or layshaft.
10 Drive the roll pin from 3rd/4th selector fork. Position the fork so that the pin has room to come out in one of the wider spaces in the teeth of the synchromesh. Withdraw the selector shaft.
11 Pull off the sleeve (A) – Fig. 6.14 – and tap out the pin (B). Slacken the screw (1) until the selector rod can be turned to set the finger pointing upwards. Pull the selector rod out towards the front of the gearbox. Retain the rollers.
12 Remove 3rd/4th selector fork.
13 Unscrew bolt (1) – Fig. 6.15 – until the reverse gear selector lever (A) can be removed.
14 Pull out reverse selector shaft (2), taking care not to lose the balls which will be displaced.
15 Prise out the nut locking cup and then unscrew the output flange nut. To do this use a deep socket which will have to be ground to reduce the thickness of its walls, as there is very little clearance. Alternatively, use a box spanner. Hold the flange from turning by making up a suitable pin wrench.
16 Pull off the output flange, using a puller if necessary.
17 Unbolt and remove the rear cover plate, take out and retain the shims.
18 Remove the mainshaft rear bearing with a bearing puller or, if the bearing is to be renewed, by inserting two hooked rods between the balls and attaching them to a slide hammer. Prise out the detent plugs.
19 Pull the shafts and geartrains out of the rear casing section, complete with 1st/2nd selector shaft and fork, and the idler gear. Retain the displaced balls and springs.
20 Unscrew the reverse lamp switch (1) and prise out the plug (2) – Fig. 6.16.
21 If any gears or synchromesh units are worn, then dismantle the shafts in the following way.

Mainshaft – dismantling

22 Remove the circlip (4), thrust washer (5), baulk ring (6), 3rd/4th synchro and the baulk ring (6) – Fig. 6.17.
23 Remove 3rd gear (11) and the needle roller bearing (12).
24 Support 2nd gear and press the shaft out of the remaining components, alternatively draw them from the shaft with a suitable puller.

Synchromesh units – inspection

25 Although a worn synchromesh unit will already be known as a result of noisy gear changing and the fact that the synchro could be easily beaten during quick gear selection, check for wear in all synchro units in the following way.

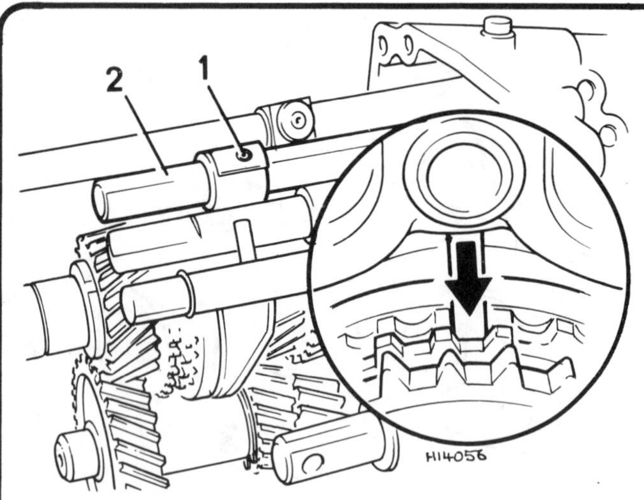

Fig. 6.13 Roll pin (1) and 3rd/4th selector fork (2) – Getrag 242 (Sec 6)

Inset: position the synchro so that the pin has enough space for removal

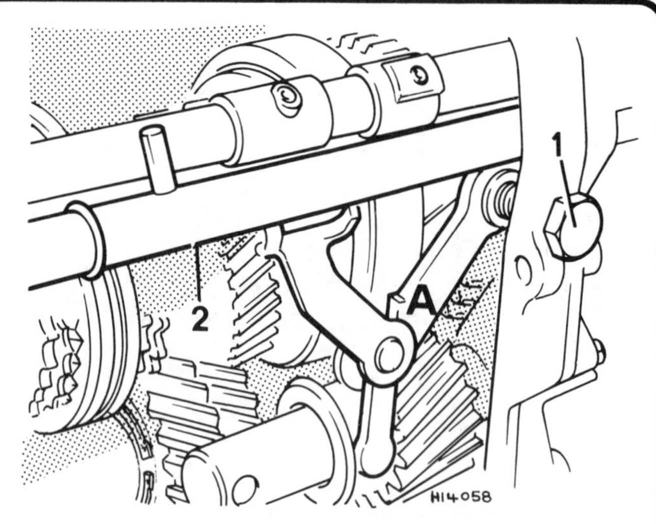

Fig. 6.15 Reverse gear selector lever (A), securing bolt (1) and reverse selector shaft (2) – Getrag 242 (Sec 6)

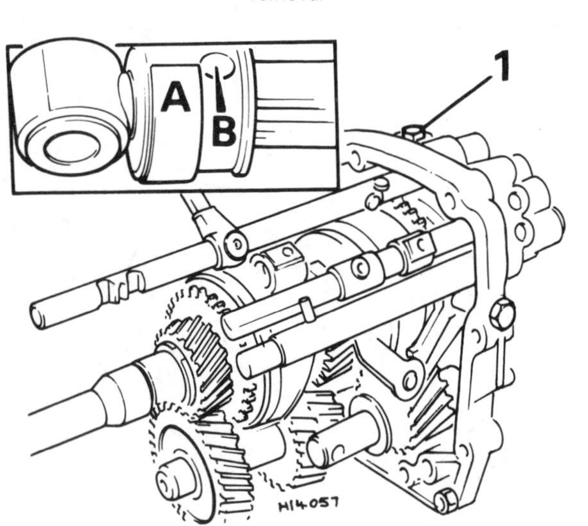

Fig. 6.14 Selector rod locking screw (1) – Getrag 242 (Sec 6)

A Sleeve *B Pin*

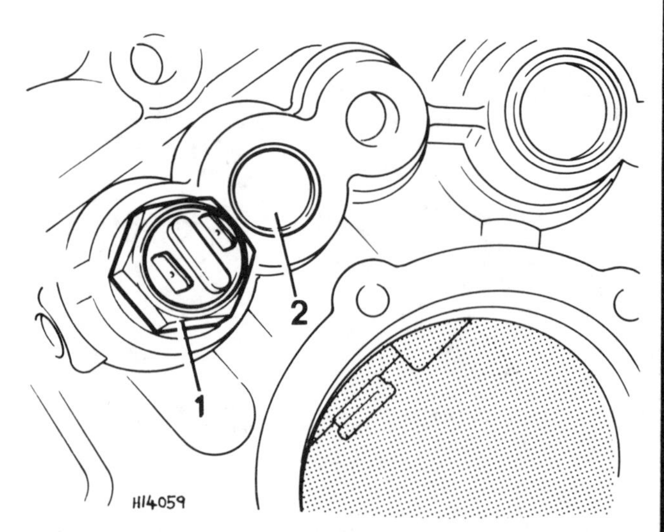

Fig. 6.16 Reverse lamp switch (1) and plug (2) – Getrag 242 (Sec 6)

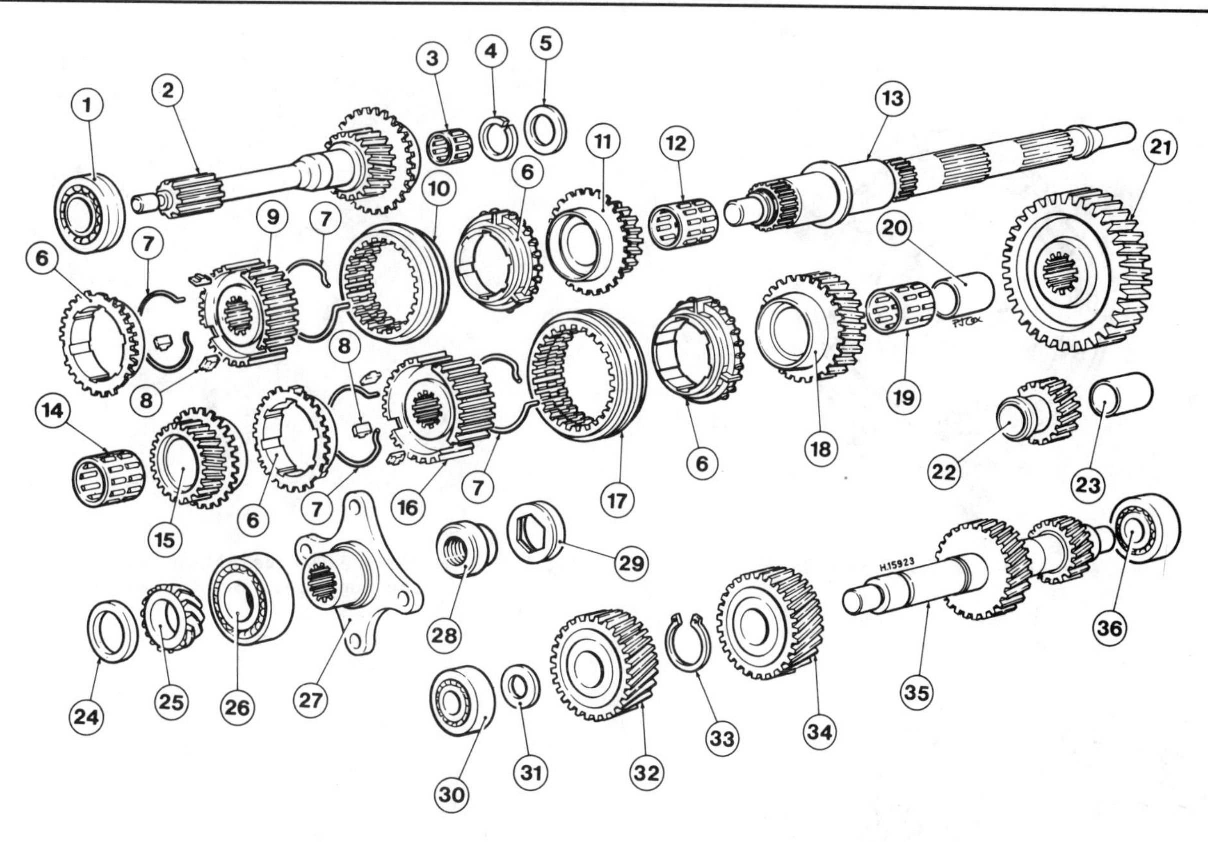

Fig. 6.17 Internal components of the Getrag 242 four-speed gearbox (Sec 6)

1 *Ball-bearing*
2 *Input shaft with 4th gear*
3 *Needle roller bearing*
4 *Circlip*
5 *Washer*
6 *Baulk ring*
7 *Synchro spring*
8 *Sliding key*
9 *Synchro-hub*
10 *Synchro sleeve*
11 *3rd gear*
12 *Needle roller bearing*
13 *Mainshaft*
14 *Needle roller bearing*
15 *2nd gear*
16 *Synchro-hub*
17 *Synchro sleeve*
18 *1st gear*
19 *Needle roller bearing*
20 *Bush*
21 *Reverse gear*
22 *Reverse idler gear*
23 *Bush*
24 *Washer*
25 *Speedometer drivegear*
26 *Bearing*
27 *Output flange*
28 *Nut*
29 *Nut locking cap*
30 *Bearing*
31 *Washer*
32 *4th gear*
33 *Circlip*
34 *3rd gear*
35 *Layshaft*
36 *Roller bearing*

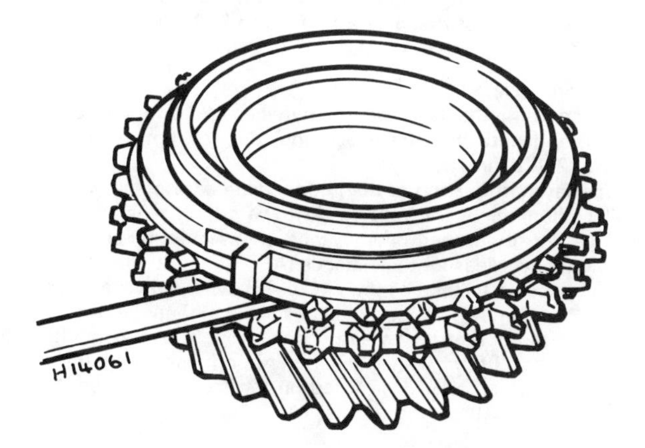

Fig. 6.18 Checking baulk ring-to-gear cone gap (Sec 6)

Fig. 6.19 Synchro-hub with spring and sliding key (Sec 6)

26 Fit the baulk ring to the gear cone and check the gap (Fig. 6.18) adjacent to the stop blocks. If the gap is less than 0.8 mm (0.032 in) renew the baulk ring.
27 If the synchro teeth are worn, renew the component concerned. When reassembling the unit engage the hooked ends of the springs in the same groove, but make sure that they run in opposite directions in relation to each other. The springs must engage in the grooves in the sliding keys.

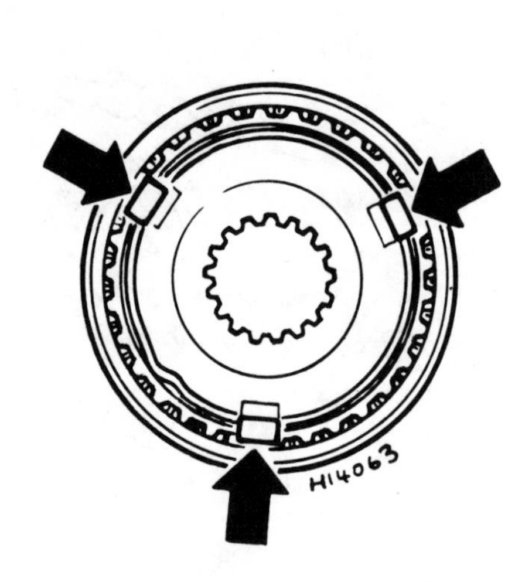

Fig. 6.20 Assemble synchro unit (Sec 6)

Sliding keys arrowed

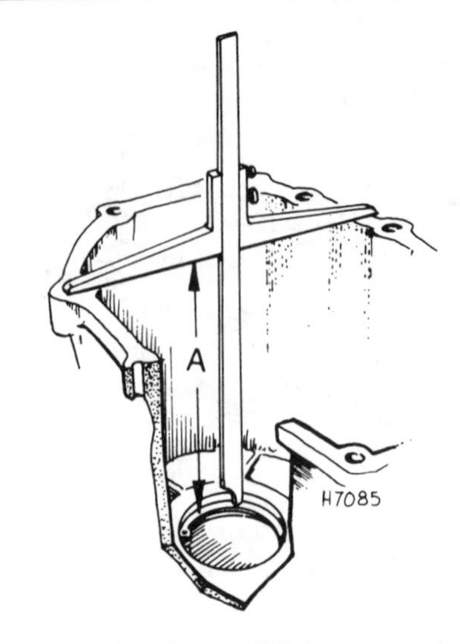

Fig. 6.22 Measuring the distance (A) from the main casing face to the bearing circlip – Getrag 242 (Sec 6)

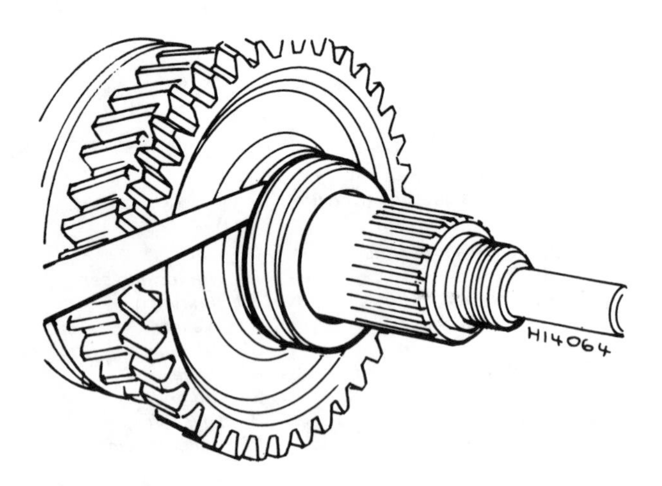

Fig. 6.21 Checking speedometer gear-to-shim clearance – Getrag 242 (Sec 6)

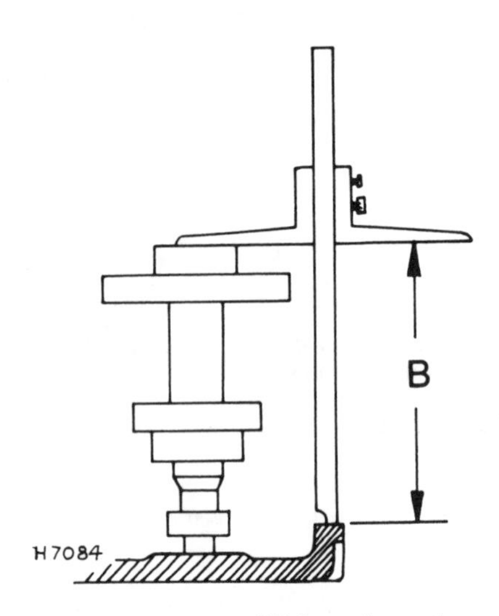

Fig. 6.23 Measuring dimension (B) from the casing gasket to the end of the layshaft – Getrag 242 (Sec 6)

28 The 1st/2nd and 3rd/4th synchros are **not** interchangeable, identify them at removal.
29 Examine the selector forks for wear and loose sliding pads. It is unlikely that the grooves in the synchro sleeves will be found to be worn.

Mainshaft – reassembly

30 To the front end of the shaft, fit the needle roller bearing, 3rd gear, the baulk ring and 3rd/4th synchro. Fit the synchro so the chamfer on the synchro sleeve is towards 4th gear.
31 Fit the thrust washer and circlip.
32 To the opposite end of the shaft fit 2nd gear with the needle roller bearing.
33 Fit the baulk ring
34 Fit 1st/2nd synchro unit and the baulk ring.
35 Fit 1st gear and the needle roller bearing with the spacer bush.
36 Fit reverse gear.
37 Locate the shim, and then press the speedometer drivegear onto the shaft, but only up to the shaft shoulder so that there is a clearance between gear and shim of 0.09 mm (0.0035 in).

Layshaft

38 The bearings may be drawn off for renewal.
39 3rd and 4th gears can be pressed from the shaft, but 3rd gear has a retaining circlip.
40 When fitting the gears, heat to between 120 and 150°C (250 and 300°F), and note that the raised shoulders on both gears must be towards 2nd gear.
41 The layshaft bearing at the intermediate casing end will have the smaller diameter of the roller cage towards the rear casing. If new bearings are fitted, then new layshaft shims must be selected in the following way. Measure the distance (A) – Fig. 6.22 – from the face of the main casing to the bearing circlip. Locate the layshaft in the rear casing. Place a new joint gasket in position and then measure from the surface of the gasket to the end of the layshaft; dimension (B) – Fig. 6.23. Subtract B from A and the difference represents the thickness of the shim(s) which should be fitted on the face of the bearing – Fig. 6.24.

Input (clutch) shaft

42 Only the needle roller and ball-bearing can be renewed. If the gearteeth are chipped or worn, renew the shaft complete. If a new ball-bearing is to be fitted, locate a 1.0 mm (0.04 in) thick shim in the casing and fit the new bearing.
43 Measure (A) – Fig. 6.25 – from end of main casing to the face of the bearing track. Note the dimensions (B) engraved on the input (clutch) shaft. Refer to the following table and read off the thickness of the shim (C) which will be required.

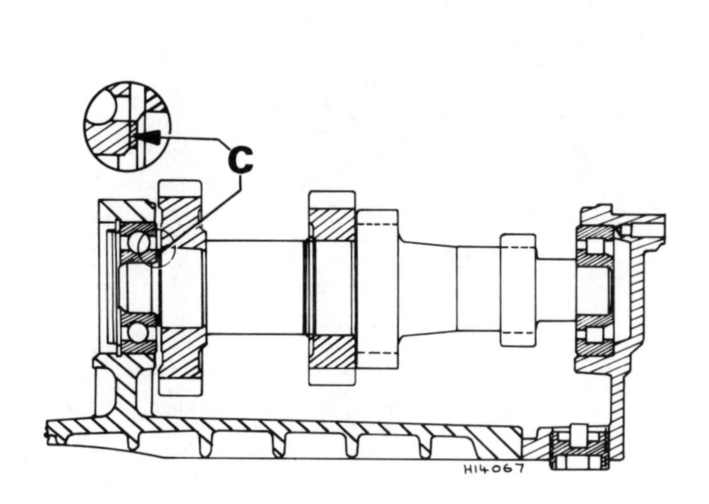

Fig. 6.24 Location of layshaft shim(s) (C) – Getrag 242 (Sec 6)

Early models

A mm (in)	B (engraved mark)	B (dimension) mm (in)	C mm (in)
159.9 (6.295)	100	23.5 (0.925)	0.5 (0.020)
159.9 (6.295)	90	23.4 (0.921)	0.6 (0.024)
159.8 (6.291)	100	23.5 (0.925)	0.4 (0.016)
159.8 (6.291)	90	23.4 (0.921)	0.5 (0.020)
159.7 (6.287)	100	23.5 (0.925)	0.3 (0.012)
159.7 (6.287)	90	23.4 (0.921)	0.4 (0.016)
159.6 (6.283)	100	23.5 (0.925)	0.3 (0.012)
159.6 (6.283)	90	23.4 (0.921)	0.3 (0.012)

Late models

A mm (in)	B (engraved mark)	B (dimension) mm (in)	C mm (in)
159.9 (6.295)	3 or 4 lines or 100	24.0 (0.945)	0.5 (0.020)
159.9 (6.295)	1 or 2 lines or 90	23.9 (0.941)	0.6 (0.024)
159.8 (6.291)	3 or 4 lines or 100	24.0 (0.945)	0.4 (0.016)
159.8 (6.291)	1 or 2 lines or 90	23.9 (0.941)	0.5 (0.020)
159.7 (6.287)	3 or 4 lines or 100	24.0 (0.945)	0.3 (0.012)
159.7 (6.287)	1 or 2 lines or 90	23.9 (0.941)	0.4 (0.016)
159.6 (6.283)	3 or 4 lines or 100	24.0 (0.945)	0.2 (0.008)
159.6 (6.283)	1 or 2 lines or 90	23.9 (0.941)	0.3 (0.012)

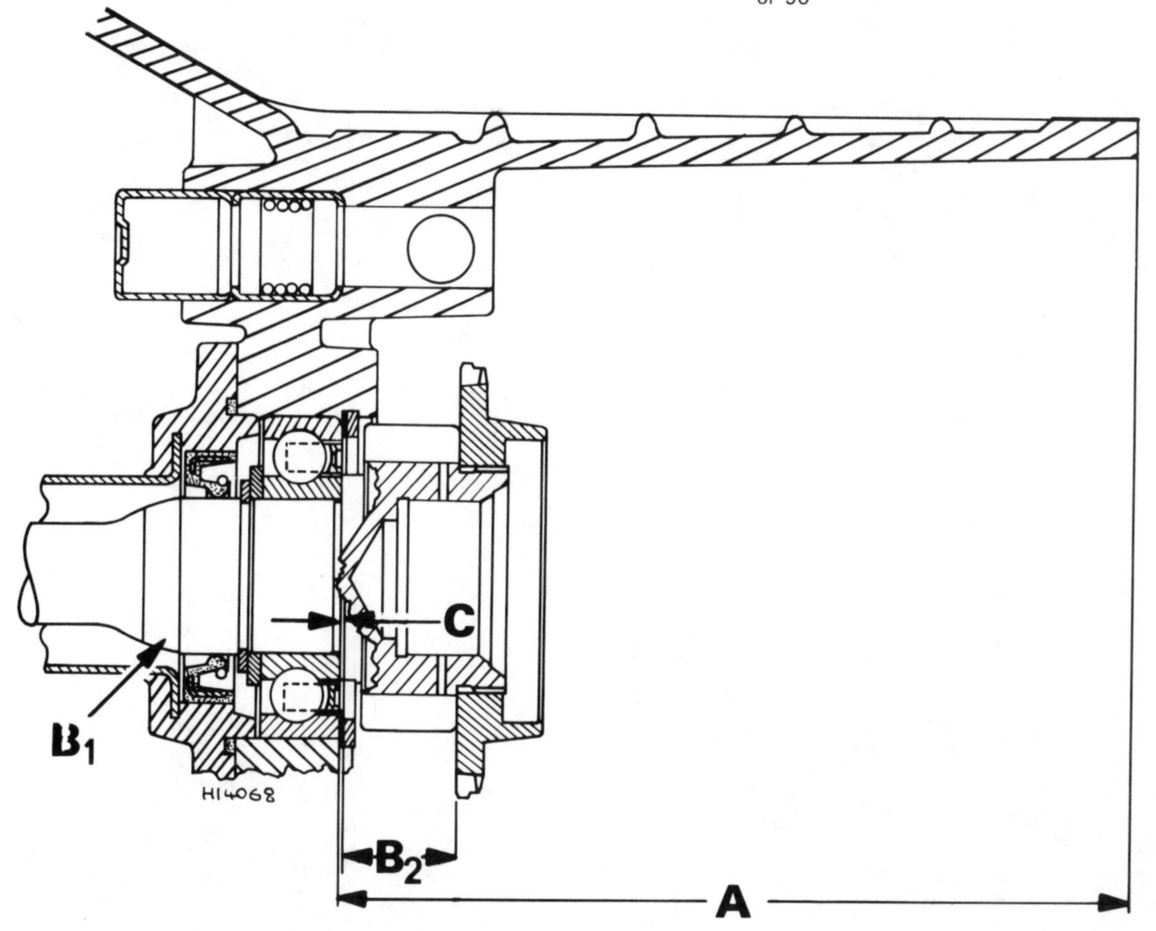

Fig. 6.25 Measuring diagram for the input shaft shim – Getrag 242 (Sec 6)

A Casing face to bearing track
B1 Engraved marks on shaft
B2 Dimension indicated by B1
C Shim

44 Now measure the thickness (D) of the input shaft bearing circlip – Fig. 6.26. Measure (E), the circlip to bearing. Subtract (D) from (E) and select a spacer washer (F) of thickness equal to the difference.

Reassembly of gearbox

45 Mesh reverse idler gear with the layshaft and fit both units into the rear casing section.
46 Connect the input (clutch) shaft to the mainshaft, making sure that the needle roller bearing is in the recess in the end of the input shaft and the baulk ring correctly located.
47 Fit the shafts to the rear casing section.
48 Locate the bearing on the rear end of the mainshaft and then tap it down the shaft and into the casing.
49 Fit the speedometer drive.
50 Using a depth gauge, measure the recess (A) – Fig. 6.30 – of the rear bearing from the casing surface.

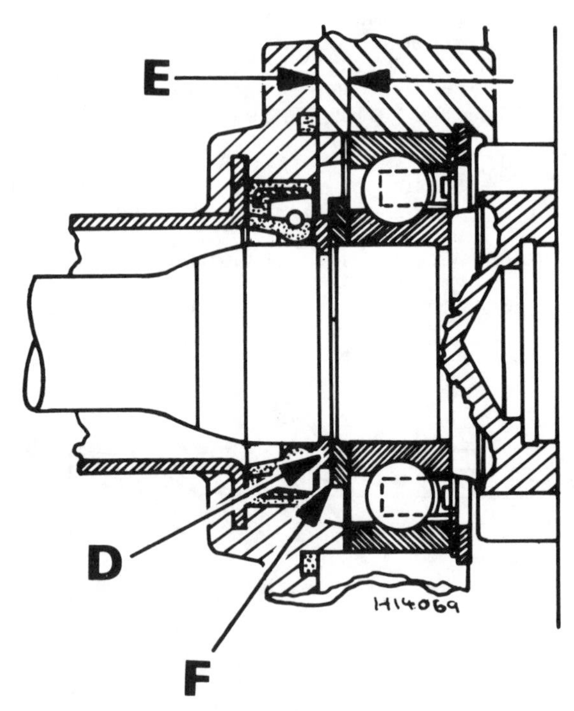

Fig. 6.26 Measuring diagram for the input shaft spacer washer – Getrag 242 (Sec 6)

D Thickness of input shaft circlip
E Circlip-to-bearing clearance
F Spacer washer

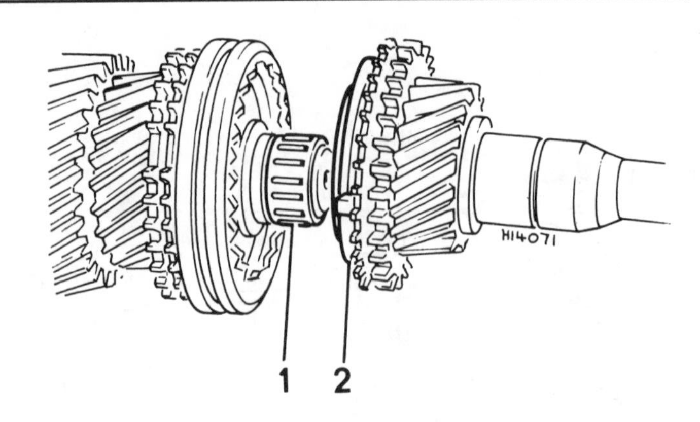

Fig. 6.28 Input shaft needle roller bearing (1) and baulk ring (2) – Getrag 242 (Sec 6)

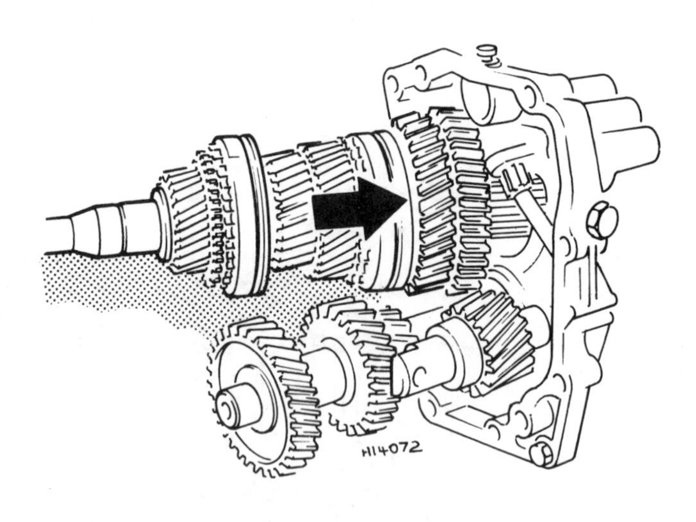

Fig. 6.29 Fitting the mainshaft/input shaft assembly to the rear casing – Getrag 242 (Sec 6)

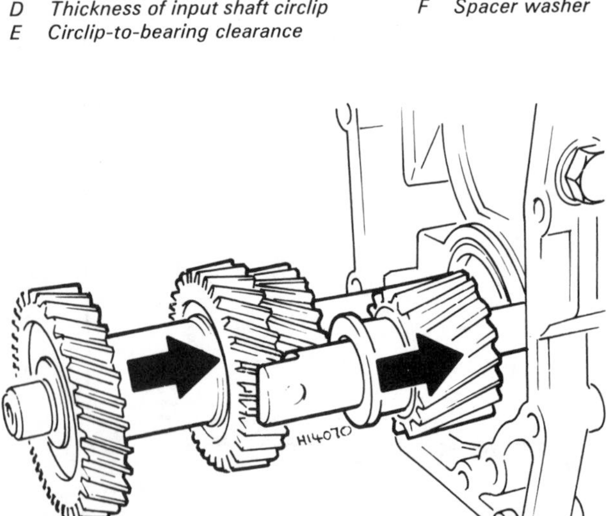

Fig. 6.27 Mesh the reverse idler gear and layshaft together and insert them into the rear casing – Getrag 242 (Sec 6)

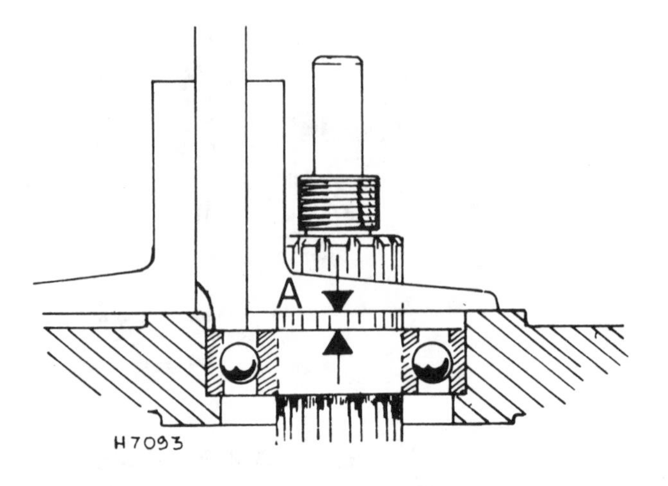

Fig. 6.30 Measuring dimension (A): casing surface to bearing (Sec 6)

51 Now measure the height (B) – Fig. 6.31 – of the end cover shoulder with a new gasket in position.
52 Subtract one measurement from the other and add a shim of thickness equal to the difference. This will eliminate all endfloat.
53 Fit a new oil seal to the end cover and bolt it to the casing.
54 Fit the output flange, and screw on the nut. Hold the flange against rotation and tighten the nut to the specified torque. Fit a new nut locking cup and stake it into the cut-out provided.
55 Insert the locking ball into the hole in the rear casing and then fit the reverse selector shaft. If there is any difficulty in inserting the shaft, hold the ball depressed with a dummy shaft which will then be displaced by the real shaft as it is pushed into position.
56 Drive out the roll pin and separate the 1st/2nd selector fork from its shaft.
57 Locate 1st/2nd selector fork in the synchro groove.
58 Insert the locking and detent balls into the hole in the rear casing and push the 1st/2nd selector shaft into position. Hold the balls depressed with a dummy shaft, if necessary. Reconnect the fork to the shaft by driving in the roll pin.
59 Locate 3rd/4th selector fork in its synchro sleeve groove. Move the sleeve to 4th gear position.
60 Push the gear selector rod into the rear casing and turn it so that the selector finger points downwards – Fig. 6.13.
61 Screw in the locking screw (1) – Fig. 6.14.
62 Fit the selector plunger, spring and plug – Fig. 6.34 – having applied thread locking fluid to the plug threads.

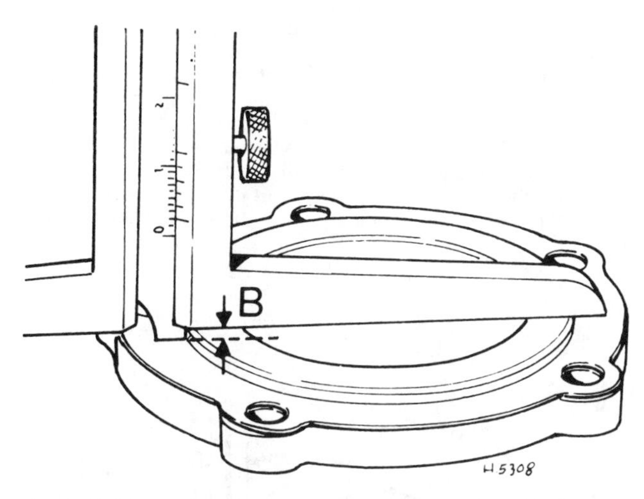

Fig. 6.31 Measuring the rear cover shoulder height (B) (Sec 6)

A new gasket is in position

Fig. 6.32 Fitting the reverse selector shaft (arrowed) – Getrag 242 (Sec 6)

63 Insert the interlock and detent balls into the rear casing and push 3rd/4th selector shaft into position, again using the dummy shaft if required. The shaft will have passed through the hole in the selector fork. Pin the fork to the shaft with a roll pin.

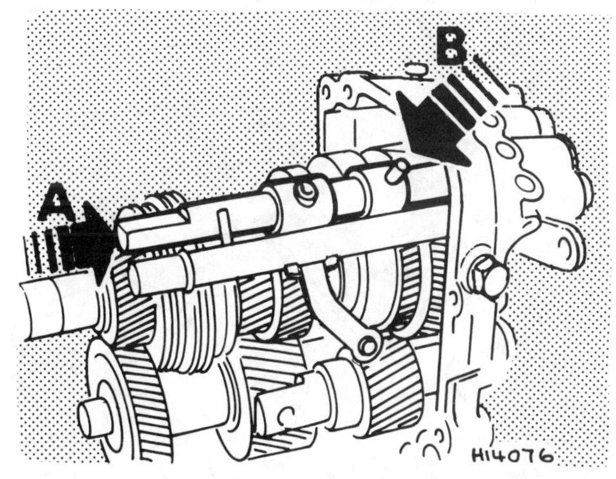

Fig. 6.33 Fitting 1st/2nd selector shaft – Getrag 242 (Sec 6)

A Push the shaft into position
B Fit the roll pin to secure the selector fork to the shaft

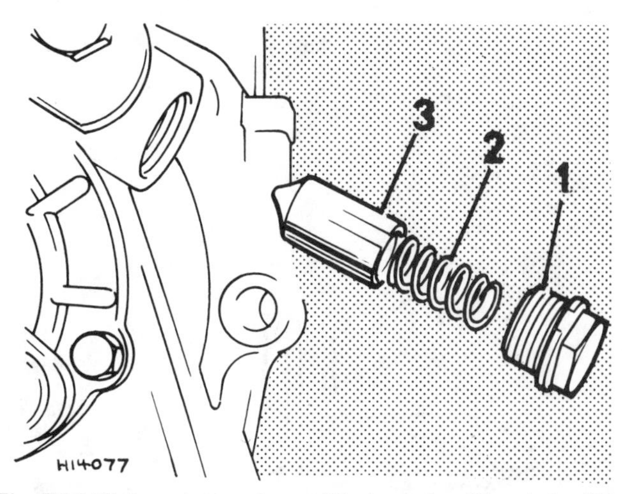

Fig. 6.34 Fit the selector plunger (3), the spring (2) and plug (1) – Getrag 242 (Sec 6)

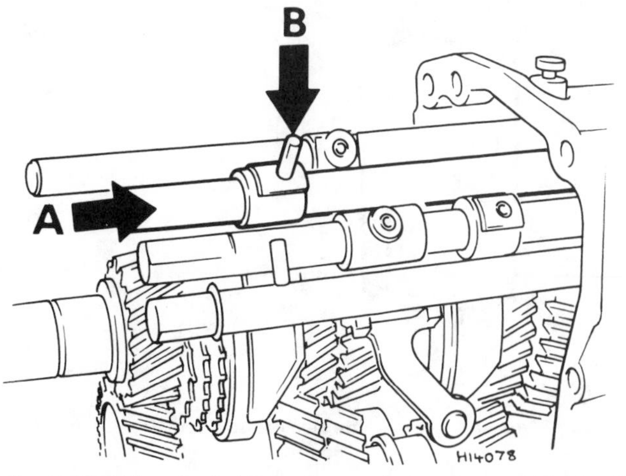

Fig. 6.35 Fitting the 3rd/4th selector shaft – Getrag 242 (Sec 6)

A Push the shaft into position
B Fit the roll pin to secure the selector fork to the shaft

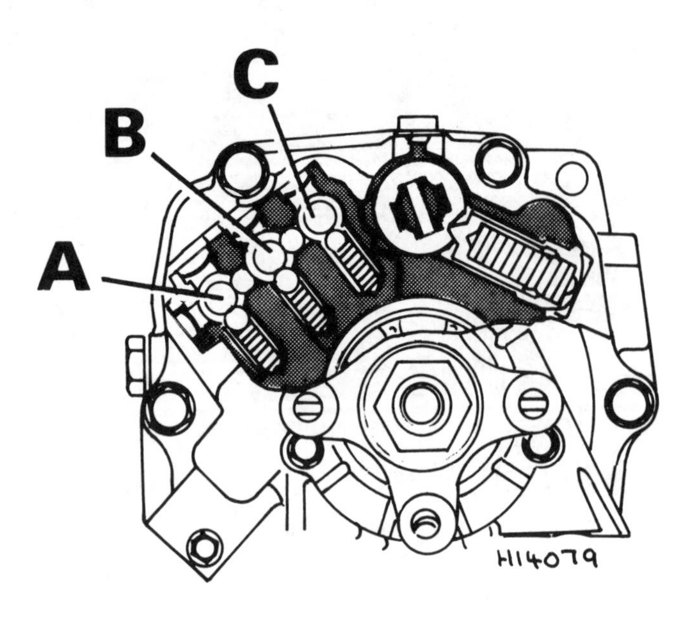

Fig. 6.36 Fitted positions of the detents – Getrag 242 (Sec 6)

A Reverse selector
B 1st/2nd selector
C 3rd/4th selector

64 Fit reverse gear selector lever, screw in the reverse lamp switch and tap in new detent plugs.
65 Push the main casing over the geartrains, making sure that the original or selected shims are in position on the shafts. Drive in the positioning dowels and screw in the casing bolts.
66 Fit the selector rod plunger spring, and cap – Fig. 6.11.
67 Tap the front bearing into position, fit the spacer washer and circlip.
68 Before bolting on the guide sleeve, measure the height (B) of its shoulder – Fig. 6.37 – and bearing depth (A) – Fig. 6.38. Subtract B from A and the difference will be equal to the thickness of the shim required. Make sure the guide sleeve is fitted with a new oil seal and flange gasket.
69 Fit the clutch release components, as described in Chapter 5, and screw in the drain plug. Fill the transmission with oil after it is fitted in the car.

7 Gearbox (Getrag 240, 5-speed) – overhaul

1 Drain the oil from the gearbox.
2 Unscrew and remove the reverse lamp switch and the selector arm lockpin assembly.
3 Using a pair of pincers, remove the selector rod lock plunger cap (1), spring (2) and plunger (3) – Fig. 6.40.
4 From inside the bellhousing, remove the clutch release components and unbolt and remove the guide sleeve.
5 Extract the circlip and shim from the front bearing.
6 Remove the bolt (1) from the side of the casing – Fig. 6.41.
7 Tap down the dowel pins between the main and the rear casing sections, then unscrew the connecting bolts and pull off the main casing. If the layshaft bearing is displaced, note that the smaller diameter of it is towards the end of the shaft.
8 Release the lockplate, hold the output flange against rotation and unscrew the output flange nut. Draw off the flange using a puller, if necessary.

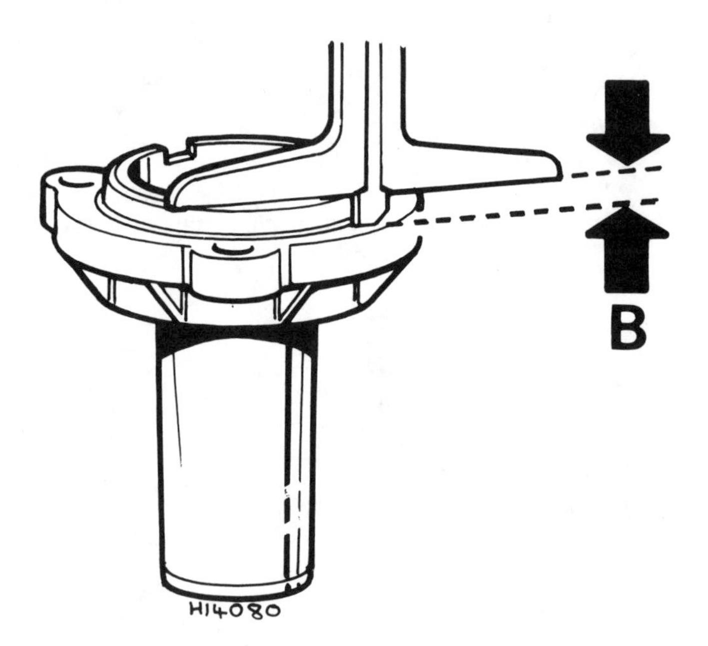

Fig. 6.37 Measuring the guide sleeve shoulder (B) – Getrag 242 (Sec 6)

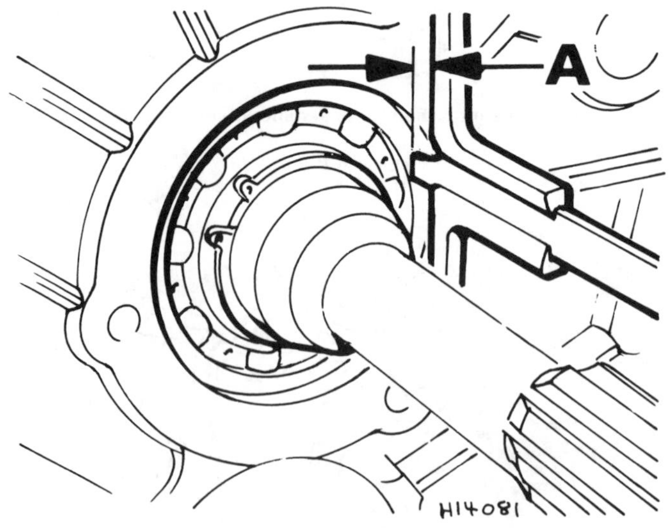

Fig. 6.38 Measuring the depth of the bearing (A) – Getrag 242 (Sec 6)

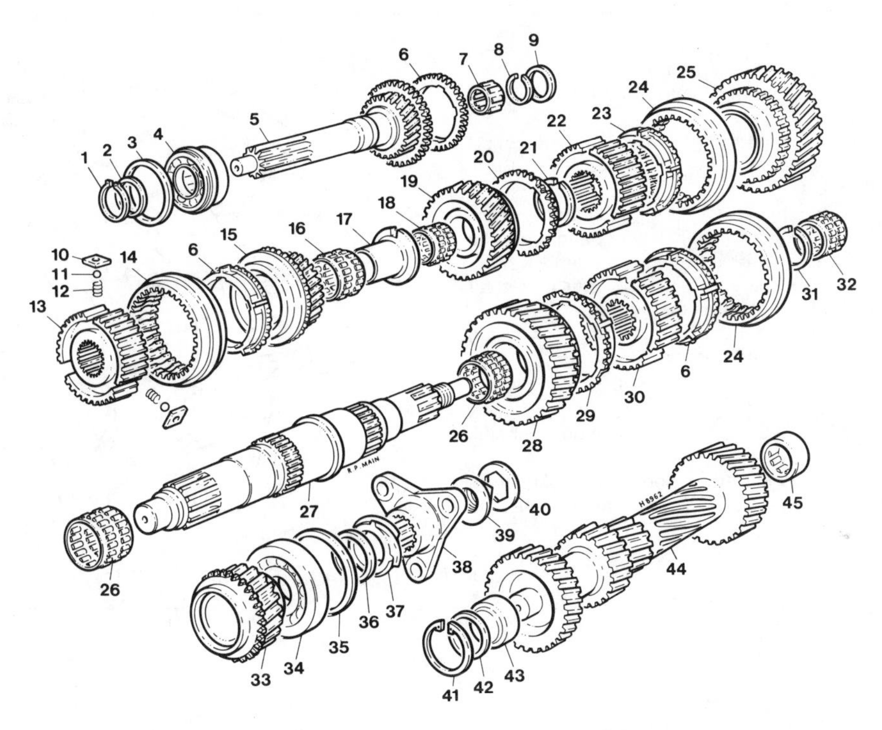

Fig. 6.39 Internal components of the Getrag 240 5-speed gearbox (Sec 7)

1 Circlip
2 Spacer
3 Spacer
4 Bearing
5 Input shaft with 4th gear
6 Baulk ring
7 Needle roller bearing
8 Circlip
9 Spacer
10 Sliding key
11 Ball
12 Spring
13 3rd/4th synchro-hub
14 3rd/4th synchro sleeve
15 3rd gear
16 Needle roller bearing
17 Bearing sleeve
18 Needle roller bearing
19 2nd gear
20 Baulk ring
21 Circlip
22 1st/2nd synchro-hub
23 Baulk ring
24 1st/2nd synchro sleeve
25 1st gear
26 Needle roller bearing
27 Mainshaft
28 Reverse gear
29 Baulk ring
30 Reverse/5th synchro-hub
31 Circlip
32 Needle roller bearing
33 5th gear
34 Bearing
35 Spacer
36 Spacer
37 Speedometer drivegear
38 Output flange
39 Nut
40 Nut locking cup
41 Circlip
42 Spacer
43 Bearing
44 Layshaft
45 Bearing

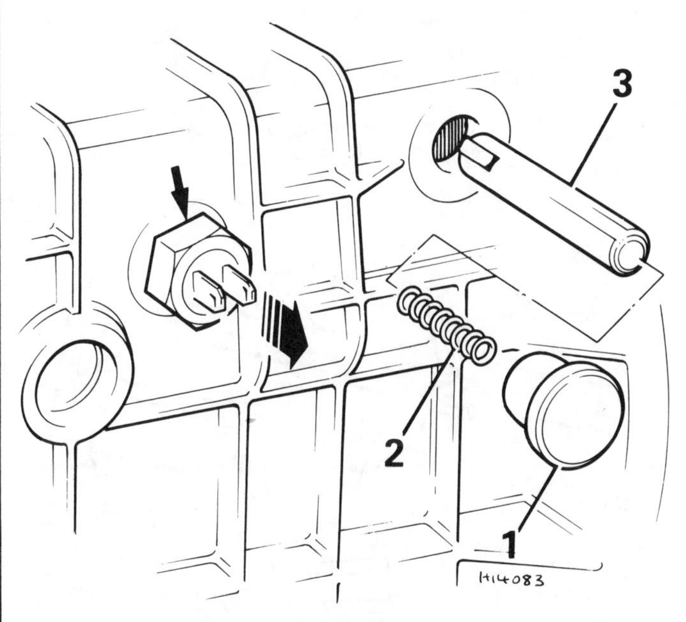

Fig. 6.40 Selector rod plunger (3), spring (2) and cap (1) – Getrag 240 (Sec 7)

Reverse switch arrowed

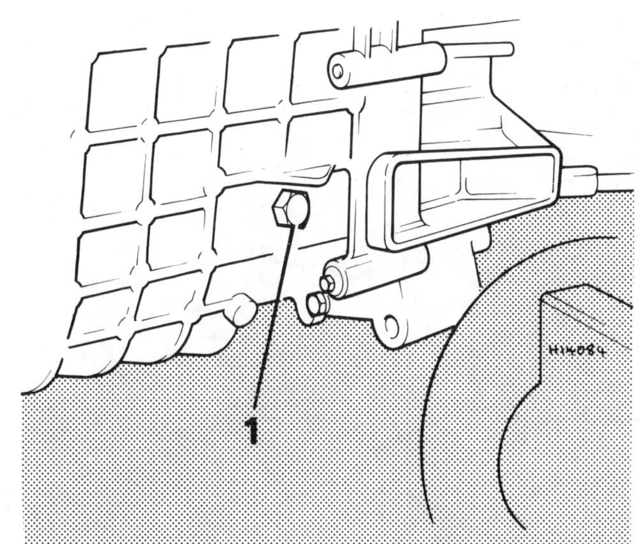

Fig. 6.41 Lockbolt (1) – Getrag 240 (Sec 7)

9 Unscrew the bolts (1 and 3) and remove the holder (2) – Fig. 6.42.
10 Remove reverse idler shaft with the gear and needle bearing.
11 Drive out the roll pin (1), pull out the selector rail (3) and take off the operating lever (2) – Fig. 6.43.
12 Move the synchro sleeve to engage 4th gear. Drive the roll pin (1) out far enough to be able to withdraw the selector rod – Fig. 6.44. Watch for the selector rod rollers.
13 Remove the detent endplate and extract the three detent springs.
14 Drive out the roll pin from the 3rd/4th selector fork and draw the shaft out towards the front of the gearbox, noting the interlock pin.
15 Select 2nd gear and reverse gears together by pushing their respective selector rods towards the front of the gearbox.
16 Press or tap the gear shafts simultaneously out of the rear casing section. Retrieve all the detent balls and springs.

Mainshaft – dismantling

17 Pull the input (clutch) shaft from the mainshaft, take off the baulk ring and extract the needle roller bearing.
18 A puller or press may be needed to remove some assemblies from the shaft. Remove 5th gear (1), the baulk ring (2), and the needle

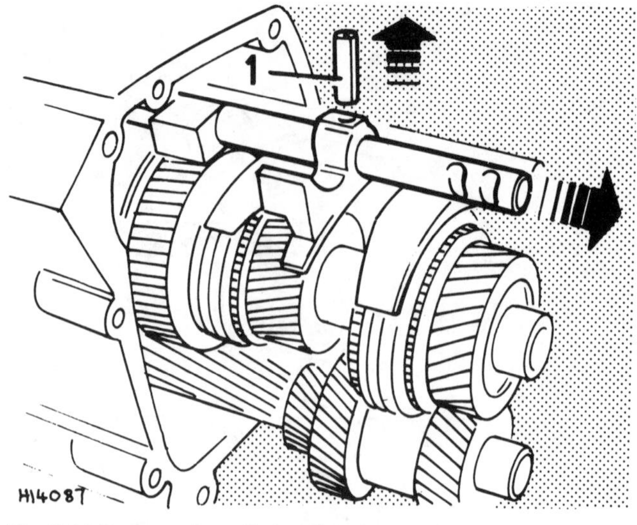

Fig. 6.44 Remove the roll pin (1) and withdraw the selector rod – Getrag 240 (Sec 7)

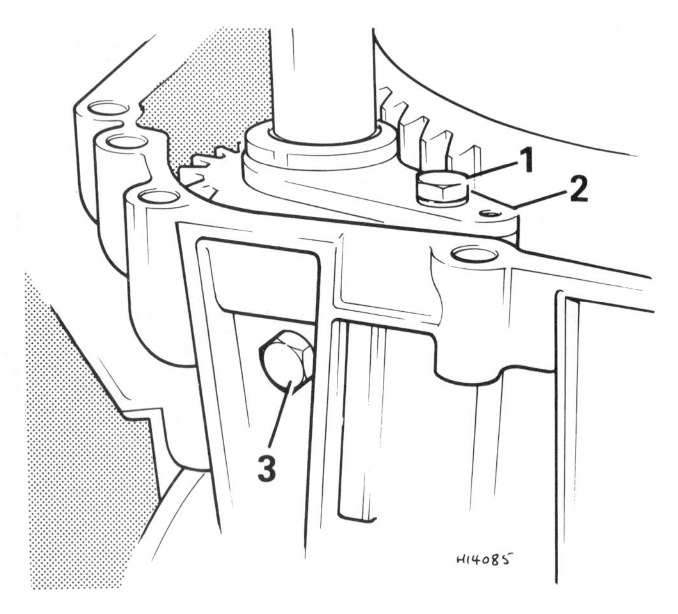

Fig. 6.42 Holder (2) and holder bolts (1 and 3) – Getrag 240 (Sec 7)

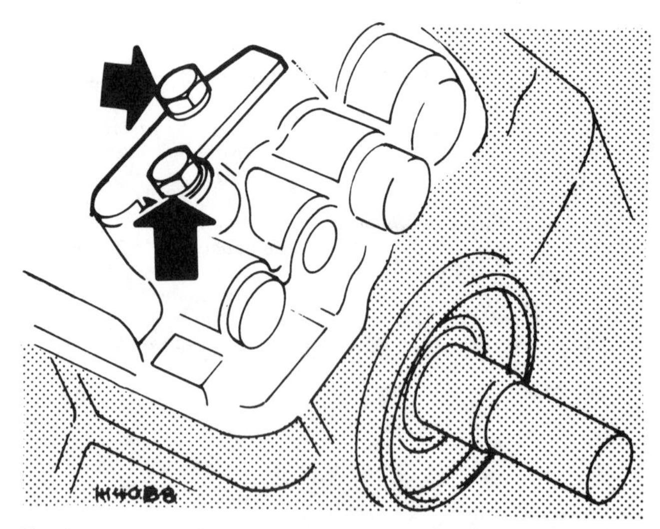
Fig. 6.45 Detent end plate securing bolts (arrowed) – Getrag 240 (Sec 7)

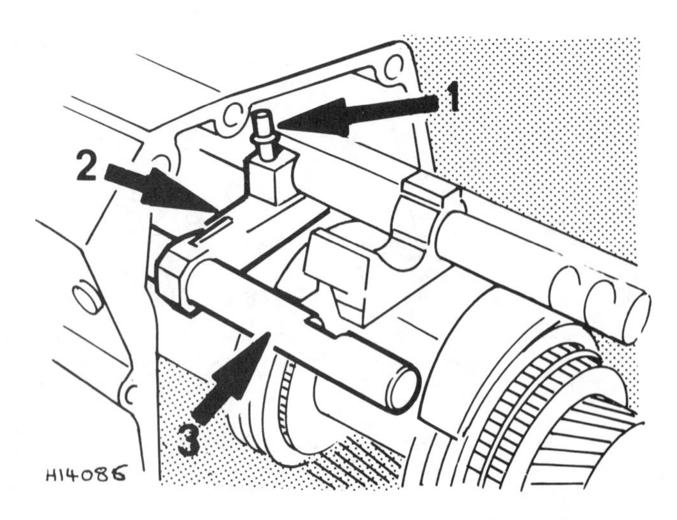

Fig. 6.43 Selector operating lever roll pin (1), operating lever (2) and selector rail (3) – Getrag 240 (Sec 7)

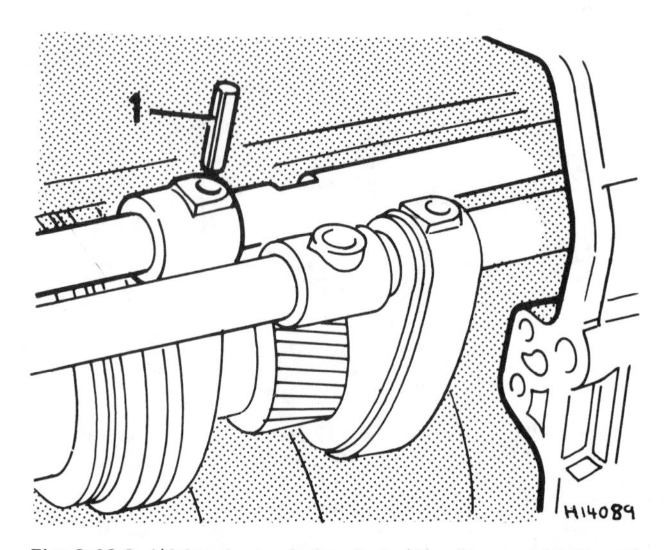

Fig. 6.46 3rd/4th selector fork roll pin (1) – Getrag 240 (Sec 7)

bearing (3) (Fig. 6.47) from the rear end of the mainshaft.

19 Extract the circlip and remove the spacer from the front end of the shaft.

20 Remove 3rd gear and the needle bearing with the 3rd/4th synchro unit.

21 Remove the bearing sleeve and 2nd gear. Take off the baulk ring and needle bearing.

22 Extract the circlip and remove 1st gear, the needle bearing and the 1st/2nd synchro unit.

23 Extract the circlip and remove reverse gear with the synchro unit and needle bearing.

Inspection

24 Renew any gears which have chipped teeth.

25 Check the gap between the baulk rings and the gear cones. If less than 0.8 mm (0.032 in) renew the baulk ring. Chipped or worn teeth in the synchro components will mean the purchase of new parts.

26 Pushing the hub out of the synchro sleeve will eject the springs, balls and sliding keys.

27 When reassembling, note the following points. Align the flat teeth on the sleeve with the sliding keys. On 3rd/4th units, the groove in the sleeve must be adjacent to the smaller projection on the hub. Make sure that the stepped side of the sliding key is towards the synchro sleeve.

28 Check the selector forks for wear and renew if worn.

Bearings – renewal

29 Wear in the shaft bearings should be rectified by renewing the bearings in the following way.

30 To remove the bearing from the main casing, extract the circlip and shim and press or draw the bearing from its seat.

31 To remove the mainshaft bearing from the rear casing section, unscrew the bolt (1) – Fig. 6.50 – and remove the spring (2).

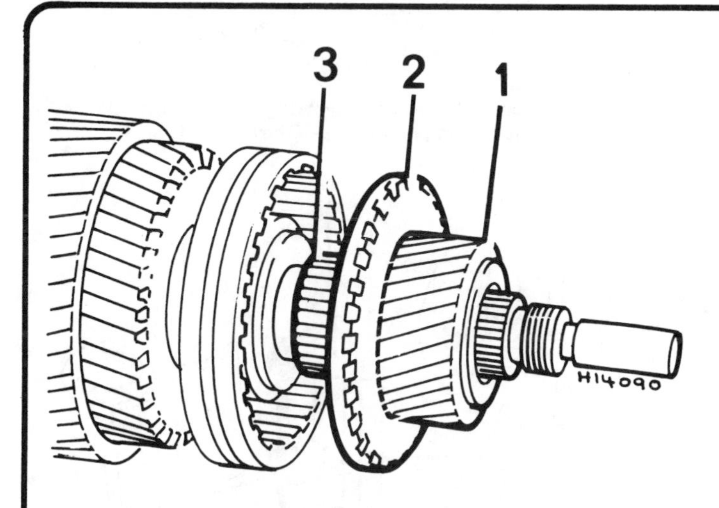

Fig. 6.47 Remove 5th gear (1), the baulk ring (2), and needle bearing (3) from the mainshaft – Getrag 240 (Sec 7)

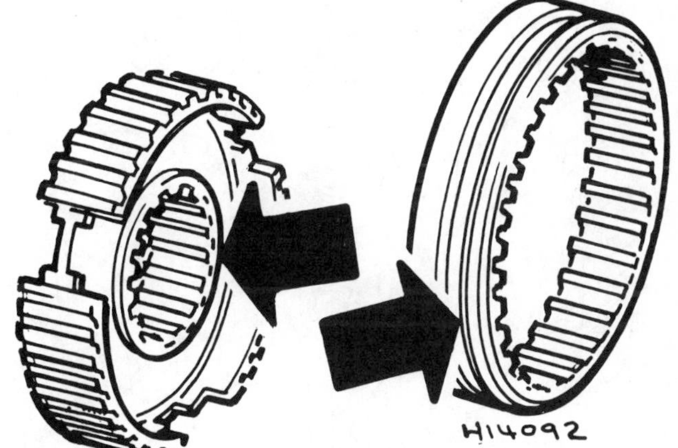

Fig. 6.49 3rd/4th synchro-hub and sleeve alignment – Getrag 240 (Sec 7)

The groove on the sleeve must be adjacent to the smaller hub projection

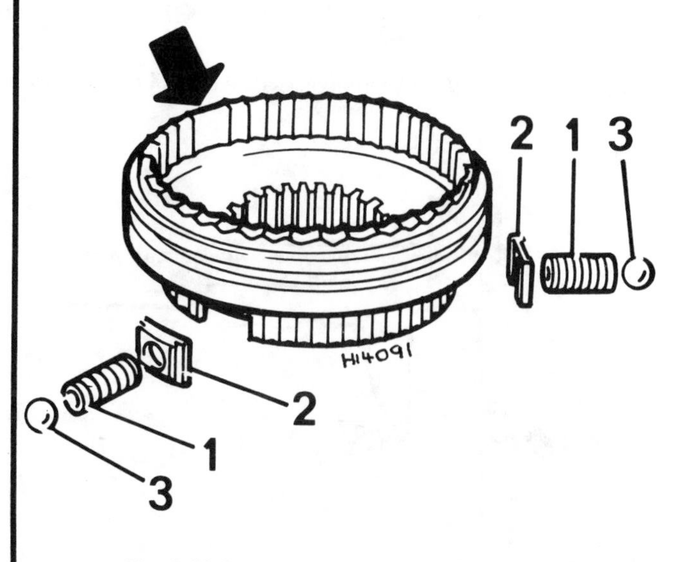

Fig. 6.48 Synchro components – Getrag 240 (Sec 7)

1 Spring
2 Sliding key
3 Ball

The flat teeth of the sleeve (arrowed) must align with the sliding keys

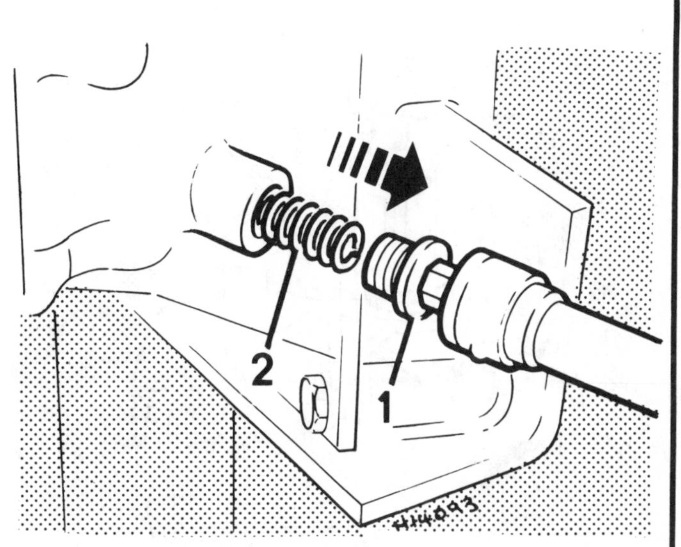

Fig. 6.50 Bolt (1) and spring (2) in the rear casing – Getrag 240 (Sec 7)

32 Remove the socket-headed bolt and the selector arm – Fig. 6.52.
33 Unbolt and remove the bolt, locking lever (1), spacer (2) and bearing holder (3) – Fig. 6.53.
34 Extract the oil seal, bearing and shim.
35 To select the shim for use with the new bearing, measure dimension (A) – Fig. 6.54 – then the width of the new bearing (B) – Fig. 6.55. Subtract B from A, the difference is the thickness of the required shim.
36 When fitting the bearing, heat the casing in boiling water, place the selected shim in the bearing seat and press in the bearing so that its sealed face enters first.
37 Refit the bearing holder and selector arm.

Layshaft

38 The gears cannot be removed from the layshaft, but to renew the layshaft bearing in the rear casing section, drive out the outer track from the casing and draw the inner race from the end of the layshaft. Fit the new bearing by reversing the removal operations, align the slot in the track with the casing lock bead.

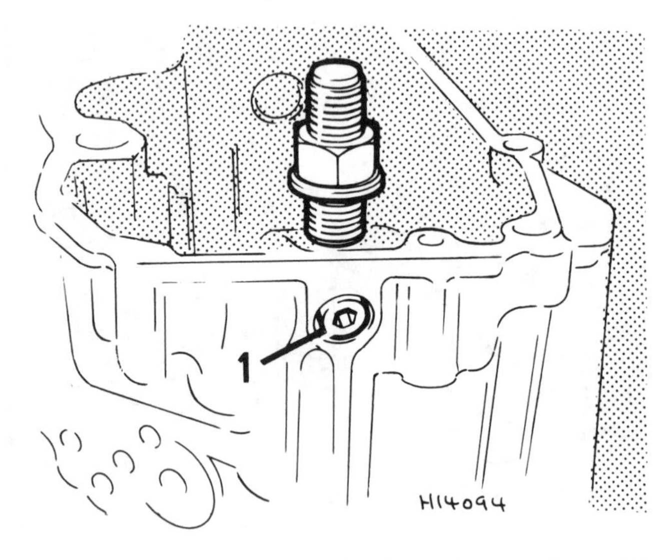

Fig. 6.51 Socket-headed bolt (1) in the rear casing – Getrag 240 (Sec 7)

Fig. 6.52 Selector arm – Getrag 240 (Sec 7)

Note the roller – arrowed

Fig. 6.53 Unbolt and remove the locking lever (1), the spacer (2) and the bearing holder (3) – Getrag 240 (Sec 7)

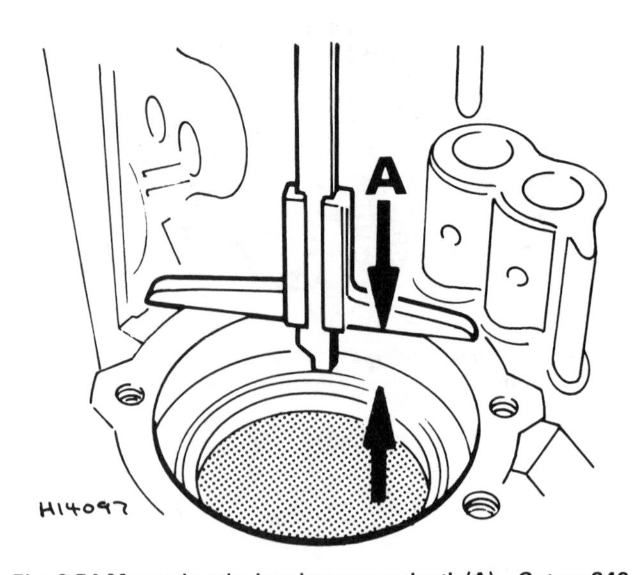

Fig. 6.54 Measuring the bearing recess depth (A) – Getrag 240 (Sec 7)

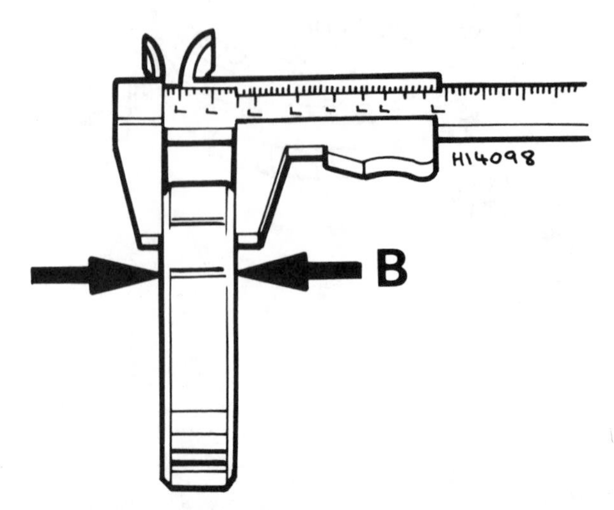

Fig. 6.55 Measuring the width of the new bearing (B) – Getrag 240 (Sec 7)

39 To renew the layshaft bearing in the main casing, remove the outer track and press in the new one, using the original spacer – making sure that the oil groove in the track aligns with the one in the casing. Remove the bearing race from the end of the layshaft.
40 The layshaft endfloat must now be checked. To do this, locate the layshaft in the rear casing bearing track.
41 Lower the main casing into position and locate it with two dowel pins and two bolts. Unscrew the oil filler/level plug.
42 Apply the stylus of a dial gauge to the end of the layshaft and then move the shaft up and down by inserting a screwdriver through the oil filler hole. If the endfloat is not between 0.13 and 0.23 mm (0.005 and 0.009 in), remove the bearing outer track from the main casing and change the shim for one of different thickness.

Reassembly

43 To the mainshaft rear end fit reverse gear, the baulk ring and 5th/reverse synchro unit.
44 On gearboxes which do not have reverse gear synchro facility, the circlip in the sleeve must face towards reverse gear. The synchro sleeve should be pushed towards reverse gear and the thickest circlip available fitted to eliminate all endfloat.
45 Fit the needle bearing, 1st gear and the baulk ring to the front end of the shaft.
46 Fit the 1st/2nd synchro. Push the sleeve towards 1st gear and fit the thickest circlip available which will eliminate all endfloat.
47 Fit the needle bearing, the baulk ring and 2nd gear.
48 Heat the bearing sleeve in boiling water and fit it to the shaft.
49 Fit the needle bearing, 3rd gear and the baulk ring.
50 Fit 3rd/4th synchro unit so that the narrow groove is towards 4th gear.
51 Fit the spacer and the circlip to the front end of the mainshaft.
52 To the rear end of the mainshaft fit 5th gear, the needle bearing and the baulk ring.
53 Insert the needle roller bearing into the recess in the input (clutch) shaft and connect it to the front end of the mainshaft.

Gearbox – reassembly

54 Locate the 1st/2nd and 5th/reverse selector shafts with all the selector forks in their mainshaft synchro sleeve grooves.
55 Make sure that all detent balls, springs and interlock pins have been removed from the rear casing.
56 Select 2nd and reverse gears simultaneously and insert the geartrains with the selector shafts all meshed together into the rear casing section.
57 Move the selector shafts to set the gears in neutral.
58 Slide 3rd/4th selector shaft through the selector fork and then stick the interlock pin in the shaft with thick grease. Note the position of the detent groove – Fig. 6.57.
59 Insert the two detent balls, holding them with a blob of thick grease and push the selector shaft into position.
60 Pin the fork to 3rd/4th selector shaft.
61 Fit the three remaining detent balls and springs, the selector arm lockpin and locking lever plunger assemblies.

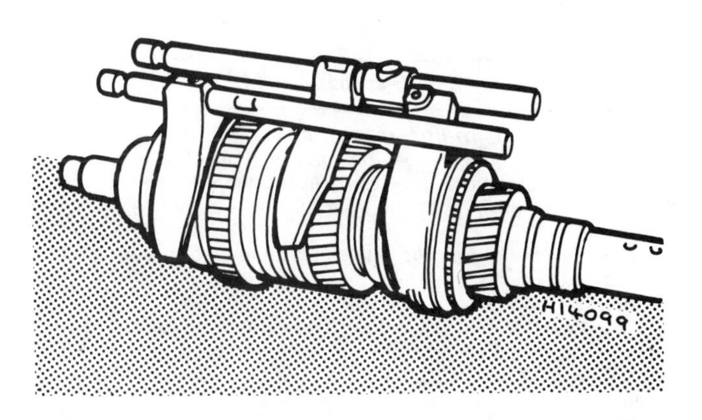

Fig. 6.56 1st/2nd and 5th/reverse selector shafts and forks located in their mainshaft synchro sleeve grooves – Getrag 240 (Sec 7)

Fig. 6.57 3rd/4th selector shaft interlock pin (1) – Getrag 240 (Sec 7)

Arrow indicates detent groove

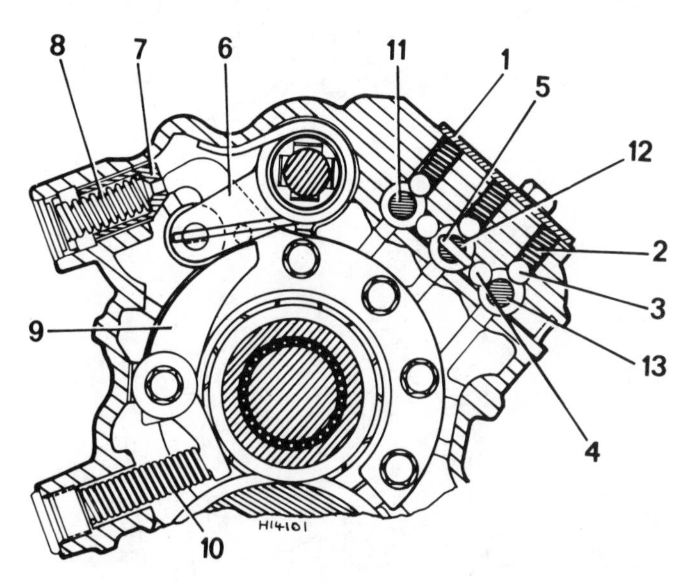

Fig. 6.58 Detent and lockpin arrangement – Getrag 240 (Sec 7)

1 Cover plate
2 Detent spring
3 Detent ball
4 Interlock ball
5 Interlock pin
6 Selector arm
7 Selector arm, lockpin and plug
8 Spring
9 Locking lever
10 Locking lever spring, plunger and cap
11 Reverse/5th selector shaft
12 3rd/4th selector shaft
13 1st/2nd selector shaft

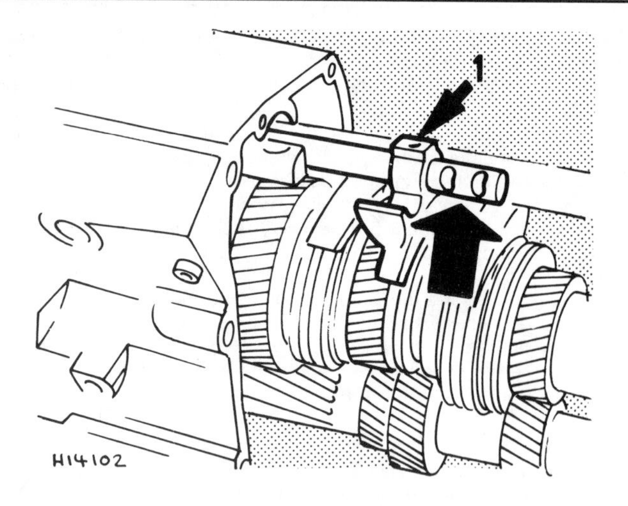

Fig. 6.59 Fit the selector arm to the selector shaft with a roll pin (1) – Getrag 240 (Sec 7)

The grooves in the shaft (arrowed) must face outwards

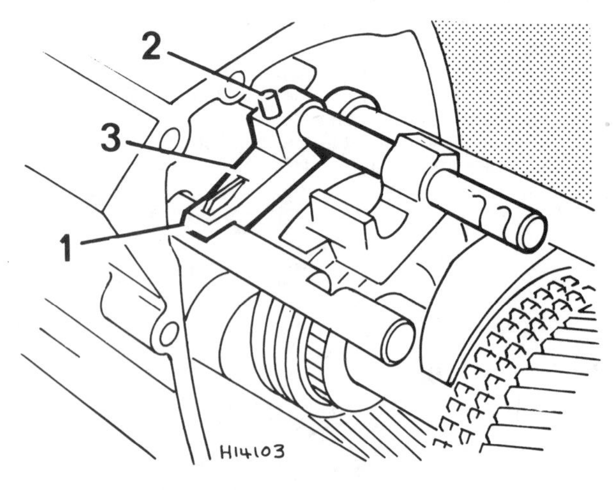

Fig. 6.60 Fitting the selector rail – Getrag 240 (Sec 7)

1 Groove
2 Roll pin
3 Operating lever

Fig. 6.61 Fit the holder (1) – Getrag 240 (Sec 7)

62 Fit the detent plate using thread locking fluid on the bolt threads.
63 Drive the pin from the selector arm and locate the four rollers in position with grease. Slide in the selector shaft while at the same time fitting the selector arm. Fit a new roll pin.
64 Fit a new selector shaft oil seal.
65 Fit the selector rod so that its groove is as arrowed – Fig. 6.60.
66 Apply thread locking fluid to the reverse idler shaft rear end and fit the shaft with the needle bearing and reverse gear. Apply thread locking fluid to the lock bolt and screw it into position.
67 Fit the holder (1) – Fig. 6.61.
68 Fit the output flange. Apply thread locking fluid and tighten the nut to the specified torque. Fit and stake a new lockplate.
69 Check if there is any clearance between the front bearing and circlip. If there is, change the shim to eliminate it.
70 Check the guide sleeve protrusion, as described in Section 7, paragraph 68, and select a suitable circlip. Bolt on the guide sleeve with new oil seal and gasket.
71 Fit the clutch release components (Chapter 5).
72 Fit the selector arm and the selector rod lock plunger assemblies.

8 Gearbox (Getrag 245, 5-speed) – overhaul

Dismantling into major assemblies

1 Drain the oil from the gearbox and then unbolt and remove the guide sleeve from inside the clutch bellhousing.
2 Extract the circlip from the front bearing and remove the spacer shim.
3 Tap down the dowel pins between the intermediate casing section and the main casing.
4 Unscrew and remove the casing connecting bolts.
5 Withdraw the main casing from the intermediate casing. Take care to catch the shaft bearings which may be displaced.
6 Prise out the locking cup and then unscrew the output flange nut. To do this use a deep socket which may have to be ground to reduce the thickness of its walls as there is very little clearance. Alternatively, use a box spanner. Hold the flange from turning by making up a suitable tool (photo). Pull off the flange using a suitable puller, if necessary.
7 Remove the lockbolt which holds the speedometer driven gear and pull out the gear.
8 Unscrew the selector arm lock plunger plug and extract the spring and plungers.
9 Unbolt and remove the rear cover and shim.
10 Remove the cap (use pincers for this) and take out the selector rod

8.6 Tool for holding output flange

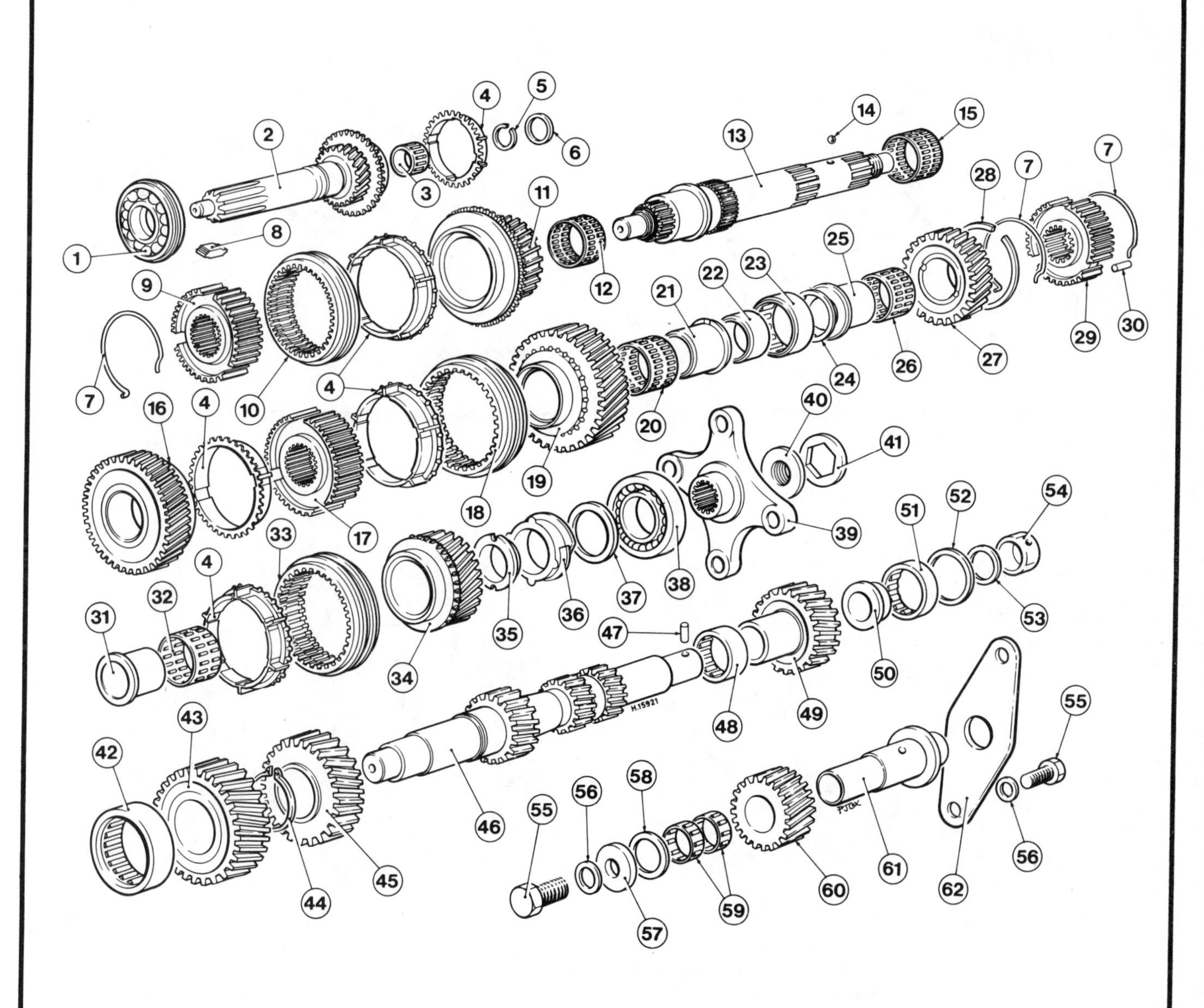

Fig. 6.62 Internal components of the Getrag 245 5-speed overdrive gearbox (Sec 8)

1 Ball-bearing
2 Input shaft
3 Needle bearing
4 Baulk ring
5 Circlip
6 Washer
7 Sychro spring
8 Sliding key
9 3rd/4th synchro-hub
10 3rd/4th synchro sleeve
11 3rd gear
12 Needle bearing
13 Mainshaft
14 Lockball (early models)
15 Needle bearing
16 2nd gear
17 1st/2nd synchro-hub
18 1st/2nd synchro sleeve
19 1st gear
20 Needle bearing
21 Bearing bush
22 Bearing inner track
23 Roller bearing
24 Shim (X)
25 Bearing bush
26 Needle bearing
27 Reverse gear
28 Circlip
29 Reverse/5th synchro-hub
30 Sliding key
31 Bearing bush
32 Needle bearing
33 Reverse/5th synchro sleeve
34 5th gear
35 Washer
36 Speedometer drivegear
37 Washer
38 Ball-bearing
39 Output flange
40 Nut
41 Nut locking cup
42 Roller bearing
43 4th gear
44 Circlip
45 3rd gear
46 Layshaft
47 Pin
48 Roller bearing
49 5th gear
50 Bearing inner track
51 Roller bearing
52 Washer
53 Washer
54 Collar
55 Reverse idler shaft bolt
56 Lockwasher
57 Washer
58 Thrust washer
59 Needle bearing
60 Reverse idler gear
61 Reverse idler shaft
62 Reverse idler shaft holder

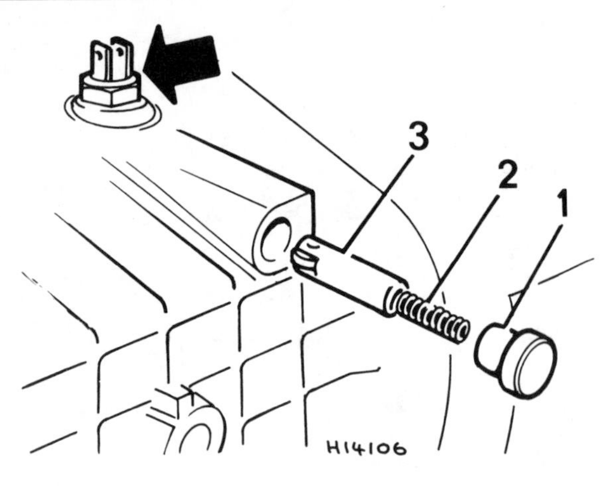

Fig. 6.63 Selector rod plunger (3), spring (2) and cap (1) – Getrag 245 (Sec 8)

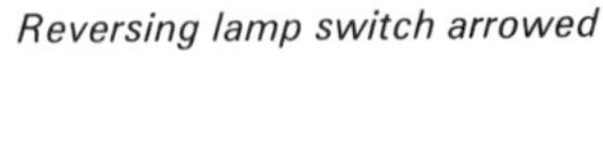
Reversing lamp switch arrowed

Fig. 6.65 Selector rail (1) and operating lever (2) – Getrag 245 (Sec 8)

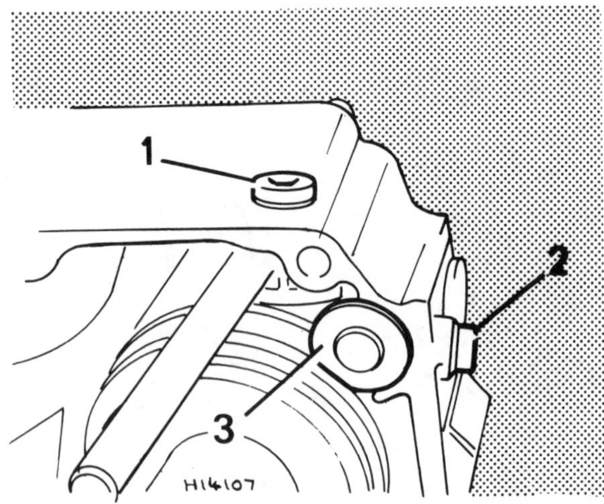

Fig. 6.64 Unscrew the two socket-headed screws (1 and 2) and remove the clamp (3) – Getrag 245 (Sec 8)

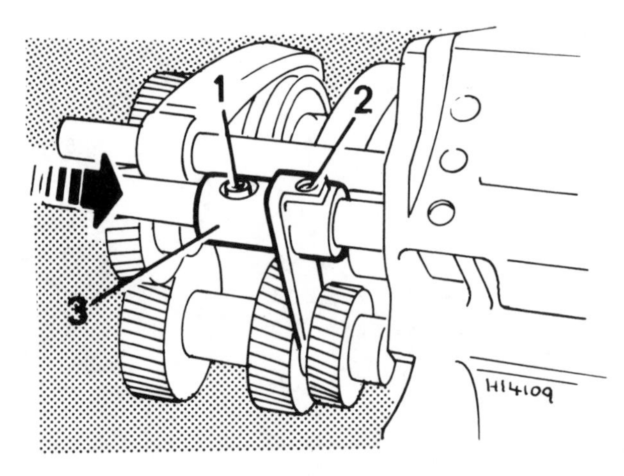

Fig. 6.66 1st/2nd selector shaft roll pins (1 and 2) – Getrag 245 (Sec 8)

3 Dog

spring and plunger – Fig. 6.63.

11 Tap down the rear casing section dowel pins, unscrew the casing connecting bolts, noting the location of the shorter one.

12 Select 2nd gear. Do this by moving 1st/2nd synchro sleeve towards the front of the gearbox. Prise out the detent plugs.

13 Draw off the rear casing section by making up a suitable puller. Be prepared for the spring-loaded selector arm and rollers to be ejected from the selector rod.

14 Unscrew the two socket-headed screws (1 and 2) and remove the clamp (3) – Fig. 6.64.

15 Withdraw the selector rail (1) towards the rear of the gearbox and remove the operating lever (2) held by a socket-headed screw – Fig. 6.65 (photo).

16 Drive out the roll pin from the dog. Pull the selector rod towards the rear of the gearbox, take off the selector arm.

17 From the end of the mainshaft, take off the speedometer drivegear and notched spacer.

18 Drive out the pin from the end of the layshaft, take off the collar, washer, shim and spacer.

19 Draw off the layshaft 5th gear with bearing race.

20 Remove 5th gear baulk ring and split bearing from the mainshaft.

21 Push 5th/reverse selector shaft towards the rear of the gearbox and then drive the roll pin from the selector fork. During this operation, the synchro sleeve will probably separate from its hub and release the sliding keys.

8.15 Operating lever socket screw

22 Slide the fork, with the synchro from 5th/reverse selector shaft, but avoid removing the shaft unless absolutely essential. If it must be done, watch for ejection of the spring-loaded balls and note that the shaft detent grooves are towards the bottom of the gearbox.
23 Knock out 1st/2nd selector fork roll pin, also the dog roll pin.
24 Engage 3rd gear by moving the synchro sleeve. Knock out the roll pin which holds the fork to the 3rd/4th selector shaft. Align the roll pin so that it passes out into the gap in the synchro teeth.
25 Withdraw 1st/2nd and 3rd/4th selector shafts until 1st/2nd and 3rd/4th selector forks can be taken off. Detent balls and springs will be ejected from the shafts. Should the detent balls jam during shaft removal, reposition them by using a length of thin wire passed into the shaft detent groove.
26 Unscrew the two socket-headed screws and remove reverse gear holder. Unscrew the reverse gear idler shaft fixing bolt.
27 Screw a bolt into the reverse idler shaft and tap out reverse gear, bearing and shaft. Note the position of the flat on the washer.
28 From the mainshaft, remove the reverse gearwheel and take off the needle bearing, flanged bush and shim.
29 Remove the layshaft and mainshaft from the intermediate casing while meshed together.
30 From the rear end of the mainshaft take off the shim. Separate the input (clutch) shaft from the mainshaft.

Mainshaft – dismantling
31 A press or puller will be required to remove some gears and synchro units from the shaft.
32 Extract the circlip from the front end of the shaft and take off the spacer washer.
33 Remove 3rd/4th synchro unit.
34 Remove 3rd gear (photo).
35 Take off the split bearing.
36 Take off the shim and remove the following parts from the rear end of the shaft. 1st gear and needle bearing, 1st/2nd synchro, the bearing track and spacer, baulk ring, needle bearing and 2nd gear.

Layshaft
37 The 3rd, 4th and 5th gears can be removed from the layshaft if the teeth show signs of wear or damage.
38 Avoid striking the gears or gripping the teeth in a vice without soft jaw protectors during any overhaul work. The roller bearings are of split type (photo).

Inspection
39 Check the synchro units, as described in Section 6, paragraphs 25 to 29, but the baulk ring-to-gear cone gap must not be less than 1.0 mm (0.040 in).

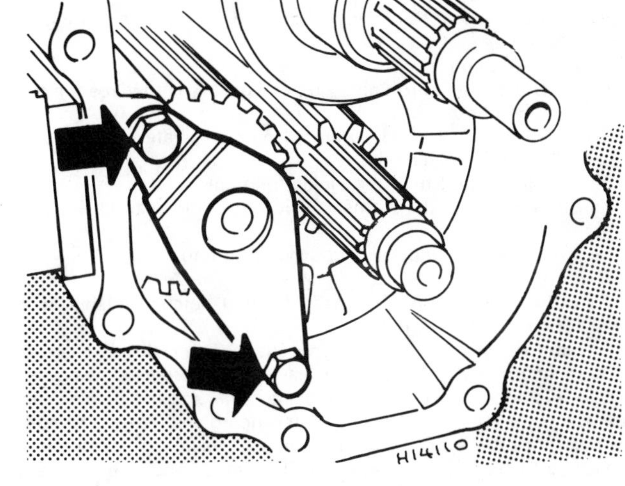

Fig. 6.67 Reverse gear holder retaining screws (arrowed) – Getrag 245 (Sec 8)

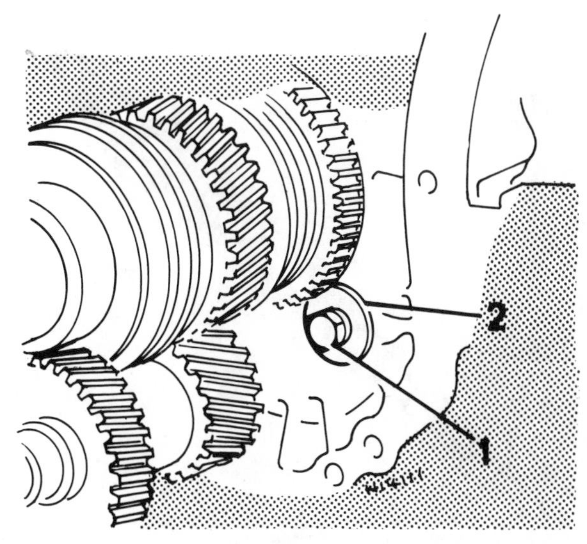

Fig. 6.68 Reverse gear idler shaft bolt (1) and washer (2) – Getrag 245 (Sec 8)

8.34 Drawing 3rd gear and synchro unit from mainshaft

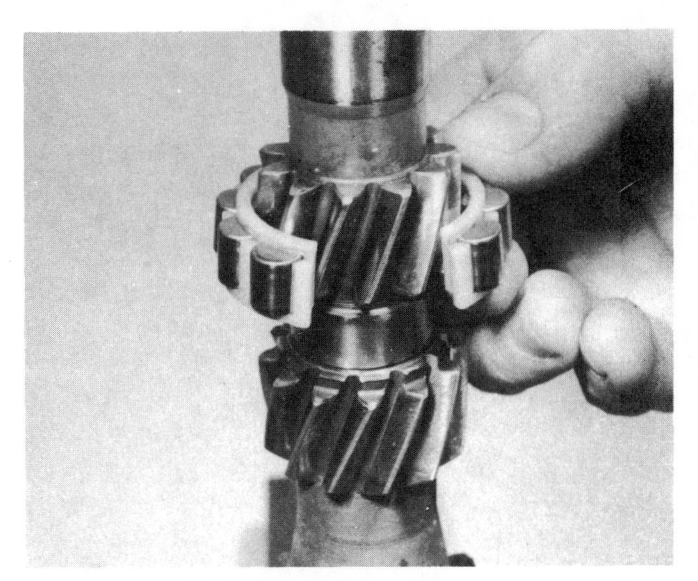

8.38 Layshaft roller bearing

Mainshaft – reassembly

40 To the front end of the mainshaft, fit 3rd gear needle bearing and the gear (photos).

41 Fit the baulk ring (photo).

42 Fit the 3rd/4th synchro unit so that its groove is towards the front of the gearbox (photo).

43 The synchro-hub should be warmed in boiling water, it can then be tapped fully onto the shaft.

44 Fit the spacer and then the circlip (photos).

45 To the rear end of the mainshaft, fit the needle bearing, bush and 2nd gear (photos).

46 Fit the baulk ring and 1st/2nd synchro (photo).

47 Fit the baulk ring (photo).

48 Fit the needle bearing, 1st gear, flanged notched bush and the roller bearing inner track (photos).

49 If new reverse/5th components have been fitted, then the thickness of the shim (X) must be calculated in the following way. Measure distance (A) between the shaft collar and the bearing inner track (Fig. 6.69). Dismantle reverse/5th synchro and then push reverse gear bush into the synchro-hub and then measure distance (B) from hub to bush (Fig. 6.70). Subtract B from A and the difference represents the thickness of the required shim.

8.40C Fitting 3rd gear to mainshaft

8.40A Mainshaft stripped

8.41 Fitting baulk ring to 3rd gear

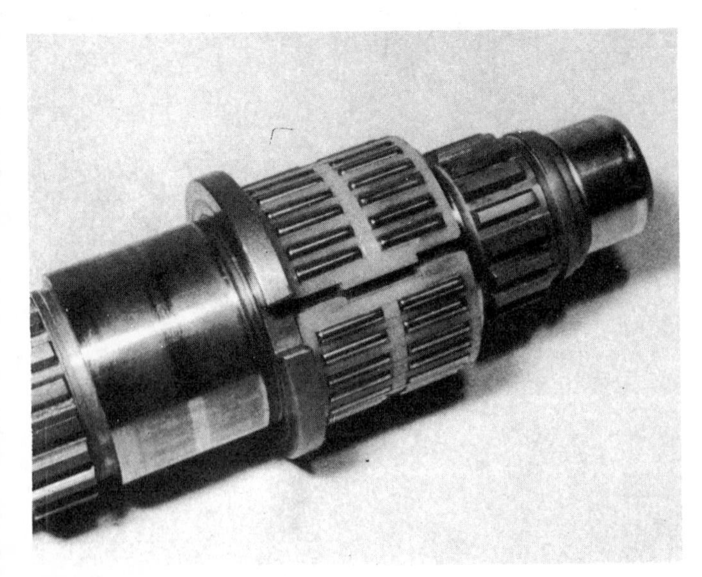

8.40B 3rd gear needle bearing

8.42 Fitting 3rd/4th synchro
Arrow indicates groove

8.44A Spacer

8.44B Fitting circlip

8.45A 2nd gear needle bearing

8.45B Fitting 2nd gear

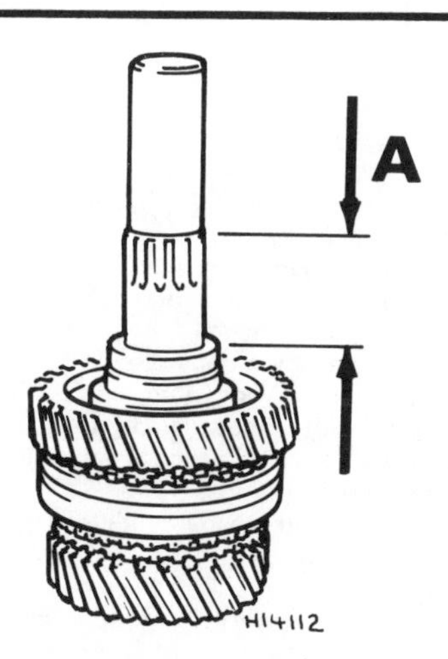

Fig. 6.69 Measuring the distance (A) between the shaft collar and the bearing inner track – Getrag 245 (Sec 8)

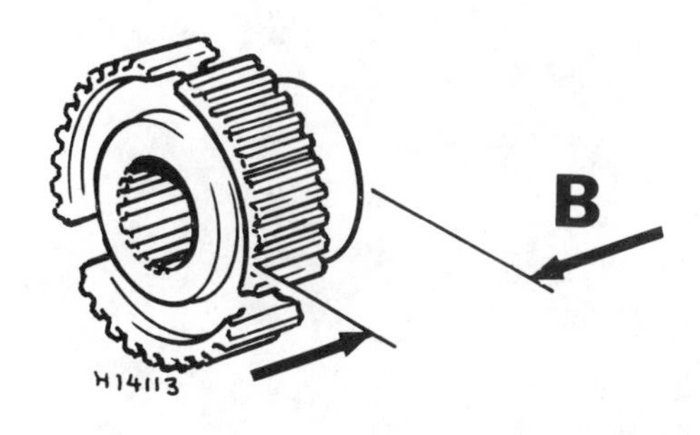

Fig. 6.70 Measuring the distance (B) from the hub to the bush – Getrag 245 (Sec 8)

8.46A Baulk ring

8.48A 1st gear, needle bearing and flanged bush

8.46B 1st/2nd synchro

8.48B Fitting roller bearing inner track

8.47 Baulk ring

Reassembly of gearbox

50 If new bearings are being fitted, then the outer tracks should be removed and refitted after the casing adjacent to the bearing recesses has been heated in boiling water.

51 Insert a 2.0 mm (0.080 in) thick shim under the mainshaft bearing track before pressing the track into the casing.

52 The clearance between layshaft bearing and its circlip in the casing must be eliminated by means of shims.

53 Commence reassembly by inserting the needle roller bearing into the recess in the end of the input (clutch) shaft. Fit the baulk ring to 3rd/4th speed synchro sleeve and then connect the input shaft to the front end of the mainshaft (photos).

54 Mesh the mainshaft and layshaft together and fit them into the intermediate casing (photo).

55 To the interior of the intermediate casing, fit the selected shim (X), the flanged bush and the needle bearing (photos).

56 Fit reverse gear to the mainshaft (photo).

57 Fit reverse idler shaft with reverse gear and bearing. Screw in the retaining bolt, noting the position of the cut-away edge of the thrust washer (photos).

58 Fit reverse gear holder (photo). Apply thread locking fluid to the threads of the socket-headed retaining screws.

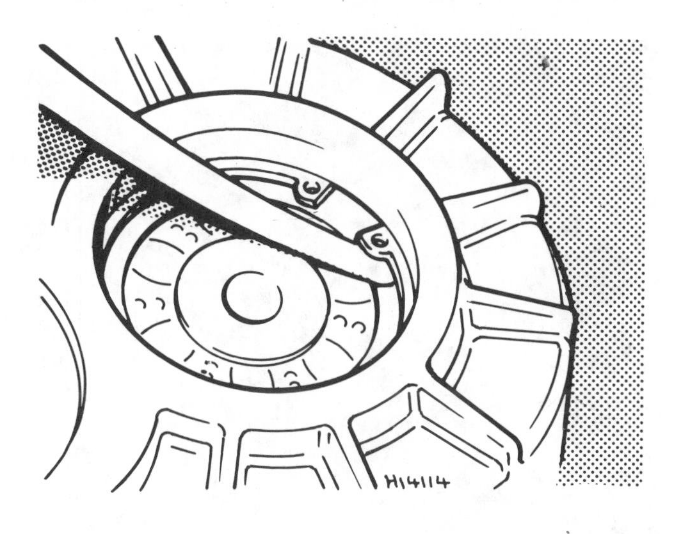

Fig. 6.71 Checking the layshaft bearing-to-circlip clearance – Getrag 245 (Sec 8)

8.53A Fitting baulk ring to 3rd/4th synchro

8.53B Connecting input shaft to mainshaft

8.54 Fitting geartrains to intermediate casing

8.55A Shim (X) on mainshaft

8.55B Flanged bush on mainshaft

8.55C Needle bearing on mainshaft

8.56 Reverse gear

8.57A Reverse gear, shaft and bearing

8.57B Reverse gear thrustwasher

8.57C Reverse shaft retaining bolt

8.58 Reverse gear holder

59 Engage the 1st/2nd and 3rd/4th selector forks in their synchro sleeve grooves (photo). Make sure that the angled corners of the forks are towards each other.
60 Insert the 1st/2nd selector shaft detent ball and spring into its hole in the intermediate casing (photo). Keep the detent ball depressed and pass the selector shaft through the dog and fork and into the casing.
61 Pin the fork and dog to the selector shaft (photo).
62 Insert the 3rd/4th selector shaft detent ball and spring (photo). Keep the detent ball depressed and pass the selector shaft through its fork and into the intermediate casing.
63 Pin the fork to the selector shaft.
64 Push the reverse/5th selector fork onto its shaft.
65 Locate the fork in the groove of the reverse/5th synchro sleeve and fit the shaft, fork and synchro as an assembly (photo), but only just enter the shaft into the intermediate casing. The boss on the fork must be towards the front of the gearbox.
66 Drop the remaining interlock ball into position, follow with the reverse/5th detent ball and spring. Hold the ball depressed and push the selector shaft into position. The shaft detent grooves must be towards the bottom of the gearbox. On no account push the shaft so far that the square cut-outs in it align with the detent ball, otherwise the ball will jam.

8.61 Selector fork pins
A 3rd/4th *B 1st/2nd* *C Dog*

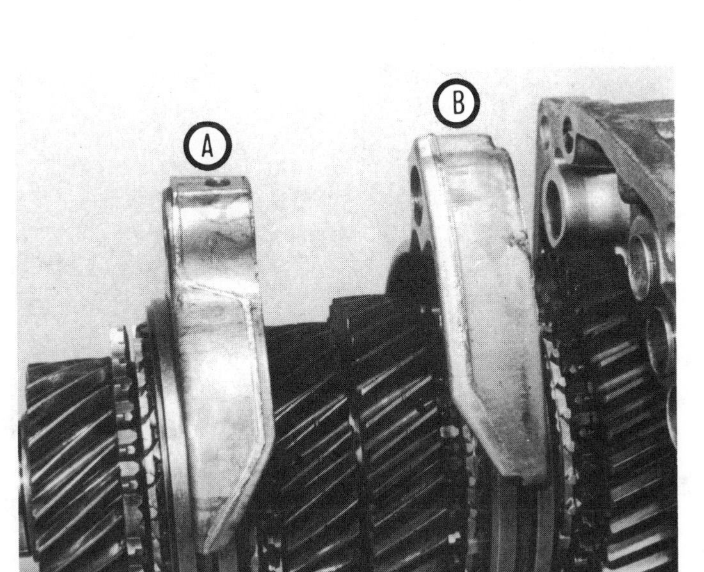

8.59 Selector forks
A 3rd/4th *B 1st/2nd*

8.62 3rd/4th detent ball

8.60 1st/2nd detent ball

8.65 5th/reverse synchro, fork and shaft

67 Pin the reverse/5th fork to the selector shaft (photo).
68 To the mainshaft, fit the flanged bush up against the synchro-hub so that the pins engage in the flange notches (photo). Make the fitting easier by warming the bush in boiling water.
69 Fit the split needle bearing, baulk rings and 5th gear to the mainshaft (photos).
70 To the layshaft, fit 5th gear, and the bearing inner track so that its flange is towards the gear (photo).
71 Pin the collar with the spacer, shim and washer to the end of the layshaft (photos). The chamfer on the collar should be towards the end of the shaft. Eliminate any play by altering the thickness of the shim, if necessary.
72 To the end of the mainshaft fit the notched spacer; chamfer to the end of the shaft (photo).
73 Heat the speedometer drivegear in boiling water and fit it to the shaft so that the thin groove is towards the end of the shaft (photo). Fit the layshaft roller race (photo).
74 Push the selector rod with a new oil seal into the intermediate casing. Make sure that the notches in the rod are away from the selector shafts and make sure that it passes through the dog as it is pushed into position. Pin the dog to the rod.

8.69A Split needle bearing

8.67 5th/reverse fork pin

8.69B 5th gear on mainshaft

8.68 Flanged bush on mainshaft

8.70 5th gear on layshaft

8.71A Spacer on layshaft

8.71B Shim on layshaft

8.71C Washer on layshaft

8.71D Collar on layshaft

8.71E Pinning collar to layshaft

8.72 Notched spacer on mainshaft

8.73A Fitting speedometer drivegear

8.75A Fitting selector rail

8.73B Layshaft roller race

8.75B Selector rail operating lever and screw

8.74 Selector rod dog and pin

75 Fit the selector rail and operating lever (photo). Screw in the lever socket-headed screw having applied thread locking fluid to the screw threads (photo).
76 Fit the clamp and screw (photos).
77 Stick the small rollers to the selector rod (photo).
78 Locate the spring-loaded selector arm on the selector rod (photo).
79 Stick the interlock plunger, using thick grease into its hole in the casing (photo). Make sure that it is not displaced as the casing is fitted.
80 Smear the casing mating flanges with gasket cement. Engage 2nd gear by pushing 1st/2nd synchro sleeve towards the front of the gearbox.
81 Join the rear casing to the intermediate casing (photo). If the casings will not close together, drive out the 1st/2nd selector fork and dog roll pins to allow the fork and dog to 'float' as the casings are joined. Refit the roll pins on completion.
82 Tap the dowel pins into position and screw in the casing bolts (photos).
83 Insert the two selector arm plungers into the hole in the rear casing (photo). It is essential that the projection on the lower plunger is aligned with the gearbox centre line and the projections where the two plungers join are opposite each other. Insert the spring and screw in the threaded plug.
84 Fit the selector rod plunger, spring and cap (photos).

8.76A Selector rail clamp

8.76B Selector rail clamp screw

8.77 Selector rod rollers

8.78 Spring-loaded selector arm

8.79 Interlock plunger

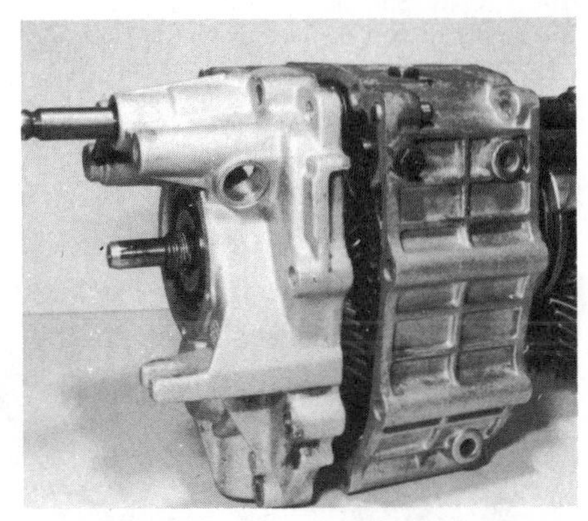
8.81 Joining rear and intermediate casings

8.82A Driving home a dowel pin

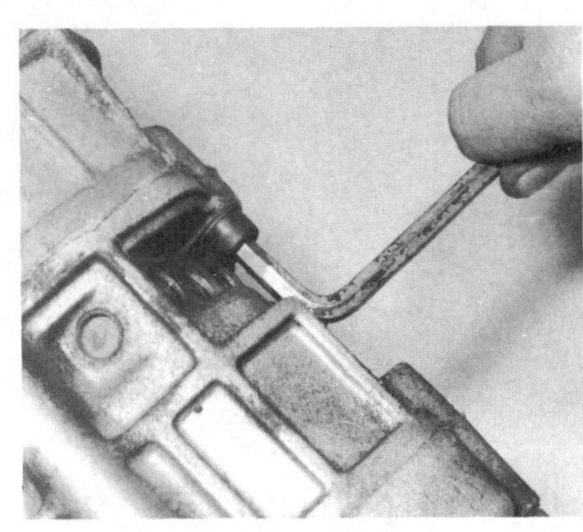
8.82B Tightening a casing bolt

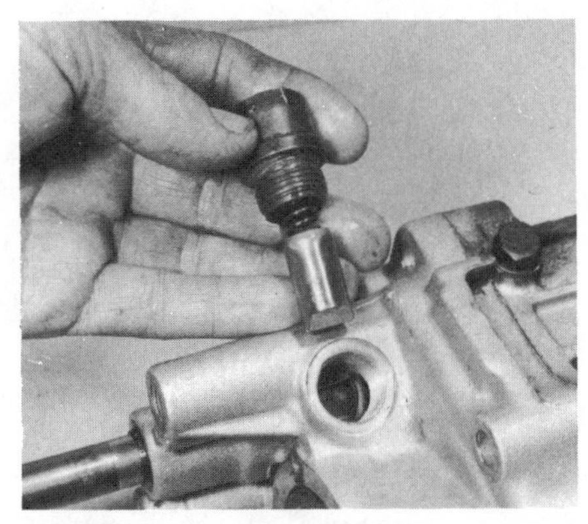
8.83 Fitting selector arm plunger, spring and plug

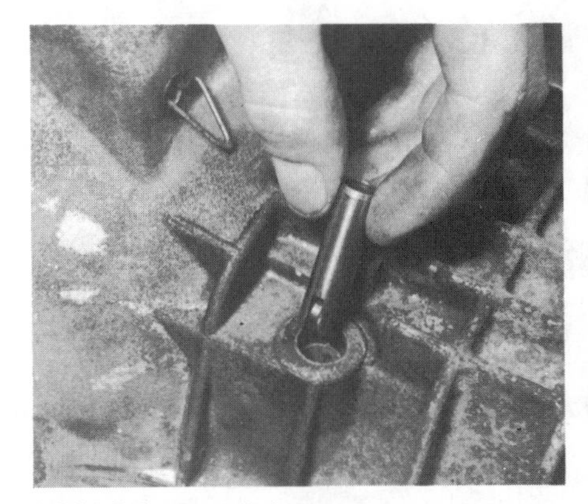
8.84A Selector rod plunger

8.84B Selector rod plunger spring

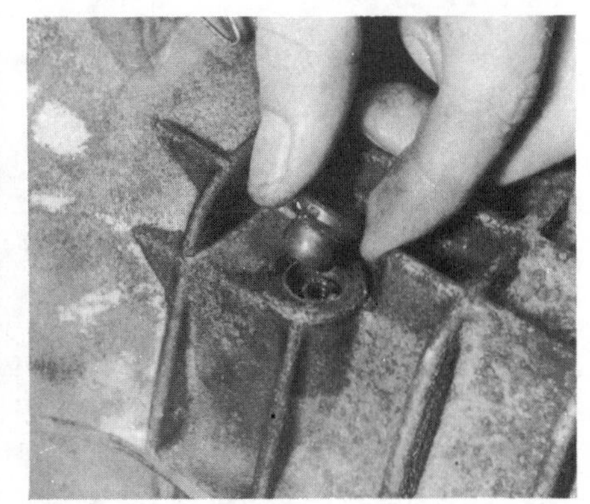
8.84C Selector rod plunger cap

85 Apply sealant to the threads of the reverse lamp switch and screw it into position (photo).
86 Apply sealant to new detent ball plugs and drive them into position (photo).
87 Drive the rear bearing into position.
88 Fit the spacer to the rear bearing (photo). If new components have been fitted, determine the shim thickness as described in Section 6, paragraphs 50 to 52.
89 Fit the rear cover with new oil seal and gasket (photo). Fill the seal lips with grease.
90 Fit the output flange, screw on the nut and tighten to the specified torque (photos).
91 Locate a new nut locking cup and stake it into the cut-out provided (photo).
92 Fit the speedometer driven gear (photo) and its lockbolt.
93 Fit the roller bearing races to the front ends of the mainshaft and the layshaft (photos).
94 Apply gasket cement to the main casing flanges and push it into position on the intermediate casing (photo). Should it not mate completely, this will probably be due to one of the shaft front split type bearings having expanded. Remove the bearing and place it in the casing instead of on the shaft.
95 Tap in the dowel pins and screw in the casing connecting bolts.

8.88 Rear bearing spacer

8.85 Applying thread sealant to reverse lamp switch

8.89 Tightening a rear cover bolt

8.86 Applying sealant to detent ball plug

8.90A Fitting output flange

8.90B Flange nut

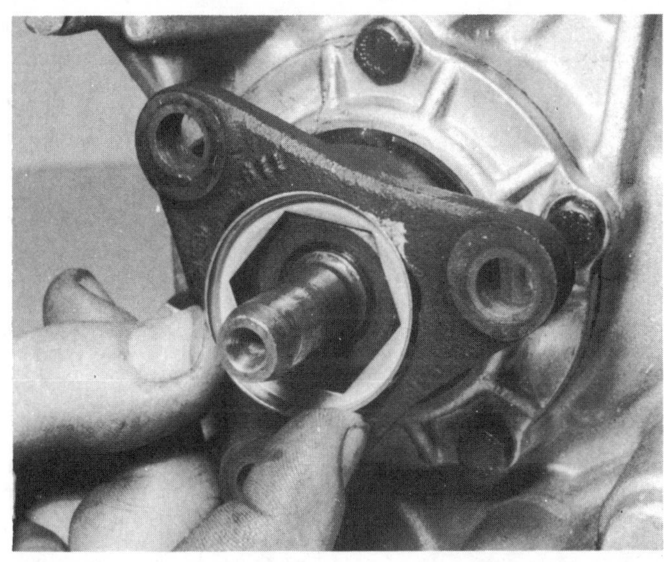

8.91 Output flange nut locking cup

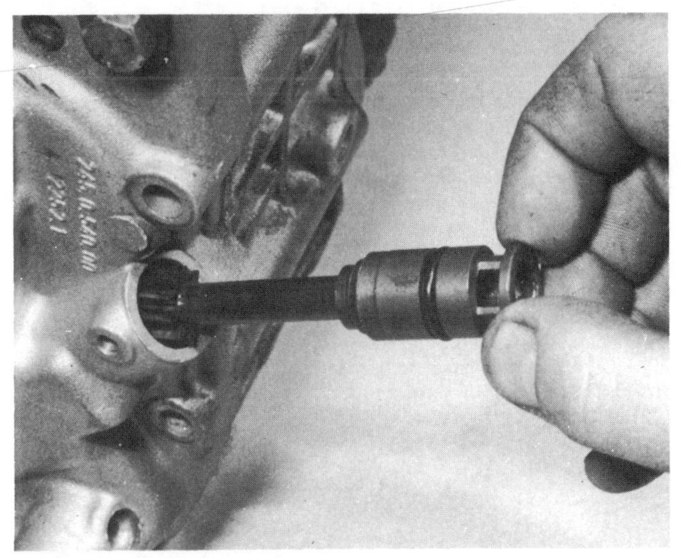

8.92 Fitting speedometer gear

8.93A Layshaft front bearing

8.93B Mainshaft front bearing

8.94 Joining main and intermediate casings

8.96A Input shaft bearing

8.96D Input shaft bearing circlip fitted

8.96B Spacer

8.96C Circlip

96 Fit the front bearing to the input shaft (photo). Fit the spacer, shim and circlip (photos).

97 If new components have been fitted, carry out the following shim selection procedure. Using a depth gauge, measure distance (A) of the bearing below the surface of the casing – Fig. 6.72. Measure dimensions (B) and (C) on the guide sleeve – Figs. 6.73 and 6.74. Subtract A from B and subtract C from the difference. This will give the thickness of the shim to be used.

98 Fit the clutch guide sleeve fitted with a new oil seal. Apply gasket cement to the sleeve flange and bolt it into position so that the oil drain channel is at the bottom.

99 Fit the clutch release components, as described in Chapter 5.

100 Refill the gearbox with oil after it has been refitted to the car.

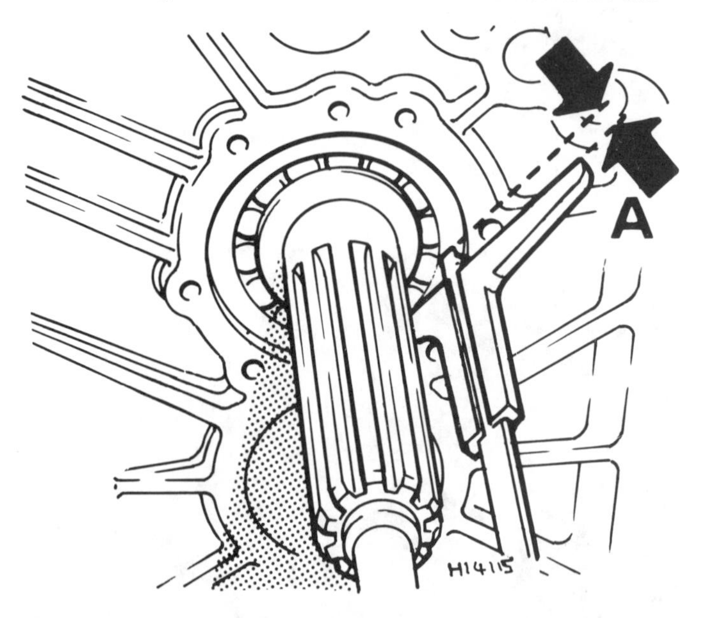

Fig. 6.72 Measuring distance (A): the depth of the bearing below the surface of the casing – Getrag 245 (Sec 8)

9 Gearbox (Getrag 245, 5-speed Sport) – overhaul

Dismantling into major assemblies

1 Remove the clutch release components, the output flange, the main casing and the rear cover, all as described in Section 8.

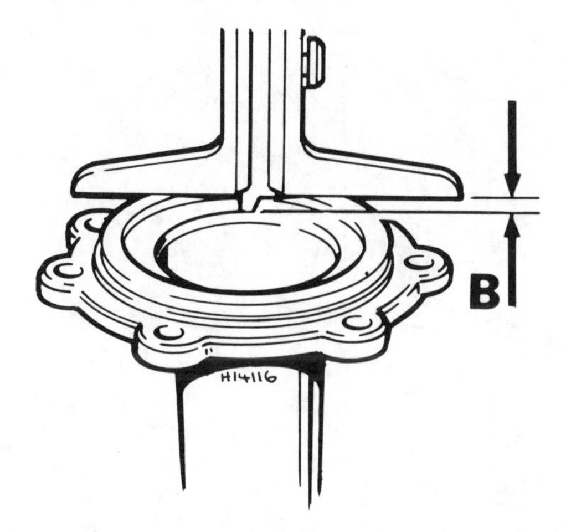

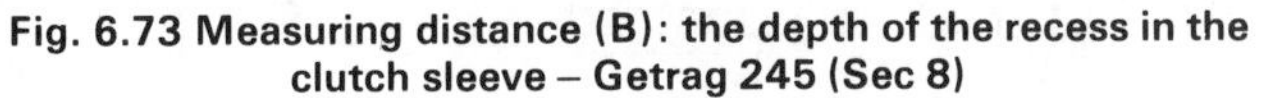

Fig. 6.73 Measuring distance (B): the depth of the recess in the clutch sleeve – Getrag 245 (Sec 8)

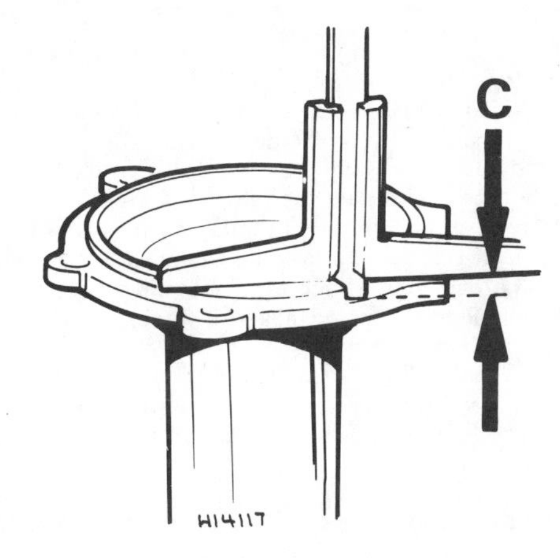

Fig. 6.74 Measuring distance (C): the depth of the clutch sleeve shoulder – Getrag 245 (Sec 8)

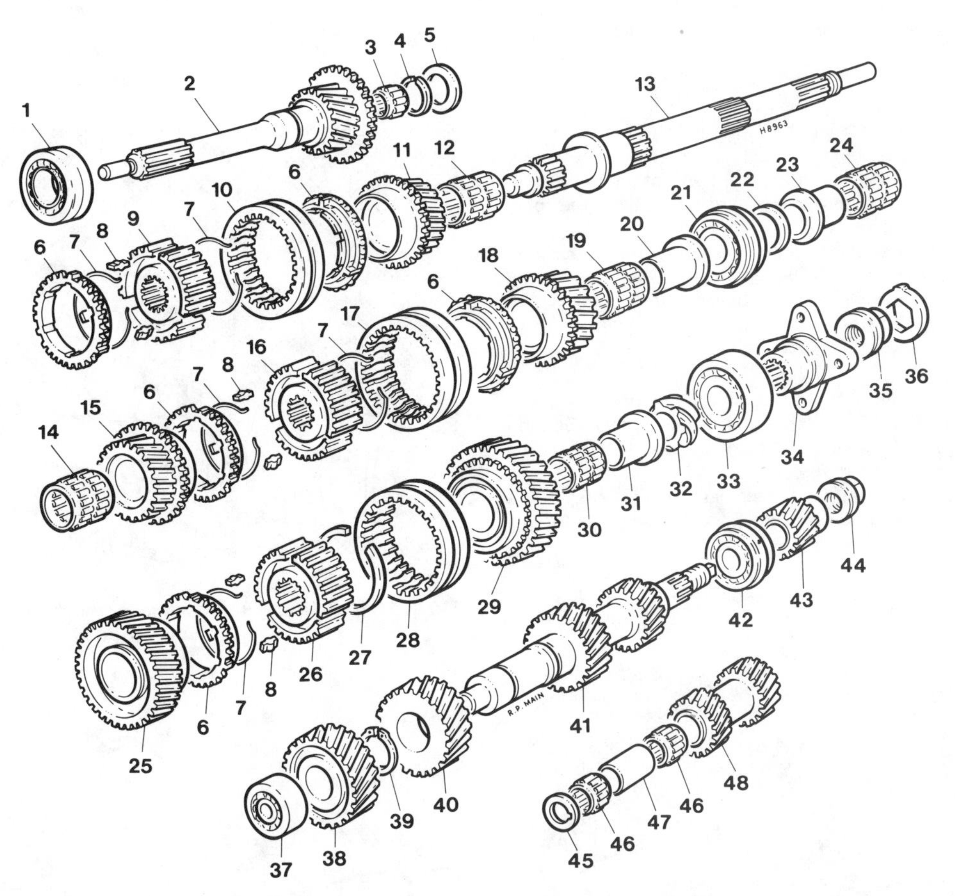

Fig. 6.75 Internal components of the Getrag 245 5-speed Sport gearbox (Sec 9)

1 *Ball-bearing*
2 *Input (clutch) shaft*
3 *Needle bearing*
4 *Circlip*
5 *Washer*
6 *Baulk ring*
7 *Spring*
8 *Sliding key*
9 *4th/5th synchro-hub*
10 *4th/5th synchro sleeve*
11 *4th gear*
12 *Needle bearing*
13 *Mainshaft*
14 *Needle bearing*
15 *3rd gear*
16 *2nd/3rd synchro-hub*
17 *2nd/3rd sychro sleeve*
18 *2nd gear*
19 *Needle bearing*
20 *Bearing bush*
21 *Bearing*
22 *Shim (X)*
23 *Bearing bush*
24 *Needle bearing*
25 *1st gear*
26 *1st/reverse synchro-hub*
27 *Lockwasher*
28 *1st/reverse synchro sleeve*
29 *Reverse gear*
30 *Needle bearing*
31 *Bearing bush*
32 *Speedometer drivegear*
33 *Ball-bearing*
34 *Output flange*
35 *Nut*
36 *Nut locking cup*
37 *Ball-bearing*
38 *5th gear*
39 *Circlip*
40 *4th gear*
41 *Layshaft*
42 *Bearing*
43 *1st gear*
44 *Nut*
45 *Washer*
46 *Needle bearing*
47 *Spacer*
48 *Double gear*

2 Select 4th gear by moving the 4th/5th synchro sleeve.
3 Rotate the input (clutch) shaft until the fork roll pin is aligned with the tooth gap – Fig. 6.76. Knock out the roll pin and withdraw the 4th/5th selector shaft. Retrieve the detent balls.
4 Cut off the lockwire from the 2nd/3rd selector fork lockbolt. Unscrew the bolt and withdraw the selector shaft.
5 From the rear end of the mainshaft, withdraw the ball-bearing using a puller or, if the bearing is to be renewed, insert two hooked rods between the balls and attach them to a slide hammer.
6 Remove the speedometer drivegear (if fitted).
7 Tap down the rear casing section dowel pins, unscrew the connecting bolts and pull the rear section from the main casing.
8 Drive out the roll pins (1 to 3) – Fig. 6.78 – and then pull the selector rod towards the rear of the gearbox. Take off the arm (4) and retrieve the rollers on the rod.
9 Using a two-legged puller, draw the speedometer drivegear (models without rear-mounted speedometer drive) with reverse gear and bush from the mainshaft.
10 Remove the dog (1) – Fig. 6.79 – and pull the selector shaft with the fork and 1st/2nd synchro towards the rear of the gearbox.
11 Take off the baulk ring, 1st gear and needle bearing.
12 Remove the bearing bush and shim from the mainshaft.
13 Warm the intermediate casing section in boiling water and then pull the geartrains, meshed together, out of the intermediate casing section.

Mainshaft – dismantling

14 From the front end of the mainshaft pull off the input (clutch) shaft, baulk ring and needle bearing. 5th gear is part of the input shaft.
15 Remove the circlip and shim from the front end of the mainshaft.
16 Remove 4th/5th synchro with 4th gear and the split needle roller bearing.
17 Press the mainshaft out of the following components or draw them from the shaft with a suitable puller. Bearing race, bush, 2nd gear, baulk ring, 2nd/3rd synchro, needle bearing, the synchromesh baulk ring and 3rd gear with needle bearing.

Inspection

18 Check all gears for chipped or worn teeth and bearings for wear.
19 Check the synchro units and selector forks, as described in Section 6; the baulk ring-to-gear cone gap must not be less than 1.0 mm (0.040 in), otherwise renew the baulk ring.
20 If new components have been fitted, calculate the thickness of the shim used at the 1st gear bearing bush. To do this, measure the

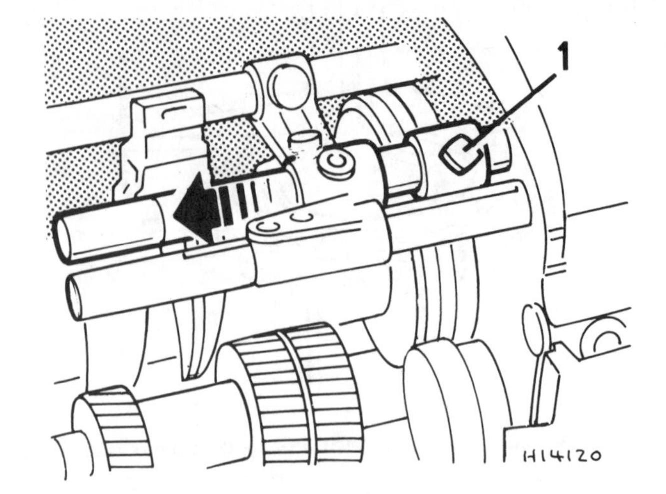

Fig. 6.77 2nd/3rd selector fork lockbolt (1) – Getrag 245 Sport (Sec 9)

Remove the shaft in the direction of the arrow

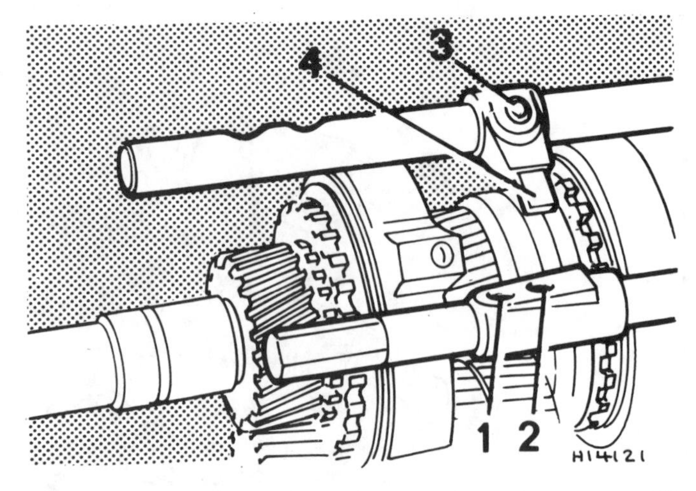

Fig. 6.78 Roll pins (1 to 3) and selector shaft arm (4) – Getrag 245 Sport (Sec 9)

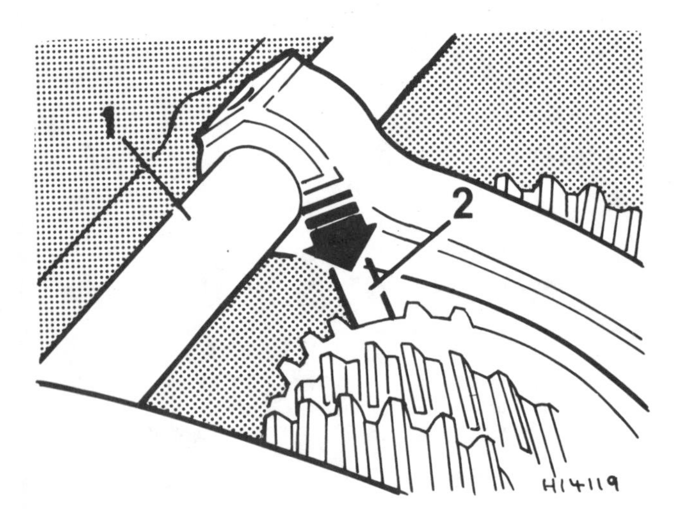

Fig. 6.76 4th/5th selector shaft (1) and roll pin (2) – Getrag 245 Sport (Sec 9)

Knock the pin out into the tooth gap

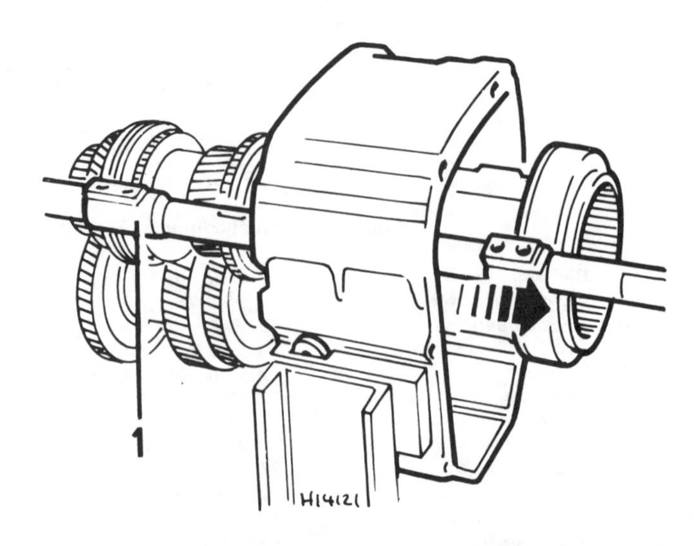

Fig. 6.79 Remove the dog (1) and pull the selector shaft towards the rear, as arrowed – Getrag 245 Sport (Sec 9)

distance (A) from the collar on the mainshaft to the bearing inner track – Fig. 6.80.

21 Remove the sleeve from 1st/reverse synchro-hub then place reverse gear bearing bush in the synchro-hub. Measure the distance (B) from the hub collar to bearing bush – Fig. 6.81. Subtract B from A and the difference represents the thickness of the shim required.

Bearings

22 If a new mainshaft rear bearing has been fitted in the rear casing section, then any clearance between the casing flange and the face of the speedometer drivegear must be eliminated by fitting a shim (X) – Fig. 6.82. To determine the shim thickness, measure distance (A) and then place the speedometer drivegear on the rear bearing and measure

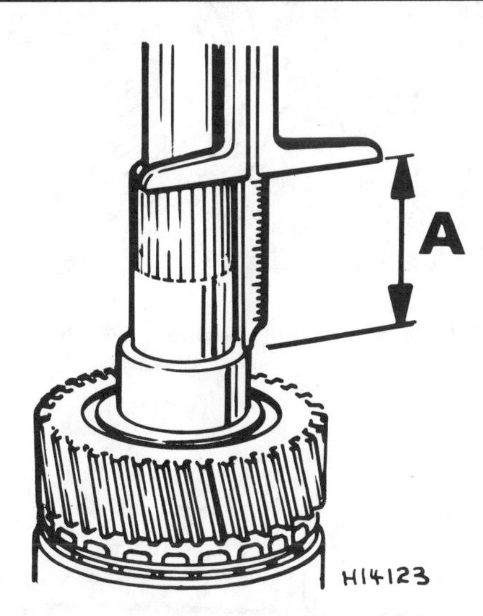

Fig. 6.80 Measuring distance (A) from the mainshaft collar to the bearing inner track – Getrag 245 Sport (Sec 9)

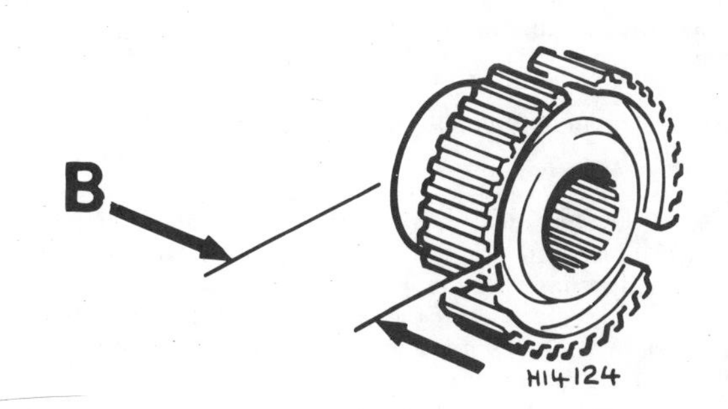

Fig. 6.81 Measuring distance (B) from the hub collar to the bush – Getrag 245 Sport (Sec 9)

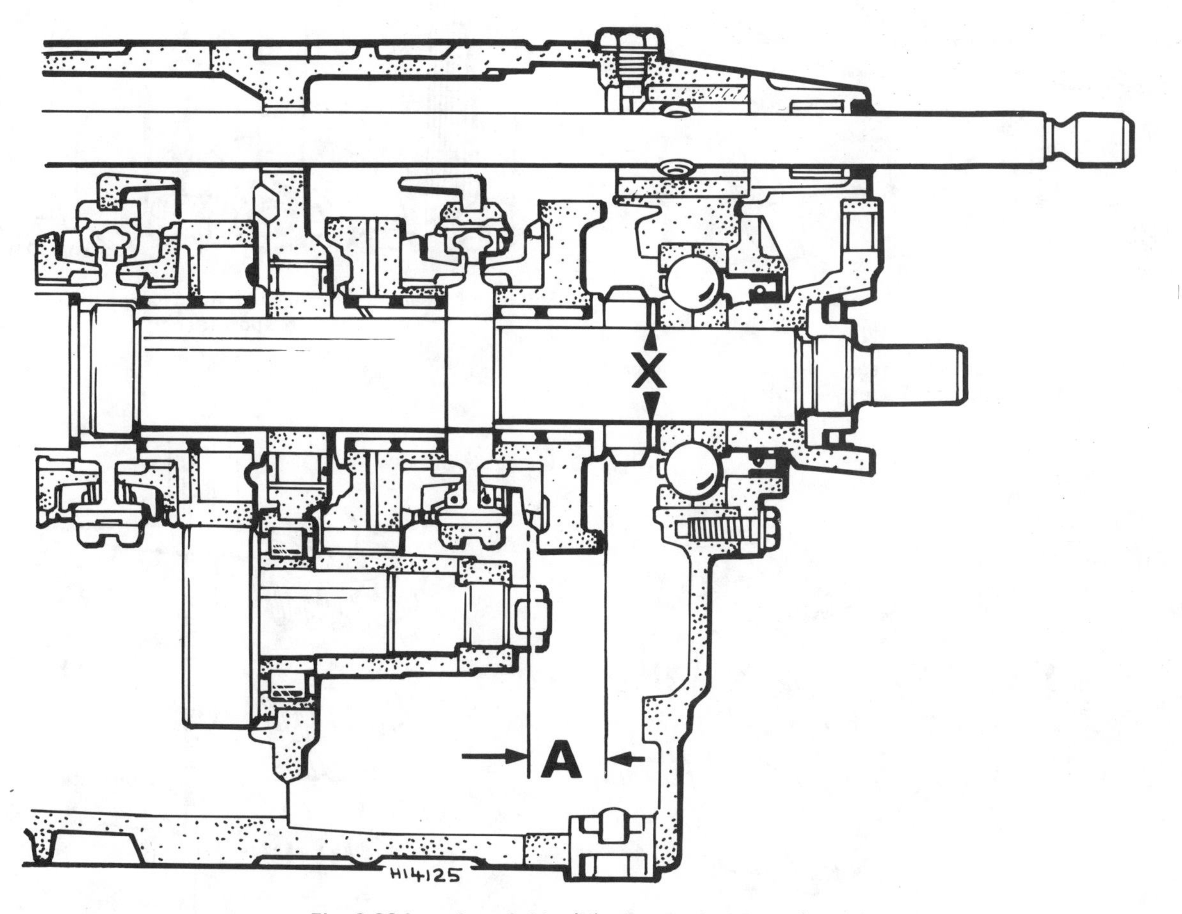

Fig. 6.82 Location of shim (X) – Getrag 245 Sport (Sec 9)

A Bearing-to-casing dimension

the distance (B) from the gear face to the casing flange – Fig. 6.83. Subtract B from A and the difference represents the thickness of the required shim.

Mainshaft – reassembly

23 Fit the needle bearing, 3rd gear and the synchro baulk ring.
24 Fit 2nd/3rd synchro, the needle bearing, baulk ring and 2nd gear.
25 Press the bearing bush onto the shaft.
26 Press on the bearing inner track.
27 Fit the needle roller bearing, 4th gear and 4th/5th synchro unit so that the shoulder on the synchro sleeve is towards 5th gear.
28 Fit the shim and circlip to the front end of the mainshaft. Check the clearance between synchro-hub and circlip and change the shim, if necessary, to eliminate any gap.

Layshaft

29 Check the layshaft gear teeth for wear or chipping. If the roller bearing is to be renewed, grip the shaft in the jaws of a vice fitted with jaw protectors and unscrew the layshaft nut.
30 Draw off the gear, take off the outer bearing race and then heat the inner track in boiling water and remove it from the shaft.
31 Reassemble by reversing the removal operations, but note that the inner track has its collar away from the end of the shaft. Apply thread locking fluid to clean threads and tighten the nut to the specified torque.

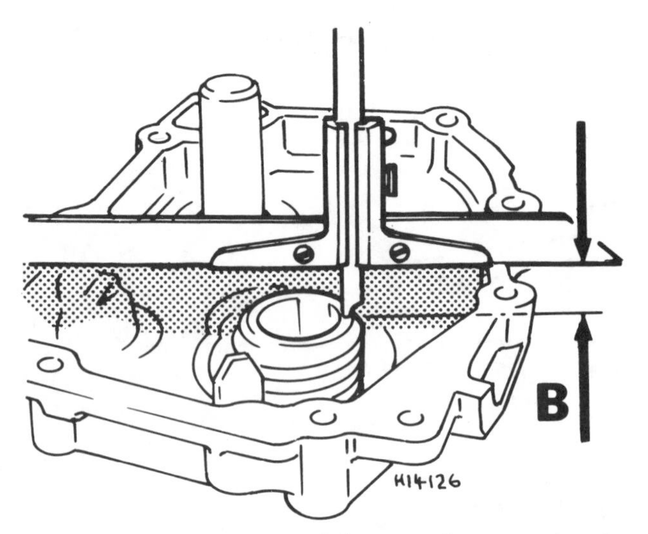

Fig. 6.83 Measuring distance (B): gear casing to speedometer gear – Getrag 245 Sport (Sec 9)

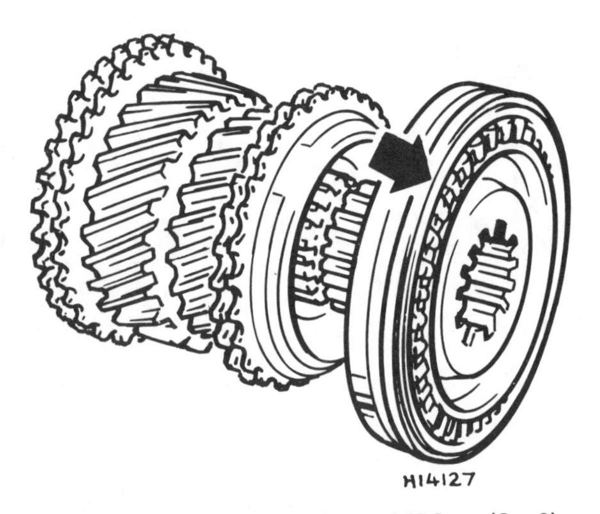

Fig. 6.84 4th/5th synchro – Getrag 245 Sport (Sec 9)

The shoulder (arrowed) must be towards 5th gear

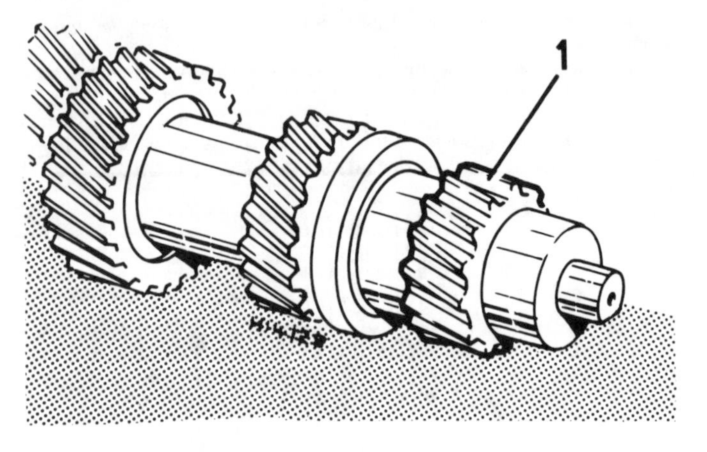

Fig. 6.85 Layshaft gear (1) – Getrag 245 Sport (Sec 9)

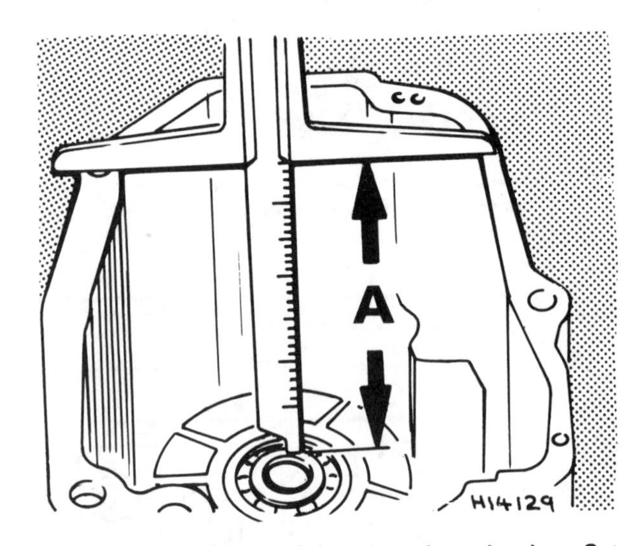

Fig. 6.86 Measuring distance (A): main casing to bearing – Getrag 245 Sport (Sec 9)

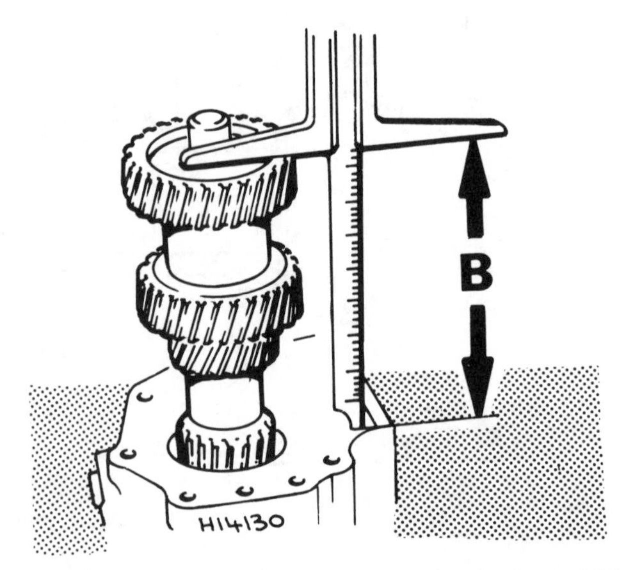

Fig. 6.87 Measuring distance (B): casing to gear – Getrag 245 Sport (Sec 9)

32 If new components have been fitted, then the layshaft endfloat must be checked and adjusted. To do this, use a depth gauge and measure the distance (A) from the flange of the main casing to the bearing – Fig. 6.86.
33 With the layshaft located in the bearing in the intermediate casing section, measure distance (B) from the casing flange to the surface of the gear – Fig. 6.87. Subtract B from A and select a shim which is between 0.1 and 0.2 mm (0.004 and 0.008 in) thinner than the difference.

Reassembly of gearbox

34 Heat the intermediate casing section in boiling water and install the geartrains meshed together.
35 Fit the selected shim (X) to the mainshaft and then heat the bearing bush in boiling water and push it onto the shaft.
36 Fit the needle bearing, 1st gear and baulk ring.
37 Fit 1st/reverse selector shaft with fork. Engage the 1st/reverse synchro sleeve with the fork so that the synchro spring faces 1st gear.
38 Push the synchro unit onto the mainshaft.
39 Fit reverse gear and the split needle bearing.
40 Heat the bearing bush in boiling water and push it onto the mainshaft.
41 Heat the speedo drivegear in a similar way and push it onto the shaft.
42 Fit the selector dog – Fig. 6.89 – and secure it with roll pins.
43 Locate 2nd/3rd and 4th/5th selector forks.
44 Push in the selector rod and fit the arm (1) to it so that the chamfer is as shown (Fig. 6.90). Pin the arm when the grooves in the rod are facing outward.
45 Stick the two rollers in the selector rod using thick grease.
46 Fit the needle bearing, spacer, needle bearing and gear to the shaft in the rear casing.
47 Apply jointing compound to clean mating flanges and push the rear casing onto the intermediate casing against detent ball spring pressure.

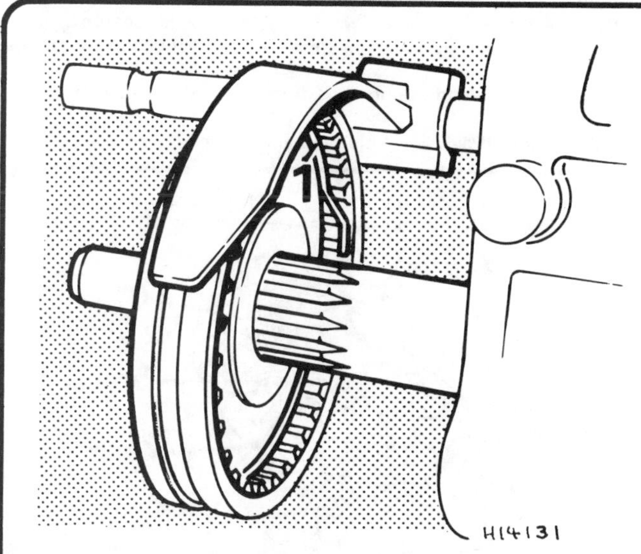

Fig. 6.88 1st/reverse synchro sleeve and selector fork – Getrag 245 Sport (Sec 9)

1 Synchro spring

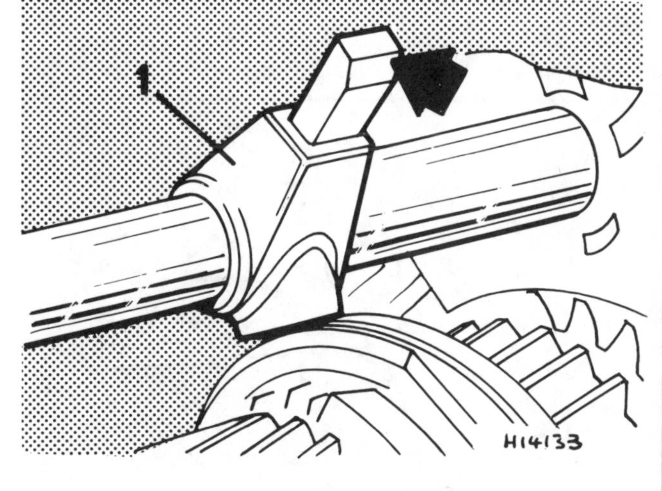

Fig. 6.90 Selector shaft arm (1) – Getrag 245 Sport (Sec 9)

Position the chamfer as arrowed

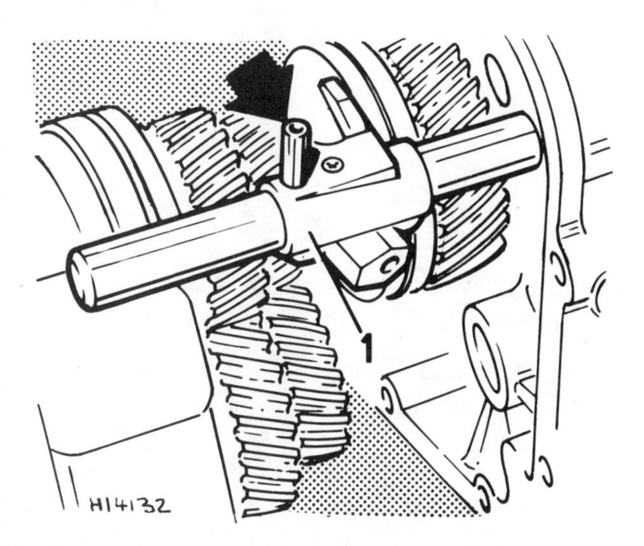

Fig. 6.89 1st/reverse selector shaft dog (1) and roll pin (arrowed) – Getrag 245 Sport (Sec 9)

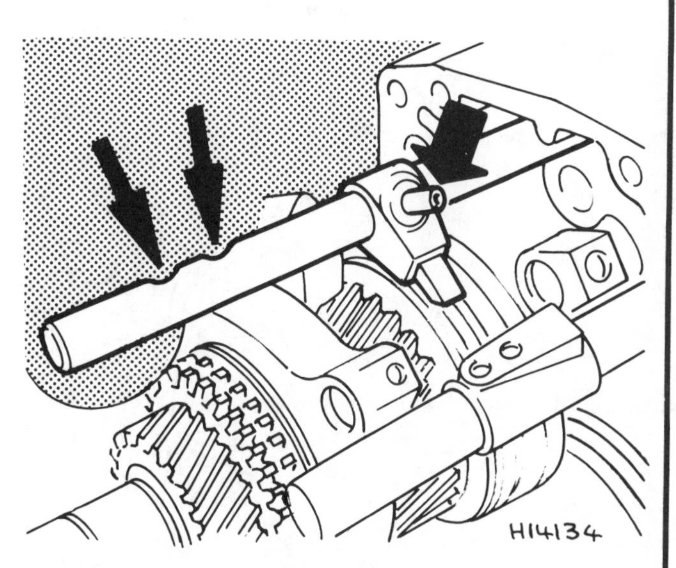

Fig. 6.91 Securing the selector arm with a roll pin – Getrag 245 Sport (Sec 9)

The grooves (arrowed) must face outwards

48 Insert the detent ball into the 1st/reverse hole – Fig. 6.92 – and bolt the rear casing into position.
49 Push in 2nd/3rd selector shaft, insert the interlock ball and then the detent ball. Depress the detent ball so that the selector shaft can be pushed into the rear casing.
50 Screw in the fork lockbolt and secure with wire.
51 Repeat the operations with the 4th/5th selector shaft, interlock ball and detent ball.
52 Pin the fork to the 4th/5th selector shaft.
53 Fit the selector rod lock plunger, spring and plug.
54 Screw in the reverse lamp switch and fit new detent ball hole plugs.
55 Fit the ball-bearing into the rear casing section.
56 Fit the new bearing spacer, the cover with new oil seal and gasket. If new components have been fitted, determine the shim thickness, as described in Section 6, paragraphs 50 to 52.
57 Fit the output flange with lockplate. Tighten the nut to the specified torque and stake the lockplate.
58 Clean the mating faces of the main casing and the intermediate casing. Apply jointing compound and locate the casings. Tap in the dowel pins and screw in the connecting bolts.
59 Fit the locking lever plunger, spring and cap – Fig. 6.94.
60 Drive the front bearing into position on the input (clutch) shaft.
61 Working within the bellhousing, check the thickness of the bearing shim required, as described in Section 8, paragraph 97. Apply jointing compound to the guide sleeve and bolt it into position. Make sure that the guide sleeve has been fitted with a new oil seal.
62 Fit the clutch release components, as described in Chapter 5.
63 Fill the gearbox with oil after it has been refitted to the car.

10 Gearbox (ZF S 5-16, 5-speed) – overhaul

Dismantling into major assemblies

1 Drain the oil from the gearbox.
2 Unbolt and remove the guide sleeve from inside the clutch bellhousing.
3 Extract the bearing circlip.
4 Unscrew the reverse lamp switch.
5 Tap out the dowel pins and unscrew and remove the bolts which hold the main casing to the rear casing.
6 Pull the main casing from the rear casing.
7 Remove the magnet from the rear casing and wipe it clean.
8 Remove the plug (1) – Fig. 6.96.
9 Remove the ball-bearing towards the front of the gearbox.
10 Remove the output flange, as described in Section 6, paragraphs 15 and 16.
11 Remove the detent spring caps from the end cover. Extract the detent springs.
12 Pull out the three detent plungers using circlip pliers.

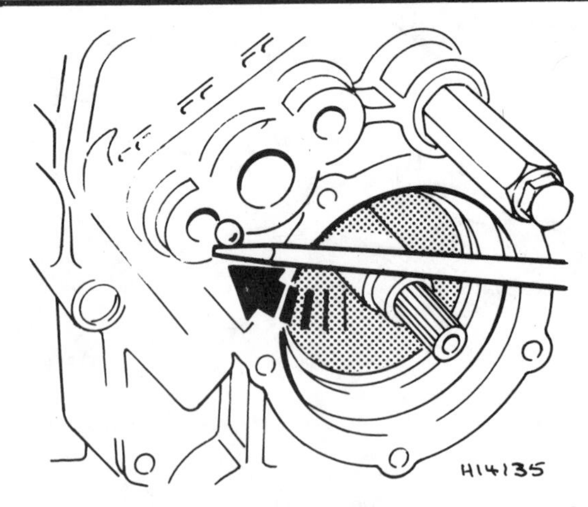

Fig. 6.92 Inserting 1st/reverse detent ball – Getrag 245 Sport (Sec 9)

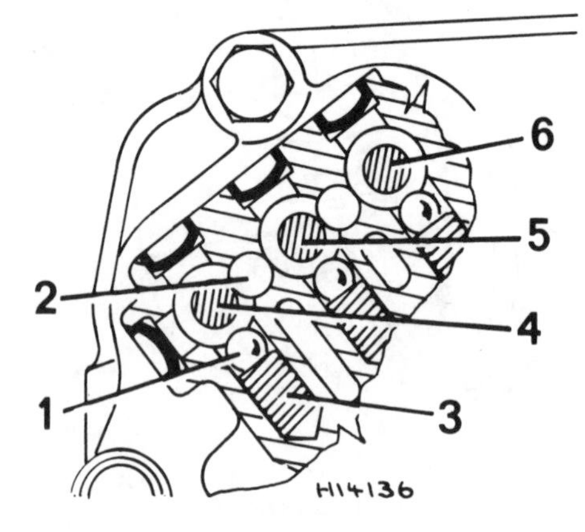

Fig. 6.93 Detent and interlock arrangement – Getrag 245 Sport (Sec 9)

1 Detent ball
2 Interlock ball
3 Spring
4 1st/reverse selector shaft
5 2nd/3rd selector shaft
6 4th/5th selector shaft

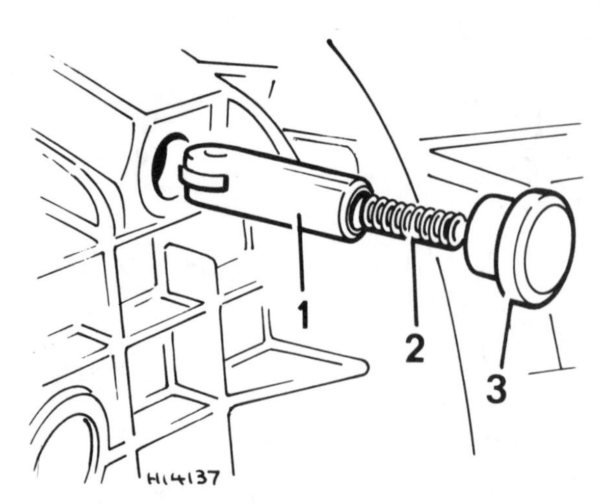

Fig. 6.94 Locking lever plunger (1), spring (2) and cap (3) – Getrag 245 Sport (Sec 9)

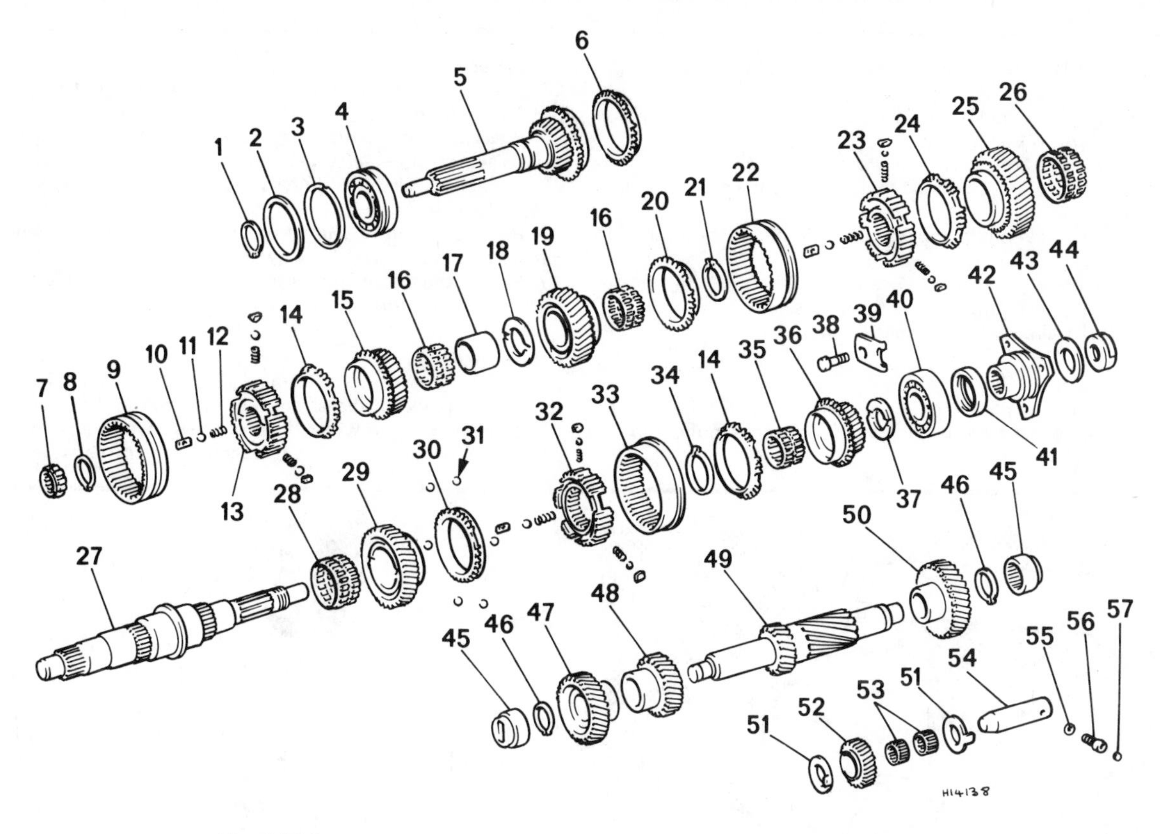

Fig. 6.95 Internal components of the ZF S 5-16 5-speed gearbox (Sec 10)

1 *Circlip*
2 *Spacer*
3 *Circlip*
4 *Ball-bearing*
5 *Input shaft*
6 *Baulk ring*
7 *Roller bearing*
8 *Circlip*
9 *Synchro sleeve*
10 *Sliding key*
11 *Ball*
12 *Spring*
13 *Synchro-hub*
14 *Baulk ring*
15 *3rd gear*
16 *Needle bearing*
17 *Bearing sleeve*
18 *Thrust washer*
19 *2nd gear*
20 *Baulk ring*
21 *Circlip*
22 *Synchro sleeve (1st/2nd)*
23 *Synchro-hub (1st/2nd)*
24 *Baulk ring*
25 *1st gear*
26 *Needle bearing*
27 *Mainshaft*
28 *Needle bearing*
29 *Reverse gear*
30 *Baulk ring*
31 *Balls (six)*
32 *Synchro-hub (reverse/5th)*
33 *Synchro sleeve (reverse/5th)*
34 *Circlip*
35 *Needle bearing*
36 *5th gear*
37 *Thrust washer*
38 *Bolt*
39 *Clamp*
40 *Ball-bearing*
41 *Oil seal*
42 *Output flange*
43 *Nut locking cup*
44 *Nut*
45 *Roller bearing*
46 *Circlip*
47 *4th gear*
48 *3rd gear*
49 *Layshaft*
50 *5th gear*
51 *Thrust washer*
52 *Reverse gear*
53 *Needle bearing*
54 *Reverse idler shaft*
55 *Seal*
56 *Bolt*
57 *Bolt lock*

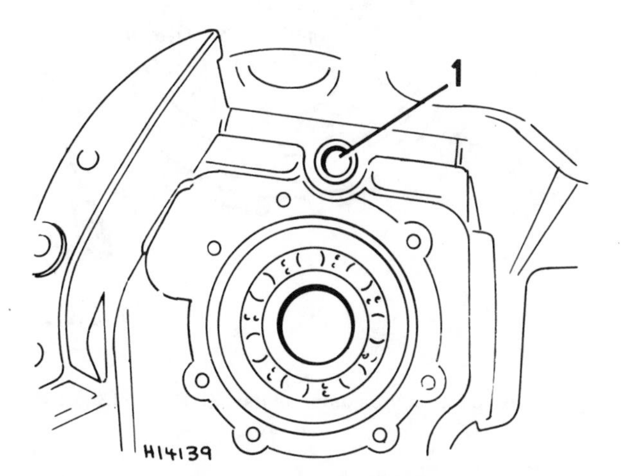

Fig. 6.96 Casing plug (1) – ZF S 5-16 (Sec 10)

Fig. 6.97 Detent spring caps (1, 2 and 3) – ZF S 5-16 (Sec 10)

13 Drive out the roll pins from the fork on 3rd/4th selector shaft – Fig. 6.98.
14 Using a small clamp, push back the reverse gear leaf spring (1) until the selector arm (2) is accessible – Fig. 6.99.
15 Swing the selector arm out of the groove in the selector shaft.
16 Pull out 3rd/4th selector shaft and then unscrew the bolt (1) – Fig. 6.100.
17 Remove reverse gear shaft, reverse gear, the needle bearing and thrust washer.
18 Remove the operating lever bolt.
19 Select reverse gear by moving the synchro sleeve.
20 Press the gear trains out of the rear casing.

Mainshaft – dismantling

21 Separate the input (clutch) shaft from the mainshaft. Take off the baulk ring and the needle roller bearing from the recess in the end of the input shaft.
22 Extract the mainshaft front synchro circlip.
23 Support 3rd gear and press the mainshaft out of the gear and 3rd/4th synchro.
24 Press the shaft out of the bearing sleeve, thrust washer and 2nd gear. Take off the needle bearing and baulk ring.
25 Extract the circlip and press the shaft from 1st gear. Remove the needle bearing.
26 Press the output shaft from 5th gear. Remove baulk ring and needle bearing.
27 Extract the circlip and press the output shaft from reverse gear and 5th/reverse synchro.

Inspection

28 Check the synchro units, as described in Section 7, but note that the stepped side of the sliding keys is towards the synchro-hub. On 1st/2nd synchro the wider band of the sleeve is towards the greater projection on the hub. On 5th/reverse synchro the wider band of the

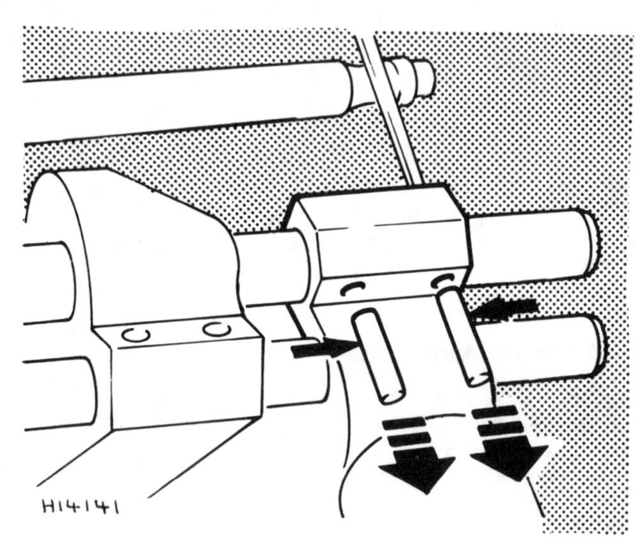

Fig. 6.98 Removing the 3rd/4th selector fork roll pins (arrowed) – ZF S 5-16 (Sec 10)

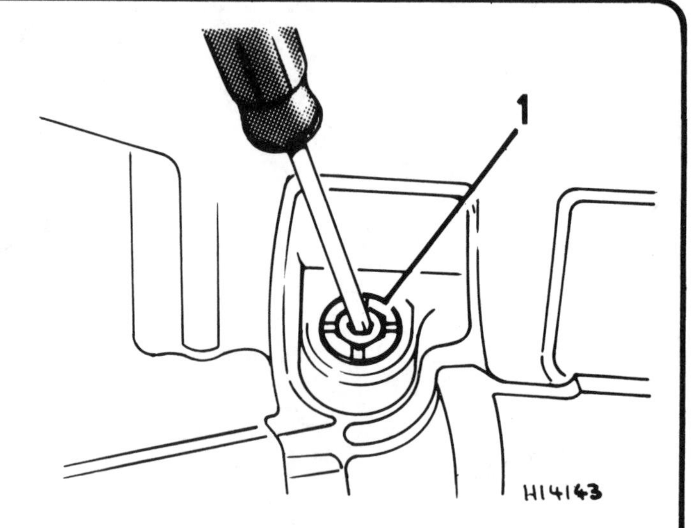

Fig. 6.100 Removing the socket-headed bolt (1) – ZF S 5-16 (Sec 10)

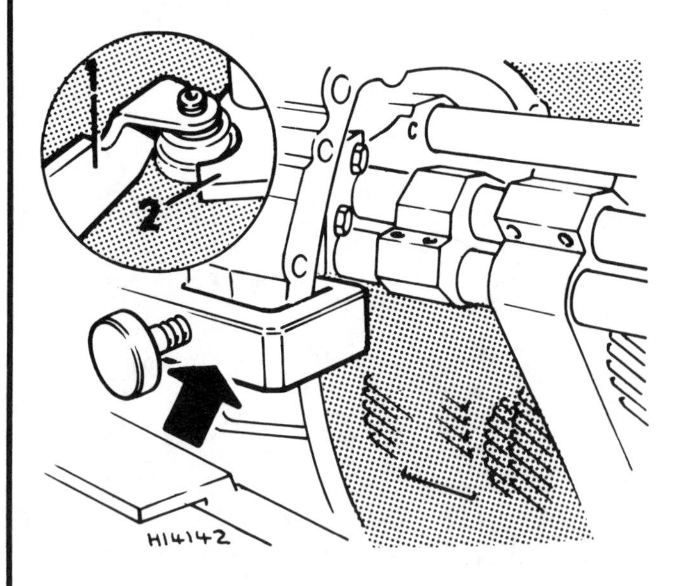

Fig. 6.99 Reverse gear leaf spring (1) and selector arm (2) – ZF S 5-16 (Sec 10)

Note use of small clamp (arrowed)

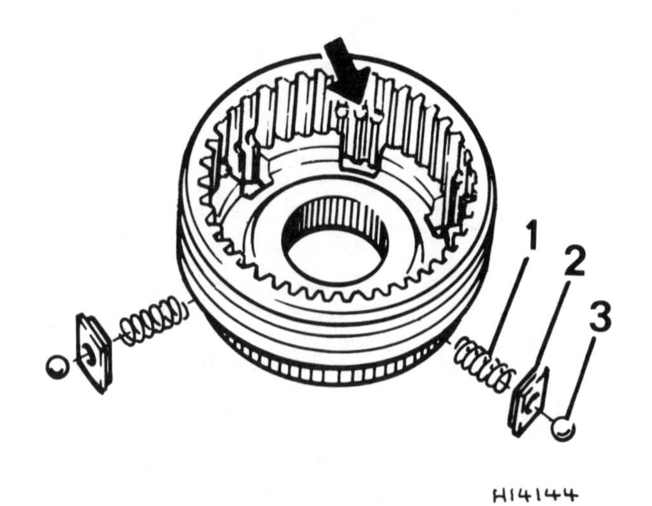

Fig. 6.101 Synchro components – ZF S 5-16 (Sec 10)

1 Spring
2 Sliding key
3 Ball

The flat teeth on the sleeve (arrowed) must align with the sliding keys

sleeve is towards the less projecting side of the hub.
29 Renew any gears which are chipped or worn. Renew all oil seals and gaskets.

Bearings – renewal

30 The bearings should be removed from, and refitted to, the casing sections after having heated the casing in boiling water. Always fill the lips of new oil seals with grease.
31 The ouput (clutch) shaft endfloat must be checked and adjusted in the following way, with the main casing in position. Using a depth gauge, measure distance (A) between the surface of the casing and the input shaft – Fig. 6.104.
32 Measure distance (A) from the surface of the casing to the bearing circlip – Fig. 6.105.
33 Measure distance (C) from the bearing outer track to the circlip – Fig. 6.106.
34 Subtract B from A and then subtract C from the difference. This will give the required endfloat. Select a suitable circlip to provide this.

Fig. 6.102 1st/2nd synchro – ZF S 5-16 (Sec 10)

The wider band of the sleeve (1) must be towards the greater projection on the hub (2)

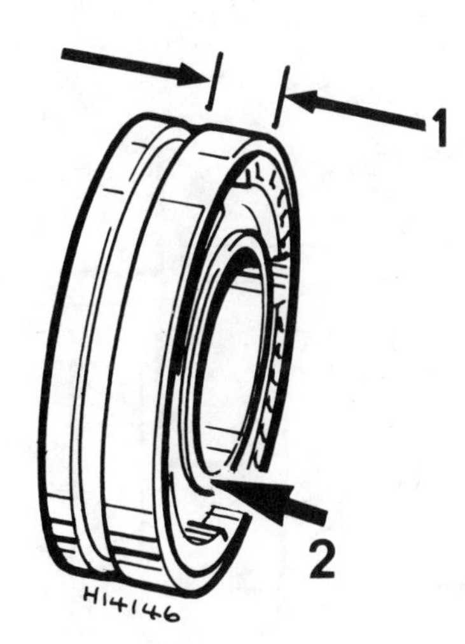

Fig. 6.103 5th/reverse synchro – ZF S 5-16 (Sec 10)

The wider band of the sleeve (1) must be towards the lesser projection on the hub (2)

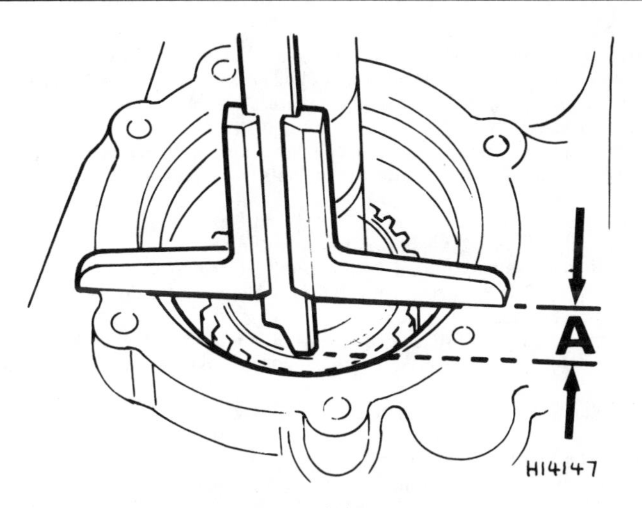

Fig. 6.104 Measuring distance (A) from the casing to the input shaft – ZF S 5-16 (Sec 10)

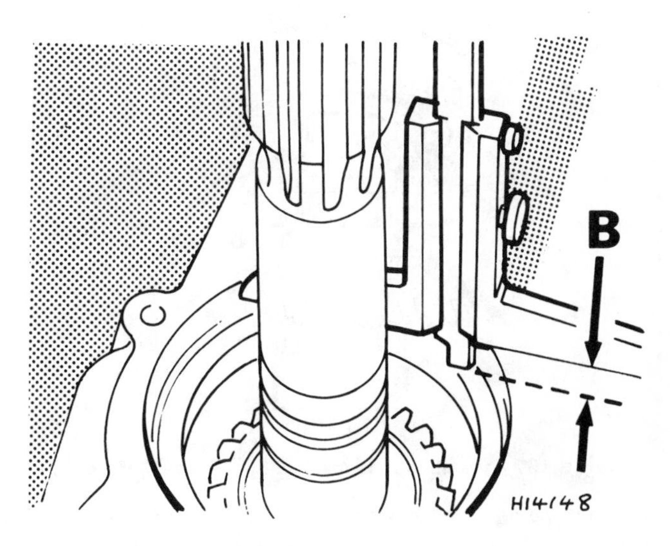

Fig. 6.105 Measuring distance (B) from the casing to the circlip – ZF S 5-16 (Sec 10)

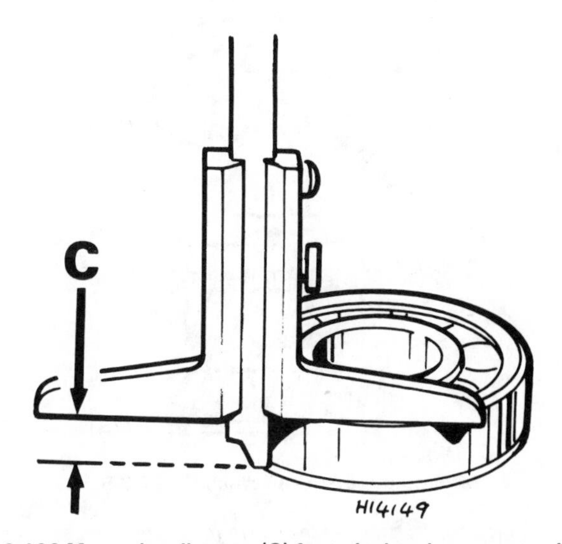

Fig. 6.106 Measuring distance (C) from the bearing outer track to the circlip – ZF S 5-16 (Sec 10)

Reassembly of mainshaft

35 Fit the needle bearing, reverse gear and, on models with reverse gear synchro, the baulk ring with six balls held in position with grease.
36 Fit the synchro so that the shorter hub projection is towards reverse gear.
37 Move the synchro sleeve in the direction of reverse gear and fit a circlip which is thick enough to eliminate all endfloat in the synchro-hub.
38 Fit the baulk ring, needle bearing and 5th gear.
39 Heat the thrust washer and fit it to the shaft.
40 Fit the needle bearing, 1st gear and baulk ring.
41 Fit 1st/2nd synchro with the less projecting side of the hub towards 1st gear.
42 Move the synchro sleeve in the direction of 1st gear and fit a circlip which is thick enough to eliminate all endfloat in the synchro-hub.
43 Fit the baulk ring, needle bearing and 2nd gear.
44 Heat the thrust washer and the bearing sleeve in boiling water and fit to the shaft.
45 Fit the needle bearing, 3rd gear and baulk ring.
46 Fit 3rd/4th synchro so that the longer projecting side of the synchro-hub faces 3rd gear. Fit the circlip.

Layshaft and input (clutch) shaft

47 The gears on the shafts are fitted during production and removal should not be attempted. Leave the removal and fitting of new gears to your dealer.
48 The 5th gear on the input shaft is an integral part of the shaft.

Gearbox – reassembly

49 Engage reverse gear.
50 Mesh together the input, output and layshafts with 1st/2nd and 5th/reverse selector shafts and the 3rd/4th fork and selector rod. Install simultaneously into the casing rear section. Make sure that the operating lever (1) is correctly located – Fig. 6.109. The leaf spring must be clamped.
51 Disengage reverse gear and then slide 3rd/4th selector shaft into place so that the detent grooves (1) are as shown – Fig. 6.110.
52 Drive in the 3rd/4th fork pins.

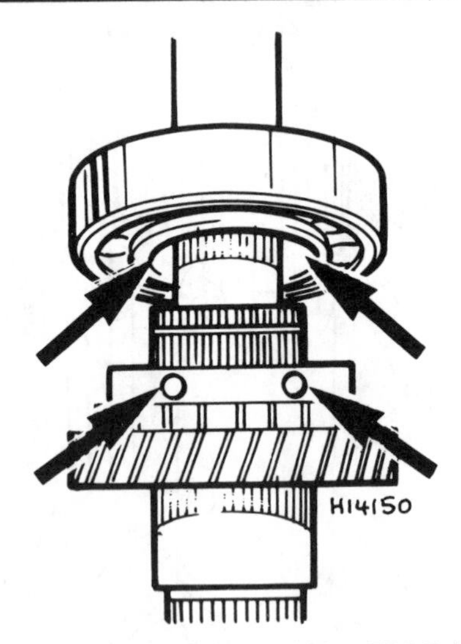

Fig. 6.107 Assembling the mainshaft – ZF S 5-16 (Sec 10)

Arrows show location of two of the six reverse gear synchro balls

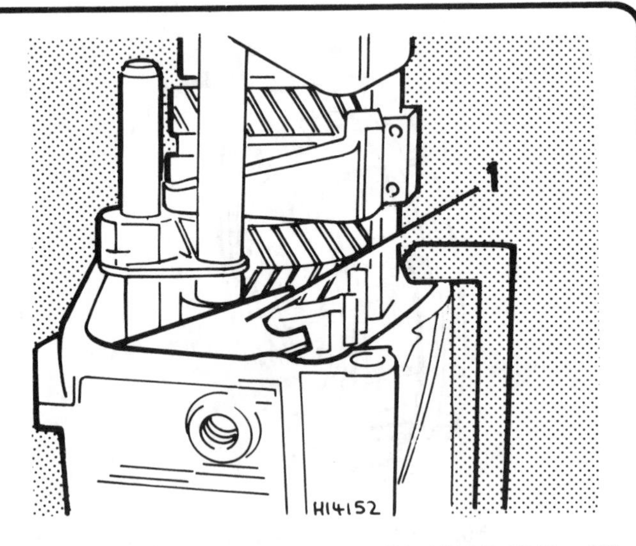

Fig. 6.109 Fitting the operating lever (1) – ZF S 5-16 (Sec 10)

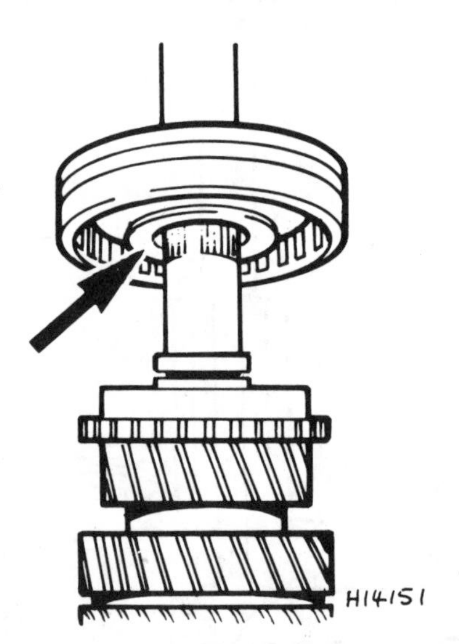

Fig. 6.108 Fitting the 3rd/4th synchro – ZF S 5-16 (Sec 10)

The greater projection on the hub (arrowed) must face 3rd gear

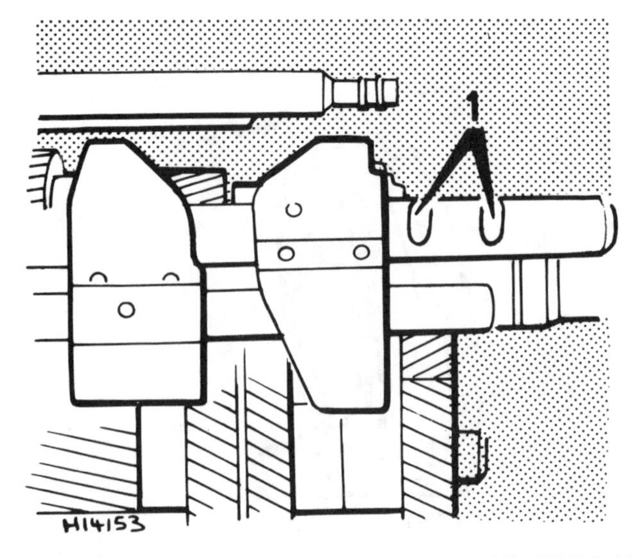

Fig. 6.110 3rd/4th selector shaft detent grooves (1) – ZF S 5-16 (Sec 10)

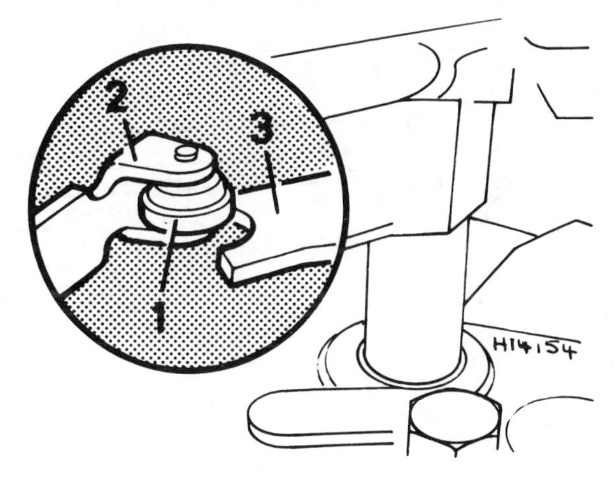

Fig. 6.111 The roller (1) on the spring (2) must engage in the selector arm (3) – ZF S 5-16 (Sec 10)

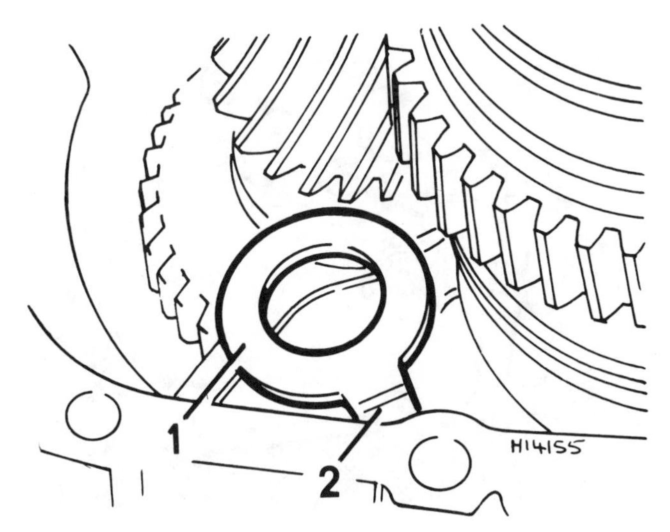

Fig. 6.112 Fit the thrust washer (1) into the casing with the angled tab (2) positioned thus – ZF S 5-16 (Sec 10)

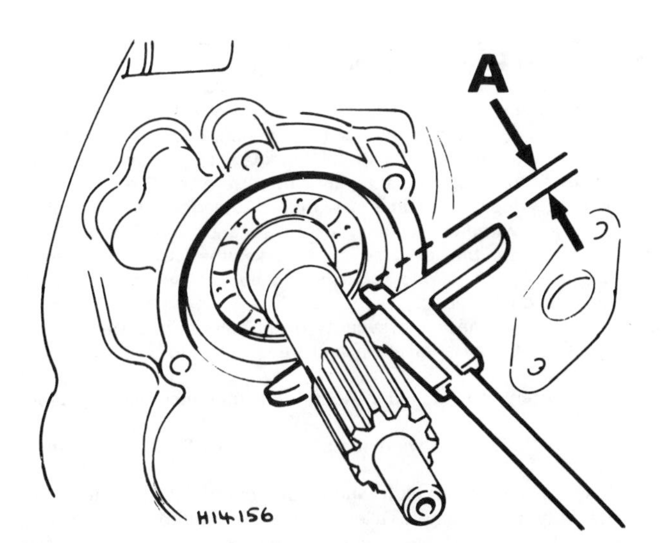

Fig. 6.113 Measuring distance (A): the input shaft bearing depth – ZF S 5-16 (Sec 10)

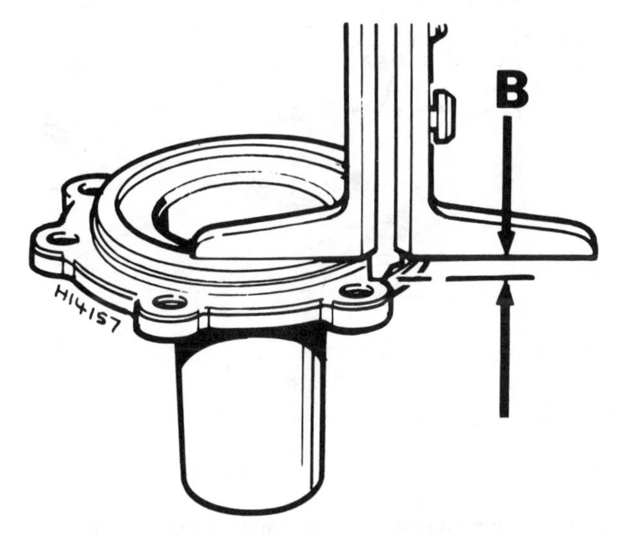

Fig. 6.114 Measuring distance (B): the height of the clutch guide sleeve shoulder – ZF S 5-16 (Sec 10)

New gasket in position

53 Release the leaf spring clamp and make sure that the roller (1) on the spring (2) engages in the selector arm (2) – Fig. 6.111.
54 Screw in the selector lever pivot bolt, making sure that the tip of the bolt engages positively.
55 Insert the three detent plungers and springs and fit new plugs.
56 Fit the thrust washer (1) into the casing so that the angled tab (2) is located as shown – Fig. 6.112.
57 Fit reverse idle gear, the two needle bearings and shaft. Make sure that the greater projecting boss on the gear is towards the casing.
58 Fit the lockbolt with a new seal.
59 Fit the output flange and nut, having applied thread locking fluid to the threads. Stake the nut lockplate.
60 Fit the magnet and a new end cap.
61 If not already fitted, install the casing bearing.
62 Fit the main casing to the rear section, tap in the dowel pins and screw in the bolts to the specified torque.
63 Warm the end of the casing and install the input shaft bearing.
64 Fit the bearing circlip and screw in the reverse lamp switch.
65 Measure the input shaft bearing recess (A) – Fig. 6.113.
66 Measure distance (B): the shoulder height of the clutch guide sleeve with the gasket in position – Fig. 6.114. Subtract B from A and the difference indicates the thickness of the spacer required.
67 Fit the clutch guide sleeve with a new oil seal and flange gasket.
68 Fill the gearbox with oil after the unit has been refitted to the car.

Part 2: AUTOMATIC TRANSMISSION

12 General description

1 This type of transmission may be optionally specified on certain models. It is fully automatic and incorporates a fluid filled torque converter and a planetary gear unit.
2 On Series 1 models, three forward and one reverse speed are provided with a kickdown facility for rapid acceleration during overtaking when an immediate change to a lower speed range is required.
3 On Series 2 models, four forward speeds are provided – also with the kickdown facility.
4 Due to the complexity of the automatic transmission unit, if performance is not up to standard, or overhaul is necessary, it is imperative that this be left to a main agent who will have the special equipment and knowledge for fault diagnosis and rectification.
5 The contents of the following Sections are therefore confined to supplying general information and any service information and instruction that can be used by the owner.

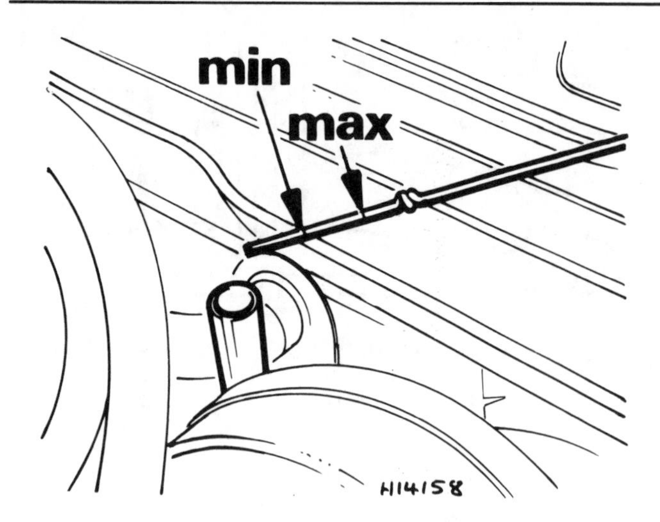

Fig. 6.115 Dipstick markings – automatic transmission (Sec 13)

Min to max = 0.3 litre (0.5 pt) approx

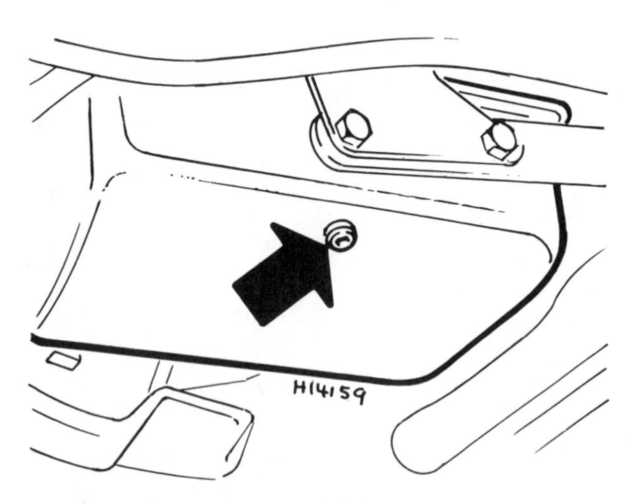

Fig. 6.116 Sump pan drain plug (arrowed) – automatic transmission (Sec 13)

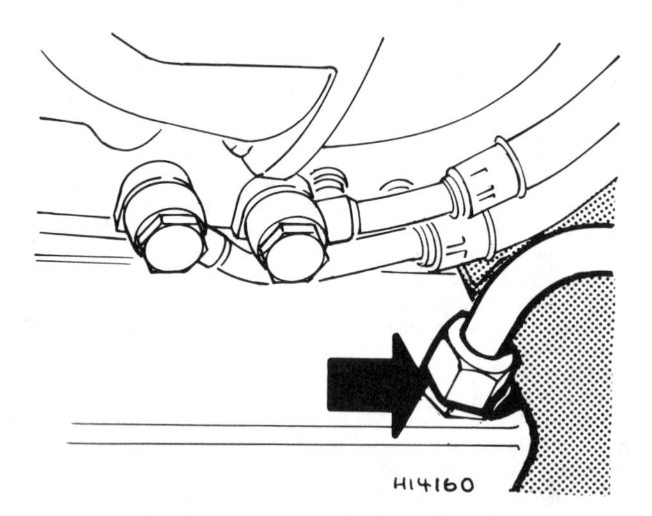

Fig. 6.117 Fluid level/dipstick guide tube bolt (arrowed) – automatic transmission (Sec 13)

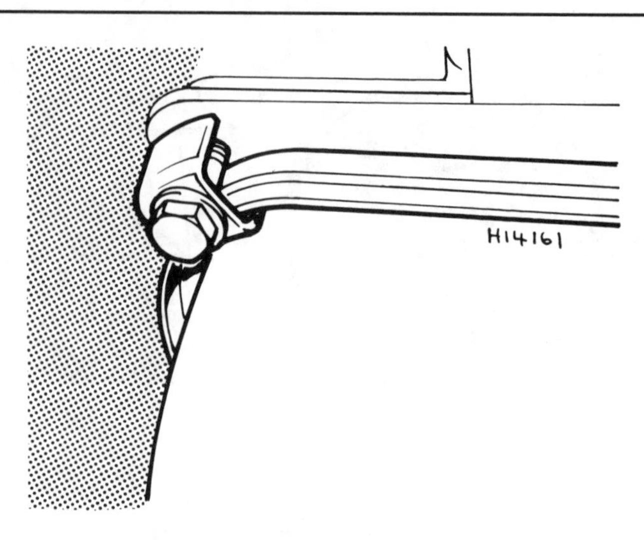

Fig. 6.118 Sump pan fixing clamps – automatic transmission (Sec 13)

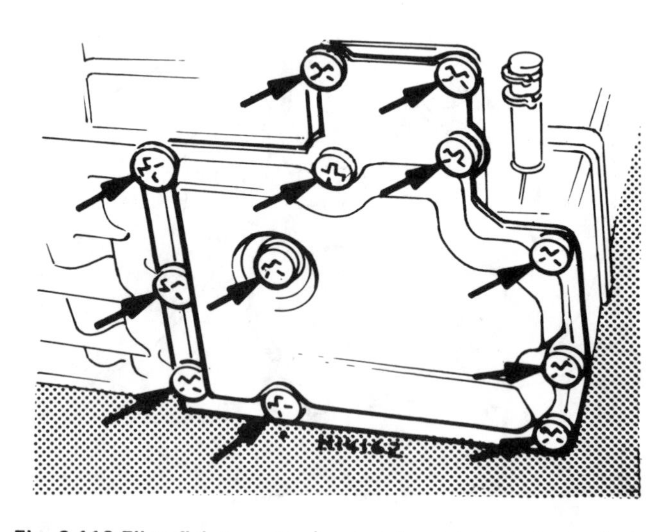

Fig. 6.119 Filter fixing screws (arrowed) – automatic transmission (Sec 13)

Later models have only three screws

13 Fluid level checking and fluid changing

1 The most important maintenance operation is the checking of the fluid level. To do this, run the car for a minimum of 5 miles (8 km), apply the handbrake and, with the engine idling, move the speed selector lever to all positions, finally setting it in the P detent.

2 With the engine still idling, withdraw the dipstick, wipe clean, reinsert it and withdraw it again for the second time. The fluid level should be between the 'low' and 'high' marks otherwise top it up to the correct level by pouring specified fluid down the combined filler/dipstick guide tube.

3 Occasionally, check the security of all bolts on the transmission unit and keep the exterior clean and free from mud or oil to prevent overheating.

4 At the intervals specified in Routine Maintenance the fluid should be changed.

5 Have the fluid hot, having completed at least five miles (8 km) on the road.

6 Unscrew the drain plug and allow the fluid to drain into a sufficiently large container. Take care that the fluid does not scald.

7 Provided the fluid has been renewed regularly, the fluid filter should not require cleaning. However, if fluid changing has been neglected, clean the filter in the following way.

8 Disconnect the fluid filler/dipstick guide tube from the transmission sump pan.
9 Unscrew the pan fixing clamps and remove the pan.
10 Extract the filter securing screws and remove the filter.
11 Clean the filter, or if it is clogged with resinous deposits, renew it complete.
12 Refit the filter, locate the magnet near to it and check that the sealing gasket is in good condition and clamp the sump pan in position (shorter clamp ends to pan).

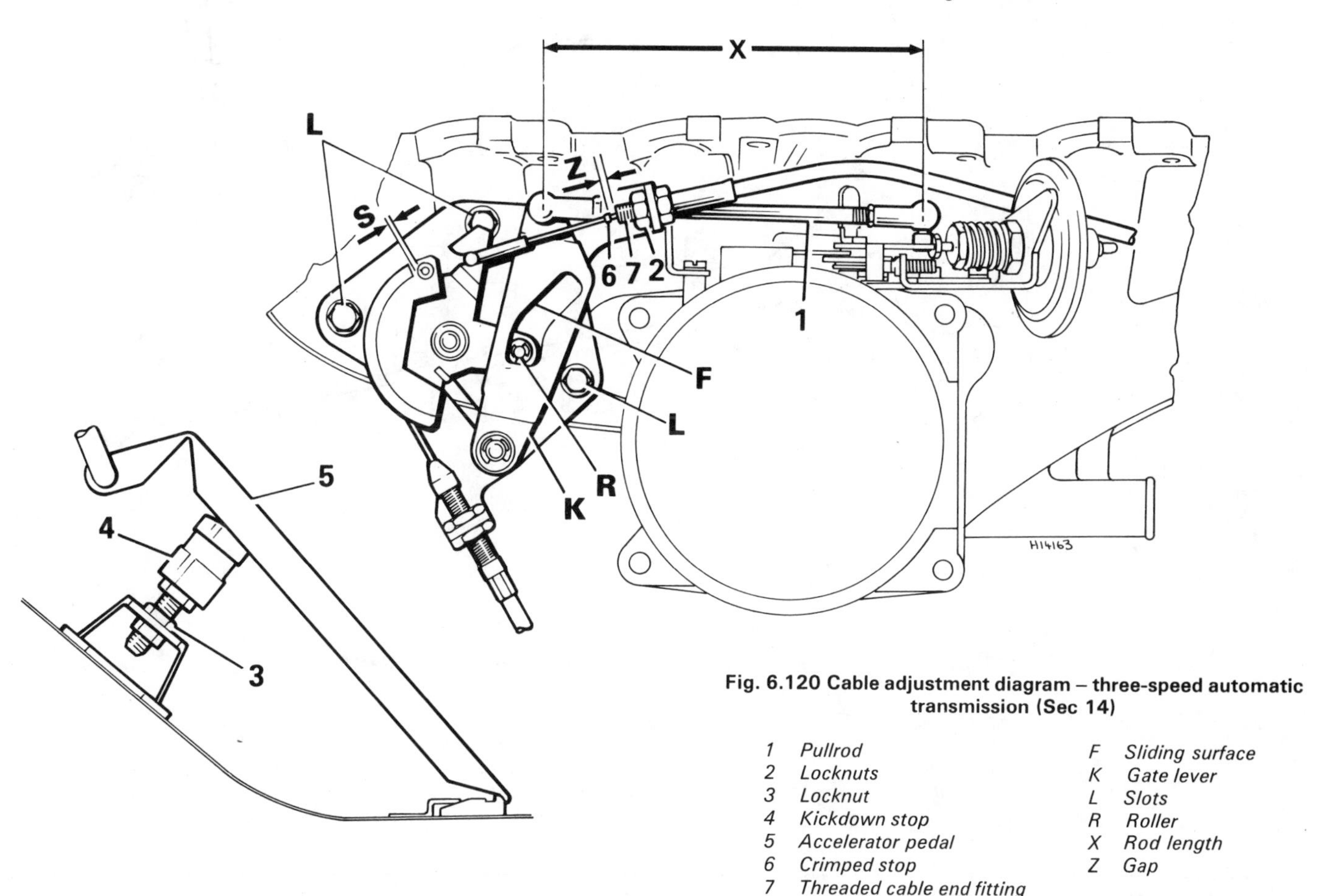

Fig. 6.120 Cable adjustment diagram – three-speed automatic transmission (Sec 14)

1 Pullrod
2 Locknuts
3 Locknut
4 Kickdown stop
5 Accelerator pedal
6 Crimped stop
7 Threaded cable end fitting
F Sliding surface
K Gate lever
L Slots
R Roller
X Rod length
Z Gap

13 Refit the drain plug and filler tube.
14 Fill the transmission with the specified type and quantity of fluid. Bring to operating temperature and top up, if necessary.

14 Throttle and kickdown cable – adjustment

Three-speed – early models

1 Release the locknut on the pullrod (1) – Fig. 6.120 – prise off one balljoint and turn it until the length of the rod (between balljoint sockets) is between 165.0 and 166.0 mm (6.496 and 6.536 in).
2 Now check that the roller (R) is in contact with the surface (F) of the gate lever (K). Any free travel evident before the throttle butterfly lever is moved must not exceed 1.5 mm (0.06 in). If necessary move the throttle mechanism in its slots (L).
3 With the engine idling, and the throttle butterfly lifter raised, turn the locknuts (2) as necessary to provide a clearance (Z) at the crimped stop (6) of between 0.25 and 0.75 mm (0.010 and 0.030 in).
4 Release the locknut (3) and screw the kickdown stop fully down. Depress the accelerator pedal until the kickdown detent position is felt. Hold the pedal in this position and unscrew the stop until it just touches the pedal.
5 Have an assistant depress the accelerator pedal fully (through the detent) and then measure the distance (Z) from the crimped stop (6) to the end of the threaded fitting (7). This should be at least 45.0 mm (1.77 in).

Three-speed – late models

6 The operations are similar to those described in earlier paragraphs, but where a throttle boost is fitted, this must be pulled out in order to be able to adjust the throttle cable.
7 The operations are as described for three-speed units, but the modified throttle cable arrangement should be noted.

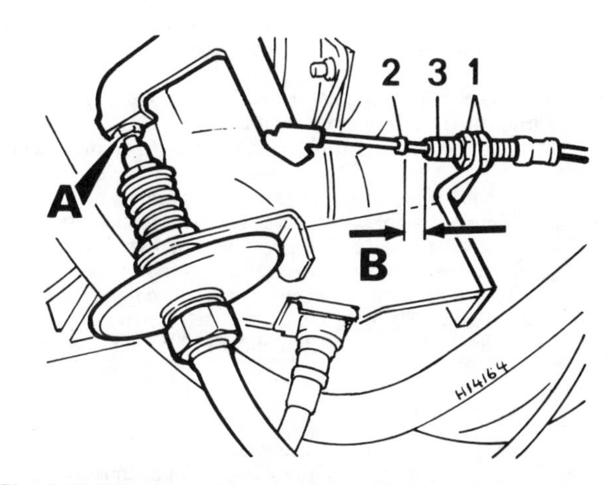

Fig. 6.121 Throttle cable – three-speed automatic transmission (late models) (Sec 14)

1 Locknuts
2 Crimped stop
3 Threaded end fitting
A Throttle boost
B Clearance

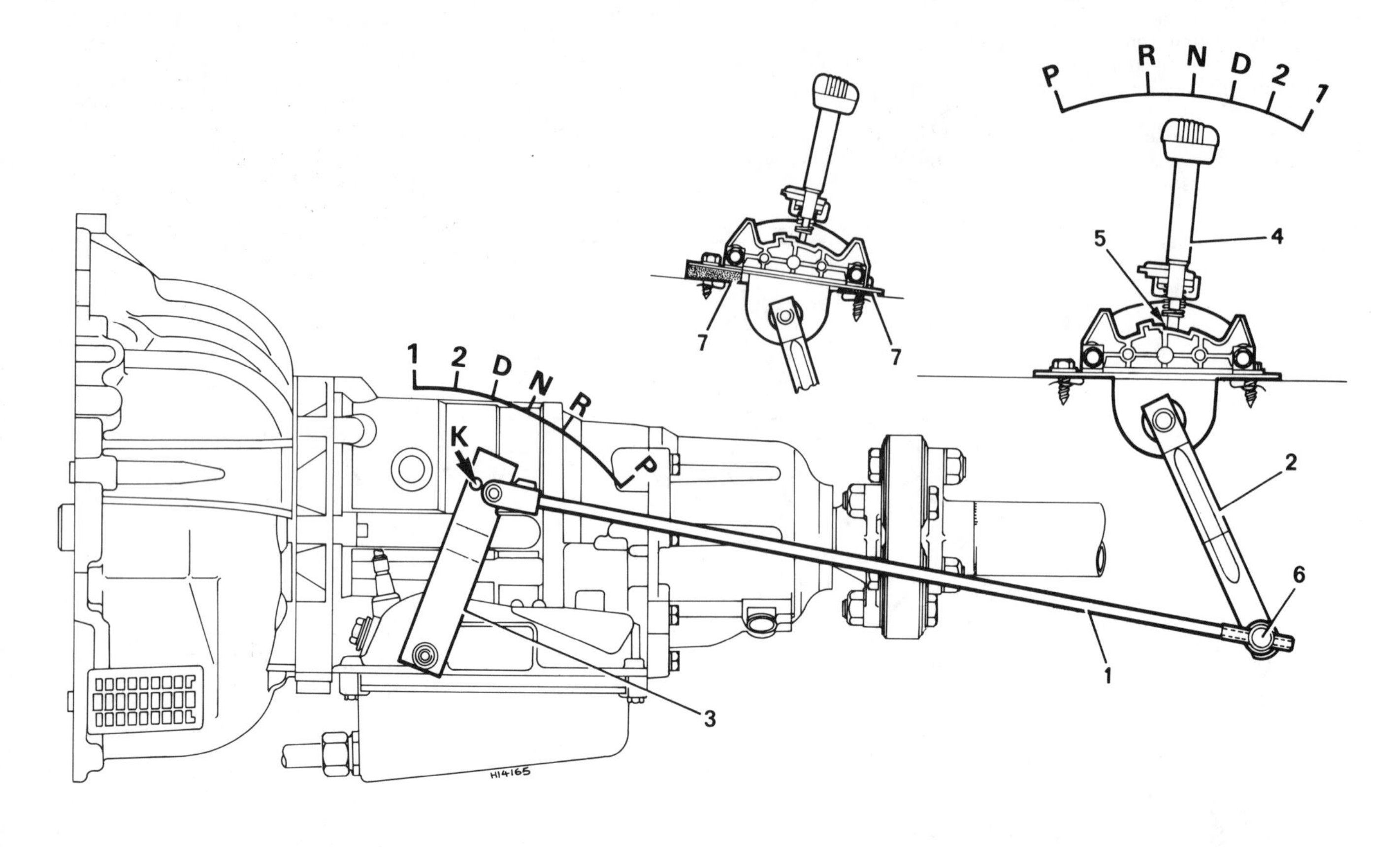

Fig. 6.122 Selector lever – three-speed automatic transmission (Sec 15)

1 Selector rod
2 Hand control lever lower section
3 Selector arm
4 Hand control lever
5 Stop
6 Trunnion pivot pin
7 Blocks
K Hole for use with air conditioned cars

15 Speed selector linkage – adjustment

Three-speed

1 Working under the car, disconnect the selector rod (1) from the base of the hand control lever (2) – Fig. 6.122.

2 Move the selector arm (3) on the side of the transmission until it clicks in the N detent. This position can be determined by counting three clicks from the fully forward position.

3 Push the hand control lever (4) against its stop (5) on the selector gate.

4 Adjust the length of the selector rod until the trunnion pivot pin (6) will just slide through the hole in the lever (2). Now reduce the length of the selector rod by screwing in the trunnion by between one and two turns. Connect the rod to the lever.

5 It is most important that the selector rod is only connected to arm (3) in the hole indicated. The hole (K) is only used if an air conditioner is fitted in order to compensate for the underlay blocks (7) which are used.

Four-speed

6 The operations are similar to those described for the three-speed unit, except that to set the lever on the side of the transmission, count four clicks from the fully forward position.

Inhibitor switch – all models

7 This is located at the base of the selector lever. If removed (one screw), make sure that the two pins on the switch engage in the holes in the selector gate when refitting.

16 Oil seals – renewal

1 Certain oil seals may be renewed without having to remove the transmission.

Output shaft oil seal

2 Disconnect the exhaust downpipes from the manifold and the transmission support.

3 Unbolt the propeller shaft centre bearing support and remove the bolts which connect the shaft flexible coupling to the output flange.

4 Compress the shaft and release it from the output shaft. Support the shaft by tying it to one side.

5 Lever out the nut locking cup and unscrew the nut. This can be held against rotation if P is selected.

6 Remove the output flange, using a puller if necessary.

7 Remove the defective oil seal using a small puller with outward facing claws.

8 Pack the lips of the new seal with grease and drive it squarely into position using a piece of tubing.

9 Fit the flange, screw on the nut to the specified torque and stake a new nut lock in position.

10 Reconnect the propeller shaft. When bolting up the centre bearing support, preload the bearing by pushing the support towards the front of the car – see Chapter 7, Section 2.

Speedometer driven gear O-ring

11 To renew the O-ring, extract the lockbolt and pull out the speedometer cable from the transmission.

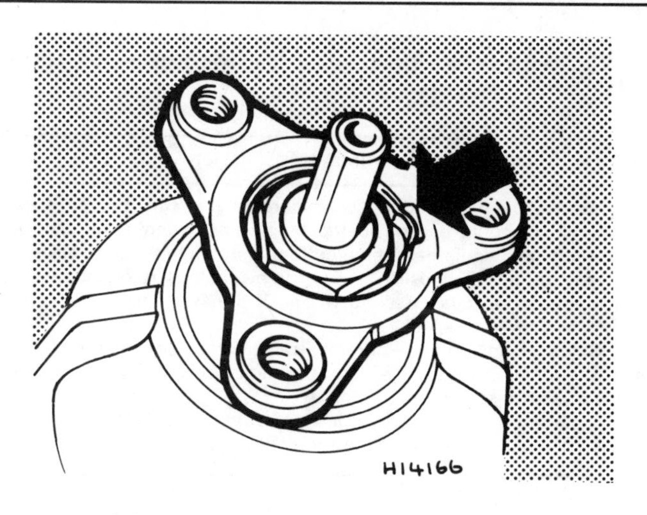

Fig. 6.123 Output shaft nut locking cup (arrowed) – automatic transmission (Sec 16)

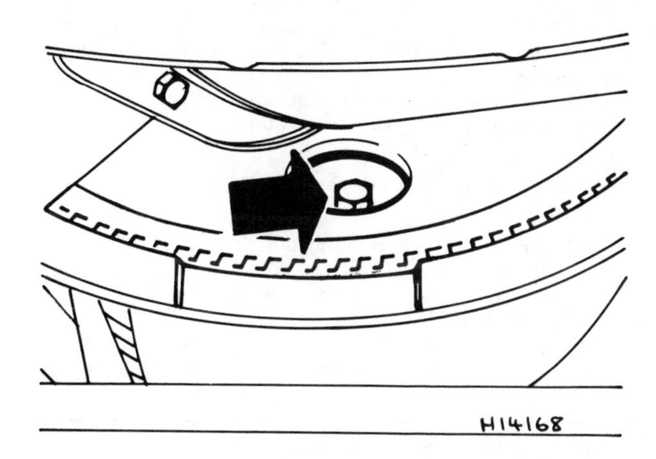

Fig. 6.125 Torque converter-to-driveplate bolt (arrowed) – automatic transmission (Sec 17)

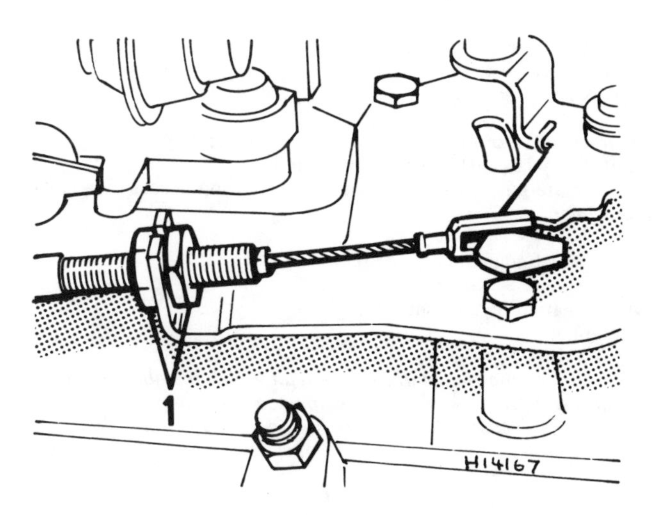

Fig. 6.124 Throttle cable locknuts (1) – automatic transmission (Sec 17)

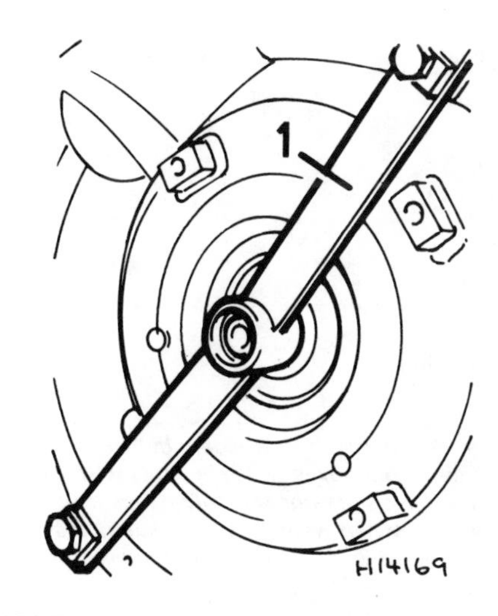

Fig. 6.126 Torque converter retaining strap (1) – automatic transmission (Sec 17)

12 Using an angled screwdriver, pull out the bush and renew the oil seal.
13 Refitting is a reversal of removal.

Selector arm shaft oil seal

14 Unscrew the nut and remove the lever from the side of the transmission.
15 Tap in one side of the oil seal to eject the opposite side. Lever out the seal and tap the new one into position.
16 Reconnect the selector arm.

17 Transmission – removal and refitting

1 Drain the transmission fluid, disconnect the battery.
2 Disconnect the exhaust downpipes from the manifold and release the pipe support from the transmission.
3 Disconnect the speedometer cable from the transmission.
4 Disconnect the propeller shaft from the transmission, as described in Section 16.
5 Disconnect the fluid filler pipe from the sump pan and the fluid cooler pipes from the transmission, also the selector rod.
6 Unbolt and remove the cover plate from the lower face of the torque converter housing.
7 Working within the engine compartment, release the locknuts (1) and disconnect the throttle cable – Fig. 6.124.
8 Take off the locknuts and pull the cable through the hole in the intake manifold.
9 Working under the car, remove the bolts which connect the torque converter to the driveplate. Turn the crankshaft while doing this to bring each bolt into view.
10 Support the rear end of the transmission and unbolt the mounting crossmember from the body.
11 Lower the transmission as far as it will go and unscrew the torque converter housing-to-engine bolts. A socket on a long extension will be required for this. Also unbolt and remove the oil filler/dipstick guide tube.
12 Prise out the protective grille and insert a prising bar between the torque converter and the driveplate.
13 Withdraw the transmission using a trolley jack and the help of assistants and, at the same time, prise the torque converter towards the rear so that it is kept in full engagement with the oil pump in the transmission. Retain the torque converter in this position by bolting a

length of flat bar to the bellhousing flange.

14 While the transmission is removed, examine the driveplate. Any cracks or distortion will indicate the need for a new one. Always fit new bolts when refitting the driveplate and apply thread locking fluid to their threads.

15 If the transmission is being exchanged, transfer the following components before parting with the old unit.

Selector arm
Rear crossmember and exhaust bracket
Cover plate

16 Refitting is a reversal of removal, but observe the following:

Blow through the fluid cooler pipes before connecting. If transmission failure has occurred, flush debris out of the cooler with two changes of ATF
Adjust the throttle cable and selector lever (Sections 14 and 15)
Preload the propeller shaft centre bearing, as described in Section 16
Tighten all bolts to the specified torque

17 Fill the transmission with the specified type and quantity of fresh fluid.

18 Fault diagnosis – automatic transmission

1 As has been mentioned elsewhere in this Chapter, no service repair work should be considered by anyone without the specialist knowledge and equipment required to undertake this work. This is also relevant to fault diagnosis. If a fault is evident, carry out the various adjustments previously described, and if the fault still exists consult the local garage or specialist.

2 Before removing the automatic transmission for repair, make sure that the repairer does not require to perform diagnostic tests with the transmission installed.

3 Most minor faults will be due to incorrect fluid level or incorrectly adjusted selector control or throttle cables.

11 Fault diagnosis – manual gearbox

Symptom	Reason(s)
Weak or ineffective synchromesh	Synchro baulk rings worn, split or damaged Synchromesh units worn, or damaged
Jumps out of gear	Gearchange mechanism worn Synchromesh units badly worn Selector fork badly worn
Excessive noise	Incorrect grade of oil in gearbox or oil level too low Gearteeth excessively worn or damaged Intermediate gear thrust washers worn allowing excessive endplay Worn bearings
Difficulty in engaging gears	Clutch pedal adjustment incorrect
Noise when cornering	Wheel bearing or driveshaft fault Differential fault

Note: *It is sometimes difficult to decide whether it is worthwhile removing and dismantling the gearbox for a fault which may be nothing more than a minor irritant. Gearboxes which howl, or where the synchromesh can be beaten by a quick gearchange, may continue to perform for a long time in this state. A worn gearbox usually needs a complete rebuild to eliminate noise because the various gears, if re-aligned on new bearings, will continue to howl when wearing surfaces are presented to each other. The decision to overhaul therefore, must be considered with regard to time and money available, relative to the degree of noise or malfunction that the driver has to suffer.*

Chapter 7 Propeller shaft, driveshafts, hubs, roadwheels and tyres

For modifications, and information applicable to later models, see Supplement at end of manual

Contents

Specifications

Propeller shaft

Type	Two section, tubular with flexible joint at front, needle bearing universal joints and flexible mounted centre bearing
Front coupling type	Giubo coupling or Jurid disc
Centre bearing preload ('A' in Fig. 7.3):	
Series 1	2 mm (0.08 in)
Series 2, pre-1985	2 to 4 mm (0.08 to 0.16 in)
Series 2, 1985 on	4 to 6 mm (0.16 to 0.24 in)

Front hub bearings

Type:	
Series 1	Double taper roller
Series 2	Double ball

Rear hub bearings

Type	Double ball

Roadwheels

Size (depending upon model):	
Pressed steel	5½J x 13 or 5½J x 14
Light alloy	5½J x 13, 6J x 13 or 6J x 14

Tyres

Sizes	185/70 HR 13, 195/60 HR 14, 195/60 SR 14, 175/70 SR 14 or 175/70 HR 14

Pressures (cold) – kgf/cm² (lbf/in²):	Front	Rear
185/70 HR 13:		
Normal load	2.0 (28)	2.0 (28)
Fully loaded	2.2 (31)	2.4 (34)
195/60 HR 14:		
Normal load	2.0 (28)	2.2 (31)
Fully loaded	2.3 (33)	2.6 (37)
195/60 SR 14:		
Normal load	2.0 (28)	2.2 (31)
Fully loaded	2.3 (33)	2.6 (37)
175/70 SR 14:		
Normal load	2.0 (28)	2.2 (31)
Fully loaded	2.3 (33)	2.6 (37)
175/70 HR 14:		
Normal load	2.1 (30)	2.3 (33)
Fully loaded	2.4 (34)	2.7 (38)

Torque wrench settings

	Nm	lbf ft
Propeller shaft flexible joint bolts:		
Giubo	70	52
Jurid	48	35
Propeller shaft sleeve	24	18
Propeller shaft centre bearing to body	24	18
Driveshaft to hub flange screws (Series 1)	34	25
Driveshaft to final drive output flange screws	34	25
Rear hub nut:		
Series 1	400	295
Series 2	450	332
Front hub nut (Series 2)	280	207
Caliper bolts:		
Series 1	65	48
Series 2	120	89
Roadwheel bolts	110	81
Roadwheel nuts	85	63

1 Description and maintenance

1 The propeller shaft is of two-piece tubular type having a flexible coupling at the front end and needle roller bearings at the centre and rear end.
2 The front hub bearings are of double taper roller type, adjustable for preload (Series 1) or double ball type (Series 2).
3 The rear driveshafts incorporate double homokinetic universal joints with axle hubs of double ball-bearing type.
4 The propeller shaft joints are of staked type and, in the event of wear occurring, they should either be repaired and balanced by a specialist firm or the shaft renewed.
5 The rear driveshaft gaiters should be inspected and checked for splits and leaks at regular intervals. Renewal of the gaiter is the limit of repair, wear can only be rectified by fitting a new shaft or renewing the one removable joint assembly.
6 The front hub bearing should be adjusted and lubricated at the intervals specified in Routine Maintenance.

2 Propeller shaft – removal and refitting

Series 1

1 Disconnect the forward end of the front silencer and tie it aside.
2 Fit a large compression clip around the shaft front flexible coupling (doughnut) and compress the coupling.
3 Unscrew the four bolts which have their heads furthest from the gearbox or automatic transmission.
4 Disconnect the rear end of the shaft from the final drive. Jack up one rear wheel so that the shaft can be turned to bring the bolts into view.

2.12 Three-legged type output flange

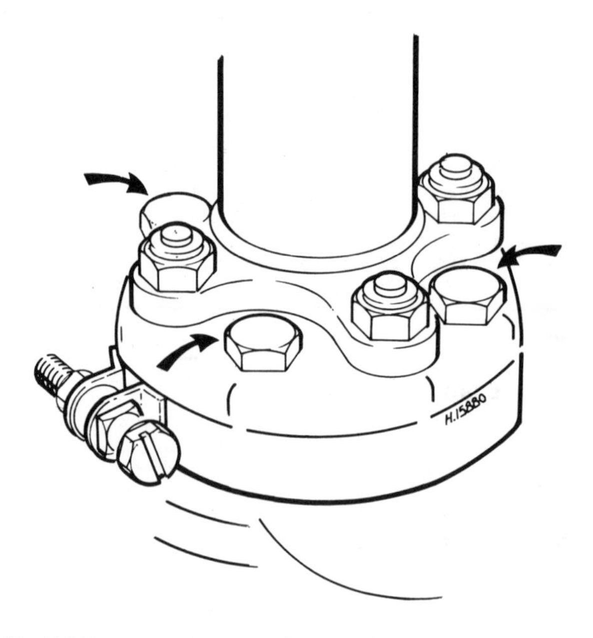

Fig. 7.1 Front coupling bolts (arrowed) and compression clip (Sec 2)

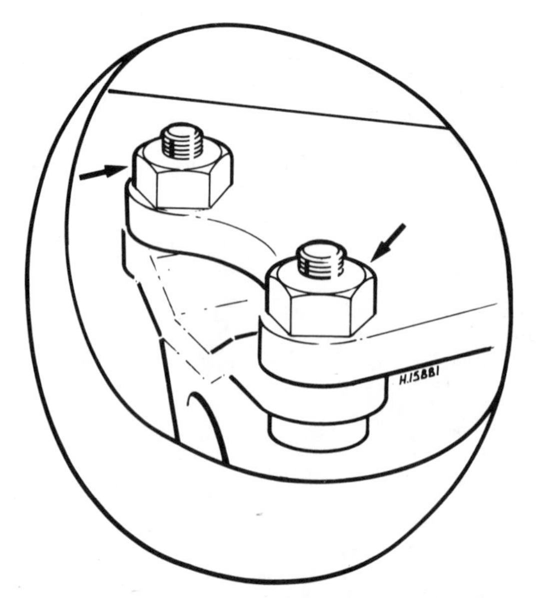

Fig. 7.2 Propeller shaft-to-final drive bolts – arrowed (Sec 2)

Viewed through crossmember

5 Unbolt and detach the centre bearing support strut from the body. Remove the propeller shaft by pulling it downwards.
6 Refitting is a reversal of removal, but observe the following.

Use new self-locking nuts on the front coupling bolts
Preload the centre bearing strut towards the front of the car (see Fig. 7.3)
Apply grease around the front sliding sleeve
Tighten all nuts/bolts to the specified torque

7 If a new propeller shaft is being fitted, its alignment at the centre bearing must be checked using the BMW special gauge 26 1 000 or something to act as a substitute. In order to maintain correct alignment, incorporate shims under the ends of the centre mounting support. The shaft must be set straight.

Fig. 7.3 Propeller shaft centre bearing setting (Sec 2)

Move the bearing strut forwards through distance 'A' (see Specifications) before tightening the nuts

Series 2

8 The operations are similar to those just described for Series 1 models, except that the rear exhaust silencer should also be dismounted and moved aside. Remove the exhaust heat shield and, on models with automatic transmission, support the rear of the transmission and unbolt the rear mounting crossmember to give access to the shaft coupling nuts.
9 Slacken the threaded sleeve at the centre bearing a few turns before removing the propeller shaft, and tighten it again after refitting.
10 On some later models, a vibration damper is fitted at the gearbox end of the shaft. After unbolting the transmission output flange from the shaft coupling, rotate the damper and pull it rearwards so that it can be removed with the shaft.
11 When refitting, whenever possible tighten coupling nuts and bolts where they bear on a metal flange, not where they bear on a rubber coupling. This will avoid distorting the coupling.

All models

12 On later models, a three-legged output flange is used, instead of the earlier four-legged type (photo).

3 Propeller shaft flexible coupling – renewal

1 Remove the propeller shaft, as described in Section 2.
2 Unbolt the old coupling and fit the new one (with a compression clamp), using new self-locking nuts.
3 On models which have automatic transmission, fit the flexible coupling so that the arrows on the edge align with the appropriate flange arms.
4 Refit the propeller shaft and tighten all nuts/bolts to the specified torque, before removing the clamp.

4 Propeller shaft centre bearing – renewal

Series 1

1 Remove the propeller shaft, as described in Section 2.
2 Mark the relative alignment of the two sections of the propeller shaft and joint yokes.

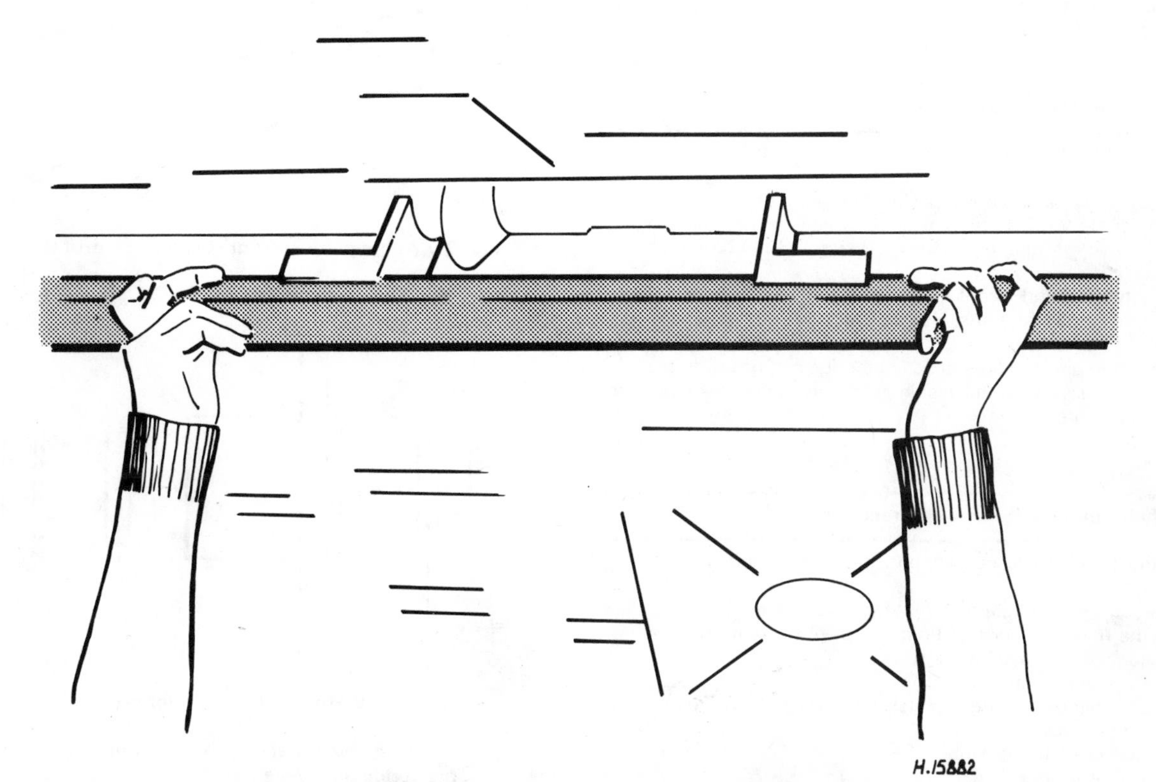

Fig. 7.4 Checking the shaft alignment using the BMW special tool (Sec 2)

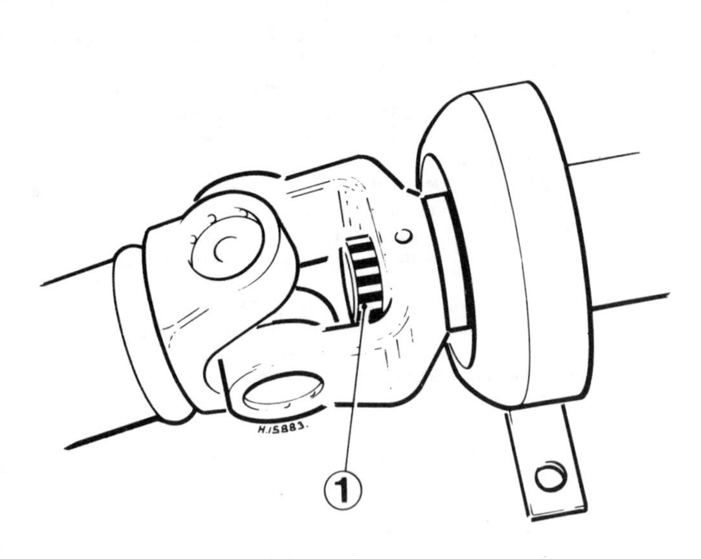

Fig. 7.5 Propeller shaft centre connecting nut (1) (Sec 4)

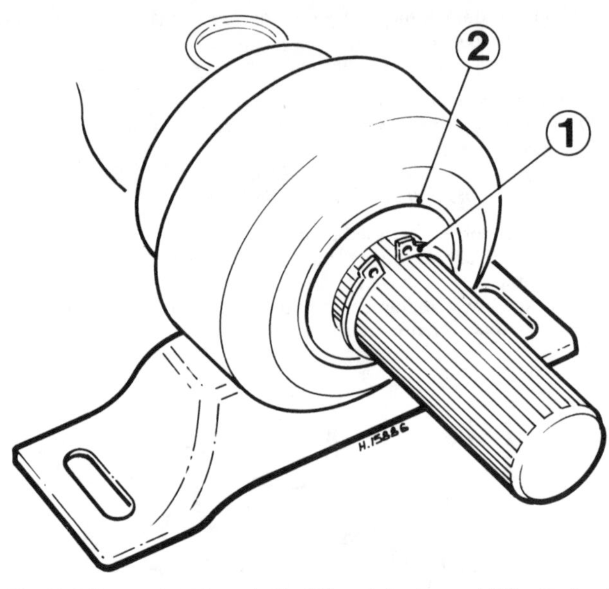

Fig. 7.6 Centre bearing circlip (1) and dust guard (2) – Series 2 (Sec 4)

3 Unscrew the connecting nut (1) – Fig. 7.5.
4 Using a suitable puller, pull off the centre bearing.
5 Refitting is a reversal of removal, apply thread locking fluid to the centre nut threads and tighten all nuts/bolts to the specified torque.

Series 2

6 With the propeller shaft removed, unscrew the threaded sleeve at the centre bearing.
7 Mark the relative alignment of the two sections of the propeller shaft and then separate them.
8 Extract the circlip (1) and remove the dust guard (2) – Fig. 7.6.
9 Using a suitable extractor, draw off the centre mounting with the grooved ball-bearing.
10 Reassembly is a reversal of dismantling. Make sure that the dust guard is flush with the centre mounting, all marks are aligned, the splines greased and the sleeve tightened to the specified torque.

5 Front hub bearings (Series 1) – adjustment

1 Raise the roadwheel and remove it.
2 Tap or lever off the grease cap.
3 Extract the split pin from the castellated nut and unscrew it.
4 Using a torque wrench, tighten the nut, while at the same time turning the hub, to a torque of between 30 and 33 Nm (22 and 24 lbf ft).
5 Unscrew the nut and turn it finger tight until all bearing play just disappears. Check that the thrust washer is just free to float and is not trapped.
6 Fit a new split pin, bend the ends around the nut, **not** over its end, and fit the grease cap, with the seal in good condition and containing 20 g (0.71 oz) of grease.
7 Fit the roadwheel.

6 Front hub bearings (Series 1) – renewal

1 Raise the front of the car, support it securely, and remove the roadwheel.
2 Disconnect the angle plate at the front suspension strut.
3 Unbolt the brake caliper and tie it up out of the way. There is no need to disconnect the hydraulic line.
4 Remove the hub grease cap.
5 Extract the split pin from the castellated nut, unscrew the nut and remove the thrust washer.
6 Pull off the disc/hub assembly.
7 Prise out the oil seal.
8 Take out the roller races.

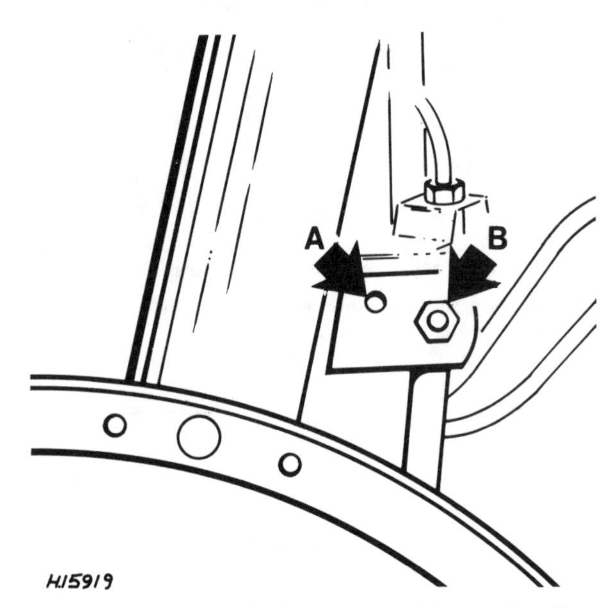

Fig. 7.7 Angle plate at front suspension strut (Sec 6)

A Engagement hole B Securing nut

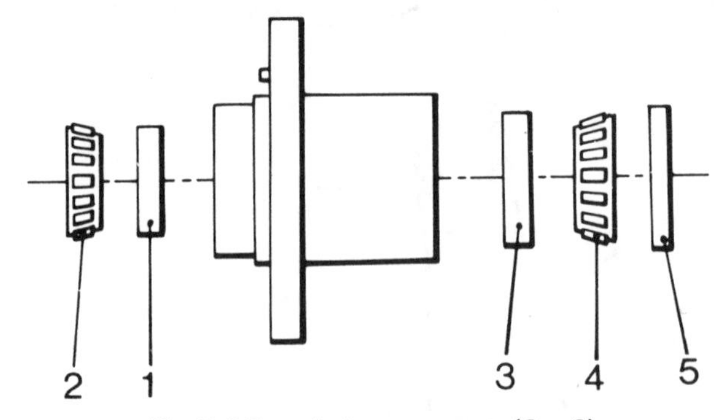

Fig. 7.8 Front hub components (Sec 6)

1 Bearing outer track
2 Bearing roller race
3 Bearing outer track
4 Bearing roller race
5 Oil seal

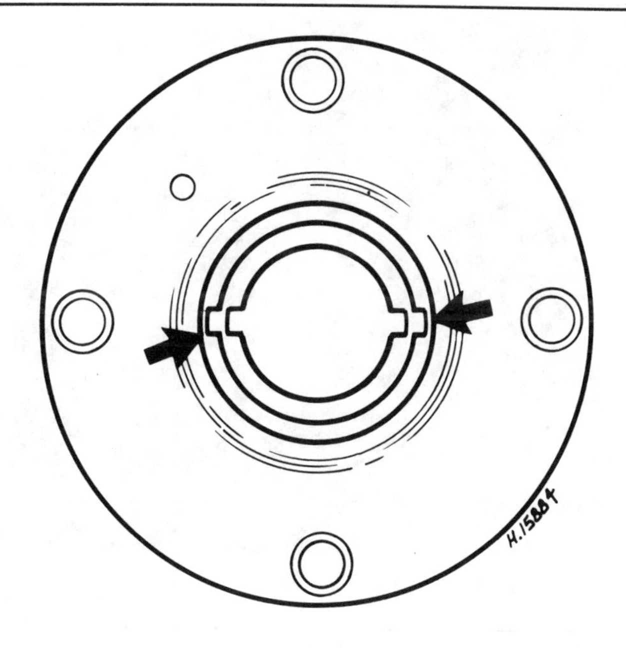

Fig. 7.9 Bearing outer track removal cut-outs – arrowed (Sec 6)

9 Drive the bearing tracks from the hub using the cut-outs provided.
10 Wipe away all old grease, drive in the new bearing outer tracks, fill the hub with 50 g (1.86 oz) of fresh grease, also grease the lips of the new oil seal, and locate the bearing inner race and the seal.
11 Offer up the hub/disc, locate the outer roller race, fit the thrust washer and nut.
12 Adjust the bearings, as described in Section 5.
13 Refit the brake caliper and the angle plate, making sure that the recess on the holder locates in the hole in the bracket.
14 On cars built up to 1980, make sure that the seal between the disc shield and the stub axle carrier is in good condition.

7 Front hub bearings (Series 2) – renewal

When undoing and tightening the hub nut it will be necessary to find a suitable method of securing the hub against rotation.

1 Raise the front of the car, support it securely and remove the roadwheel.
2 Unbolt the brake caliper and tie it up out of the way.
3 Prise off the hub grease cap.
4 Extract the socket-headed screw from the hub flange and take off the brake disc.
5 Relieve the staked hub nut and unscrew it.
6 Pull off the hub/bearing assembly with a suitable puller.
7 Remove the dust guard if the inboard bearing track stays on the stub axle and pull off the track with an extractor.
8 Renew the dust guard if destroyed.
9 Remove the bearing from the hub and press in the new one.
10 Fit the hub/bearing assembly which will have to be drawn onto the stub axle using the special tool 31-2-120 or by making up a suitably threaded sleeve to screw onto the axleshaft.
11 Fit a new nut and tighten to the specified torque. Stake the nut.
12 Fit the brake disc, caliper, grease cap and roadwheel.

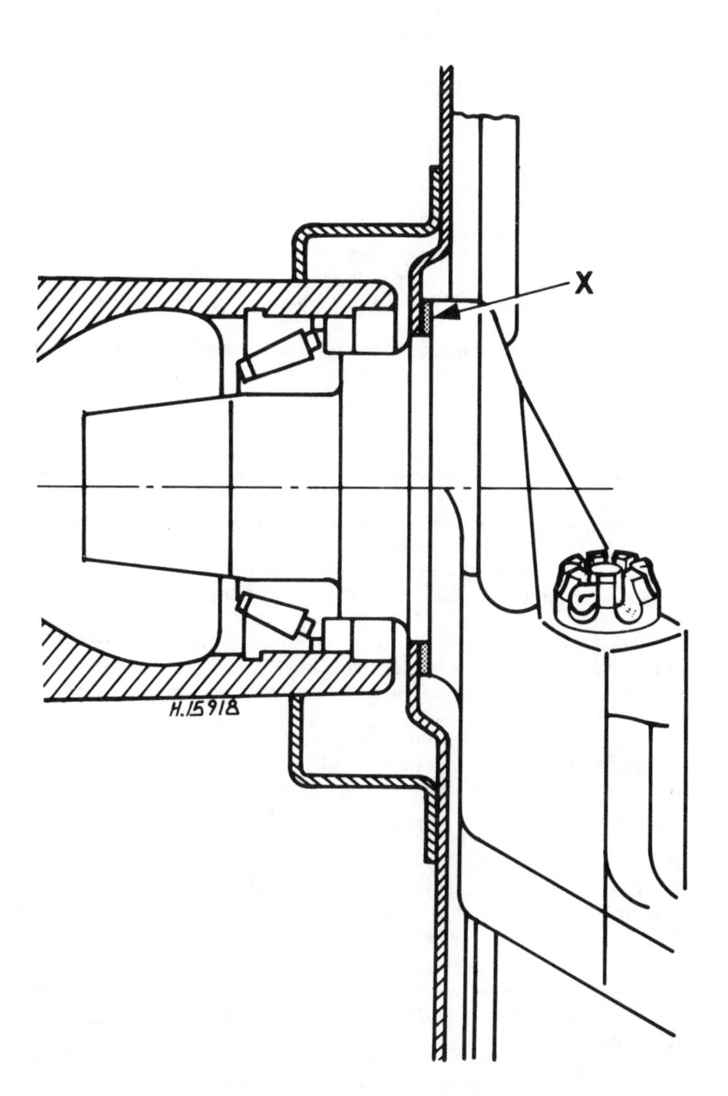

Fig. 7.10 Disc shield seal (X) (Sec 6)

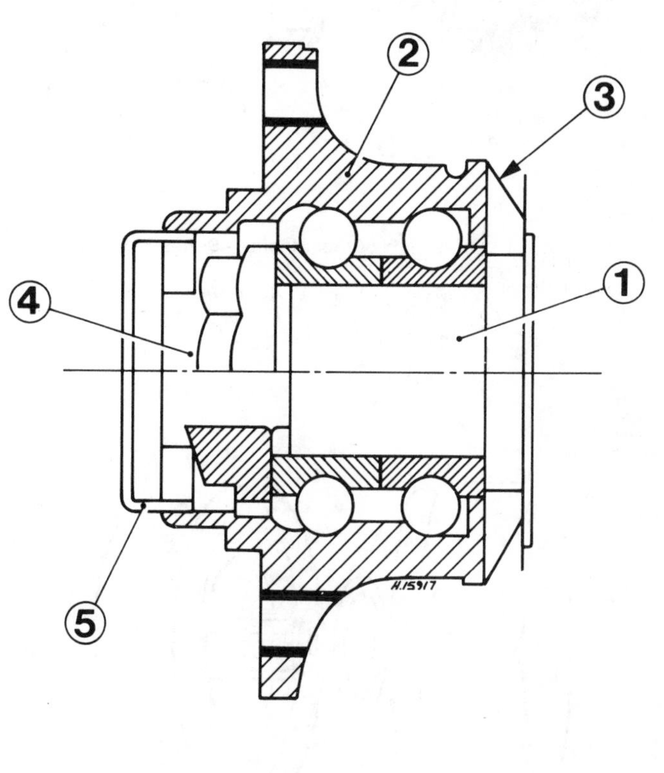

Fig. 7.11 Sectional view of front hub bearings – Series 2 (Sec 7)

1 *Stub axle*
2 *Hub*
3 *Disc shield*
4 *Nut*
5 *Grease cap*

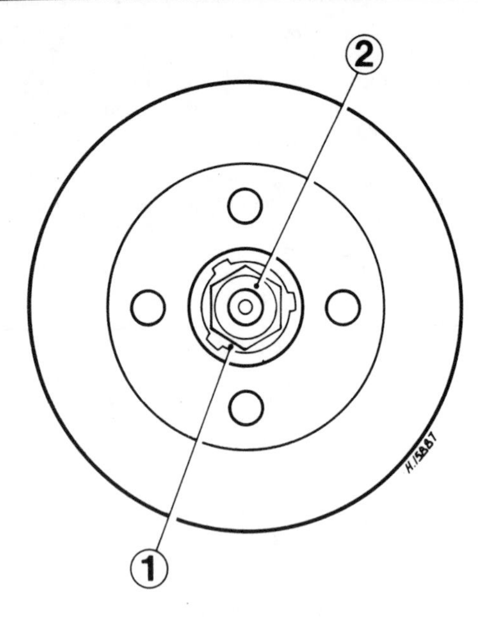

Fig. 7.12 Rear driveshaft lockplate (1) and nut (2) – Series 2 (Sec 8)

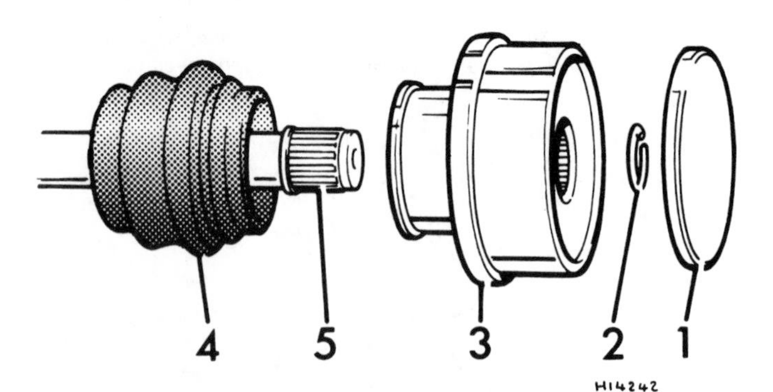

Fig. 7.13 Driveshaft outboard joint – Series 1 (Sec 9)

1 Sealing cover
2 Circlip
3 CV joint
4 Gaiter
5 Driveshaft

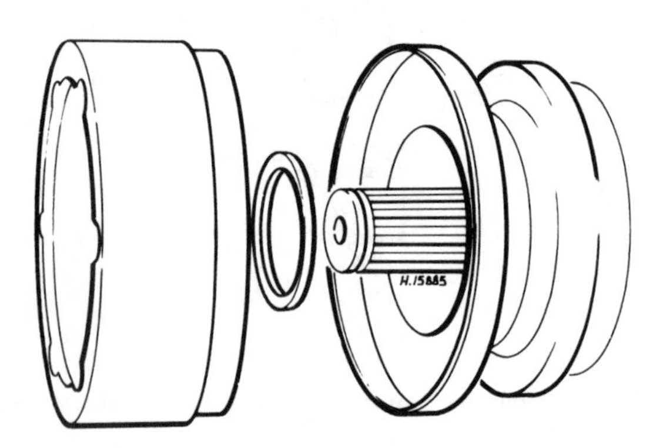

Fig. 7.14 Driveshaft clamp ring (1) – Series 1 (Sec 9)

8.1 Unscrewing a driveshaft flange screw

8 Rear driveshaft – removal and refitting

Series 1

1 Unscrew the socket-headed screws which hold the driveshaft flanges to the wheel hub and final drive flanges (photo).
2 Lift away the shaft.
3 When refitting, tighten the socket-headed screws to the specified torque.

Series 2

4 Disconnect the driveshaft from the final drive, as described for Series 1 models.
5 Remove the lockplate (1) and unscrew the nut (Fig. 7.12).
6 Using a suitable extractor, press the shaft out of the rear hub.
7 When connecting the shaft to the hub, draw it into position using the special tool (33 2 110) or make up a suitably threaded sleeve to do the job.
8 Tighten the nut and the inboard flange screws to the specified torque and fit and stake a new nut lockplate.

9 Rear driveshaft gaiter – renewal

Series 1

1 With the driveshaft removed (Section 8), take off the sealing cover (1) – Fig. 7.13 – from the outboard end.
2 Extract the circlip (2) and release the gaiter clip.
3 Press the driveshaft out of the CV joint (3) and remove the gaiter (4).
4 Reassembly is a reversal of removal, but note that the convex side of the clamp ring (1) is towards the joint (Fig. 7.14).
5 Fill the joint with the sachet of grease supplied with the repair kit (80 g/2.8 oz).
6 Fit the gaiter and tighten the clips.
7 The gaiter from the opposite end of the shaft is renewable by sliding it down and off the shaft once the outboard joint has been removed.

Series 2

8 The operations are similar to those described for Series 1, except that the removable joint is at the inboard end of the shaft.
9 The CV joint is renewable, as a repair kit, on certain models.

10 Rear stub axle and drive flange (Series 1) – removal and refitting

1 Chock the front wheels. Raise the rear wheel and remove it.
2 Extract the socket-headed screw and remove the brake drum.

3 Remove the hub grease cap and the split pin, and unscrew the nut.
4 Using a suitable puller, draw off the drive flange.
5 Disconnect the outboard end of the driveshaft, as described in Section 8.
6 Drive out the stub axle shaft using a plastic or copper-faced hammer.
7 Refitting is a reversal of removal, tighten all nuts and screws to the specified torque and insert a new spit pin.

11 Rear hub bearings (Series 1) – renewal

1 Remove the stub axle shaft as previously described (Section 10).
2 Using a suitable drift, drive out the oil seal (1) and bearing (2) – Fig. 7.15.
3 Remove the shim (3) and spacer (4).
4 If new bearings are being installed, measure the length of the spacer sleeve (A).
5 Fit the inner bearing and then use a depth gauge to measure dimension (B) from the face of the bearing outer track in the hub to the outer track of the inner ball-bearing (Fig. 7.16). Calculate the shim thickness required (C) from the following formula:

(A – B) – 0.1 mm (0.004 in) clearance = C

6 Fill the hub interior with 35 g (1.2 oz) of grease, and fit the stub axle shaft, as described in Section 11.

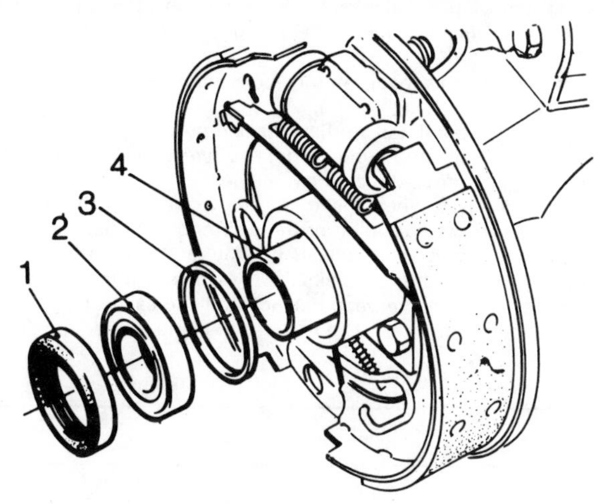

Fig. 7.15 Rear hub components – Series 1 (Sec 11)

1 Oil seal
2 Bearing
3 Shim
4 Spacer sleeve

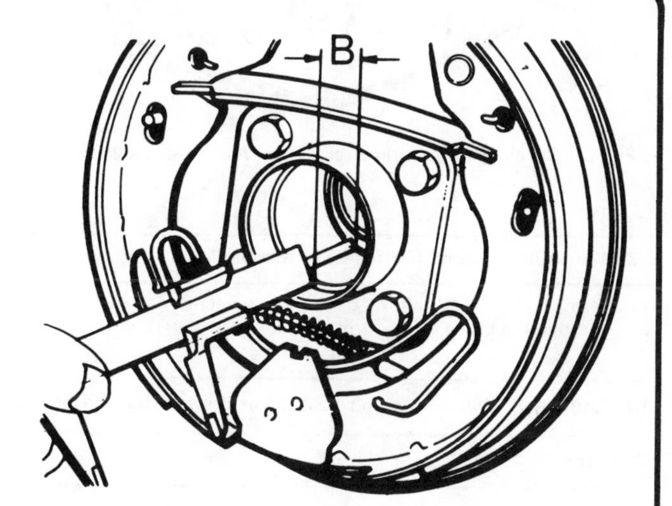

Fig. 7.16 Measuring hub recess (B) – Series 1 (Sec 11)

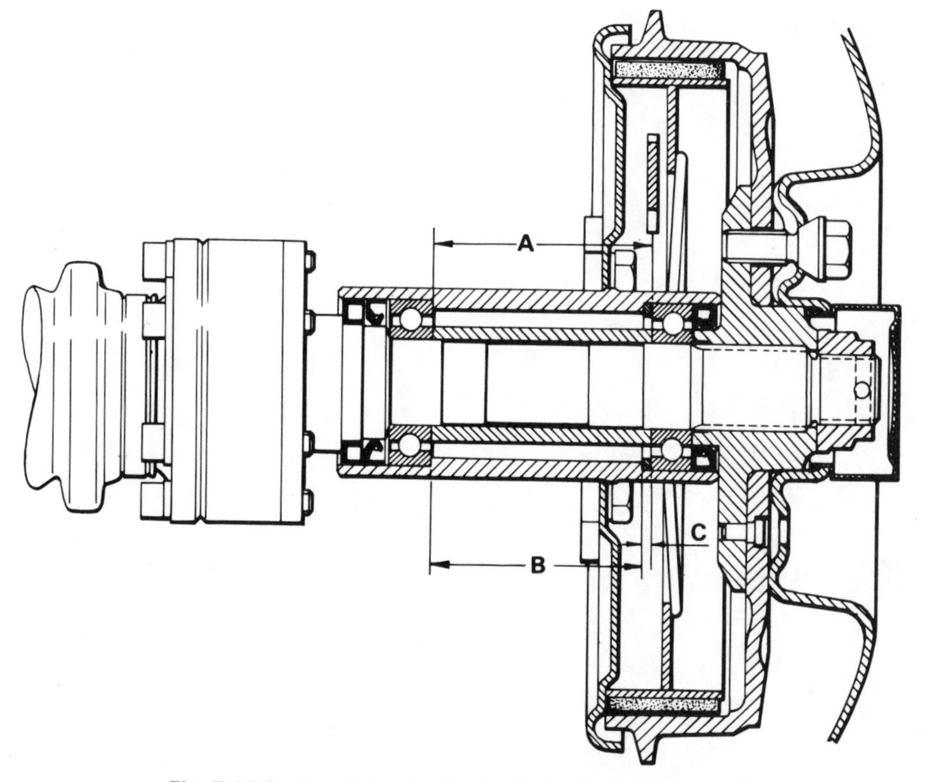

Fig. 7.17 Sectional view of the rear hub – Series 1 (Sec 11)

A Spacer sleeve length
B Hub recess depth
C = (A-B) – 0.1 mm (0.004 in)

Fig. 7.18 Rear hub bearing circlip (arrowed) – Series 2 (Sec 12)

12 Rear hub bearings (Series 2) – renewal

1 Remove the driveshaft, as described in Section 8.
2 Remove the brake drum or disc (Chapter 9), then drive out the hub with a suitable drift.
3 Extract the circlip and remove the hub bearings with an extractor or slide hammer.
4 Fit the new bearings and circlip, and the hub.
5 Refit the driveshaft, brake drum/disc and roadwheel.

13 Roadwheels and tyres

1 Before removing a roadwheel, establish whether it has been balanced on or off the car. If it has been balanced on the car, mark it in relation to its mounting hub before removing it.
2 Keep the roadwheels clean (both inner and outer rims) and protected against rust or corrosion.
3 When removing a roadwheel, release the wheel nuts/bolts before raising the car. Similarly, lower the car to the ground before carrying out the final tightening.
4 Depending upon model, nuts or bolts may be used, keep to the specified torque when tightening.
5 Keep the tyres inflated to the specified pressure.
6 Remove all nails and stones from the tyre tread and inspect the carcass generally for splits, cuts and bulges.
7 Renew the tyres when the tread has worn down the minimum permitted by current legislation or the wear indicator bars are visible.
8 To even out tread wear, wheels may be moved from front to rear and rear to front on the same side of the car (**not** from side to side) provided the wheels have been balanced off the car.
9 Periodic rebalancing may be required to compensate for lost tread rubber.

14 Fault diagnosis – propeller shaft, rear driveshafts and hub bearings

Symptom	Reason(s)
Vibration	Driveshaft bent Worn universal joints Out-of-balance roadwheels
'Clonk' on taking up drive or on overrun	Worn universal joints Worn splines on shaft, hub carrier or differential side gears Loose driveshaft (rear hub) nut Loose roadwheel bolts/nuts
Noise or roar, especially when cornering	Worn hub bearings Incorrectly adjusted hub bearings

Chapter 8 Final drive and differential

Contents

Specifications

Type ... Hypoid bevel pinion with open driveshafts. Optional limited slip differential (ZF Lok o matic)

Ratios

320	3.64 : 1
320i	3.45 : 1 (optional 3.64 : 1)
323i	3.45 : 1
323i with sport gearbox	3.25 : 1

Lubrication

Lubricant type/specification	BMW approved hypoid gear oil, viscosity SAE 90 (Duckhams D12001)
Lubricant capacity (drain and refill):	
320, 320i and 323i (except as below)	0.9 litre (1.6 Imp pts)
323i (side cover with 6 bolts) and 325i	1.7 litre (3.0 Imp pts)

Torque wrench settings	**Nm**	**lbf ft**
Series 1		
Rear axle carrier to body	150	111
Flexible mounting to rear axle carrier	100	74
Pendulum support to body	85	63
Pendulum support to final drive	85	63
Cover plate bolts	45	33
Oil filler and drain plugs	60	44
Pinion nut (nominal)	150	111
Semi-trailing arm to rear axle carrier	85	63
Side bearing cover bolts	24	18
Series 2		
Rear axle carrier to body	150	111
Final drive to rear axle carrier:		
320i	81	60
323i	110	81
Flexible mounting to rear axle carrier	90	66
Final drive to flexible mounting:		
Models up to 1982	80	59
Models 1983 on	85	63
Final drive to vibration damper	90	66
Final drive casing flexible mounting to body	85	63
Oil filler and drain plugs	60	44
Trailing arm to rear axle carrier	75	55
Support to body	28	21
Pinion nut (nominal)	150	111

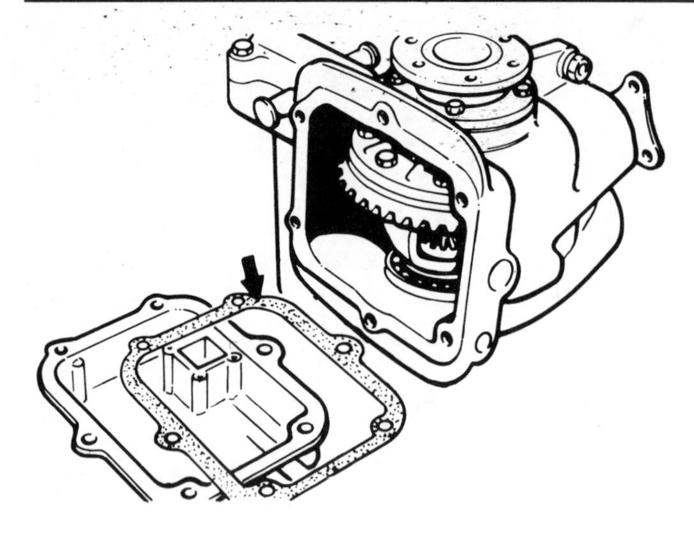

Fig. 8.1 Final drive cover plate and gasket – arrowed (Sec 3)

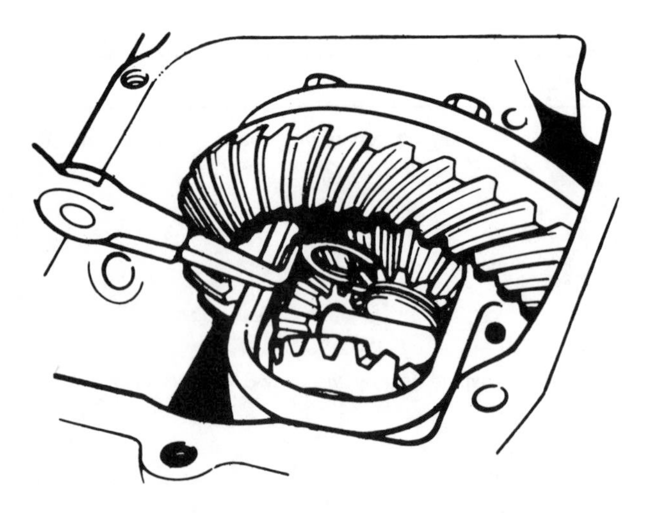

Fig. 8.2 Extract the driving flange keepers (Sec 3)

1 General description

1 The differential/final drive is of hypoid bevel gear type, flexibly mounted at the rear of the car.
2 Power is transmitted from it to the roadwheels through two universally-jointed open driveshafts to give the rear roadwheels their independent characteristics.
3 A disc type limited slip differential is available as an option.
4 Due to the need for special tools and gauges, it is recommended that only the operations described in this Chapter are carried out, and, where a complete overhaul of the final drive unit is required, that either this work is left to a BMW dealer, or a new or reconditioned unit is obtained.

2 Maintenance

1 At the intervals specified in Routine Maintenance, remove the oil level/filler plug. The oil should just be seen to dribble from the hole.
2 Top up, if required, using oil of the specified grade (see *Recommended lubricants and fluids)*.
3 At the specified mileage intervals, with the oil hot, remove the oil level/filler and drain plugs and allow the oil to drain thoroughly.
4 Clean any swarf from the drain plug and refit it.
5 Fill the final drive unit until it just starts to dribble out of the level/filler hole.
6 Periodically check the areas around the casing oil seals for leaks and, if necessary, renew the seals, as described in this Chapter.
7 If a new final drive has been fitted, renew the oil after the initial 1200 miles (2000 km).

3 Drive flange oil seals – renewal

Early models (four bolt bearing cap)

1 Remove the final drive/differential from the car, as described in Section 11.
2 Drain the oil.
3 Unbolt the cover plate.
4 Extract the driving flange keepers and withdraw the flanges.
5 Using a suitable tool, prise out the defective oil seal.
6 Dip the new seal in gear oil and drive it squarely into position using a piece of tubing.
7 Refit the driving flange and keeper.
8 Refit the cover plate with new gasket.
9 Tighten the bolts evenly to the specified torque.
10 Refit the final drive unit to the car and refill it with oil.

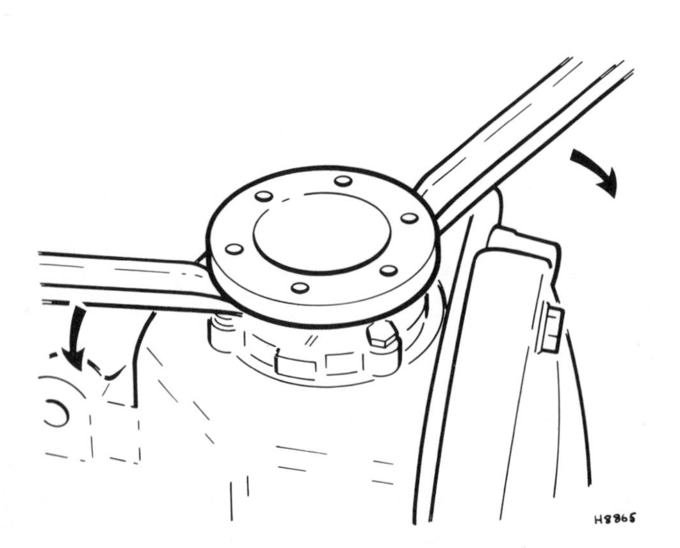

Fig. 8.3 Prise out the drive flange (Sec 3)

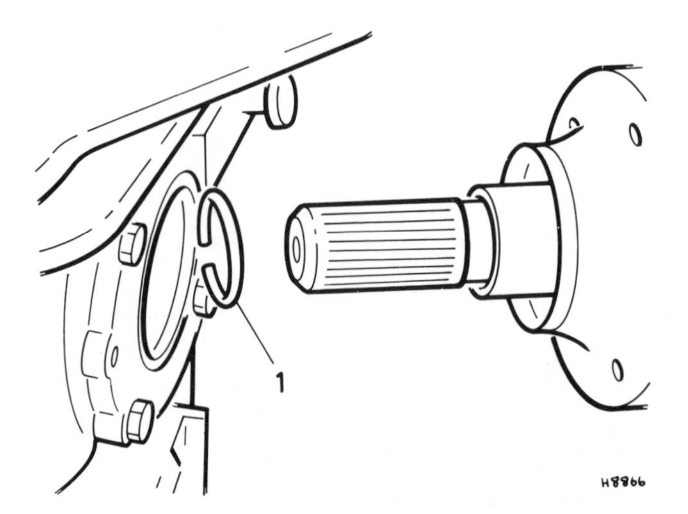

Fig. 8.4 Drive flange retaining circlip (1) (Sec 3)

Later models (six bolt bearing cap)

11 Disconnect the driveshaft from the flange on the final drive.

12 Using two levers, prise out the flange against the resistance of its retaining circlip.

13 Renew the oil seal, as described in paragraphs 5 and 6.

14 Before refitting the driving flange, locate the circlip in the groove in the differential housing. Push the drive flange in by hand, turning it at the same time until the circlip is felt to engage.

4 Pinion oil seal – renewal

1 Drain the oil from the final drive unit.

2 Remove the final drive/differential unit, as described in Section 11.

3 Accurately mark the relationship of the pinion nut to the pinion flange.

4 Hold the flange still with a pin wrench, remove the nut lockplate and unscrew the nut.

5 Now accurately mark the relationship of the pinion flange to the pinion shaft.

6 Remove the flange. If this is tight, use a suitable puller or place two bolts with nuts at opposite points between the rear face of the flange and the final drive casing. Unscrew the nuts evenly and the flange will be forced off.

7 Pull out the defective oil seal using a claw type extractor or by levering.

8 Dip the new seal in gear oil and drive it squarely into the casing until it is flush.

9 Fit the flange so that the marks made before removal are in alignment.

10 Screw on the pinion nut, hold the flange still and tighten the nut to 136 Nm (100 lbf ft). Turn the nut slightly more until the nut and shaft marks are in alignment. **Do not** overtighten, otherwise the collapsible spacer will have to be renewed and this will mean removing the cover plate, pinion shaft and taper roller bearing to obtain access to it.

11 Fit a new lockplate and stake it.

12 Refit the final drive unit to the car.

5 Pendulum support (Series 1) – renewal

1 Support the final drive unit on a jack, unscrew the bolts and remove them from the flexible bushes of the pendulum support. Remove the support.

2 When refitting, use new self-locking nuts and tighten to the specified torque.

6 Rear axle carrier flexible mounting (Series 1) – renewal

1 Unscrew the socket-headed screws on the reinforcement plate and the self-locking nuts from the pins.

2 Remove the rear seat (Chapter 12) and drive the pins out upwards.

3 Unscrew the socket-headed bolts which hold the flexible mounting. Remove the flexible mounting.

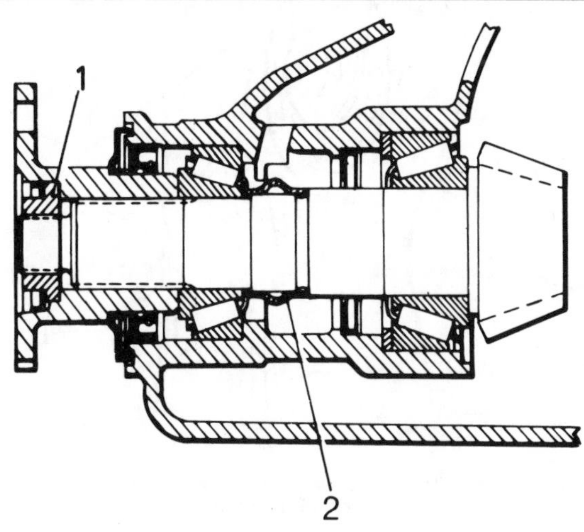

Fig. 8.5 Sectional view of the final drive (Sec 4)

1 Nut 2 Collapsible spacer

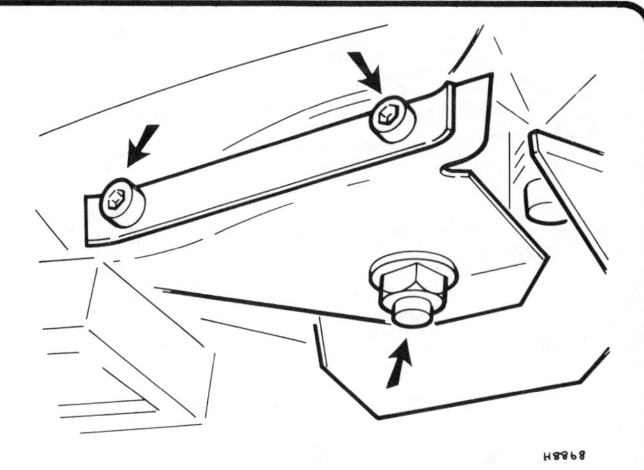

Fig. 8.7 Reinforcement plate socket-headed screws and self-locking nut (arrowed) Series 1 (Sec 6)

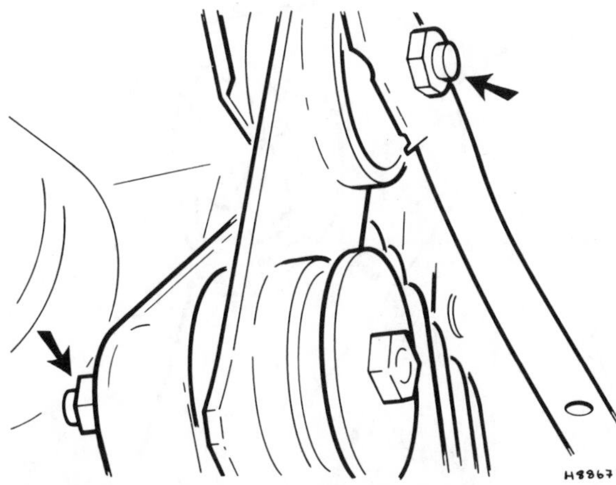

Fig. 8.6 Pendulum support securing nuts (arrowed) – Series 1 (Sec 5)

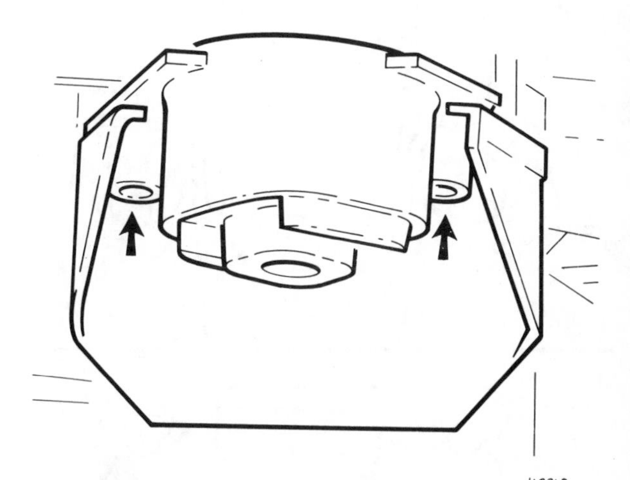

Fig. 8.8 Flexible mounting bolts (arrowed) – Series 1 (Sec 6)

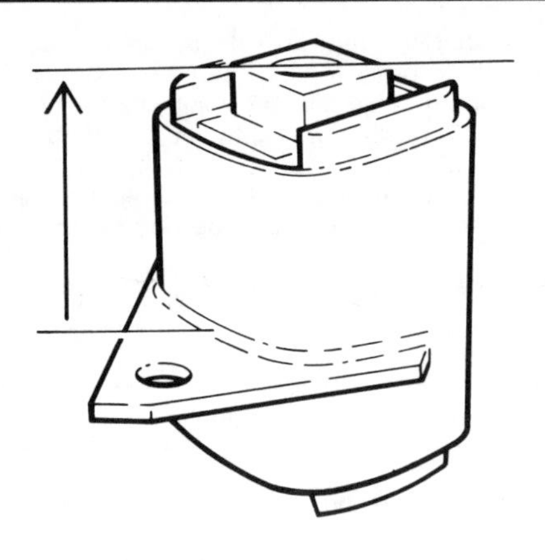

Fig. 8.9 The longer side of the flexible mounting must be towards the body – Series 1 (Sec 6)

Fig. 8.10 Semi-trailing arm bolts (arrowed) – Series 1 (Sec 7)

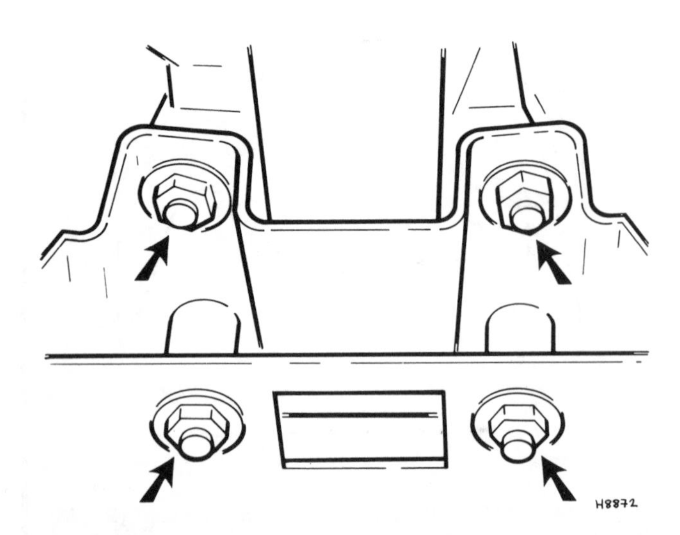

Fig. 8.11 Final drive-to-carrier bolts (arrowed) – Series 1 (Sec 7)

4 When refitting the flexible mounting, make sure that the colour markings (white – hard, plain – soft) are the same on both sides and the grey coloured mounting goes on the left-hand side with the black one on the right-hand side.
5 The longer side of the mounting must be towards the body. Tighten all bolts to the specified torque.

7 Rear axle carrier (Series 1) – removal and refitting

1 Remove the rear anti-roll bar, as described in Chapter 11.
2 Remove the bolts which secure the semi-trailing arm.
3 Unbolt the final drive housing from the carrier with the housing supported on a jack.
4 Remove the nuts and bolts at the flexible mounting.
5 Remove the carrier and detach the flexible mounting.
6 Refitting is a reversal of removal. Tighten all nuts and bolts to the specified torque.

8 Final drive housing flexible mounting (Series 2) – renewal

1 Support the final drive housing on a jack.
2 Release the nuts on the rear axle carrier.
3 Disconnect the leads from the speed pulse sensor.
4 Unscrew the flexible mounting bolt.

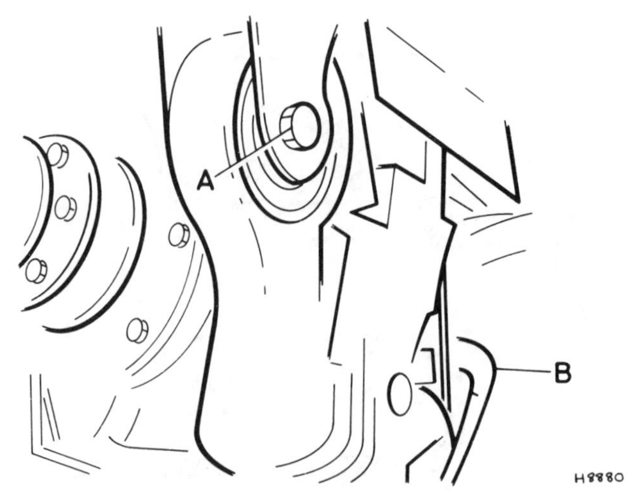

Fig. 8.12 Flexible mounting bolt (A) and speed pulse sensor (B) – Series 2 (Sec 8)

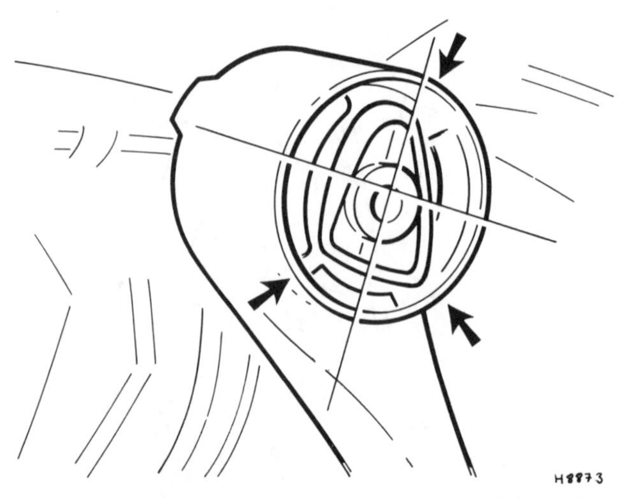

Fig. 8.13 Flexible mounting alignment – Series 2 (Sec 8)

Ensure the rubber mounts (arrowed) are correctly positioned

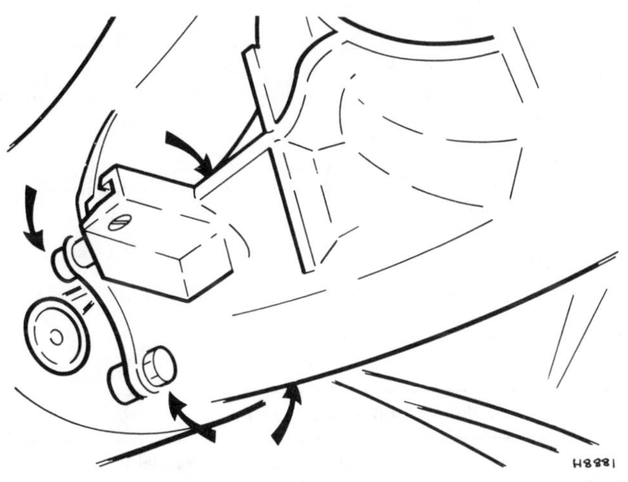

Fig. 8.14 Propeller shaft-to-final drive bolts (arrowed) – Series 2 (Sec 9)

5 Lower the final drive.
6 Mark the located position of the eccentric flexible mounting bush and remove it using a bolt, nut, washers and a distance piece.
7 Draw in the new bush so that it takes on the same eccentric alignment as the original.
8 Raise the final drive, fit the bolt and carrier nuts, connect the electrical leads and remove the jack.

9 Rear axle carrier (Series 2) – removal and refitting

1 Remove the exhaust system (Chapter 3) and the heat shield.
2 Disconnect the propeller shaft from the final drive and lower it, after releasing the centre bearing.
3 Disconnect the handbrake cable control rod.
4 Disconnect the left and right-hand rear brake hydraulic pipes and quickly cap the pipes.
5 Support the final drive housing and then disconnect the thrust strut on both sides.
6 Disconnect the leads from the speed pulse sensor.
7 On models with rear wheel disc brakes, disconnect the brake wear sensor plug and support both rear trailing arms with the roadwheels resting on the floor.
8 Disconnect both rear shock absorber lower mountings.
9 Lower the rear axle carrier and pull the handbrake cables from their protective tube. Be prepared for the suspension coil springs to be released.
10 Refitting is a reversal of removal, but observe the following:

Renew all self-locking nuts
Tighten all nuts and bolts to the specified torque
Bleed the brake hydraulic system (Chapter 9)
Adjust the handbrake (Chapter 9)

10 Rear axle carrier flexible mounting (Series 2) – renewal

1 Remove the rear seat (Chapter 12).
2 Support the semi-trailing arms, and unscrew and remove the thrust strut nuts – Fig. 8.15.
3 Drive out the threaded pin upwards.
4 Note the installed position of the flexible bush and withdraw it using a bolt, nut, washers and distance piece.
5 Draw the new bush into positon having applied brake fluid or soapy water to it. Make sure that it takes up the same position as the original one in the carrier.
6 Reconnect the pin and screw on new self-locking nuts.

11 Final drive/differential – removal and refitting

Series 1
1 Disconnect the propeller shaft (Chapter 7).

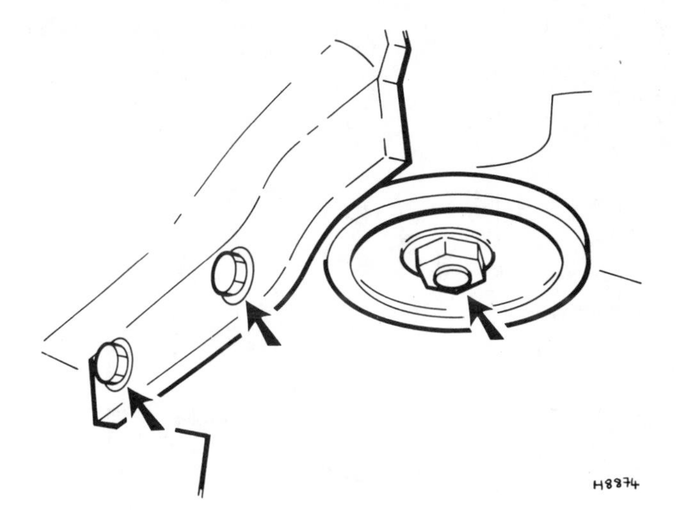

Fig. 8.15 Thrust strut nuts (arrowed) – Series 2 (Secs 9 and 10)

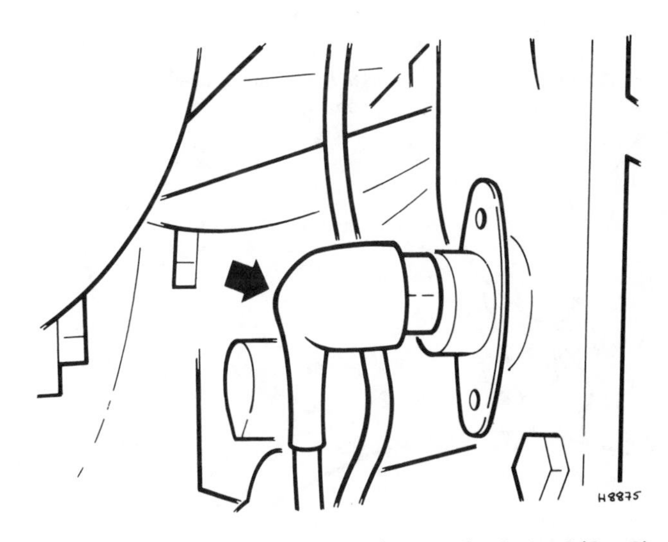

Fig. 8.16 Speed pulse sensor leads (arrowed) – Series 2 (Sec 9)

Fig. 8.17 Rear axle carrier bush alignment – Series 2 (Sec 10)

Position the opening in the rubber mount correctly (arrow)

2 Disconnect the driveshafts from the flanges on the final drive and tie them up with wire. Support the final drive on a jack.
3 Disconnect the pendulum flexible support from the final drive housing.
4 Unbolt the final drive housing from the rear axle carrier.

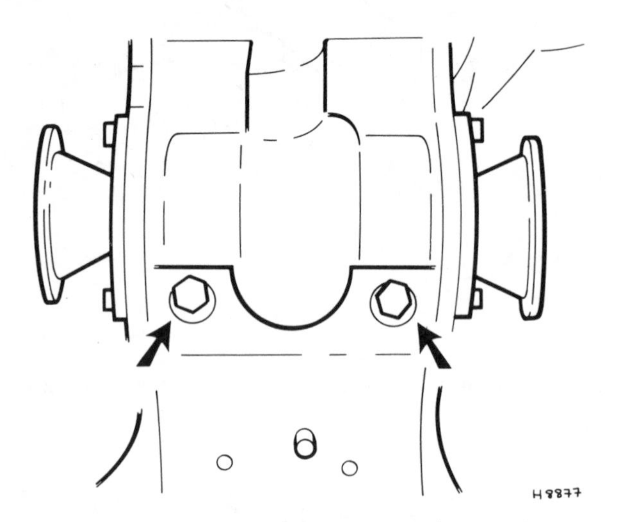

Fig. 8.18 Final drive-to-rear axle carrier bolts (arrowed) – Series 2 (Sec 11)

Series 2

5 Carry out the operations described in paragraphs 1 and 2.
6 Support the final drive housing on a jack.
7 Unscrew the top bolts which hold the final drive housing to the rear axle carrier.
8 Unscrew the front facing bolts from both sides.
9 Pull the leads from the speed pulse sensor.
10 Unscrew and remove the bolt from the flexible mounting and lower the final drive/differential.

All models

11 Refitting is a reversal of removal, tighten all nuts and bolts to the specified torque.
12 Check the oil level on completion.

12 Limited slip differential – description

1 The limited slip differential is optionally available and can be identified by the letter S cast into the casing.
2 This type of differential gives the following advantages.

Prevention of wheel slip on wet or rough surfaces when the surfaces under the rear wheels differ in their traction characteristics
Prevention of wheel slip on inside curve when driving fast into bends

3 Due to the complexity of this type of differential it is not recommended that it is dismantled by the home mechanic.

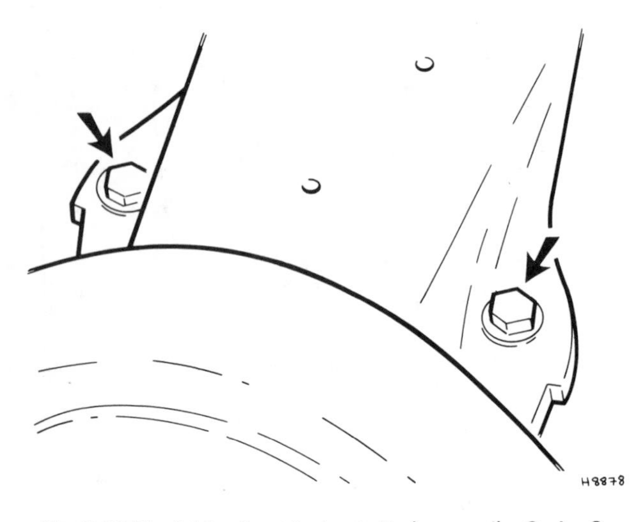

Fig. 8.19 Final drive front facing bolts (arrowed) – Series 2 (Sec 11)

Fig. 8.20 The limited slip differential has S cast into the casing (Sec 12)

13 Fault diagnosis – final drive and differential

Symptom	Reason(s)
Knock when moving off or shifting under load	Loose drive flange Excessive backlash Play in propeller shaft splines
Noise – general	Defective flexible mountings General gear or bearing wear
Vibration	Roadwheels out of balance Propeller shaft or driveshafts out of balance or worn joints Output shaft bearings worn
Oil leaks	Defective oil seals Overfilling or clogged breather

Chapter 9 Braking system

For modifications, and information applicable to later models, see Supplement at end of manual

Contents

Specifications

System type .... Four wheel hydraulic dual-circuit with vacuum servo unit. Discs front, drums rear except 323i models which have discs front and rear. Handbrake mechanical to rear wheels. Pressure regulating valve to rear brakes. Anti-lock braking system option on certain models

Hydraulic fluid

Type/specification .... Hydraulic fluid to SAE J 1703 or DOT 4 (Duckhams Universal Brake and Clutch Fluid)

Front discs

Type
- 320 .... Non-ventilated
- 320i, 323i .... Ventilated

Disc diameter .... 255.0 mm (10.039 in)

Thickness (new):
- 320 .... 12.7 mm (0.5 in)
- 323i .... 22.0 mm (0.866 in)

Minimum thickness (after refinishing):
- 320 .... 11.7 mm (0.461 in)
- 323i .... 21.0 mm (0.827 in)

Maximum disc run-out .... 0.05 mm (0.002 in)
Minimum pad lining thickness .... 2.0 mm (0.08 in)
Caliper piston diameter .... 48.0 mm (1.89 in)

Brake drums

Drum internal diameter .... 250.0 mm (9.843 in)
Maximum internal diameter (after refinishing) .... 251.0 mm (9.882 in)
Maximum ovality .... 0.05 mm (0.002 in)
Minimum friction lining thickness .... 3.0 mm (0.118 in)
Wheel cylinder piston diameter .... 19.05 mm (0.750 in)

Rear discs

Type .... Non-ventilated
Disc diameter .... 258.0 mm (10.57 in)
Thickness (new) .... 10.0 mm (0.394 in)
Minimum thickness (after refinishing) .... 9.0 mm (0.354 in)
Maximum disc run-out .... 0.2 mm (0.008 in)
Minimum pad lining thickness .... 2.0 mm (0.078 in)
Caliper piston diameter .... 27.0 mm (1.063 in)

Master cylinder

Piston diameter .... 20.64 mm (0.8126 in)

Vacuum servo unit

Type .... ATE 52/225

Rear handbrake (323i)

Drum diameter	160.0 mm (6.299 in)	

Torque wrench settings

	Nm	lbf ft
Front caliper to stub axle carrier	90	66
Rear wheel cylinder to backplate	10	7
Brake backplate to trailing arm	60	44
Rear caliper to trailing arm	60	44
Disc shield	45	33
Master cylinder mounting nut (LHD)	20	15
Master cylinder mounting nut (RHD)	25	18
Brake pipe union nut	15	11
Flexible hose end fitting	15	11
Bleed screw	5	4
Caliper guide pin bolt	34	25
Vacuum servo mounting bolts	25	18
Pedal pivot bolt nut	28	21

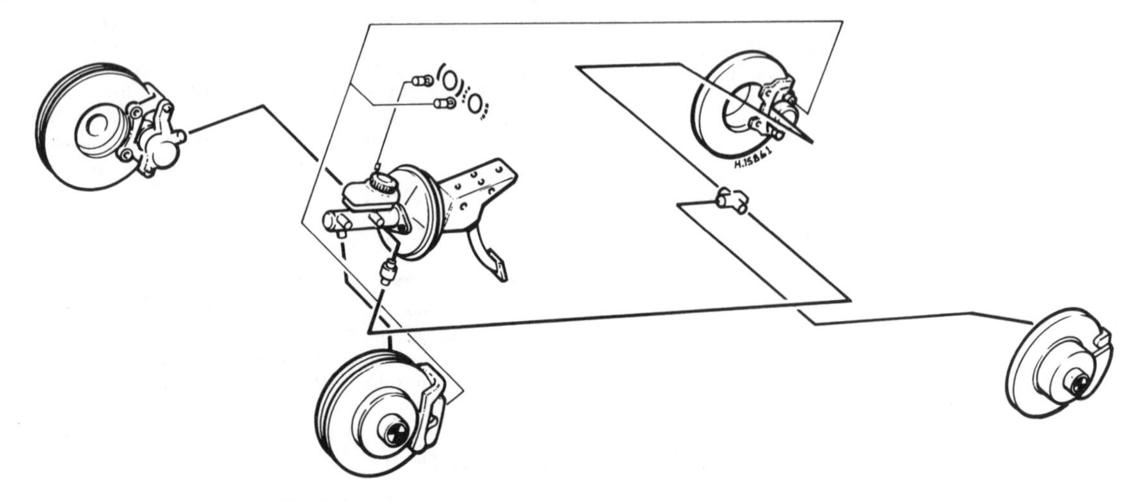

Fig. 9.1 Brake hydraulic system – 323i models with rear discs (Sec 1)

1 General description

The braking system is of four wheel dual-circuit, hydraulic type with discs at the front and drums on the rear, except on 323i models which also have disc brakes at the rear.

A vacuum servo unit is fitted to all models and a pressure regulator incorporated in the hydraulic system to limit pressure to the rear wheels.

The handbrake is operated mechanically on the rear wheels.

On Series 2 models, fluid level and pad wear sensors are incorporated in the system.

On Series 1 models, the calipers are of fixed dual piston type. On Series 2 models, the calipers are of single piston sliding type.

The anti-lock brake system (ABS) is described in Section 27.

2 Maintenance and adjustment

1 Even though a fluid level sensor is incorporated in the master cylinder reservoir, at the weekly maintenance check inspect the level of the hydraulic fluid through the translucent reservoir. Topping-up should seldom be required, if it is, suspect a leak.

2 Inspect all system pipes and unions at regular intervals for leaks.

3 Check the wear in disc pads and shoe linings, as described in the following Sections.

4 On 320 models adjust the rear brakes, as described in the following paragraphs.

5 Raise the rear roadwheels and fully release the handbrake.

6 Turn the roadwheel and then turn the leading shoe adjuster, which is the one nearest the front of the car, towards the front of the car until the wheel locks. Release the adjuster until the wheel is just free to spin.

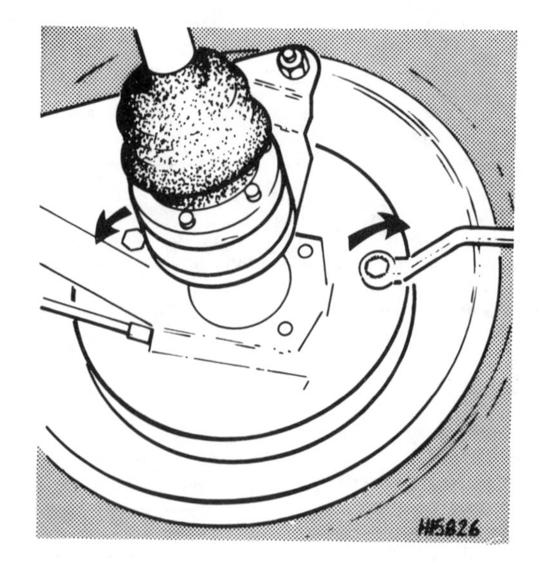

Fig. 9.2 Brake shoe adjusters (Sec 2)

Arrows show direction of rotation to take up wear. Right-hand side shown – left-hand side is mirror image

7 Now turn the adjuster on the trailing shoe in the opposite direction until the wheel locks and then release it until the wheel is just free to turn.
8 Repeat on the opposite wheel and lower the car to the floor.

3 Front disc pads (Series 1) – inspection and renewal

1 Raise the front of the car, support it securely and remove the roadwheel(s).
2 On ATE calipers, drive out the spring collar retaining pins and take off the cross spring (1) – Fig. 9.3.
3 On Girling calipers, extract the clips (photo) and drive out the retaining pins. Take off the cross spring (1) – Fig. 9.4.
4 Inspect the thickness of the friction material of the disc pads. If it is below the specified minimum, renew the pads as an axle set (four pads).
5 Withdraw the pads by gripping them with a pair of pliers. Note the anti-squeal shims on Girling pads.
6 Brush out the caliper jaws **without** inhaling any dust, as *this is injurious to health.*
7 The caliper pistons must now be depressed in order to be able to accommodate the new thicker pads. Do this using a broad blade, such

3.3 Front disc pad pin clip (Girling)

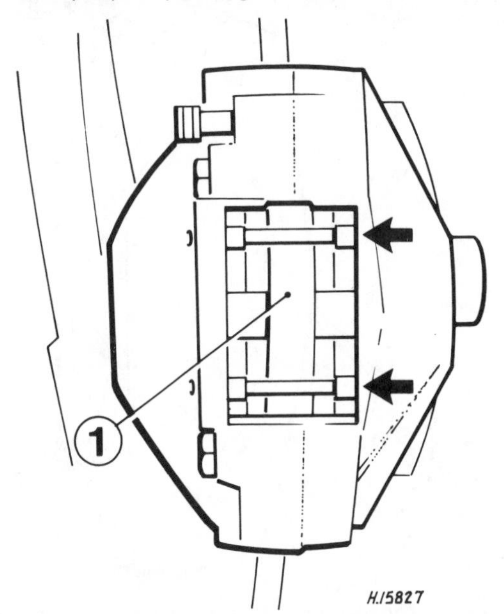

Fig. 9.3 Drive out the pins (arrowed) and take off the cross spring (1) – Series 1, ATE caliper (Sec 3)

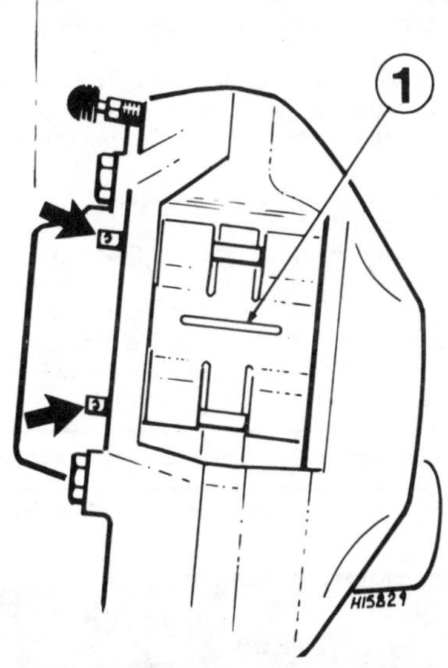

Fig. 9.4 Drive out the pins (arrowed) and take off the cross spring (1) – Series 1 Girling caliper (Sec 3)

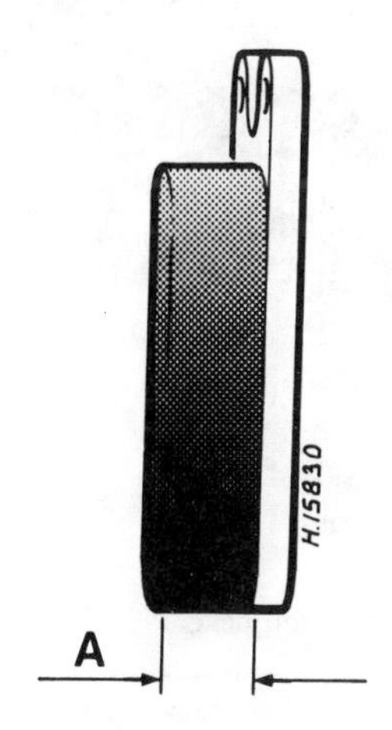

Fig. 9.5 Disc pad thickness (A) (Sec 3)

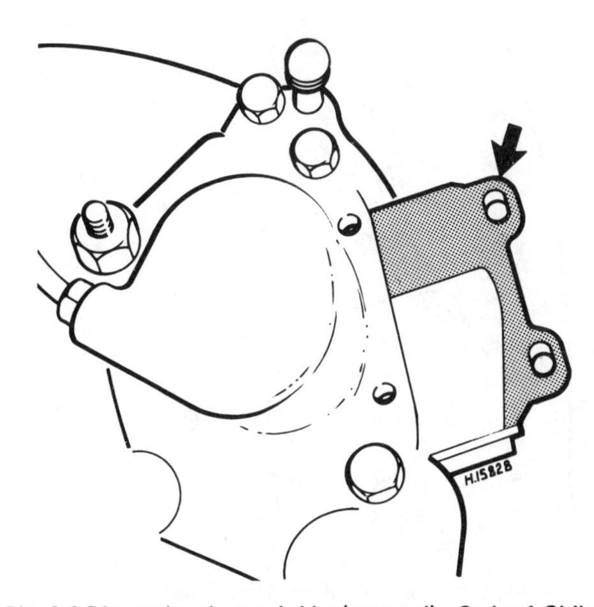

Fig. 9.6 Disc pad anti-squeal shim (arrowed) – Series 1 Girling caliper (Sec 3)

as a tyre lever. As the piston is depressed, the fluid will rise in the master cylinder reservoir. Anticipate this by removing some fluid with a clean syringe.
8 Smear the surface of the pad backplates with anti-seize grease and insert the pads into the caliper (friction surface to disc). With Girling brakes, place the anti-squeal shims on the backplates the correct way up.
9 Refit the retaining pins and clips (Girling).
10 Repeat on the opposite brake.
11 Apply the brake pedal hard two or three times to position the pads against the discs.
12 Fit the roadwheels and lower the car to the floor.
13 Check the hydraulic fluid level and top up if necessary.
14 Avoid harsh braking as far as possible for a few hundred miles to allow the new pads to bed in.

4 Front disc pads (Series 2) – inspection and renewal

1 Raise the front of the car, support it securely and remove the roadwheel(s).
2 Inspect the thickness of the friction material of the disc pads. If it is below the specified minimum, renew the pads as an axle set (four pads).
3 Disconnect the pad wear sensor plug.
4 Counterhold the guide pin, unscrew and remove the guide pin bolt, and swivel the caliper upwards (photos).
5 Withdraw the disc pads (photo).
6 Brush out all dust from the caliper, but avoid inhaling it as *it is injurious to health.*
7 The caliper piston must now be depressed in order to be able to accommodate the new thicker pads. Do this using a broad blade such as a tyre lever. As the piston is depressed, the fluid will rise in the master cylinder reservoir. Anticipate this by removing some fluid with a clean syringe.
8 Smear the surface of the pad backplates with anti-seize grease and refit the pads.
9 Make sure that the springs are correctly located – Fig. 9.7.
10 Transfer the wear sensor pin to the new pad. If the plastic coating of the pin has been worn away, renew the pin. Also check the condition of the pin retaining circlip.

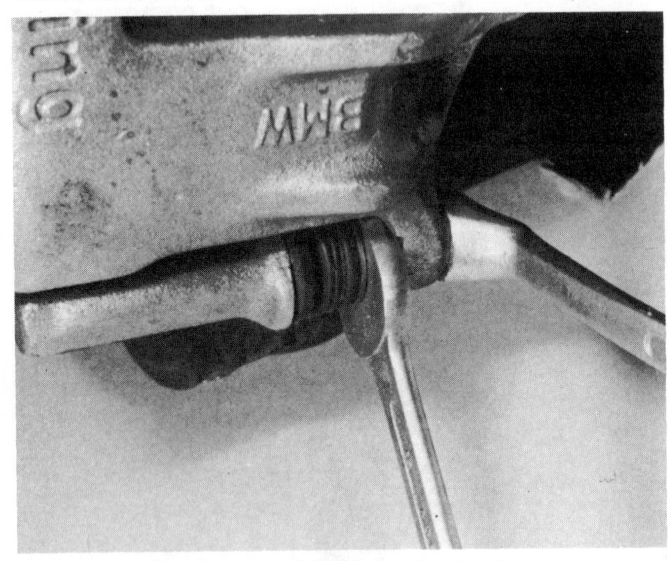

4.4A Unscrewing single piston caliper guide pin bolt

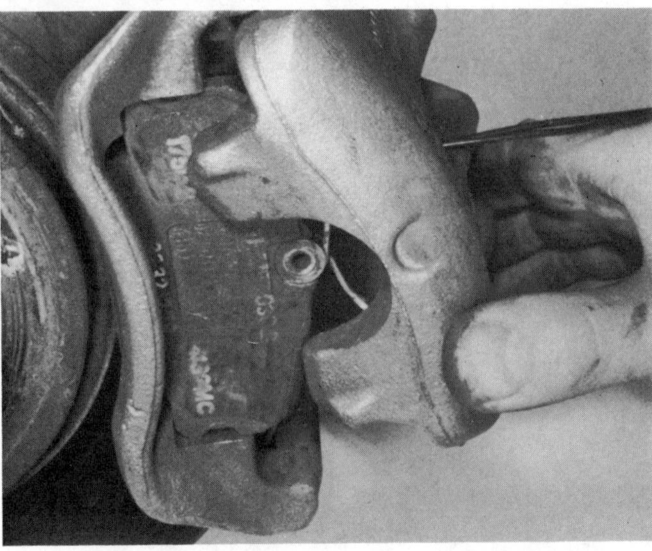
4.4B Swivelling caliper upwards

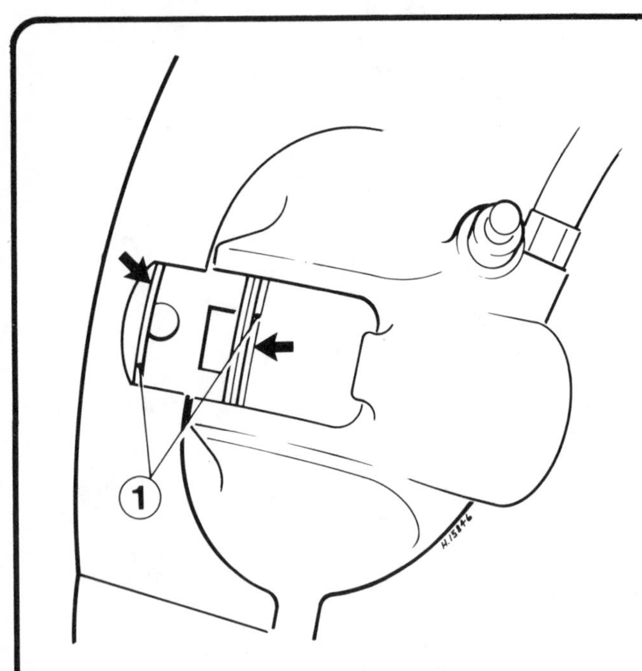

Fig. 9.7 Disc pad springs (1) – Series 2 (Sec 4)

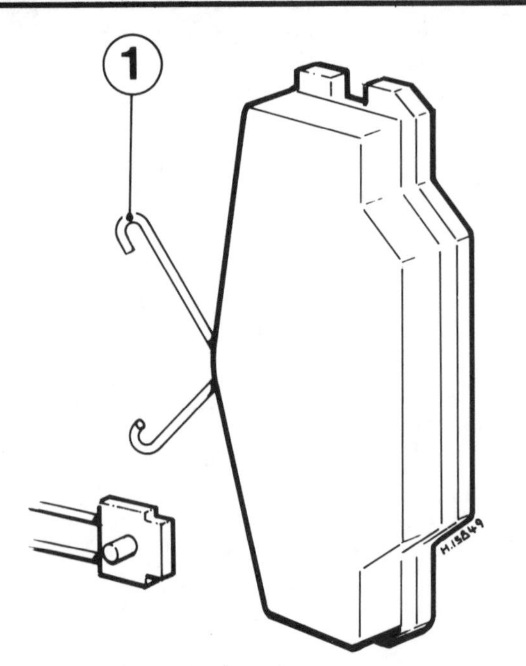

Fig. 9.8 Pad wear sensor pin and anti-rattle spring (1) – Series 2 (Sec 4)

4.5 Removing disc pad

11 Swivel the caliper down over the pads and secure it with a new guide pin bolt, tightened to the specified torque.
12 Reconnect the pad wear sensor plug.
13 Follow paragraphs 10 to 14 of the previous Section.

5 Rear disc pads (323i) – inspection and renewal

Series 1

1 Raise the rear of the car, support it securely and remove the roadwheel.
2 The operations are very similar to those described for the front brakes in the preceding Sections except that the caliper is of single piston sliding type.
3 Before fitting the new pads, clean the guide faces (A) – Fig. 9.9 – and make sure that the guide spring (arrowed) – Fig. 9.10 – is pushed fully in.

Series 2

4 Remove the roadwheel and then inspect the thickness of the friction material of the pads. If it has worn below its specified minimum, renew the pads as an axle set.
5 Remove the plastic caps (1) – Fig. 9.11 – and disconnect the leads from the pad wear sensor.
6 Unscrew the guide bolts (1) – Fig. 9.12.

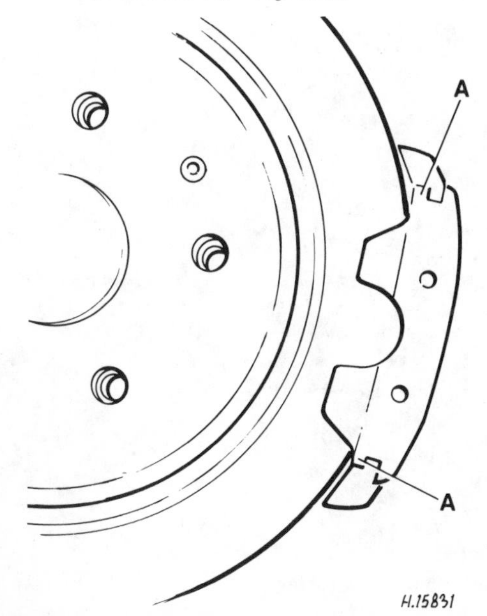

Fig. 9.9 Rear caliper guide faces (A) – 323i models (Sec 5)

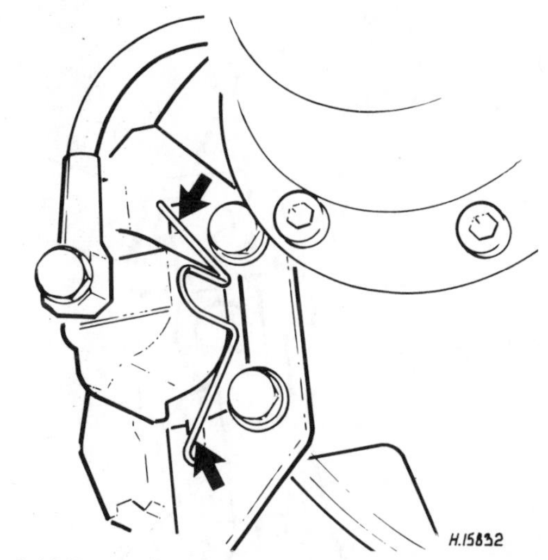

Fig. 9.10 Rear caliper guide spring (arrowed) – 323i models (Sec 5)

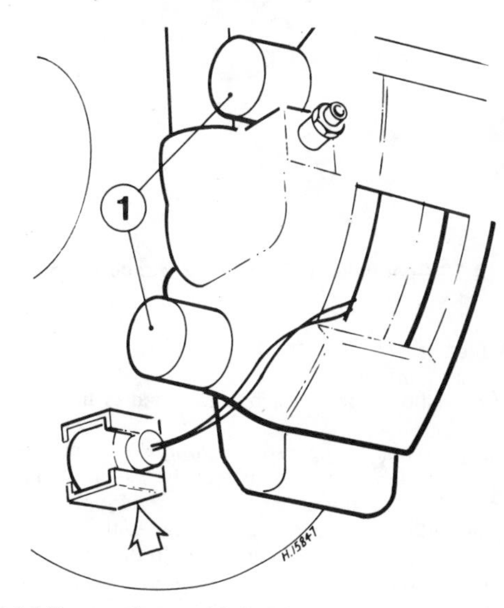

Fig. 9.11 Rear caliper guide bolt plastic caps (1) and pad wear sensor lead plug (arrowed) – 323i models (Sec 5)

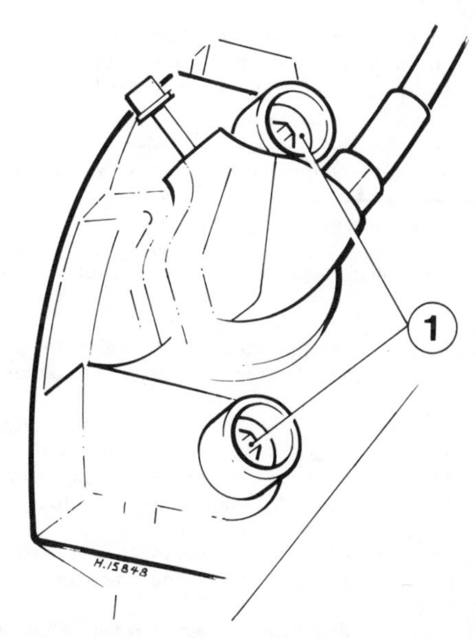

Fig. 9.12 Rear caliper guide bolts (1) – 323i models (Sec 5)

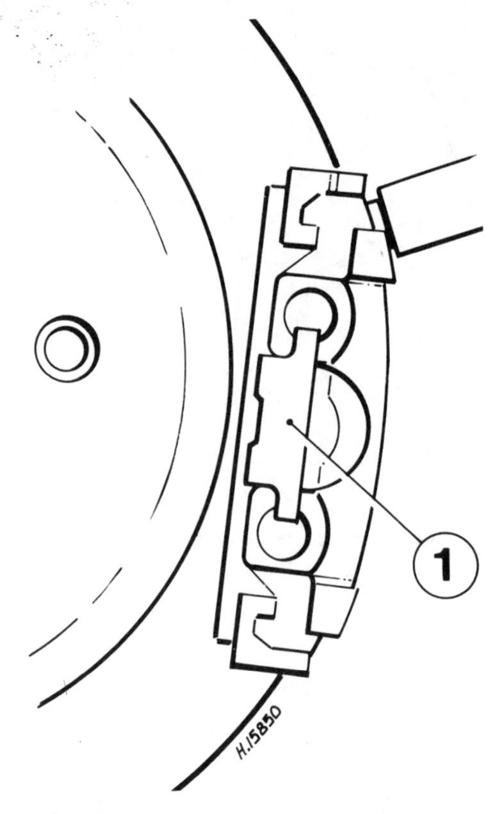

Fig. 9.13 Rear caliper clip (1) – 323i models (Sec 5)

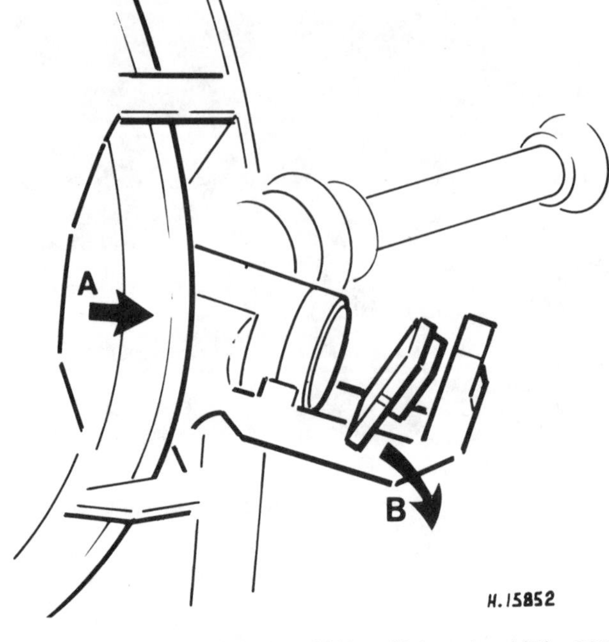

Fig. 9.14 Remove outboard pad (A) and inboard pad (B) – 323i models (Sec 5)

The inboard pad is engaged in the piston with a spring

7 Pull out the clip (1) – Fig. 9.13.
8 Withdraw the outboard pad.
9 Remove the inboard pad, which is engaged in the piston with a spring.
10 Clean away all dust *taking care not to inhale it* and then depress the piston fully into the caliper. Anticipate the rise in fluid level in the master cylinder reservoir by removing some fluid with a syringe.
11 Smear the surface of the pad backplates with anti-seize grease and fit the pads to the caliper (friction face to disc).
12 Fit the guide bolts (clean, but not greased) and tighten to the specified torque.
13 Fit the plastic caps and connect the wear sensor leads.

All models

14 Repeat on the opposite brake and then apply the brakes two or three times to position the pads against the discs.
15 Fit the roadwheels and lower the car to the floor.

6 Rear shoe linings (Series 1) – inspection and renewal

1 Raise the rear of the car, support it securely and remove the roadwheel.
2 Extract the small retaining screw and pull off the brake drum (photo).
3 If the drum is stuck tight and tapping with a plastic-faced mallet will not dislodge it, suspect that the shoes are caught in grooves worn in the drums and slacken off both shoe adjusters completely to release them.
4 If the linings have worn down to the rivets or nearly flush with their heads, renew the shoes as an axle set (four shoes) using factory lined shoes. Do not attempt to reline the old shoes yourself.
5 Twist and release the shoe steady springs (photo).
6 Disconnect the shoe lower return spring.
7 Pull the upper ends of the shoes outwards from the piston tappets.
8 Unhook the upper spring and disconnect the handbrake cable and shoe strut (photos).
9 Transfer the handbrake lever to the new trailing shoe and then lay the shoes out in their correct relative positions, the leading shoe nearer the front of the car. Apply a smear of grease to the highpoints on the backplate (photo).
10 Connect the strut and shoe upper return spring (longer end to handbrake lever) and pass the shoes over the hub flange and engage the handbrake cable with the lever on the trailing shoe.
11 Expand the tops of the shoes and place them on the piston tappets.
12 Engage the lower ends of the shoes in the anchor block (photo) and fit the lower return spring. Fit the shoe steady springs.
13 Clean out the drum, refit and adjust, as described in Section 2.
14 Repeat the operations on the opposite wheel, refit the roadwheels and lower the car.

6.2 Extracting brake drum screw

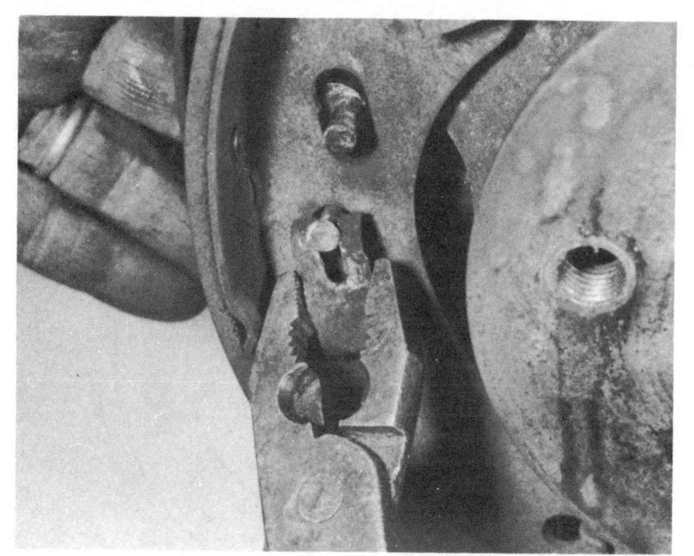
6.5 Removing shoe steady clip

6.8A Shoe upper return spring

6.8B Shoe upper strut connection

6.8C Handbrake cable connection to shoe lever

6.9 Backplate high points greased – arrowed

6.12 Shoe lower anchor block

7 Rear shoe linings (Series 2) – inspection and renewal

1 Raise the rear of the car, support it securely and remove the roadwheel.
2 Extract the retaining screw and pull off the brake drum. If it is stuck tight and it will not come off with reasonable blows from a plastic-faced mallet, slacken the handbrake cable and pass a thin screwdriver through one of the roadwheel bolt holes to engage the automatic adjuster star wheel. Turn the star wheel to back off the shoes from the drum.
3 If the linings have worn down to the rivets or nearly flush with their heads, renew the shoes as an axle set (four shoes) using factory lined shoes. Do not attempt to reline the old shoes yourself.
4 Remove the shoe steady springs. To do this, grip the edges of the spring retaining cups, depress and turn them through 90° and then release them.
5 Disconnect the shoe lower return spring.
6 Disconnect the shoe upper return spring.
7 Remove the leading shoe, complete with automatic adjuster strut.
8 Disconnect the handbrake cable from the trailing shoe, and remove the shoe.
9 Transfer the handbrake lever to the new trailing shoe, clean and grease the automatic adjuster. The left-hand adjuster has right-hand threads while the right-hand one has left-hand threads.
10 Offer the trailing shoe to the backplate and engage the handbrake cable to the shoe lever.
11 Connect the automatic adjuster in its fully contracted state and connect the shoe return springs. Make sure the automatic adjuster clip is correctly positioned – Fig. 9.17.
12 Turn the adjuster star wheel to expand the shoes until the brake drum will only just pass over them. Fit the drum and screw.
13 Apply the brake foot pedal several times to bring the shoes to their maximum adjustment by means of the automatic adjuster.
14 Repeat the operations on the opposite brake.
15 Adjust the handbrake (Section 29) on completion.

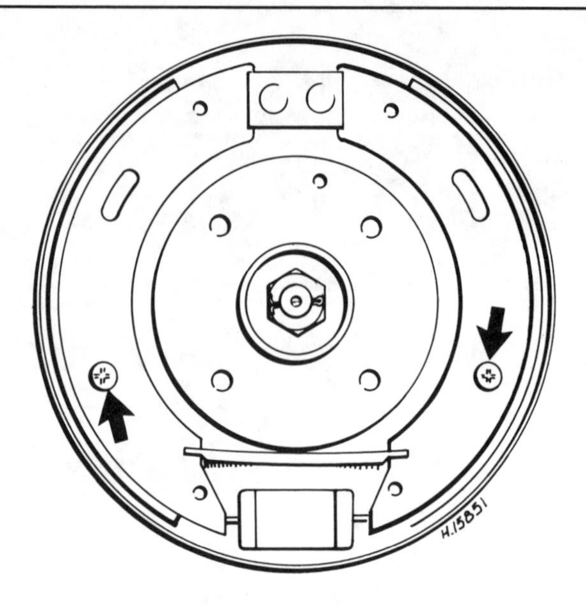

Fig. 9.15 Shoe steady springs (arrowed) – Series 2 (Sec 7)

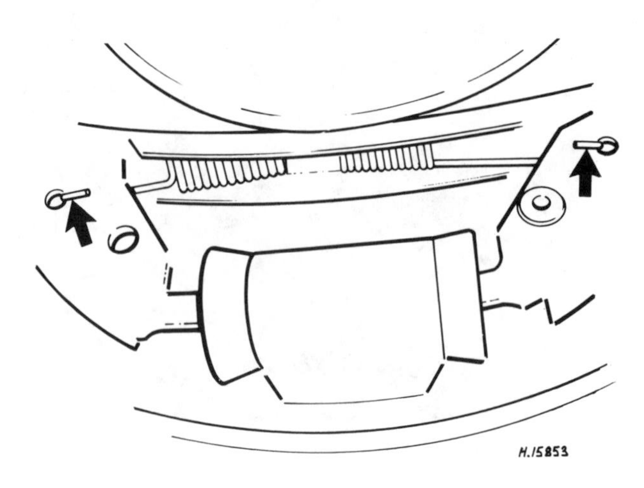

Fig. 9.16 Shoe lower return spring connection (arrowed) – Series 2 (Sec 7)

8 Handbrake shoes (323i) – removal and refitting

1 Shoes are used in conjunction with rear disc brakes to provide an entirely separate handbrake facility.
2 It is very unlikely that the handbrake shoe linings, which are of bonded type, will ever require renewal as their application is usually to a static drum.
3 Raise the rear of the car, support it securely and remove the roadwheel.
4 Unbolt the caliper and tie it to one side. Do not disconnect the hydraulic line.
5 Extract the securing screw and remove the brake disc.
6 With the handbrake shoes now exposed, disconnect the shoe lower return spring.
7 Release the shoe steady springs, as described in Section 7.
8 Expand the shoes, pull their upper ends from the adjuster tappets and withdraw the shoes upwards.
9 Disconnect the shoe upper return spring and take out the automatic adjuster.
10 Clean the automatic adjuster and grease it.
11 Refit the shoes by reversing the removal operations.
12 Turn the adjuster star wheel to expand the shoes until the disc/drum will just pass over them.
13 Fit the drum and screw.
14 Adjust the handbrake as described in Section 29.
15 Refit the caliper, tightening the fixing bolts to the specified torque.
16 Refit the roadwheel and lower the car.
17 Bed in new linings as described in Chapter 13, Section 10.

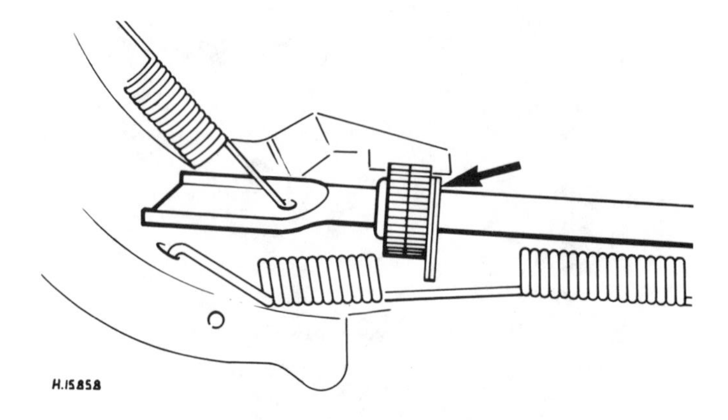

Fig. 9.17 Shoe automatic adjuster (Sec 7)

The clip (arrowed) must be correctly positioned

9 Front caliper (Series 1) – removal, overhaul and refitting

1 Raise the front of the car, support it securely and remove the roadwheel.
2 Using a syringe, remove the hydraulic fluid from the master cylinder reservoir.
3 Unscrew the pipe union from the caliper and then unbolt and

Fig. 9.18 Front caliper dust excluder retaining ring (1), dust excluder (2) and piston (3) – Series 1 (Sec 9)

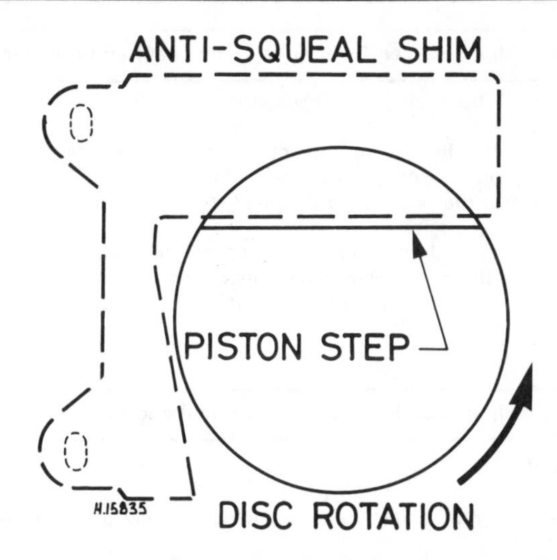

Fig. 9.20 Girling caliper piston step positioned using the anti-squeal shim as a template – Series 1 (Sec 9)

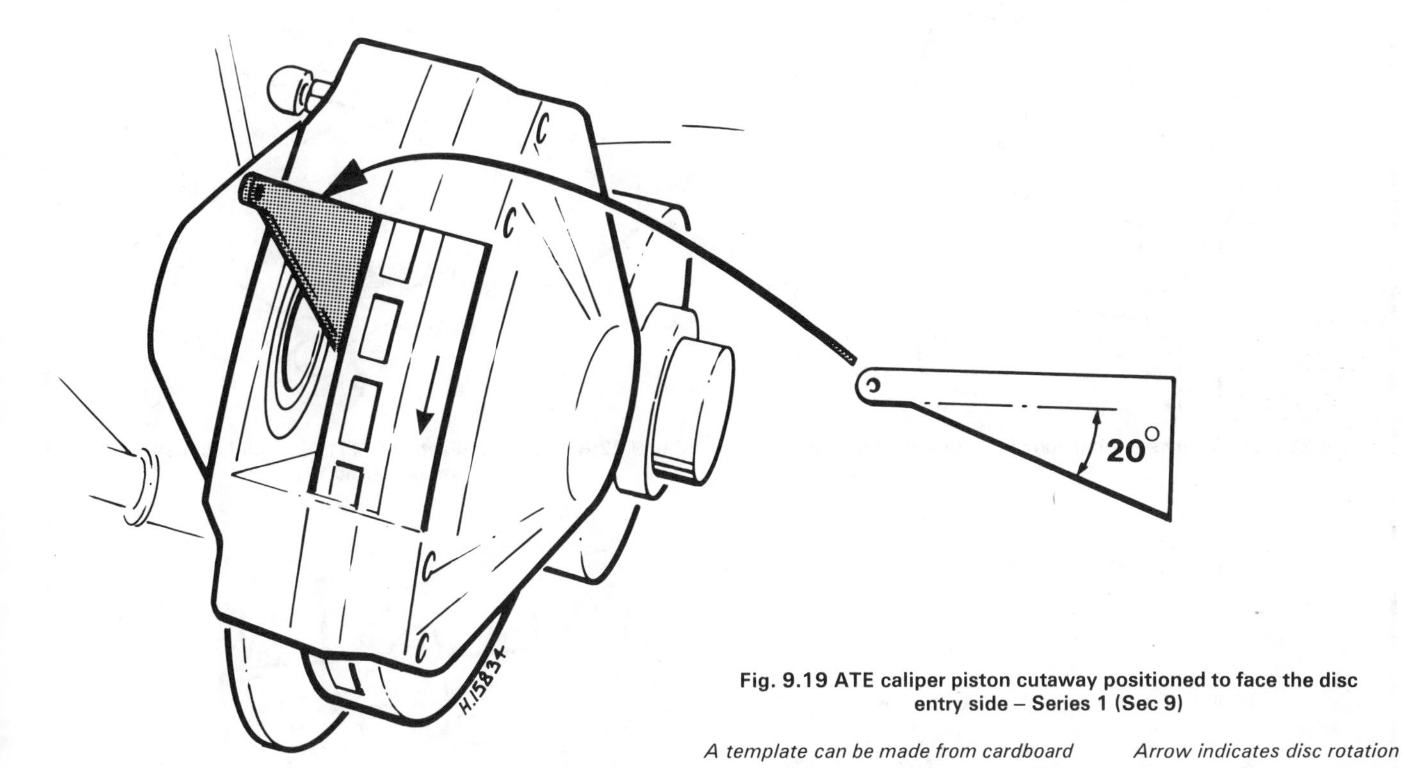

Fig. 9.19 ATE caliper piston cutaway positioned to face the disc entry side – Series 1 (Sec 9)

A template can be made from cardboard *Arrow indicates disc rotation*

remove the caliper.

4 Clean away external dirt and remove the brake pads.

5 Remove the dust excluder retaining ring and the dust excluder.

6 Retain one piston with a small clamp and then apply air pressure to the fluid inlet and eject the free piston. Only low air pressure is required, such as obtained from a foot or hand pump.

7 Examine the surface of the piston and cylinder bore. If it is corroded or scored, renew the caliper complete. If the components are in good condition, obtain a repair kit for the particular caliper – Girling or ATE which will contain all the necessary new seals and other renewable items.

8 Extract the old piston seal and fit the new one without scratching the piston. Any cleaning required should only be done with hydraulic fluid or methylated spirit – nothing else.

9 Dip the piston/seal in clean hydraulic fluid and insert it carefully into the cylinder bore. Before pushing the piston down the bore, twist it so that the cutaway or step is set in the following way, according to make of caliper.

ATE: 20° cutaway must face the brake disc entry side as shown – Fig. 9.19.

Girling: The step should be aligned with the edge of the anti-squeal shim which, in fact, should be used as a template – Fig. 9.20.

10 Depress the piston fully, fit the new dust excluder and retaining ring.

11 Clamp the reconditioned piston, apply air pressure and eject the remaining one. Repeat the reconditioning operations, remembering to set the piston step or cutaway.

12 Refit the caliper, tightening the fixing bolts to specified torque. Fit the pads.

13 Reconnect the brake pipe and fill the master cylinder reservoir with fresh fluid.

14 Bleed the system, as described in Section 22.

15 **Warning**: If both calipers are being overhauled together, make sure that they go back to their respective sides so that the bleed screws are at the top. If a new caliper is being purchased, make sure that it is of the same make as the opposite one.

10 Front caliper (Series 2) – removal, overhaul and refitting

1 Raise the front of the car, support it securely and remove the roadwheel.
2 Remove the fluid from the master cylinder reservoir, using a syringe and then disconnect the brake pipe from the caliper.
3 Disconnect the pad sensor plug and then unbolt and remove the caliper.
4 Overhaul procedure is very similar to that described in Section 9, but of course the caliper is of single piston type.
5 Refit, tighten the bolts to the specified torque and bleed the front hydraulic circuit.

11 Rear caliper (323i) – removal, overhaul and refitting

Removal

Series 1

1 Raise the rear of the car, support it securely and remove the roadwheel.
2 Disconnect the brake hydraulic hose and plug the banjo union. Two rubber washers and self-locking grips are useful for this purpose.
3 Unbolt and remove the caliper.

Series 2

4 With the roadwheel removed, unscrew the bolts (1) – Fig. 9.21.
5 Disconnect the pad wear sensor plug and remove the caliper.

Overhaul

Series 1

6 Refer to Section 9.

Series 2

7 Remove the plastic caps (1) and unscrew the guide bolts (2) – Fig. 9.22. Remove the pads and separate the cylinder from the caliper.
8 Remove the dust excluder retaining ring and the dust excluder.
9 Apply low air pressure to the fluid entry port and eject the piston. Examine the surface of the piston and cylinder bore. If corroded or scored, renew the cylinder assembly complete.
10 If the components are in good condition, obtain a repair kit which will contain all the renewable items, including seals and dowel sleeves.
11 Clean components in hydraulic fluid or methylated spirit – nothing else.

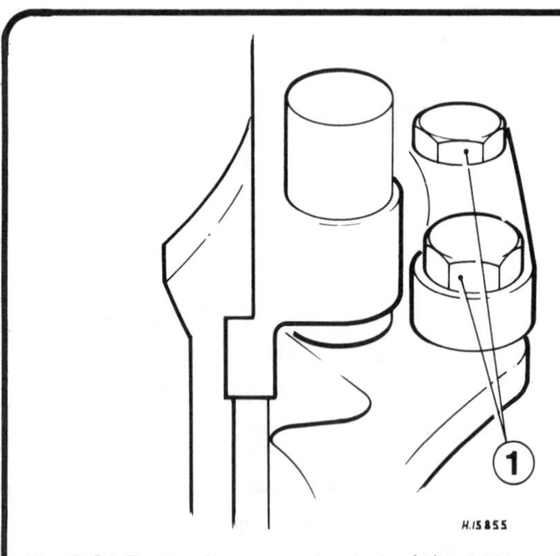

Fig. 9.21 Rear caliper securing bolts (1) – 323i models (Sec 11)

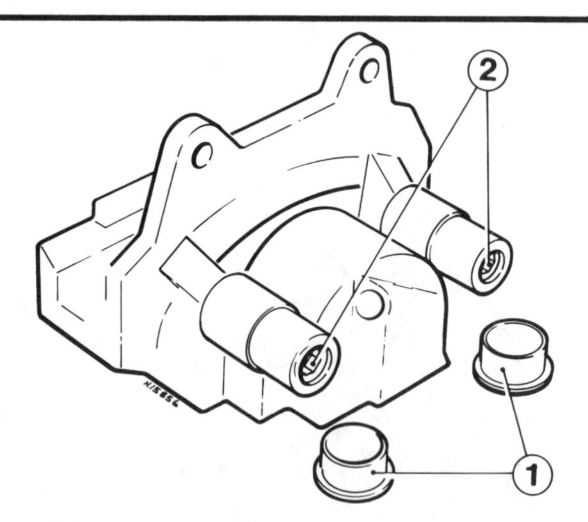

Fig. 9.22 Rear caliper plastic caps (1) and guide bolts (2) – 323i models (Sec 11)

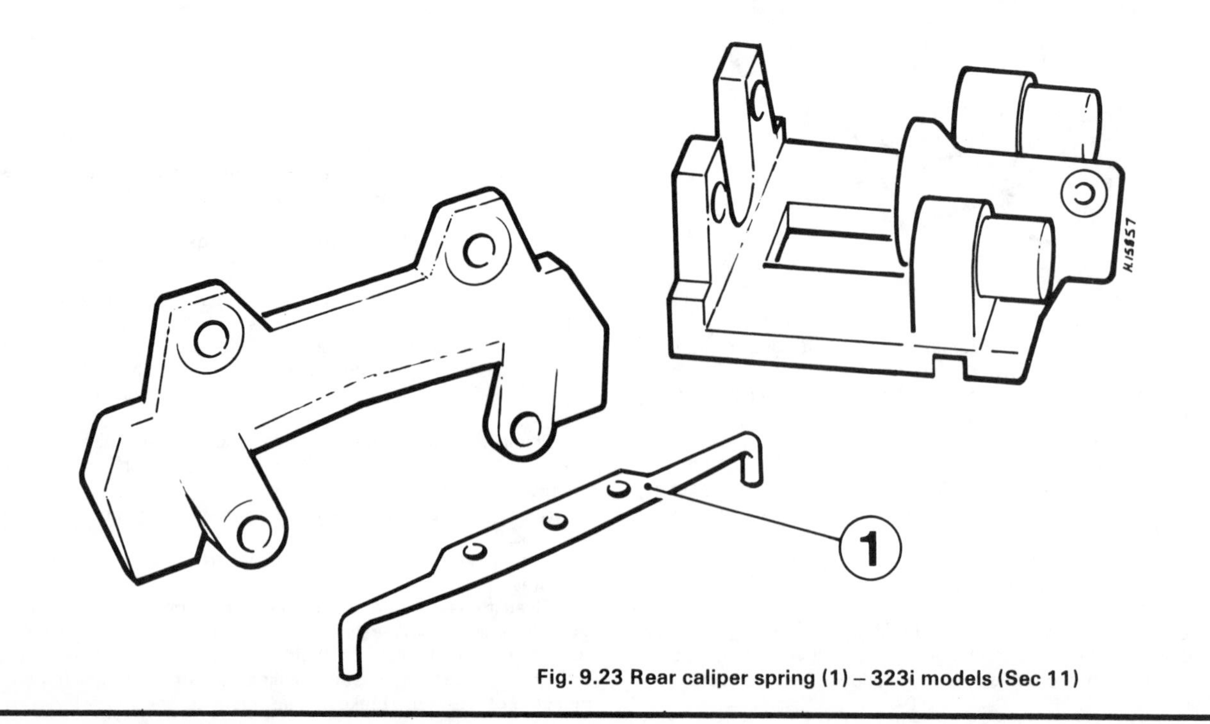

Fig. 9.23 Rear caliper spring (1) – 323i models (Sec 11)

12 Fit the new piston seal using the fingers only, dip the piston in clean hydraulic fluid and insert it into the cylinder bore.
13 Before pushing the piston fully into the bore, engage the dust excluder and fit the retaining ring.
14 Assemble the cylinder to the carrier and fit the disc pads. Push the outboard pad fully to one side before inserting the spring – Fig. 9.23.

Refitting

All models

15 Use new sealing rings at the banjo union, tighten all bolts to the specified torque and fill and bleed the hydraulic circuit.

12 Front disc – removal, renovation and refitting

1 Raise the front of the car, support it securely and remove the roadwheel.
2 If the disc is scored, cracked or deeply grooved, it should be removed for renovation or renewal.
3 If the disc is suspected of being out-of-true, check it with a dial gauge while turning the disc or by using feeler blades between the disc and a fixed point. If the run-out exceeds the specified maximum, renew **both** discs.
4 Light scoring or grooving is normal. Deep grooving can be removed by surface grinding on both sides, and on both discs at the same time to maintain balance. Take care that any balance weights on the discs are not removed during the operations and the overall thickness of the disc is not reduced below specification.
5 To remove the disc, unbolt the caliper and tie it to one side, there is no need to disconnect the hydraulic line.
6 Remove the angular plate from the suspension strut.
7 Extract the small retaining screw and withdraw the disc.
8 Refitting is a reversal of removal.

13 Rear disc – removal, renovation and refitting

1 The operations are very similar to those described for the front discs in the preceding Section.

14 Front disc shield – removal and refitting

1 Remove the roadwheel, disc and hub (Chapter 7).
2 A ventilated or non-ventilated disc shield may be encountered to match the type of disc fitted.
3 Unscrew the fixing screws and remove the shield.
4 When refitting, tighten the screws to specified torque.

15 Rear brake backplate – removal and refitting

1 Remove the roadwheel, brake drum and shoes.
2 Remove the hydraulic wheel cylinder, as described in Section 17.
3 Remove the hub/flange (Chapter 7).
4 Unbolt the backplate and withdraw it, passing the handbrake cable through the grommet.
5 Refitting is a reversal of removal, tighten bolts to the specified torque, bleed the hydraulic circuit (Section 22) and adjust the handbrake (Section 29).

16 Brake drum – inspection and renovation

1 Whenever the brake drums are removed to inspect the lining wear, take the opportunity to inspect the interior of the drum for grooving or cracks.
2 The drum may be machined out provided the maximum internal diameter is not exceeded (see Specifications).
3 Ovality or out-of-round, detected as the result of brake judder or binding, may also be rectified in the same way.
4 Always re-machine or regrind **both** drums at the same time.

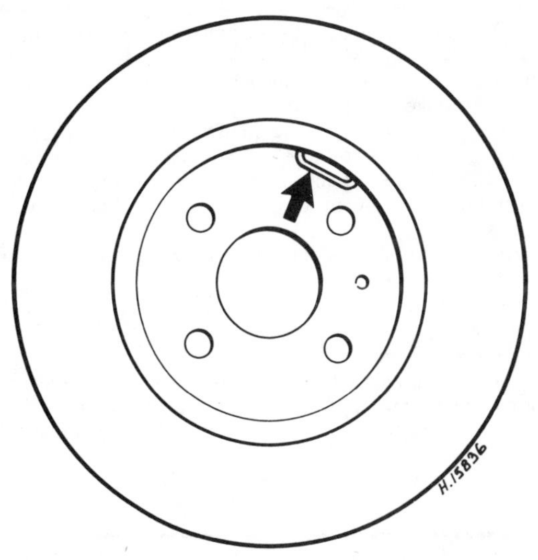

Fig. 9.24 Front disc balance weight – arrowed (Sec 12)

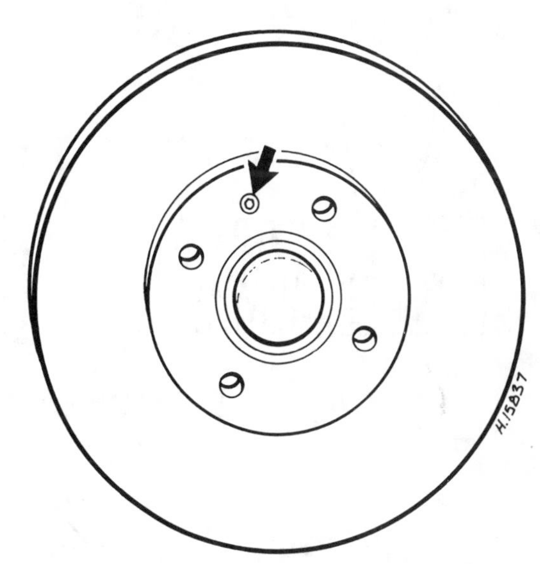

Fig. 9.25 Front disc retaining screw – arrowed (Sec 12)

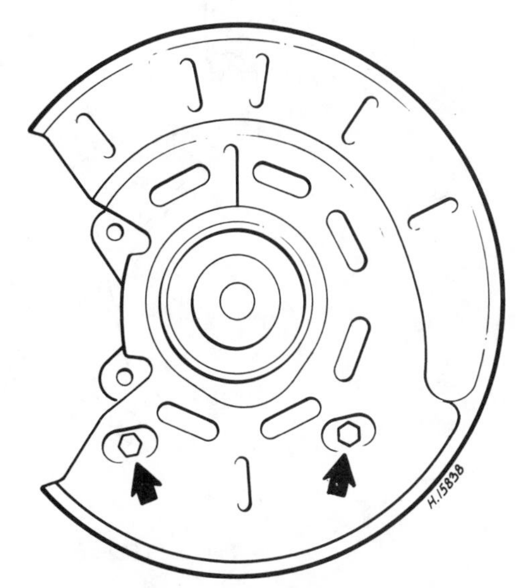

Fig. 9.26 Ventilated type disc shield fixing screws – arrowed (Sec 14)

17 Rear wheel hydraulic cylinder – removal, overhaul and refitting

1 Raise the rear of the car, support it securely and remove the roadwheel and brake drum.
2 Turn the shoe adjusters to the point of maximum adjustment.
3 Working on the rear of the brake backplate, unbolt the wheel cylinder, unscrew the bleed screw and disconnect the brake hydraulic pipe. Cap the pipe to prevent loss of fluid. A bleed screw dust cap is useful for this.
4 Expand the shoes slightly and slide the hydraulic cylinder sideways and out of the backplate.
5 Clean away external dirt and apply air pressure to the fluid entry hole while holding the finger over the bleed screw hole. The pistons and springs will be ejected.
6 Examine the surfaces of the piston and cylinder bore. If they are corroded or scored, renew the cylinder complete. Where the components are in good condition, clean them in hydraulic fluid or methylated spirit – nothing else, and obtain a repair kit which will contain all the new seals and renewable items.
7 Discard the old seals and fit the new ones, using the fingers only to manipulate them into position.
8 Dip the first piston in clean hydraulic fluid and insert it into the cylinder bore, fit the spring and the second piston.
9 Apply some brake grease to the ends of the pistons and to the interior of the dust excluders and fit them to the cylinder.
10 Refit the wheel cylinder to the brake backplate, reconnect the brake pipe and screw in the bleed screw.
11 Refit the brake drum (after contracting the shoes) and the roadwheel.
12 Adjust the brake shoes and bleed the hydraulic circuit (Section 22).

18 Master cylinder (Series 1) – removal, overhaul and refitting

1 Remove the fluid from the master cylinder reservoir and then remove the reservoir by 'rocking' it upwards out of its seals. Unscrew the master cylinder fixing nuts.
2 Unbolt and remove the support plate from the wing valance.

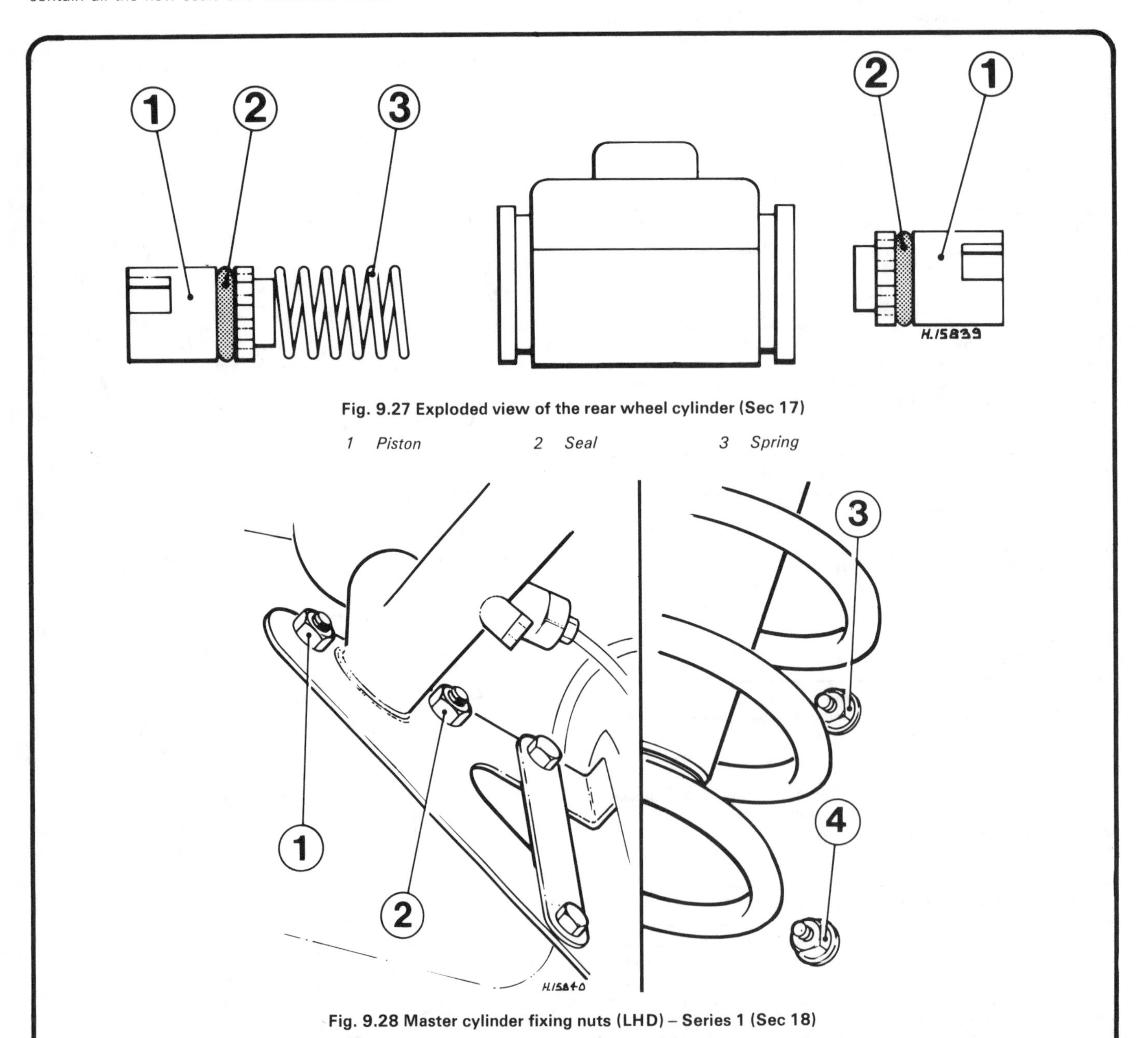

Fig. 9.27 Exploded view of the rear wheel cylinder (Sec 17)

1 Piston 2 Seal 3 Spring

Fig. 9.28 Master cylinder fixing nuts (LHD) – Series 1 (Sec 18)

1 Servo nut 2 Servo nut 3 Wing valance nut 4 Wing valance nut

3 Disconnect the brake hydraulic pipes from the master cylinder. Be prepared for some loss of fluid.
4 Remove the master cylinder from its mounting studs on the servo unit.
5 Apply finger pressure to the rod (1), unscrew the stop bolt (2) and extract the circlip (3) – Fig. 9.31. The primary piston will be ejected.
6 Shake out the secondary piston.
7 Examine the surfaces of the cylinder bores and pistons. If corroded or scored, renew the master cylinder complete.
8 If the components are in good condition, obtain a repair kit which will contain all the necessary seals and other renewable items. Discard the old seals and clean the components in hydraulic fluid or methylated spirit – nothing else.
9 The primary piston can be dismantled by removing the connecting screw.
10 Manipulate all seals into position using the fingers only and note carefully the fitted direction of the seal lips.
11 Dip the secondary piston in clean hydraulic fluid and push it into the cylinder.
12 Fit the primary piston with a new copper sealing washer, apply

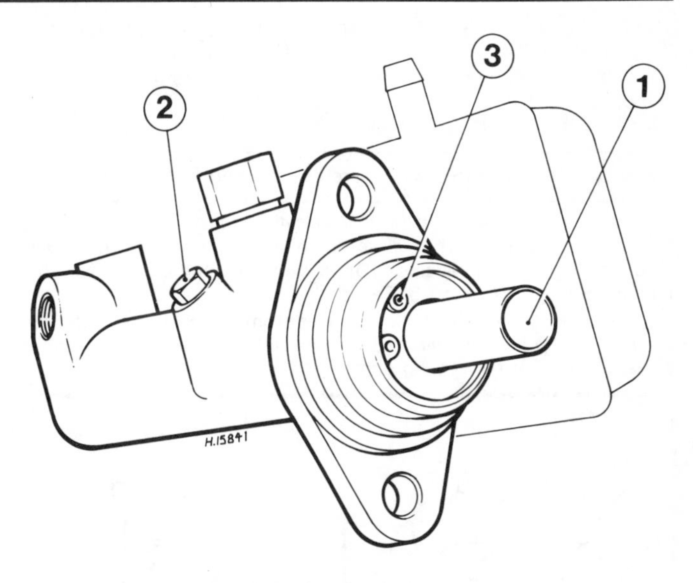

Fig. 9.31 Master cylinder – Series 1 (Sec 18)

1 Rod
2 Stop bolt
3 Circlip

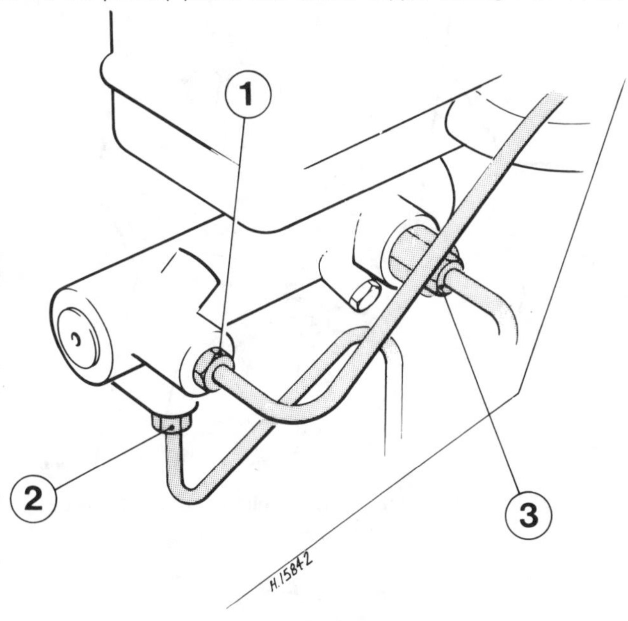

Fig. 9.29 Master cylinder hydraulic pipelines (LHD) – Series 1 (Sec 18)

1 To front right-hand caliper
2 To front left-land caliper
3 To rear brakes

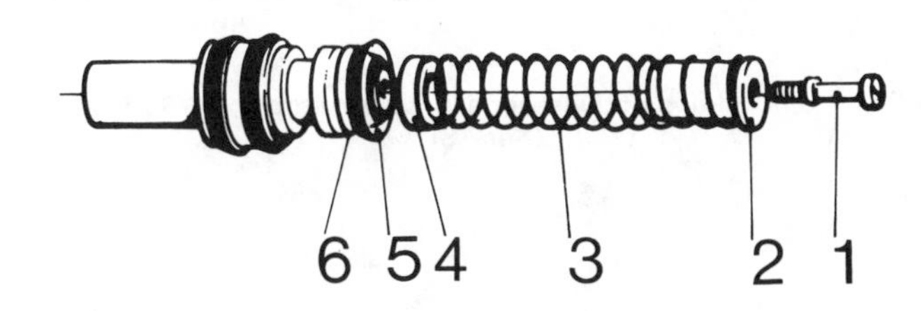

Fig. 9.32 Exploded view of primary piston – Series 1 (Sec 18)

1 Connecting bolt
2 Spring cup
3 Spring
4 Support ring
5 Seal
6 Washer

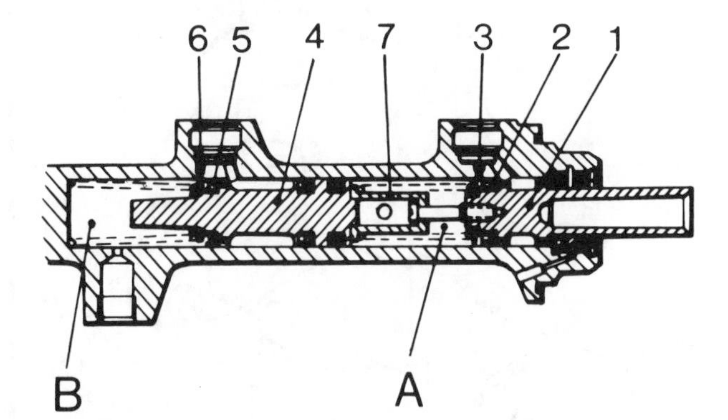

Fig. 9.30 Sectional view of the master cylinder – Series 1 (Sec 18)

1 Primary piston
2 Seal
3 Compensating passage
4 Secondary piston
5 Seal
6 Compensating passage
7 Spring cap
A Primary cylinder
B Secondary cylinder

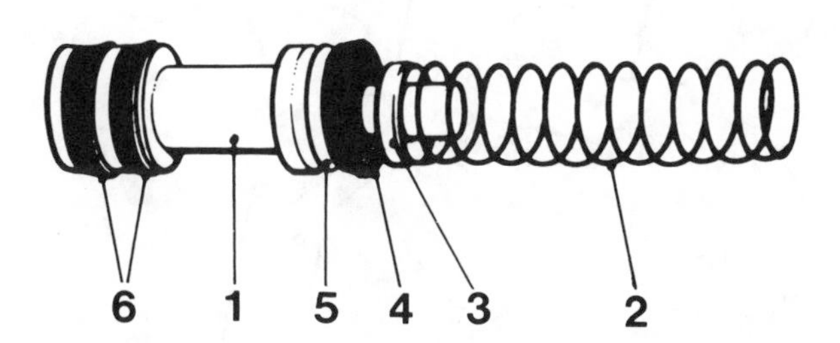

Fig. 9.33 Exploded view of the secondary piston – Series 1 (Sec 18)

1 Piston
2 Spring
3 Support ring
4 Seal
5 Washer
6 Seals

light pressure to the piston rod and screw in the secondary piston stop bolt. Fit the circlip.
13 Refitting is a reversal of removal, observe all torque tightening figures.
14 Bleed the complete brake hydraulic circuit (Section 22).

19 Master cylinder (Series 2) – removal, overhaul and refitting

1 Remove the fluid from the master cylinder reservoir.
2 Disconnect the fluid level sensor plug and the clutch hydraulic feed hose (when applicable). On K-Jetronic models, remove the mixture regulator (Chapter 3, Section 30).
3 Disconnect the brake hydraulic lines from the master cylinder.
4 Pull off the master cylinder reservoir tank using a 'rocking' action to release it from the sealing rings.
5 Unscrew the master cylinder mounting bolts and remove the cylinder.
6 The overhaul operations are as described in Section 18.
7 Refit by reversing the removal operations and then bleed the complete hydraulic circuit.

20 Pressure regulating valve – removal and refitting

1 This valve reduces the hydraulic pressure to the rear brakes during heavy applications of the brake pedal and so prevents rear wheel lock up.
2 No repair or adjustment is possible, but in the event of a fault developing, renew the valve complete.
3 Disconnect the brake lines from the valve, noting their locations

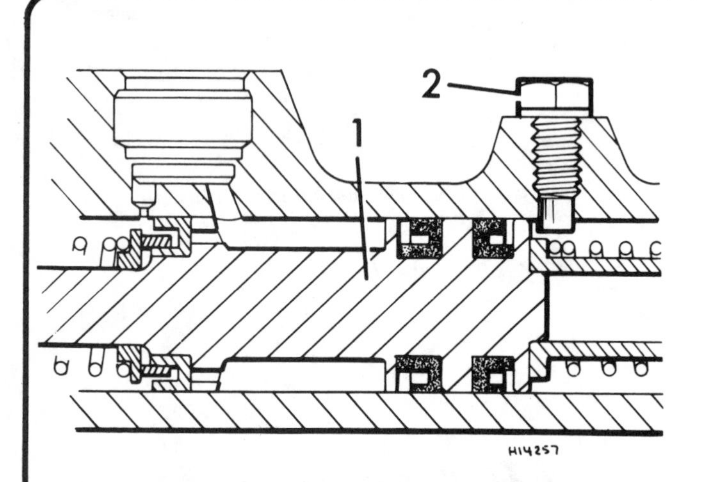

Fig. 9.34 Location of the secondary piston stop bolt – Series 1 (Sec 18)

1 Piston 2 Stop bolt

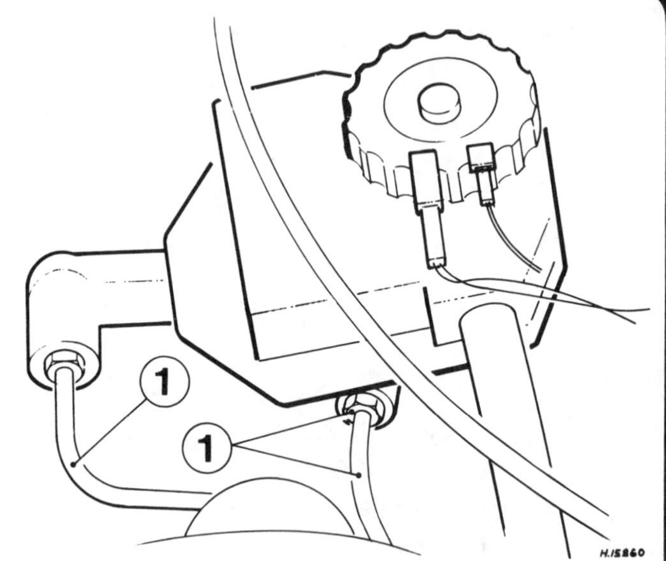

Fig. 9.36 Master cylinder hydraulic pipelines (1) – Series 2 (Sec 19)

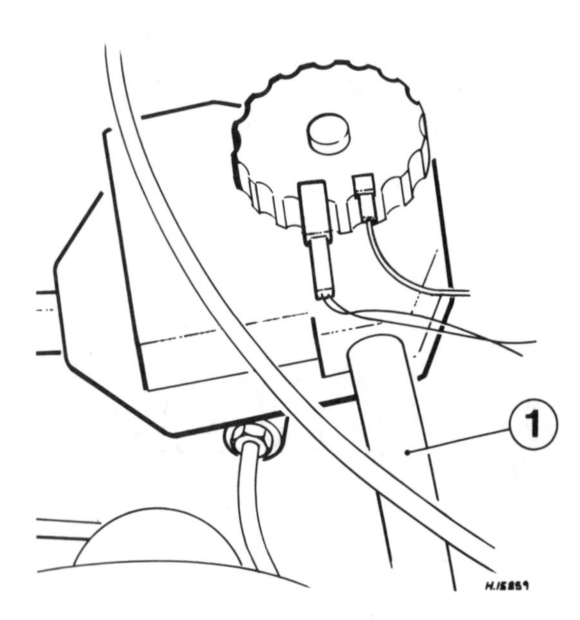

Fig. 9.35 Master cylinder clutch hydraulic feed hose (1) – Series 2 (Sec 19)

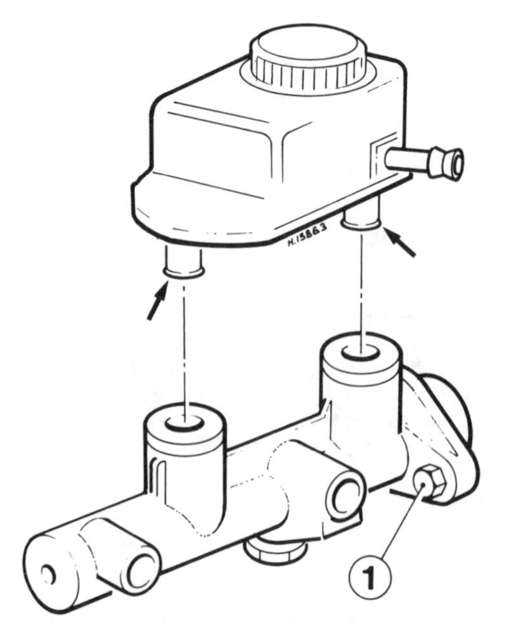

Fig. 9.37 Master cylinder reservoir and mounting bolts (1) – Series 2 (Sec 19)

Arrows indicate reservoir locating pipes

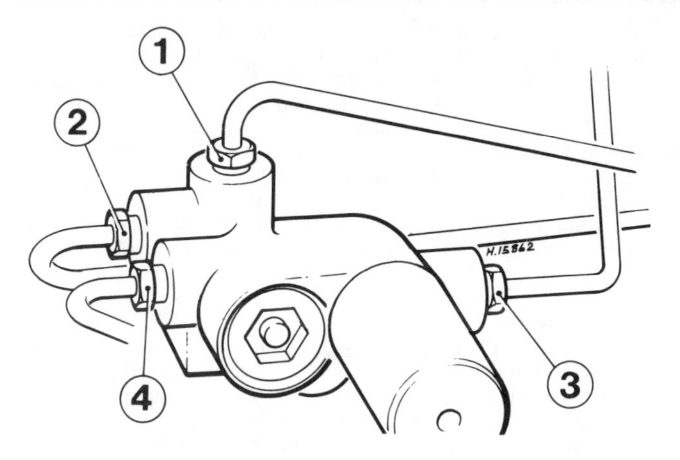

Fig. 9.38 Pressure regulating valve – Series 1 (Sec 20)

1 *Front brake inlet*
2 *Front brake outlet*
3 *Rear brake inlet*
4 *Rear brake outlet*

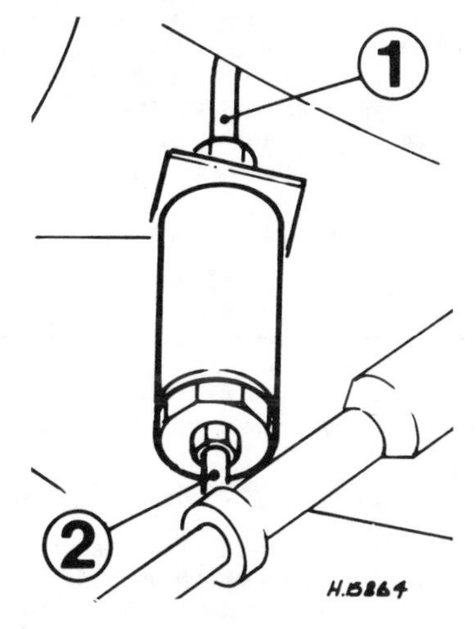

Fig. 9.39 Pressure regulating valve – Series 2 (Sec 20)

1 *Hydraulic pipeline* 2 *Hydraulic pipeline*

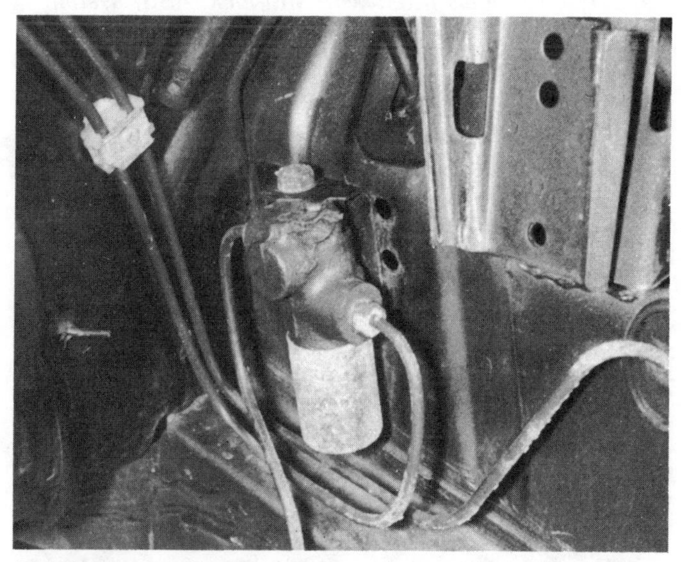

20.4 Pressure regulator (Series 1)

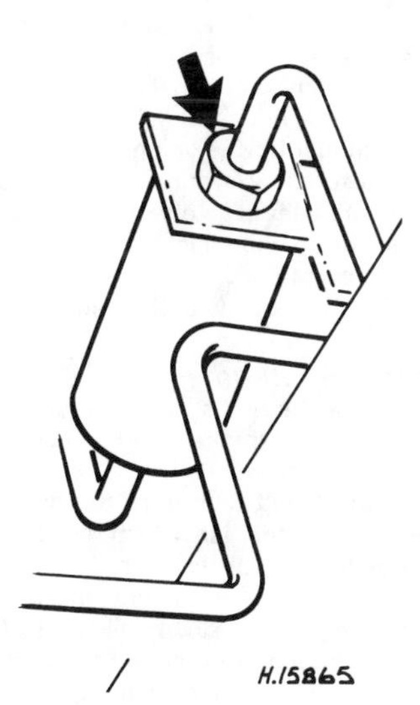

Fig. 9.40 Pressure regulating valve securing nut (arrowed) – Series 2 (Sec 20)

and allowing the hydraulic fluid to drain into a container.
4 On Series 1 models, unbolt the pressure regulator valve from the engine compartment rear bulkhead (photo).
5 On Series 2 models, unclamp and remove the valve from under the rear of the car.
6 Refitting is a reversal of removal. Bleed the hydraulic circuit, as described in Section 22.

21 Flexible hoses and rigid pipelines

1 Periodically check the condition of the flexible hydraulic hoses. Any sign of rot, splitting or tiny cracks when bent with the fingers will indicate the need for a new hose.
2 To remove a hose, unscrew the rigid pipeline union from it, holding the hose end fitting against rotation with another open-ended spanner.
3 A special brake union spanner is to be preferred to release the unions, but if one is not available, self-locking grips are better than rounding off the union with an open-ended spanner.
4 The hose end fittings are secured in brackets and the 'set' is given to the hose to keep it away from adjacent components by a spring clip which can be pulled out with a pair of pliers.
5 On 323i rear hoses, the hose is attached to the caliper by means of a banjo union.

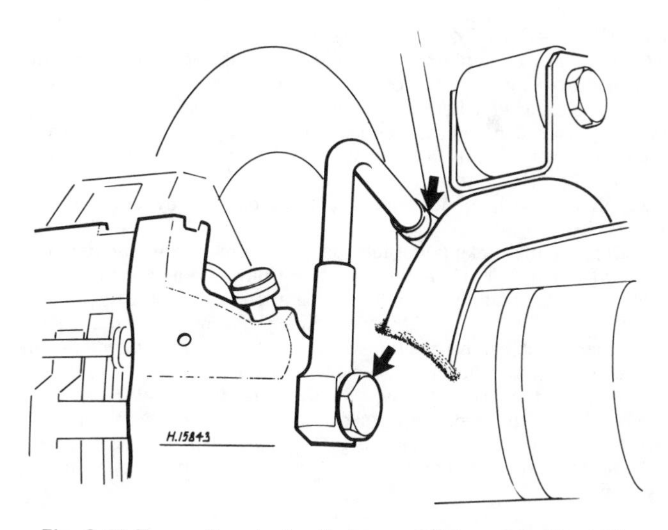

Fig. 9.41 Rear caliper hydraulic hose – 323i models (Sec 21)

Banjo unions arrowed

6 Regularly inspect the condition of the rigid hydraulic lines. If they are corroded or have been damaged by flying stones then they must be renewed.
7 New pipes are available from BMW dealers or can be made to pattern by most garages and motor stores.
8 Always make sure that the pipe fixing clips are secure and tight to prevent rattle.
9 The system will of course have to be bled on completion of the work (Section 22).

22 Hydraulic system – bleeding

1 The two independent hydraulic circuits are as follows:

(a) Front disc brakes
(b) Rear drum brakes (320 and 320i) or rear disc brakes (323i)

2 If the master cylinder has been disconnected and reconnected then the complete system (both circuits) must be bled.
3 If only a component of one circuit has been disturbed then only that particular circuit need be bled.
4 If the entire system is being bled, the sequence of bleeding should be carried out by starting at the bleed screw furthest from the master cylinder and finishing at the one nearest to it. Unless the pressure bleeding method is being used, do not forget to keep the fluid level in the master cylinder reservoir topped up to prevent air from being drawn into the system which would make any work done worthless.
5 Before commencing operations, check that all system hoses and pipes are in good condition with the unions tight and free from leaks.
6 Take great care not to allow hydraulic fluid to come into contact with the vehicle paintwork as it is an effective paint stripper. Wash off any spilled fluid immediately with cold water.
7 As the system incorporates a vacuum servo, destroy the vacuum by giving several applications of the brake pedal in quick succession.

Bleeding – two man method
8 Gather together a clean jar and a length of rubber or plastic tubing which will be a tight fit on the brake bleed screws.
9 Engage the help of an assistant.
10 Push one end of the bleed tube onto the first bleed screw and immerse the other end in the jar which should contain enough hydraulic fluid to cover the end of the tube.
11 Open the bleed screw one half a turn and have your assistant depress the brake pedal fully, then slowly release it. Tighten the bleed screw at the end of each pedal downstroke to obviate any chance of air or fluid being drawn back into the system.
12 Repeat this operation until clean hydraulic fluid, free from air bubbles, can be seen coming through into the jar.
13 Tighten the bleed screw at the end of a pedal downstroke and remove the bleed tube. Bleed the remaining screws in a similar way.

Bleeding – using one-way valve kit
14 There are a number of one-man, one-way brake bleeding kits available from motor accessory shops. It is recommended that one of these kits is used wherever possible as it will greatly simplify the bleeding operation and also reduce the risk of air or fluid being drawn back into the system, quite apart from being able to do the work without the help of an assistant.
15 To use the kit, connect the tube to the bleed screw and open the screw one half a turn.
16 Depress the brake pedal fully and slowly release it. The one-way valve in the kit will prevent expelled air from returning at the end of each pedal downstroke. Repeat this operation several times to be sure of ejecting all air from the system. Some kits include a translucent container which can be positioned so that the air bubbles can actually be seen being ejected from the system.
17 Tighten the bleed screw, remove the tube and repeat the operations on the remaining brakes.
18 On completion, depress the brake pedal. If it still feels spongy repeat the bleeding operations, as air must still be trapped in the system.

Bleeding – using a pressure bleeding kit
19 These kits are available from motor accessory shops and are usually operated by air pressure from the spare tyre.
20 By connecting a pressurised container to the master cylinder fluid reservoir, bleeding is then carried out simply by opening each bleed screw in turn and allowing the fluid to run out, rather like turning on a tap, until no air is visible in the expelled fluid.
21 By using this method, the large reserve of hydraulic fluid provides a safeguard against air being drawn into the master cylinder during bleeding which may occur if the fluid level in the reservoir is allowed to fall too low.
22 Pressure bleeding is particularly effective when bleeding 'difficult' systems or when bleeding the complete system at time of routine fluid renewal.

All methods
23 When bleeding is completed, check and top up the fluid level in the master cylinder reservoir.
24 Check the feel of the brake pedal. If it feels at all spongy, air must still be present in the system and further bleeding is indicated. Failure to bleed satisfactorily after a reasonable repetition of the bleeding operations may be due to worn master cylinder seals.
25 Discard brake fluid which has been expelled. It is almost certain to be contaminated with moisture, air and dirt making it unsuitable for further use. Clean fluid should always be stored in an airtight container as it absorbs moisture readily (hygroscopic) which lowers its boiling point and could affect braking performance under severe conditions.

Bleeding on models fitted with anti-lock (ABS) system
26 On models equipped with this device, it is recommended that the pressure bleeding system is used. Have an assistant depress the brake pedal and hold it down.
27 Open the right rear bleed screw, release and depress the brake pedal twelve times fully, hold the pedal down and then close the bleed screw.
28 Repeat the procedure on the left rear, front right and front left brakes in that order.
29 If a pressure bleeding device is not used, the manual bleeding procedure will be as for a brake system without ABS, but include the twelve strokes of the pedal as just described at each bleed screw.

23 Vacuum servo unit – description and maintenance

1 A vacuum servo unit is fitted into the brake hydraulic circuit in series with the master cylinder, to provide assistance to the driver when the brake pedal is depressed. It reduces the effort, required by the driver, to operate the brakes under all braking conditions, whilst the engine is running.
2 The unit operates by vacuum obtained from the induction manifold and is composed of, basically, a booster diaphragm and non-return valve. The servo unit piston does not fit tightly into the cylinder, but has a strong diaphragm to keep its edges in constant contact with the cylinder wall, so assuring an airtight seal between the two parts. The forward chamber is held under vacuum conditions created in the inlet manifold of the engine and, during periods when the brake pedal is not in use, the controls open a passage to the rear chamber so placing it under vacuum conditions as well. When the brake pedal is depressed, the vacuum passage to the rear chamber is cut off and the chamber opened to atmospheric pressure. The consequent rush of air pushes the servo piston forward in the vacuum chamber and operates the main pushrod.
3 The controls are designed so that assistance is given under all conditions and, when the brakes are not required, vacuum in the rear chamber is established when the brake pedal is released. All air from the atmosphere entering the rear chamber is passed through a small air filter.
4 Under normal operating conditions the vacuum servo unit is very reliable and does not require overhaul except at very high mileage. In this case it is far better to obtain a service exchange unit, rather than repair the original unit.
5 It is emphasised that the servo unit assists in reducing the braking effort required at the foot pedal and, in the event of its failure, the hydraulic braking system is in no way affected except that the need for higher pedal pressures will be noticed.
6 Maintenance consists of periodically checking the condition of the vacuum hose and, at the specified intervals, renewing the servo air filter element, as described in the next Section.

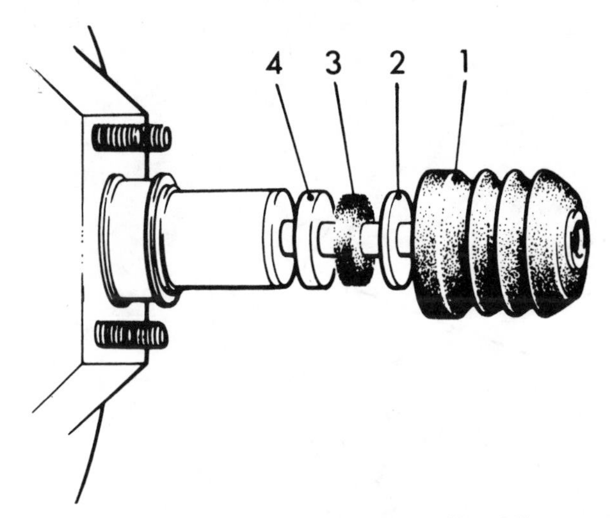

Fig. 9.42 Vacuum servo unit pushrod (Sec 24)

1 Dust excluding gaiter
2 Retainer
3 Silencer
4 Filter element

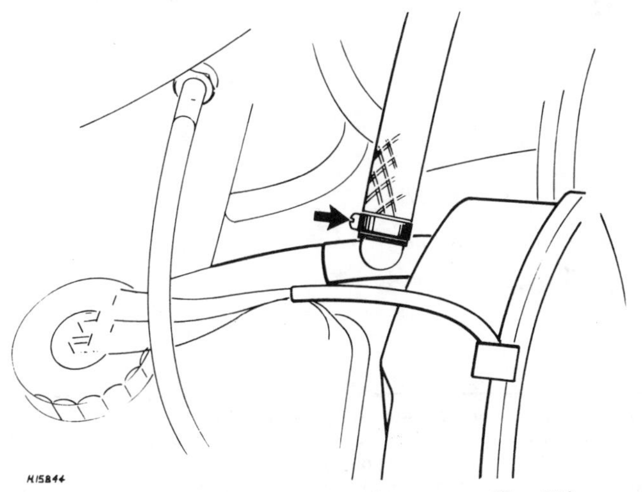

Fig. 9.43 Vacuum hose connection to servo (Sec 25)

Securing clip arrowed

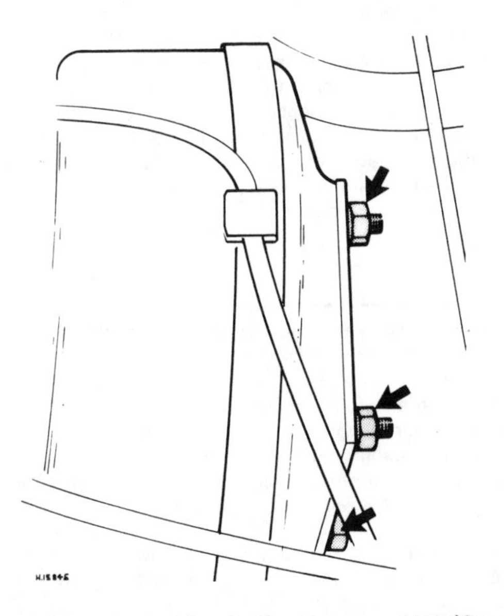

Fig. 9.44 Servo-to-bulkhead securing nuts – LHD (Sec 25)

24 Vacuum servo air filter element – renewal

Left-hand drive

1 Disconnect the servo pushrod from the brake pedal and remove the clevis fork.

2 Pull off the dust excluding gaiter (1) the retainer (2), silencer (3) and the filter element (4) – Fig. 9.42.

3 Fit the new element and refit other components, reconnect the pushrod and check the pedal adjustment, as described in Section 32.

Right-hand drive

Series 1

4 The servo and master cylinder are mounted at the front right-hand corner of the engine compartment and operated by a remote control rod and lever. Access to the servo filter element is obtained after disconnecting the lever from the servo pushrod.

Series 2

5 The servo and master cylinder are mounted on the left-hand side of the engine compartment rear bulkhead, the servo pushrod being operated by a cross-shaft located inside the car.

6 Access to the servo filter is obtained by disconnecting the cross-shaft lever from the pushrod.

25 Vacuum servo unit – removal and refitting

1 Remove the hydraulic fluid from the master cylinder reservoir.

2 On 323i LHD models, remove the mixture regulator unit, as described in Chapter 3.

3 Disconnect the pushrod, or remote control rod, from the brake pedal or servo lever.

4 Disconnect the hydraulic pipes from the master cylinder.

5 Disconnect the vacuum hose from the servo unit.

6 Unbolt the servo unit from the engine compartment bulkhead (or, with Series 1 LHD, unbolt it from the support member) and wing valance.

7 The master cylinder may be unbolted from the servo unit.

8 It is not recommended that the servo is overhauled, but if faulty fit a new unit.

9 When fitting the master cylinder to the servo use a new sealing ring and tighten the nuts to specified torque.

10 Bleed the hydraulic system, as described in Section 22.

Fig. 9.45 Servo support plate-to-wing valance nuts (arrowed) Series 1, LHD (Sec 25)

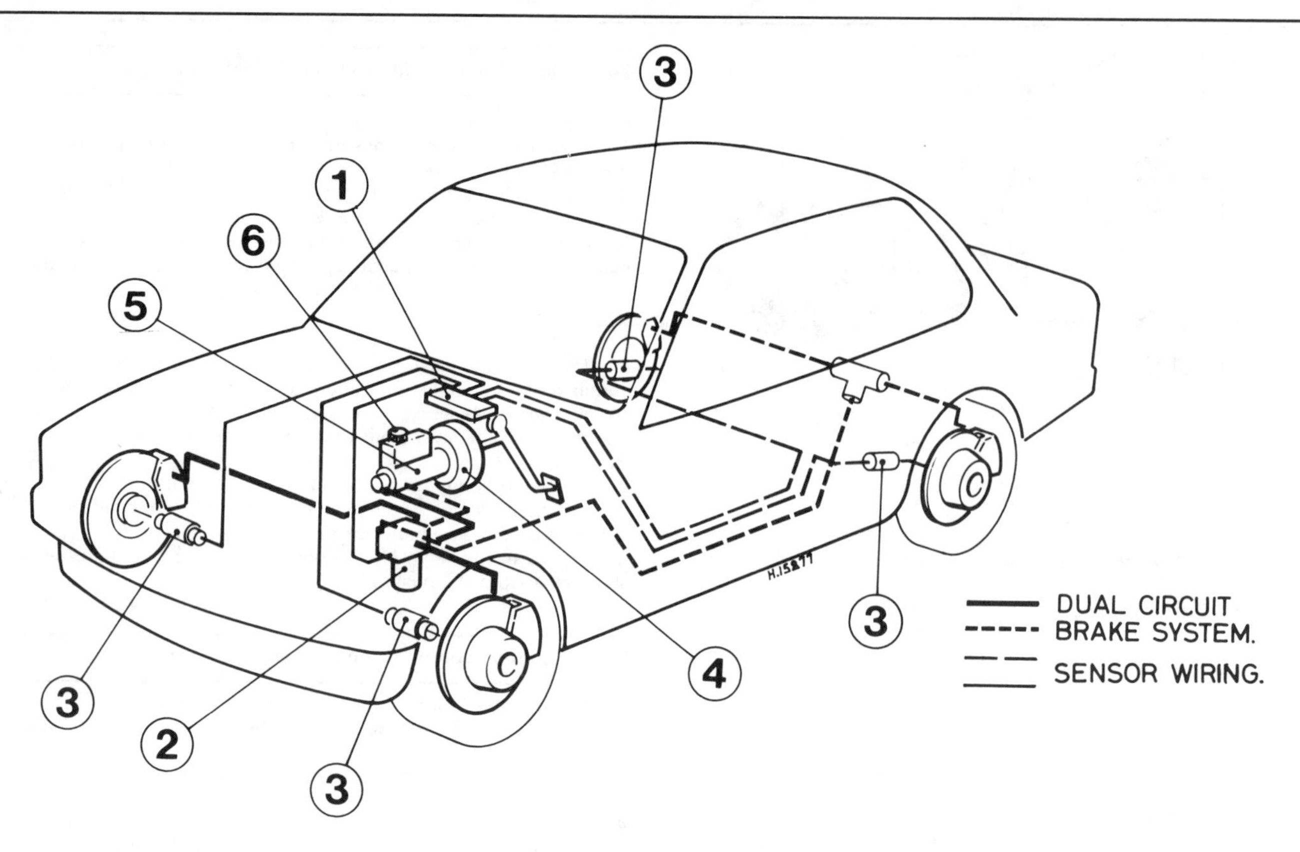

Fig. 9.46 Anti-lock brake system (ABS) – LHD (Sec 27)

1 Control unit
2 Hydraulic unit
3 Speed sensors
4 Vacuum servo unit
5 Master cylinder
6 Fluid reservoir

26 Servo one-way valve – renewal

1 This is simply a matter of releasing the hose clips and taking out the old valve and fitting the new one. Make sure that the arrow or the black side of the valve faces the intake manifold (photo).

26.1 Vacuum servo one-way valve

27 Anti-lock brake system (ABS) – description

1 This optional system is designed to give the car the shortest possible braking distances in a straight line or on a turn on any road surface.
2 The system incorporates a control unit, hydraulic assembly and speed sensors in addition to the normal brake units.
3 These devices regulate the braking pressure to each of the front wheels independently, and to the rear wheels as a pair.
4 The brake pressure regulating cycle begins if the peripheral speed of a roadwheel is not equal to the car's roadspeed which will indicate that wheel lock is about to occur.
5 The regulating action takes place irrespective of the force being applied to the foot pedal so that the repeated 'dabbing' action often recommended when braking on slippery surfaces is not required.

28 Anti-lock brake system components – removal and refitting

Hydraulic unit

1 Disconnect the battery negative lead.
2 Remove the air cleaner.
3 Remove the headlamp cover panel.
4 Disconnect the hydraulic lines (1 and 2) – Fig. 9.47. Cap the pipes.
5 Disconnect the hydraulic lines (1, 3 and 4) – Fig. 9.48. Cap the pipes.
6 Unscrew the bolt (2) and remove the cover.
7 Remove the bolts (1 and 2) – Fig. 9.49 – and disconnect the earth lead (3) and multi-pin plug.
8 Release the nut (1) – Fig. 9.50 – and withdraw the hydraulic unit.

Control unit

9 Remove the facia under cover.

10 Push back the clamp (1) and pull out the multi-pin plug (2) – Fig. 9.51.

11 Unscrew and remove the control unit.

12 If the control unit must be renewed, always use one with the same code number.

Wiring harness

13 Disconnect the battery negative and positive leads.

14 Remove the cover from the hydraulic unit. Unscrew bolts (1 and 2) – Fig. 9.49 – and then disconnect the multi-pin plug from the hydraulic unit.

15 Remove the headlamp cover panels and disconnect the plugs from the pulse sensors in the engine compartment.

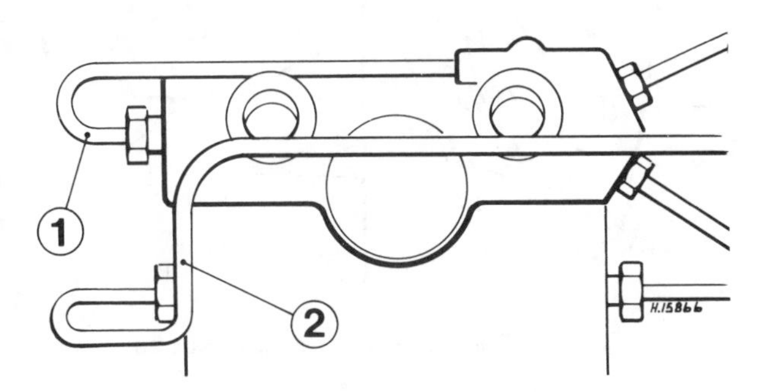

Fig. 9.47 Anti-lock system hydraulic unit pipelines (Sec 28)

1 To pressure regulator 2 To master cylinder

Fig. 9.50 Anti-lock system hydraulic unit mounting bolt (1) (Sec 28)

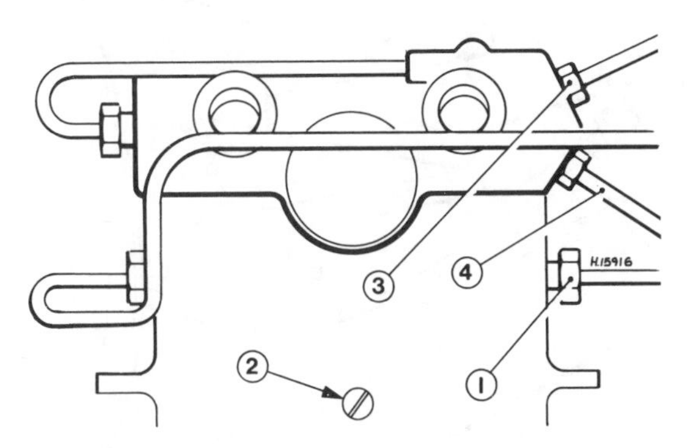

Fig. 9.48 Anti-lock system hydraulic unit pipelines (Sec 28)

1 To master cylinder 3 To left front caliper
2 Cover bolt 4 To right front caliper

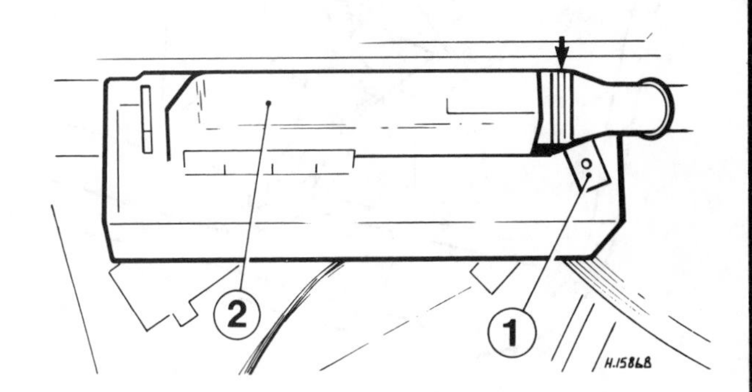

Fig. 9.51 Anti-lock system control unit (Sec 28)

1 Clamp 2 Multi-pin plug

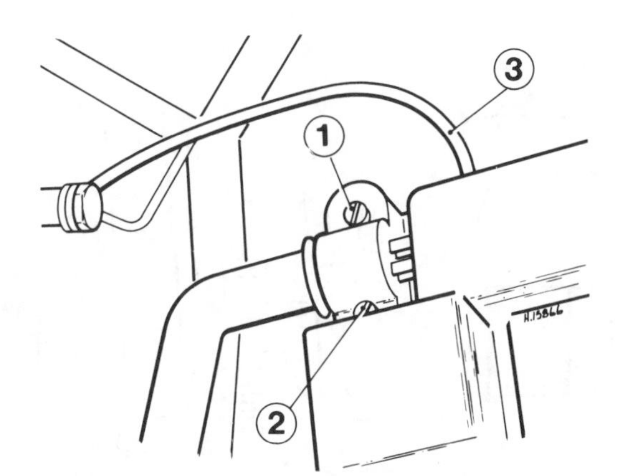

Fig. 9.49 Anti-lock system hydraulic unit mounting bolts (Sec 28)

1 Bolt 3 Earth wire
2 Bolt

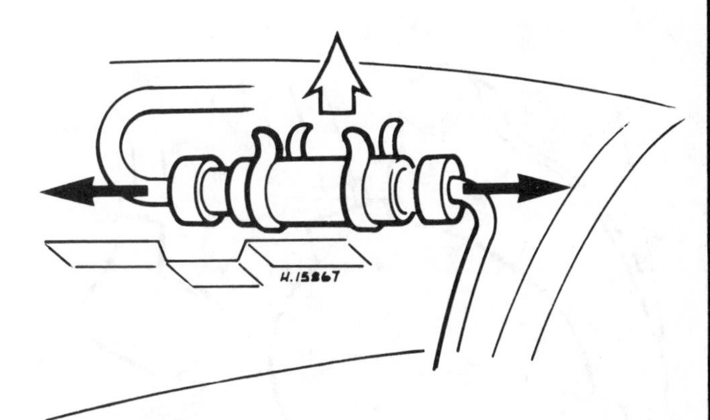

Fig. 9.52 Disconnect the plugs from the sensor (Sec 28)

16 Release the wiring harness within the engine compartment.
17 Remove the front and rear seats and disconnect the plugs from the pulse sensors.
18 Lift the carpets and trim panels as necessary to withdraw the harness.
19 Disconnect the multi-pin plug from the control unit.
20 Disconnect the earth wire from the body immediately above the control unit, then pull off the plugs and remove the electronic relay located immediately below the unit.
21 Reach up behind the instrument panel and pull out the ABS indicator lamp and holder.
22 Remove the fusebox and push the wiring harness into the passenger compartment.

Front speed pulse sensor

23 Make sure that the ignition is off and then extract the sensor screw.
24 Pull out the sensor, release the wiring and disconnect the plug.
25 The pulse wheel can only be renewed with the front hub bearing (Chapter 7).
26 When refitting the sensor, apply molybdenum disulphide grease.

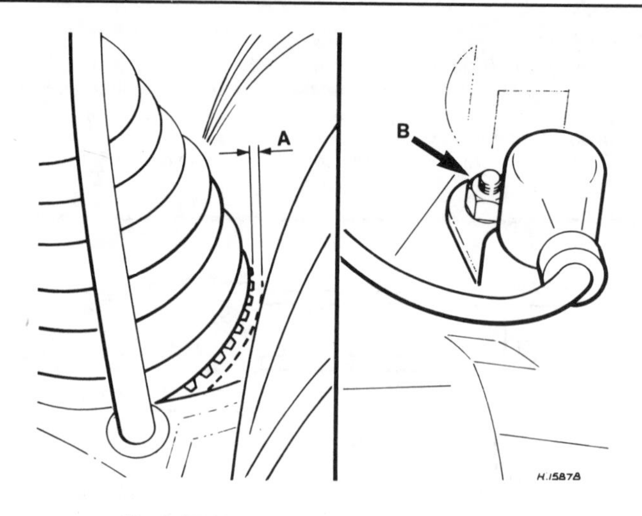

Fig. 9.55 Rear speed pulse sensor (Sec 28)

A Fixed clearance *B Securing screw*

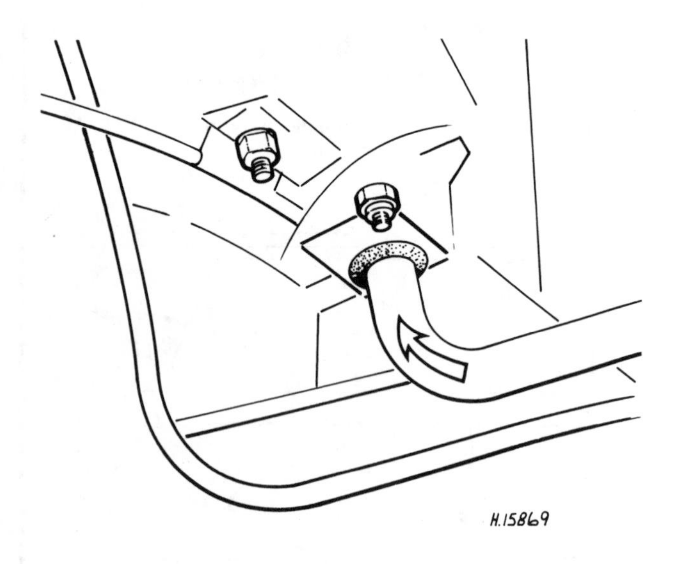

Fig. 9.53 Push the ABS system harness into the passenger compartment (Sec 28)

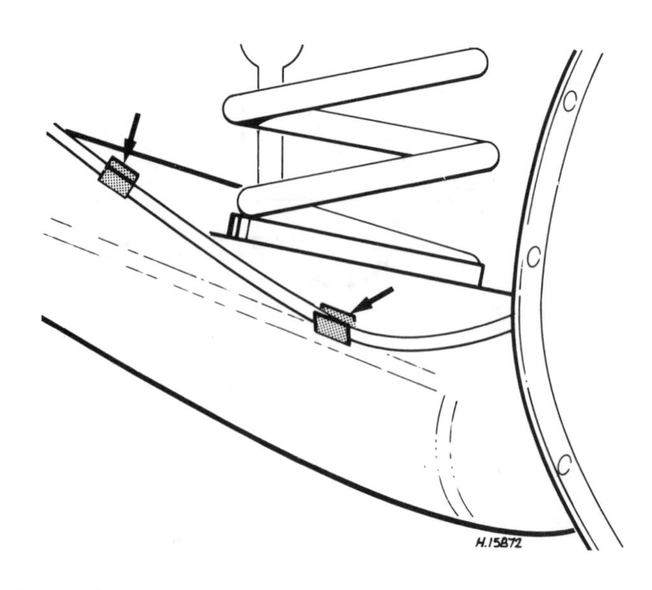

Fig. 9.56 Rear speed pulse sensor wiring clips – arrowed (Sec 28)

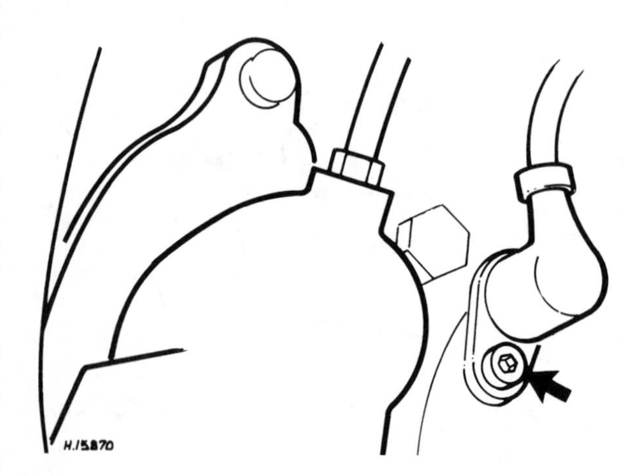

Fig. 9.54 Front speed pulse sensor screw – arrowed (Sec 28)

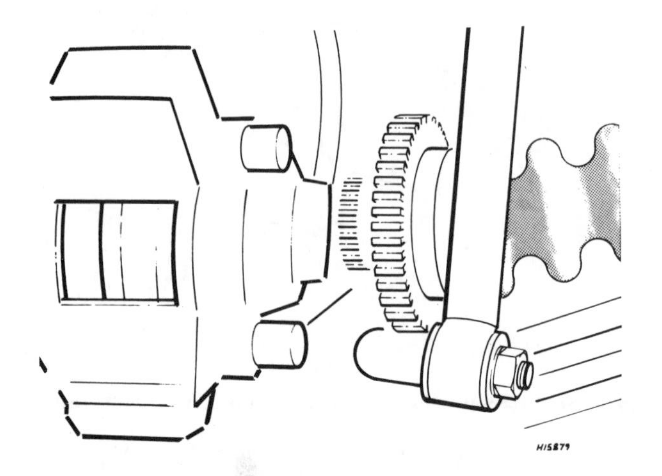

Fig. 9.57 Rear pulse wheel (Sec 28)

Rear speed pulse sensor

27 Make sure that the ignition is off then remove the rear roadwheel.
28 Extract the socket-headed screw and withdraw the sensor, release the wiring and disconnect the plug. The rear seat will have to be removed to reach the plug.
29 The pulse wheel can only be renewed with the driveshaft (Chapter 7).

Hydraulic unit relays

30 Extract the screw and remove the cover from the hydraulic unit.
31 Withdraw the motor relay (2) and the valve relay (3) – Fig. 9.58.

All components

32 Refitting is a reversal of removal. Bleed the hydraulic system where necessary.

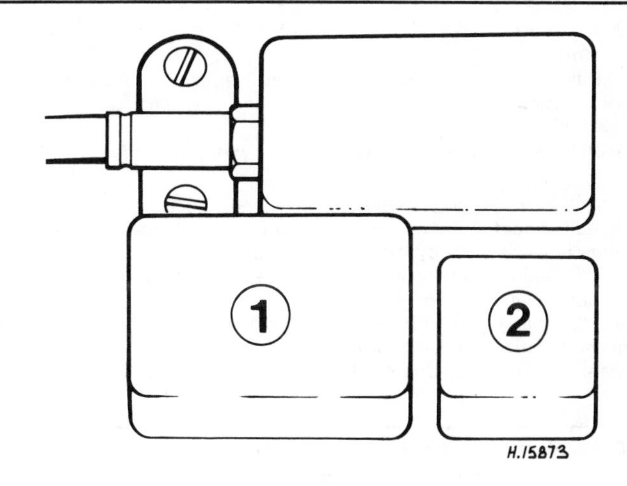

Fig. 9.58 Anti-lock system hydraulic unit relays (Sec 28)

1 Motor relay 2 Valve relay

29 Handbrake – adjustment

Series 1 (rear drum brakes)

1 This will only be necessary if the handbrake lever can be pulled up more than six clicks to fully apply the brakes.
2 Raise the rear of the car, chock the front wheels and release the handbrake fully.
3 Adjust the brakes, as described in Section 2.
4 Pull the gaiter up the handbrake control lever to expose the adjuster nuts (photo).
5 Slacken both locknuts and then pull the lever over four notches (clicks).
6 Tighten both adjuster nuts until the rear wheels just start to bind when turned. Release the lever and then check that the rear wheels are locked when the lever is pulled over five notches. Adjust further, if required, and then make sure that the wheels turn freely when the handbrake lever is fully released.
7 Tighten the locknuts without altering the position of the adjuster nuts, pull down the gaiter.

Series 2 (rear drum brakes)

8 The action of the brake pedal will normally keep the handbrake in correct adjustment through the medium of the automatic shoe adjuster.
9 However, if the handbrake control lever requires pulling over more than eight notches (clicks) to fully apply the brakes, then the cables have stretched.
10 Lift out the front clamp, pull off the gaiter (1) and disconnect the rear clamp – Fig. 9.60 – at the hand control lever.
11 Unscrew the adjuster nuts at the lever several turns and fully release the handbrake lever. Raise the rear of the car.

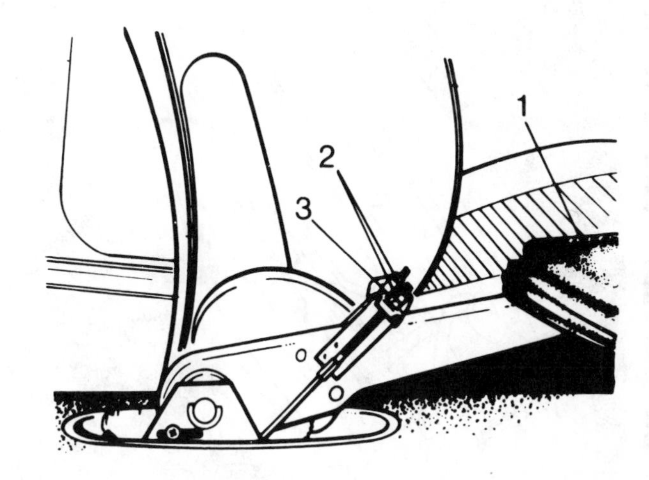

Fig. 9.59 Handbrake adjuster nuts – Series 1 (Sec 29)

1 Gaiter 3 Adjuster nut
2 Locknut

29.4 Handbrake control lever (Series 1)

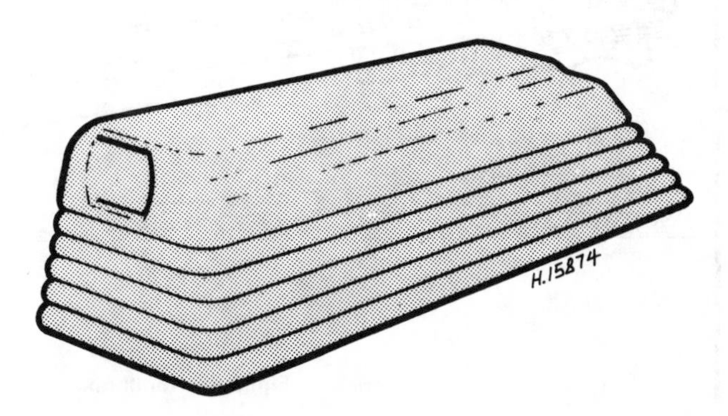

Fig. 9.60 Handbrake gaiter – Series 2 (Sec 29)

12 Apply the footbrake several times to bring the shoes to maximum adjustment.
13 Pull the handbrake control lever over five notches (clicks) and then turn the nuts at the lever until the rear roadwheels can just be turned very stiffly.
14 Release the lever and check that the wheels turn freely.

Series 2 (rear disc brakes)

15 Adjustment of the cables which actuate the shoes in the separate drums is carried out by means of the nuts at the hand control lever until the brakes are fully applied when the lever is pulled over between five and seven notches.
16 Adjustment to compensate for lining wear, or after fitting new shoes, is carried out using the star wheel adjuster, accessible through a wheel bolt hole. See Chapter 13, Section 10, for further details.

30 Handbrake control lever – removal and refitting

Series 1

1 Pull up the lever gaiter, unscrew the nuts and disconnect the cables.
2 Remove the pivot bolt and take out the lever.
3 The sector may be renewed if the teeth of the ratchet are worn.
4 Refitting is a reversal of removal.

Series 2

5 Release the clamps and pull the gaiter up the lever.
6 Remove the ashtray and unscrew the bolt now exposed.
7 Remove the console towards the rear.
8 Unscrew the nuts from the ends of the handbrake cables.
9 Unscrew the bolts (1, 2 and 3) – Fig. 9.64 – and remove the handbrake lever.

All models

10 Check the operation of the handbrake warning switch and adjust its setting if necessary so that it operates correctly (Section 29).

31 Handbrake cables – renewal

Rear drum brakes

1 Slide up the gaiter, release the handbrake and disconnect the cables from the control lever.
2 Remove the brake drum.
3 Disconnect the shoe assembly, as described in Section 6 or 7.
4 Disconnect the cable from the lever on the trailing shoe.
5 Withdraw the cable through the brake backplate and from the reaction strut and clamps.
6 Refitting is a reversal of removal. Adjust the handbrake (Section 29).

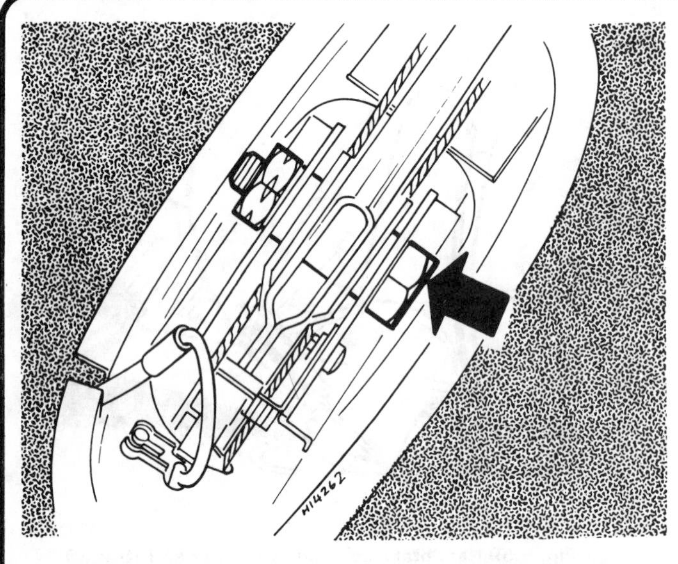

Fig. 9.61 Handbrake lever pivot bolt – arrowed (Sec 30)

Fig. 9.63 Console bolt under ashtray (arrowed) – Series 2 (Sec 30)

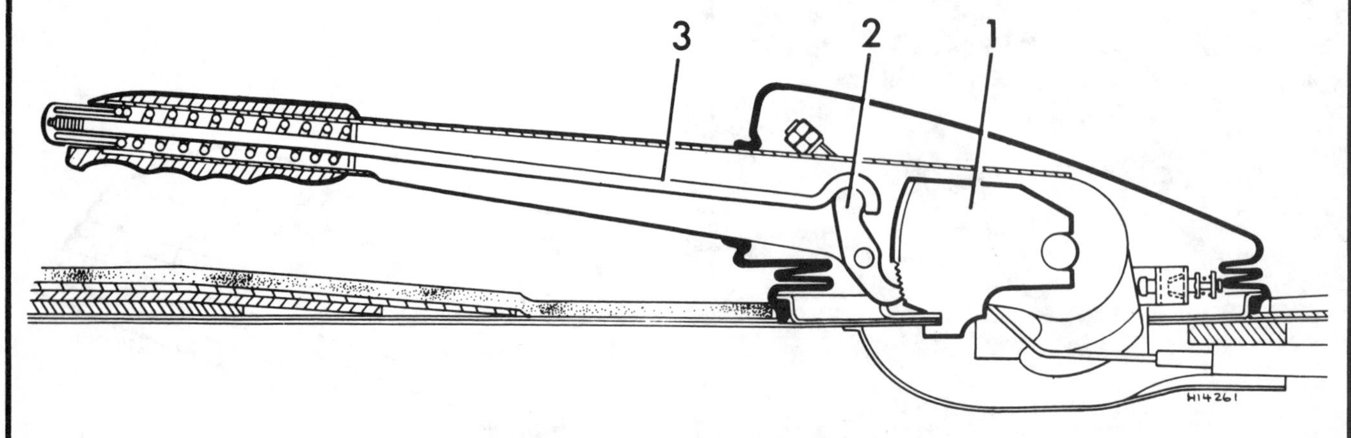

Fig. 9.62 Handbrake lever components – Series 1 (Sec 30)

1 Sector 2 Pawl 3 Rod

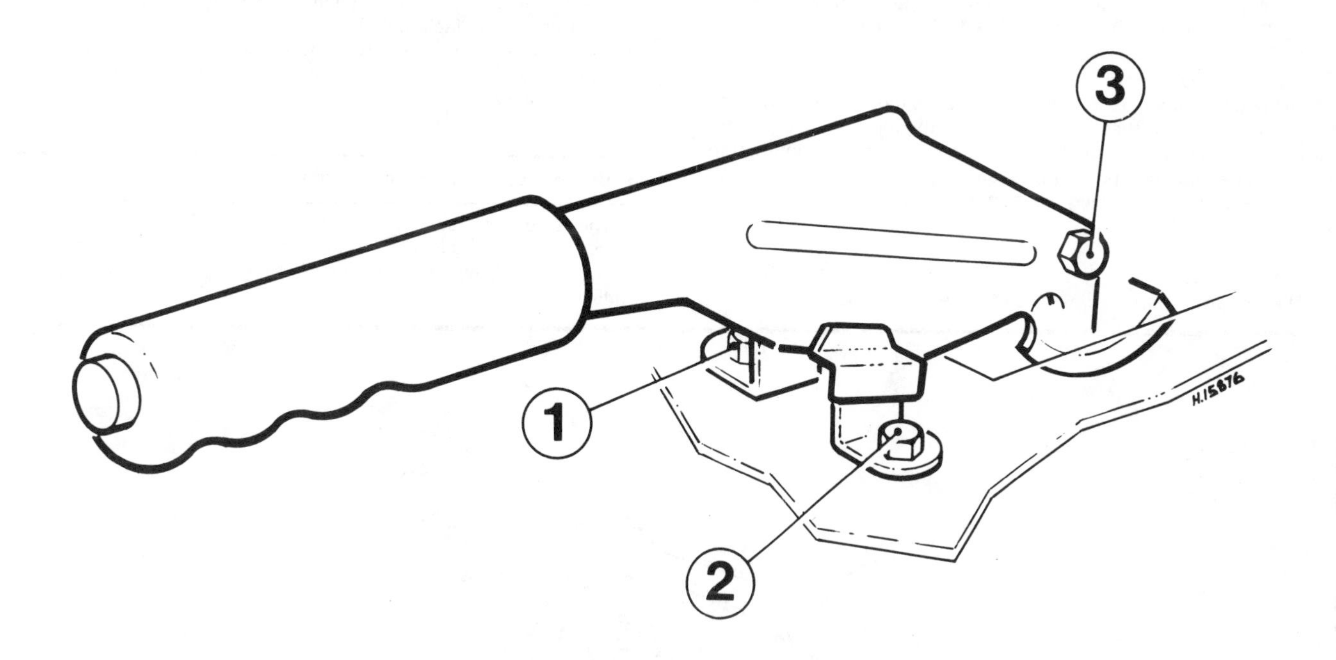

Fig. 9.64 Handbrake lever bolts (1, 2 and 3) – Series 2 (Sec 30)

Fig. 9.65 Handbrake cable support bolts (arrowed) – 323i models (Sec 31)

32.6 Brake servo control rod and lever (RHD, Series 1)

Rear disc brakes

7 Disconnect the cables at the hand control lever, as described in paragraph 1.

8 Withdraw the shoes, as described in Section 8.

9 Unbolt the handbrake cable support and pull out the handbrake cable.

10 Release the cable from the reaction strut and the retaining clamps.

11 Refitting is a reversal of removal. Adjust the handbrake (Section 29).

32 Brake pedal – removal and refitting

Series 1 (LHD)

1 Remove the facia under cover panel.

2 Disconnect the pedal return spring.

3 Remove the clip and the clevis pin and disconnect the pushrod from the pedal arm.

4 Unscrew the self-locking nut from the pedal arm pivot bolt and then withdraw the bolt sufficiently to withdraw the pedal.

5 The pivot bushes can be renewed – apply grease when reassembling and adjust the pedal to conform with the diagram (Fig. 9.66) by turning the pushrod with the clevis fork locknut released.

Series 1 (RHD)

6 The pedal removal operations are similar to those described for the LHD versions, except that the pushrod is in the form of a long remote control rod which connects with the vacuum servo unit mounted at the front of the engine compartment (photo).

7 Set the pedal by releasing the locknut at the clevis fork and turning the remote control rod.

Series 2 (LHD)

8 The operations are as described for Series 1 models.

Series 2 (RHD)

9 The pedal must be disconnected from the cross-shaft which is mounted under the facia panel.

10 The cross-shaft in turn is connected by means of a crank to the servo pushrod mounted on the left-hand side of the engine compartment rear bulkhead.

33 Brake stop-lamp switch – adjustment

1 The stop-lamp switch must be kept in correct adjustment by means of the nut and locknut so that between 5.0 and 6.0 mm (0.197 and 0.236 in) of the switch plunger is exposed when the brake pedal is fully released.

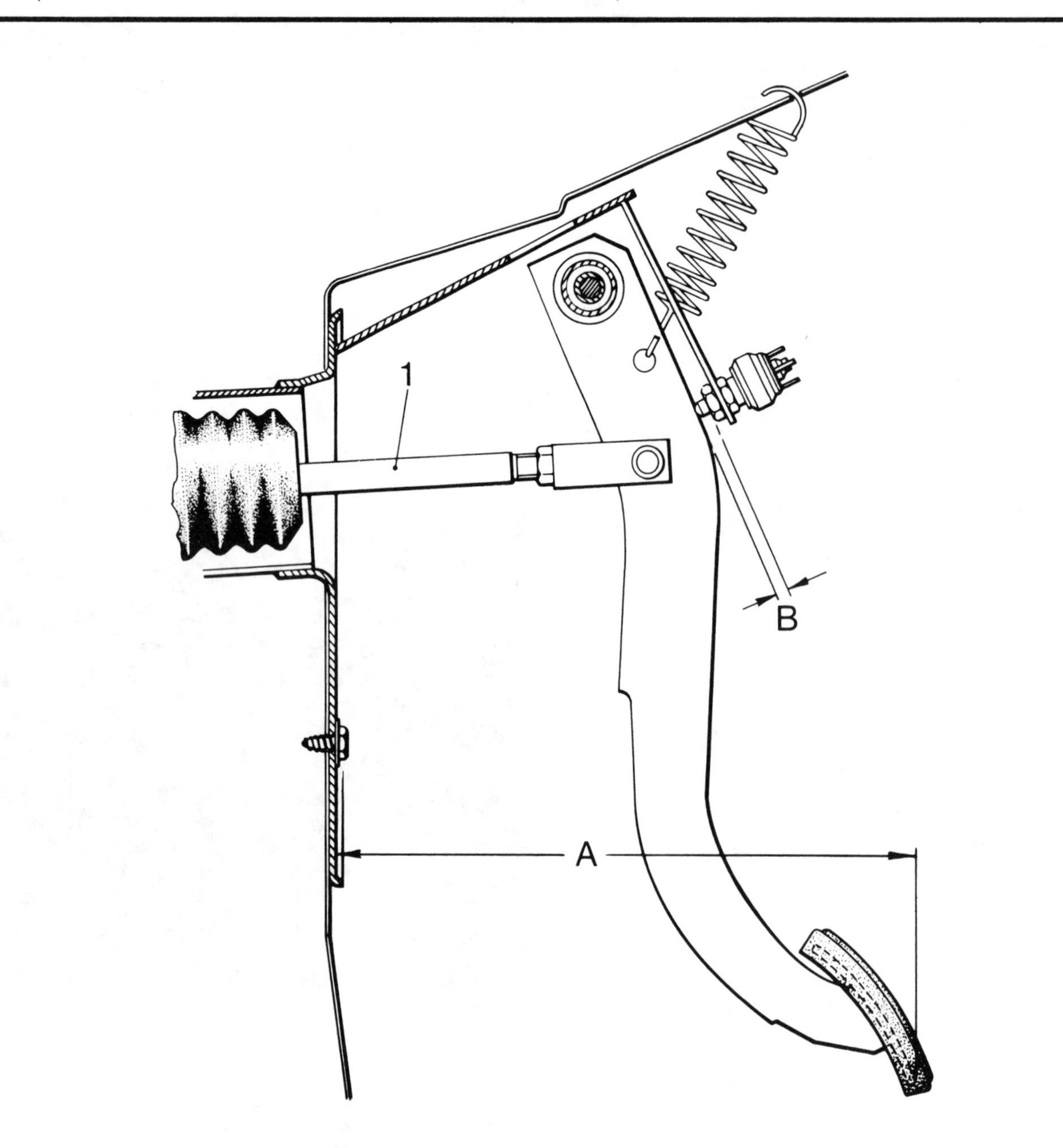

Fig. 9.66 Brake pedal setting diagram (Sec 32)

1 Pushrod
A (LHD) = 239.0 to 249.0 mm (9.41 to 9.80 in)
A (RHD) = 258.0 to 268.0 mm (10.15 to 10.55 in)
B = 5.0 to 6.0 mm (0.20 to 0.24 in)

34 Fault diagnosis – braking system

Symptom	Reason(s)
Pedal travels almost to floorboards before brakes operate	Brake fluid level too low Caliper leaking Master cylinder leaking (bubbles in master cylinder fluid) Brake flexible hose leaking Brake line fractured Brake system unions loose Rear brakes need adjustment Defective master cylinder seals
Brake pedal feels springy	New linings not yet bedded-in Brake discs or drums badly worn or cracked Master cylinder securing nuts loose
Brake pedal feels spongy and soggy	Caliper or wheel cylinder leaking Master cylinder leaking (bubbles in master cylinder reservoir) Brake pipe line or flexible hose leaking Unions in brake system loose Air in system Automatic adjusters on rear shoes not working
Excessive effort required to brake car	Pad or shoe linings badly worn New pads or shoes recently fitted – not yet bedded-in Harder linings fitted than standard causing increase in pedal pressure Linings and brake drums contaminated with oil, grease or hydraulic fluid Servo unit inoperative or faulty
Brakes uneven and pulling to one side	Linings and discs or drums contaminated with oil, grease or hydraulic fluid Tyre pressures unequal Brake caliper loose Brake pads or shoes fitted incorrectly Different type of linings fitted at each wheel Anchorages for front suspension or rear suspension loose Brake discs or drums badly worn, cracked or distorted Setting of caliper piston step incorrect
Brakes tend to bind, drag or lock-on	Air in hydraulic system Wheel cylinders seized Handbrake cables too tight
Pulsating action when brake pedal applied	Play in hub bearings Brake disc distorted Brake drum distorted
Disc pads worn at an angle	Weak pad cross spring Play in hub bearing Pad lining below minimum specified thickness Caliper piston steps incorrectly set

Chapter 10 Electrical system

For modifications, and information applicable to later models, see Supplement at end of manual

Contents

Specifications

System type	12V negative earth with battery, alternator and pre-engaged starter
Battery	
320	44 Ah
323i	55 Ah
Alternator	
Type	Bosch
Output	14V, 65A
Brush wear limit (minimum projection)	5.0 mm (0.197 in)
Regulator voltage	13.5 to 14.6V
Starter motor	
Type	Bosch
Minimum brush length	11.0 mm (0.433 in)
Bulbs	**Wattage**
Headlamp:	
Main beam (Halogen)	55
Dipped beam (Halogen)	50 (55 on Series 2)
Front sidelight	4
Front direction indicator lamp	21
Rear direction indicator lamp	21
Tail lamp	10
Stop-lamp	21
Rear foglamp	21
Reversing lamp	21
Rear number plate lamp	5
Luggage boot lamp	10
Interior lamp	10
Glovebox lamp	5
Side repeater lamp	5
Indicator and warning (wedge base)	1.2
Front foglamps	55
Ignition (charge) warning lamp	3

Fuses (Series 1)

Number	Circuit protected	Amperage
1	RH front foglamp	8
2	LH front foglamp	8
3	Electric fuel pump	16
4	RH headlamp (dipped)	8
5	LH headlamp (dipped)	8
6	Tail, RH sidelight, rear number plate, instruments, rear foglamp, engine compartment	8
7	RH headlamp (main beam)	8
8	LH headlamp (main beam)	8
9	Tail, LH sidelight	8
10	Heated rear window	16
11	Heater blower, air conditioner fan	25
12	Stop-lamps, radio	8
13	Auxiliary electric fan	25
14	Reversing lamps, tachometer, instrument and indicator lamps	8
15	Horn, direction indicators, wash/wipe	16
16	Cigar lighter, electric aerial	16
17	Hazard warning, interior and boot lamps, clock, glovebox	8
18	Auxiliary fan	16

Fuses (Series 2)

Number	Circuit protected	Amperage
1	LH headlamp (main beam)	7.5
2	RH headlamp (main beam)	7.5
3	Auxiliary fan	15
4	Direction indicators	15
5	Wash/wipe systems	25
6	Stop-lamps, cruise control	7.5
7	Horns	15
8	Heated rear window	25
9	Engine electrics (carburettor), reversing lamp	15
10	Instruments	7.5
11	Fuel pump	15
12	Radio, check control	7.5
13	LH headlamp (dipped)	7.5
14	RH headlamp (dipped)	7.5
15	Rear foglamps	7.5
16	Heated front seats	15
17	Sliding roof	25
18	Auxiliary fan	30
19	Exterior rear view mirror	7.5
20	Heater blower	30
21	Interior lamps	7.5
22	LH tail and front sidelight	7.5
23	RH tail and front sidelight, rear number plate, instruments	7.5
24	Hazard warning lamps	15
25	Spare	
26	Spare	
27	Central locking system, door lock heating, anti-theft system	25
28	Cigar lighter, electric aerial	25
29	LH fog lamp	7.5
30	RH foglamp	7.5

Relays

Relay	Function
K1	Auxiliary fan
K2	Horns
K3	Headlamp main beam
K4	Headlamp dipped beam
K5	Heated front seats
K6	Auxiliary fan
K7	Heater blower
K8	Front foglamps
K9	Electric windows
K10	Wipers (intermittent)

Torque wrench settings

	Nm	lbf ft
Alternator adjuster link and mounting bolts	22	16
Starter mounting bolts	46	34

1 General description

1 The system is of 12 volt, negative earth type with battery, alternator and pre-engaged starter.
2 The system is fully fused and various options are available, including electric front windows, central door locking and a cruise control system.

2 Battery – maintenance and inspection

1 The modern battery seldom requires topping-up, nevertheless the electrolyte level should be inspected weekly as a means of providing the first indication that the alternator is overcharging or that the battery casing has developed a leak. The battery plates should always be covered to a depth of 6.0 mm (0.25 in) with electrolyte.
2 When topping-up is required, use only distilled water or melted ice from a refrigerator (frosting, not ice cubes).
3 Acid should never be required if the battery has been correctly filled from new, unless spillage has occurred.
4 Inspect the battery terminals and mounting tray for corrosion. This is the white fluffy deposit which grows at these areas. If evident, clean it away and neutralise it with ammonia or baking soda. Apply petroleum jelly to the terminals and paint the battery tray with anti-corrosive paint.
5 Keep the top surface of the battery casing dry.
6 An indication of the state of charge of a battery can be obtained by checking the electrolyte in each cell using a hydrometer. The specific gravity of the electrolyte for fully charged and fully discharged conditions at the electrolyte temperature indicated, is listed below.

Fully discharged	Electrolyte temperature	Fully charged
1.098	38°C (100°F)	1.268
1.102	32°C (90°F)	1.272
1.106	27°C (80°F)	1.276
1.110	21°C (70°F)	1.280
1.114	16°C (60°F)	1.284
1.118	10°C (50°F)	1.288
1.122	4°C (40°F)	1.292
1.126	-1.5°C (30°F)	1.296

7 There should be very little variation in the readings between the different cells, but if a difference is found in excess of 0.025 then it will probably be due to an internal fault indicating impending battery failure. This assumes that electrolyte has not been spilled at some time and the deficiency made up with water only.
8 If electrolyte is accidentally spilled at any time, mop up and neutralise the spillage at once. Electrolyte attacks and corrodes metal rapidly; it will also burn holes in clothing and skin. Leave the addition of acid to a battery to your dealer or service station, as the mixing of acid with distilled water can be dangerous.
9 Never smoke or allow naked lights near the battery; the hydrogen gas which it gives off is explosive.
10 With normal motoring, the battery should be kept in a good state of charge by the alternator and never need charging from a mains charger.
11 However, if the daily mileage is low, with much use of starter and electrical accessories, it is possible for the battery to become discharged due to the fact that the alternator is not in use long enough to replace the current consumed.
12 Also, as the battery ages, it may not be able to hold its charge and some supplementary charging may be needed. Before connecting the charger, disconnect the battery terminals or better still, remove the battery from the vehicle.
13 Specially rapid 'boost' charges which are claimed to restore the power of the battery in 1 to 2 hours are most dangerous as they can cause serious damage to the battery plates through overheating.
14 While charging the battery note that the temperature of the electrolyte should never exceed 37.8°C (100°F).

3 Battery – removal and refitting

1 Disconnect the negative lead then the positive lead (photos).
2 Unscrew the battery clamp bolt, remove the clamp and lift the battery from its tray.

3.1A Early type battery

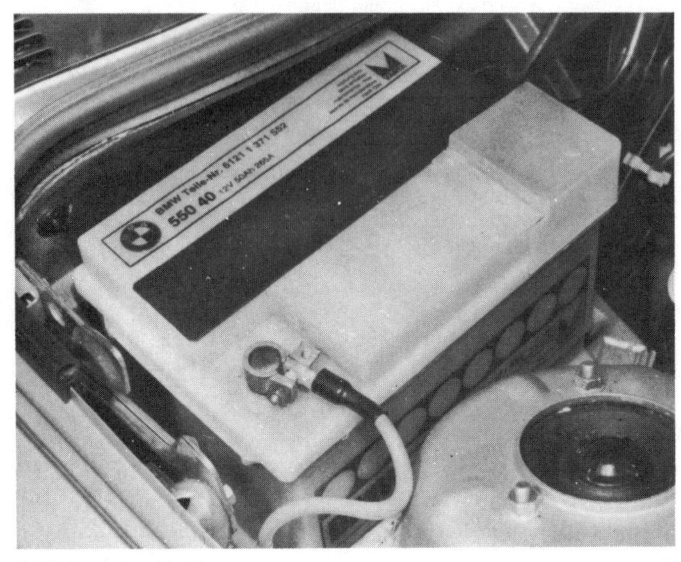

3.1B Later type battery

3 Refitting is a reversal of removal, smear the terminals with petroleum jelly to prevent corrosion.

4 Alternator – maintenance and precautions

1 Maintenance consists of occasionally wiping away any dirt or oil which may have collected on the unit.
2 Check the tension of the alternator driving belt at the intervals specified in Routine Maintenance. If adjustment is required, refer to Chapter 2.
3 Take extreme care when making circuit connections to a vehicle fitted with an alternator and observe the following. When making connections to the alternator from a battery always match correct polarity. Before using electric-arc welding equipment to repair any part of the vehicle, disconnect the connector from the alternator and disconnect the positive battery terminal.
4 Never disconnect a battery lead while the engine is running.

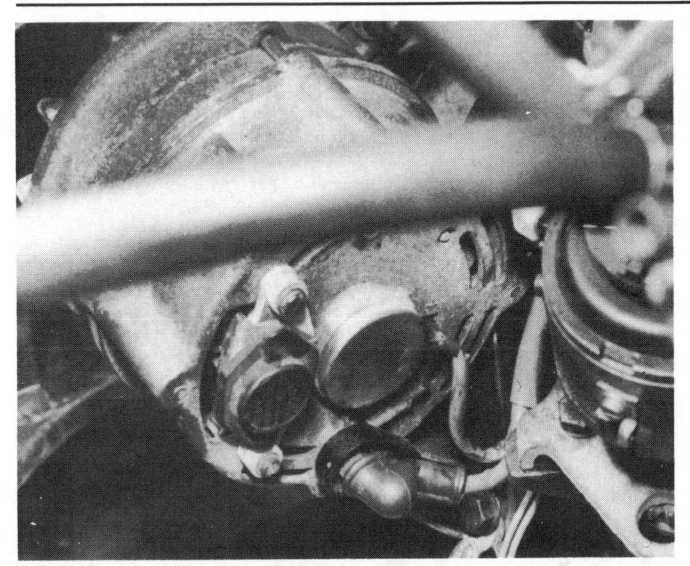

5.3 Typical alternator connections

6.2A Releasing regulator/brush holder screw

5.4 Alternator belt adjuster link

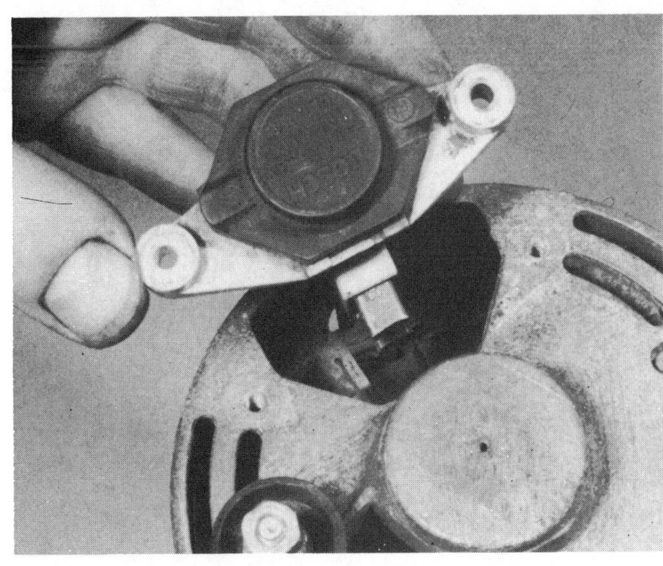

6.2B Removing regulator/brush holder from alternator

5 Alternator – removal and refitting

1 Disconnect the battery negative lead.
2 On fuel injection models, remove the air cleaner and the airflow sensor.
3 Disconnect the leads from the rear cover of the alternator (photo).
4 Remove the bolt from the adjuster link (photo), push the unit in towards the engine and remove the drivebelt.
5 Unscrew the alternator mounting bolts and remove the unit.
6 Refitting is a reversal of removal. Tension the drivebelt, as described in Chapter 2.

6 Alternator – overhaul

1 Overhaul of the alternator should be limited to the following operations. If an alternator has been in service for a long time and is generally worn, it is more satisfactory and will prove more economical to obtain a new or factory exchange unit.

Carbon brushes – renewal

2 With the alternator removed, extract the screws which secure the externally mounted voltage regulator and remove the regulator/brush assembly (photos).

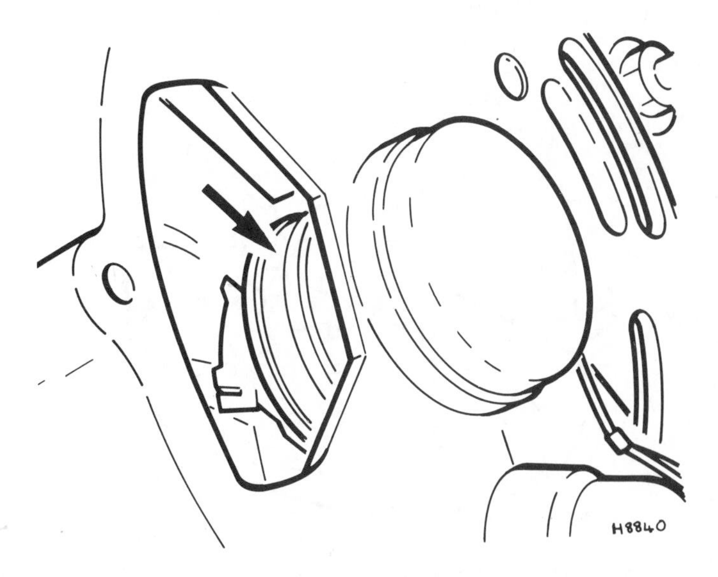

Fig. 10.1 Alternator slip rings – arrowed (Sec 6)

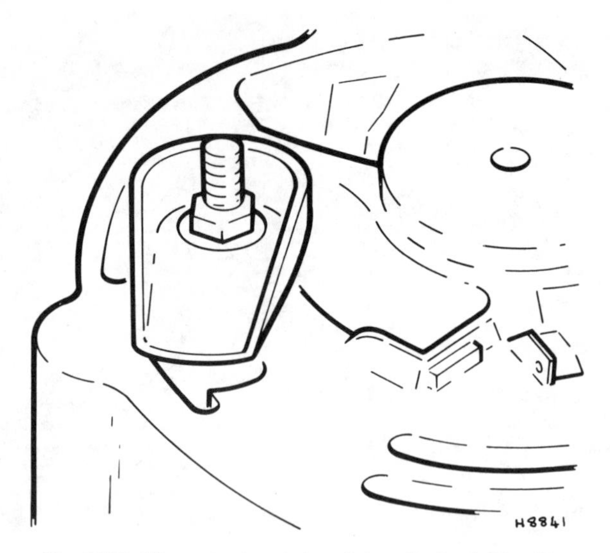

Fig. 10.2 Alternator insulator plate – Series 1 (Sec 6)

3 The worn brushes should be unsoldered and the new ones soldered in position. Do not allow the solder to run down the leads or their flexibility will be ruined.
4 While the brush holder is removed take the opportunity to clean the slip rings with a fuel-moistened cloth. If badly marked, use a piece of fine glass paper.
5 Refit the regulator/brush holder and refit the alternator.

Diode plate – renewal

6 If testing of the alternator by your dealer indicates that the diode plate is faulty, renew it in the following way.

Series 1

7 With the alternator removed, take off the insulator plate.
8 Unscrew the diode plate fixing screws and remove the plate.
9 Fit the new plate, but check the condition of the insulating sleeve.

Series 2

10 With the alternator removed, unscrew the nuts and pull off the plug for the capacitor.
11 Extract the screws and remove the diode plate.
12 When fitting the new diode plate, make sure that the insulating sleeves are correctly located.

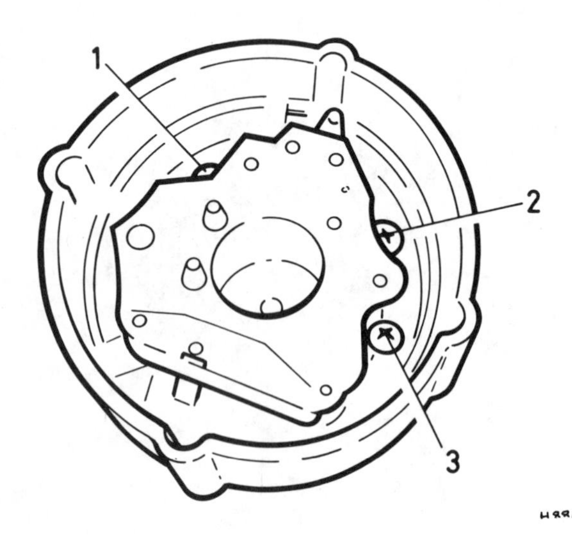

Fig. 10.3 Alternator diode plate fixing screws (1, 2 and 3) – Series 1 (Sec 6)

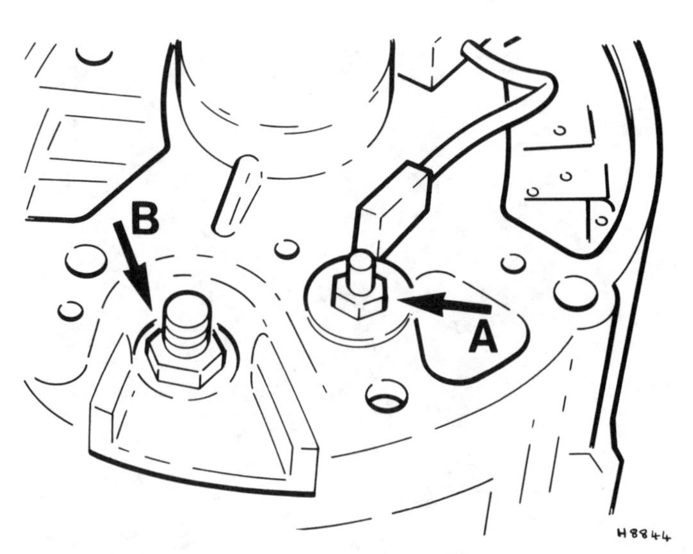

Fig. 10.5 Alternator capacitor plug (A) and diode plate nut (B) – Series 2 (Sec 6)

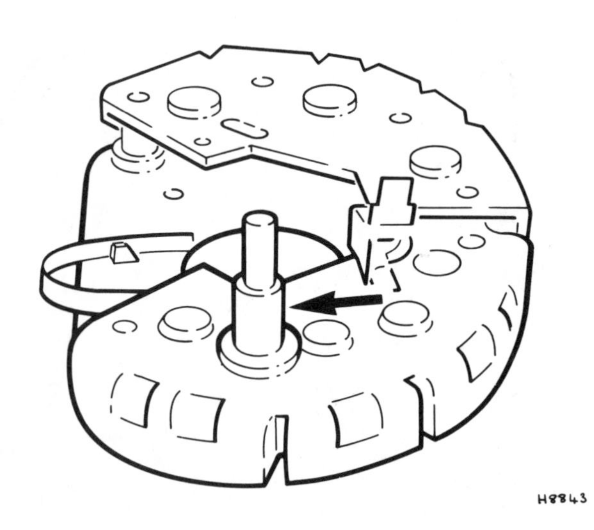

Fig. 10.4 Diode plate insulating sleeve (arrowed) – Series 1 (Sec 6)

Fig. 10.6 Diode plate fixing screws (arrowed) – Series 2 (Sec 6)

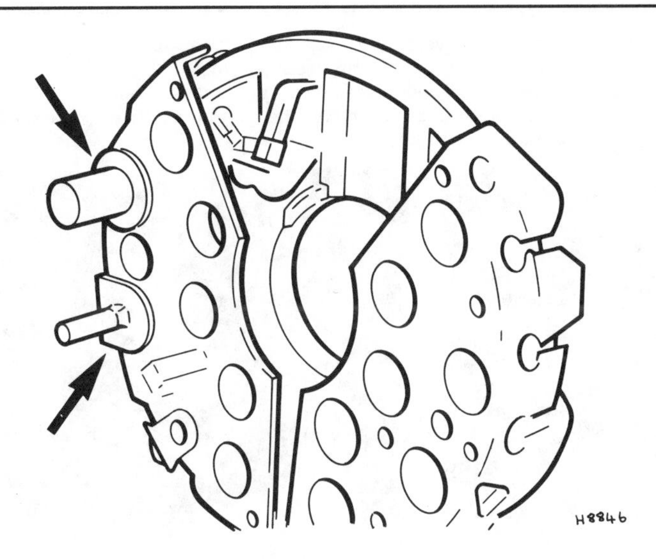

Fig. 10.7 Diode plate insulating sleeves (arrowed) – Series 2 (Sec 6)

8.3 Starter motor leads

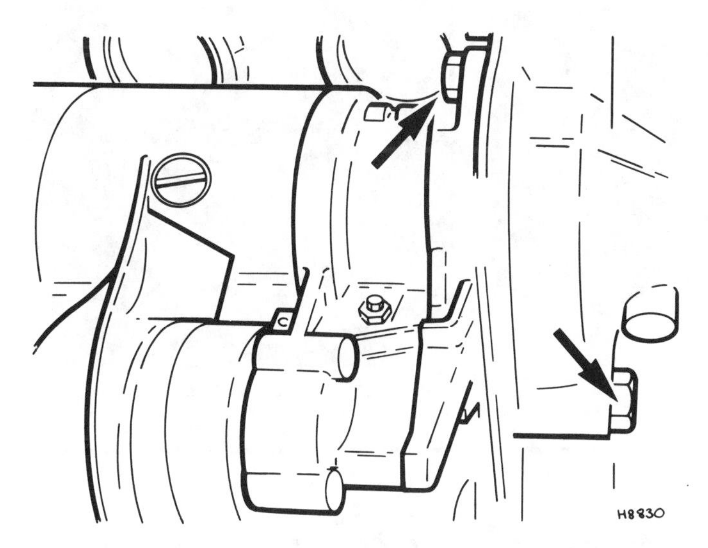

Fig. 10.8 Starter motor rear mounting bolts – arrowed (Sec 8)

8.4A Starter motor front bracket

7 Voltage regulator – removal and refitting

1 As described in Section 6, the voltage regulator is one assembly with the brush holder.

8 Starter motor – removal and refitting

1 Disconnect the battery negative lead.
2 Remove the air cleaner (on 320 models).
3 Disconnect the leads from the starter motor solenoid terminals (photo).
4 Unscrew the starter motor mounting bolts (photo and Fig. 10.8) and withdraw it from the transmission bellhousing (photo).
5 Refitting is a reversal of removal.

9 Starter motor – overhaul

1 The pre-engaged type of starter motor normally has a very long life and when it does eventually become worn it is recommended that it is renewed or a factory reconditioned unit fitted.
2 The following operations should be regarded as the limit of economical home repair operations.

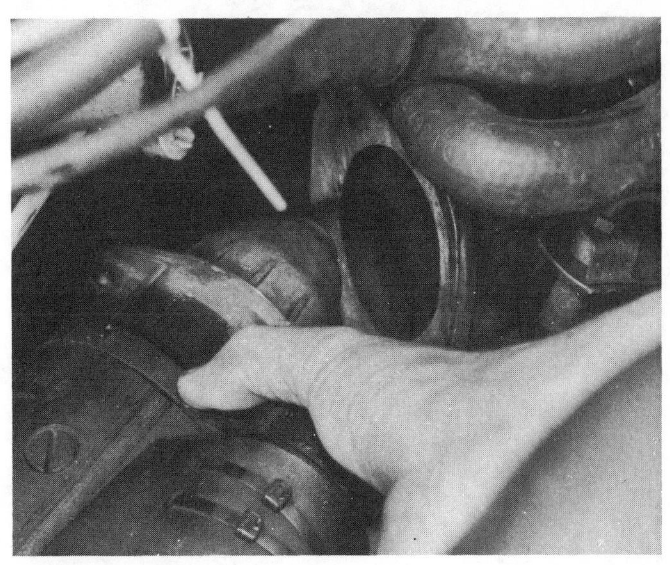
8.4B Removing starter motor

Brush renewal

3 With the starter removed, remove the screws, or nuts and bolts, securing the solenoid (as necessary) and withdraw the solenoid. As it is removed, unhook the engagement lever.

4 On 320 models, unbolt and remove the front bracket (photo).

5 Extract the screws and take off the dust cap (photo).

6 Remove the circlip, shim and seal (photo).

7 Unscrew the tie-bolts and remove the end cap (photos).

8 Pull back the springs, lift the brushes from their slides and remove the brush holder plate (photo).

9.4 Unbolting starter front bracket

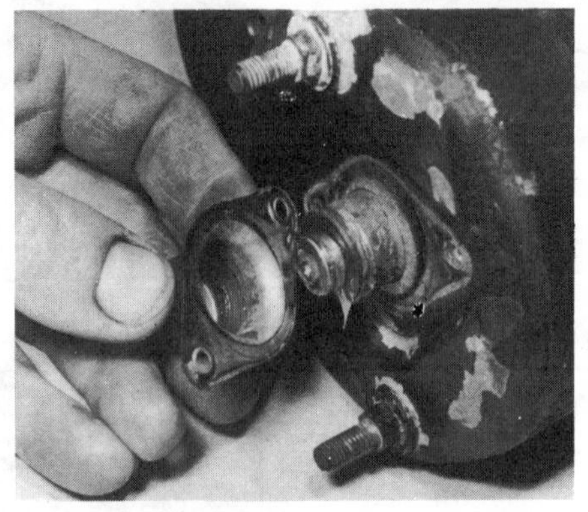

9.5 Removing starter dust cap

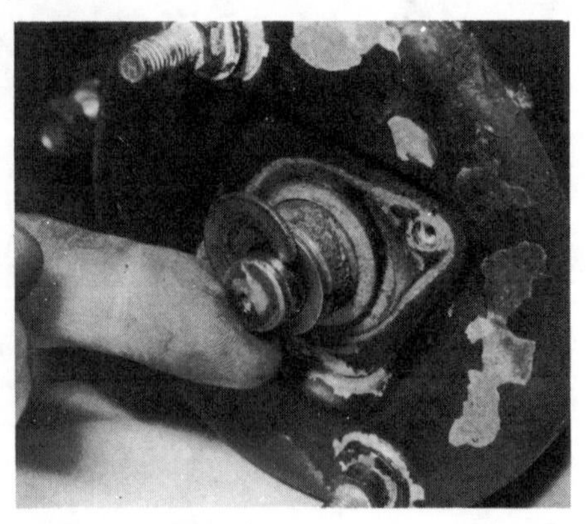

9.6 Removing circlip

9.7A Removing starter motor tie-bolt

9.7B Removing end cap

9.8 Starter brush holder plate

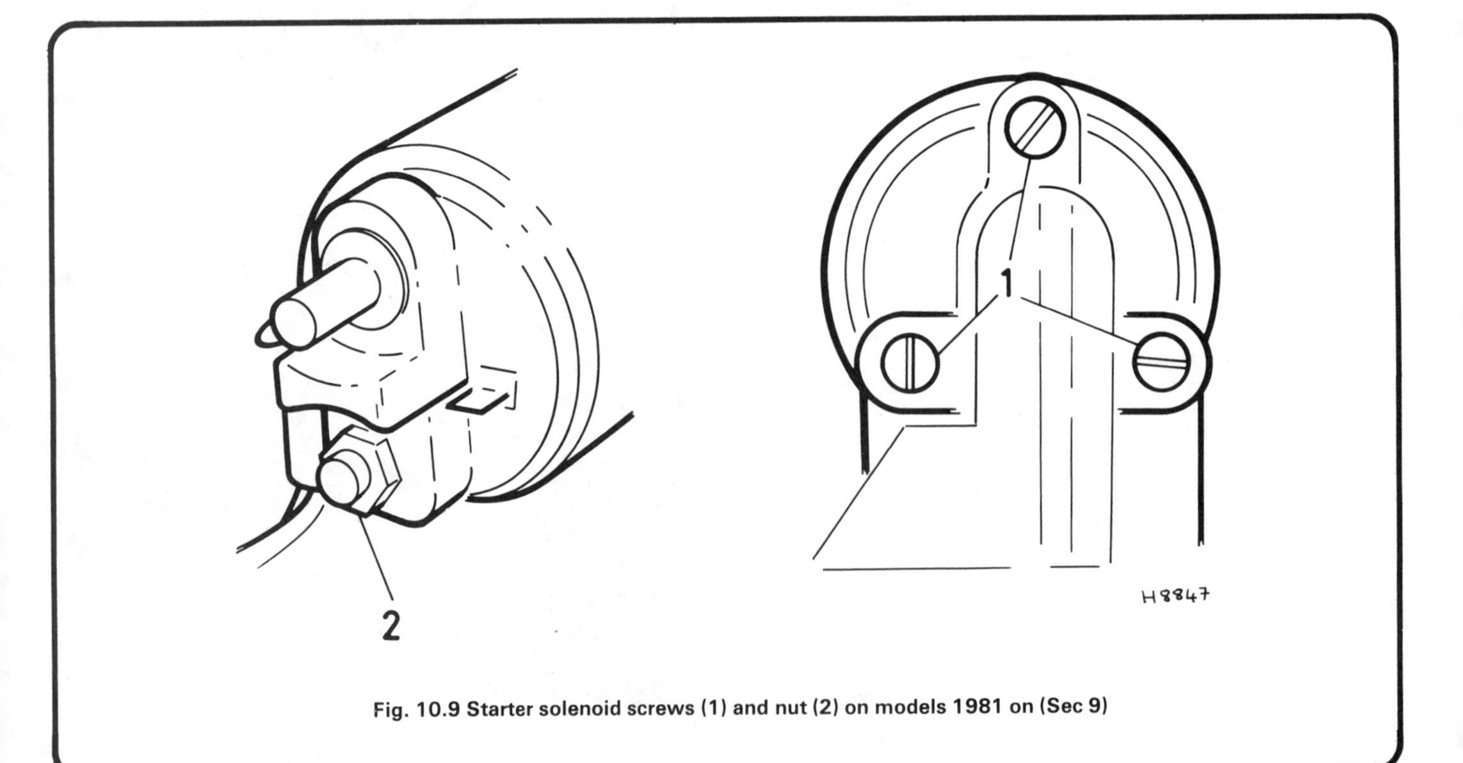

Fig. 10.9 Starter solenoid screws (1) and nut (2) on models 1981 on (Sec 9)

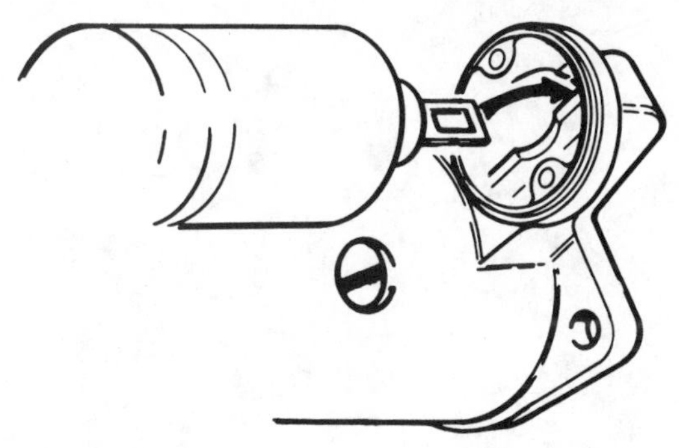

Fig. 10.10 **Removing the starter solenoid (Sec 9)**
Unhook the engagement lever (arrowed)

9 Unsolder the old brush leads and solder the new ones into position. Do not allow solder to run down the leads or their flexibility will be ruined.

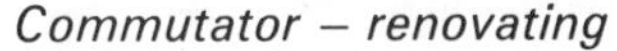

Commutator – renovating

10 If the carbon brushes have been removed for renewal, take the opportunity to inspect the commutator.
11 Clean it with a fuel-soaked rag or, if necessary, use fine glass paper.
12 Check that the insulators between the segments are 0.5 mm (0.02 in) lower than the segments, otherwise cut them back squarely using a hacksaw.
13 Reassembly is a reversal of dismantling. If the armature endplay is between 0.10 and 0.15 mm (0.004 to 0.006 in) this is correct, otherwise alter the shims used to bring it within that tolerance.

10 Fuses and relays

1 The fuse and relay block is mounted within the engine compartment.

Fuses

2 The circuits protected are given on the fusebox lid on Series 1 models (photo).
3 On Series 2 models, refer to Specifications or owner's handbook (photo).
4 To renew a blown fuse, pull it from its contacts or pull it from its socket, according to type. Never use a fuse with a different rating from the original or substitute anything else, such as a piece of wire.
5 If a new fuse blows immediately, find the cause before renewing it again. Faulty insulation is usually the reason, so inspect all the particular circuit wiring.

Relays

6 The starter inhibitor relay (automatic transmission) is located under the facia panel as is the wiper intermittent relay on Series 1 models (photo). On Series 2 models, this relay is in the fusebox, with the other relays.

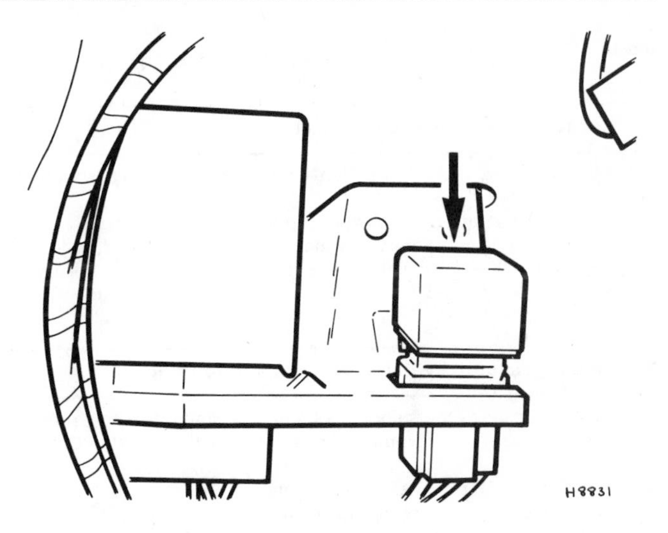

Fig. 10.11 Starter inhibitor switch relay (arrowed) – automatic transmission (Sec 10)

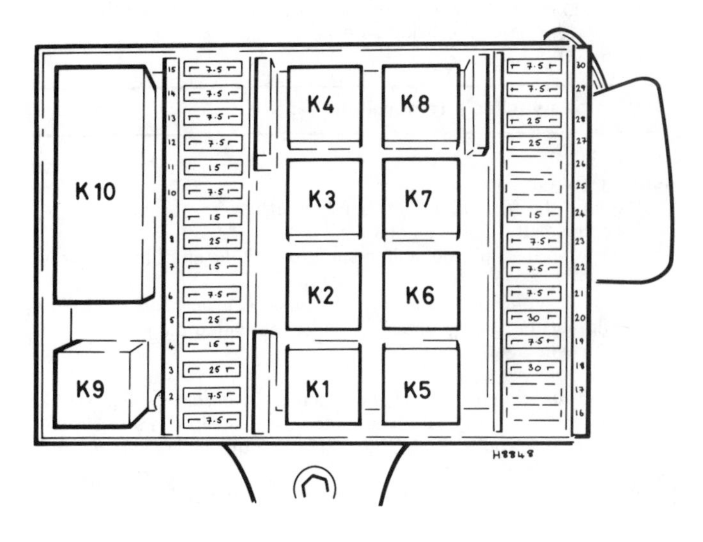

Fig. 10.12 Relays in the fusebox – Series 2 (Sec 10)

K1 Auxiliary fan
K2 Horns
K3 Headlamp main beam
K4 Headlamp dipped beam
K5 Heated front seats
K6 Auxiliary fan
K7 Heater blower
K8 Front foglamps
K9 Electric windows
K10 Wipers (intermittent)

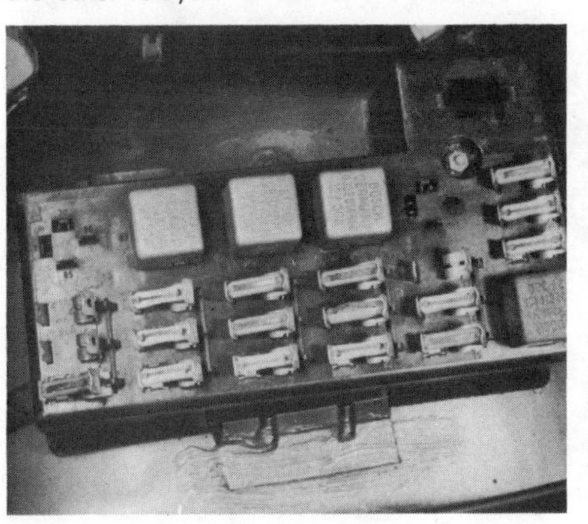

10.2 Series 1 fusebox, with relays

10.3 Series 2 fusebox, with relays

10.6 Wiper intermittent relay (Series 1)

7 The direction indicator relay is under the facia panel, at the side of the steering column.

11 Direction indicator flasher (relay) unit

1 Rapid flashing of the direction indicators may be caused by a blown bulb.
2 Failure to operate may be due to poor earth at the lamp.
3 If everything is in order, renew the relay which is located under the facia panel at the side of the steering column. The facia under cover will have to be removed to give access to the relay (photo).

12 Steering column switch – removal and refitting

1 To give access to the steering column combination switch, remove the steering wheel and column lower shroud, as described in Chapter 11.
2 Remove the facia panel under cover.
3 Disconnect the battery negative lead.
4 Disconnect the wiring plug from the combination switch.
5 Pull the direction indicator flasher relay from its clips and disconnect the wiring plug.
6 Release all column wiring harness straps.
7 Extract the fixing screws (photo) and remove the switches (wiper or direction/dipper).
8 Refitting is a reversal of removal. Make sure that the earth wire is located under one of the fixing screws.

13 Control switches – removal and refitting

Series 1

Lighting switch

1 Remove the facia panel left-hand under cover.
2 Disconnect the battery negative lead.
3 Pass a pin through the switch shaft to hold the shaft and unscrew the knob.
4 Unscrew the switch retaining bezel, using circlip pliers or similar.
5 Withdraw the switch and disconnect the wiring plug.

Heater blower switch

6 Disconnect the battery.
7 Pull off the switch knob (1) and unscrew the bezel (2) – Fig. 10.13.
8 Unscrew the switch retaining plate, using circlip pliers or similar.
9 Pull off the knobs from the heater control levers, extract the screws and withdraw the panel.
10 Pull the plug from the switch and remove the switch.

Fig. 10.13 Heater blower switch – Series 1 (Sec 13)

1 Knob 2 Bezel

11.3 Direction indicator flasher (relay) unit

12.7 Combination switch screws

13.15 Courtesy lamp switch

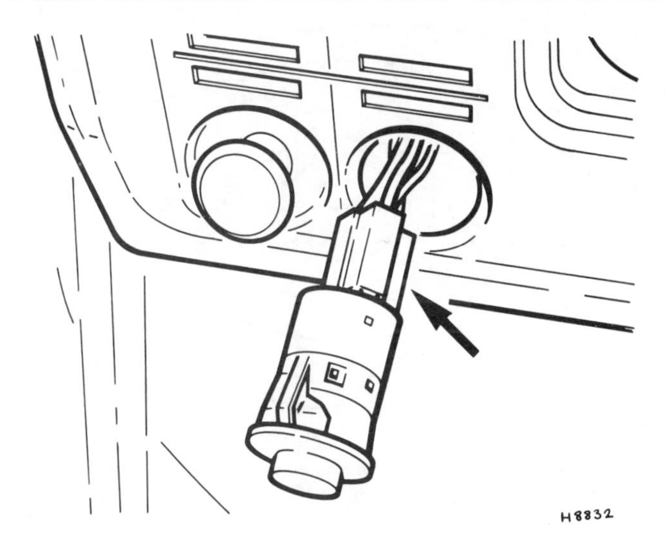

Fig. 10.14 Heated rear window switch – Series 1 (Sec 13)

Disconnect the wiring plug (arrowed)

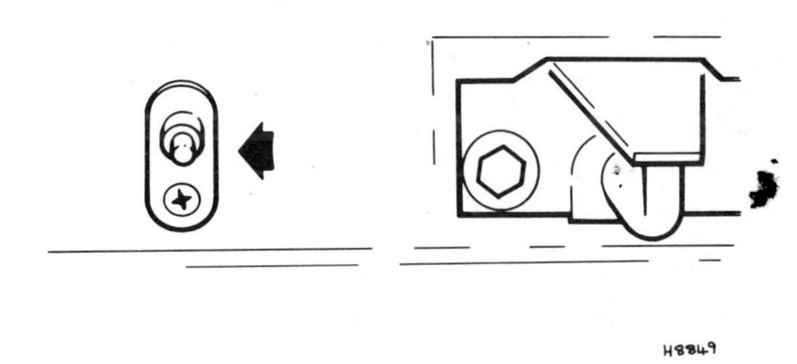

Fig. 10.15 Boot lamp switch (arrowed) – Series 2 (Sec 13)

Heated rear window switch

11 Disconnect the battery.

12 Pull the switch from the instrument panel and disconnect the wiring plug.

Hazard warning switch

13 The procedure is as for the heated rear window switch.

Courtesy lamp switch

14 Open the door fully and pull out the rubber plug from the rubber switch cover on the body pillar.

15 Extract the screw and withdraw the switch (photo).

16 If the leads are to be detached, tape them to the pillar to prevent them from slipping into the interior.

17 Apply petroleum jelly to the switch contacts to prevent corrosion.

All switches

18 Refitting of all switches is a reversal of removal.

Series 2

Lighting switch

19 Disconnect the battery and remove the facia panel under cover.

20 Unscrew the control knob and pull the switch from the panel. Disconnect the wiring plug.

Rocker and pushbutton switches

21 The switches for the heated rear window and foglamps are simply prised from their panel and the wiring plugs disconnected.

22 The switch for the hazard warning lamps is removed in a similar way.

Courtesy and boot lamp switches

23 These are of plunger type and are secured with a single screw.

Glovebox lamp switch

24 Open the glovebox and prise the switch from its seat. Disconnect the wiring plug.

All switches

25 Refitting is a reversal of removal.

14 Horns and switches

1 The horns are located, one each side, behind the radiator (photos).

2 The horn switches are located in the spokes of the steering wheel.

14.1A Horn and bracket

14.1B Horn wiring connections

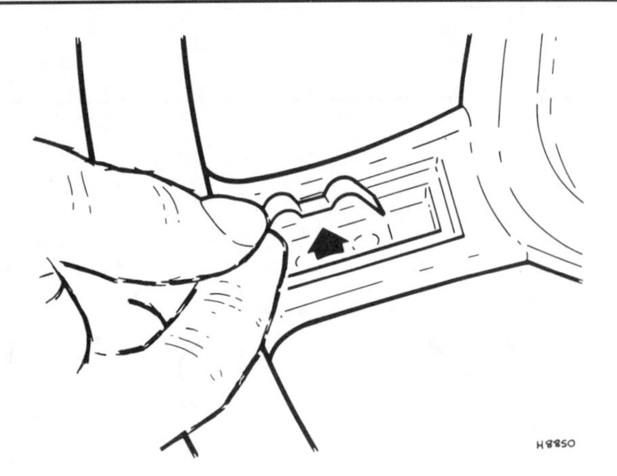

Fig. 10.16 Horn switch spring contact pin – arrowed (Sec 14)

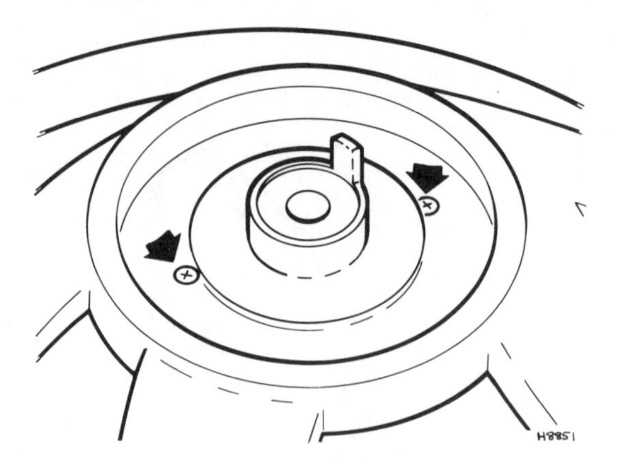

Fig. 10.17 Horn contact slip ring securing screws – arrowed (Sec 14)

3 To remove a horn switch button, prise it out with a small screwdriver.
4 Fit with the spring contact pin facing downwards.
5 The carbon brush contact slip ring may be removed after having taken off the steering wheel and extracted the fixing screws. When refitting the wheel, guide the contact lug into its recess.

15 Electrically-operated windows

1 These are an option on Series 2 front and rear door windows.
2 The windows are operated from pushbutton switches on the centre console.
3 Switches are fitted under the rear windows and they can be isolated by the driver.
4 As a protection against fault or overload, a circuit breaker is incorporated and a manual winding facility is provided.
5 The operating pushbutton switches and the automatic cut-out are removed by prising them from their locations.
6 Access to, and removal of, the power-operated regulator is described in Section 20 of Chapter 12.
7 For further information see Chapter 13, Section 11.

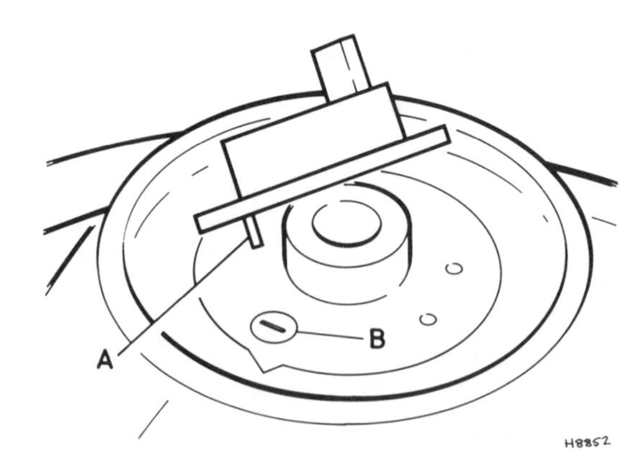

Fig. 10.18 Horn switch contact lug (A) and recess (B) (Sec 14)

16 Windscreen wiper arm and blade – removal and refitting

1 To remove a wiper blade, pull the arm fully away from the glass until it locks.
2 Swivel the blade through 90°, press the locking tab with the finger nail and slide the plastic block and blade out of the hooked end of the wiper arm (photo).
3 Before removing the wiper arm, stick a piece of masking tape along the blade on the glass. This will facilitate alignment of the arm when refitting.
4 Flip up the cover, unscrew the nut and pull the arm from the splined drive spindle (photo). If necessary, use a large screwdriver blade to prise off the arm.
5 Refitting of blade and arm are reversals of removal, do not overtighten the arm retaining nut.

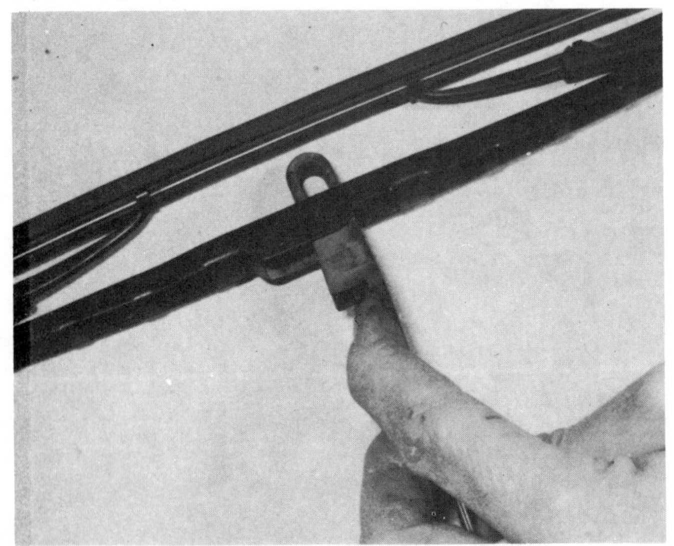

16.2 Removing a wiper blade

16.4 Wiper arm nut and cover

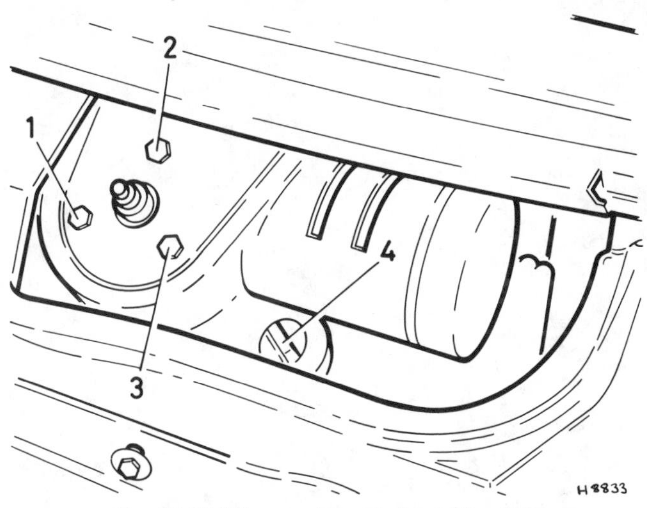

Fig. 10.19 Wiper motor – Series 1 (Sec 17)

1 Mounting bolt
2 Mounting bolt
3 Mounting bolt
4 Stop buffer

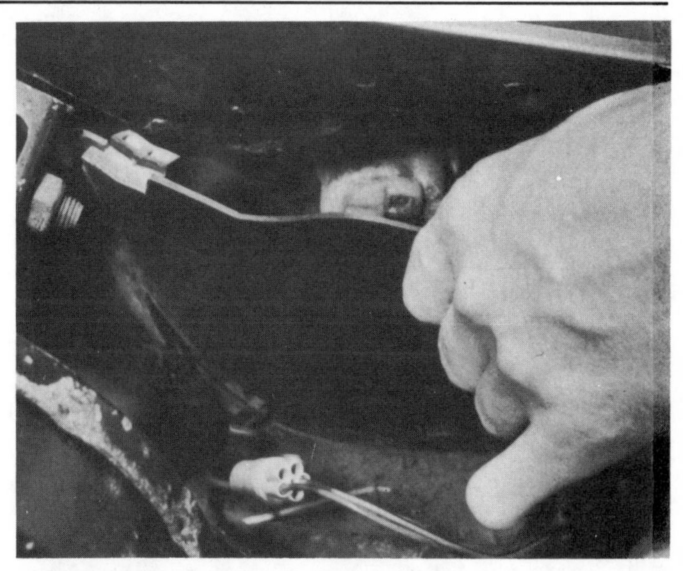

17.2A Bulkhead cover plate

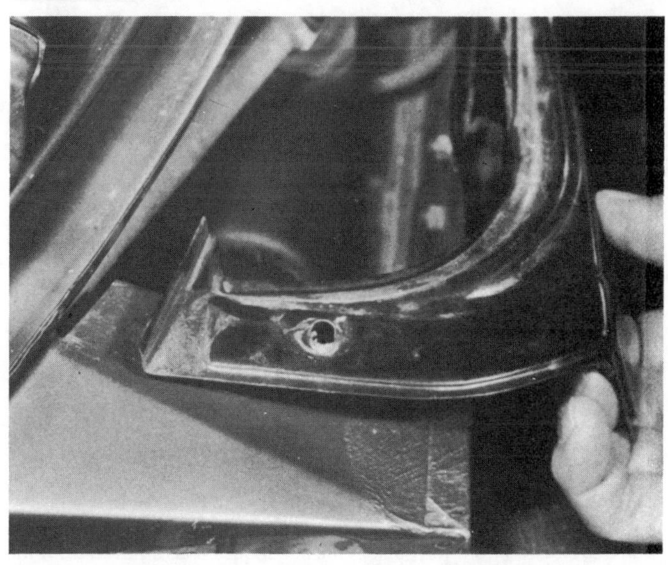

17.2B Bulkhead cover plate

17.3 Wiper motor and crankarm

17 Windscreen wiper motor and linkage – removal and refitting

Series 1

1 Disconnect the battery negative lead.
2 Extract the screws and remove the cover panels from the engine compartment rear bulkhead (photos).
3 Mark the position of the linkage crankarm in relation to the wiper gearbox drive spindle, unscrew the nut and disconnect the crankarm from the spindle (photo).
4 Disconnect the wiper motor wiring plug.
5 Unscrew the mounting bolts and withdraw the motor.
6 To remove the linkage, remove the wiper arms, as previously described (Section 16), and then unscrew the drive spindle (wheelbox) retaining nuts. Push the spindles into the bulkhead cavity and withdraw the linkage through one of the large apertures.
7 Refitting is a reversal of removal, but note that the stop buffer must be tightened until the motor is felt to be supported.

Series 2

8 Disconnect the battery.
9 Remove the heater motor, as described in Chapter 2.
10 Working at the engine compartment rear bulkhead, remove the bracket securing the wiper motor assembly.
11 Disconnect the wiring plug from the motor.
12 Lift out the grille from the scuttle panel in front of the windscreen.
13 Remove both wiper arms, as previously described (Section 16).
14 Disconnect both link-rods from the spindle mounting (wheelbox).
15 Remove the wiper motor assembly.

18 Windscreen washer pump – removal and refitting

Models up to 1979

1 Detach the hoses from the pump.
2 Pull the pump from its mounting and disconnect the wiring plug.
3 The pump on these earlier models can be dismantled by extracting the screws and taking off the cover.
4 Clean out any dirt and reassemble, checking that the gasket is in good order.

Models 1980 on

5 Disconnect the wiring plug and remove the pump by pulling it upwards.
6 Disconnect the hose from the pump.
7 Refit by reversing the removal operations.

Jets

8 These can be adjusted by inserting a pin into the washer nozzles.

19 Heated rear window

1 The element on the rear window should be treated with care. Clean it only with water and detergent, rub in the direction of the filaments.
2 Avoid scratching with rings on the fingers or articles placed on the rear parcels shelf.
3 Never stick labels over the element.

20 Headlamp wash/wipe

1 Fitted as standard to some models and as an option on others. A separate fluid reservoir is used with the necesssary wiper motors, pumps and jets.
2 Access to the wiper motors is obtained by removing the radiator air intake side grilles (Chapter 12).

21 Instrument panel – removal and refitting

Series 1

1 Disconnect the battery.
2 Remove the facia panel under cover from the driver's side.
3 Reach under the instrument panel at the side of the steering column and unscrew the knurled retaining nut (photo).
4 Disconnect the speedometer cable at its remote connector.
5 Remove the steering wheel, as described in Chapter 11.
6 Withdraw the instrument panel (photo) and disconnect the wiring plugs.
7 Refitting is a reversal of removal.

Series 2

8 Disconnect the battery and remove the steering wheel, as described in Chapter 11.
9 Remove the facia panel under cover.
10 Remove the retaining nuts and trim – Fig. 10.21.
11 Extract the screws from under the top edge of the instrument panel and remove the trim.
12 Extract the instrument panel fixing screws.
13 Withdraw the instrument panel until the wiring plugs and speedometer cable can be disconnected.
14 Refitting is a reversal of removal.

Series 1 and Series 2

15 The individual instruments, including the digital clock control unit, can be removed from the back of the panel once it is removed from the facia (photo).

Fig. 10.20 Windscreen and headlamp washer fluid reservoirs (Sec 20)

21.3 Instrument panel fixing nut (arrowed)

21.6 Withdrawing the instrument panel

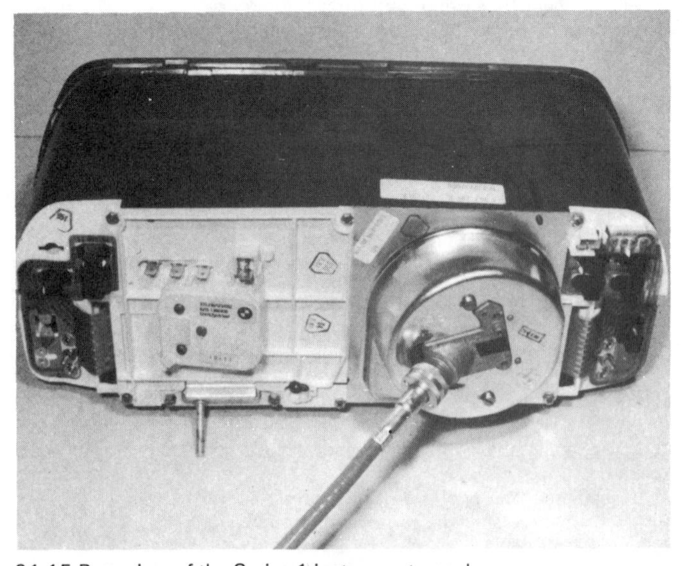

21.15 Rear view of the Series 1 instrument panel

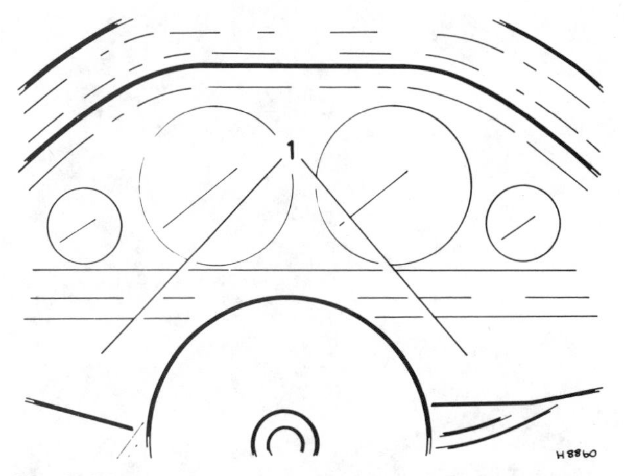

Fig. 10.21 Remove the nuts securing the trim (1) – Series 2 (Sec 21)

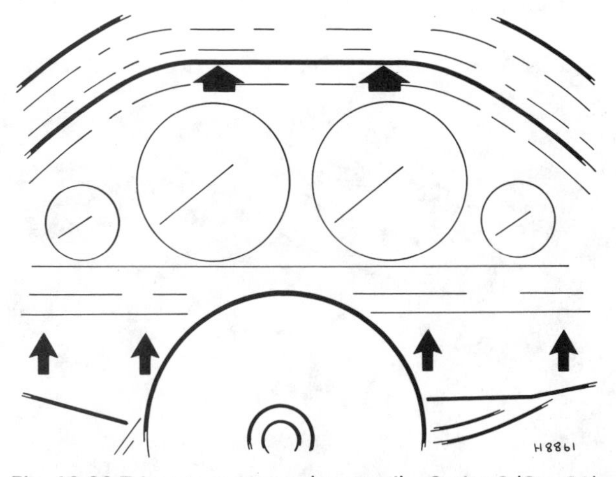

Fig. 10.22 Trim upper screws (arrowed) – Series 2 (Sec 21)

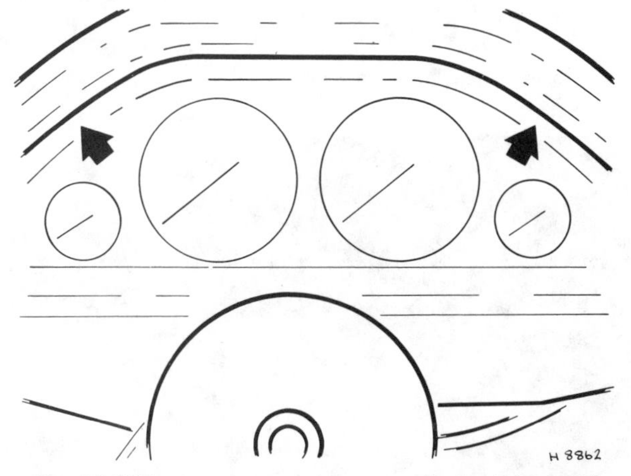

Fig. 10.23 Instrument panel screws – Series 2 (Sec 21)

16 The printed circuit board is also detachable, but handle with great care.

22 Clock – removal and refitting

Series 1, up to 1980

1 On these models, remove the heater control lever knobs and withdraw the panel, as described in Chapter 2.

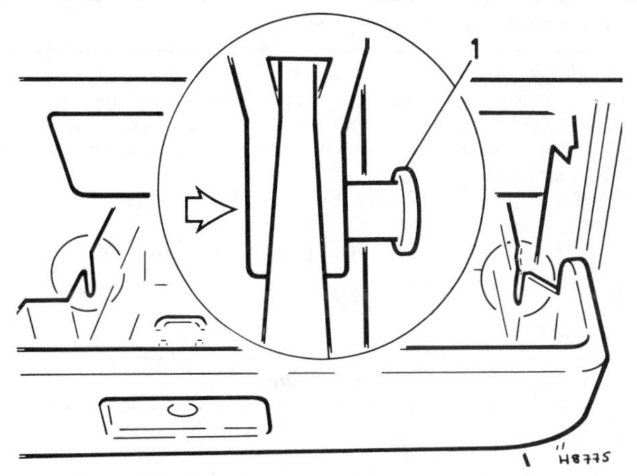

Fig. 10.24 Glovebox lid retaining straps (Sec 22)

Remove securing pin (1) in direction of arrow

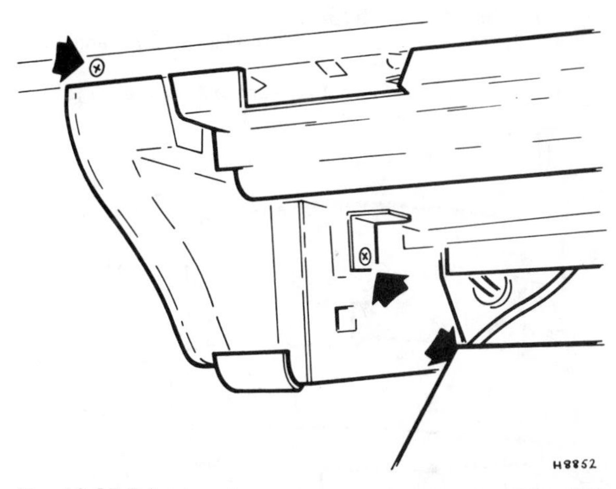

Fig. 10.25 Trim panel securing screws – arrowed (Sec 22)

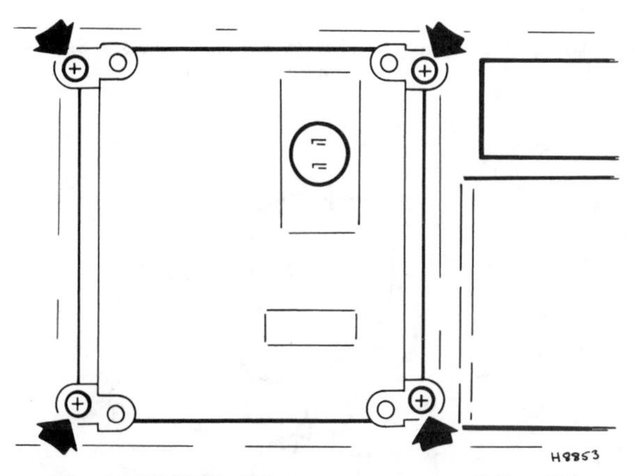

Fig. 10.26 Clock fixing screws – arrowed (Sec 22)

2 Disconnect the leads from the clock and then unscrew the knurled retaining nuts and withdraw the clock.

Later (fuel injection) models

3 On later models, disconnect the retaining straps and remove the glovebox lid and the trim panel.

4 Disconnect the wiring plug, extract the fixing screws and remove the clock.

5 Refitting is a reversal of removal.

23 Speedometer drive cable – renewal

1 Disconnect the battery.
2 Disconnect the speedometer cable from the transmission.
3 Withdraw the instrument panel (Section 21) until the speedometer cable can be disconnected from the speedometer head by unscrewing the knurled ring nut.
4 On Series 1 models, the cable is in two sections having a connector, a short distance from the head.
5 Release the cable from its clips and withdraw it through the bulkhead grommet.
6 Refitting is a reversal of removal.

24 Headlamps – removal and refitting

Series 1

1 Remove the radiator side grille (photo).
2 Extract the screws from the headlamp retaining rim (photo).
3 Withdraw the headlamp until the plug at its rear can be disconnected (photo).

Series 2 (outer dipped beam)

4 Turn the swivel retainers (1, 2 and 3) – Fig. 10.27 – and withdraw the headlamp.
5 Unscrew the cap (1) – Fig. 10.28 – and pull off the plugs (2, 3 and 4)

24.1 Removing a side grille screw

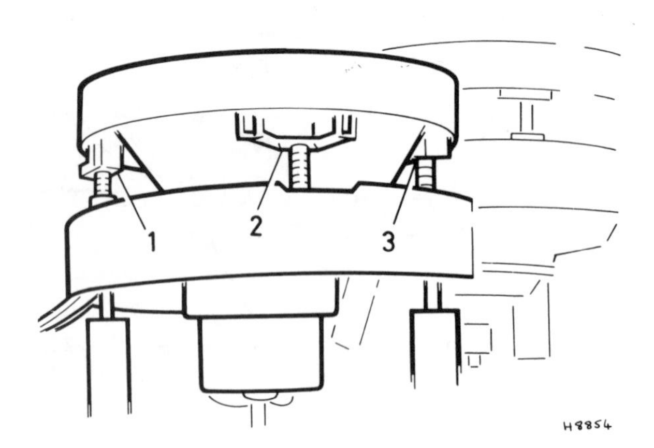

Fig. 10.27 Headlamp swivel retainers (1, 2 and 3) – Series 2 (Sec 24)

24.2 Removing a headlamp rim screw

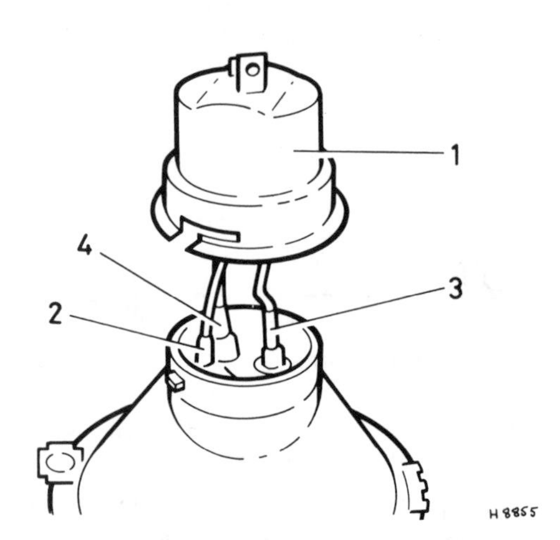

Fig. 10.28 Rear of headlamp (dipped beam) – Series 2 (Sec 24)

1 Cap
2 Earth plug (brown)
3 Sidelight plug (grey)
4 Dipped beam plug (yellow)

24.3 Headlamp withdrawn

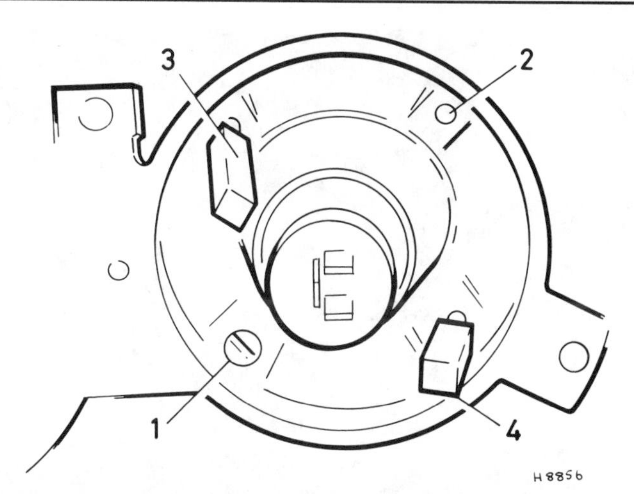

Fig. 10.29 Rear of headlamp (main beam) – Series 2 (Sec 24)

1 Swivel retainer
2 Spring
3 Vertical adjuster
4 Horizontal adjuster

Series 2 (inner main beam)

6 Turn the swivel retainer (1) through a $\frac{1}{4}$ turn – Fig. 10.29.
7 Disconnect the spring (2) and unscrew the adjusters (3 and 4).
8 Withdraw the headlamp, unscrew the cap and pull off the plug.

All models

9 Refitting is a reversal of removal, check the beam alignment on completion (Section 25).

25 Headlamp beam alignment

1 This should be carried out by a service station having suitable alignment equipment. Make sure that the tyres are correctly inflated with the car at normal kerb weight.
2 In an emergency, the horizontal and vertical adjusters may be used to align the headlamp beams accordingly. These are reached from within the engine compartment and are located at the rear of the headlamps.
3 On Series 2 models, remove the cover for access to the adjusters.

26 Exterior lamp bulbs (Series 1) – renewal

Headlamp

1 Open the bonnet and remove the cover panel.
2 Twist and remove the cap.
3 Release the spring clip and withdraw the bulb holder (photo).
4 Do not finger the halogen type bulb; if it is touched inadvertently, clean it with methylated spirit.

Front sidelight

5 The bulb is located in the headlamp unit, the holder being simply pulled from its socket (photo).

Front direction indicator

6 Extract the lens screws (photo).
7 Push in and twist to release the bayonet type bulb (photo).

Rear lamp cluster

8 Unscrew the knurled nuts, tap the ends of the studs gently and withdraw the lens (photos).
9 Renew the individual bulbs as necessary.

Rear number plate

10 Extract the screws, release the complete lamp assembly, remove the lens and take out the festoon type bulb (photo).

All lamps

11 Refitting is a reversal of removal.

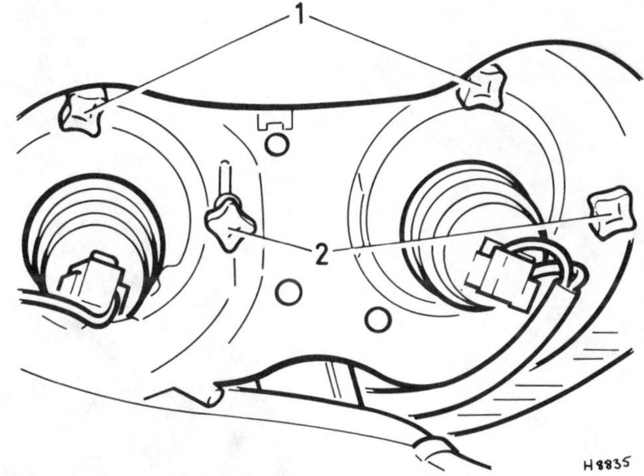

Fig. 10.30 Headlamp beam adjusters – Series 1 (Sec 25)

1 Vertical
2 Horizontal

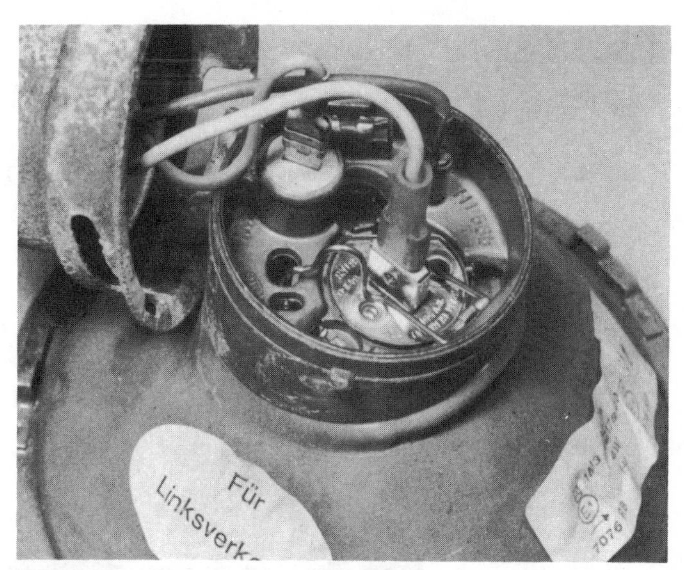

26.3 Headlamp bulb holder

26.5 Front sidelight bulb

26.6 Front direction indicator lamp lens screw

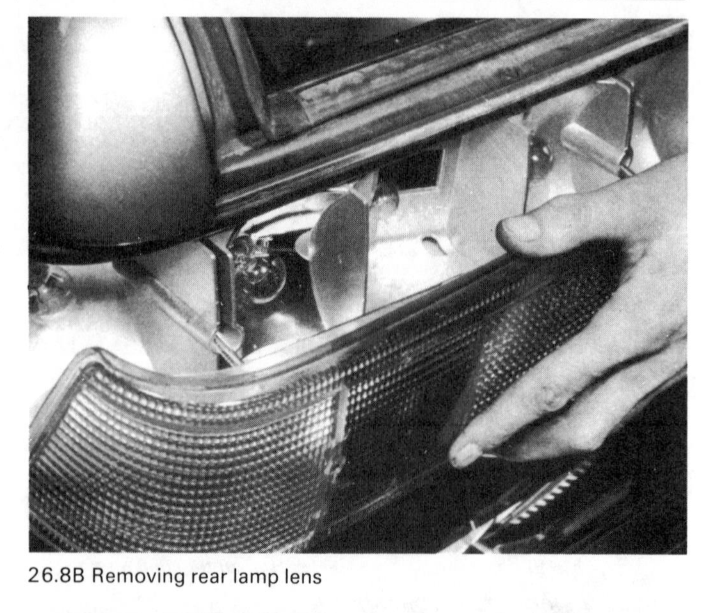
26.8B Removing rear lamp lens

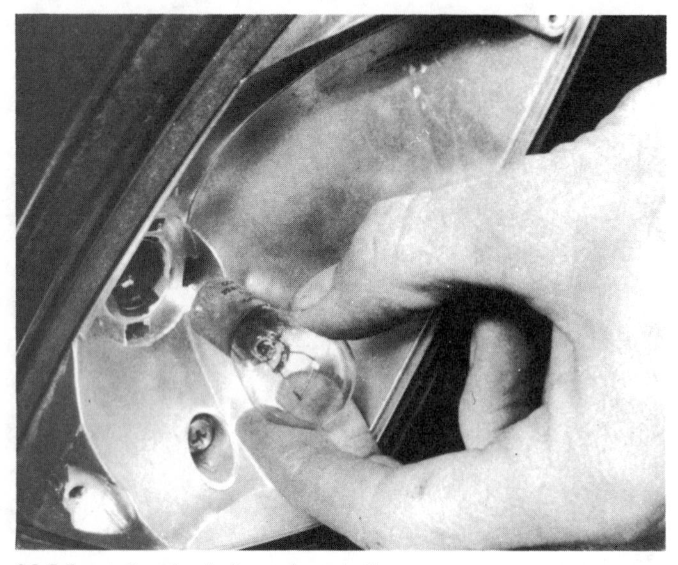
26.7 Front direction indicator lamp bulb

26.10 Rear number plate lamp

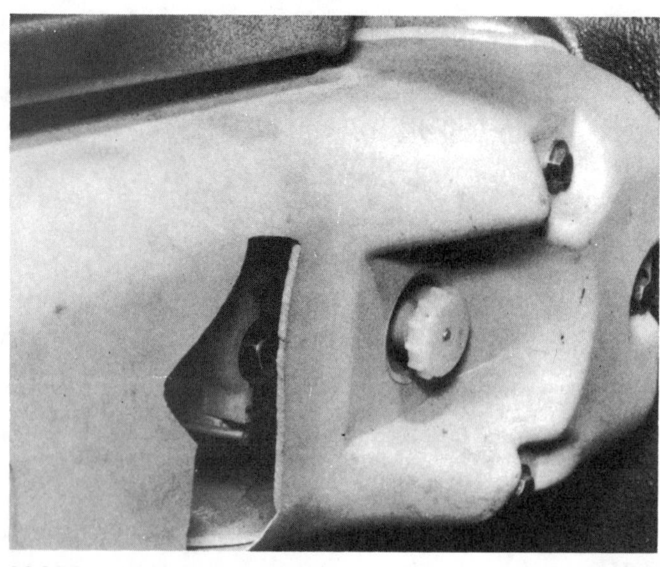
26.8A Rear lamp cluster securing nut

27 Exterior lamp bulbs (Series 2) – renewal

Headlamp

1 The operations are as described in the preceding Section, but remove the rear covers.

Front sidelight

2 The operations are as described in the preceding Section.

Front direction indicator

3 The lamps are located in the front bumper.
4 Extract the screws, withdraw the lens and depress and twist the bayonet fitting type bulb (photo).

Side repeater

5 Extract the screws and push the lamp body forwards out of its aperture.
6 Pull the bulb from the rear of the lamp.

Front foglamp

7 Extract the screws and withdraw the lamp.
8 Release the bulb holder spring clip and withdraw the holder and bulb.

Rear lamp cluster

9 Open the boot lid, release the quick-action fasteners by twisting them.

10 Withdraw the bulb holder/reflector assembly. Remove the bayonet type bulbs as necessary (photos).

Rear number plate

11 Remove as described in the preceding Section.

All lamps

12 Refitting is the reversal of removal.

28 Interior lamp bulbs – renewal

Courtesy lamp

1 Prise out the lamp assembly and pull the festoon type bulb from its contacts (photo).

Boot lamp

2 On Series 1 models, extract the two fixing screws. On Series 2 models, simply pull the lamp from its recess.

3 A festoon type bulb is used.

Warning and indicator lamps

4 Withdraw the instrument panel far enough to be able to pull out

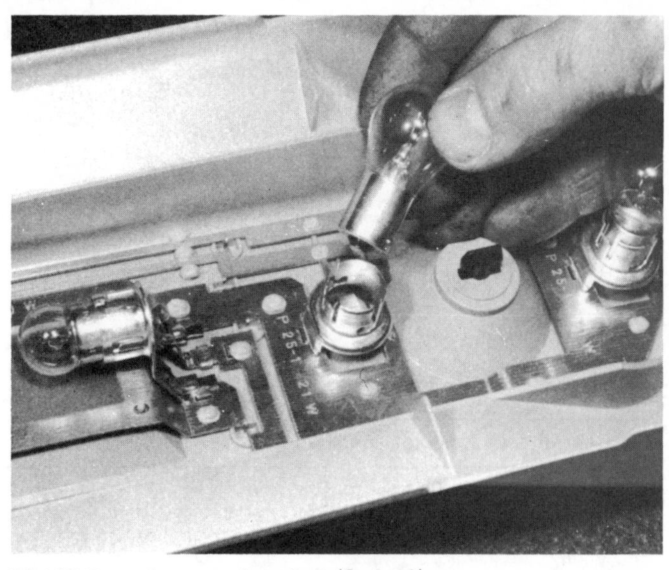

27.10B Removing a rear lamp bulb (Series 2)

27.4 Front direction indicator lamp lens screw (Series 2)

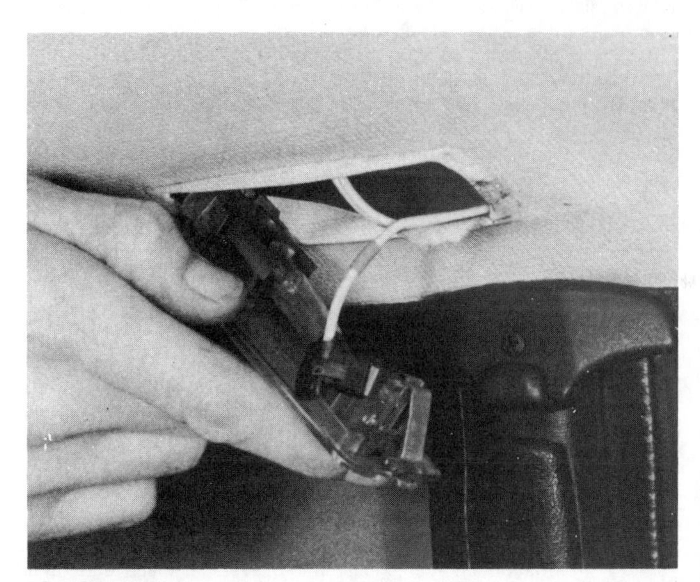

28.1 Courtesy lamp

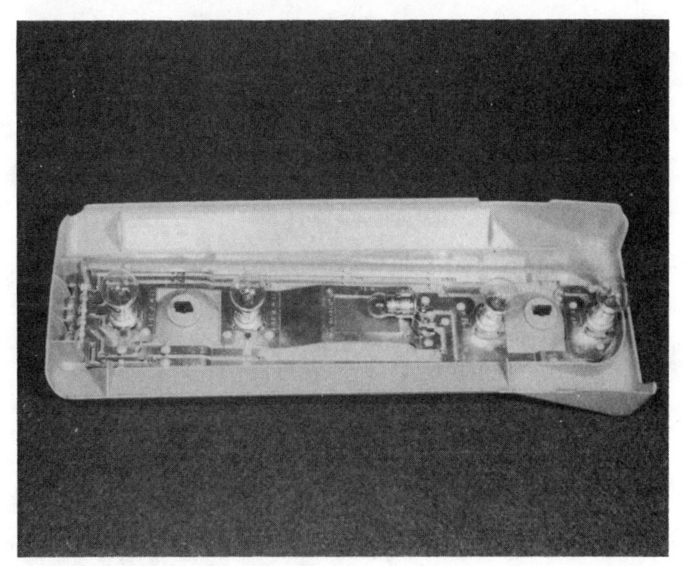

27.10A Rear lamp cluster (Series 2)

28.4 Instrument panel bulb

the bulb holders (Section 21). The bulbs are of wedge-base type and are simply pulled from the holders (photo).

5 The check control has light emitting diodes to monitor the function of the following:

Dipped headlamps
Rear lamps
Stop-lamps
Rear number plate lamp
Engine oil level
Coolant level
Washer fluid level

6 The check control can be removed by prising the upper lip outwards and then withdrawing the unit upwards.

7 On later models, the check control is located above the interior rear view mirror.

29 Central door locking system

1 This may be fitted on Series 2 models.

2 The system consists of solenoids to operate the door locks, fuel tank filler flap and boot lid lock with the necessary control switches and wiring.

3 Whenever a lock is operated, or the door lock plunger is pressed down, all the system locks are operated at the same time. The doors can still be locked or unlocked from inside the car.

4 The boot can be locked independently with the key and it must then be unlocked by using the key.

5 The door lock solenoids are accessible after removing the trim panel, as described in Chapter 12.

6 The solenoid for the fuel filler flap is located behind the side trim panel within the luggage compartment. The solenoid for the boot lid lock is accessible as described in Section 12 of Chapter 13.

30 Energy control gauge

1 This is built into the tachometer on certain models. At speeds in excess of approximately 13 mph (20 kph) the needle of the gauge indicates the fuel consumption.

2 As a general rule, the lowest fuel consumption will be achieved by changing to the highest possible gear as soon as possible to give the lowest engine revolutions.

31 Computer

1 An in-car computer is fitted to some models. This device will supply information on fuel consumption, average speed and other factors.

2 Information cen be fed into the computer using the input buttons.

3 If the battery is disconnected, all stored data will be erased.

4 Operation of the computer is outside the scope of this manual. Reference should be made to the driver's handbook or your local dealer for further information.

32 Cruise control system

1 This device is optionally available on later models and, once set by the steering column control lever, will maintain a constant roadspeed.

2 The cruise control system cuts out if the brakes or clutch pedals are depressed.

3 The accelerator pedal is still effective when the cruise control is engaged. When the pedal is released, the cruise control system will resume its preset speed level.

4 When switched off by the steering column control, the last setting can be restored if the control is moved to the RECALL/ABRUF position. Once the ignition is switched off, the last speed setting will be cancelled.

33 Service indicator

1 This visual device, located in the instrument cluster, is used to remind the driver that certain service operations and inspections are due.

Fig. 10.31 Cruise control lever (Sec 32)

RECALL/ABRUF Recalls last setting
OFF/AUS Turns the system off
CONST/ENGAGE/KONST Sets the system at the current roadspeed

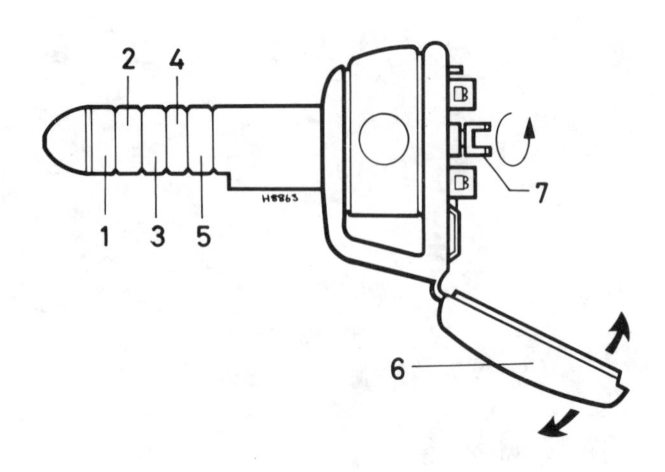

Fig. 10.32 Anti-theft system key (Sec 34)

1	*Variable code disc*	*5*	*Owner's private code disc*
2	*Variable code disc*	*6*	*Cover*
3	*Owner's private code disc*	*7*	*Guide screw*
4	*Owner's private code disc*		

2 The indicator lights can only be cancelled by inserting the special tool (62 11 00) into the diagnostic socket.

34 Anti-theft system

1 This is a system which gives an audible alarm if the doors, boot or bonnet are tampered with.

2 If an attempt is made to start the engine then the ignition circuit is interrupted.

3 The system is activated and de-activated by inserting a special key in a magnetic lock.

4 The key code can be altered by slackening the guide screw (7) – Fig. 10.32 – through five turns and turning the code discs.

5 When the battery negative lead is disconnected the magnetic lock code will be erased. Once the battery has been reconnected and the newly coded key inserted, the lock and system will be reprogrammed for the new code.

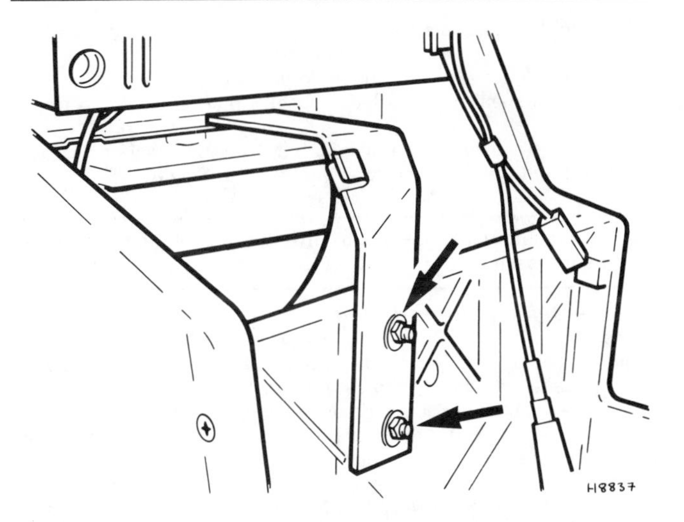

Fig. 10.33 Radio rear support bracket nuts (arrowed) – Series 1 (Sec 36)

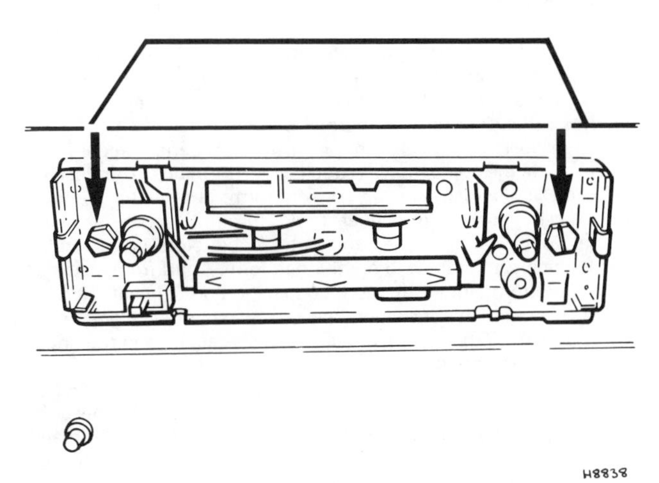

Fig. 10.34 Radio front fixing screws (arrowed) – Series 1 (Sec 36)

35 Electrically-heated front seats

1 On certain models, the driver's and passenger's seats are heated electrically.
2 The control switches are located on the centre console at the side of the handbrake, and a relay is fitted.

36 Radio/cassette player (factory-fitted equipment, Series 1) – removal and refitting

1 Disconnect the battery negative lead.
2 Pull off the radio control knobs and the switch levers, and unscrew the ring nuts using a box spanner.
3 Extract the centre console fixing screws and withdraw the console until the rear support bracket can be unbolted.
4 Disconnect the power, earth, aerial and speaker leads from the radio.
5 Take off the radio escutcheon panel and unscrew the radio fixing screws.
6 Remove the radio.
7 The radio speakers may be located under a facia grille, under the rear parcel shelf grilles or in the footwell side panels, according to whether they are for mono or stereo reproduction.
8 The aerial is located on the front wing, and access to its mounting is obtained after removal of the under-wing rear shield.
9 Refitting is a reversal of removal, make sure that the in-line fuse in the power feed is in good condition.
10 If a new radio receiver has been fitted, trim the aerial. This is usually done by inserting a small screwdriver in the small hole just below the right-hand control knob. With the receiver tuned to a weak station around the 200 m (1500 kHz) wavelength, turn the screw until maximum volume is obtained.

37 Radio/cassette player (factory-fitted equipment, Series 2) – removal and refitting

1 Disconnect the battery negative lead.
2 Pull off the control knobs and the bezels.
3 Push the spring catches upwards and take off the escutcheon plate.
4 Unscrew the screws and take off the retaining plates.
5 Pull the radio from the facia panel until the power, earth, aerial and loudspeaker leads can be disconnected.

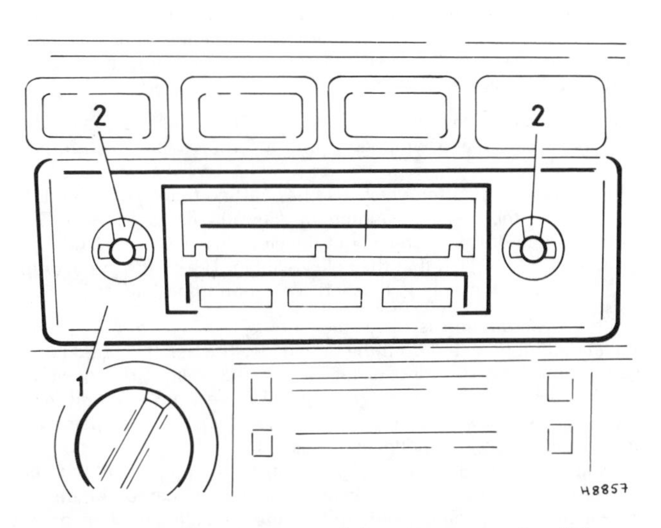

Fig. 10.35 Radio escutcheon (1) and spring catches (2) – Series 2 (Sec 37)

Fig. 10.36 Radio retaining plates (1) and screws (2) – Series 2 (Sec 37)

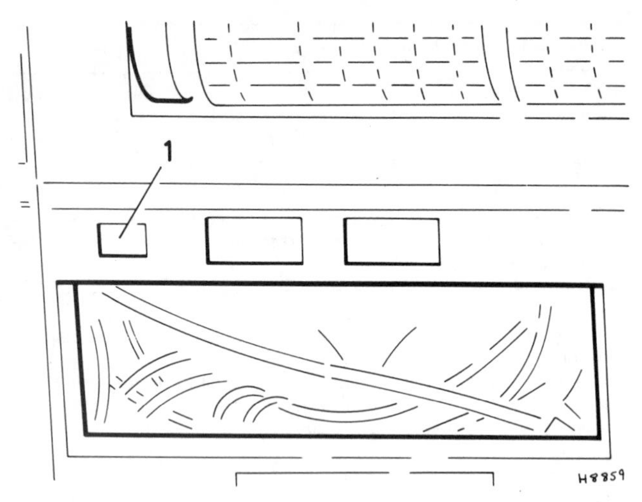

Fig. 10.37 Loudspeaker balance control (1) (Sec 37)

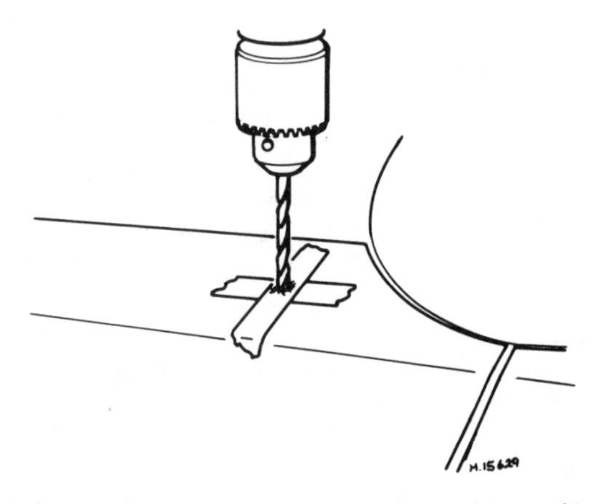

Fig. 10.38 Drilling the bodywork for aerial installation (Sec 38)

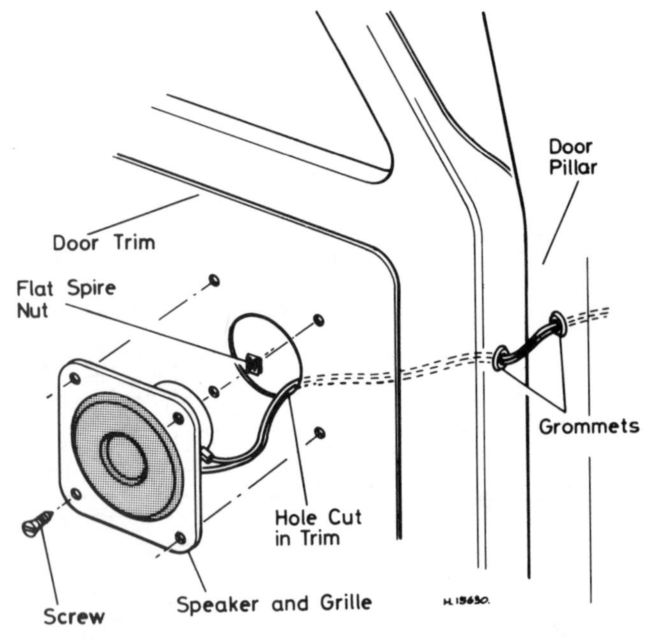

Fig. 10.39 Door-mounted speaker installation (Sec 38)

6 The electrically-operated aerial is located behind the side trim panel within the boot.

7 The front loudspeakers are mounted in the trim panels at the sides of the footwells.
8 The rear loudspeakers are mounted on the rear parcel shelf.
9 Where four speakers are fitted, a speaker balance control is fitted in the facia panel.
10 Refitting is a reversal of removal, but if a new aerial or receiver have been fitted, trim the aerial, as described in Section 36.

38 Radio equipment (not factory-fitted) – installation and interference suppression

Aerials – selection and fitting

The choice of aerials is now very wide. It should be realised that the quality has a profound effect on radio performance, and a poor, inefficient aerial can make suppression difficult.

A wing-mounted aerial is regarded as probably the most efficient for signal collection, but a roof aerial is usually better for suppression purposes because it is away from most interference fields. Stick-on wire aerials are available for attachment to the inside of the windscreen, but are not always free from the interference field of the engine and some accessories.

Motorised automatic aerials rise when the equipment is switched on and retract at switch-off. They require more fitting space and supply leads, and can be a source of trouble.

There is no merit in choosing a very long aerial as, for example, the type about three metres in length which hooks or clips on to the rear of the car, since part of this aerial will inevitably be located in an interference field. For VHF/FM radios the best length of aerial is about one metre. Active aerials have a transistor amplifier mounted at the base and this serves to boost the received signal. The aerial rod is sometimes rather shorter than normal passive types.

A large loss of signal can occur in the aerial feeder cable, especially over the Very High Frequency (VHF) bands. The design of feeder cable is invariably in the co-axial form, ie a centre conductor surrounded by a flexible copper braid forming the outer (earth) conductor. Between the inner and outer conductors is an insulator material which can be in solid or stranded form. Apart from insulation, its purpose is to maintain the correct spacing and concentricity. Loss of signal occurs in this insulator, the loss usually being greater in a poor quality cable. The quality of cable used is reflected in the price of the aerial with the attached feeder cable.

The capacitance of the feeder should be within the range 65 to 75 picofarads (pF) approximately (95 to 100 pF for Japanese and American equipment), otherwise the adjustment of the car radio aerial trimmer may not be possible. An extension cable is necessary for a long run between aerial and receiver. If this adds capacitance in excess of the above limits, a connector containing a series capacitor will be required, or an extension which is labelled as 'capacity-compensated'.

Fitting the aerial will normally involve making a $\frac{7}{8}$ in (22 mm) diameter hole in the bodywork, but read the instructions that come with the aerial kit. Once the hole position has been selected, use a centre punch to guide the drill. Use sticky masking tape around the area for this helps with marking out and drill location, and gives protection to the paintwork should the drill slip. Three methods of making the hole are in use:

(a) Use a hole saw in the electric drill. This is, in effect, a circular hacksaw blade wrapped round a former with a centre pilot drill.
(b) Use a tank cutter which also has cutting teeth, but is made to shear the metal by tightening with an Allen key.
(c) The hard way of drilling out the circle is using a small drill, say $\frac{1}{8}$ in (3 mm), so that the holes overlap. The centre metal drops out and the hole is finished with round and half-round files.

Whichever method is used, the burr is removed from the body metal and paint removed from the underside. The aerial is fitted tightly ensuring that the earth fixing, usually a serrated washer, ring or clamp, is making a solid connection. *This earth connection is important in reducing interference.* Cover any bare metal with primer paint and topcoat, and follow by underseal if desired.

Aerial feeder cable routing should avoid the engine compartment and areas where stress might occur, eg under the carpet where feet will be located. Roof aerials require that the headlining be pulled back and that a path is available down the door pillar. It is wise to check with the vehicle dealer whether roof aerial fitting is recommended.

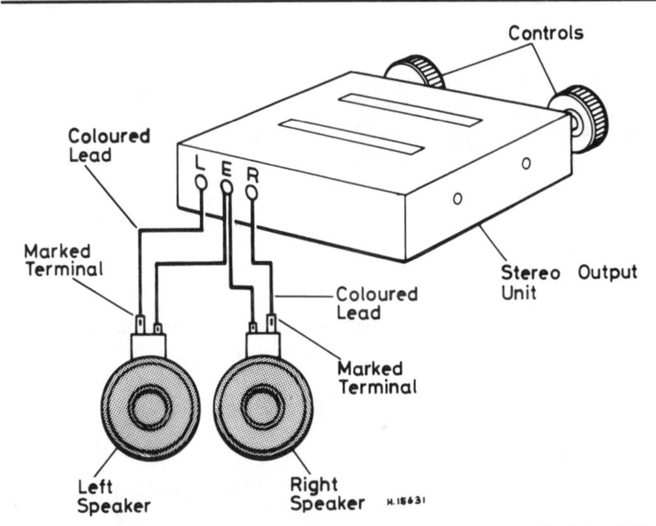

Fig. 10.40 Speaker connections must be correctly made (Sec 38)

Loudspeakers

Speakers should be matched to the output stage of the equipment, particularly as regards the recommended impedance. Power transistors used for driving speakers are sensitive to the loading placed on them.

Before choosing a mounting position for speakers, check whether the vehicle manufacturer has provided a location for them. Generally door-mounted speakers give good stereophonic reproduction, but not all doors are able to accept them. The next best position is the rear parcel shelf, and in this case speaker apertures can be cut into the shelf, or pod units may be mounted.

For door mounting, first remove the trim, which is often held on by poppers' or press studs, and then select a suitable gap in the inside door assembly. Check that the speaker would not obstruct glass or winder mechanism by winding the window up and down. A template is often provided for marking out the trim panel hole, and then the four fixing holes must be drilled through. Mark out with chalk and cut cleanly with a sharp knife or keyhole saw. Speaker leads are then threaded through the door and door pillar, if necessary drilling 10 mm diameter holes. Fit grommets in the holes and connect to the radio or tape unit correctly. Do not omit a waterproofing cover, usually supplied with door speakers. If the speaker has to be fixed into the metal of the door itself, use self-tapping screws, and if the fixing is to the door trim use self-tapping screws and flat spire nuts.

Rear shelf mounting is somewhat simpler but it is necessary to find gaps in the metalwork underneath the parcel shelf. However, remember that the speakers should be as far apart as possible to give a good stereo effect. Pod-mounted speakers can be screwed into position through the parcel shelf material, but it is worth testing for the best position. Sometimes good results are found by reflecting sound off the rear window.

Unit installation

Many vehicles have a dash panel aperture to take a radio/audio unit, a recognised international standard being 189.5 mm x 60 mm. Alternatively a console may be a feature of the car interior design and this, mounted below the dashboard, gives more room. If neither facility is available a unit may be mounted on the underside of the parcel shelf; these are frequently non-metallic and an earth wire from the case to a good earth point is necessary. A three-sided cover in the form of a cradle is obtainable from car radio dealers and this gives a professional appearance to the installation; in this case choose a position where the controls can be reached by a driver with his seat belt on.

Installation of the radio/audio unit is basically the same in all cases, and consists of offering it into the aperture after removal of the knobs (*not* push buttons) and the trim plate. In some cases a special mounting plate is required to which the unit is attached. It is worthwhile supporting the rear end in cases where sag or strain may occur, and it is usually possible to use a length of perforated metal strip attached between the unit and a good support point nearby. In general it is recommended that tape equipment should be installed at or nearly horizontal.

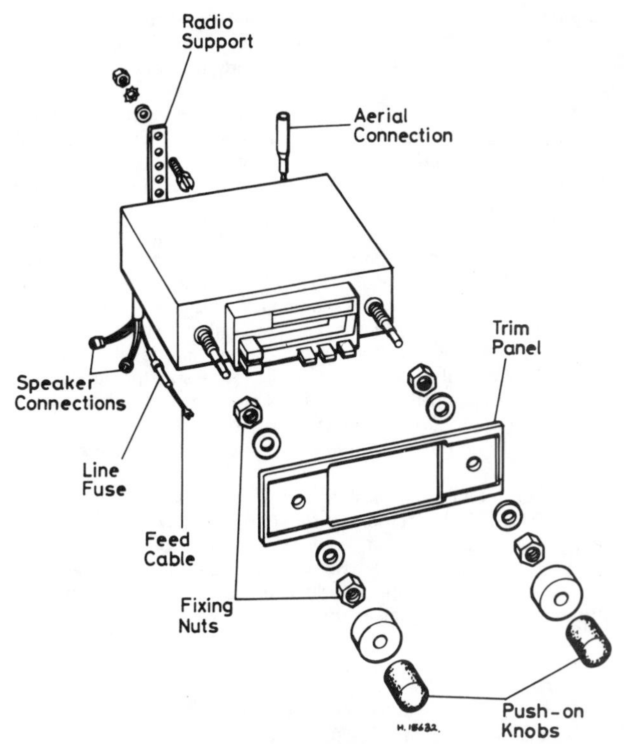

Fig. 10.41 Mounting component details for radio/cassette unit (Sec 38)

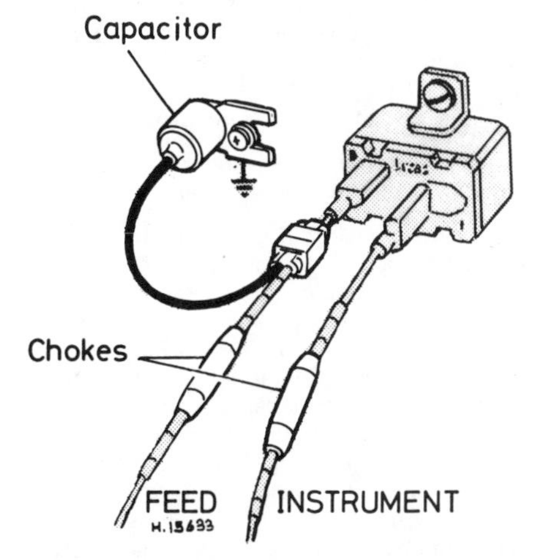

Fig. 10.42 Voltage stabiliser interference suppression (Sec 38)

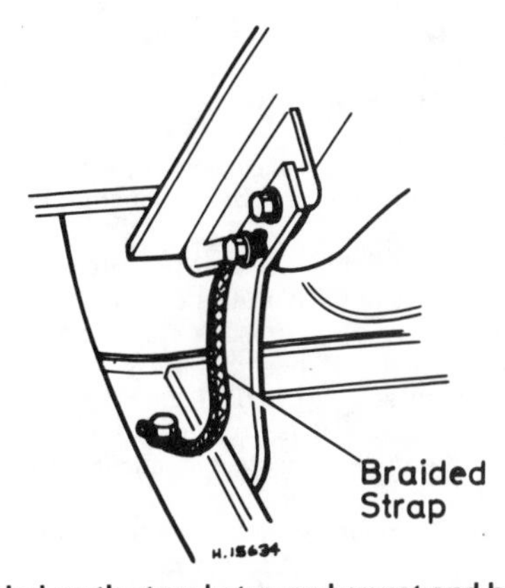

Fig. 10.43 Braided earth strap between bonnet and body (Sec 38)

Connections to the aerial socket are simply by the standard plug terminating the aerial downlead or its extension cable. Speakers for a stereo system must be matched and correctly connected, as outlined previously.

Note: *While all work is carried out on the power side, it is wise to disconnect the battery earth lead.* Before connection is made to the vehicle electrical system, check that the polarity of the unit is correct. Most vehicles use a negative earth system, but radio/audio units often have a reversible plug to convert the set to either + or – earth. *Incorrect connection may cause serious damage.*

The power lead is often permanently connected inside the unit and terminates with one half of an in-line fuse carrier. The other half is fitted with a suitable fuse (3 or 5 amperes) and a wire which should go to a power point in the electrical system. This may be the accessory terminal on the ignition switch, giving the advantage of power feed with ignition or with the ignition key at the 'accessory' position. Power to the unit stops when the ignition key is removed. Alternatively, the lead may be taken to a live point at the fusebox with the consequence of having to remember to switch off at the unit before leaving the vehicle.

Before switching on for initial test, be sure that the speaker connections have been made, for running without load can damage the output transistors. Switch on next and tune through the bands to ensure that all sections are working, and check the tape unit if applicable. The aerial trimmer should be adjusted to give the strongest reception on a weak signal in the medium wave band, at say 200 metres.

Interference

In general, when electric current changes abruptly, unwanted electrical noise is produced. The motor vehicle is filled with electrical devices which change electric current rapidly, the most obvious being the contact breaker.

When the spark plugs operate, the sudden pulse of spark current causes the associated wiring to radiate. Since early radio transmitters used sparks as a basis of operation, it is not surprising that the car radio will pick up ignition spark noise unless steps are taken to reduce it to acceptable levels.

Interference reaches the car radio in two ways:

(a) by conduction through the wiring.
(b) by radiation to the receiving aerial.

Initial checks presuppose that the bonnet is down and fastened, the radio unit has a good earth connection *(not* through the aerial downlead outer), no fluorescent tubes are working near the car, the aerial trimmer has been adjusted, and the vehicle is in a position to receive radio signals, ie not in a metal-clad building.

Switch on the radio and tune it to the middle of the medium wave (MW) band off-station with the volume (gain) control set fairly high. Switch on the ignition (but do not start the engine) and wait to see if irregular clicks or hash noise occurs. Tapping the facia panel may also produce the effects. If so, this will be due to the voltage stabiliser, which is an on-off thermal switch to control instrument voltage. It is located usually on the back of the instrument panel, often attached to the speedometer. Correction is by attachment of a capacitor and, if still troublesome, chokes in the supply wires.

Switch on the engine and listen for interference on the MW band. Depending on the type of interference, the indications are as follows.

A harsh crackle that drops out abruptly at low engine speed or when the headlights are switched on is probably due to a voltage regulator.

A whine varying with engine speed is due to the alternator. Try temporarily taking off the fan belt – if the noise goes this is confirmation.

Regular ticking or crackle that varies in rate with the engine speed is due to the ignition system. With this trouble in particular and others in general, check to see if the noise is entering the receiver from the wiring or by radiation. To do this, pull out the aerial plug, (preferably shorting out the input socket or connecting a 62 pF capacitor across it). If the noise disappears it is coming in through the aerial and is *radiation noise.* If the noise persists it is reaching the receiver through the wiring and is said to be *line-borne.*

Interference from wipers, washers, heater blowers, turn-indicators, stop lamps, etc is usually taken to the receiver by wiring, and simple treatment using capacitors and possibly chokes will solve the problem. Switch on each one in turn (wet the screen first for running wipers!)

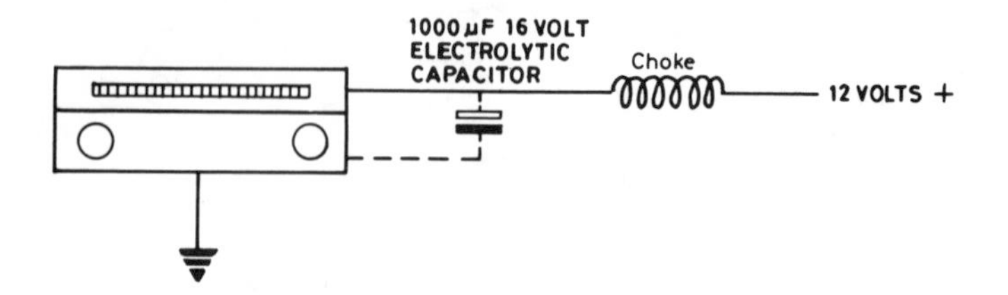

Fig. 10.44 Line-borne interference suppression (Sec 38)

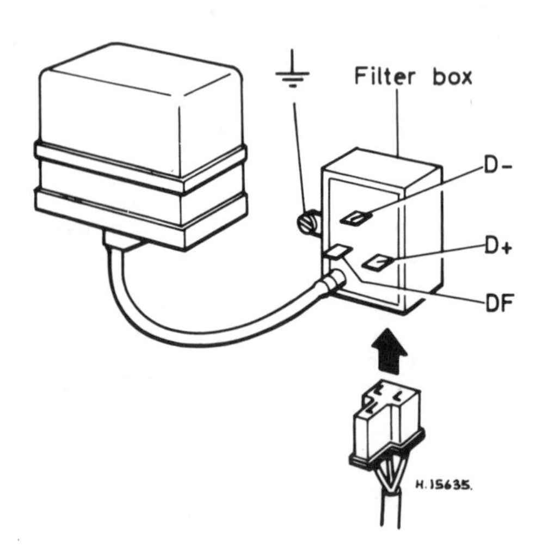

Fig. 10.45 Typical filter box for vibrating contact voltage regulator (alternator equipment) (Sec 38)

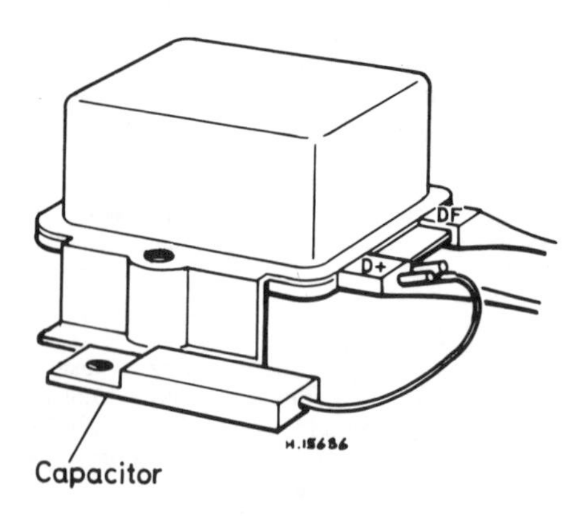

Fig. 10.46 Suppression of AM interference by vibrating contact voltage regulator (alternator equipment) (Sec 38)

and listen for possible interference with the aerial plug in place and again when removed.

Electric petrol pumps are now finding application again and give rise to an irregular clicking, often giving a burst of clicks when the ignition is on but the engine has not yet been started. It is also possible to receive whining or crackling from the pump.

Note that if most of the vehicle accessories are found to be creating interference all together, the probability is that poor aerial earthing is to blame.

Component terminal markings

Throughout the following sub-sections reference will be found to various terminal markings. These will vary depending on the manufacturer of the relevant component. If terminal markings differ from those mentioned, reference should be made to the following table, where the most commonly encountered variations are listed.

Alternator	*Alternator terminal (thick lead)*	*Exciting winding terminal*
DIN/Bosch	B+	DF
Delco Remy	+	EXC
Ducellier	+	EXC
Ford (US)	+	DF
Lucas	+	F
Marelli	+B	F

Ignition coil	*Ignition switch terminal*	*Contact breaker terminal*
DIN/Bosch	15	1
Delco Remy	+	–
Ducellier	BAT	RUP
Ford (US)	B/+	CB/–
Lucas	SW/+	–
Marelli	BAT/+B	D

Voltage regulator	*Voltage input terminal*	*Exciting winding terminal*
DIN/Bosch	B+/D+	DF
Delco Remy	BAT/+	EXC
Ducellier	BOB/BAT	EXC
Ford (US)	BAT	DF
Lucas	+/A	F
Marelli		F

Suppression methods – ignition

Suppressed HT cables are supplied as original equipment by manufacturers and will meet regulations as far as interference to neighbouring equipment is concerned. It is illegal to remove such suppression unless an alternative is provided, and this may take the form of resistive spark plug caps in conjunction with plain copper HT cable. For VHF purposes, these and 'in-line' resistors may not be effective, and resistive HT cable is preferred. Check that suppressed cables are actually fitted by observing cable identity lettering, or measuring with an ohmmeter – the value of each plug lead should be 5000 to 10 000 ohms.

A 1 microfarad capacitor connected from the LT supply side of the ignition coil to a good nearby earth point will complete basic ignition interference treatment. *NEVER fit a capacitor to the coil terminal to the contact breaker – the result would be burnt out points in a short time.*

If ignition noise persists despite the treatment above, the following sequence should be followed:

(a) Check the earthing of the ignition coil; remove paint from fixing clamp.
(b) If this does not work, lift the bonnet. Should there be no change in interference level, this may indicate that the bonnet is not electrically connected to the car body. Use a proprietary braided strap across a bonnet hinge ensuring a first class electrical connection. If, however, lifting the bonnet increases the interference, then fit resistive HT cables of a higher ohms-per-metre value.
(c) If all these measures fail, it is probable that re-radiation from metallic components is taking place. Using a braided strap between metallic points, go round the vehicle systematically – try the following: engine to body, exhaust system to body, front suspension to engine and to body, steering column to body, gear lever to engine and to body, Bowden cable to body, metal parcel shelf to body. When an offending component is located it should be bonded with the strap permanently.
(d) As a next step, the fitting of distributor suppressors to each lead at the distributor end may help.
(e) Beyond this point is involved the possible screening of the distributor and fitting resistive spark plugs, but such advanced treatment is not usually required for vehicles with entertainment equipment.

Electronic ignition systems have built-in suppression components, but this does not relieve the need for using suppressed HT leads. In some cases it is permitted to connect a capacitor on the low tension supply side of the ignition coil, but not in every case. Makers' instructions should be followed carefully, otherwise damage to the ignition semiconductors may result.

Suppression methods – generators

Alternators should be fitted with a 3 microfarad capacitor from the B+ main output terminal (thick cable) to earth. Additional suppression may be obtained by the use of a filter in the supply line to the radio receiver.

It is most important that:

(a) Capacitors are never connected to the field terminals of an alternator.
(b) Alternators must not be run without connection to the battery.

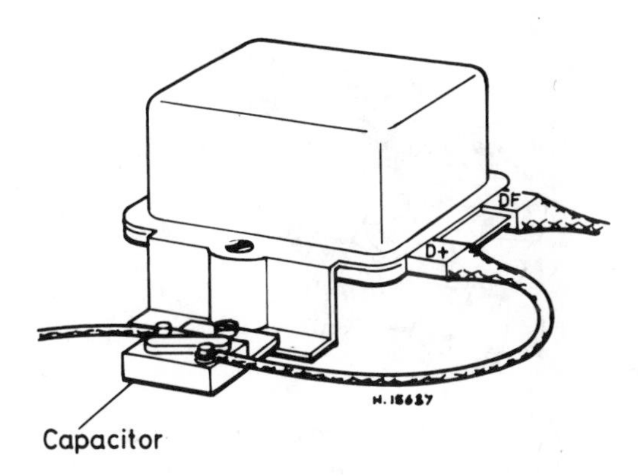

Fig. 10.47 Suppression of interference from electronic voltage regulator when integral with alternator (Sec 38)

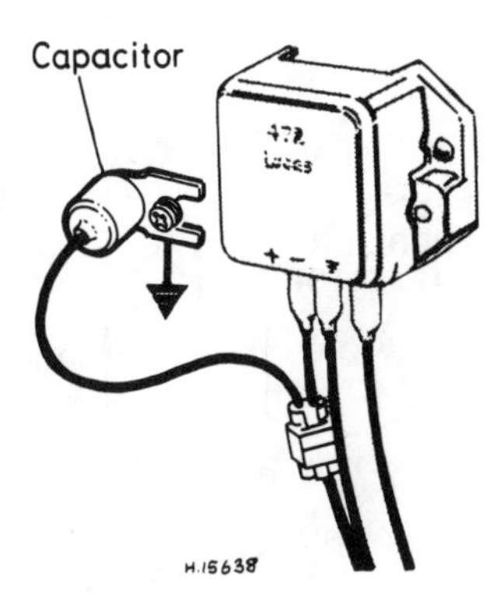

Fig. 10.48 Electronic voltage regulator suppression (Sec 38)

Suppression methods – voltage regulators

Alternator regulators come in three types:

(a) Vibrating contact regulators separate from the alternator. Used extensively on continental vehicles.
(b) Electronic regulators separate from the alternator.
(c) Electronic regulators built-in to the alternator.

In case (a) interference may be generated on the AM and FM (VHF) bands. For some cars a replacement suppressed regulator is available. Filter boxes may be used with non-suppressed regulators.

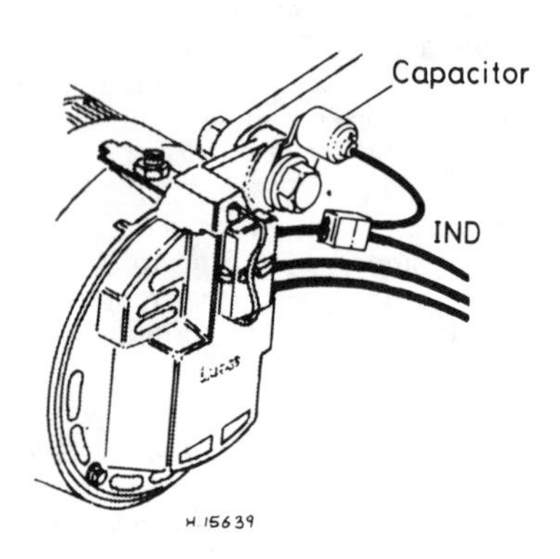

Fig. 10.49 Suppression of interference from electronic voltage regulator when integral with alternator (Sec 38)

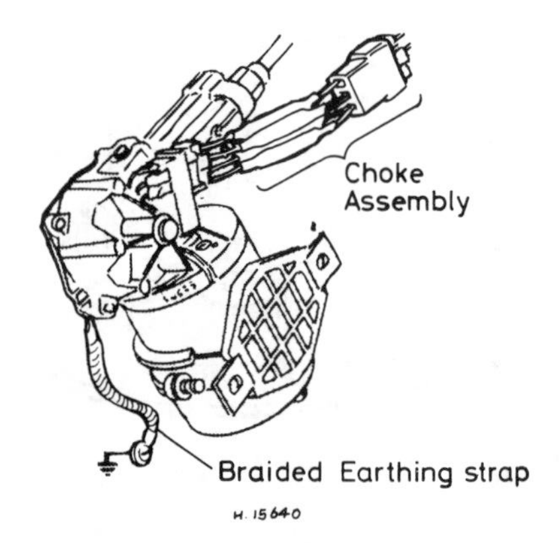

Fig. 10.50 Wiper motor suppression (Sec 38)

But if not available, then for AM equipment a 2 microfarad or 3 microfarad capacitor may be mounted at the voltage terminal marked D+ or B+ of the regulator. FM bands may be treated by a feed-through capacitor of 2 or 3 microfarad.

Electronic voltage regulators are not always troublesome, but where necessary, a 1 microfarad capacitor from the regulator + terminal will help.

Integral electronic voltage regulators do not normally generate much interference, but when encountered this is in combination with alternator noise. A 1 microfarad or 2 microfarad capacitor from the warning lamp (IND) terminal to earth for Lucas ACR alternators and Femsa, Delco and Bosch equivalents should cure the problem.

Suppression methods – other equipment

Wiper motors – Connect the wiper body to earth with a bonding strap. For all motors use a 7 ampere choke assembly inserted in the leads to the motor.

Heater motors – Fit 7 ampere line chokes in both leads, assisted if necessary by a 1 microfarad capacitor to earth from both leads.

Electronic tachometer – The tachometer is a possible source of ignition noise – check by disconnecting at the ignition coil CB terminal. It usually feeds from ignition coil LT pulses at the contact breaker terminal. A 3 ampere line choke should be fitted in the tachometer lead at the coil CB terminal.

Horn – A capacitor and choke combination is effective if the horn is directly connected to the 12 volt supply. The use of a relay is an alternative remedy, as this will reduce the length of the interference-carrying leads.

Electrostatic noise – Characteristics are erratic crackling at the receiver, with disappearance of symptoms in wet weather. Often shocks may be given when touching bodywork. Part of the problem is the build-up of static electricity in non-driven wheels and the acquisition of charge on the body shell. It is possible to fit spring-loaded contacts at the wheels to give good conduction between the rotary wheel parts and the vehicle frame. Changing a tyre sometimes helps – because of tyres' varying resistances. In difficult cases a trailing flex which touches the ground will cure the problem. If this is not acceptable it is worth trying conductive paint on the tyre walls.

Fuel pump – Suppression requires a 1 microfarad capacitor between the supply wire to the pump and a nearby earth point. If this is insufficient a 7 ampere line choke connected in the supply wire near the pump is required.

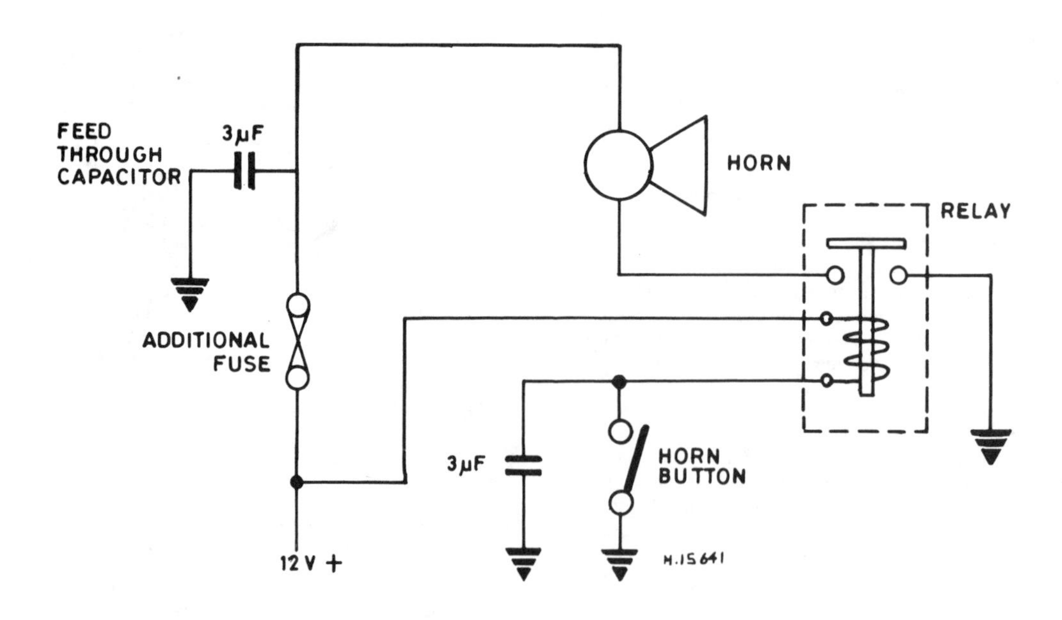

Fig. 10.51 Use of relay to reduce horn interference (Sec 38)

Fluorescent tubes – Vehicles used for camping/caravanning frequently have fluorescent tube lighting. These tubes require a relatively high voltage for operation and this is provided by an inverter (a form of oscillator) which steps up the vehicle supply voltage. This can give rise to serious interference to radio reception, and the tubes themselves can contribute to this interference by the pulsating nature of the lamp discharge. In such situations it is important to mount the aerial as far away from a fluorescent tube as possible. The interference problem may be alleviated by screening the tube with fine wire turns spaced an inch (25 mm) apart and earthed to the chassis. Suitable chokes should be fitted in both supply wires close to the inverter.

Radio/cassette case breakthrough

Magnetic radiation from dashboard wiring may be sufficiently intense to break through the metal case of the radio/cassette player. Often this is due to a particular cable routed too close and shows up as ignition interference on AM and cassette play and/or alternator whine on cassette play.

The first point to check is that the clips and/or screws are fixing all parts of the radio/cassette case together properly. Assuming good earthing of the case, see if it is possible to re-route the offending cable – the chances of this are not good, however, in most cars.

Next release the radio/cassette player and locate it in different positions with temporary leads. If a point of low interference is found, then if possible fix the equipment in that area. This also confirms that local radiation is causing the trouble. If re-location is not feasible, fit the radio/cassette player back in the original position.

Alternator interference on cassette play is now caused by radiation from the main charging cable which goes from the battery to the output terminal of the alternator, usually via the + terminal of the starter motor relay. In some vehicles this cable is routed under the dashboard, so the solution is to provide a direct cable route. Detach the original cable from the alternator output terminal and make up a new cable of at least 6 mm^2 cross-sectional area to go from alternator to battery with the shortest possible route. *Remember – do not run the engine with the alternator disconnected from the battery.*

Ignition breakthrough on AM and/or cassette play can be a difficult problem. It is worth wrapping earthed foil round the offending cable run near the equipment, or making up a deflector plate well screwed down to a good earth. Another possibility is the use of a suitable relay to switch on the ignition coil. The relay should be mounted close to the ignition coil; with this arrangement the ignition coil primary current is not taken into the dashboard area and does not flow through the ignition switch. A suitable diode should be used since it is possible that at ignition switch-off the output from the warning lamp alternator terminal could hold the relay on.

Connectors for suppression components

Capacitors are usually supplied with tags on the end of the lead, while the capacitor body has a flange with a slot or hole to fit under a nut or screw with washer.

Connections to feed wires are best achieved by self-stripping connectors. These connectors employ a blade which, when squeezed down by pliers, cuts through cable insulation and makes connection to the copper conductors beneath.

Chokes sometimes come with bullet snap-in connectors fitted to the wires, and also with just bare copper wire. With connectors, suitable female cable connectors may be purchased from an auto-accessory shop together with any extra connectors required for the cable ends after being cut for the choke insertion. For chokes with bare wires, similar connectors may be employed together with insulation sleeving as required.

VHF/FM broadcasts

Reception of VHF/FM in an automobile is more prone to problems than the medium and long wavebands. Medium/long wave transmitters are capable of covering considerable distances, but VHF transmitters are restricted to line of sight, meaning ranges of 10 to 50 miles, depending upon the terrain, the effects of buildings and the transmitter power.

Because of the limited range it is necessary to retune on a long journey, and it may be better for those habitually travelling long distances or living in areas of poor provision of transmitters to use an AM radio working on medium/long wavebands.

When conditions are poor, interference can arise, and some of the suppression devices described previously fall off in performance at very high frequencies unless specifically designed for the VHF band. Available suppression devices include reactive HT cable, resistive distributor caps, screened plug caps, screened leads and resistive spark plugs.

For VHF/FM receiver installation the following points should be particularly noted:

(a) Earthing of the receiver chassis and the aerial mounting is important. Use a separate earthing wire at the radio, and scrape paint away at the aerial mounting.
(b) If possible, use a good quality roof aerial to obtain maximum height and distance from interference generating devices on the vehicle.
(c) Use of a high quality aerial downlead is important, since losses in cheap cable can be significant.
(d) The polarisation of FM transmissions may be horizontal, vertical, circular or slanted. Because of this the optimum mounting angle is at 45° to the vehicle roof.

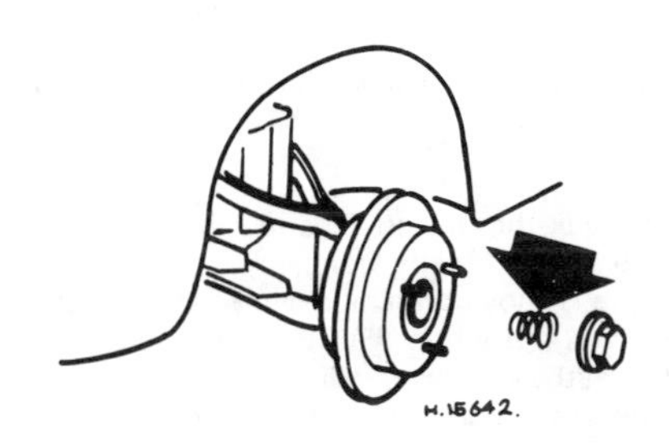

Fig. 10.52 Use of spring contacts at wheels (Sec 38)

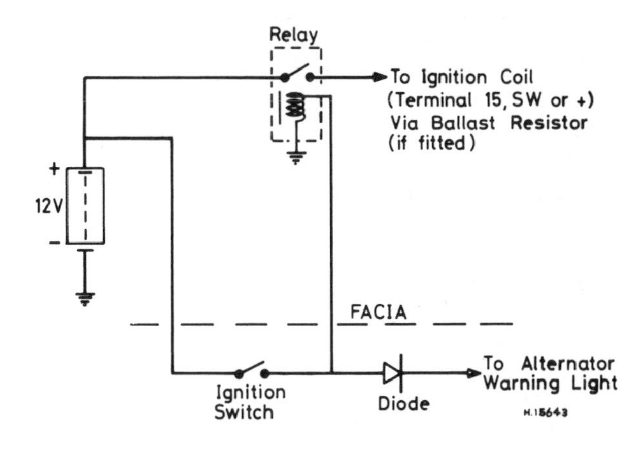

Fig. 10.53 Use of ignition coil relay to suppress case breakthrough (Sec 38)

Citizens' Band radio (CB)

In the UK, CB transmitter/receivers work within the 27 MHz and 934 MHz bands, using the FM mode. At present interest is concentrated on 27 MHz where the design and manufacture of equipment is less difficult. Maximum transmitted power is 4 watts, and 40 channels spaced 10 kHz apart within the range 27.60125 to 27.99125 MHz are available.

Aerials are the key to effective transmission and reception. Regulations limit the aerial length to 1.65 metres including the loading coil and any associated circuitry, so tuning the aerial is necessary to obtain optimum results. The choice of a CB aerial is dependent on whether it is to be permanently installed or removable, and the performance will hinge on correct tuning and the location point on the vehicle. Common practice is to clip the aerial to the roof gutter or to employ wing mounting where the aerial can be rapidly unscrewed. An alternative is to use the boot rim to render the aerial theftproof, but a popular solution is to use the 'magmount' – a type of mounting having a strong magnetic base clamping to the vehicle at any point, usually the roof.

Aerial location determines the signal distribution for both transmission and reception, but it is wise to choose a point away from the engine compartment to minimise interference from vehicle electrical equipment.

The aerial is subject to considerable wind and acceleration forces. Cheaper units will whip backwards and forwards and in so doing will alter the relationship with the metal surface of the vehicle with which it forms a ground plane aerial system. The radiation pattern will change correspondingly, giving rise to break-up of both incoming and outgoing signals.

Interference problems on the vehicle carrying CB equipment fall into two categories:

(a) Interference to nearby TV and radio receivers when transmitting.
(b) Interference to CB set reception due to electrical equipment on the vehicle.

Problems of break-through to TV and radio are not frequent, but can be difficult to solve. Mostly trouble is not detected or reported because the vehicle is moving and the symptoms rapidly disappear at the TV/radio receiver, but when the CB set is used as a base station any trouble with nearby receivers will soon result in a complaint.

It must not be assumed by the CB operator that his equipment is faultless, for much depends upon the design. Harmonics (that is, multiples) of 27 MHz may be transmitted unknowingly and these can fall into other user's bands. Where trouble of this nature occurs, low pass filters in the aerial or supply leads can help, and should be fitted in base station aerials as a matter of course. In stubborn cases it may be necessary to call for assistance from the licensing authority, or, if possible, to have the equipment checked by the manufacturers.

Interference received on the CB set from the vehicle equipment is, fortunately, not usually a severe problem. The precautions outlined previously for radio/cassette units apply, but there are some extra points worth noting.

It is common practice to use a slide-mount on CB equipment enabling the set to be easily removed for use as a base station, for example. Care must be taken that the slide mount fittings are properly earthed and that first class connection occurs between the set and slide-mount.

Vehicle manufacturers in the UK are required to provide suppression of electrical equipment to cover 40 to 250 MHz to protect TV and VHF radio bands. Such suppression appears to be adequately effective at 27 MHz, but suppression of individual items such as alternators, clocks, stabilisers, flashers, wiper motors, etc, may still be necessary. The suppression capacitors and chokes available from auto-electrical suppliers for entertainment receivers will usually give the required results with CB equipment.

Other vehicle radio transmitters

Besides CB radio already mentioned, a considerable increase in the use of transceivers (ie combined transmitter and receiver units) has taken place in the last decade. Previously this type of equipment was fitted mainly to military, fire, ambulance and police vehicles, but a large business radio and radio telephone usage has developed.

Generally the suppression techniques described previously will suffice, with only a few difficult cases arising. Suppression is carried out to satisfy the 'receive mode', but care must be taken to use heavy duty chokes in the equipment supply cables since the loading on 'transmit' is relatively high.

39 Fault diagnosis – electrical system

Symptom	Reason(s)
No voltage at starter	Battery discharged Battery defective internally Battery terminals loose or earth lead not securely attached to body Loose or broken connections in starter motor circuit Starter motor switch or solenoid faulty
Voltage at starter motor – faulty motor	Starter brushes badly worn, sticking, or brush wires loose Commutator dirty, worn or burnt Starter motor armature faulty Field coils earthed
Electrical defects	Battery in discharged condition Starter brushes badly worn, sticking, or brush wires loose Loose wires in starter motor circuit Starter motor pinion sticking on the screwed sleeve Dirt or oil on drivegear
Starter motor noisy or rough in engagement	Pinion or flywheel gear teeth broken or worn Starter drive main spring broken Starter motor retaining bolts loose
Alternator not charging*	Drivebelt loose and slipping, or broken Brushes worn, sticking, broken or dirty Brush springs weak or broken

** If all appears to be well but the alternator is still not charging, take the car to an automobile electrician for checking of the alternator*

Symptom	Reason(s)
Battery will not hold charge for more than a few days	Battery defective internally Electrolyte level too low or electrolyte too weak due to leakage Plate separators no longer fully effective Battery plates severely sulphated Drivebelt slipping Battery terminal connections loose or corroded Alternator not charging properly Short in lighting circuit causing continual battery drain

Symptom	Reason/s
Ignition light fails to go out, battery runs flat in a few days	Drivebelt loose and slipping, or broken Alternator faulty

Failure of individual equipment to function correctly is dealt with alphabetically below

Symptom	Reason/s
Fuel gauge gives no reading	Fuel tank empty Electric cable between tank sender unit and gauge earthed or loose Fuel gauge case not earthed Fuel gauge supply cable interrupted Fuel gauge unit broken
Fuel gauge registers full all the time	Electric cable between tank unit and gauge broken or disconnected
Horn operates all the time	Horn push either earthed or stuck down Horn cable to horn push earthed
Horn fails to operate	Blown fuse Cable or cable connection, broken or disconnected Horn has an internal fault
Horn emits intermittent or unsatisfactory noise	Cable connections loose Horn incorrectly adjusted
Lights do not come on	If engine not running, battery discharged Light bulb filament burnt out or bulbs broken Wire connections loose, disconnected or broken Light switch shorting or otherwise faulty
Lights come on but fade out	If engine not running, battery discharged
Lights give very poor illumination	Lamp glasses dirty Reflector tarnished or dirty Lamps badly out of adjustment Incorrect bulb with too low wattage fitted Existing bulbs old and badly discoloured Electrical wiring too thin not allowing full current to pass
Lights work erratically, flashing on and off, especially over bumps	Battery terminals or earth connections loose Lights not earthing properly
Wiper motor fails to work	Blown fuse Wire connections loose, disconnected or broken Brushes badly worn Armature worn or faulty Field coils faulty
Wiper motor works very slowly and takes excessive current	Commutator dirty, greasy or burnt Drive to spindles bent or unlubricated Drive spindle binding or damaged Armature bearings dry or unaligned Armature badly worn or faulty
Wiper motor works slowly and takes little current	Brushes badly worn Commutator dirty, greasy or burnt Armature badly worn or faulty
Wiper motor works, but wiper blades remain static	Linkage disengaged or faulty Drive spindle damaged or worn Wiper motor gearbox parts badly worn

Chapter 11 Suspension and steering

Contents

Specifications

Type

Front suspension	MacPherson strut, track control arms and anti-roll bar
Rear suspension	Independent, hydraulic shock absorbers, coil springs, semi-trailing links. Anti-roll bar
Steering	Rack and pinion with safety column. Power-assistance option

Steering and suspension angles

Series 1:	
Toe-in:	
To March 1981	1.0 to 2.5 mm (0.039 to 0.099 in)
April 1981 on	1.4 to 2.6 mm (0.055 to 0.102 in)
Camber	–30′ to 30′
Castor	7°50′ to 8°50′
Kingpin inclination	10°24′ to 11°24′
Wheel turning angle (full lock):	
Inner wheel	41°
Outer wheel	36°
Series 2:	
Toe-in	1.4 to 2.6 mm (0.055 to 0.102 in)
Camber	0°10′ to 1°10′
Castor angle	8°30′ to 9°30′
Kingpin inclination	13°30′ to 14°30′
Wheel turning angle (full lock):	
Inner wheel	41°
Outer wheel	34°

Rear suspension angles

Series 1:	
Toe-in	1.2 to 2.8 mm (0.047 to 0.110 in)
Camber	1°30′ to 2°30′ negative
Series 2:	
Toe-in	1.2 to 2.8 mm (0.047 to 0.110 in)
Camber	1°20′ to 2°20′ negative

Steering

Ratio:	
Manual	21.4 : 1
Power assisted	20.5 : 1
Steering wheel diameter	380.0 mm (15.0 in)
Turns (lock to lock)	4.05
Turning circle (between kerbs):	
Left	9.40 m (30 ft 10 in)
Right	9.60 m (31 ft 6 in)

Lubrication

Manual steering:	
Type	Special BMW or molybdenum disulphide grease (Duckhams LBM 10)
Quantity	20 to 30 g (0.7 to 1.1 oz)
Power-assisted steering:	
Type	Dexron II type ATF (Duckhams D-Matic)
Quantity	1.2 litre (2.1 Imp pints)
Strut tube (engine oil)	30 cc

Torque wrench settings

	Nm	lbf ft
Series 1		
Front suspension		
Crossmember to body side-members	45	33
Control arm pivot bolt	85	63
Control arm to stub axle carrier	65	48
Strut top mounting nuts	24	18
Strut spindle self-locking nut	80	59
Strut ring nut	120	89
Anti-roll bar clamp bolts	65	48
Anti-roll bar to control arm	75	55
Rear suspension		
Semi-trailing arm to crossmember	85	63
Shock absorber lower mounting	50	37
Shock absorber upper mounting	25	18
Anti-roll bar clamp bolts	24	18
Anti-roll bar to trailing arm	24	18
Steering		
Steering gear mounting bolts	50	37
Steering gear damper mounting nuts	18	13
Tie-rod end locknut	60	44
Tie-rod end ball-stud nut	40	30
Steering shaft coupling pinch-bolt	25	18
Flexible disc bolt	23	17
Steering wheel nut	85	63
Series 2		
Front suspension		
Anti-roll bar clamp bolts	48	35
Anti-roll bar to track control arm	120	89
Control arm pivot bracket bolts	45	33
Strut top mounting nuts	24	18
Strut piston self-locking nut	80	59
Strut tube ring nut	120	89
Crossmember bolts	45	33
Track control arm to strut	85	63
Rear suspension		
Rear axle carrier to body	140	103
Semi-trailing arm to rear axle carrier	70	52
Shock absorber top mounting nuts	25	18
Shock absorber lower mounting	50	37
Anti-roll bar to semi-trailing arm	25	18
Steering		
Steering wheel nut	80	59
Shaft coupling pinch-bolt	25	18
Shaft flexible disc bolts	25	18
Tie-rod clamp bolt	15	11
Tie-rod balljoint stud nut	40	30
Steering gear to crossmember	45	33
Steering column clamp	25	18
Power steering hoses	45	33

1 General description

The front suspension is of MacPherson strut type with lower track control arm wishbones and trailing links. An anti-roll bar is fitted.

The rear suspension is of independent type with double-acting hydraulic shock absorbers, coil springs and semi-trailing arms. The final drive/differential is flexibly-mounted to the bodyshell and power is transmitted through open driveshafts. An anti-roll bar is fitted.

There are considerable design and component differences between Series 1 and 2 models, particularly with the rear suspension. On Series 2 models, a box-section subframe is used to support the trailing links and final drive unit. The subframe is flexibly-mounted. The coil springs are mounted remotely from the shock absorbers.

The steering is of rack and pinion type with a safety steering column. Power steering is an option on all models.

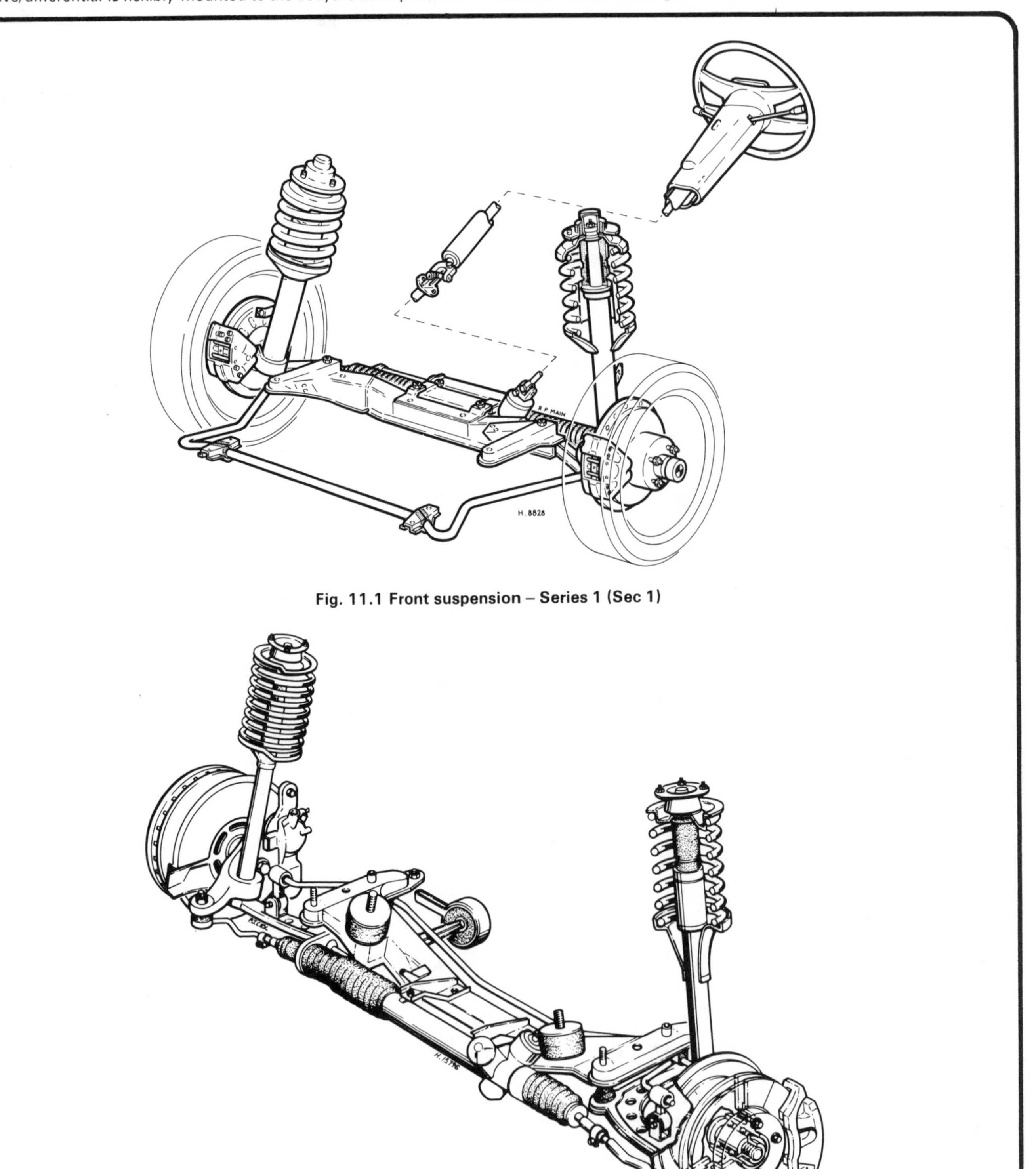

Fig. 11.1 Front suspension – Series 1 (Sec 1)

Fig. 11.2 Front suspension – Series 2 (Sec 1)

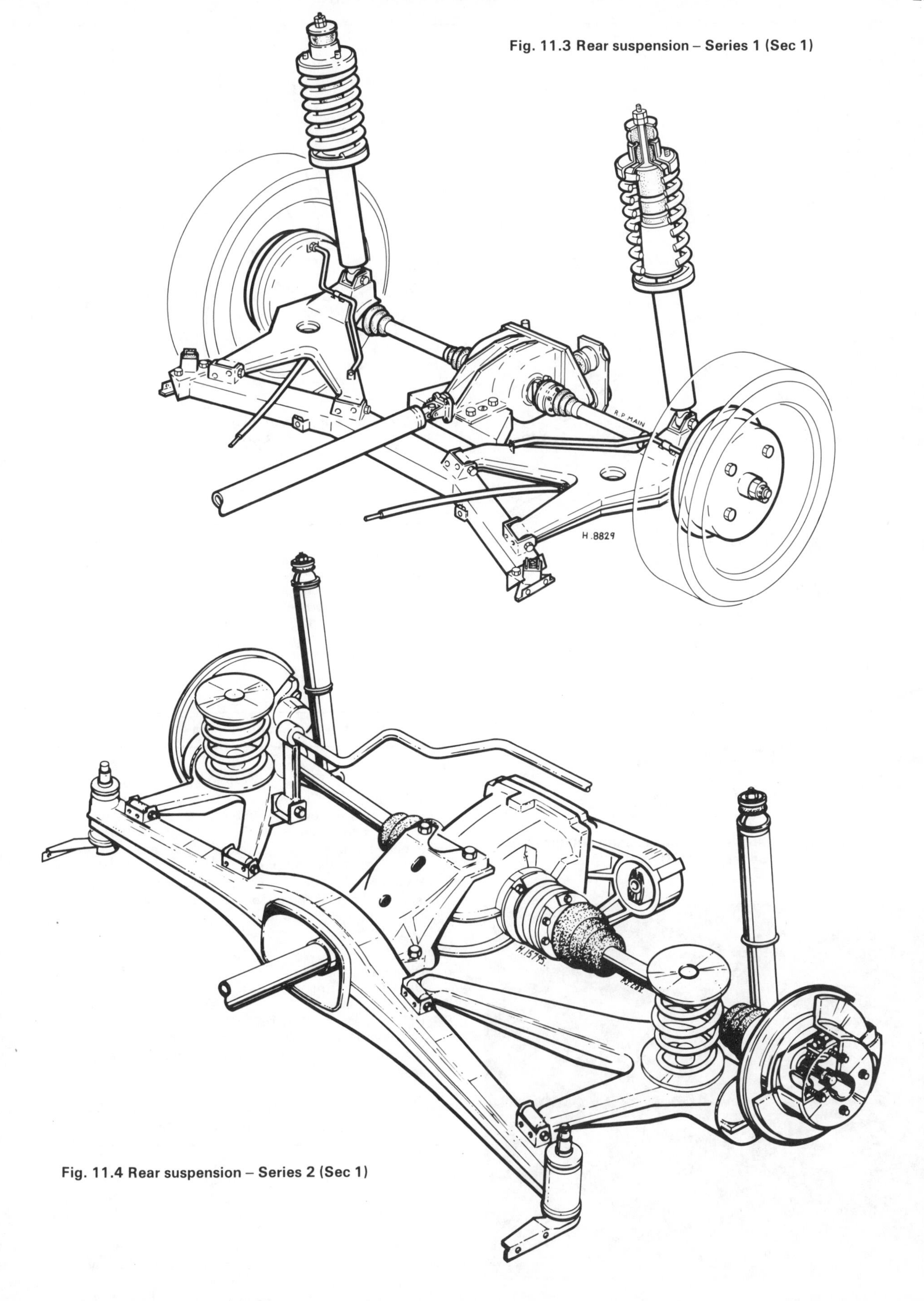

Fig. 11.3 Rear suspension – Series 1 (Sec 1)

Fig. 11.4 Rear suspension – Series 2 (Sec 1)

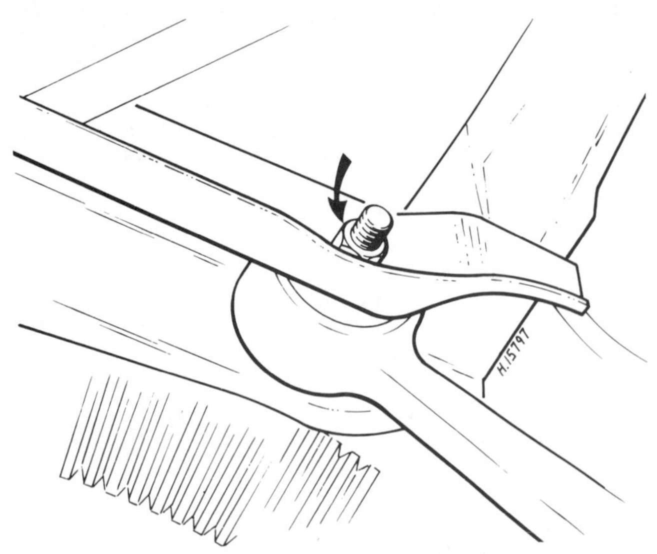

Fig. 11.5 Track control arm pivot bolt (arrowed) – Series 1 (Sec 3)

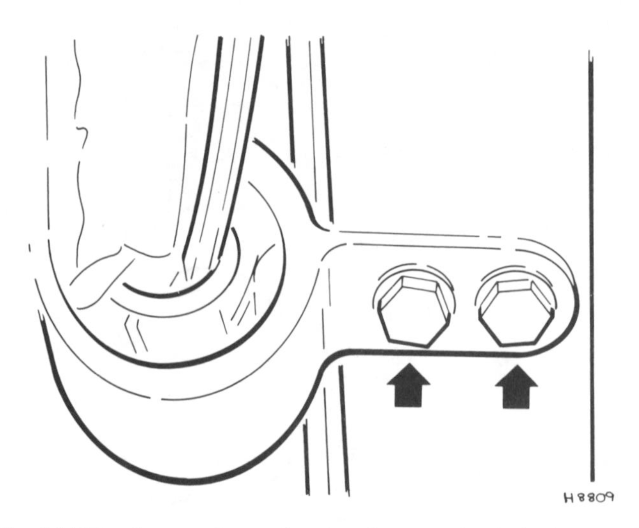

Fig. 11.7 Track control arm pivot bracket securing bolts (arrowed) – Series 2 (Sec 3)

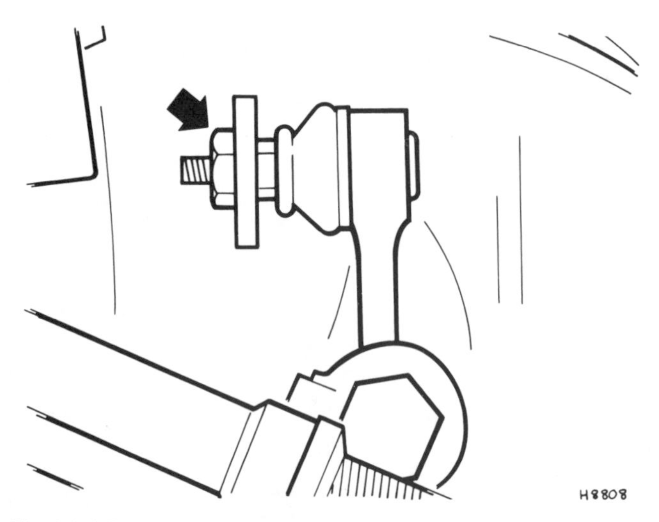

Fig. 11.6 Front anti-roll bar-to-thrust rod securing nut (arrowed) – Series 2 (Sec 3)

3.2 Front anti-roll bar clamp

2 Maintenance

1 At the intervals specified in Routine Maintenance, inspect all steering and suspension joints for wear.
2 Check the steering rack gaiters for splits.
3 Check the suspension struts and shock absorbers for leaks and failure of damping properties.
4 At the specified intervals, check the front wheel alignment (tracking) – see Section 33.
5 Refer to Section 30 for details of power-assisted steering maintenance.

3 Front anti-roll bar – removal and refitting

Series 1

1 Unscrew and remove the self-locking nut from both ends of the anti-roll bar.
2 Unbolt and remove the rubber bushed clamps (photo).
3 On one side, disconnect the inboard end of the track control arm (wishbone) from the crossmember (bolt head to rear of car).
4 Remove the anti-roll bar.
5 Refitting is a reversal of removal. Make sure that the clamp rubbers are in good condition and use new self-locking end nuts. Tighten to the specified torque.

Series 2

6 Disconnect the thrust rods from both ends of the anti-roll bar.
7 Unbolt the left-hand end bracket for the track control arm from the body side-member.
8 Unbolt the anti-roll bar clamps.
9 Refitting is a reversal of removal, make sure that the clamp rubbers are in good condition and tighten all bolts to the specified torque.

4 Track control arm – removal and refitting

Series 1

1 Remove the self-locking nut from the end of the anti-roll bar.
2 Disconnect the track control arm from the crossmember.
3 Working at the stub axle carrier, extract the split pin and unscrew the castellated nut.
4 The long ball-stud of the control arm must be pressed downwards out of the stub axle carrier. A special tool (311100) is available for this, but it may be possible to adapt an engineer's clamp to do the job.
5 If the control arm ball-stud has an endfloat exceeding 1.4 mm (0.055 in), then the control arm must be renewed complete.

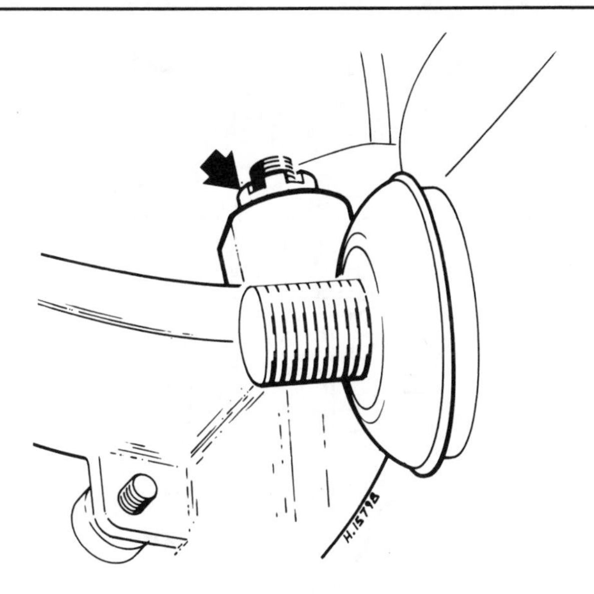

Fig. 11.8 Track control arm ball-stud castellated nut (arrowed) – Series 1 (Sec 4)

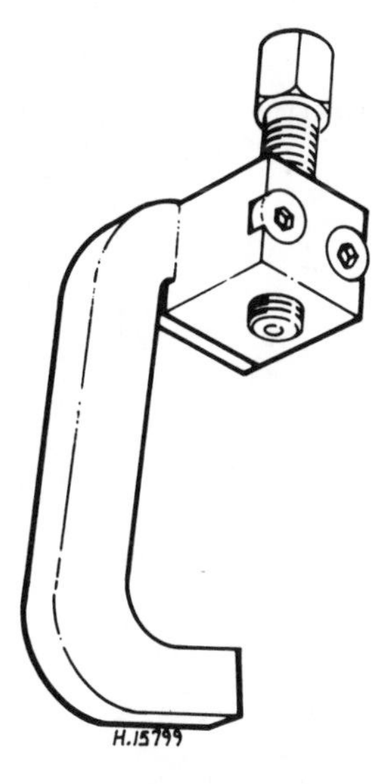

Fig. 11.9 BMW tool for separating the control arm ball-stud from the stub axle carrier – Series 1 (Sec 4)

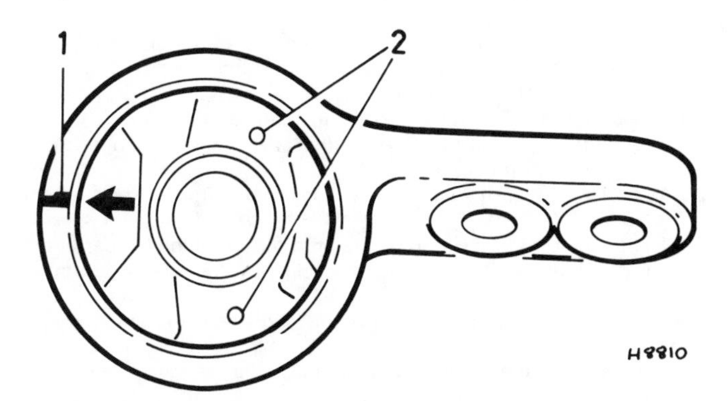

Fig. 11.10 Track control arm flexible mounting – Series 2 (Sec 4)

1 Cast boss (to align with arrow) 2 Orange paint marks

6 The control arm flexible bushes can be renewed if necessary by using a bolt, nut, washer and distance piece to draw out the old bush and pull in the new. Smearing the bush with soapy water or brake fluid will assist fitting.
7 Refitting is a reversal of removal, **do not** grease the hole in the stub axle carrier, tighten all fixings to the specified torque and use a new self-locking nut on the end of the anti-roll bar.

Series 2

8 Remove the front roadwheel.
9 Unbolt the track control arm rear bracket from the body side-member.
10 Disconnect the thrust rod from the end of the anti-roll bar.
11 Unscrew the nut from the control arm centre balljoint and tap the ball-pin loose with a plastic hammer.
12 Unscrew the nut which holds the control arm out-board balljoint to the stub axle carrier. Use a balljoint extractor or similar tool to disconnect the ball-stud from the stub axle carrier.
13 Wear in the balljoint can only be rectified by renewal of the track control arm.
14 The flexible mounting in the end bracket can be renewed by drawing the bracket from the control arm. The rubber mounting will be destroyed in the process.
15 Remove the flexible mounting from the bracket. When refitting, note that the arrow is aligned with the cast boss on the bracket.
16 Refitting is a reversal of removal, use a new self-locking nut on the end of the anti-roll bar, tighten all fixings to the specified torque and the end bracket bolts when the weight of the car is again on its roadwheels.

5 Front suspension strut – removal, overhaul and refitting

Series 1

1 Raise the front of the car and remove the roadwheel.
2 Unbolt and remove the strut angle bracket.
3 Unbolt the brake caliper and tie it up out of the way, there is no need to disconnect the hydraulic line.
4 Extract the split pin from the castellated nut on the tie-rod end.
5 Disconnect the tie-rod end balljoint from the steering arm of the stub axle carrier, using a suitable splitter tool (photo).
6 Extract the split pin, unscrew the castellated nut and, using a suitable tool, press the track control arm outboard balljoint stud out of the stub axle carrier.
7 Slacken the self-locking nut on the end of the anti-roll bar.
8 Disconnect the inboard end of the track control arm from the body crossmember.
9 Working at the strut turret within the engine compartment, unscrew and remove the three upper bearing nuts.

5.5 Balljoint splitter tool

Fig. 11.11 Front strut angle bracket securing nut (arrowed) – Series 1 (Sec 5)

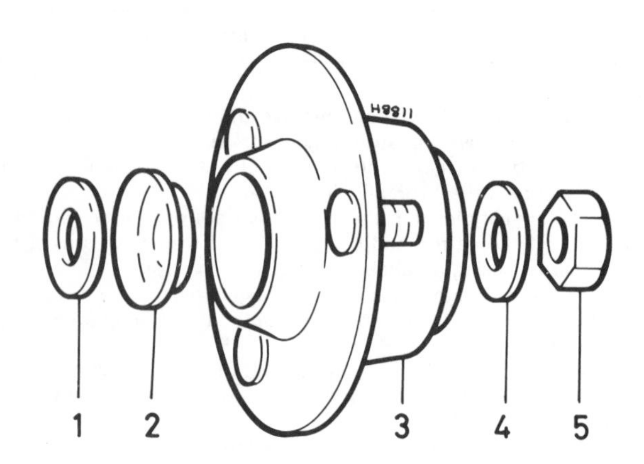

Fig. 11.12 Strut top mounting components – Series 1 (Sec 5)

1	*Washer*	4	*Washer*
2	*Seal*	5	*Self-locking nut*
3	*Bearing*		

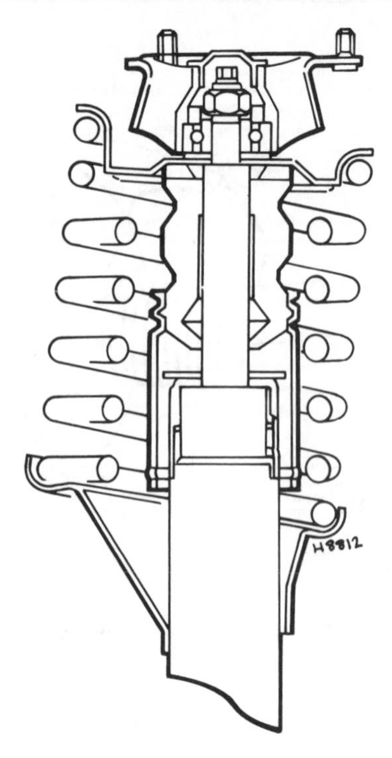

Fig. 11.13 Sectional view of the front strut top mounting – Series 2 (Sec 5)

1	*Cap*	9	*Strut tube*
2	*Flexible mounting*	10	*Insulating ring*
3	*Self-locking nut*	11	*Spring upper retainer*
4	*Washer*	12	*Coil spring*
5	*Insulator*	13	*Piston rod*
6	*Washer*	14	*Insulating ring*
7	*Buffer*	15	*Ring nut*
8	*Protective sleeve*		

10 Withdraw the strut, complete with coil spring, from under the front wing.
11 Fit suitable spring compressors. These are obtainable from motor stores or may be hired. Compress the spring and check that tension has been released from the upper spring retainer.
12 Prise off the strut end cap, hold the piston rod against rotation and unscrew the self-locking nut.
13 Remove the upper bearing.
14 Gently release the spring compressor, take off the spring retaining plate, spring, bump stop and gaiter.
15 Unscrew the ring nut from the top of the strut and withdraw the shock absorber cartridge. Tip out the oil from the strut tube.
16 Reassembly and refitting are reversals of removal and dismantling, but observe the following points.
17 Pour the specified quantity of engine oil into the strut tube. The oil acts as a heat transfer medium.
18 Use new self-locking nuts and tighten all fixings to the specified torque.
19 If the coil spring is to be renewed, always renew both front springs.
20 Make sure that the spring ends butt up tightly against the retaining plate stops.

Series 2

21 Raise the front of the car and remove the roadwheel.
22 Disconnect the disc pad wear sensor plug and the earth connection and then slip the wires and brake hose out of the clips on the suspension strut.
23 Unbolt the caliper and tie it up out of the way, there is no need to disconnect the hydraulic line.
24 Disconnect the connecting rod on the end of the anti-roll bar.
25 Disconnect the end of the track control arm from the stub axle carrier, as described in Section 4.
26 Disconnect the tie-rod end balljoint from the steering arm.
27 Working at the strut turret within the engine compartment, unscrew the three mounting nuts.
28 Withdraw the strut, complete with coil spring, from under the front wing.
29 Removal of the coil spring is similar to that described in paragraph 11 to 14, but note the different design of the upper mounting components.
30 The coil spring is fitted with upper and lower rubber insulating rings.
31 Overhaul of the strut is carried out in a similar way to that described in paragraphs 15 to 20.
32 Refitting is a reversal of removal.
33 Struts should be stored vertically for at least 24 hours before fitting, with their piston rods fully extended. Failure to do this after the struts have been stored horizontally may cause temporary loss of damping.

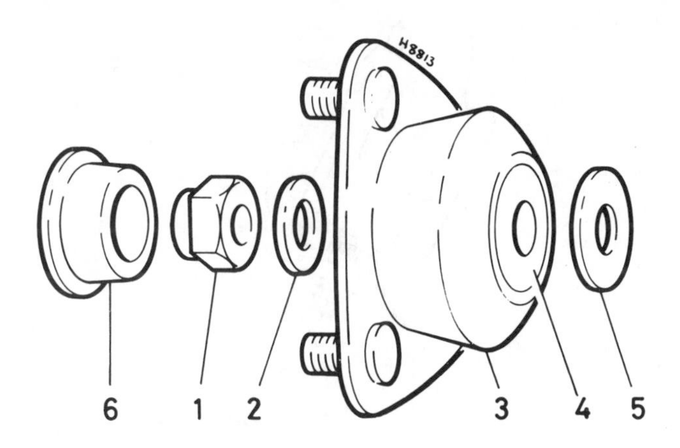

Fig. 11.14 Strut top mounting components – Series 2 (Sec 5)

1 Self-locking nut
2 Washer
3 Flexible mounting
4 Insulator
5 Washer
6 Cap

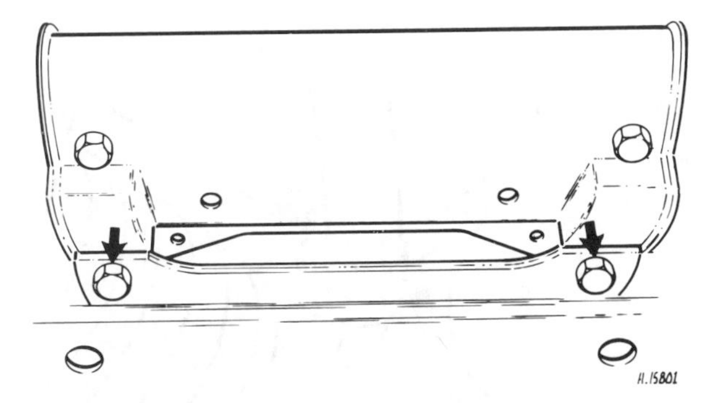

Fig. 11.15 Steering rack housing mounting bolts (arrowed) – Series 1 (Sec 6)

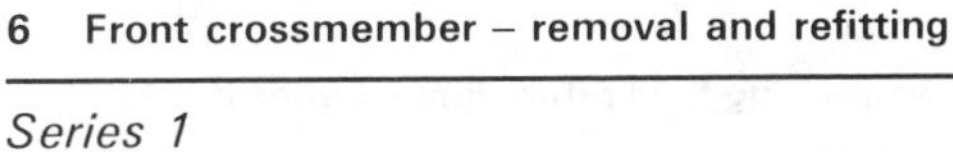

6 Front crossmember – removal and refitting

Series 1

1 Remove the front anti-roll bar as previously described (Section 3).
2 Disconnect the inboard ends of both track control arms.
3 Unbolt the steering rack from the front crossmember.
4 Support the weight of the engine on a jack or hoist and disconnect the left-hand and right-hand engine mountings.
5 Unbolt and remove the crossmember.
6 Refitting is a reversal of removal. Make sure that the steps in the engine mountings locate in their cut-outs, use new self-locking nuts and tighten all fixings to the specified torque.

Series 2

7 Raise the front of the car and support under the front sill jacking points.
8 Unbolt both track control arm rear pivot brackets from the side-members.
9 Disconnect both ends of the anti-roll bar.
10 Unscrew the nuts from both track control arm centre balljoints. Loosen the ball-studs by striking with a plastic-faced hammer.
11 Remove the anti-roll bar.
12 Unbolt the steering gear from the crossmember.
13 Support the engine on a jack or hoist and disconnect both engine mountings.
14 Unbolt and remove the crossmember.
15 Refitting is a reversal of removal, but make sure that the engine mounting twist lock engages correctly in its bore.

Fig. 11.16 Left-hand engine mounting – Series 1 (Sec 6)

1 Nut 2 Step

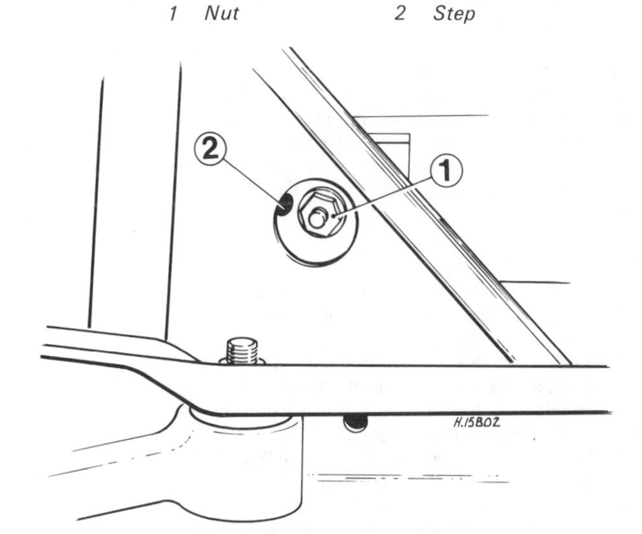

Fig. 11.17 Right-hand engine mounting – Series 1 (Sec 6)

1 Nut 2 Step

Fig. 11.18 Engine mounting twist lock (1) must engage correctly – Series 2 (Sec 6)

16 Renew self-locking nuts and tighten all fixings to the specified torque.
17 Check the front wheel alignment on completion (see Section 33).

7 Front suspension (complete) – removal and refitting

Series 1

1 Raise the front of the car and support it securely under the front sill jacking points. The front of the car must be raised high enough to allow the suspension to be withdrawn. Remove the roadwheels.
2 Unbolt the brake calipers and tie them up out of the way. Do not disconnect the hydraulic hoses. On 1980 and later models, disconnect the pad sensor plug.
3 Remove the angle bracket from the lower end of the suspension strut.
4 Unbolt the anti-roll bar clamps.
5 Attach the engine to a hoist and just take its weight. Disconnect the left and right-hand engine mountings.
6 Unscrew the suspension strut top mounting nuts and remove them.
7 Place a jack (preferably trolley type) under the centre of the crossmember.
8 Unbolt the crossmember from the body side-members.
9 Unscrew the pinch-bolt on the steering shaft coupling, lower the jack until the suspension can be tilted backwards and withdrawn from under the front of the car.
10 Refitting is a reversal of removal, but observe the following points. Set the steering wheel in the straight-ahead position and set the pinion so that the mark on the dust seal is between the two marks on the rack housing before engaging the pinion shaft with the coupling.
11 Renew all self-locking nuts and tighten all fixings to the specified torque.

Series 2

12 Raise the front end sufficiently high to permit removal of the front suspension. Support under the sill front jacking points.
13 Remove the front roadwheels.
14 Disconnect the pad wear sensor and earth wire.
15 Release the wires and brake hoses from the strut clips.
16 Unbolt both front calipers and tie them up out of the way. Do not disconnect the hydraulic hoses.
17 Remove the steering shaft coupling bolts and separate the coupling from the rack pinion shaft.
18 On cars equipped with power-assisted steering, drain the fluid from the reservoir and disconnect the fluid return line.
19 Disconnect the fluid pressure line. Cap the disconnected lines.
20 Unbolt both track control arm rear brackets from the body side-members, also remove the heat shield.
21 Support the weight of the engine on a hoist and disconnect the left-hand and right-hand engine mountings.
22 Place a jack, preferably of trolley type under the centre of the crossmember and unbolt both ends from the body members.
23 Unscrew the suspension strut top mounting nuts.
24 Lower the jack, tilt the suspension rearwards and withdraw it from under the car. Avoid pulling the suspension struts out sideways.
25 When refitting, observe the following points. Set front wheels and steering wheel in the straight-ahead position. The shaft and housing marks should be in alignment, and the slot in the coupling aligned with the mark on the steering gear. Make sure that the twist lock of the engine mounting engages in its hole. Renew all self-locking nuts and tighten all fixings to the specified torque.
26 On cars with power-assisted steering, discard the drained fluid, fill with fresh fluid of the specified type and bleed the system, as described in Section 32.

8 Rear anti-roll bar – removal and refitting

1 Disconnect the ends of the anti-roll bar from the semi-trailing arms (photo).
2 Unbolt the clamps which hold the anti-roll bar to the rear crossmember (photo).
3 Refitting is a reversal of removal. Check that the clamp rubbers are in good condition and tighten all fixings to the specified torque.

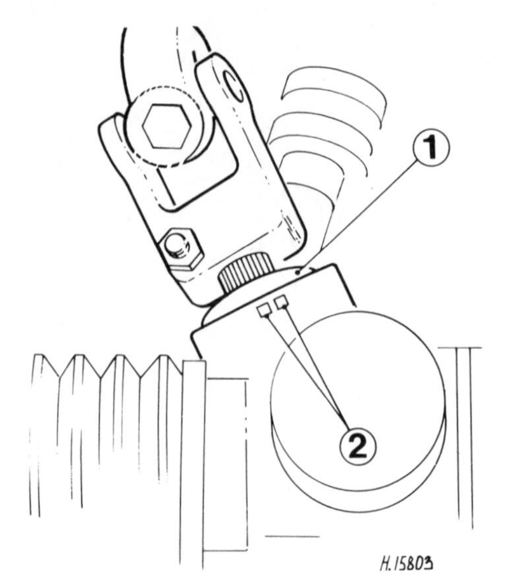

Fig. 11.19 Steering alignment marks – Series 1 (Sec 7)

1 Dust shield 2 Rack housing

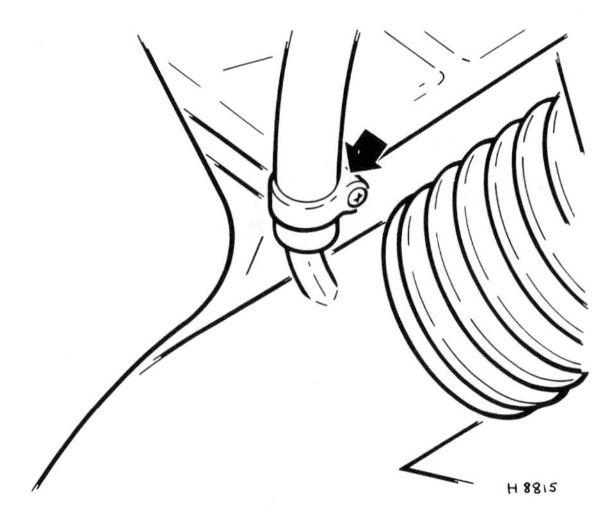

Fig. 11.20 Power steering fluid return line – Series 2 (Sec 7)

Arrow indicates securing clip

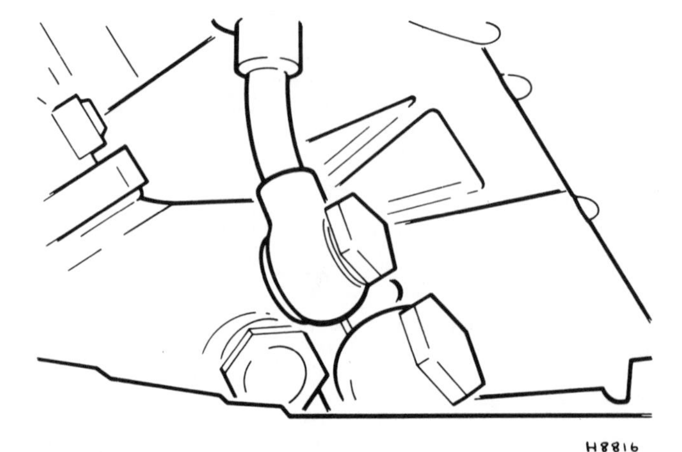

Fig. 11.21 Power steering pressure line – Series 2 (Sec 7)

8.1 Rear semi-trailing arm and anti-roll bar connection – arrowed

8.2 Rear anti-roll bar clamp

Fig. 11.22 Rear strut spring cup – Series 1 (Sec 9)

The pin must locate in the cut-out (arrowed)

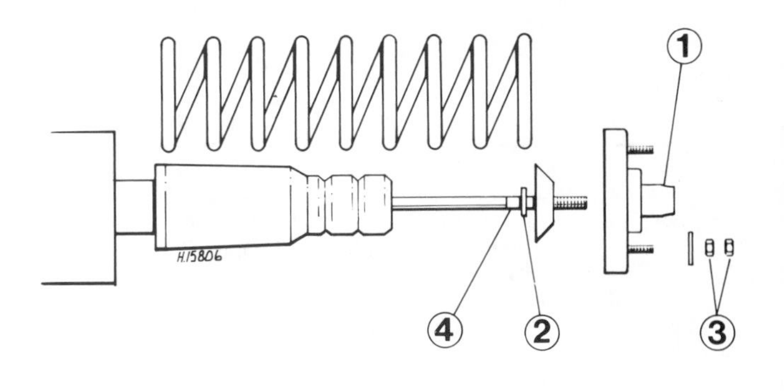

Fig. 11.23 Rear strut top mounting components – Series 1 (Sec 9)

1 Flexible mounting
2 Disc
3 Nuts
4 Lockring

9 Rear suspension strut (Series 1) – removal and refitting

1 Support the semi-trailing arm by placing a jack under it. Remove the roadwheel.
2 Unscrew and remove the suspension strut lower mounting bolt.
3 Working within the luggage compartment, unscrew the three strut upper mounting nuts.
4 Withdraw the strut, complete with coil spring, from under the wheel arch.
5 If the coil spring must be removed, compress the spring and dismantle the upper mounting, as described in Section 5.
6 The strut damper cannot be overhauled but if it is leaking or has lost its damping properties, renew the strut tube.
7 When reassembling, check the condition of the rubber insulators in the centering cup and make sure that the pins locate correctly in the cut-outs in the rubber underlay.
8 When fitting the upper mounting, make sure that the sequence of components is as shown (Fig. 11.23). Make sure that the ends of the coil spring butt against the end stops.
9 Tighten all fixings to the specified torque.

10 Rear shock absorber (Series 2) – removal, testing and refitting

1 Without raising the rear wheel, disconnect the shock absorber lower mounting.
2 Working within the luggage compartment, partially remove the trim panel and unscrew the two shock absorber mounting nuts.
3 Withdraw the shock absorber downwards, noting the mounting flange gasket.
4 Grip the shock absorber lower mounting in the jaws of a vice, with the unit held vertically. Fully extend and contract the unit several times. Any loss of damping action, jerkiness or seizure can only be rectified by renewal of the unit.
5 Refitting is a reversal of removal, but note that if a new unit has been stored horizontally, it must be positioned vertically, fully extended, for 24 hours before fitting to the car.

11 Rear coil spring (Series 2) – removal and refitting

1 Disconnect the rear end of the exhaust system, lower it a few

inches and support it on a piece of wire.
2 Unscrew the final drive flexible mounting bolts on the side from which the spring is being removed and push downwards by inserting a wedge.
3 Disconnect the anti-roll bar.
4 Remove the roadwheel and then support the trailing arm by placing a jack underneath it.
5 Lower the trailing arm enough to be able to remove the coil spring.
6 Refitting is a reversal of removal. Make sure that the rubber insulating ring is in good condition and tighten all fixings to the specified torque.

12 Rear semi-trailing arm (Series 1) – removal and refitting

1 Working inside the car, disconnect the handbrake cables from the handbrake control lever.
2 Disconnect the driveshaft from the roadwheel hub flange.
3 Disconnect the suspension strut lower mounting. Remove the roadwheel.
4 Disconnect the rigid brake pipe from the flexible hose. Cap the open ends to prevent loss of fluid.
5 Disconnect the anti-roll bar from the semi-trailing arm.
6 Unscrew and remove both pivot bolts from the semi-trailing arm and withdraw the complete suspension arm/hub assembly.
7 Remove the brake assembly, as described in Chapter 9.
8 Remove the hub bearings and stub shaft, as described in Chapter 7.
9 The flexible bushes in the semi-trailing arm may be removed using a press or a bolt, nut, washers and distance pieces.
10 When refitting, observe the following points. Tighten all bolts and nuts to the specified torque. Tighten the semi-trailing arm pivot bolts only when the weight of the car is on the roadwheels.
11 Adjust the handbrake and bleed the brake circuit, as described in Chapter 9.

13 Rear semi-trailing arm (Series 2) – removal and refitting

1 Raise the rear end and support securely. Remove the roadwheel.
2 Remove the driveshaft, as described in Chapter 7.
3 Disconnect the handbrake cable and the rigid hydraulic pipe from the rear brake flexible hose (Chapter 9).
4 Place a jack under the semi-trailing arm and disconnect the shock absorber lower mounting.
5 Disconnect the anti-roll bar and links.
6 Unbolt the trailing arm pivots and remove the arm/hub/brake assembly.
7 Remove the brake (Chapter 9) and hub bearings (Chapter 7), and renew the flexible bushes using a press or a bolt, nut, washer and distance pieces.
8 Refitting is a reversal of removal, tighten all nuts and bolts to the specified torque, tighten the trailing arm bolts only when the weight of the car is on the roadwheels.
9 Adjust the handbrake and bleed the brake circuit (Chapter 9).

14 Steering rack gaiters – inspection and renewal

1 During the Routine Maintenance check, pay special attention to the rack gaiters. Splits at the base of the pleats can easily be overlooked, unless the gaiters are fully extended by turning the steering to full lock.
2 To remove defective gaiters, remove the tie-rod ends, as described in Section 15. Unclip the gaiters and pull them from the rack housing. If there has been loss of lubricant, it may require making good.
3 Slide the new gaiters into position, fit the retaining clips and refit the tie-rod ends.

15 Tie-rod end balljoint – renewal

Series 1

1 Raise the front end and remove the roadwheel.

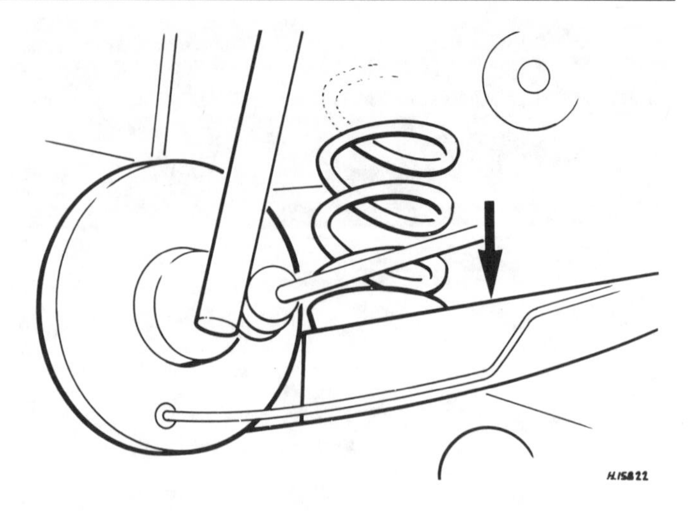

Fig. 11.24 Pushing down the final drive flexible mounting – Series 2 (Sec 11)

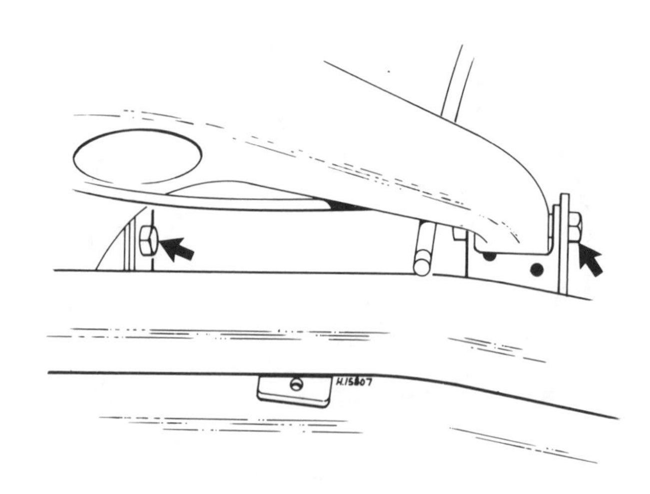

Fig. 11.25 Semi-trailing arm pivot bolts (arrowed) – Series 1 (Sec 12)

2 Hold the flats on the balljoint with a spanner and release the locknut.
3 Extract the split pin and unscrew the castellated nut on the balljoint stud.
4 Using a balljoint splitter, disconnect the balljoint from the steering arm.
5 Measure the length of exposed threads on the tie-rod and then unscrew the balljoint from the rod.
6 Clean the threads and apply a smear of grease to them. Screw on the new tie-rod end balljoint until the same length of threads is exposed as before removing the old one.
7 Fit the tapered ball-stud into the eye of the steering arm. **Do not** apply any grease. Screw on the nut to the specified torque and insert a new split pin. If difficulty is experienced in tightening (or loosening) a balljoint taper stud, due to the stud turning in the eye, place a jack or long lever against the joint socket to force the taper further into its conical seat.
8 Tighten the locknut while holding the balljoint in the centre of its arc of travel.
9 Refit the roadwheel and check the front wheel alignment, as described in Section 33.

15.10 Track control arm (Series 2)
Tie-rod end clamp arrowed

16.2 Steering wheel hub motif

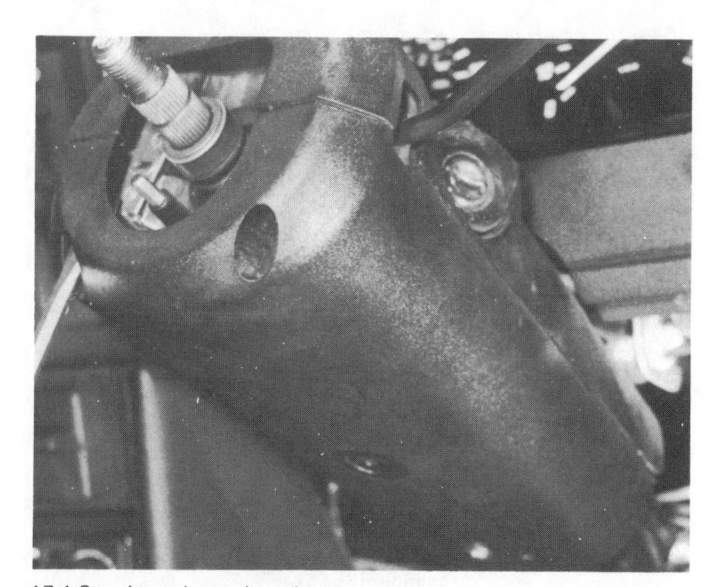

17.1 Steering column shrouds
Wheel removed for photographic access

Series 2

10 The operations are similar to those just described, except that a clamp is used instead of a locknut to secure the balljoint to the tie-rod (photo).

16 Steering wheel – removal and refitting

Series 1

1 Set the steering in the straight-ahead attitude.
2 Prise out the motif from the centre of the steering wheel hub (photo).
3 Unscrew the retaining nut and remove the steering wheel. This should be achieved by thumping the wheel rim with the palms of the hands at two opposite points simultaneously.
4 If reasonable impact does not release it, then a puller will have to be used.
5 When refitting, check that the marks on the steering shaft and the rack housing are in alignment. This will confirm that the steering is centred.
6 Fit the steering wheel with the spokes correctly angled and tighten the nut to the specified torque. Fit the motif.

Series 2

7 The operations are similar to those just described, except that a thrust washer is used under the nut and the wheel can only be pulled off if the steering column is unlocked.

17 Steering column lower shroud – removal and refitting

1 The lower section of the steering column upper shroud can be removed after releasing the facia lower trim panel and extracting the shroud screws (photo).
2 Refitting is a reversal of removal.

18 Steering column upper shroud and lock (Series 1) – removal and refitting

1 Disconnect the battery negative lead.
2 Remove the steering wheel and shroud lower section (Sections 16 and 17).
3 Extract the combination switch fixing screws.

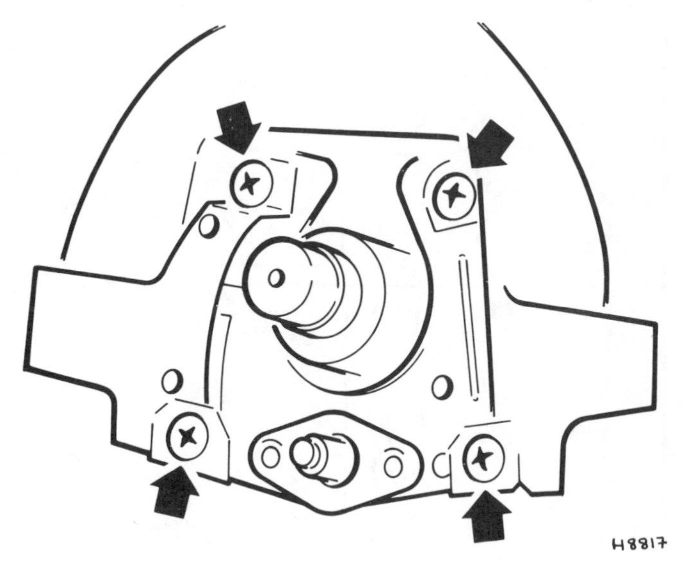

Fig. 11.26 Combination switch fixing screws (arrowed) – Series 1 (Sec 18)

4 Release the hazard warning relay.
5 Extract the screw and withdraw the ignition switch. Release the wiring harness switch.
6 Chisel off or drill out the shear-head screws.
7 Lift off the upper section of shroud from the steering column.
8 Chisel off or drill out the shear-head screw (arrowed) – Fig. 11.31. Remove the plate (1) and withdraw the steering lock.
9 The lock cylinder can be pulled out after depressing the spring plunger.
10 Refit by reversing the removal operations. When fitting the ignition switch, remove the key, turn the switch anti-clockwise against its stay, push it into position and lock the setscrew with a blob of thick paint.
11 Tighten new shear-head screws until their heads break off.

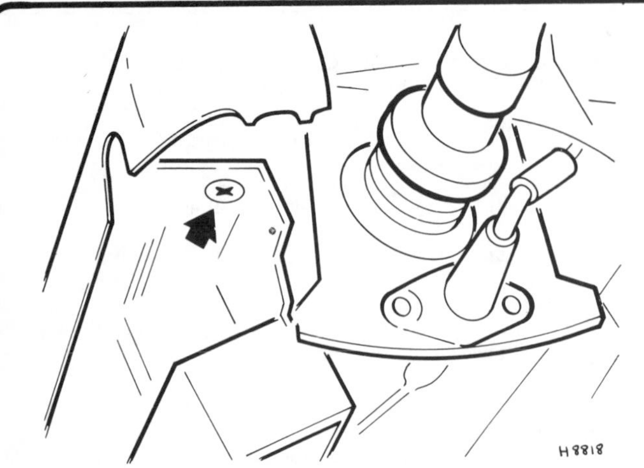

Fig. 11.27 Hazard warning relay fixing screw (arrowed) – Series 1 (Sec 18)

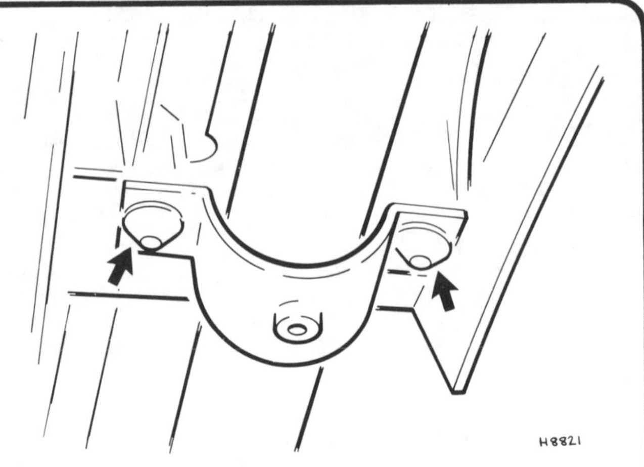

Fig. 11.30 Upper column shroud shear-head screws (arrowed) – Series 1 (Sec 18)

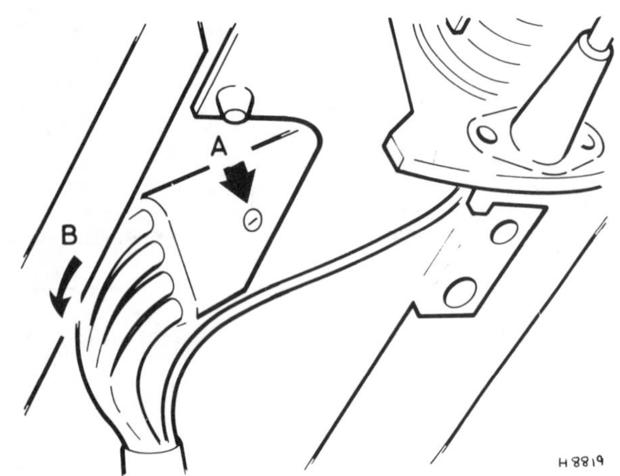

Fig. 11.28 Withdrawing the ignition switch – Series 1 (Sec 18)

A Remove the securing screw
B Withdraw the switch in this direction

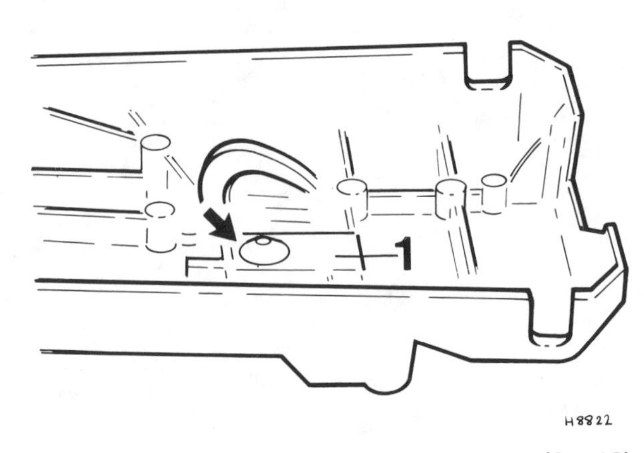

Fig. 11.31 Removing the steering lock – Series 1 (Sec 18)

Chisel off or drill out the shear-head screw (arrowed) and remove the plate (1)

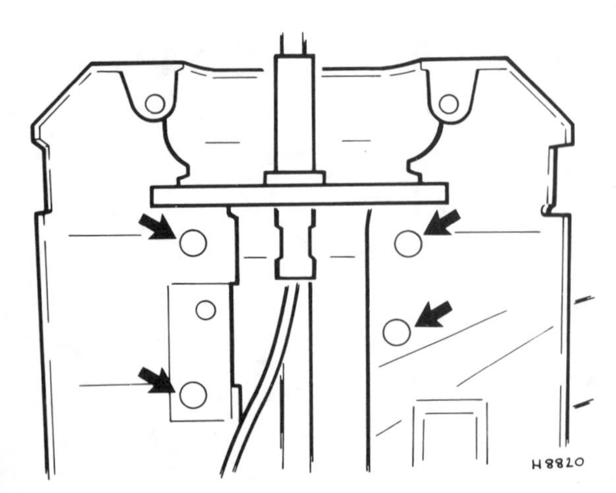

Fig. 11.29 Shear-head screws (arrowed) – Series 1 (Secs 18 and 23)

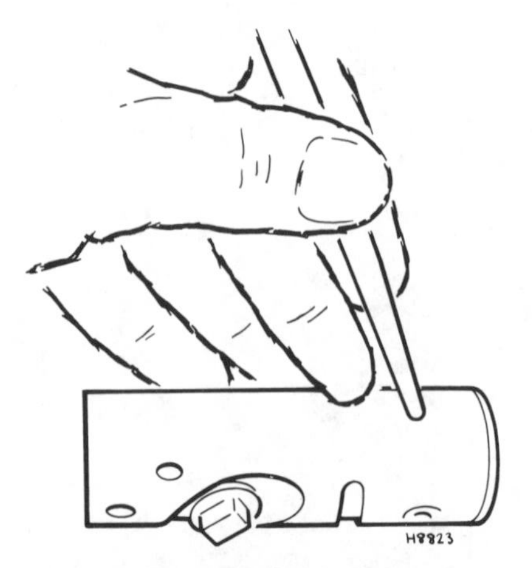

Fig. 11.32 Depress the spring plunger to release the steering lock cylinder (Sec 18)

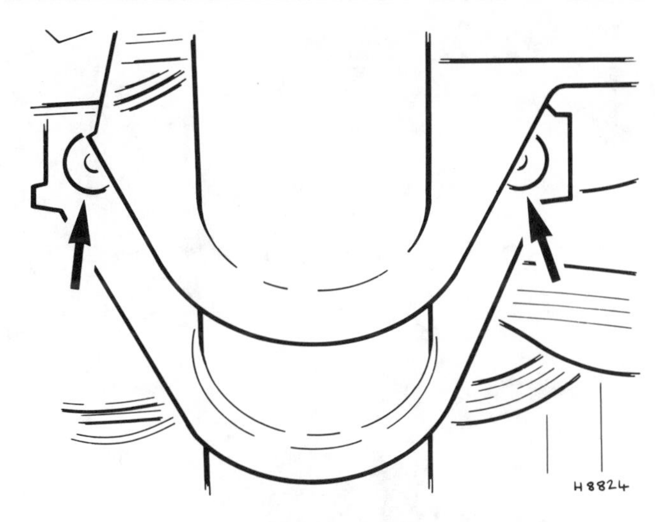

Fig. 11.33 Upper column shroud shear-head screws (arrowed) – Series 2 (Secs 19 and 25)

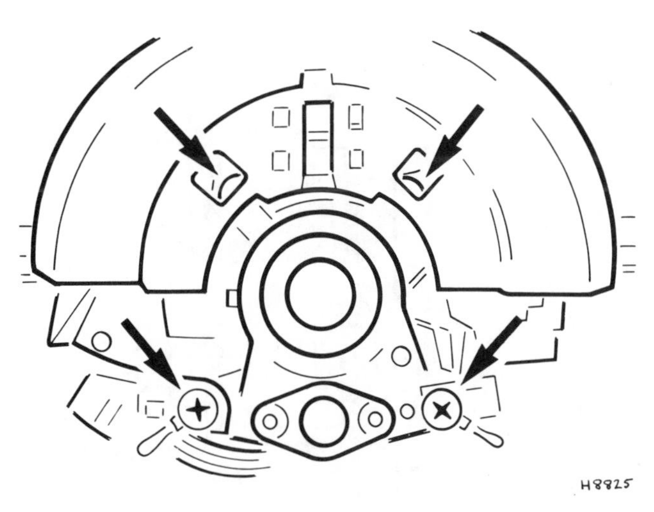

Fig. 11.34 Combination switch fixing screws (arrowed) – Series 2 (Sec 20)

19 Steering column upper shroud (Series 2) – removal and refitting

1 Remove the steering wheel (Section 16).
2 Disconnect the battery negative lead.
3 Release the facia lower centre trim, extract the screws and remove the column shroud lower section.
4 Chisel off or drill out the shear-head screws and remove the steering column upper section of shroud.
5 Refit by reversing the removal operations and tighten the new shear-head screws until their heads break off.

20 Steering column lock (Series 2) – removal and refitting

1 Disconnect the battery, remove the steering wheel (Section 16) and take off the column shroud lower section.
2 Extract the combination switch screws.
3 Remove the collar from the steering shaft.
4 Extract the circlip (1), washer (2), spring (3) and ring (4) – Fig. 11.36.
5 Prise out the steering shaft upper bearings and then disconnect the central wiring plug.
6 Chisel off or drill out the screw (1) – Fig. 11.37 – and then pull the casing and lock off the column tube.

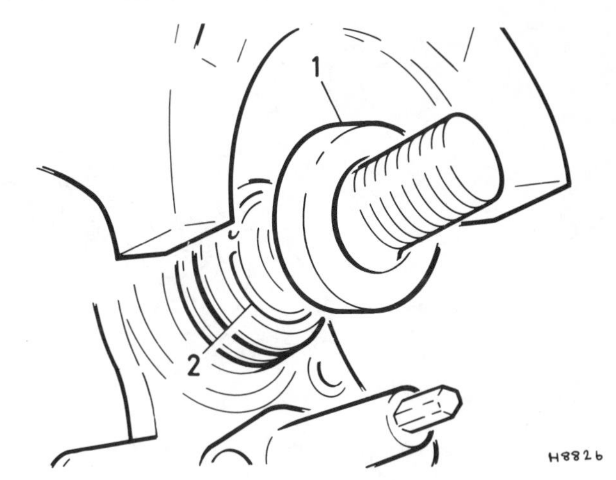

Fig. 11.35 Steering shaft collar (1) and circlip (2) – Series 2 (Sec 20)

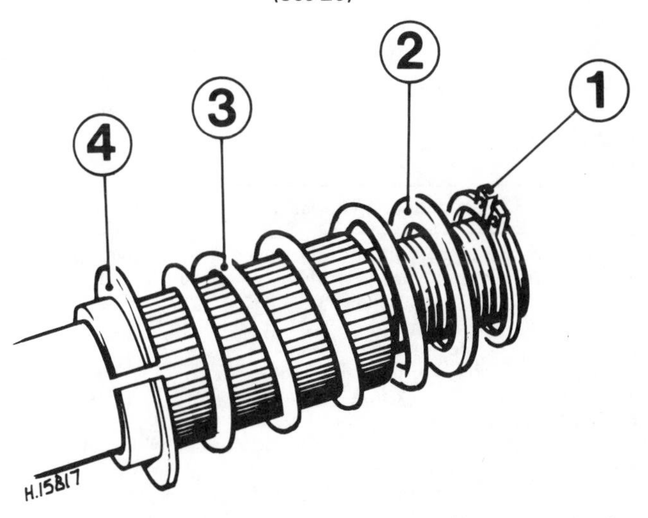

Fig. 11.36 Steering shaft upper components (Secs 20 and 24)

1	*Circlip*	3	*Spring*
2	*Washer*	4	*Ring*

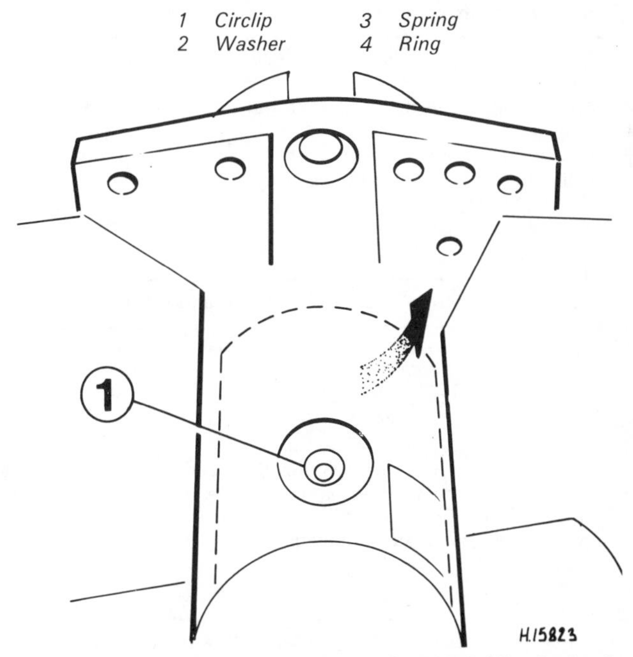

Fig. 11.37 Steering column lock shear-head bolt (1) – Series 2 (Sec 20)

Pull steering lock and casing off in direction of arrow

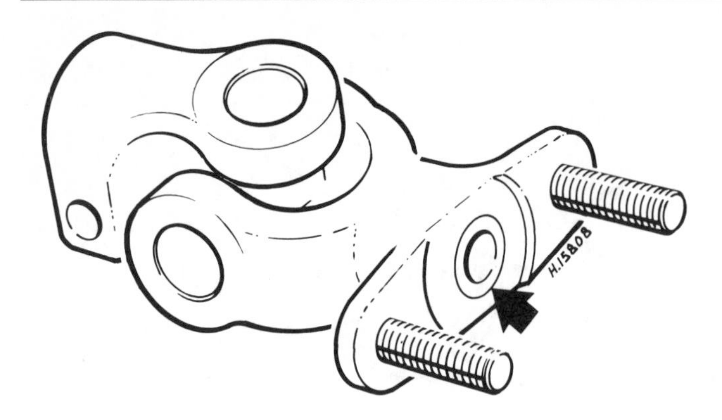

Fig. 11.38 Steering shaft coupling plastic disc (arrowed) – Series 1 (Sec 21)

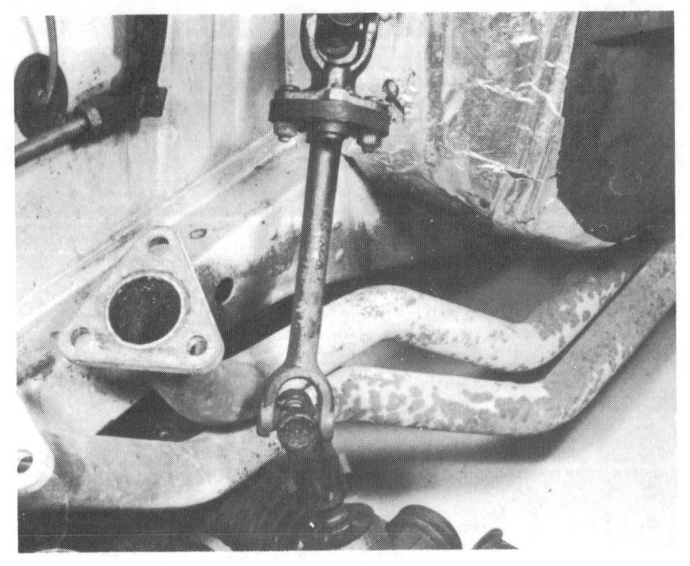

21.1 Steering shaft (engine removed)

7 Refit by reversing the removal operations, but observe the following points. Tighten new Torx type shear-head screws until their heads shear off. Fit the circlip using a hammer and piece of tubing and make sure that the notch in the collar locks the circlip.

21 Steering shaft coupling (Series 1) – removal and refitting

1 Remove the pinch-bolt from the upper universal joint (photo).
2 Remove the pinch-bolt from the lower universal joint.
3 Unscrew the rack housing bolts to release it from the crossmember.
4 Remove the steering lower shaft.
5 Unbolt the coupling from the flexible disc.
6 When refitting, check that the coupling plastic bush is not worn, otherwise renew it.
7 Set the steering in the straight-ahead position with shaft and rack housing marks in alignment.
8 Tighten all nuts to the specified torque.

22 Steering shaft coupling (Series 2) – removal and refitting

1 The lower steering shaft and coupling are an assembly on later models.
2 Remove the coupling pinch-bolt and remove the steering lower shaft assembly.
3 Centre the steering before refitting (marks on rack housing and shaft aligned) and make sure that spring washers (Fig. 11.39) are correctly located if a new shaft is being fitted. Tighten the pinch-bolts to the specified torque.

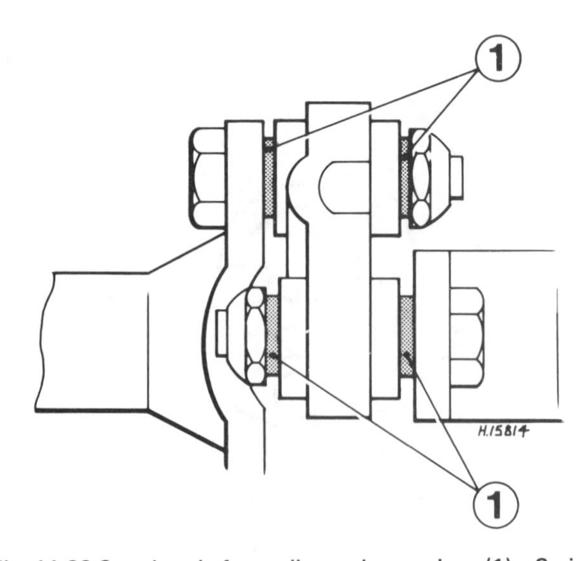

Fig. 11.39 Steering shaft coupling spring washers (1) – Series 2 (Sec 22)

23 Steering column (Series 1) – removal and refitting

1 Carry out the operations described in Section 18, paragraphs 1 to 5.
2 Chisel off or drill out the shear-head screws from the column saddle bracket (Fig. 11.29).
3 Unscrew the column tube clamp.
4 Unscrew the upper pinch-bolt from the steering shaft coupling and withdraw the column/shaft assembly into the car interior.
5 The refitting operations are a reversal of removal. Tighten all fixings to the specified torque and tighten new shear-head screws until their heads break off.

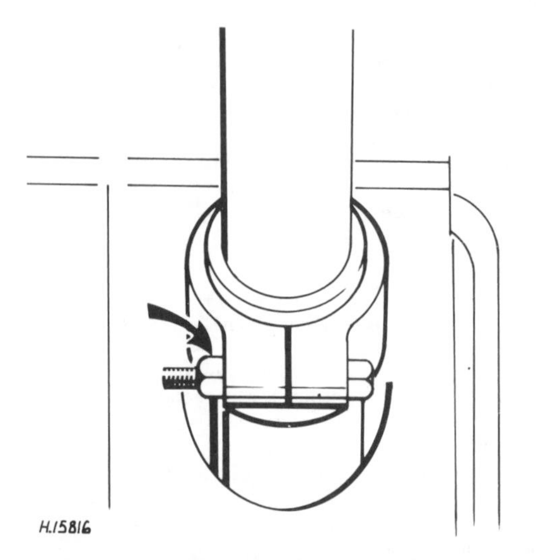

Fig. 11.40 Steering column tube clamp pinch-bolt (arrowed) – Series 1 (Sec 23)

24 Steering shaft and bearings (Series 1) – removal and refitting

Upper bearing

1 The upper bearing can be removed and refitted without removing the column.

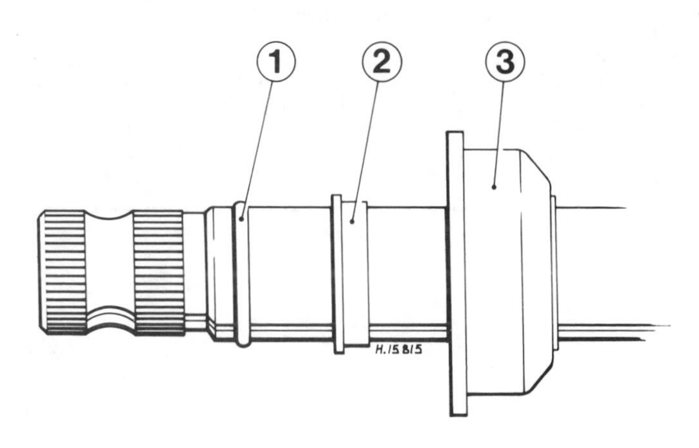

Fig. 11.41 Steering shaft lower components – Series 1 (Sec 24)

1 Circlip 3 Bearing
2 Ring

2 Remove the steering wheel, the column shroud lower section and the combination switch (Sections 16, 17 and 18).
3 From the shaft, take off the collar and the circlip.
4 Take off the washer (2), coil spring (3) and ring (4) – Fig. 11.36. Withdraw the upper bearing.
5 When refitting the new bearing, press it in flush.

Lower bearing and shaft

6 With the column removed, as described in Section 23, remove the collar and other components from the top of the shaft as described in paragraphs 3 and 4.
7 Using a plastic-faced hammer, tap the shaft downwards. It will come out complete with bearing.
8 Extract the circlip (1), ring (2) and take off the bearing (3) – Fig. 11.41.
9 Reassemble by reversing the dismantling operations, but note that the flange on the ring is away from the bearing.

25 Steering column (Series 2) – removal and refitting

1 Disconnect the battery, remove the steering wheel (Section 16) and take off the column lower shroud section (Section 7).
2 Disconnect the main wiring plug.
3 Disconnect the steering shaft coupling by removing the pinch-bolt.
4 Chisel off or drill out the screw heads (Fig. 11.33). Remove the column upper shroud.
5 Loosen the clamp and remove the steering column.
6 Refitting is a reversal of removal, tighten the Torx type screws until their heads shear off.

26 Steering shaft and bearings (Series 2) – removal and refitting

Upper bearing

1 The operations are described in Section 20, and can be carried out without having to remove the column.

Lower bearing and shaft

2 Carry out the operations 1 to 5 in Section 20.
3 Tap the shaft down until the circlip (1), collar (2) and ring (3) – Fig. 11.42 – can be removed.
4 Withdraw the shaft out of the top of the column. Drive the lower bearing and retainer out of the lower end of the column.
5 When refitting, make sure that the notch in the collar locks the circlip and also that the flange on the ring is towards the bearing.

27 Steering gear (manual) – removal and refitting

1 Raise the front end and remove the roadwheels.

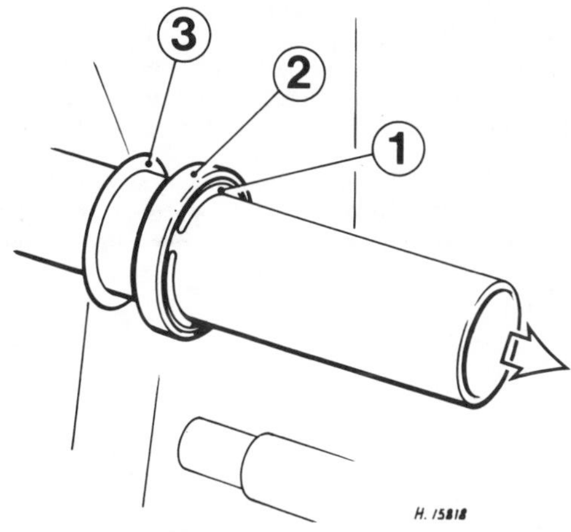

Fig. 11.42 Steering shaft upper components – Series 2 (Sec 26)

1 Circlip 3 Ring
2 Collar

2 Disconnect the tie-rod ends from the steering arms and the steering column shaft coupling, as described in earlier Sections.
3 Unbolt the gear housing from the crossmember and remove it.
4 When refitting, centre the steering gear (shaft and housing marks in alignment), tighten all fixings to the specified torque and check and adjust the front wheel alignment (Section 33).

28 Steering gear (power-assisted) – removal and refitting

1 The operations are very similar to those described in the preceding Section, except that the fluid lines must be disconnected from the steering gear housing and the pipes plugged.
2 When refitting is completed, fill and bleed the system, as described in Section 32.

29 Steering gear – overhaul

1 It is not recommended that the steering gear is overhauled; a worn unit should be changed for a new or factory reconditioned assembly.
2 Adjustment to a steering gear may be carried out in the following way to eliminate rack knock or slackness.
3 Remove the steering gear and secure it in a vice.
4 Unscrew the nut (arrowed) – Fig. 11.43 – and push back the damper.
5 Remove the end cap and slacken the screw using an Allen key so

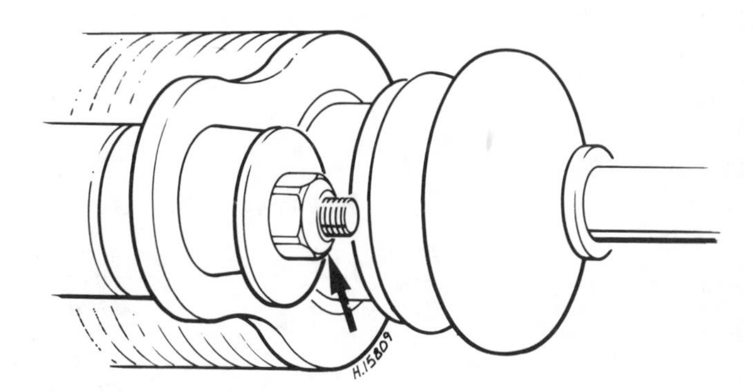

Fig. 11.43 Steering damper nut – arrowed (Sec 29)

that A – Fig. 11.45 – is 12.0 mm (0.47 in).

6 Pull out the split pin.

7 The adjuster ring nut should now be tightened to 6 Nm (4.3 lbf ft) or with light hand pressure. In the absence of the special tool, a box spanner can usually be found to fit the centre hexagon cut-out. Insert a new split pin and bend the ends over.

8 The rack should now be turned from lock to lock and any stiffness or jerkiness noted. It is permisslble to unscrew the ring nut one castellation but no more. If the movement is still not smooth then the gear is worn.

9 Finally check the turning force by winding a cord round the pinion shaft and attach it to a spring balance. If the force required to turn the pinion is not between 4.5 and 5.4 kg (10 and 12 lbs) turn the self-locking centre socket-headed adjuster screw to bring the friction within specification. Turning clockwise increases friction, anti-clockwise decreases it.

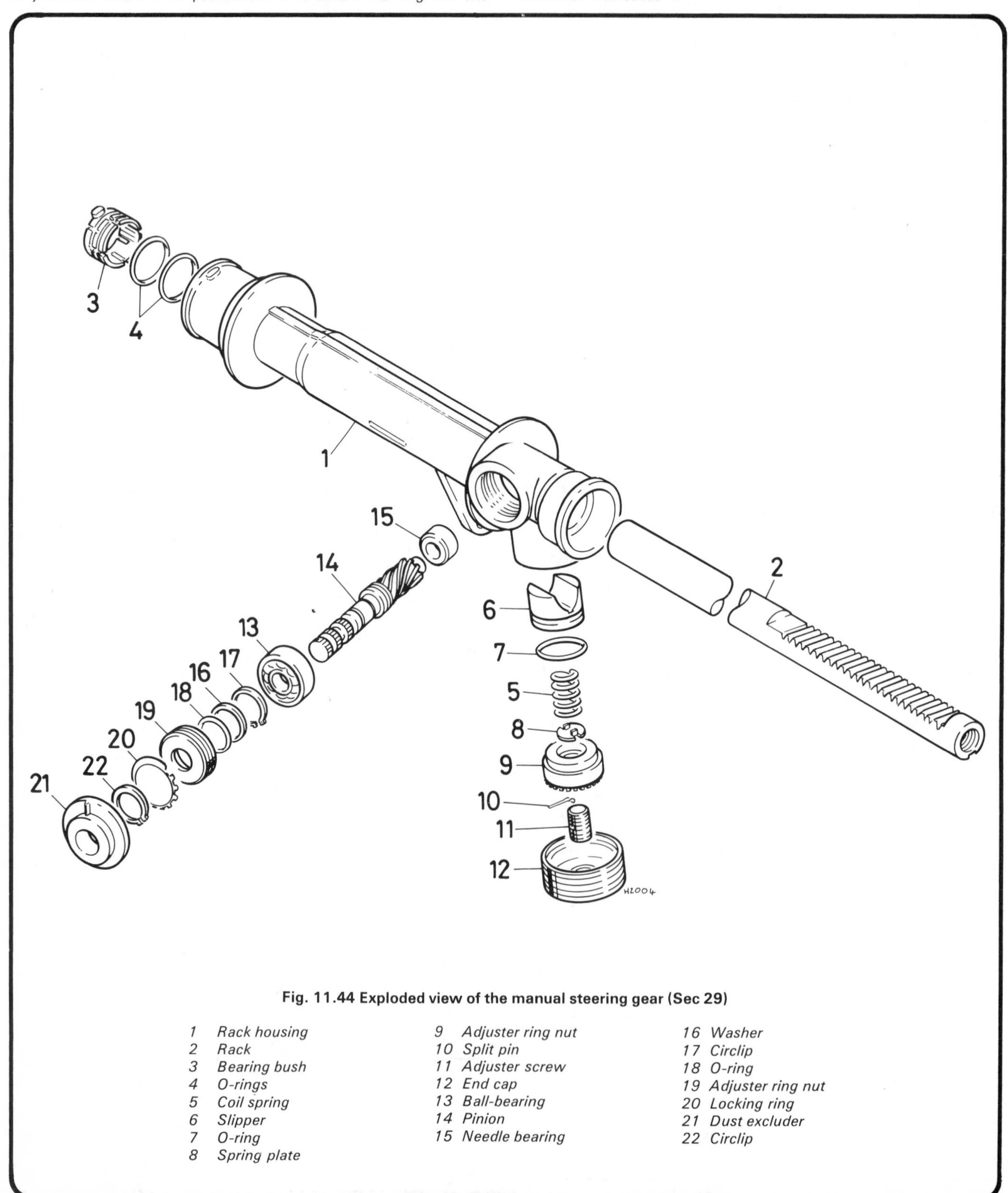

Fig. 11.44 Exploded view of the manual steering gear (Sec 29)

1 Rack housing
2 Rack
3 Bearing bush
4 O-rings
5 Coil spring
6 Slipper
7 O-ring
8 Spring plate
9 Adjuster ring nut
10 Split pin
11 Adjuster screw
12 End cap
13 Ball-bearing
14 Pinion
15 Needle bearing
16 Washer
17 Circlip
18 O-ring
19 Adjuster ring nut
20 Locking ring
21 Dust excluder
22 Circlip

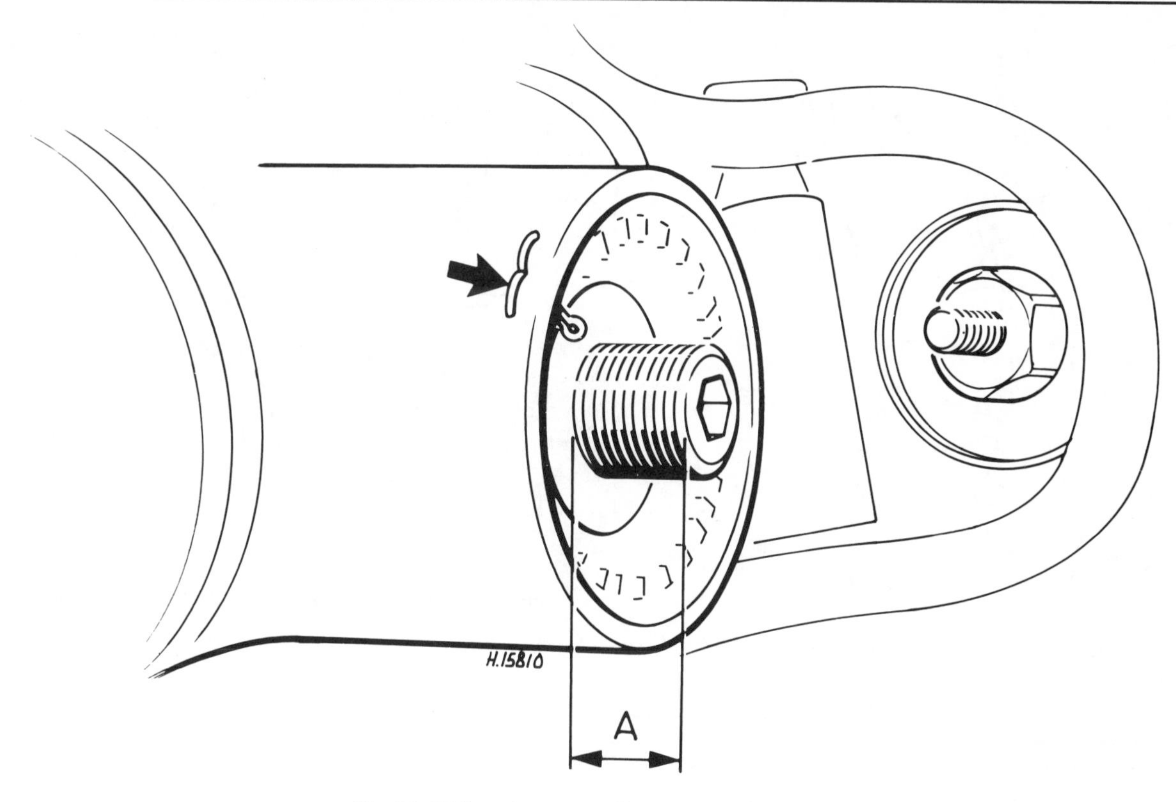

Fig. 11.45 Steering gear adjuster screw (Sec 29)

A = 12.0 mm (0.47 in) *Split pin arrowed*

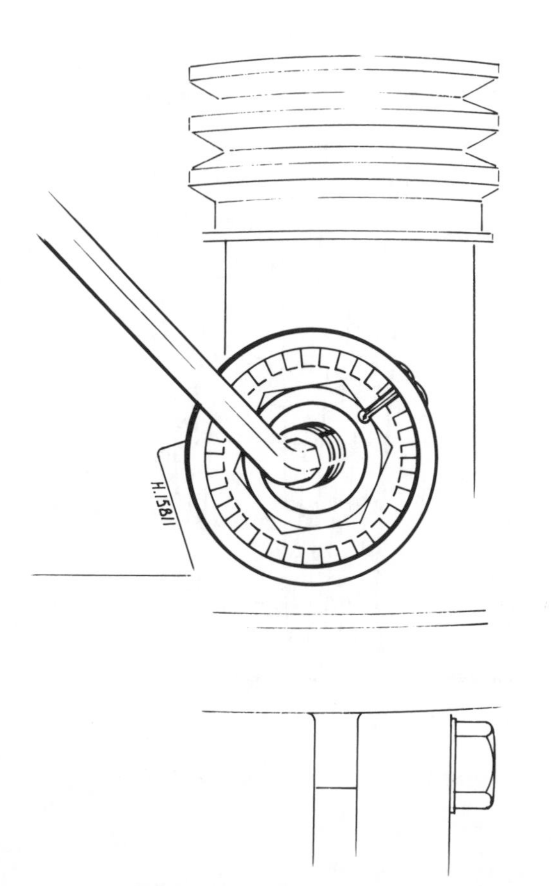

Fig. 11.46 Adjusting the steering gear turning friction (Sec 29)

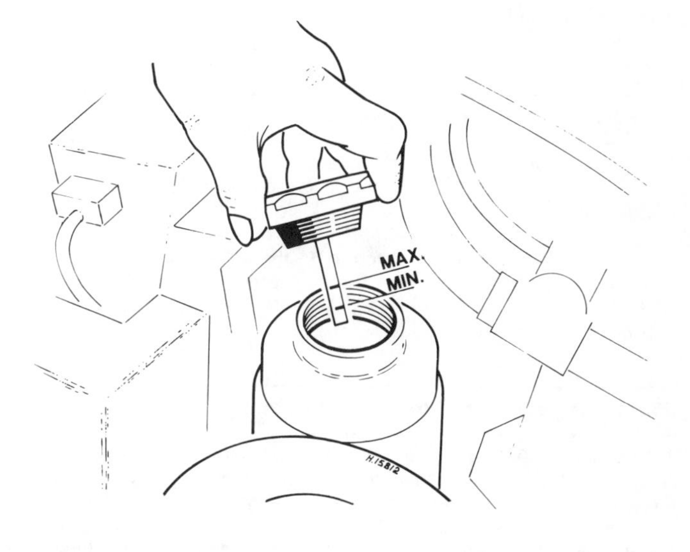

Fig. 11.47 Checking the power steering fluid level (Sec 30)

30 Power steering – maintenance

1 The oil level should be maintained between the MAX and MIN marks on the dipstick. Use only oil of specified type.

2 Periodically inspect the condition of the pump drivebelt. If it is frayed, renew it, as described in Chapter 2.

3 Maintain the correct drivebelt tension by adjusting, if necessary, as described in Chapter 2, Section 7.

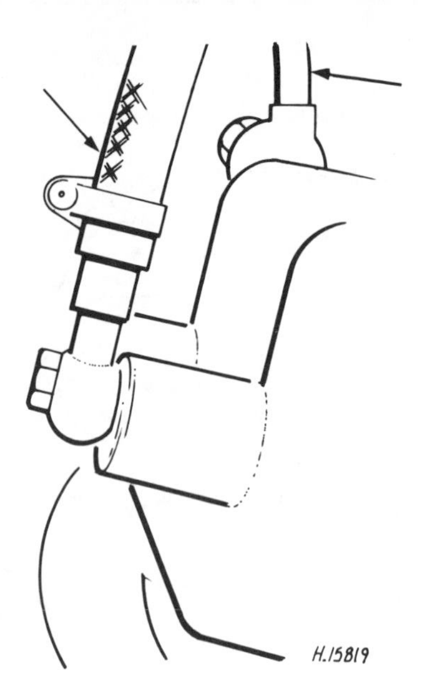

Fig. 11.48 Power steering fluid lines – arrowed (Sec 31)

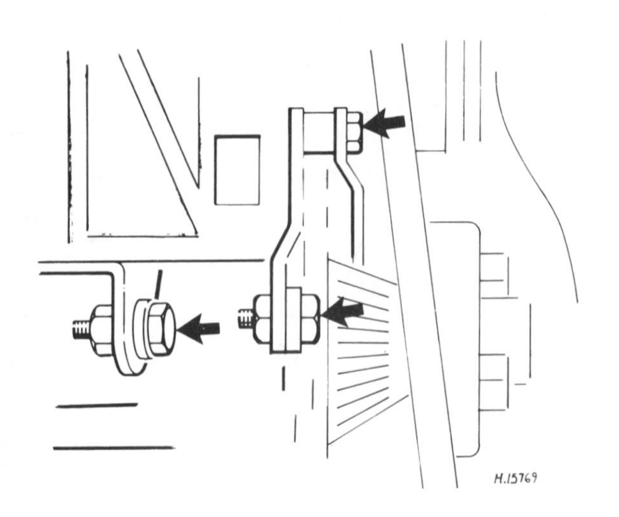

Fig. 11.49 Steering pump mounting bolts – arrowed (Sec 31)

31 Power steering pump – removal and refitting

1 Syphon the fluid from the pump reservoir.
2 Disconnect the fluid lines and plug or cap their open ends.
3 Release the pump adjuster nut and move the pump in as far as possible towards the engine. Slip the belt off the pulleys.
4 Unscrew the mounting bolts and remove the pump.
5 It is not recommended that a worn or faulty pump is overhauled, but exchange it for a new or factory reconditioned unit.
6 Refit the pump, connect the fluid lines and adjust the drivebelt, as described in Chapter 2, Section 7.
7 Fill and bleed the system, as described in the next Section.

32 Power assisted steering system – filling and bleeding

1 Raise the front end with the roadwheels off the ground.
2 Fill the pump reservoir with the specified fluid to the MAX mark on the dipstick.
3 Start the engine and turn the steering from lock to lock twice.
4 Switch off the engine and top up to the MAX mark.
5 It may be found that when the engine is switched off, the fluid level rises about 12.5 mm (0.5 in) above the MAX mark. This is normal, **do not** reduce the level.

33 Steering angles and front wheel alignment

1 Accurate front wheel alignment is essential to provide good steering and roadholding characteristics and to ensure slow and even tyre wear. Before considering the steering angles, check that the tyres are correctly inflated, that the front wheels are not buckled, the hub bearings are not worn or incorrectly adjusted and that the steering linkage is in good order, without slackness or wear at the joints.
2 Wheel alignment consists of four factors:
Camber: this is the angle at which the road wheels are set from the vertical when viewed from the front, or rear, of the vehicle. Positive camber is the angle (in degrees) that the wheels are tilted outwards at the top from the vertical.
Castor: this is the angle between the steering axis and a vertical line when viewed from each side of the vehicle. Positive castor is indicated when the steering axis is inclined towards the rear of the vehicle at its upper end.
Steering axis inclination: this is the angle when viewed from the front, or rear, of the vehicle between vertical and an imaginary line drawn between the top and bottom strut mountings.

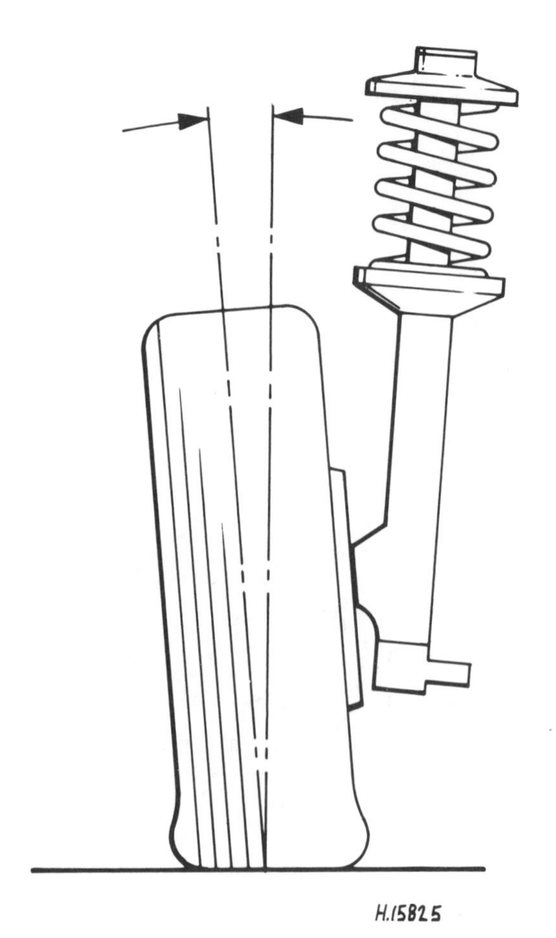

Fig. 11.50 Positive camber (Sec 33)

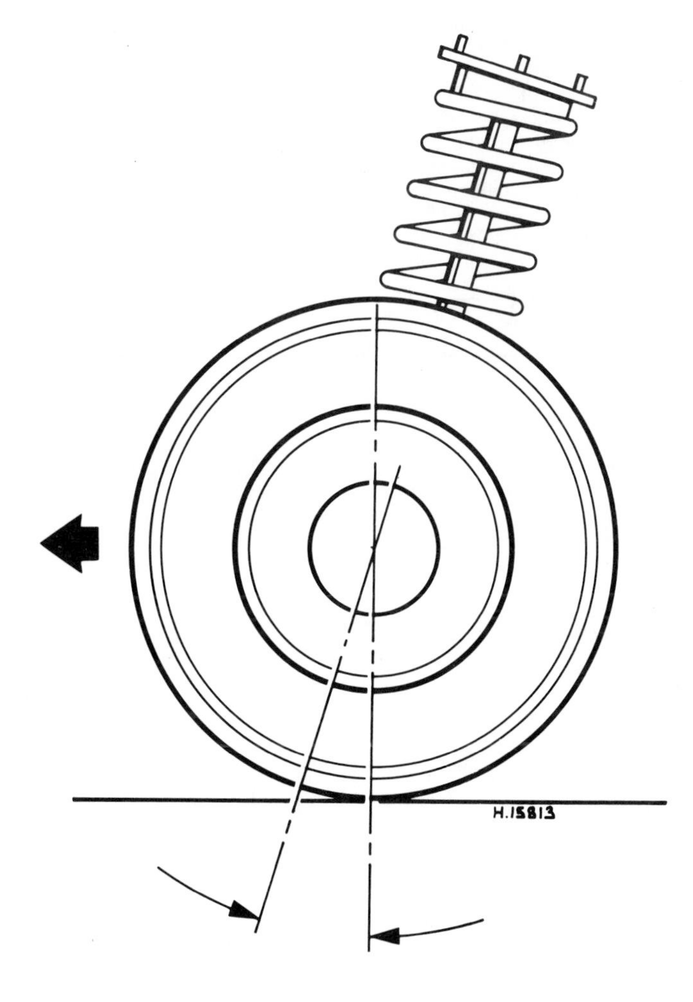

Fig. 11.51 Castor (Sec 33)

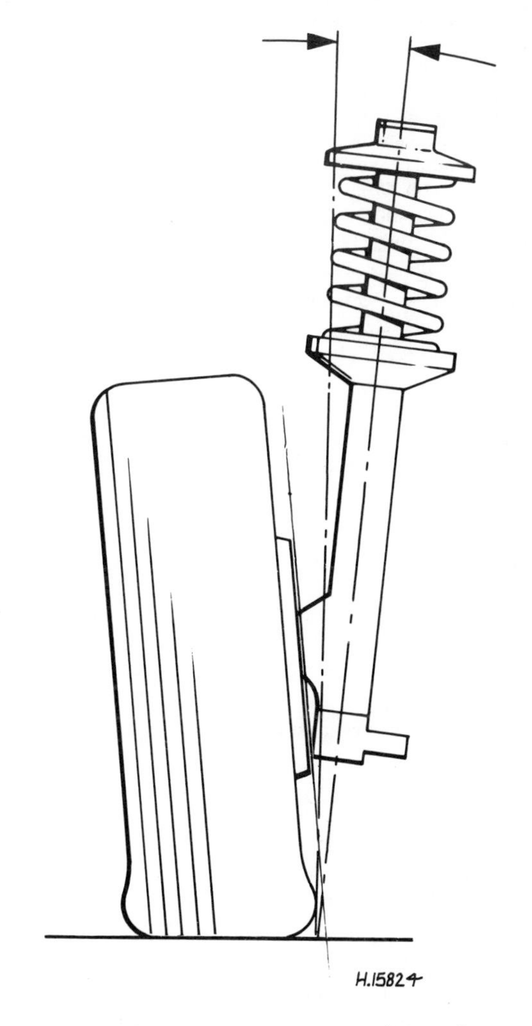

Fig. 11.52 Steering axis inclination (Sec 33)

Toe: this is the amount by which the distance between the front inside edges of the roadwheel rims differs from that between the rear inside edges. If the distance between the front edges is less than that at the rear, the wheels are said to toe-in. If the distance between the front inside edges is greater than that at the rear, the wheels toe-out.

3 Due to the need for precision gauges to measure the small angles of the steering and suspension settings, it is preferable that adjustment of camber and castor are left to a service station having the necessary equipment.

4 For information purposes, however, adjustment of camber and castor is carried out in the following way:

Camber: By changing the suspension strut top mountings for eccentric ones which are available in different + or – increments.

Castor: Set in production, this angle is not adjustable but an incorrect angle must be due to worn lower track control arm bushes or balljoints. Rectify by renewal of the worn components.

5 To check the front wheel alignment, first make sure that the lengths of both tie-rods are equal when the steering is in the straight-ahead position. Measuring the lengths of the exposed threads on the balljoints is a good way to do this. If adjustment is needed, release the locknut (Series 1) or the clamp (Series 2) and turn the tie-rods with a pair of grips.

6 Obtain a tracking gauge. These are available in various forms from accessory stores or one can be fabricated from a length of steel tubing suitably cranked to clear the sump and bellhousing and having a setscrew and locknut at one end.

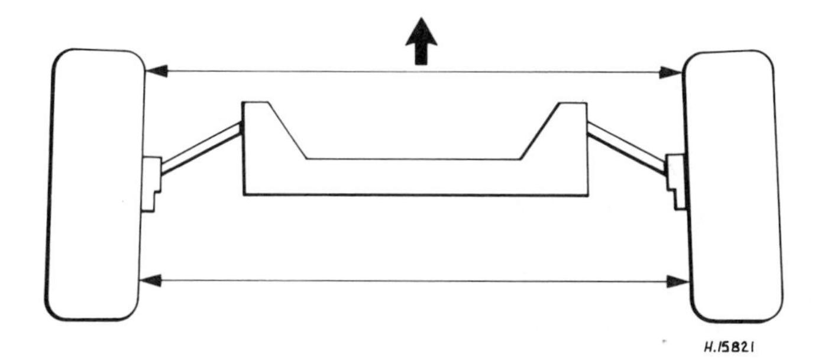

Fig. 11.53 Front wheel toe-in (Sec 33)

7 With the gauge, measure the distance between the two wheel inner rims (at hub height) at the front of the wheel. Push the vehicle forward to rotate the wheel through 180° (half a turn) and measure the distance between the wheel inner rims, again at hub height, at the rear of the wheel. This last measurement should differ from the first by the appropriate toe-in, according to Specification.

8 Where the toe-in is found to be incorrect release the tie-rod balljoint locknuts (Series 1) or the clamps (Series 2) and turn the tie-

rods equally. Only turn them a quarter of a turn at a time before re-checking the alignment. Do not grip the threaded part of the tie-rod during adjustment and make sure that the bellows outboard clip is released, otherwise the gaiters will twist as the tie-rod is rotated.
9 When viewed from the centre line of the car on Series 1 models, turning a tie-rod clockwise will decrease the toe-in. On Series 2 models, turning the rod clockwise will increase the toe-in.
10 Always turn both rods in the same direction when viewed from the centre line of the vehicle, otherwise the rods will become unequal in length. This would cause the steering wheel spoke position to alter and cause problems on turns with tyre scrubbing.
11 On completion, tighten the tie-rod end locknuts or clamps without disturbing their setting, check that the balljoint is at the centre of its arc of travel. Retighten the gaiter clips.

34 Rear wheel alignment

1 The toe-in and camber angle are set in production and any deviation from specified figures will be due to worn suspension flexible bushes or deformed components.
2 If the components are in good condition and it is positively established that the toe-in setting is out of adjustment, then it is possible for eccentric flexible bushes to be fitted to the trailing arms. This is a job for your dealer who will be able to calculate the setting of the eccentric to bring the toe-in within tolerance.

35 Fault diagnosis – suspension and steering

Symptom	Reason(s)
Front suspension	
Vehicle wanders	Incorrect wheel alignment Worn front control arm balljoints
Heavy or stiff steering	Incorrect front wheel alignment Incorrect tyre pressures
Wheel wobble or vibration	Roadwheels out of balance Roadwheel buckled Incorrect front wheel alignment Faulty strut Weak coil spring
Excessive pitching or rolling on corners or during braking	Faulty strut Weak or broken coil spring
Tyre squeal when cornering	Incorrect front wheel alignment Incorrect tyre pressures
Abnormal tyre wear	Incorrect tyre pressures Incorrect front wheel alignment Worn hub bearing
Rear suspension	
Poor roadholding and wander	Faulty shock absorber Weak coil spring Worn or incorrectly adjusted hub bearing Worn trailing arm bush
Manual steering	
Stiff action	Lack of rack lubrication Seized tie-rod end balljoints Seized suspension lower balljoint
Free movement at steering wheel	Wear in tie-rod balljoints Wear in rack teeth
Knocking when traversing uneven surface	Incorrectly adjusted rack slipper Faulty steering damper
Power-assisted steering	
The symptoms and reasons applicable to manual steering gear will apply, plus the following	
Stiff action or no return action	Slipping pump drivebelt Air in fluid Steering column out of alignment Castor angle incorrect due to damage or gross wear in bushes and mountings
Steering effort on both locks unequal	Leaking seal in steering gear Clogged fluid passage within gear assembly
Noisy pump	Loose pulley Kinked hose Clogged filter in fluid reservoir Low fluid level

Chapter 12 Bodywork and fittings

For modifications, and information applicable to later models, see Supplement at end of manual

Contents

1 General description

The body and underframe is of unitary, all welded construction, and is designed with safety cells at the front and rear of the car. All models have an integral roll-over bar built into the side pillars and roof, and the fuel tank is positioned beneath the floor of the rear seats in order to be protected from any rear impact damage. The versions covered by this manual have two or four-door bodywork.

2 Maintenance – bodywork and underframe

1 The general condition of a vehicle's bodywork is the one thing that significantly affects its value. Maintenance is easy but needs to be regular. Neglect, particularly after minor damage, can lead quickly to further deterioration and costly repair bills. It is important also to keep watch on those parts of the vehicle not immediately visible, for instance the underside, inside all the wheel arches and the lower part of the engine compartment.

2 The basic maintenance routine for the bodywork is washing – preferably with a lot of water, from a hose. This will remove all the loose solids which may have stuck to the vehicle. It is important to flush these off in such a way as to prevent grit from scratching the finish. The wheel arches and underframe need washing in the same way to remove any accumulated mud which will retain moisture and tend to encourage rust. Paradoxically enough, the best time to clean the underframe and wheel arches is in wet weather when the mud is thoroughly wet and soft. In very wet weather the underframe is usually cleaned of large accumulations automatically and this is a good time for inspection.

3 Periodically, it is a good idea to have the whole of the underframe of the vehicle steam cleaned, engine compartment included, so that a thorough inspection can be carried out to see what minor repairs and renovations are necessary. Steam cleaning is available at many garages and is necessary for removal of the accumulation of oily grime which sometimes is allowed to become thick in certain areas. If steam cleaning facilities are not available, there are one or two excellent grease solvents available which can be brush applied. The dirt can then be simply hosed off.

4 After washing paintwork, wipe off with a chamois leather to give an unspotted clear finish. A coat of clear protective wax polish will give

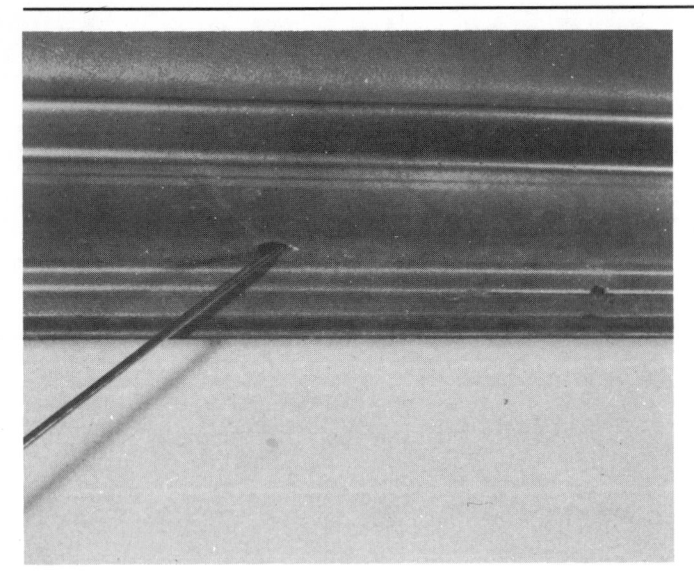

2.4A Door drain hole

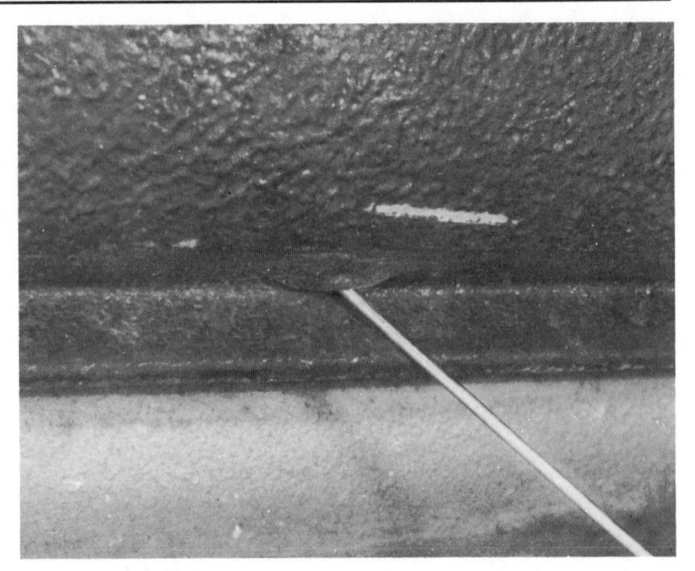

2.4B Sill drain hole

added protection against chemical pollutants in the air. If the paintwork sheen has dulled or oxidised, use a cleaner/polisher combination to restore the brilliance of the shine. This requires a little effort, but such dulling is usually caused because regular washing has been neglected. Always check that the door and ventilator opening drain holes and pipes are completely clear so that water can be drained out. Bright work should be treated in the same way as paintwork. Windscreens and windows can be kept clear of the smeary film which often appears, by adding a little ammonia to the water. If they are scratched, a good rub with a proprietary metal polish will often clear them. Never use any form of wax or other body or chromium polish on glass (photos).

3 Maintenance – upholstery and carpets

Mats and carpets should be brushed or vacuum cleaned regularly to keep them free of grit. If they are badly stained remove them from the vehicle for scrubbing or sponging and make quite sure they are dry before refitting. Seats and interior trim panels can be kept clean by wiping with a damp cloth. If they do become stained (which can be more apparent on light coloured upholstery) use a little liquid detergent and a soft nail brush to scour the grime out of the grain of the material. Do not forget to keep the headlining clean in the same way as the upholstery. When using liquid cleaners inside the vehicle do not over-wet the surfaces being cleaned. Excessive damp could get into the seams and padded interior causing stains, offensive odours or even rot. If the inside of the vehicle gets wet accidentally it is worthwhile taking some trouble to dry it out properly, particularly where carpets are involved. *Do not leave oil or electric heaters inside the vehicle for this purpose.*

4 Minor body damage – repair

The photographic sequences on pages 258 and 259 illustrate the operations detailed in the following sub-sections.

Repair of minor scratches in bodywork

If the scratch is very superficial, and does not penetrate to the metal of the bodywork, repair is very simple. Lightly rub the area of the scratch with a paintwork renovator, or a very fine cutting paste, to remove loose paint from the scratch and to clear the surrounding bodywork of wax polish. Rinse the area with clean water.

Apply touch-up paint to the scratch using a fine paint brush; continue to apply fine layers of paint until the surface of the paint in the scratch is level with the surrounding paintwork. Allow the new paint at least two weeks to harden: then blend it into the surrounding paintwork by rubbing the scratch area with a paintwork renovator or a very fine cutting paste. Finally, apply wax polish.

Where the scratch has penetrated right through to the metal of the bodywork, causing the metal to rust, a different repair technique is required. Remove any loose rust from the bottom of the scratch with a penknife, then apply rust inhibiting paint to prevent the formation of rust in the future. Using a rubber or nylon applicator fill the scratch with bodystopper paste. If required, this paste can be mixed with cellulose thinners to provide a very thin paste which is ideal for filling narrow scratches. Before the stopper-paste in the scratch hardens, wrap a piece of smooth cotton rag around the top of a finger. Dip the finger in cellulose thinners and then quickly sweep it across the surface of the stopper-paste in the scratch; this will ensure that the surface of the stopper-paste is slightly hollowed. The scratch can now be painted over as described earlier in this Section.

Repair of dents in bodywork

When deep denting of the vehicle's bodywork has taken place, the first task is to pull the dent out, until the affected bodywork almost attains its original shape. There is little point in trying to restore the original shape completely, as the metal in the damaged area will have stretched on impact and cannot be reshaped fully to its original contour. It is better to bring the level of the dent up to a point which is about $\frac{1}{8}$ in (3 mm) below the level of the surrounding bodywork. In cases where the dent is very shallow anyway, it is not worth trying to pull it out at all. If the underside of the dent is accessible, it can be hammered out gently from behind, using a mallet with a wooden or plastic head. Whilst doing this, hold a suitable block of wood firmly against the outside of the panel to absorb the impact from the hammer blows and thus prevent a large area of the bodywork from being 'belled-out'.

Should the dent be in a section of the bodywork which has a double skin or some other factor making it inaccessible from behind, a different technique is called for. Drill several small holes through the metal inside the area – particularly in the deeper section. Then screw long self-tapping screws into the holes just sufficiently for them to gain a good purchase in the metal. Now the dent can be pulled out by pulling on the protruding heads of the screws with a pair of pliers.

The next stage of the repair is the removal of the paint from the damaged area, and from an inch or so of the surrounding 'sound' bodywork. This is accomplished most easily by using a wire brush or abrasive pad on a power drill, although it can be done just as effectively by hand using sheets of abrasive paper. To complete the preparation for filling, score the surface of the bare metal with a screwdriver or the tang of a file, or alternatively, drill small holes in the affected area. This will provide a really good 'key' for the filler paste.

To complete the repair see the Section on filling and re-spraying.

Repair of rust holes or gashes in bodywork

Remove all paint from the affected area and from an inch or so of the surrounding 'sound' bodywork, using an abrasive pad or a wire brush on a power drill. If these are not available a few sheets of abrasive paper will do the job just as effectively. With the paint removed you will be able to gauge the severity of the corrosion and therefore decide whether to renew the whole panel (if this is possible) or to repair the affected area. New body panels are not as expensive as most people think and it is often quicker and more satisfactory to fit a new panel than to attempt to repair large areas of corrosion.

Remove all fittings from the affected area except those which will act as a guide to the original shape of the damaged bodywork (eg headlamp shells etc). Then, using tin snips or a hacksaw blade, remove all loose metal and any other metal badly affected by corrosion. Hammer the edges of the hole inwards in order to create a slight depression for the filler paste.

Wire brush the affected area to remove the powdery rust from the surface of the remaining metal. Paint the affected area with rust inhibiting paint; if the back of the rusted area is accessible treat this also.

Before filling can take place it will be necessary to block the hole in some way. This can be achieved by the use of aluminium or plastic mesh, or aluminium tape.

Aluminium or plastic mesh is probably the best material to use for a large hole. Cut a piece to the approximate size and shape of the hole to be filled, then position it in the hole so that its edges are below the level of the surrounding bodywork. It can be retained in position by several blobs of filler paste around its periphery.

Aluminium tape should be used for small or very narrow holes. Pull a piece off the roll and trim it to the approximate size and shape required, then pull off the backing paper (if used) and stick the tape over the hole; it can be overlapped if the thickness of one piece is insufficient. Burnish down the edges of the tape with the handle of a screwdriver or similar, to ensure that the tape is securely attached to the metal underneath.

Bodywork repairs – filling and re-spraying

Before using this Section, see the Sections on dent, deep scratch, rust holes and gash repairs.

Many types of bodyfiller are available, but generally speaking those proprietary kits which contain a tin of filler paste and a tube of resin hardener are best for this type of repair. A wide, flexible plastic or nylon applicator will be found invaluable for imparting a smooth and well contoured finish to the surface of the filler.

Mix up a little filler on a clean piece of card or board – measure the hardener carefully (follow the maker's instructions on the pack) otherwise the filler will set too rapidly or too slowly.

Using the applicator apply the filler paste to the prepared area; draw the applicator across the surface of the filler to achieve the correct contour and to level the filler surface. As soon as a contour that approximates to the correct one is achieved, stop working the paste – if you carry on too long the paste will become sticky and begin to 'pick up' on the applicator. Continue to add thin layers of filler paste at twenty-minute intervals until the level of the filler is just proud of the surrounding bodywork.

Once the filler has hardened, excess can be removed using a metal plane or file. From then on, progressively finer grades of abrasive paper should be used, starting with a 40 grade production paper and finishing with 400 grade wet-and-dry paper. Always wrap the abrasive paper around a flat rubber, cork, or wooden block – otherwise the surface of the filler will not be completely flat. During the smoothing of the filler surface the wet-and-dry paper should be periodically rinsed in water. This will ensure that a very smooth finish is imparted to the filler at the final stage.

At this stage the 'dent' should be surrounded by a ring of bare metal, which in turn should be encircled by the finely 'feathered' edge of the good paintwork. Rinse the repair area with clean water, until all of the dust produced by the rubbing-down operation has gone.

Spray the whole repair area with a light coat of primer – this will show up any imperfections in the surface of the filler. Repair these imperfections with fresh filler paste or bodystopper, and once more smooth the surface with abrasive paper. If bodystopper is used, it can be mixed with cellulose thinners to form a really thin paste which is ideal for filling small holes. Repeat this spray and repair procedure until you are satisfied that the surface of the filler, and the feathered edge of the paintwork are perfect. Clean the repair area with clean water and allow to dry fully.

The repair area is now ready for final spraying. Paint spraying must be carried out in a warm, dry, windless and dust free atmosphere. This condition can be created artificially if you have access to a large indoor working area, but if you are forced to work in the open, you will have to pick your day very carefully. If you are working indoors, dousing the floor in the work area with water will help to settle the dust which would otherwise be in the atmosphere. If the repair area is confined to one body panel, mask off the surrounding panels; this will help to minimise the effects of a slight mis-match in paint colours. Bodywork fittings (eg chrome strips, door handles etc) will also need to be masked off. Use genuine masking tape and several thicknesses of newspaper for the masking operations.

Before commencing to spray, agitate the aerosol can thoroughly, then spray a test area (an old tin, or similar) until the technique is mastered. Cover the repair area with a thick coat of primer; the thickness should be built up using several thin layers of paint rather than one thick one. Using 400 grade wet-and-dry paper, rub down the surface of the primer until it is really smooth. While doing this, the work area should be thoroughly doused with water, and the wet-and-dry paper periodically rinsed in water. Allow to dry before spraying on more paint.

Spray on the top coat, again building up the thickness by using several thin layers of paint. Start spraying in the centre of the repair area and then, using a circular motion, work outwards until the whole repair area and about 2 inches of the surrounding original paintwork is covered. Remove all masking material 10 to 15 minutes after spraying on the final coat of paint.

Allow the new paint at least two weeks to harden, then, using a paintwork renovator or a very fine cutting paste, blend the edges of the paint into the existing paintwork. Finally, apply wax polish.

5 Major body damage – repair

Where distortion of the underbody members has occurred repair should be left to your dealer or a bodywork establishment who will have the necessary alignment jigs, and welding and hydraulic bending equipment.

Without correct alignment, the steering and suspension will be adversely affected.

6 Front bumper – removal and refitting

1 Reach under the front wings and unscrew the end fixing bolts.

2 Unscrew the centre bracket nuts and remove the complete bumper bar.

3 If necessary, the bumper can be separated into the centre and end sections.

Fig. 12.1 Front bumper end fixing bolt – arrowed (Sec 6)

This sequence of photographs deals with the repair of the dent and paintwork damage shown in this photo. The procedure will be similar for the repair of a hole. It should be noted that the procedures given here are simplified – more explicit instructions will be found in the text

In the case of a dent the first job – after removing surrounding trim – is to hammer out the dent where access is possible. This will minimise filling. Here, the large dent having been hammered out, the damaged area is being made slightly concave

Now all paint must be removed from the damaged area, by rubbing with coarse abrasive paper. Alternatively, a wire brush or abrasive pad can be used in a power drill. Where the repair area meets good paintwork, the edge of the paintwork should be 'feathered', using a finer grade of abrasive paper

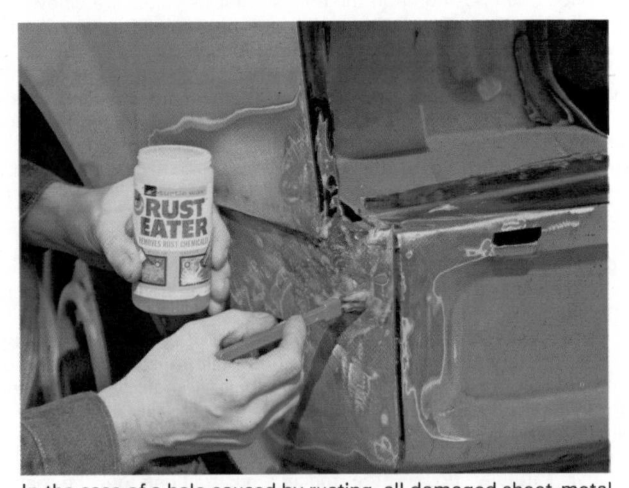

In the case of a hole caused by rusting, all damaged sheet-metal should be cut away before proceeding to this stage. Here, the damaged area is being treated with rust remover and inhibitor before being filled

Mix the body filler according to its manufacturer's instructions. In the case of corrosion damage, it will be necessary to block off any large holes before filling – this can be done with aluminium or plastic mesh, or aluminium tape. Make sure the area is absolutely clean before ...

... applying the filler. Filler should be applied with a flexible applicator, as shown, for best results; the wooden spatula being used for confined areas. Apply thin layers of filler at 20-minute intervals, until the surface of the filler is slightly proud of the surrounding bodywork

Initial shaping can be done with a Surform plane or Dreadnought file. Then, using progressively finer grades of wet-and-dry paper, wrapped around a sanding block, and copious amounts of clean water, rub down the filler until really smooth and flat. Again, feather the edges of adjoining paintwork

The whole repair area can now be sprayed or brush-painted with primer. If spraying, ensure adjoining areas are protected from over-spray. Note that at least one inch of the surrounding sound paintwork should be coated with primer. Primer has a 'thick' consistency, so will find small imperfections

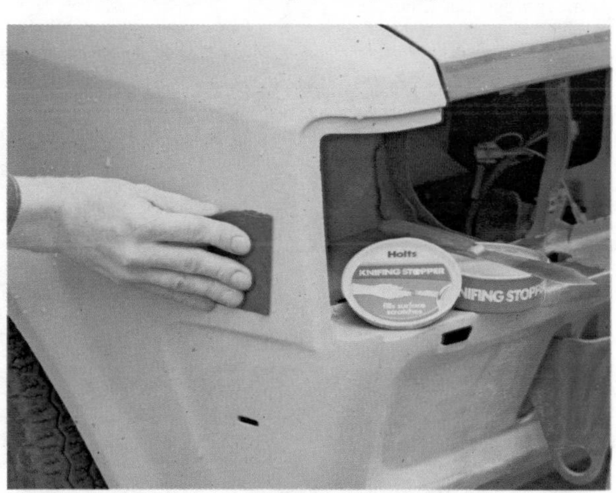

Again, using plenty of water, rub down the primer with a fine grade wet-and-dry paper (400 grade is probably best) until it is really smooth and well blended into the surrounding paintwork. Any remaining imperfections can now be filled by carefully applied knifing stopper paste

When the stopper has hardened, rub down the repair area again before applying the final coat of primer. Before rubbing down this last coat of primer, ensure the repair area is blemish-free – use more stopper if necessary. To ensure that the surface of the primer is really smooth use some finishing compound

The top coat can now be applied. When working out of doors, pick a dry, warm and wind-free day. Ensure surrounding areas are protected from over-spray. Agitate the aerosol thoroughly, then spray the centre of the repair area, working outwards with a circular motion. Apply the paint as several thin coats

After a period of about two weeks, which the paint needs to harden fully, the surface of the repaired area can be 'cut' with a mild cutting compound prior to wax polishing. When carrying out bodywork repairs, remember that the quality of the finished job is proportional to the time and effort expended

6.4 Bumper bracket on side-member

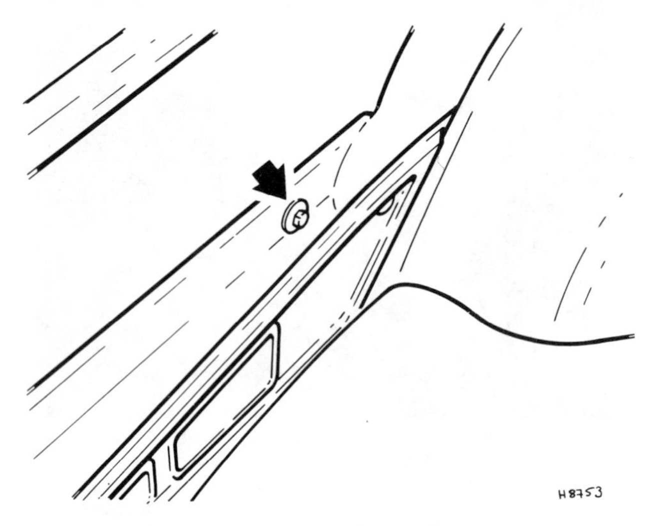

Fig. 12.2 Rear bumper end fixing bolt – arrowed (Sec 7)

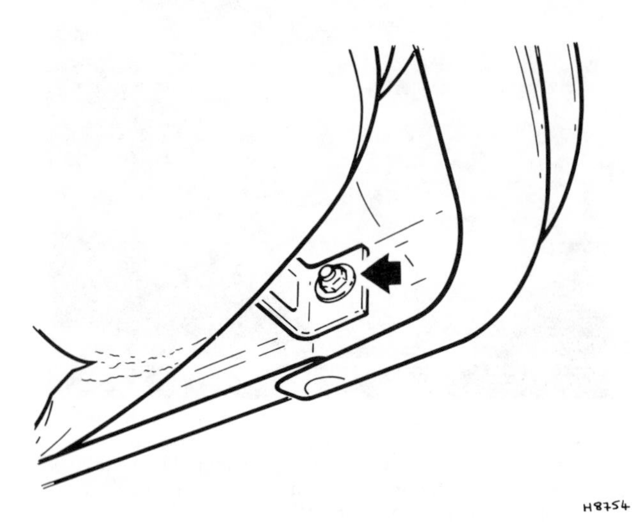

Fig. 12.3 Rear bumper bracket bolt – arrowed (Sec 7)

4 The bumper support brackets may be unbolted from the body members (photo).

5 Refitting is a reversal of removal, but check that the end fitting rubber cushions are in good condition.

7 Rear bumper – removal and refitting

1 Open the boot lid and unscrew the bumper end fitting bolts.

2 Disconnect the rear number plate lamp leads.

3 Unscrew the nuts from the support brackets and lift the bumper bar away.

4 Refitting is a reversal of removal. Check that the end fitting rubber cushions are in good condition.

8 Radiator grille – removal and refitting

1 Open the bonnet, extract the centre grille screws and clips, and remove the grille (photos).

2 To remove the side grille, first detach the direction indicator lamp, as described in Chapter 10, then extract the fixing screws and clips, and remove the grille.

8.1A Radiator grille screw

8.1B Side grille clip

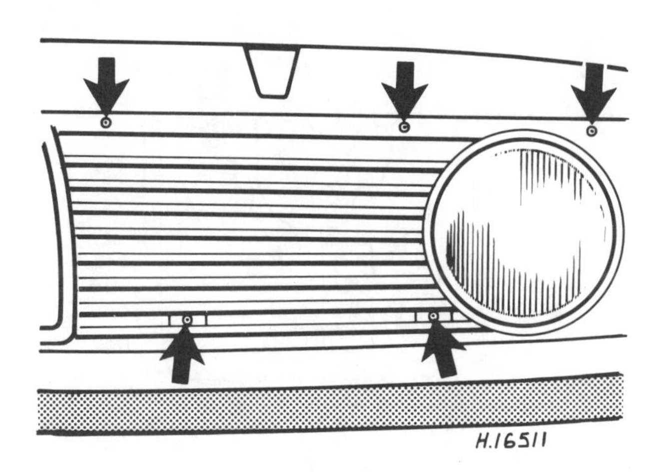

Fig. 12.4 Series 1 side grille screws – arrowed (Sec 8)

8.1C Grille locating tongues

9.2 Bonnet hinge bolts

9.5 Bonnet lid strut (Series 2)

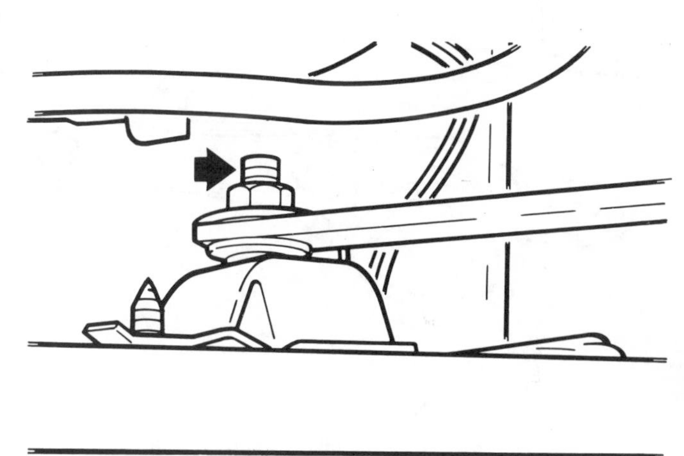

Fig. 12.5 Bonnet strut nut – arrowed (Sec 9)

9 Bonnet – removal and refitting

1 Open the bonnet and mark the position of the hinges on the underside of it with a soft pencil.
2 Unscrew and remove three bolts from each hinge and loosen the remaining one (photo).
3 With an assistant supporting the weight of the bonnet, disconnect the supporting struts from the bonnet.
4 Remove the remaining hinge bolts and lift the bonnet away.
5 The hinge assembly, the support struts and the gas-filled strut pistons (Series 2) may be removed from the engine compartment if required (photo).
6 Refitting is a reversal of removal, but do not fully tighten the hinge bolts until the bonnet has been gently closed and the alignment checked.
7 The bonnet can be moved within the limits of the elongated hinge bolt holes.
8 Adjust the strikers and rollers, as described in the next Section.

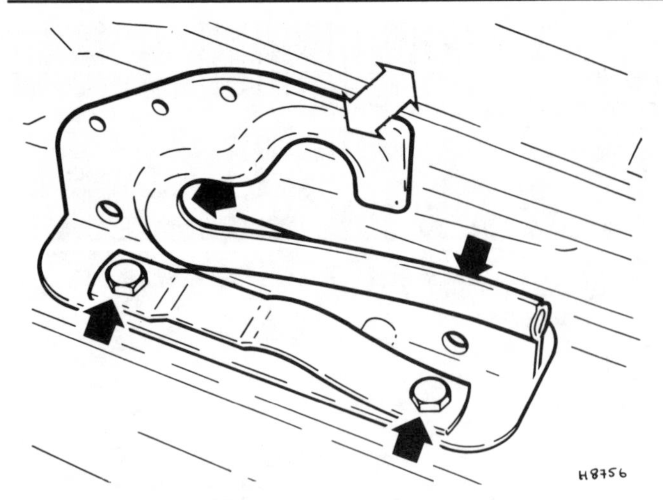

Fig. 12.6 Bonnet striker – Series 1 (Sec 10)

Solid arrows show the securing screws
Hollow arrows show direction of adjustment

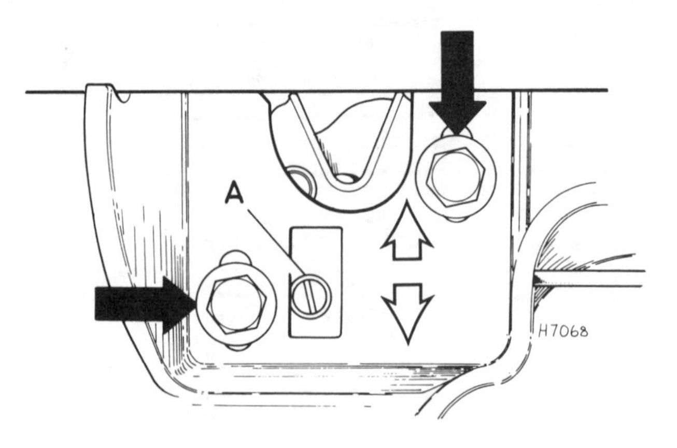

Fig. 12.8 Bonnet lid latch (Secs 10 and 11)

Solid arrows show the securing screws
Hollow arrows show direction of adjustment
A Bonnet release screw

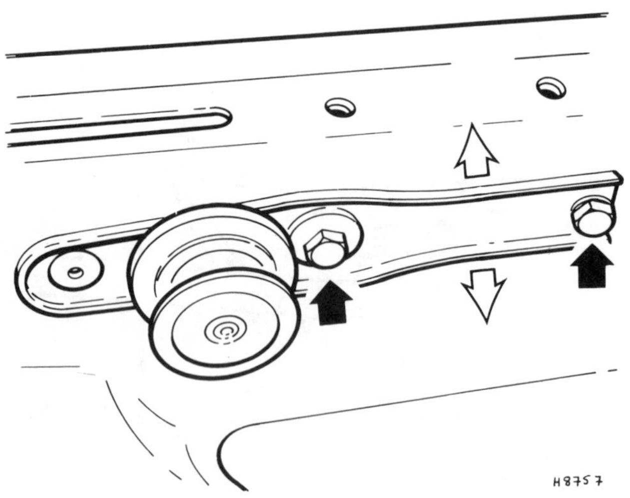

Fig. 12.7 Bonnet guide roller – Series 1 (Sec 10)

Solid arrows show the securing screws
Hollow arrows show direction of adjustment

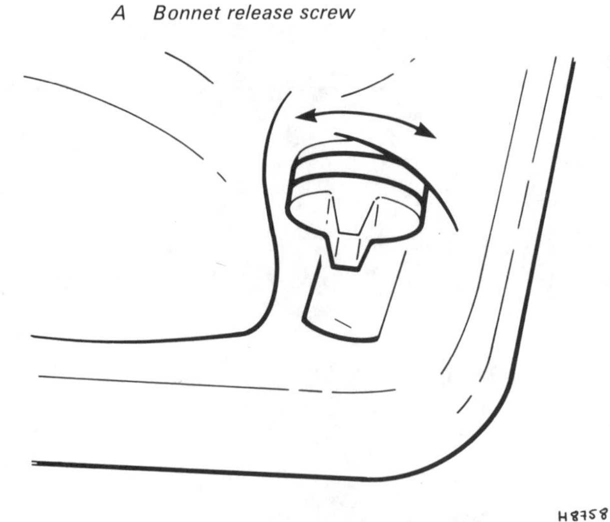

Fig. 12.9 Bonnet buffers (Sec 10)

Arrows show direction of adjustment

10 Bonnet striker and latch – adjustment

1 The strikers can be moved sideways after loosening the bolts.
2 The rear end of the bonnet can be raised or lowered to align with the front door contour by releasing the bolts and sliding the guide roller.
3 The latch is adjustable by sliding it, after having released the fixing bolts.
4 Make sure that the rubber buffers are turned out sufficiently to support the bonnet firmly without rattle.

11 Bonnet release cable – removal and refitting

1 Remove the facia panel under cover.
2 Open the bonnet and disconnect the cable from the latch.
3 Pull the cable through the bulkhead and detach it from the control handle under the facia.
4 Fit the new cable by reversing the removal operations. Eliminate all cable slack before tightening the pinch screw at the latch. Bend over the end of the cable.
5 It is worth remembering that, in the event of the bonnet release cable breaking, the bonnet can be opened by inserting a screwdriver into the small screw on the face of the latch (Fig. 12.8) and turning it.

12 Bonnet release latch – removal and refitting

1 Remove the radiator centre grille and disconnect the release cable.
2 Mark the set position of the latch and unbolt and remove it.
3 Refit by reversing the removal operations.

13 Front wing – removal and refitting

1 Remove the front bumper.
2 Remove the radiator grille.
3 Remove the direction indicator lamp.
4 Remove the front roadwheel.
5 Working at the rear of the wheel arch, remove the sealing panel (Series 2; undershield).
6 Extract the self-tapping screws from just ahead of the wheel arch and along the wing upper edge.
7 Remove the screws from the sill, and the inner panel.
8 Cut through the mastic flange joint and remove the wing.
9 Clean the body mating flanges and apply a thick bead of mastic or the special sealing strip available from BMW dealers.
10 Fit the new wing, but before tightening the self-tapping screws, check the alignment with the adjacent body panels. Make sure that the

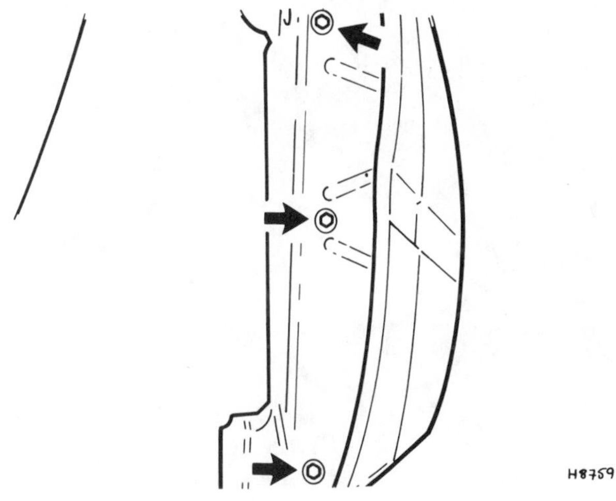

Fig. 12.10 Wing inner screws – arrowed (Sec 13)

gap between the rear edge of the wing and the leading edge of the door is even.

11 Apply underseal to the underside of the wing and, as the new wing is supplied in primer, refinish it to match the body colour.

14 Door trim panel – removal and refitting

Front door

1 Remove the armrest. These are secured by end screws covered by a sliding sleeve or blanking plate, according to model. Screws are also located underneath (photos).

2 On models which have the exterior mirror switch built into the armrest, withdraw and unplug the switch to give access to the armrest screw (photo).

3 Prise off the window regulator handle cover, extract the screw and remove the handle and escutcheon plate (photo).

4 Note the setting of the door interior remote control handle, extract the screw and remove it (photo). On later models with a flush fitting handle, prise out the escutcheon by sliding it rearwards and lifting it out (photos).

5 Remove the panel-mounted mirror control switch (if fitted) and unplug it (photo).

6 Insert the fingers or a wide-bladed screwdriver under the trim panel and pull the panel clips from their holes (photo). Note the conical spring behind the regulator handle which has its larger coils towards the trim panel.

7 Peel away the waterproof sheet.

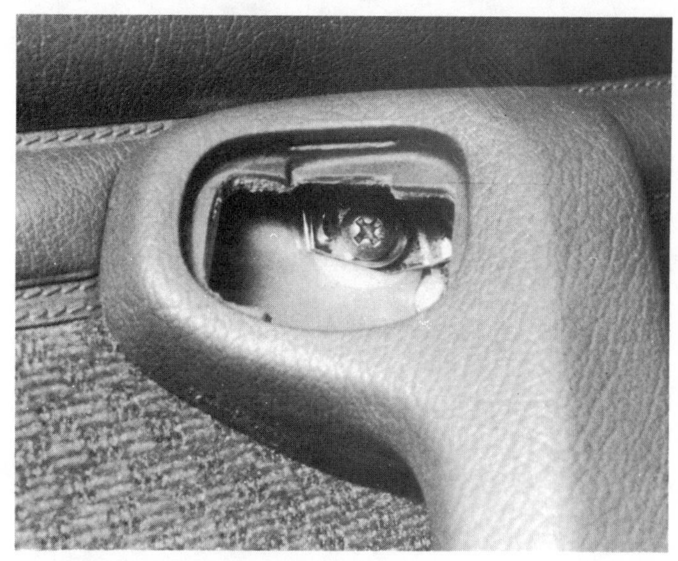

14.1B Armrest fixing screw

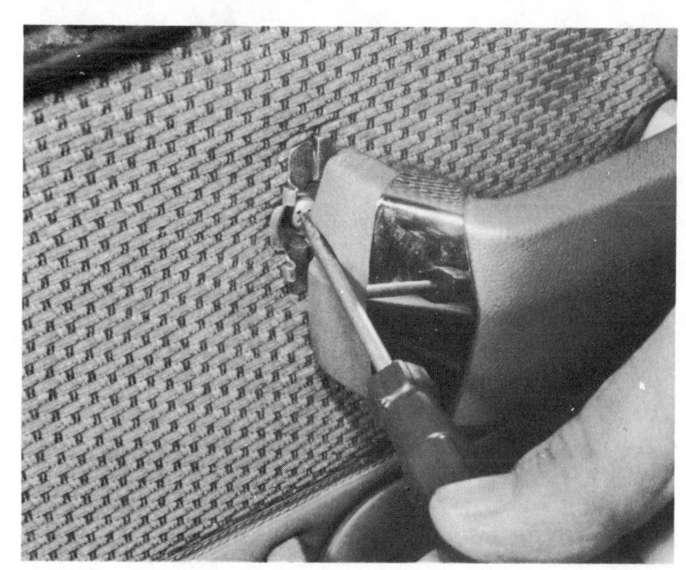

14.1C Armrest fixing screw

14.1A Armrest blanking plate

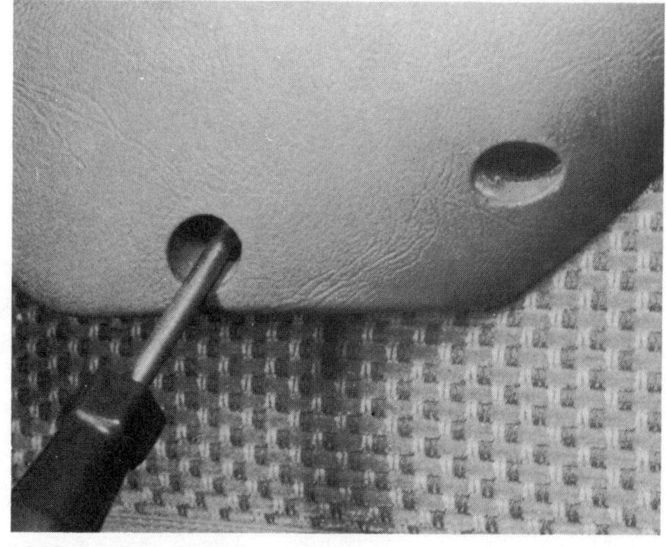

14.1D Armrest base screws

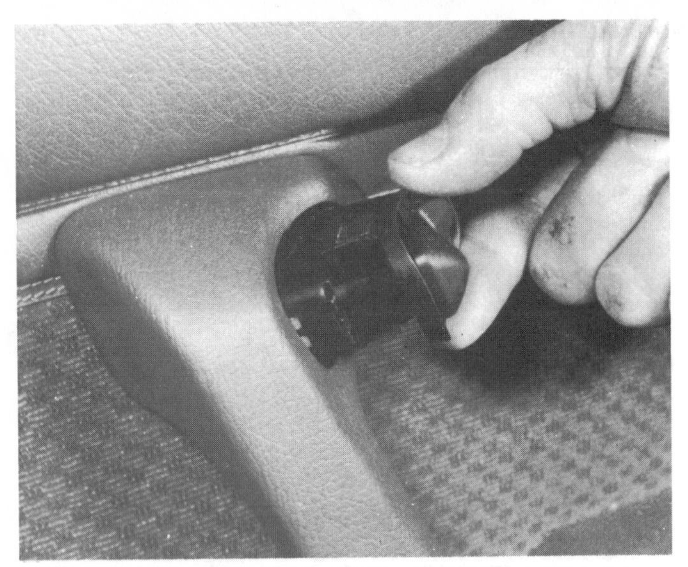

14.2 Exterior mirror switch (Series 2)

14.3 Window regulator handle screw

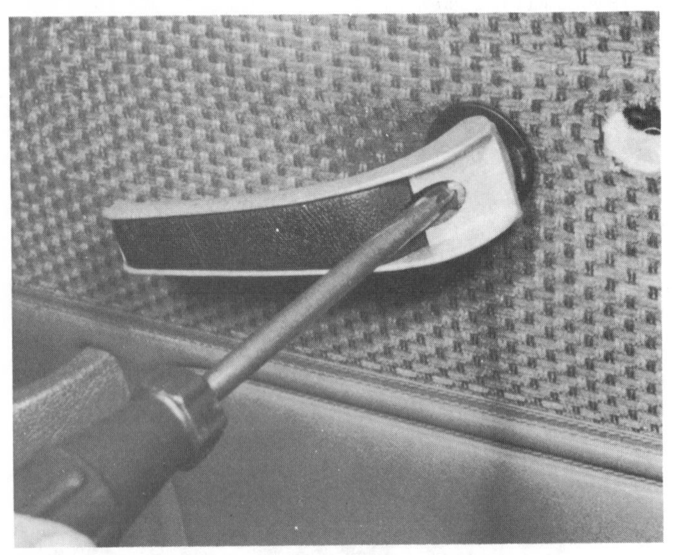

14.4A Door handle screw (Series 1)

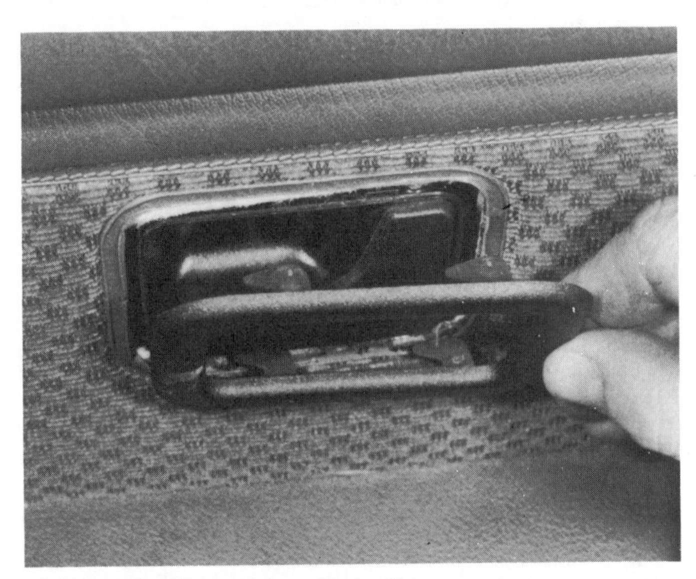

14.4B Door handle escutcheon (Series 2)

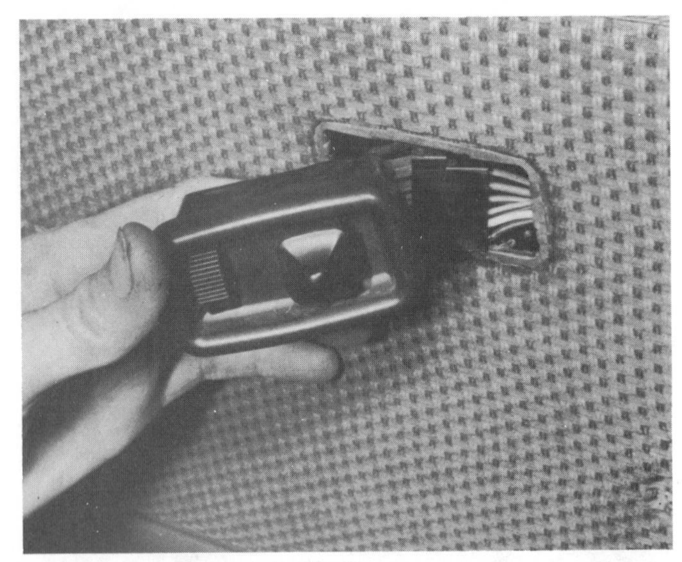

14.5 Exterior mirror switch (Series 1)

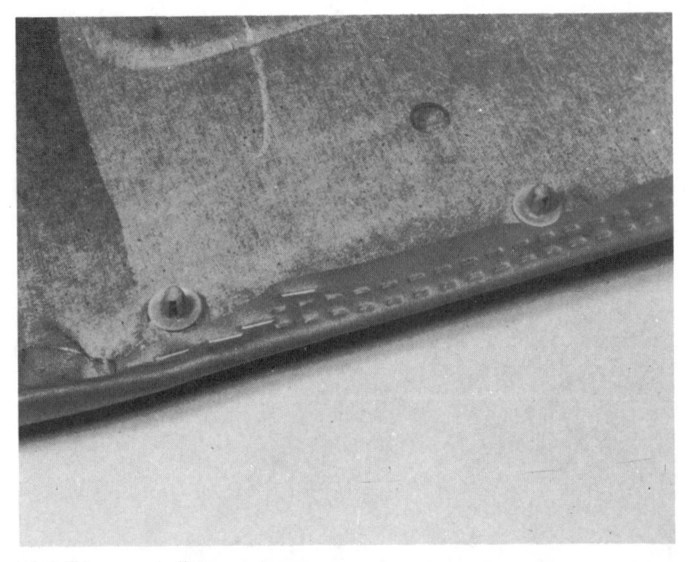

14.6 Trim panel clips

Rear door

8 The operations are similar to those just described, but the lock plunger knob must be unscrewed. A foam plastic disc is located behind the regulator handle.

9 When removing the trim panel hold the glass inner weatherstrip cover to prevent it being removed as well.

All doors

10 Refitting is a reversal of removal.

15 Door lock – removal and refitting

Series 1

1 Remove the door trim panel, as described in the preceding Section.

2 Peel back the waterproof sheet.

3 Unscrew and remove the glass guide rail bolt.

4 Disconnect the link rod between the door lock and the cylinder.

5 Unscrew and remove the bolts which hold the remote mechanism (photo).

6 Disconnect the connecting rod from the guide clip F – Fig. 12.12.

7 Using an Allen key, extract the screws and remove the clamp plate (photo).

8 Close the rotary striker with the fingers, remove the lock screws and withdraw the lock from the door cavity.

9 Refitting is a reversal of removal.

Series 2

10 With the trim panel removed, as previously described, unscrew the remote control assembly.

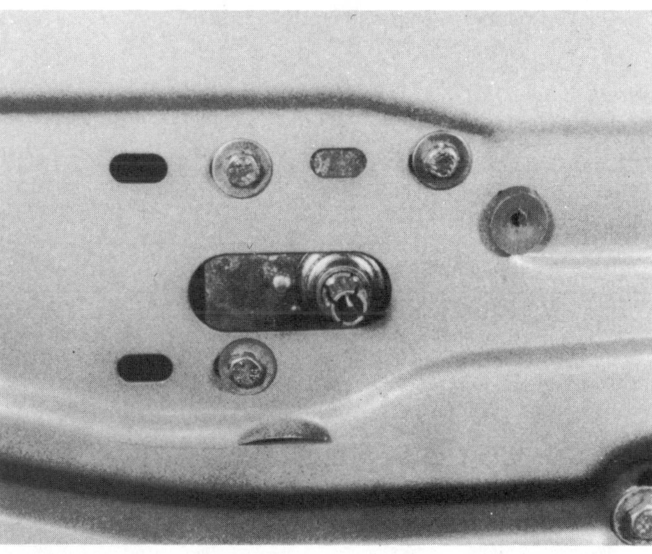

15.5 Lock remote control bolts

15.7 Door clamp plate and rotary striker

Fig. 12.11 Glass guide rail bolt – arrowed (Sec 15)

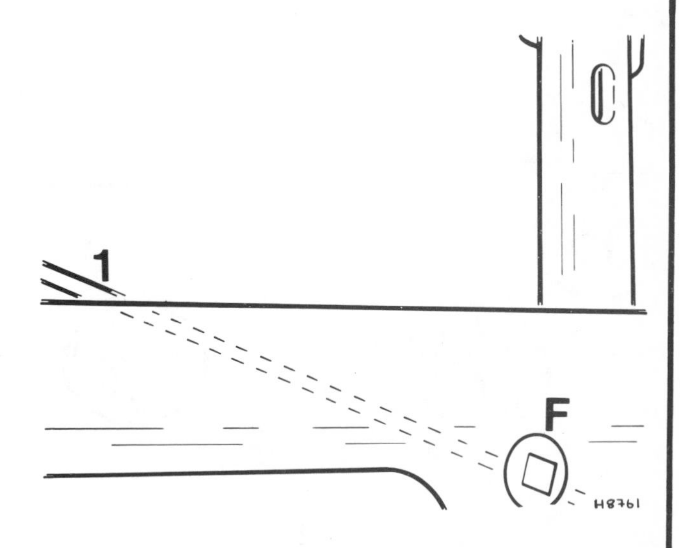

Fig. 12.12 Lock remote control connecting rod (Sec 15)

1 Rod *F Guide clip*

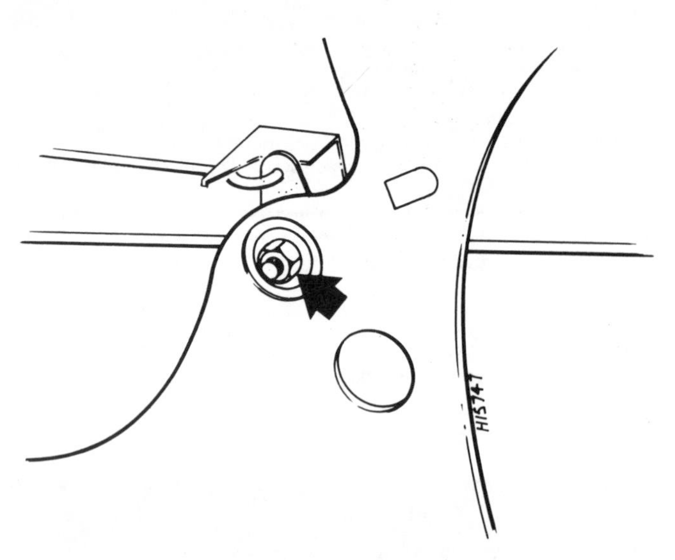

Fig. 12.13 Operating lever nut – arrowed (Sec 15)

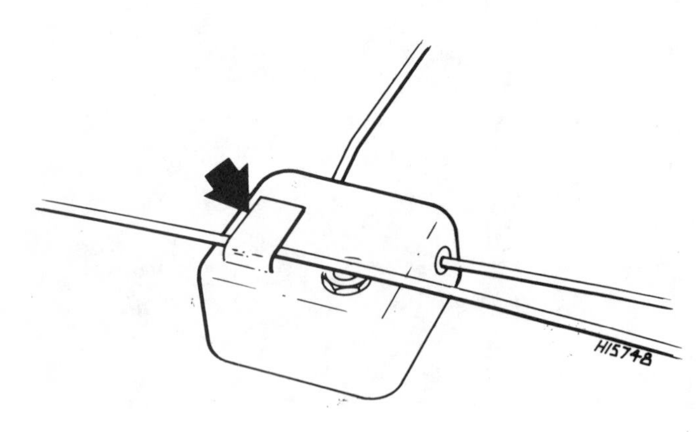

Fig. 12.14 Remote control rod operating lever cap holder – arrowed (Sec 15)

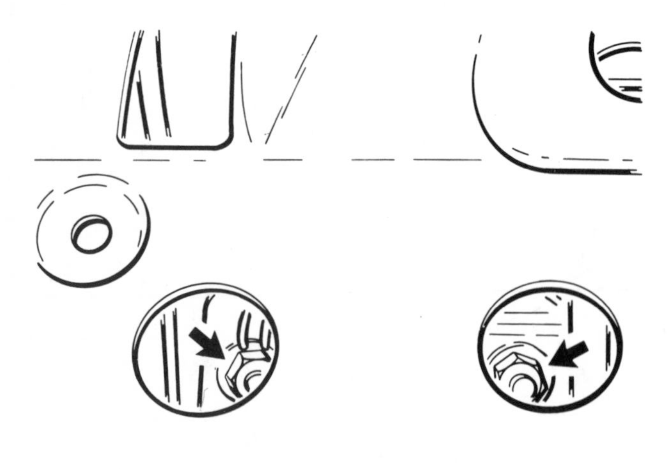

Fig. 12.15 Door lock operating mechanism securing nuts – arrowed (Sec 17)

11 Unscrew the operating lever.
12 Unscrew the lock bolts at the door edge.
13 Disconnect the link from the cylinder and remove the lock mechanism, complete with remote control.
14 Refitting is a reversal of removal, but engage the remote control rod in the operating lever cap holder.
15 For cars equipped with central door locking, refer to Chapter 10.

16 Door lock cylinder – removal and refitting

Series 1
1 Remove the door trim panel, as previously described (Section 14). Peel back the waterproof sheet.
2 Unscrew and remove the rear window guide rail.
3 Partially lift the window guide out of the rail and remove the rail downwards.
4 Disconnect the lock-to-cylinder link rod.
5 Pull out the lock cylinder retainer and pull out the cylinder.
6 The key number is engraved on the cylinder.
7 Refitting is a reversal of removal.

Series 2
8 The operations are similar to those just described, but a washer is located behind the retainer.
9 Some models have a lock cylinder heater which comes off with the retainer.

17 Door exterior handle – removal and refitting

1 Remove the door trim panel and peel back the waterproof sheet.
2 Disconnect the operating mechanism from the handle and then extract the two fixing screws. Remove the handle.
3 The lock operating mechanism can be removed after unscrewing the two nuts.

18 Door window – removal and refitting

Series 1
1 Remove the door trim panel and waterproof sheet.
2 Unscrew and remove the retaining bolts from the holder (3) – Fig. 12.16.
3 Disconnect the glass from the lifting arm, tilt the glass and remove it upwards from the door cavity.

Fig. 12.16 Door window holder (Sec 18)

1 Bolt
2 Bolt
3 Holder

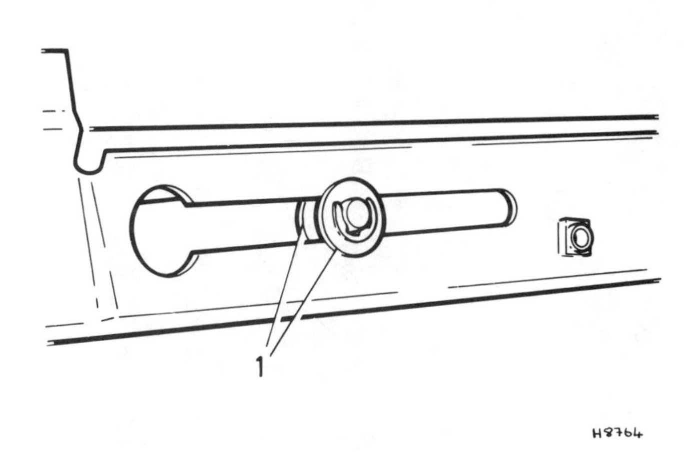

Fig. 12.17 Window lift rail (Sec 18)

1 Plastic discs

Fig. 12.18 Window holder bolts – arrowed (Sec 18)

4 Refitting is a reversal of removal, but make sure that the lift rail runs between the two plastic discs (1) – Fig. 12.17.

Series 2

5 With the trim panel removed, pull off the inner weatherstrip.
6 Remove the bolts (arrowed) – Fig. 12.18 – but hold the glass from dropping.
7 Swing the front end of the glass out of the guide roller and remove the glass upwards.
8 Refitting is a reversal of removal.

Adjustment

9 Before tightening the holder bolts, adjust the glass and holder to give an even closure at the top edge. If necessary, the glass guide channel rails can be moved to provide smooth up and down operation.

19 Door window regulator (manual) – removal and refitting

Series 1

1 Remove the interior trim panel and waterproof sheet, as described earlier (Section 14).
2 Temporarily fit the regulator handle and close the window.
3 Remove the bolts which hold the window regulator to the door (photo).
4 Support the glass and detach the lifting arm by using the large hole in the lifting plate.
5 Withdraw the mechanism from the door cavity.
6 Refitting is a reversal of removal, but apply grease to the toothed sector of the regulator.

Series 2

7 With the trim panel and waterproof sheet removed, remove the screws from the glass holder and swing the forward end of the glass out of the guide roller. Lower the glass as far as it will go.
8 Unscrew and remove the regulator fixing bolts and cut through the conduit clip.
9 Unscrew the remaining bolts and withdraw the regulator mechanism from the door cavity.
10 Refitting is a reversal of removal.

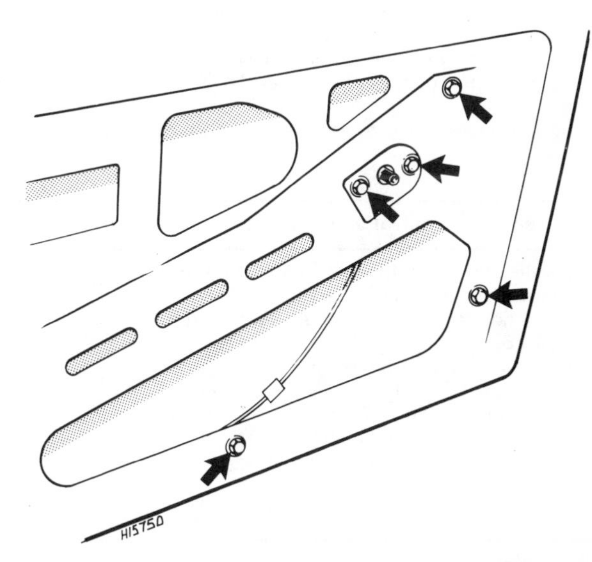

Fig. 12.19 Window regulator fixing bolts – arrowed (Sec 19)

19.3 Window regulator bolts

20 Powered window regulator – removal and refitting

1 On cars equipped with this type of window, the removal operations are as described for the manually-operated type, except that the wiring plugs for the winder motors must be disconnected.

21 Door check strap – removal and refitting

1 Remove the door interior trim panel and waterproof sheet as described earlier (Section 14).
2 Drill out the check strap pivot pin from below (photo).
3 Unscrew the bolts from the door edge and withdraw the check strap into the door cavity.
4 When refitting the check strap, rivet the pivot pin and set the strap to its second notch.

21.2 Door check strap

22 Door – removal and refitting

1 Remove the door trim panel and waterproof sheet, as previously described (Section 14).
2 Open the door to its fullest extent and support it on jacks or blocks with pads of rag to prevent damage to the paintwork.
3 Disconnect the check strap (Section 21).
4 Unplug the wiring from the door mirror, electric windows and central door lock, as applicable, and draw the wires through the flexible duct which runs between the door hinged edge and the body pillar.
5 Unscrew the door hinge bolts and lift the door from the car.
6 Transfer all internal components to the new door.
7 External components should not be fitted until the door has been finished in the matching body colour.
8 Adjust the position of the door as necessary before tightening the hinge bolts. Shims may be used under the hinges to bring the door flush with the wing.
9 Adjust the lock catch to provide smooth positive closure of the door.

23 Door catch – removal and refitting

1 Mark the position of the catch on the door pillar with a soft pencil before removing the fixing screws (photo).
2 On two-door models, remove the rear quarter panel, as described in Section 25.
3 Remove the catch screws and the catch. On two-door models, hold the threaded plate from falling as it is not of captive type.
4 When refitting, fit the screws finger tight and then shut the door very gently to position the catch.
5 Tighten the screws and check that the door closes smoothly and does not rattle.

23.1 Door catch

24 Door rubbing strip

1 The ends are held by plastic cap nuts which should be unscrewed to remove it (photo).
2 Locating pegs are used in the centre run of the strip.

25 Rear quarter trim panel (2-door) – removal and refitting

1 Remove the rear seat cushion and back, as described in Section 41.
2 Pull the panel clips out of their holes by inserting the fingers under the edge of the panel.
3 Slide the seat belt guide out of the panel and remove the panel (photo).
4 Refitting is a reversal of removal.

26 Rear quarter fixed window (2-door) – removal and refitting

1 Remove the rear quarter trim panel, as described in the preceding Section.
2 With an assistant restraining the glass from outside the car, lie inside and press the glass out with the feet. If the glass is broken, clean all glass crystals out of the car and from the rubber weatherseal channels.
3 Check that the rubber weatherseal is in good condition and refit the glass using the cord method described in Section 28.

24.1 Rubbing strip cap nut

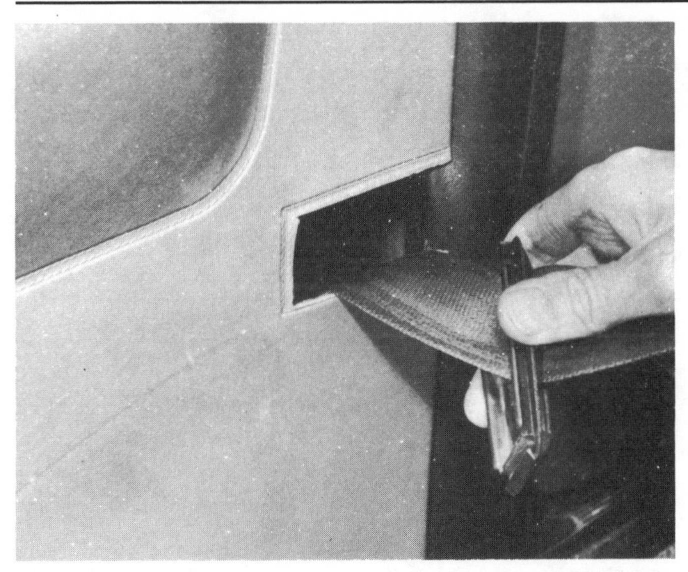

25.3 Trim panel seat belt guide

27 Door quarter light (4-door) – removal and refitting

1 Remove the interior trim panel from the rear door, as described in Section 25.
2 Peel away the waterproof sheet.
3 Pull off the interior weatherstrip.
4 Remove the exterior weatherstrip upwards from its clips using a wooden wedge, or similar.
5 Wind the window fully down and pull out the flexible glass channel.
6 Release the door lock remote control and allow it to hang down.
7 Unscrew the bolts (arrowed) – Fig. 12.21.
8 Disconnect the guide rail of the fixed glass from the top retainer.
9 Tilt the quarter light with frame out of the door frame and remove.
10 Refitting is a reversal of removal. Apply soapy water to the rubber channel to ease fitting.

28 Windscreen – removal and refitting

1 It is recommended that both these operations are left to professionals. Where the work is to be attempted, however, proceed in the following way.
2 Remove the wiper arms and the interior mirror.
3 Prise the bright trim from the rubber surround.
4 Run a blade round the lips of the rubber surround to ensure that it is not stuck to the body.

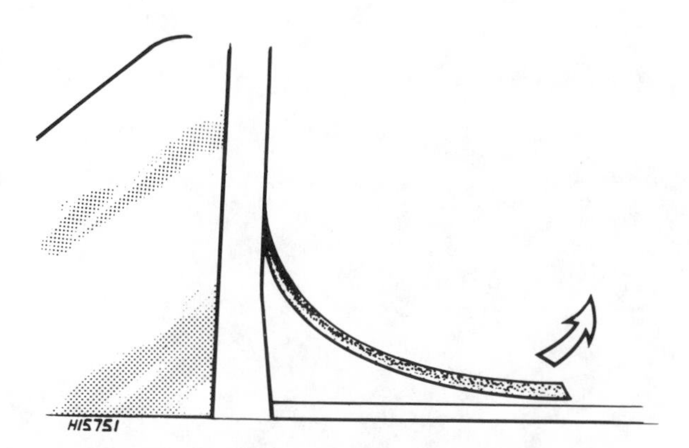

Fig. 12.20 Pulling out the flexible glass channel (Sec 27)

5 Have an assistant press one corner of the glass outwards while you pull the lip of the rubber over the body flange and restrain the glass from being ejected too violently. The pressure is best applied by sitting in the seats and wearing soft soled shoes, placing the feet on the glass.
6 Unless the rubber surround is in perfect condition, renew it. Apply black mastic or sealant to the glass channel in the rubber surround and fit the surround to the glass. With the windscreen it is recommended that the bright trim is inserted into the rubber at this stage but with the rear window it is best to fit it after the glass has been installed. The use of a tool will make the fitting of this trim easy.

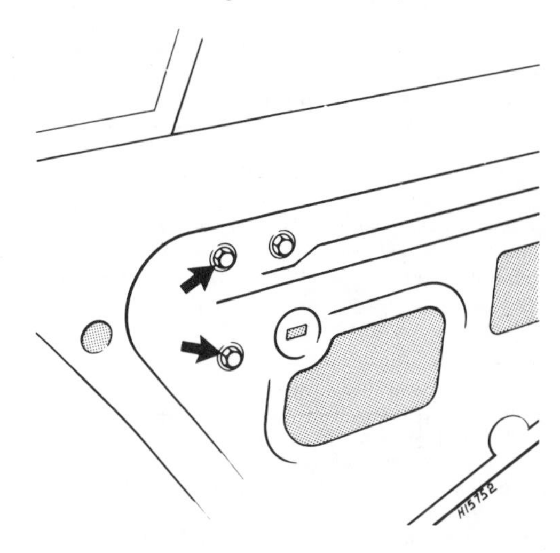

Fig. 12.21 Guide channel bolts – arrowed (Sec 27)

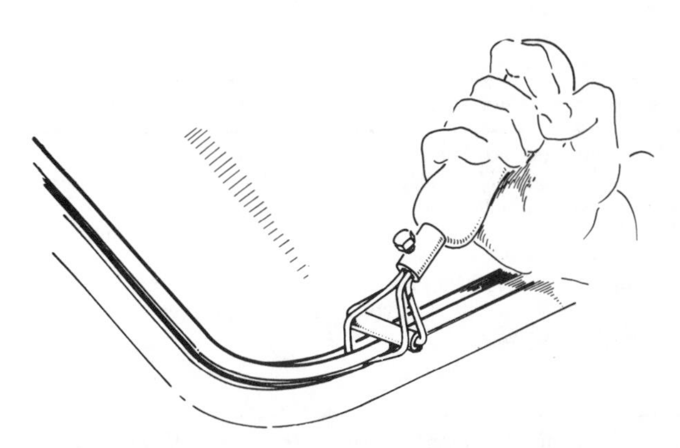

Fig. 12.22 Removing the windscreen trim (Sec 28)

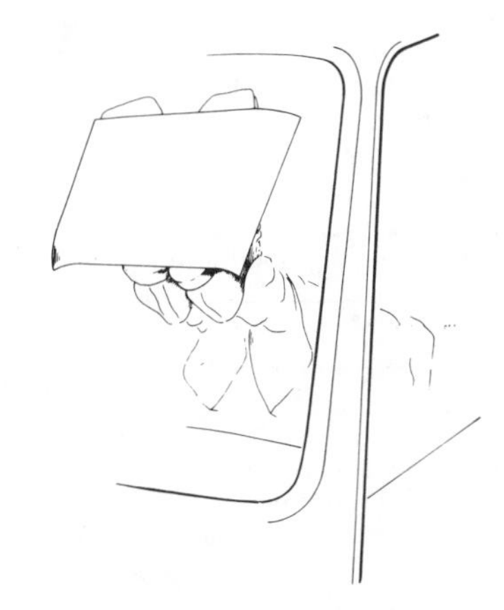

Fig. 12.23 Pushing out the windscreen (Sec 28)

7 Locate a length of cord in the rubber surround, in the groove which will engage with the body. Allow the ends of the cord to cross over and hang out of the groove at the bottom of the glass.
8 Offer up the glass and surround to the body aperture, engaging the bottom groove. Push the glass downwards and inwards and have your assistant pull the ends of the cords evenly which will have the effect of pulling the lip of the surround over the body flange.
9 If necessary the nozzle of a mastic gun can be inserted under the outer lip of the rubber surround and a bead of sealant supplied all round to make a positive seal. Clean off any sealant according to the manufacturer's instructions and then refit the wiper arms and interior mirror.

29 Rear window – removal and refitting

1 The operations are similar to those described in the preceding Section for the windscreen, except that the leads for the heating element must be disconnected.
2 The rear window glass is of toughened type as opposed to the laminated glass of the windscreen. If the reason for removal is because of breakage, make sure that all glass crystals are removed, particularly from the groove in the rubber weatherseal.

30 Boot lid – removal and refitting

1 Open the boot lid and mark the position of the hinges on its underside. Masking tape is useful for this (photo).
2 With the help of an assistant, support the lid and unscrew and remove the hinge bolts. Lift the lid away.
3 Refitting is a reversal of removal, but do not fully tighten the bolts until the lid has been gently closed and its alignment checked. Move the lid as necessary to achieve an even gap all round, then tighten the bolts. Adjust the striker and the rubber closure buffers as necessary to achieve smooth positive closure.

31 Boot lid lock and striker – removal, refitting and adjustment

1 Open the boot lid. The striker and lock are retained by bolts.
2 Once the lock is removed, the lock cylinder can be taken out by inserting a box spanner and unscrewing the ring nut.
3 Withdraw the cylinder, which should bear the same number as the door lock cylinder.
4 Refitting is a reversal of removal, but move the position of the lock and striker as necessary to achieve smooth positive closure before tightening the bolts.

32 Boot lid counterbalance spring – removal and refitting

1 Open the boot lid and release the spring ends from the slots in the mountings. Do this with care, using a cranked lever or large adjustable spanner, as there is considerable tension in the torsion rod. Have an assistant support the weight of the lid during the operation (photo).
2 Refitting is a reversal of removal, but make sure that the rods cross over each other.

33 Centre console – removal and refitting

Series 1
1 Extract the fixing screws from both sides of the console.
2 Remove the gear lever knob.
3 Remove the gaiter and console top cover.
4 Disconnect the radio leads.
5 Unscrew the nut and remove the retaining plate.
6 Disconnect the ashtray lamp lead and pull the console out rearwards.

Series 2
7 Release the trim panel under the facia.

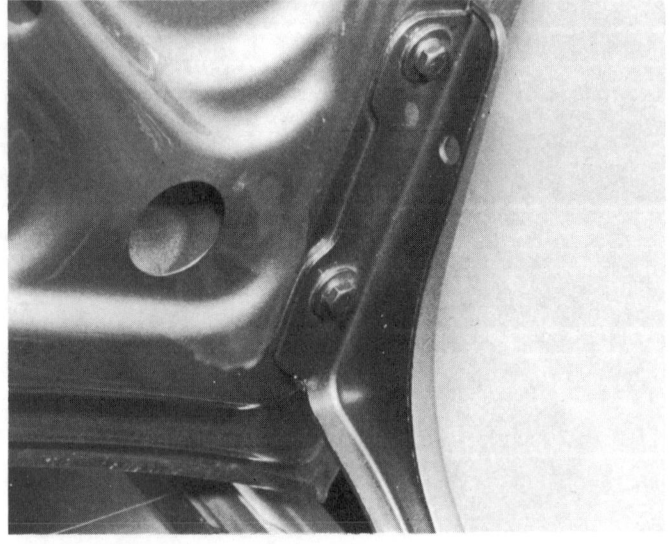

30.1 Boot lid hinge

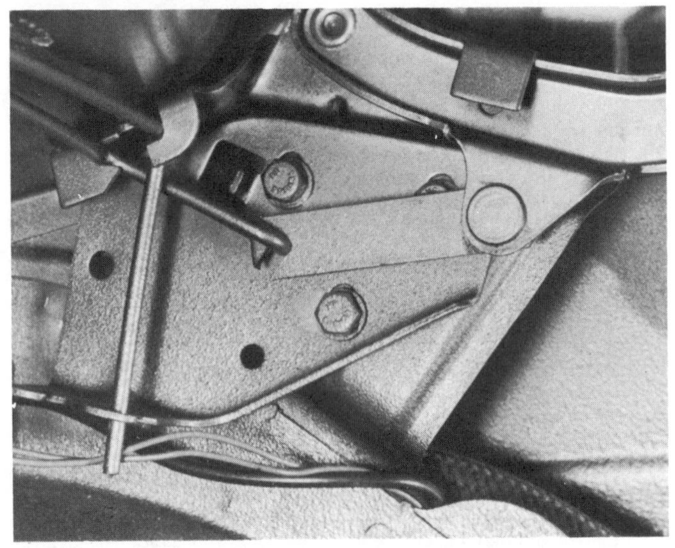

32.1 Boot lid torsion rods

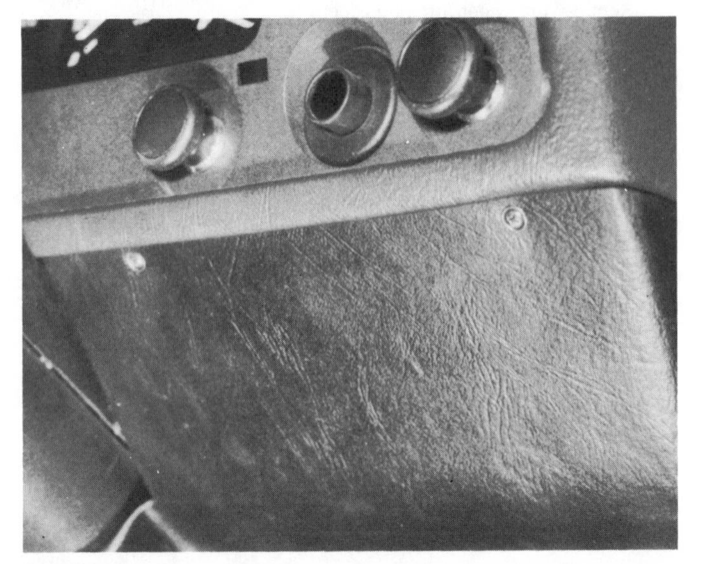

35.1 Facia under cover

8 Remove the ashtray and unscrew the nut exposed.
9 Pull the console rearwards and over the handbrake lever.

Manual transmission
10 Remove the gear lever knob and slide the gaiter off the lever.

Automatic transmission
11 Remove the cover plate at the control lever; unscrew the bolts now exposed.

All models (Series 2)
12 If power operated windows are fitted, lift out the control switch and disconnect the wiring plug.
13 Remove the insulation sheet and unscrew the nut.
14 Unscrew the screws and remove the ashtray housing.
15 Disconnect the ashtray lamp and leads for the cigar lighter.
16 Unscrew the screw from the upper front edge of the console.
17 Remove the retainers by turning them through 90°.
18 Pull the console out rearwards.

All models
19 Refitting is a reversal of removal.

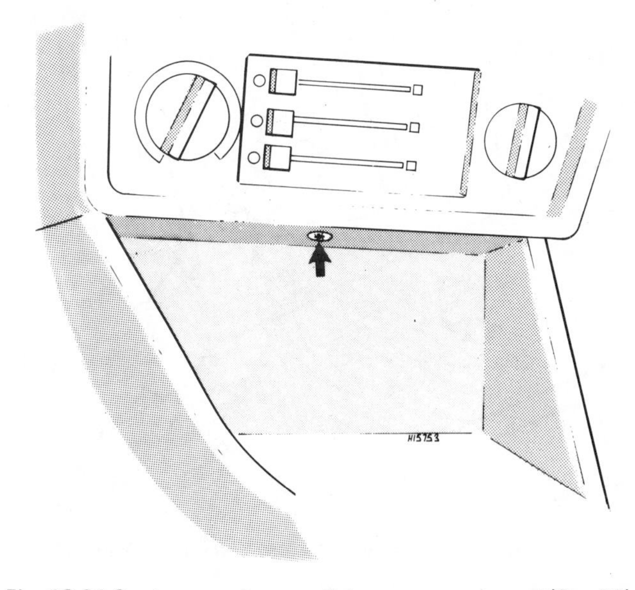

Fig. 12.24 Centre console upper fixing screw – arrowed (Sec 33)

34 Glovebox – removal and refitting

1 Open the lid and remove the hinge bolts.
2 Pinch the ends of the plastic rivets together and remove them. Withdraw the glovebox.
3 Disconnect the lamp wiring plug.
4 Refitting is a reversal of removal.

35 Facia under cover – removal and refitting

1 The covers are located under the length of the facia and are secured in sections by screws (photo).
2 On certain models, trim may have to be removed after disconnecting the glovebox pivots.

36 Facia panel (Series 1, up to 1980) – removal and refitting

1 Disconnect the battery negative lead and remove the centre console, as described in Section 33.
2 Remove the instrument panel, as described in Chapter 10.
3 Remove the under covers, as described in Section 35.
4 Pull off the heater control knobs and extract the switch panel screws.
5 Pull the switch panel forward and disconnect the wiring plugs.
6 Extract the control lever mounting screws.
7 Withdraw the pushbutton switches and disconnect their leads.
8 Unscrew the rheostat bezel nut without allowing the switch to turn and remove and disconnect the switch.
9 Disconnect the hazard warning switch wiring plug.
10 Pull out the indicator lamp bulb holders.
11 From the left-hand side of the facia unscrew the nut – Fig. 12.25.
12 From the right-hand side of the facia remove the screw (1) – Fig. 12.26.
13 Disconnect the glovebox hinge and lamp.
14 Unscrew the nuts at the angular support brackets.
15 Unscrew the nut from the extreme right-hand corner.
16 Release the left and right-hand toggle fasteners.
17 Pull one end of the facia panel outwards and remove it.
18 With the facia panel removed, the demisting ducts and outlets may be unbolted and removed, if required.
19 Refitting is a reversal of removal, but observe the following points.
20 Make sure that the heater ducts are connected to the demister outlets and all cables are clipped neatly in position.
21 Apply pressure to the facia before tightening the fixing nuts and screws.
22 Reconnect the battery.

Fig. 12.25 Facia left-hand fixing nut – arrowed (Secs 36 and 37)

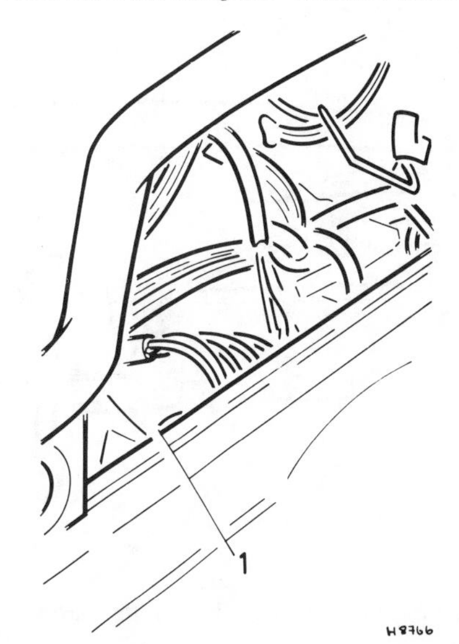

Fig. 12.26 Facia right-hand fixing screw (1) (Secs 36 and 37)

Fig. 12.27 Facia corner nut – arrowed (Secs 36 and 37)

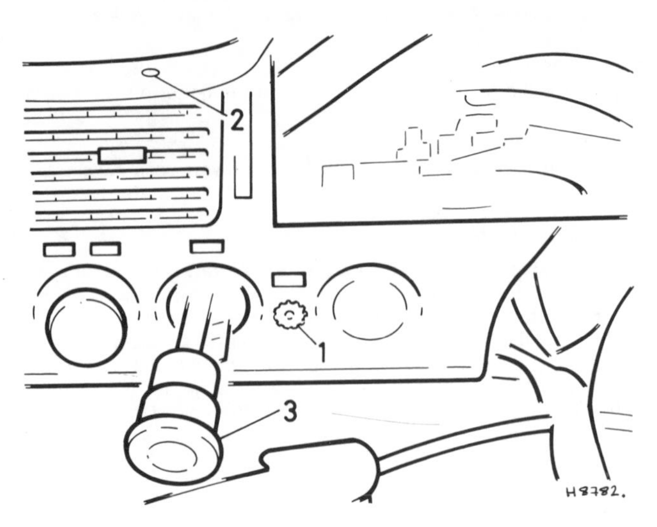

Fig. 12.30 Panel knurled nut (1) and screw (2) (Sec 37)

3 Demister switch

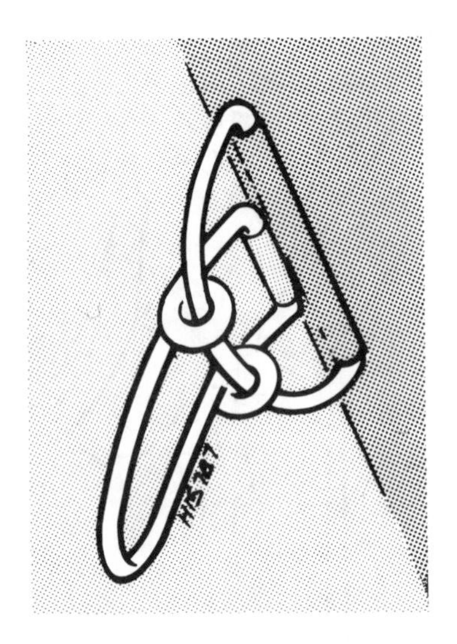

Fig. 12.28 Facia toggle clip (Secs 36 and 37)

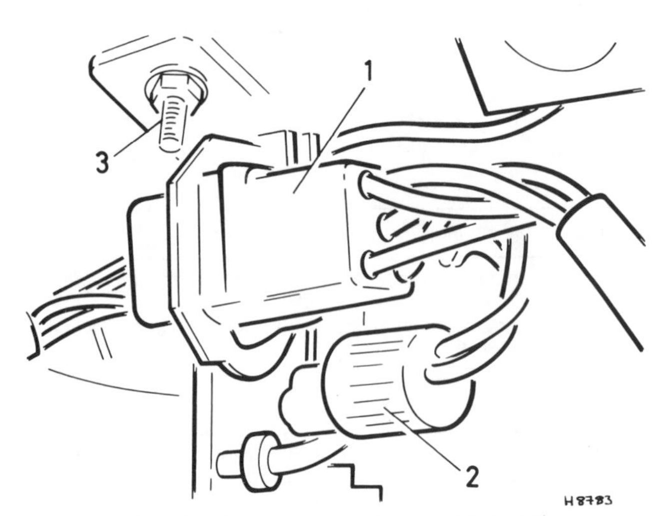

Fig. 12.31 Wiring plugs (1 and 2) (Sec 37)

3 Securing nut

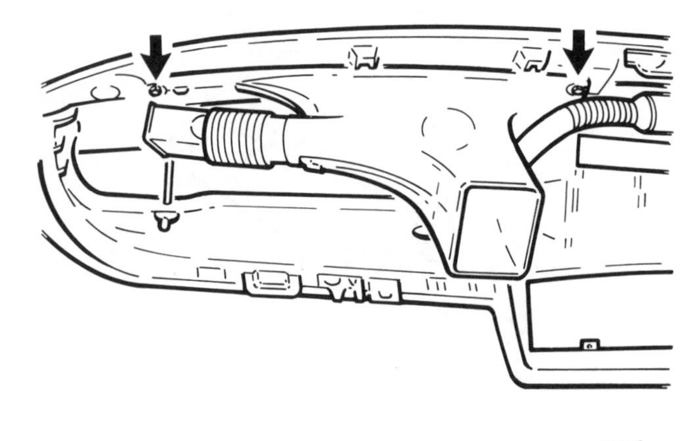

Fig. 12.29 Demister duct securing bolts – arrowed (Sec 36)

37 Facia panel (Series 1, 1980 on) – removal and refitting

1 This job should not be entertained lightly as it entails removing the windscreen.
2 Once this has been done, remove the centre console and instrument panel as described in Section 33.
3 Remove the instrument panel under cover. Disconnect the battery.
4 Pull off the heater control knobs and extract the switch panel screws.
5 Unscrew the knurled nut (1) – Fig. 12.30. Pull out the heated rear window switch and disconnect the wiring plug.
6 Remove the lighting switch, but do not disconnect the multi-plug.
7 Push out the digital clock control unit.
8 Pull out the switch plate and disconnect the wiring plugs.
9 Open the clips and release the wiring.
10 Tilt the heater control unit forward and disconnect the heater temperature (coolant valve) cable and lighting plugs.
11 Release the left- and right-hand toggle clips – see Fig. 12.28.
12 Disconnect the plugs (1 and 2) – Fig. 12.31 – and unscrew the nut (3).
13 Pull out the instrument panel bulb holders.
14 Disconnect the glovebox lamp.
15 Unscrew the nuts on the left-hand side of the panel (Fig. 12.25).

16 Unscrew the screw and nut on the right-hand side of the panel (Figs. 12.26 and 12.27).
17 Remove the facia directly upwards.
18 Refitting is a reversal of removal; make sure that the demister ducts are securely connected and all wiring is neatly clipped.

38 Facia panel (Series 2) – removal and refitting

1 Disconnect the battery negative lead.
2 Remove the steering wheel, as described in Chapter 11.
3 Remove the facia under cover (Section 35) and the lower section of the steering column shroud.
4 Remove the centre console (Section 33).
5 Remove the instrument panel (Chapter 10).
6 Disconnect the wiring plugs from the lighting switch.
7 Open the glovebox and unscrew the bolts arrowed – Fig. 12.32.
8 Disconnect the glovebox lamp and take off the trim.
9 Pull out the pins from the glovebox lid check straps.
10 Unscrew the bolt (2) – Fig. 12.33 – and remove the trim (1).
11 Remove the retaining clips (1) – Fig. 12.34 – and push the headlamp socket out of the glovebox.
12 Loosen the glovebox hinge bolts and remove the glovebox.
13 Remove the radio (Chapter 10).
14 Remove and disconnect the switches from their panel.
15 Unscrew the heater control lever panel mounting screws and withdraw the panel until all cables and wires can be disconnected.
16 Unscrew all the bolts shown in Figs. 12.35 to 12.39 which secure the facia.
17 Working at the windscreen pillars, pull off the channel edging and withdraw the pillar casings upwards.
18 Open the wiring clips and withdraw the wiring harnesses from under the facia into the footwell.
19 Remove the ignition switch bezel.
20 Remove the steering column shroud upper section.
21 Remove the combination switch control lever screws and levers; according to the equipment fitted.
22 Withdraw the facia panel.
23 Refitting is a reversal of removal, but make sure that the demister ducts are securely connected and all wiring neatly taped into position.

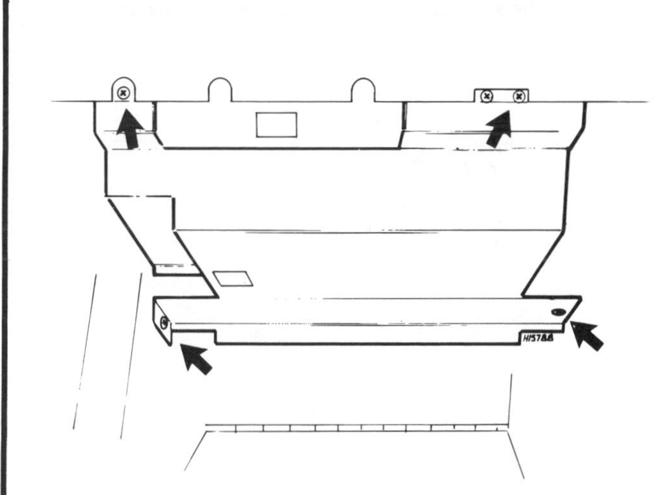

Fig. 12.32 Glovebox bolts – arrowed (Sec 38)

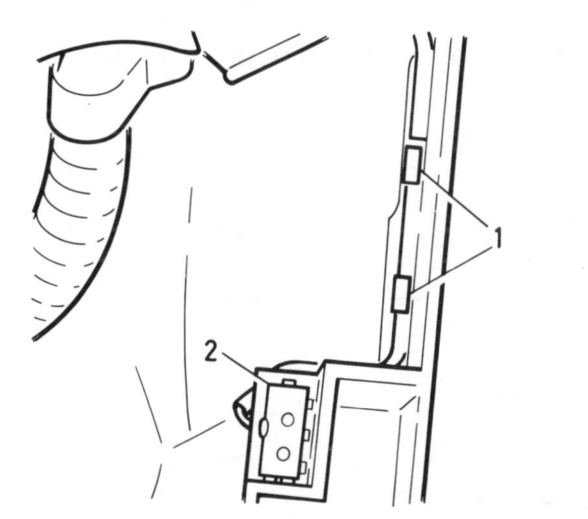

Fig. 12.34 Retaining clips (1) and handlamp socket (2) (Sec 38)

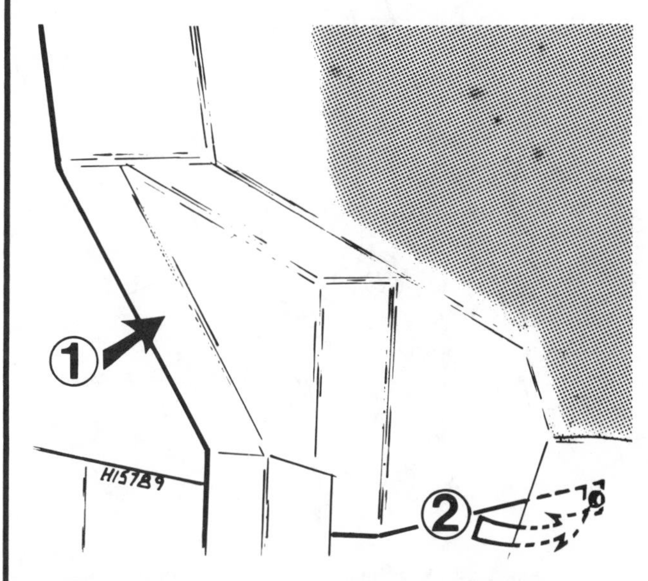

Fig. 12.33 Facia trim (1) and fixing bolt (2) (Sec 38)

Fig. 12.35 Facia end bracket bolts – arrowed (Sec 38)

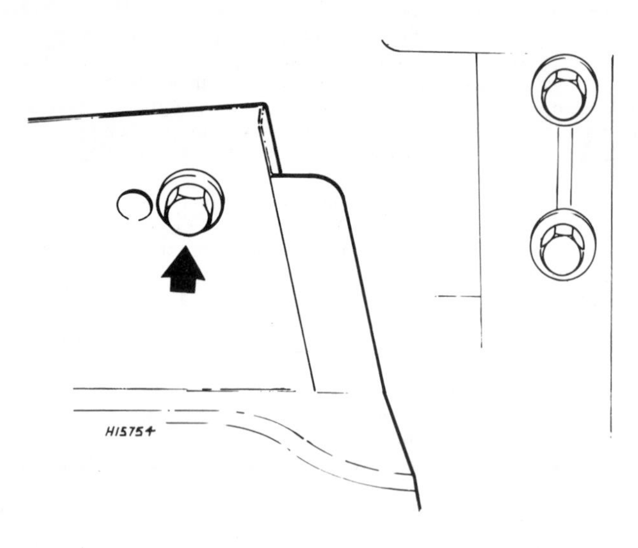

Fig. 12.36 Facia centre bolt – arrowed (Sec 38)

Fig. 12.37 Facia edge screws – arrowed (Sec 38)

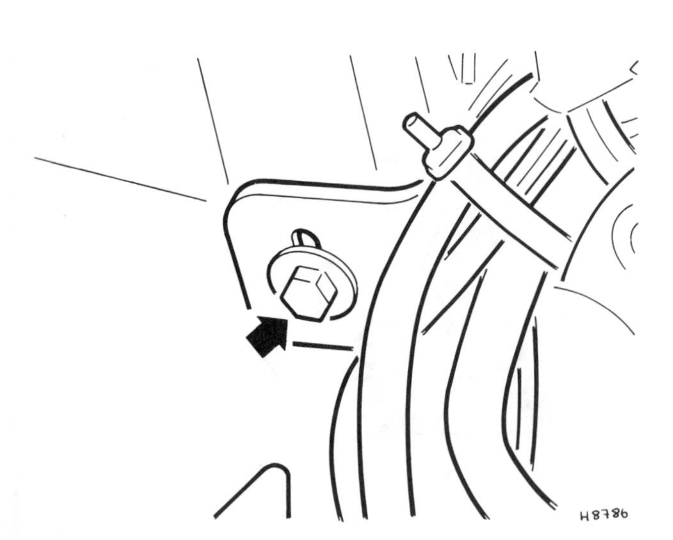

Fig. 12.38 Facia angle bracket bolt – arrowed (Sec 38)

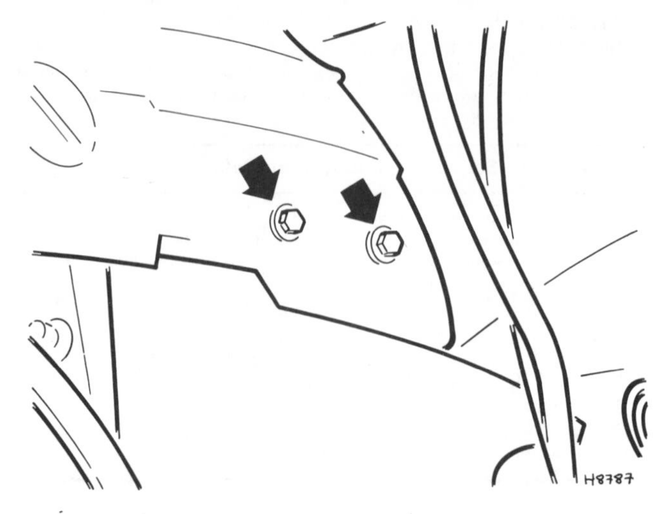

Fig. 12.39 Facia upper mounting bolts – arrowed (Sec 38)

39 Front seats – removal and refitting

Series 1, up to 1980

1 Push the seat fully forward and unscrew the bolt from the rear end of the seat runner (photo).
2 Push the seat fully to the rear and remove the front bolt.
3 Lift the seat out of the car.
4 Refitting is a reversal of removal, but slide the seat fully back and forth in its runners before fully tightening the bolts.
5 If necessary, the seat catch may be adjusted after releasing the fixing bolts.
6 On two-door models the seat back locking mechanism is accessible after extracting the screws and pulling the rear panel downwards.
7 Release the locknuts (1) – Fig. 12.40 – and turn the sleeves to adjust the cables evenly.

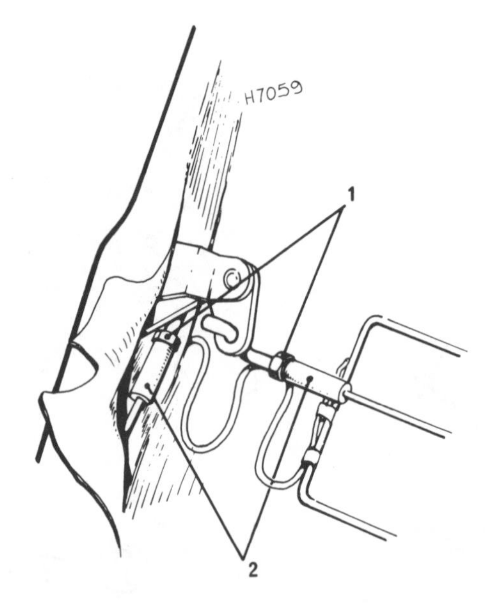

Fig. 12.40 Seat back locking cable (Sec 39)

1 Locknuts *2 Adjusting sleeves*

Series 1, 1980 on

8 The seat removal operations are similar to those just described, but the left and right-hand seat rails are removable after unscrewing the bolts (arrowed) – Fig. 12.41.

Series 2 (two-door)

9 Slide the seat fully rearwards, pull off the plastic caps and unscrew the nuts (1) – Fig. 12.42.

10 Repeat on the rear nuts with the seat pushed fully forward.

Series 2 (four-door)

11 Pull off the plastic caps and unscrew the seat belt bolt; otherwise the seat removal is as for two-door models.

All series 2 models

12 The seat rails on Series 2 models can be removed by compressing the springs and pulling out the pins. Unscrew the bolt (arrowed) – Fig. 12.44.

13 Disconnect the link rod, pull the connecting tube from the square hole in the control lever using a screwdriver.

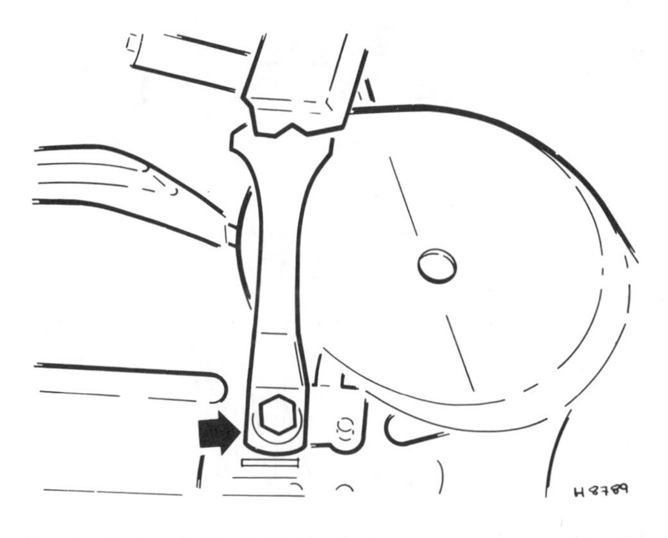

Fig. 12.43 Seat belt bolt (Series 2, four-door) – arrowed (Sec 39)

Fig. 12.41 Front seat rail bolts (Series 1, 1980 on) – arrowed (Sec 39)

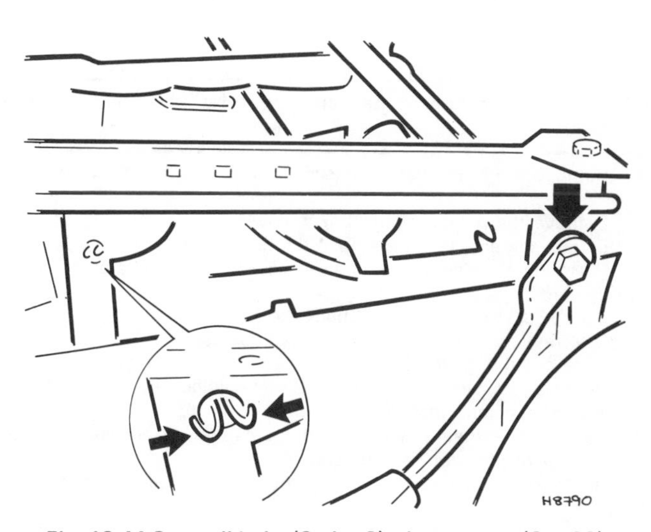

Fig. 12.44 Seat rail bolts (Series 2) – large arrow (Sec 39)

Small arrows indicate the springs

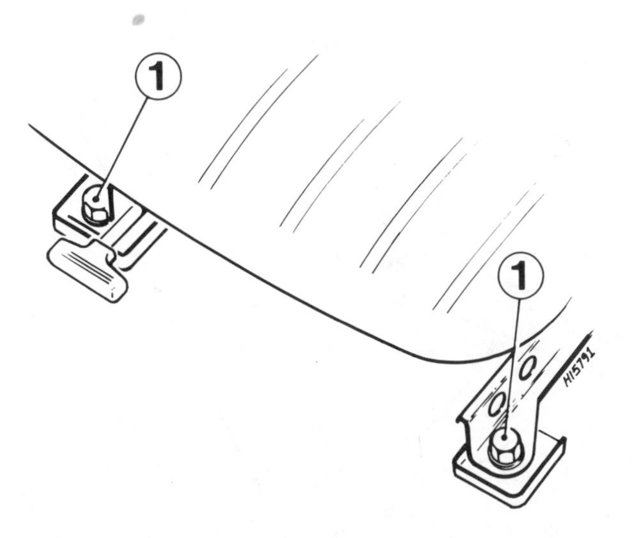

Fig. 12.42 Seat runner nuts (Series 2) (1) (Sec 39)

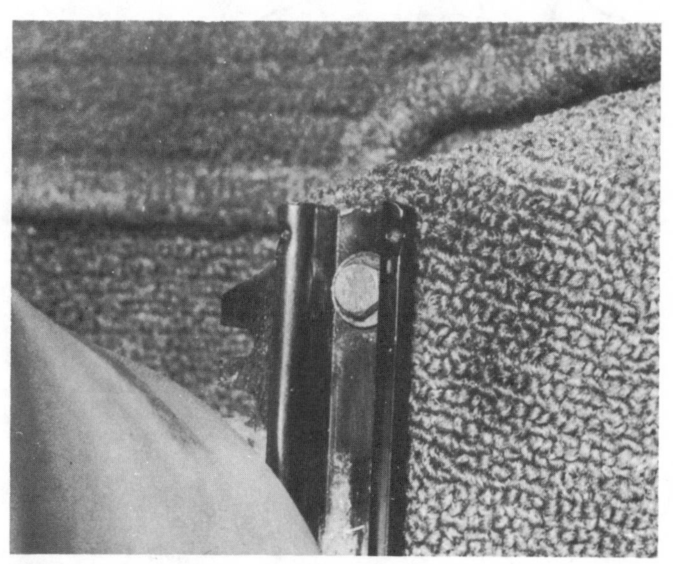

39.1 Front seat rail bolt

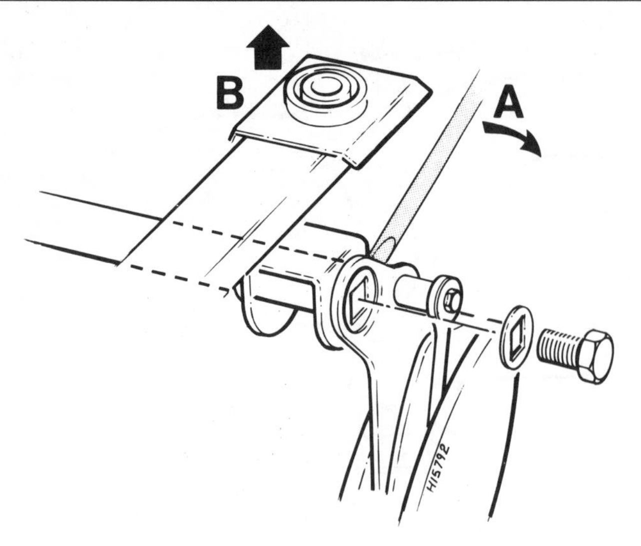

Fig. 12.45 Seat connecting tube disconnection (Sec 39)

A Lever control lever away from the connecting tube
B Release the connecting tube

40 Front seat reclining mechanism (Series 2) – removal and refitting

1 Remove the front seat, as described in Section 39, also the seat rails.
2 Remove the reclining mechanism covers.
3 Extract the screws and remove the back panels.
4 Disconnect the seat back lock cables. Press the cable guides from the holders.
5 Extract the screw and peel back the seat cover.
6 Unscrew the bolts and remove the backrest.
7 Prise out the lever – Fig. 12.48 – with a screwdriver.
8 Remove the circlip (1) – Fig. 12.49 – unlock the backrest and remove the reclining mechanism.
9 Remove the retainer and then compress the gas-pressurised strut until the pivot pins can be removed.
10 Refitting is a reversal of removal, the lever tab must engage in the lever.

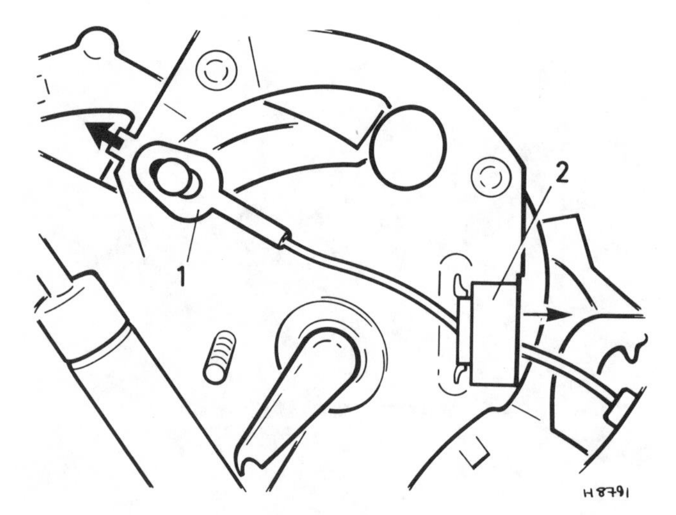

Fig. 12.46 Seat back lock cables (Series 2) (Sec 40)

1 Lock cables *2 Cable guides*

Arrows indicate movement required for disconnection

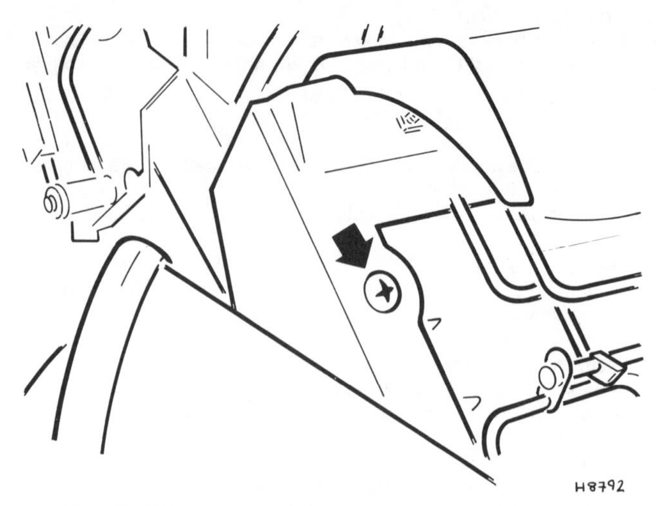

Fig. 12.47 Seat cover fixing screw – arrowed (Sec 40)

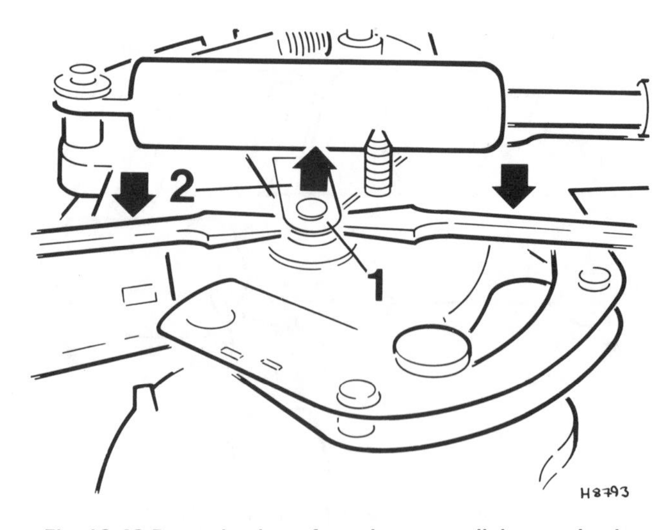

Fig. 12.48 Removing lever from the seat reclining mechanism (Sec 40)

1 Lever tab *2 Lever*

Arrows show movement of screwdrivers

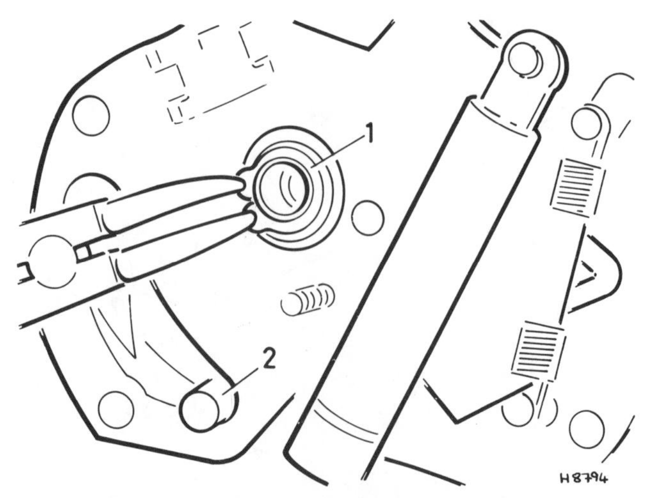

Fig. 12.49 Removing circlip from the reclining mechanism (Sec 40)

1 Circlip *2 Backrest lever*

41 Rear seat – removal and refitting

1 Prise off the plastic covers and then unscrew the two bolts from just below the lower edge of the seat cushion (photo). Lift out the cushion.
2 Unscrew the bolts from the base of the seat back and lift the back upwards off the retaining hooks (photo).
3 Refitting is a reversal of removal.

42 Interior rear view mirror – removal and refitting

1 Hold the mirror and pull it rearwards. The stem will break away from the base.
2 The base can be removed after extracting the fixing screws.

43 Exterior rear view mirror – removal and refitting

Series 1

1 Early models have the mirror held to the base by a screw accessible from outside.
2 Later models are secured by a bolt exposed when the triangular corner trim plate is removed (photo).
3 The switch for the electrically-operated mirror is a press fit in the door interior trim panel.

Series 2

4 The mirror control switch is located in the door armrest.

All models

5 The driver's side switch also operates the mirror on the passenger door subject to moving the left/right rocker switch incorporated in the switch panel.
6 The mirror wiring harness is routed through the flexible duct which runs between the leading edge of the door and the body A-pillar.
7 An optional heated exterior mirror is available.

44 Grab handles

1 Prise off the covers at the ends of the handles to expose the fixing screws (photo).
2 Remove the screws.
3 Refitting is a reversal of removal.

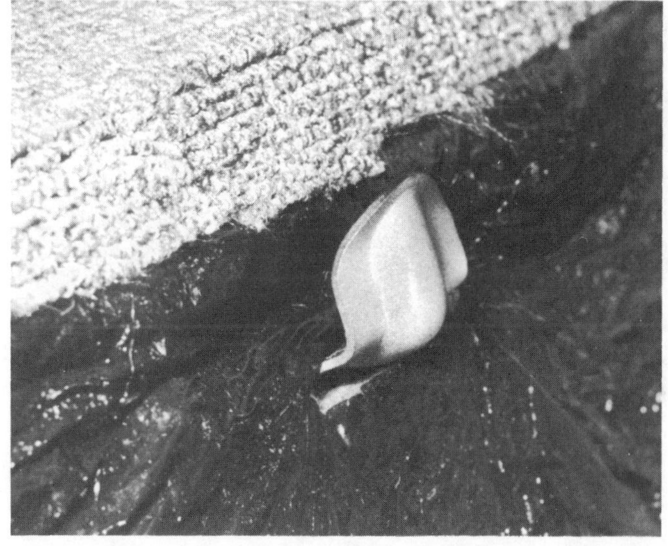

41.2 Seat back retaining hook

43.2 Mirror mounting trim plate

41.1 Unscrewing rear seat cushion bolt

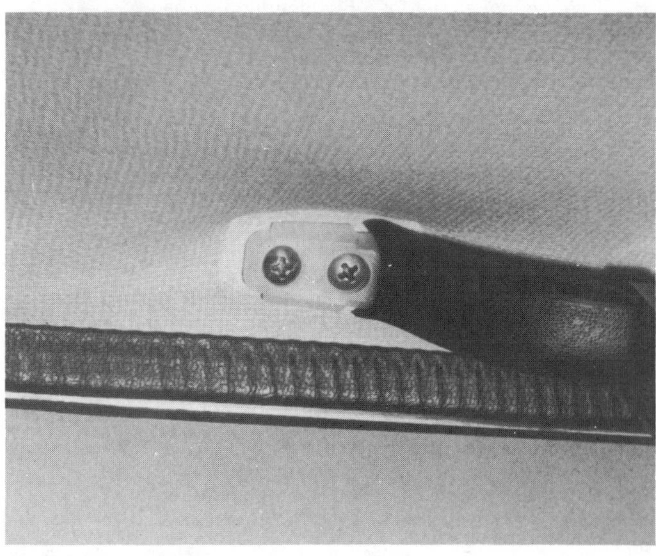

44.1 Grab handle screws

45.4 Unscrewing seat belt reel bolt (2-door)

45.5 Rear belt reel (2-door)

45 Seat belts

1 Front and rear seat belts are fitted to all models. Inspect the belts regularly for fraying or other damage and renew if evident.
2 To clean a belt, use a damp cloth and household detergent, **never** solvents.
3 Never alter the anchorage points of a belt and always maintain the original fitted sequence of the components (bolt, washers, spacers and anchor plate).
4 On two-door models, the front seat belt reels are located behind the quarter trim panels. To remove a reel, unscrew the bolt (photo), push the reel towards the outside of the car and then downwards to release the belt guard top lip.
5 The rear seat belt reels are located under small covers behind the seat back (photo).

46 Sunroof (Series 1) – dismantling, reassembly, adjustment

1 The sunroof has two functions, to lift and to slide.

Lid – removal and refitting

2 Open the roof fully and remove the left and right upper guide rails.
3 Close the roof except for a 50.0 mm (2.0 in) gap.
4 Press off the roof liner frame at the front end and push it back.
5 Close the roof completely.
6 Unscrew the left-hand and right-hand nuts and remove the sunroof lid.
7 When refitting, observe the following points.
8 When lowering the lid into position, attach the rear end to the holder and push back the holder by pressing on the gearbox.
9 Lubricate the guide rails with petroleum jelly. Use sealing strip at the front corners.

Liner frame – removal and refitting

10 With the lid removed, as previously described, pull the roof liner frame forward and disconnect the linkage at both water drains.
11 Drill out the liner frame rivets and transfer the clips to the new frame.

Gearbox – removal and refitting

12 Open the sunroof lid and remove the front cover strip.
13 Partially detach the roof liner at the centre.
14 Close the roof, but not as far as the lift position.
15 Remove the escutcheon, extract the screws and remove the winder handle.
16 Remove the winder recess plate.
17 Extract the screws and remove the gearbox.

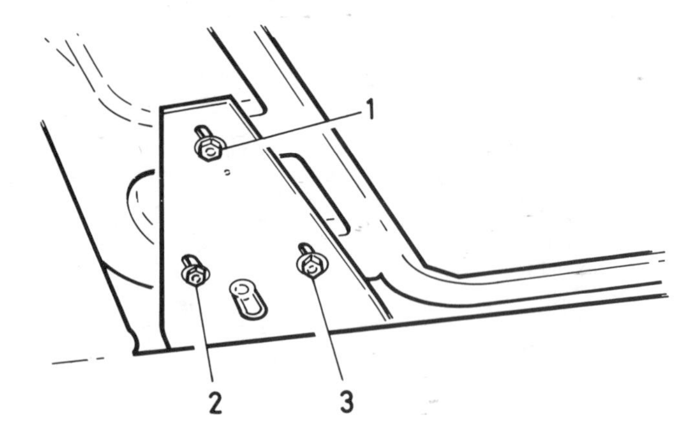

Fig. 12.50 Sunroof lid nuts (1, 2 and 3) (Sec 46)

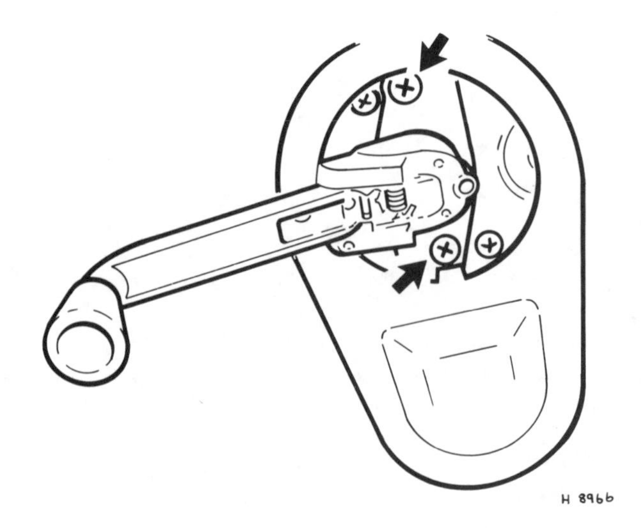

Fig. 12.51 Sunroof winder securing screws – arrowed (Sec 46)

18 Observe the following points when refitting.
19 The step (A) – Fig. 12.52 – in the winder holder must face to the left.
20 Set the gearbox to the off position (turn clockwise) before installing the gearbox.
21 Place sealing strip under the cover strip and apply adhesive to the roof liner.

Drive cables – renewal

22 Remove the lid and gearbox, as previously described.
23 Push both guides forward and remove upwards.
24 Withdraw the cables from the guide tube.
25 Pull off the circlip (1) – Fig. 12.53 – and remove the gate holder (2).
26 Observe the following points when refitting.
27 Lightly smear the gate holder with grease.
28 Tighten the gearbox screws with the gearbox in the off position.
29 Set the dimension A – Fig. 12.54 – to 2.0 mm (0.080 in) between the mark and the rear edge of the guide.
30 Lightly smear the guide and cables with grease.

Adjustment

31 Adjustment can be carried out after opening the sunroof by about 50.0 mm (2.0 in) and pressing off the liner frame at the front and pushing it back slightly.
32 Ideally, the front of the sunroof lid should be 1.0 mm (0.040 in) lower than the surrounding roof panel.
33 Release the screws (1) – Fig. 12.55 – and adjust the height with screw (2). Tighten the screw while applying pressure to the lid.
34 To adjust the height at the rear, release the gate holder screws and adjust the lid within its slots. Ideally, the rear of the lid should be 1.0 mm (0.040 in) above the surrounding roof panel.

Lift adjustment

35 Centralise the left-hand and right-hand guide pins (1) – Fig. 12.56 – in their slots.
36 Set the dimension A to 2.0 mm (0.080 in).

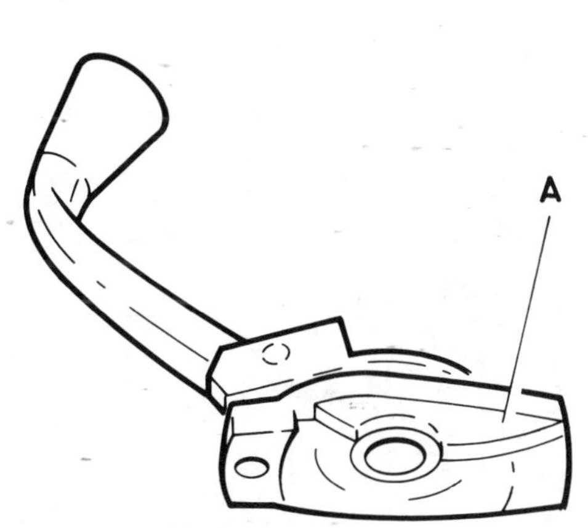

Fig. 12.52 Sunroof winder – Series 1 (Sec 46)

Step (A) to be to the left

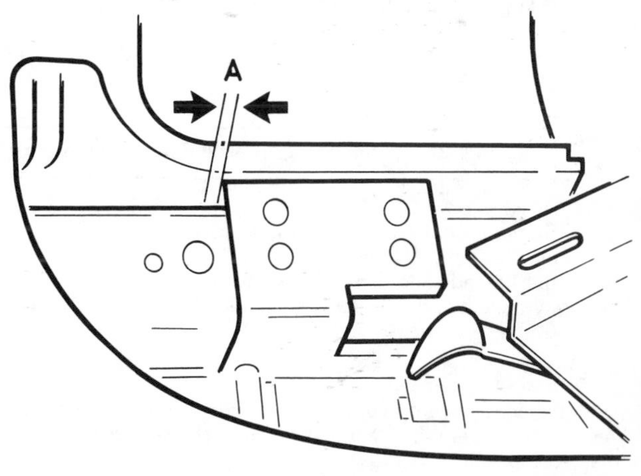

Fig. 12.54 Sunroof guide setting diagram (Sec 46)

A = 2.0 mm (0.080 in)

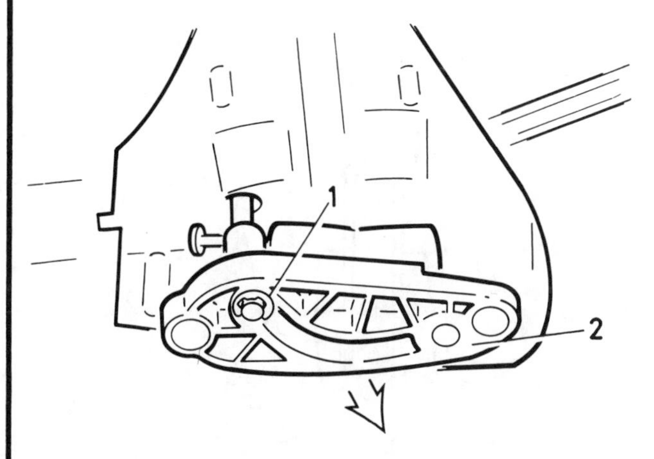

Fig. 12.53 Sunroof drive cable renewal (Sec 46)

1 Circlip
2 Gate holder
Remove gate holder in direction indicated

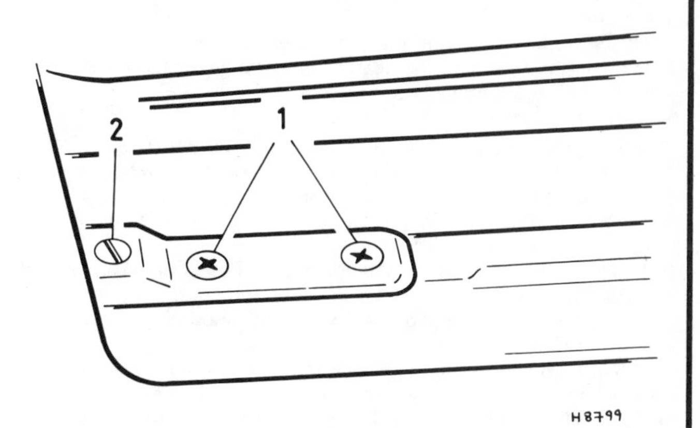

Fig. 12.55 Sunroof adjustment (Sec 46)

1 Clamp screws
2 Height setting screw

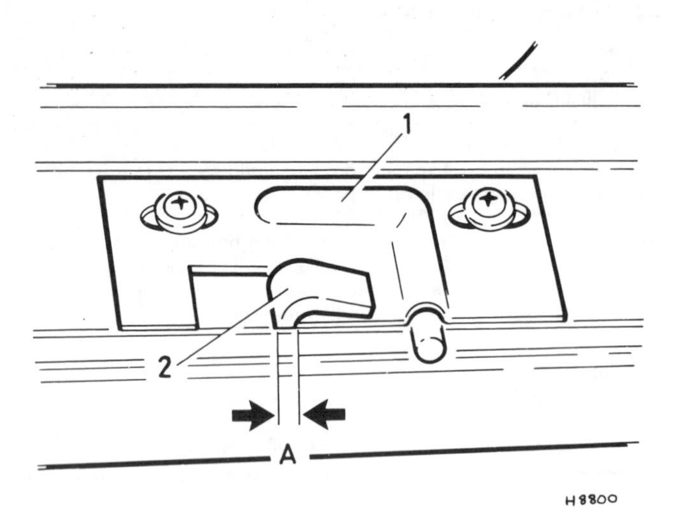

Fig. 12.56 Sunroof lift adjustment (Sec 46)

1 Guide pin
2 Deflector plate
A = 2.0 mm (0.080 in)

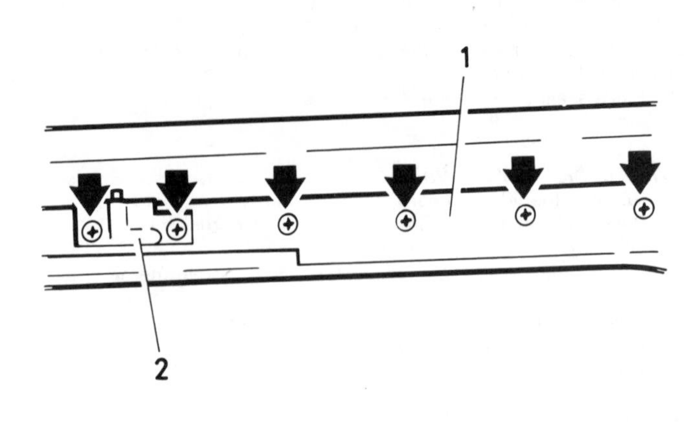

Fig. 12.57 Sunroof cover rail screws – arrowed (Sec 47)

1 Cover rail *2 Guide pin*

47 Sunroof (Series 2) – dismantling, reassembly, adjustment

Lid – removal and refitting

1 Close the lid except for 50.0 mm (2.0 in).
2 Press off the front roof liner frame.
3 Close the lid and slide back the roof liner.
4 Unscrew the left and right-hand bolts and lift off the lid. Adjust the lid after refitting.

Liner frame – removal and refitting

5 With the lid removed, as previously described, unscrew the screws and remove the cover rails (1) and guide pins (2) – Fig. 12.57. The pins are marked L and R.
6 Pull the cables from the guides, pull the liner frame forward and remove it. If necessary, drill out the connecting rod rivets. Refitting is a reversal of removal.

Gearbox (manual) – removal and refitting

7 Remove the clamping strip.
8 Peel away the trim carefully and remove the screws from both sides.
9 Close the roof, remove the escutcheon, winder handle and the winder recess plate.
10 Remove the sun visors with their holders and partially pull off the edge guard.
11 Unscrew the fixing bolt and remove the gearbox.
12 When refitting ensure the gearbox is in the off position. The larger section (A) on the handle must face the rear – Fig. 12.59.

Gearbox (electrically-operated) – removal and refitting

13 Remove the clamping strip and carefully peel away the trim. Remove the left and right-hand screws.
14 Remove the control switch, the sun visors and their holders and then pull off the edge guard.
15 Close the sunroof, by loosening the nut (1) – Fig. 12.60 – and turning the driveshaft (2) by means of an Allen key.
16 Disconnect the wiring plugs, extract the mounting screws and remove the motor/gearbox.
17 When refitting, grease the pinion and gear teeth and set the mark on the switching gear (1) opposite the mark on the control gear (2) – Fig. 12.61. Do this by turning the driveshaft with an Allen key.

Drive cables – renewal

18 Remove the lid and winder recess plate, as previously described.
19 Release the screw (arrowed) – Fig. 12.58.
20 Remove the screws from both sides and remove the cover rails and guide pins. The guide pins are marked L and R.

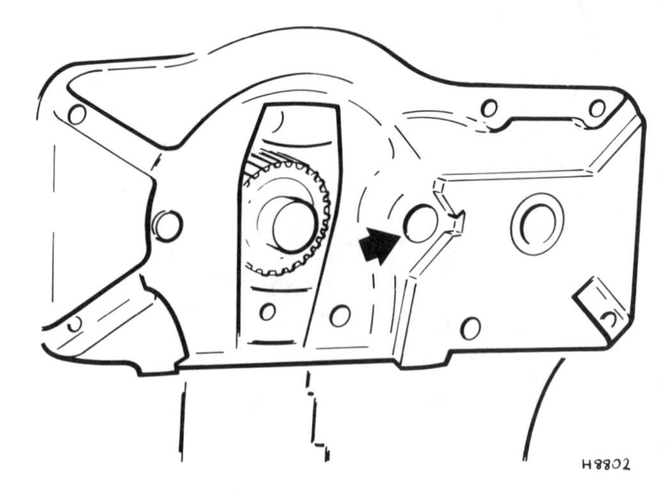

Fig. 12.58 Sunroof gearbox fixing bolt – arrowed (Sec 47)

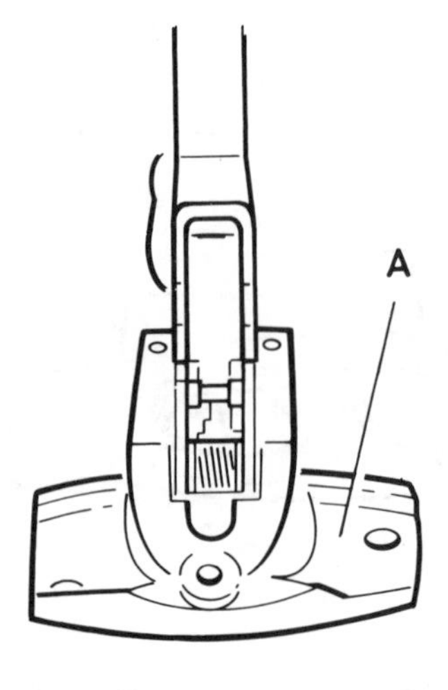

Fig. 12.59 Sunroof winder – Series 2 (Sec 47)

Larger section (A) to be to the rear

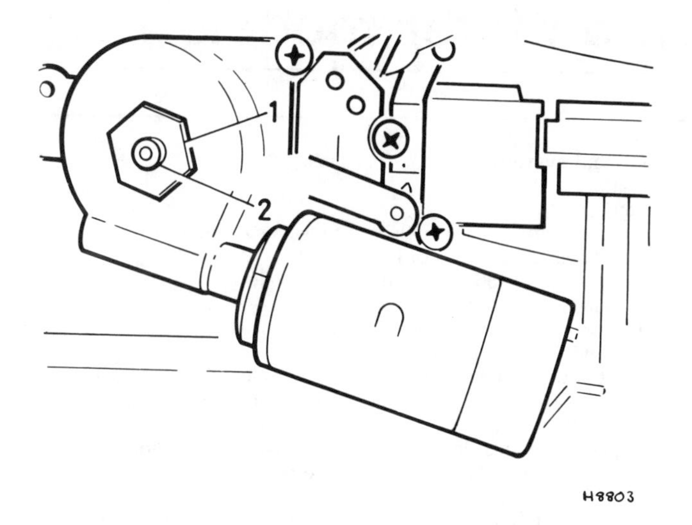

Fig. 12.60 Sunroof gearbox (electrically-operated) (Sec 47)

1 Nut 2 Driveshaft

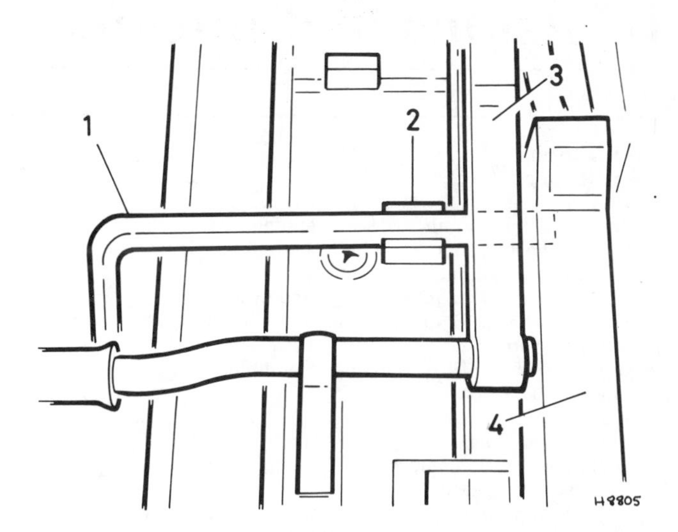

Fig. 12.62 Sunroof guide pin and holder alignment (Sec 47)

1 Allen key 3 Operating lever
2 Guide pin holder 4 Gate

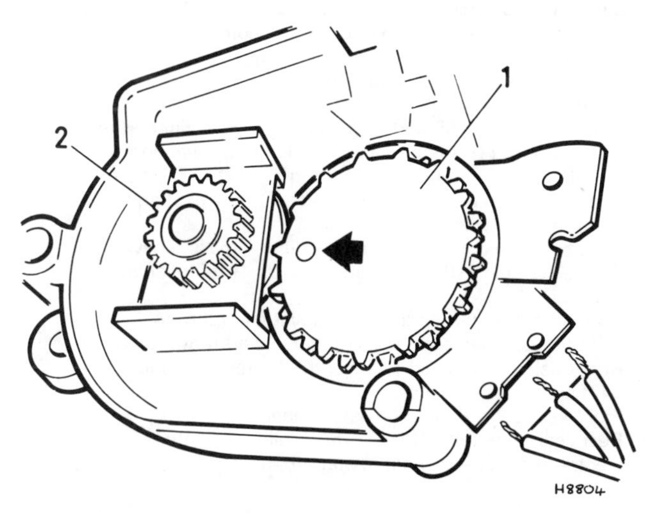

Fig. 12.61 Sunroof gearbox (electrically-operated) alignment marks (Sec 47)

1 Switching gear 2 Control gear

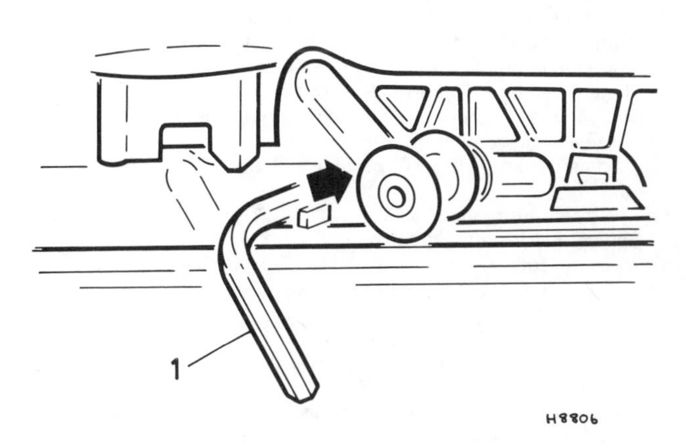

Fig. 12.63 Using an Allen key (1) to lock the sunroof (Sec 47)

21 Pull the cables from the guide tubes. It may be necessary to loosen the gearbox mounting screws to free the cables.
22 Press the gate off the drive cables.
23 Refitting is a reversal of removal, but use an Allen key (1) in guide pin holder (2) – Fig. 12.62 – on both sides and insert it into the holes of the operating lever (3) and gate (4). Grease the cables, slide and gate.

Adjustment

24 The sunroof lid should be adjusted so that at the front it is 1.0 mm (0.040 in) below the surrounding roof panel and at the rear the same distance above the roof panel. The gaps at front and rear edges must be equal.
25 To adjust, open the lid 50.0 mm (2.0 in), press off the front liner frame, close the lid and slide back the liner frame completely.
26 Insert an Allen key and lock both sides of the sunroof.
27 Now place the Allen key in the guide pin holder and push it through into the operating lever and gate – Fig. 12.62.
28 Release the screws (1, 2 and 3) – Fig. 12.64 – on both sides and adjust the lid height by moving it within its slots. Renew the Torx type self-locking screws on completion.

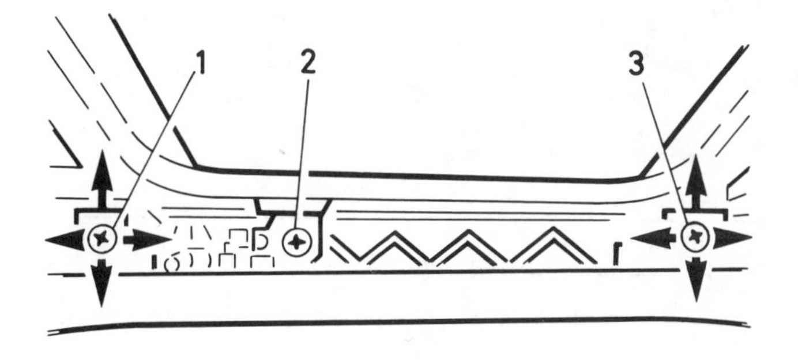

Fig. 12.64 Sunroof self-locking adjustment screws (Sec 47)

1 Torx screw 3 Torx screw
2 Torx screw

Chapter 13 Supplement
Revisions and information on later models

Contents

1 Introduction

This Supplement contains information which is additional to, or a revision of, material in the first twelve Chapters.

Most of the material relates to 1984 and later models, and includes major changes such as the engine management system.

The Sections in the Supplement follow the same order as the Chapters to which they relate.

It is recommended that before any particular operation is undertaken, reference is made to the appropriate Section(s) of the Supplement. In this way, any changes to procedure or components can be noted before referring to the main Chapters of the Manual.

Project vehicle

The vehicle used in the preparation of this Supplement, and appearing in many of the photographic sequences, was a 1987 model BMW 325i Saloon.

2 Specifications

The Specifications below are supplementrary to, or revisions of, those at the beginning of the preceding Chapters

Engine (2494 cc)

General

Engine type	Six-cylinder in-line, ohc, with Motronic engine management system
Bore	84.0 mm (3.31 in)
Stroke	75.0 mm (2.96 in)
Capacity	2494 cc (152.1 cu in)
Compression ratio	9.7:1
Power output	126 kW (171 bhp) at 5800 rpm
Maximum torque	226 Nm (167 lbf ft) at 4000 rpm

Cylinder block

Bore size:	
Standard	84.00 to 84.01 mm (3.3096 to 3.3100 in)
First rebore	84.25 to 84.26 mm (3.3195 to 3.3198 in)
Second rebore	84.50 to 84.51 mm (3.3293 to 3.3297 in)
Maximum out-of-round	0.03 mm (0.0012 in)
Maximum taper	0.02 mm (0.0008 in)

Pistons and rings

Piston diameter:	
Standard	83.98 mm (3.3088 in)
Oversizes	0.25, 0.50 mm (0.010, 0.020 in)
Top compression ring:	
End gap	0.20 to 0.50 mm (0.0079 to 0.0197 in)
Groove clearance	0.04 to 0.08 mm (0.0016 to 0.0032 in)
Second compression ring:	
End gap	0.20 to 0.50 mm (0.0079 to 0.0197 in)
Groove clearance	0.03 to 0.07 mm (0.0012 to 0.0028 in)
Oil control ring:	
End gap	0.20 to 0.50 mm (0.0079 to 0.0197 in)
Groove clearance	0.02 to 0.05 mm (0.0008 to 0.0020 in)

Cylinder head

Minimum depth after resurfacing	124.7 mm (4.913 in)
Valve guide bore in head:	
Standard	13.2 mm (0.520 in)
Oversizes	13.3, 13.4 mm (0.524, 0.528 in)
Valve guide protrusion	14.5 mm (0.57 in)
Valve guide installation temperatures:	
Cylinder head	50°C (122°F)
Valve guide	−150°C (−238°F)

Valves

Head diameter:	
Inlet	42.0 mm (1.65 in)
Exhaust	36.0 mm (1.42 in)
Stem diameter:	
Standard	7.0 mm (0.276 in)
Oversizes	7.1, 7.2 mm (0.280, 0.284 in)

Torque wrench settings

	Nm	lbf ft
Distributor adaptor to camshaft	60	44
Oil cooler pipe unions	35	26
Throttle housing/inlet manifold to cylinder head	32	24

Fuel system

General

Type	Bosch Motronic
Application	325i, 1985 on

Data

Idle speed (not adjustable)	720 to 800 rpm
CO content	0.5 to 1.5%
Fuel pressure	2.5 bar (36 lbf/in²)
Fuel delivery	1.7 litres (3.0 pints) per minute

Torque wrench setting

	Nm	lbf ft
Fuel injector	11	8

Ignition system

Ignition timing – E30 (Series 2) models

Model	Approx date	Distributor No	°BTDC @ rpm
320	To 2/83	0 237 302 037	22 @ 3000 ± 50
	2/83 to 9/84	0 237 302 039	23 @ 5000 ± 50
	9/84 on	0 237 304 024	23 @ 5000 ± 50
323	To 3/83	0 237 302 038	19 @ 3000 ± 50
	3/83 to 9/84	0 237 302 040	16 @ 5000 ± 50
	9/84 on	0 237 304 025	16 @ 5000 ± 50
325	All	Not applicable	9 ± 3 at idle*

**Motronic system – timing not adjustable*

Spark plugs

320i	Bosch W8DC, Beru 14-8 DU, Champion N9YC
323i	Bosch W8DC, Beru R533, Champion N9YC
325i	Bosch W7DCR, Beru 14-7 DUR, Champion RN7YC
Electrode gap	0.7 to 0.8 mm (0.028 to 0.032 in)

Manual gearbox

General

Gearbox type	Getrag 260
Application	323i, 325i (late 1982 on)

Ratios

1st	3.83:1
2nd	2.20:1
3rd	1.40:1
4th	1.00:1
5th	0.81:1
Reverse	3.46:1
Oil capacity	1.25 litre (2.2 pts)

Final drive (later models)

Ratio

325i (manual gearbox)	3.64:1
325i (automatic transmission)	3.46:1

Wheels and tyres

Tyre pressures – bar (lbf/in²) – later models

Model	Tyre size	Normal load: Front	Normal load: Rear	Full load: Front	Full load: Rear
320	175/70 SR 14	2.2 (31)	2.4 (34)	2.5 (36)	2.9 (41)
	195/65 HR 14	1.9 (27)	2.1 (30)	2.2 (31)	2.6 (37)
323	185/70 HR 13	2.0 (28)	2.0 (28)	2.2 (31)	2.4 (34)
	195/65 VR 14	2.2 (31)	2.2 (31)	2.3 (33)	2.6 (37)
325	195/65 VR 14	2.2 (31)	2.2 (31)	2.3 (33)	2.6 (37)
	200/60 VR 365 TD	2.2 (31)	2.2 (31)	2.3 (33)	2.6 (37)

Roadwheels

Sizes, depending on model:	
Pressed steel	5 1/2J x 14 H2, or 365 x 150 TD
Light alloy	6J x 14 H2, 7J x 15 H2, or 365 x 150 TD

Electrical system

Battery (low-maintenance type)

320i	50 Ah
325i	66 Ah

Alternator (later models)	80A type

Relays (later models) – typical

K3 (1)	LH headlamp main beam
K3 (2)	RH headlamp main beam
K1 (3)	Auxiliary fan
K10 (5)	Wash/wipe
K2 (7)	Horn
K4 (13)	LH headlamp dipped beam
K4 (14)	RH headlamp dipped beam
K4 (15)	Rear foglamp
K9 (15)	Rear foglamp (headlamp main beam interrupt)
K5 (16)	Seat heating
K5 (17)	Electric sunroof (alternative position)
K6 (18)	Auxiliary fan
K7 (19)	Exterior mirror (control and heating)
K7 (20)	Heater blower and air conditioner
K8 (29)	LH rear foglamp
K8 (30)	RH rear foglamp

General dimensions and weights

Dimensions

Height (unladen) – Convertible models	1370 mm (54.0 in)

Weights

320i manual	1080 kg (2381 lb)
320i automatic	1100 kg (2426 lb)
320i (convertible) manual	1230 kg (2712 lb)
320i (convertible) automatic	1250 kg (2756 lb)
325i manual	1125 kg (2481 lb)
325i automatic	1145 kg (2525 lb)
325i (convertible) manual	1255 kg (2767 lb)
325i (convertible) automatic	1275 kg (2811 lb)

Engine compartment – 325i

1 *Front suspension strut turret*
2 *Cooling system expansion tank*
3 *Oil filler cap*
4 *Air intake manifold*
5 *Engine wiring harness multi-plug*
6 *Brake vacuum servo unit*
7 *Brake master cylinder reservoir*
8 *Fuse and relay block*
9 *Power steering fluid reservoir*
10 *Throttle cable*
11 *Engine oil dipstick*
12 *Rotary idle adjuster*
13 *Airflow sensor*
14 *Air cleaner*
15 *Relays*
16 *ABS hydraulic control unit*
17 *Radiator*
18 *Washer fluid reservoir*
19 *Bonnet gas strut*
20 *Bonnet catch*
21 *Fuel pressure regulator*
22 *Ignition coil*
23 *Clutch fluid reservoir*

Front end viewed from underneath – 325i

1 Power steering pump
2 Engine oil cooler hoses
3 Engine oil cooler
4 Crankshaft vibration damper
5 Power steering gear
6 Horn
7 Foglamp
8 Brake hydraulic pipes
9 Gearbox drain plug
10 Suspension track control arm
11 Anti-roll bar
12 Brake caliper
13 Tie-rod
14 Crossmember
15 Engine sump pan
16 Radiator drain plug
17 Fan
18 Steering shaft flexible coupling
19 Exhaust pipe

3 Engine

Engine (2494 cc) – removal and refitting

1 The operations are similar to those described in Chapter 1, Section 15, but some differences occur due to the Motronic engine management system which is used. It is therefore recommended that this sequence of component disconnection is followed (gearbox removal).
2 Drain the cooling system.
3 Disconnect the battery negative lead (in the boot). Also disconnect the lead at the terminal block on the engine compartment rear bulkhead (photo).
4 Disconnect the exhaust downpipe and remove it.
5 Disconnect the oil cooler pipes from the engine.
6 Disconnect the radiator coolant hoses, remove the radiator.
7 Disconnect the heater hoses from the bulkhead stubs (photo).
8 Disconnect the coil HT lead.
9 Disconnect the starter motor leads.
10 Disconnect the expansion tank hose.
11 Disconnect the engine wiring harness at the multi-plug on the engine compartment rear bulkhead.
12 Remove the air cleaner and airflow sensor (paragraph 27).
13 Disconnect the vacuum hose from the brake servo unit.
14 Disconnect the alternator leads.
15 Disconnect the leads from the temperature sensors and oil pressure switch.
16 Disconnect the throttle cable.
17 Remove the TDC sensor from its clip.
18 Disconnect the speed and reference sensors at their wiring plugs on the left-hand side of the engine.
19 Disconnect and plug the fuel flow and return hoses.
20 Unbolt the power steering pump and move it to one side.
21 Working under the car, disconnect the engine earth strap.
22 With the weight of the engine supported on a hoist, disconnect the mountings and remove the engine from the car.
23 Refitting is a reversal of removal, but tension the power steering pump drivebelt, and fill and bleed the cooling system.

Cylinder head (all models with L-Jetronic fuel injection) – removal and refitting

Note: *This procedure applies specifically to the 2494 cc engine fitted to 325i models, but is broadly applicable to 320i and later 323i models also*

24 Disconnect the battery.
25 Drain the cooling system.
26 Disconnect the exhaust downpipes from the manifold, and release the exhaust support bracket from the transmission.
27 The air cleaner should be removed complete with airflow sensor, after first having disconnected the adjacent relay and multi-plug, and also having loosened the clamp on the connecting duct.
28 Disconnect the throttle cable and on automatic transmission models, the kickdown cable (photo).
29 Unscrew the nut and take out the TDC sensor.
30 Remove the diagnostic plug (photo).
31 Disconnect and plug the fuel supply line.
32 Disconnect the coolant hoses from the cylinder head (photo).
33 Remove the coolant expansion tank.
34 Disconnect the HT lead from the ignition coil.
35 Unbolt and remove the throttle valve housing.
36 Pull the plugs from fuel injectors 4, 5 and 6, and withdraw the wiring harness.
37 Disconnect the lead from the oil pressure switch. Unbolt the air intake manifold support (photos).
38 Pull the plugs from fuel injectors 1, 2 and 3, and withdraw the wiring harness.
39 Remove the rocker cover.
40 On 325i models only, remove the distributor as described in Section 6 of this Supplement.
41 Release the tension from the timing belt, and slip it from the camshaft sprocket as described in Chapter 1, Section 6.
42 Removal, cleaning, decarbonising and reassembly and refitting are all as described in Chapter 1, Sections 7 and 18, and by reversing the disconnection procedure described in this Section. Always use new gaskets, and tighten nuts and bolts to the specified torque.

3.3 Battery terminal block on engine bulkhead

3.7 Heater hose connections at bulkhead

3.28 Throttle cable details

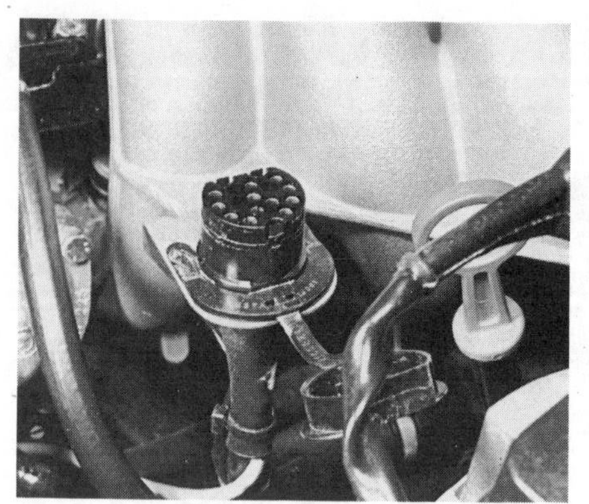
3.30 Diagnostic plug

3.32 Cylinder head coolant hoses

3.37A Oil pressure switch

3.37B Air intake manifold support

3.49 Disconnecting oil cooler line from filter base

3.50 Oil cooler mounting

TDC sensor and diagnostic plug – renewal

43 To remove the diagnostic plug (only of use to BMW dealers having the appropriate test equipment), prise back the clips and also disconnect the earth wire.

44 Using a thin rod, press the female plugs 1 (P+) yellow, 2 (S) shield and 3 (P–) black, out of their sockets (Fig. 13.1).

45 Lift the TDC sensor from its clamp.

46 Connect the new TDC sensor by reversing the removal operations, but make sure that the gap between the sensor and vibration damper is between 0.2 and 2.0 mm (0.008 and 0.08 in).

Engine oil cooler (2494 cc) – removal and refitting

47 The engine oil cooler is located behind the air intake grille in the front spoiler.

48 Remove the spoiler as described in Section 11 of this Supplement.

49 Disconnect the oil cooler lines from the oil filter mounting base on the right-hand side of the engine (photo).

50 Disconnect the oil cooler mountings and withdraw the assembly (photo).

51 Refitting is a reversal of removal. On completion, run the engine and check for oil leaks.

52 Check the oil level and top up if necessary.

4 Cooling system

Coolant pump (325i) – removal and refitting

1 In order to remove the coolant pump from these models, it is recommended that the radiator, the distributor cap, and the crankshaft pulley/damper are first removed.

2 The operations are otherwise as described in Chapter 2, Section 12.

Stale air extraction

3 Flap valves are located at the bottom sides of the luggage boot to act as stale air extractors. Water drain pipes from the sunroof are connected to the flap valve housings (photo).

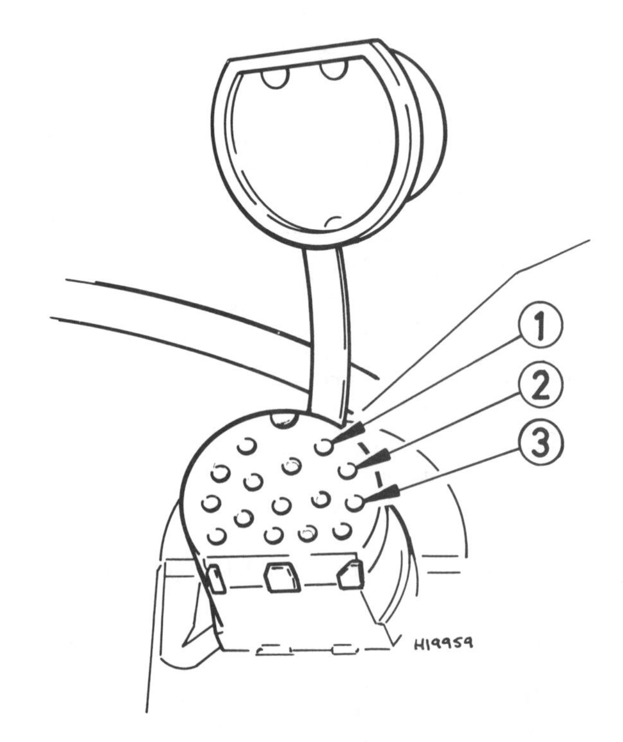

Fig. 13.1 TDC sensor wires at diagnostic plug (Sec 3)

For key see text

4.3 Air extractor flap valve. Sunroof drain tube arrowed

5 Fuel system

Carburettor (Solex 4A1) – choke spring renewal

1 Remove the air cleaner.

2 Unscrew the bolt (21) (Fig. 13.2), and pull out the pin (2).

3 Remove the choke spring.

4 To fit the new choke spring, locate the sliding sleeve (1) on the guide pin (Fig. 13.3).

5 Locate the spring (2) in the groove in the sliding sleeve, and offer the spring assembly from below and behind the adjusting pin opening.

6 Insert the pin, and then check that the bent end of the choke spring engages in the groove in the adjusting screw.

7 Turn the adjusting pin (1) (Fig. 13.4) in an anti-clockwise direction until the choke valve plate just reaches the horizontal position. Now give the pin a further half a turn. Tighten the lockbolt (3).

8 Check for correct operation with the engine idling. The lever (1) (Fig. 13.5) should be seen to be pulled against its stop by the diaphragm.

9 Pinch the hose (2) and actuate the choke valve plate several times. The setting is correct and the diaphragm is in good order if, after each time that the hose is pinched, the lever (1) returns to its stop.

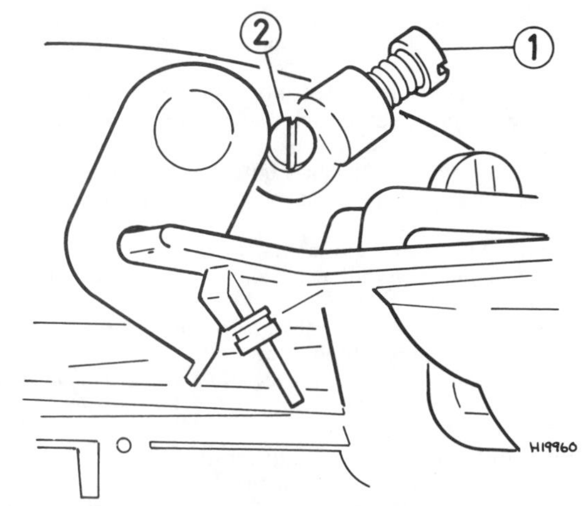

Fig. 13.2 Choke spring components – Solex 4A1 carburettor (Sec 5)

1 Lockbolt 2 Actuating pin

Fig. 13.3 Choke spring components – Solex 4A1 carburettor (Sec 5)

1 Sliding sleeve 2 Choke spring

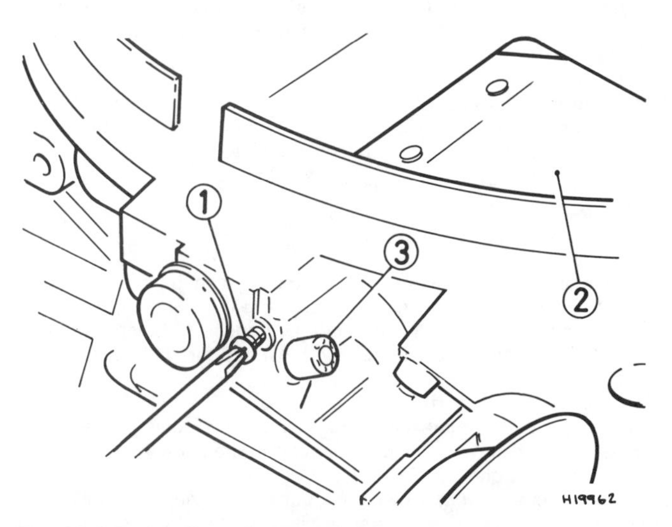

Fig. 13.4 Preloading choke spring on Solex 4A1 carburettor (Sec 5)

1 Adjusting pin
2 Choke valve plate
3 Lockbolt

Fig. 13.5 Checking choke movement (Sec 5)

1 Lever
2 Hose
3 Choke valve plate

Fuel tank (325i) – removal and refitting

10 Proceed as described in Chapter 3, Section 8. Note that on this model, there are two hoses connected to the fuel level transmitter (photo).

Exhaust system section joints

11 The exhaust pipe couplings on later models are of two-bolt flange type, with a central sealing ring (photo).

5.10 Fuel tank transmitter connections

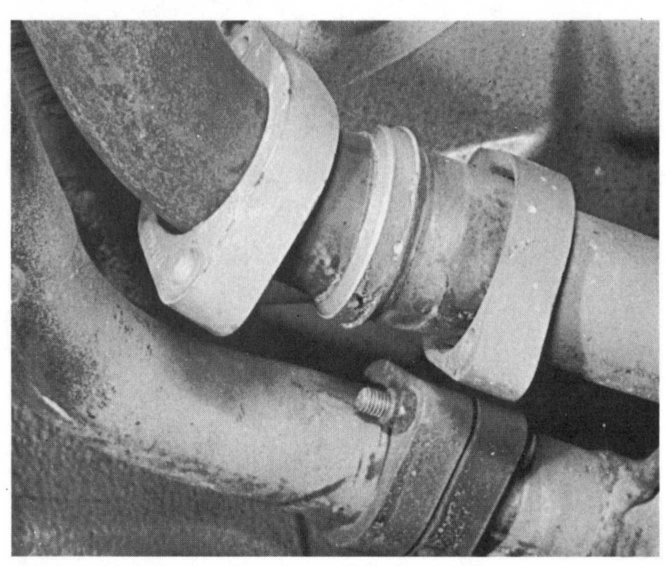

5.11 Exhaust pipe couplings

6 Engine management system

Motronic engine management system – description

1 This Bosch system is fitted to later 325i models, and controls both the fuel and ignition timing requirements of the engine through an electronic control unit (ECU). The fuel injection system is still the Bosch L-Jetronic type (Chapter 3, Section 22).

2 The volume of fuel injected and the ignition timing are constantly varied according to engine speed and load, to provide the optimum fuel economy consistent with performance.

3 Various sensors are located on the engine, and these signal the control unit which in turn converts the information to compute the ideal ignition timing, dwell angle and period of fuel injection for any operating circumstance.

4 In view of the fact that the ignition distributor acts purely as a means of passing HT current to the spark plugs without any advance capability, the assembly comprises only a camshaft-driven rotor and cap.

Motronic engine management system – precautions

5 Disconnect the battery before working on any part of the system.

6 Never actuate the starter motor if the distributor cap is off, or if the lead has been disconnected from terminal 15 on the ignition coil.

7 Never earth terminal 1 of the ignition coil.

8 If checking the engine cylinder compressions, withdraw the fuel system master relay (under a cover on the left-hand side of the engine bay) before actuating the starter motor.

9 During body repair work, if the car is to enter a paint baking oven, first remove the ECU.

Motronic system (fuel section) – tests and adjustments

Idle speed and mixture adjustment

10 There is no provision for adjusting the idle speed. The rotary idle adjuster is basically a motor-driven rotary valve, which adjusts the air volume as signalled by the engine speed section of the ECU to maintain a constant idle speed automatically, irrespective of engine temperature. If the speed is not within the specified range when the engine is at normal operating temperature, check for a leak in the air intake system, and check the operation of the rotary idler adjuster valve (paragraph 21).

11 The idle mixture should only be adjusted if an exhaust gas analyser is available.

12 With the engine idling at normal operating temperature, prise out the tamperproof plug which covers the mixture screw in the air flow sensor (photo).

13 Turn the screw with an Allen key until the CO percentage is within the specified range. Fit a new tamperproof cap on completion if required.

Throttle initial setting – adjustment

14 Prise off the tamperproof cap from the screw on the throttle crankarm on the throttle body.

15 Release the locknut and turn the screw until the throttle lever just loses contact with the end of the screw.

16 Turn the screw inwards until the lever just starts to move, and then give it a further 1/4 of a turn. Tighten the locknut and fit a new tamperproof cap.

Throttle switch – testing and adjustment

17 An ohmmeter will be required for this operation.

18 Disconnect the switch multi plug. Connect an ohmmeter between terminals 2 and 18 of the throttle switch. With the throttle closed, the reading should be 0 ohms. As soon as the throttle begins to open, the reading should rise to infinity (open circuit).

19 Now connect the ohmmeter between terminals 3 and 18. With the throttle fully open, there should be a reading of 0 ohms. If the readings are not as stated, release the switch screws and turn the switch as necessary.

20 Tighten the screws and recheck.

Rotary idle adjuster – checking

21 Disconnect the multi-plug (photo) and check the resistance between the terminals on the idle adjuster as follows.

Terminals 1 and 3 – 40 ohms
Terminals 2 and 3 – 20 ohms
Terminals 2 and 1 – 20 ohms

22 Where necessary, the rotary idle adjuster can be removed with multi-plug still connected simply by releasing the clamping ring.

23 Fully open or close the piston with the fingers, and then switch on the ignition and check that the piston moves to the mid-open/closed position.

Cold start valve – testing

24 Disconnect the multi-plug from the valve and connect an ohmmeter between the valve plug terminals. The resistance should be between 3 and 5 ohms at 20°C.

25 A fuel ejection test may be carried out by removing the valve. With the engine cold, operating the starter will cause fuel to be ejected from the valve. (Take appropriate fire precautions.) If the engine is at normal operating temperature, no fuel should be ejected when the starter motor is operated. When conducting these tests, the fuel and electrical supplies to the valve must of course be connected.

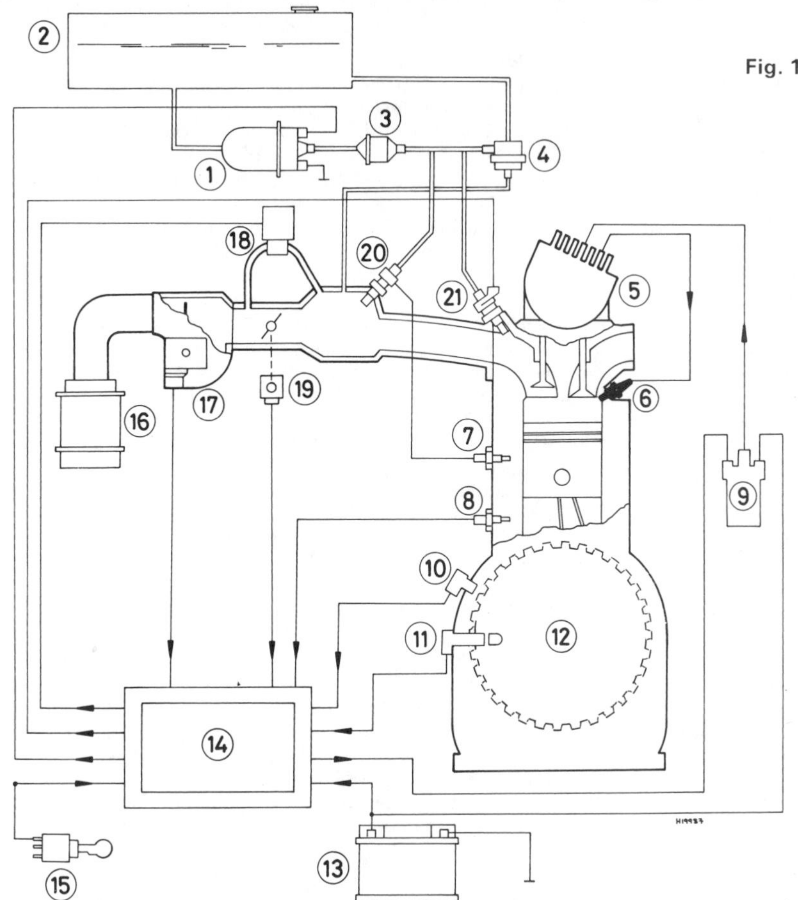

Fig. 13.6 Diagrammatic view of Motronic engine management system (Sec 6)

1 *Electric fuel pump*
2 *Fuel tank*
3 *Fuel filter*
4 *Fuel pressure regulator*
5 *Ignition distributor*
6 *Spark plugs*
7 *Coolant temperature sensor*
8 *Coolant temperature sensor*
9 *Ignition coil*
10 *Speed sensor*
11 *Reference mark sensor (timing)*
12 *Flywheel ring gear*
13 *Battery*
14 *Control unit*
15 *Ignition lock*
16 *Air cleaner*
17 *Airflow meter*
18 *Idle speed control*
19 *Throttle butterfly switch*
20 *Cold start valve*
21 *Fuel injectors*

6.12 Mixture control screw (arrowed)

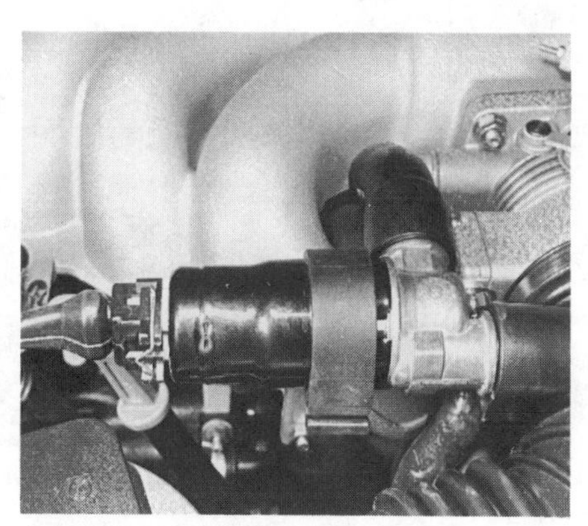

6.21 Rotary idle adjuster

Fig. 13.7 Throttle switch terminals (Sec 6)

Fig. 13.8 Rotary idle adjuster plug terminals (Sec 6)

Fuel injectors – testing

26 Disconnect the multi-plug from each of the fuel injectors and check the resistance between the terminals with an ohmmeter. This should be as follows:

Injector code	Resistance
0280150126, 0280150152 or 0280150201	*2 to 3 ohms*
All others	*15 to 17.5 ohms*

Motronic system (fuel section) – component removal and refitting

27 The reason for removal of a component will probably be due to the need for renewal after carrying out the tests described earlier.

28 Before carrying out the removal operation, disconnect the battery and (when appropriate) depressurise the fuel system. Do this with the engine cold by disconnecting the fuel inlet hose, and immediately placing its open end into a small container. Fuel under pressure may spray out as the hose is disconnected.

29 The location of the various system components is shown in the photographs here and in Chapter 3, and in the view of the engine compartment earlier in this Supplement. The ECU is fitted under the facia on the driver's side. Access is obtained after first removing the facia lower cover (photos).

30 To remove a component, disconnect the wiring plug and hoses and release its fixings. With certain items such as coolant temperature sensors, the cooling system must be partially drained.

31 When renewing the air cleaner element, unclip the casing toggles, loosen but do not remove the two screws, and lift the airflow housing until the filter element can be removed.

32 If the wiring plug is being disconnected from a temperature sensor or a fuel injector, depress the spring catch before pulling on the plug (photos).

33 Refitting is a reversal of removal, but renew all gaskets, seals and 'O' rings.

Motronic system (ignition section) – description and maintenance

34 The ignition system is an integral part of the engine management system as previously described, and comprises a distributor driven from the front end of the camshaft, a coil located on the right-hand side of the engine compartment and the spark plugs.

35 A speed sensor and a reference sensor are mounted in the flywheel housing.

36 No adjustments are provided for, but periodically check all connecting wires and plugs for security, and inspect the distributor cap and rotor for cracks or erosion of the metal-to-metal conduction areas.

Distributor – removal and refitting

37 Remove the protective cover (photo).

38 Remove the three fixing screws and take off the distributor cap. Place it to one side with HT leads still attached (photo).

39 Using an Allen key, extract the three socket-headed screws and take off the rotor which incorporates a centrifugal type speed limiter (photo).

40 Remove the dust shield (photo).

41 Refitting is a reversal of removal.

42 If the HT leads are being renewed, make sure that the new ones are connected in accordance with Fig. 13.9.

Reference and speed sensors – removal and refitting

43 Disconnect the wiring plugs (left-hand side of the engine block).

44 Working under the vehicle, remove the sensor heat shield (when fitted). Remove the fixing screw and withdraw the sensor from the flywheel housing (photos).

45 When fitting, make sure that the reference and speed sensors are not interchanged, and transfer the protective sleeve with clips to the new sensor. The reference sensor has the grey plug.

46 Smear the sensor seal with molybdenum disulphide grease, but do not allow grease to contaminate the face of the sensor.

6.29A Fuel pressure regulator

6.29B Fuel system ECU

6.32A Coolant temperature sensors (arrowed)

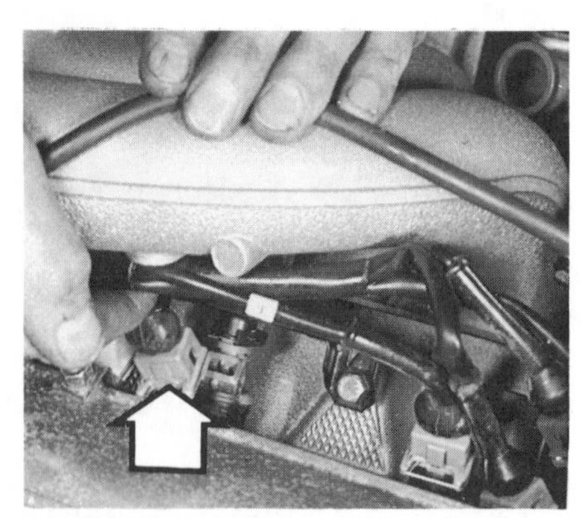

6.32B Disconnecting fuel injector wiring plug (arrowed)

6.37 Distributor protective cover

6.38 Interior of distributor cap. Note central carbon brush

6.39 Removing distributor rotor

6.40 Removing distributor dust shield

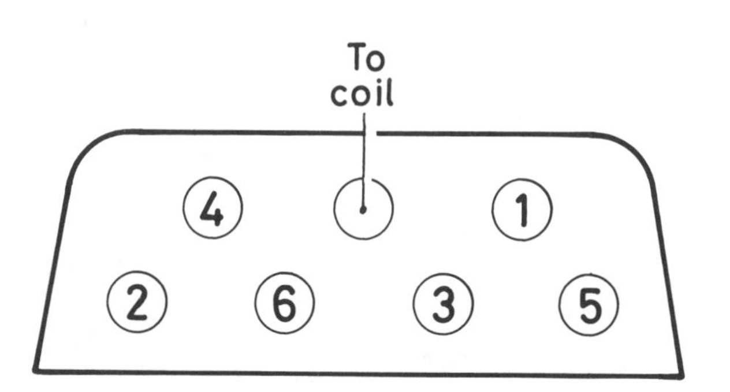

Fig. 13.9 HT leads at distributor cap (Sec 6)

6.44A Releasing reference and speed sensor screws

6.44B Sensor withdrawn

7 Manual gearbox and automatic transmission

Manual gearbox (Getrag 260) – removal and refitting

1 The operations are essentially as described in Chapter 6, Section 4, but note the additional procedure associated with the 325i Motronic engine management system.

2 Remove the heat shield (if fitted) from the speed and reference mark (TDC) sensors, and then unbolt and remove the sensors.

3 When refitting, take great care not to interchange the sensor positions, check the condition of the 'O' rings and apply molybdenum disulphide grease to the sensors before fitting, but not to their pick-up faces.

Manual gearbox (Getrag 260) – overhaul

4 The operations are as described for the Getrag 240 version in Chapter 6, Section 7, but observe the following special points.

5 Apply thread locking fluid to the clutch release bearing guide sleeve bolts, which must be clean.

6 The input shaft bearing must be fitted so that the projection on the inner track is towards the gears.

7 When reassembling the synchronisers, note that there is no groove on 3rd/4th synchro sleeve on this gearbox.

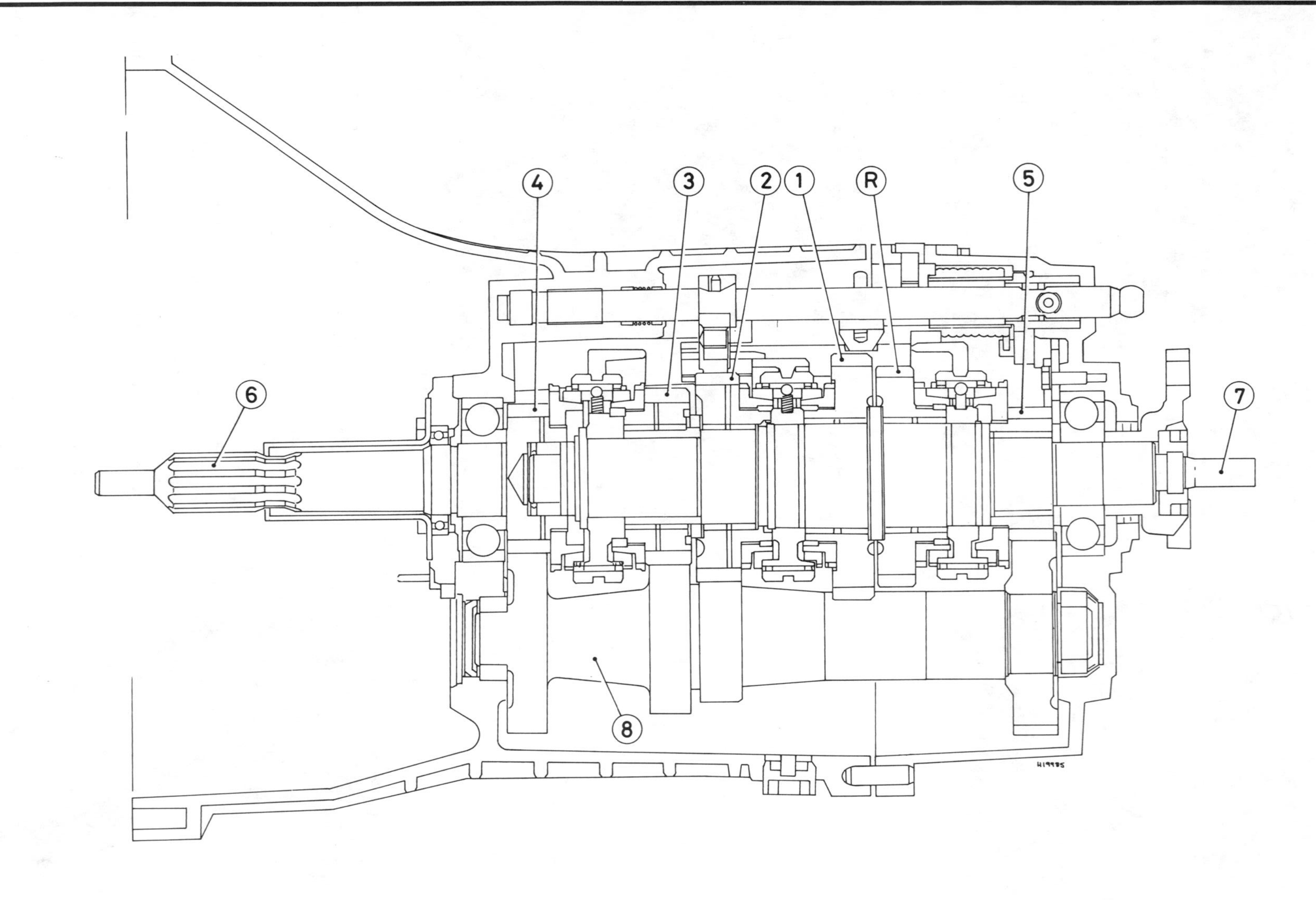

Fig. 13.10 Sectional view of Getrag 260 gearbox (Sec 7)

1 1st speed gear
2 2nd speed gear
3 3rd speed gear
4 4th speed gear
5 5th speed gear
6 Input shaft
7 Mainshaft
8 Layshaft
R Reverse gear

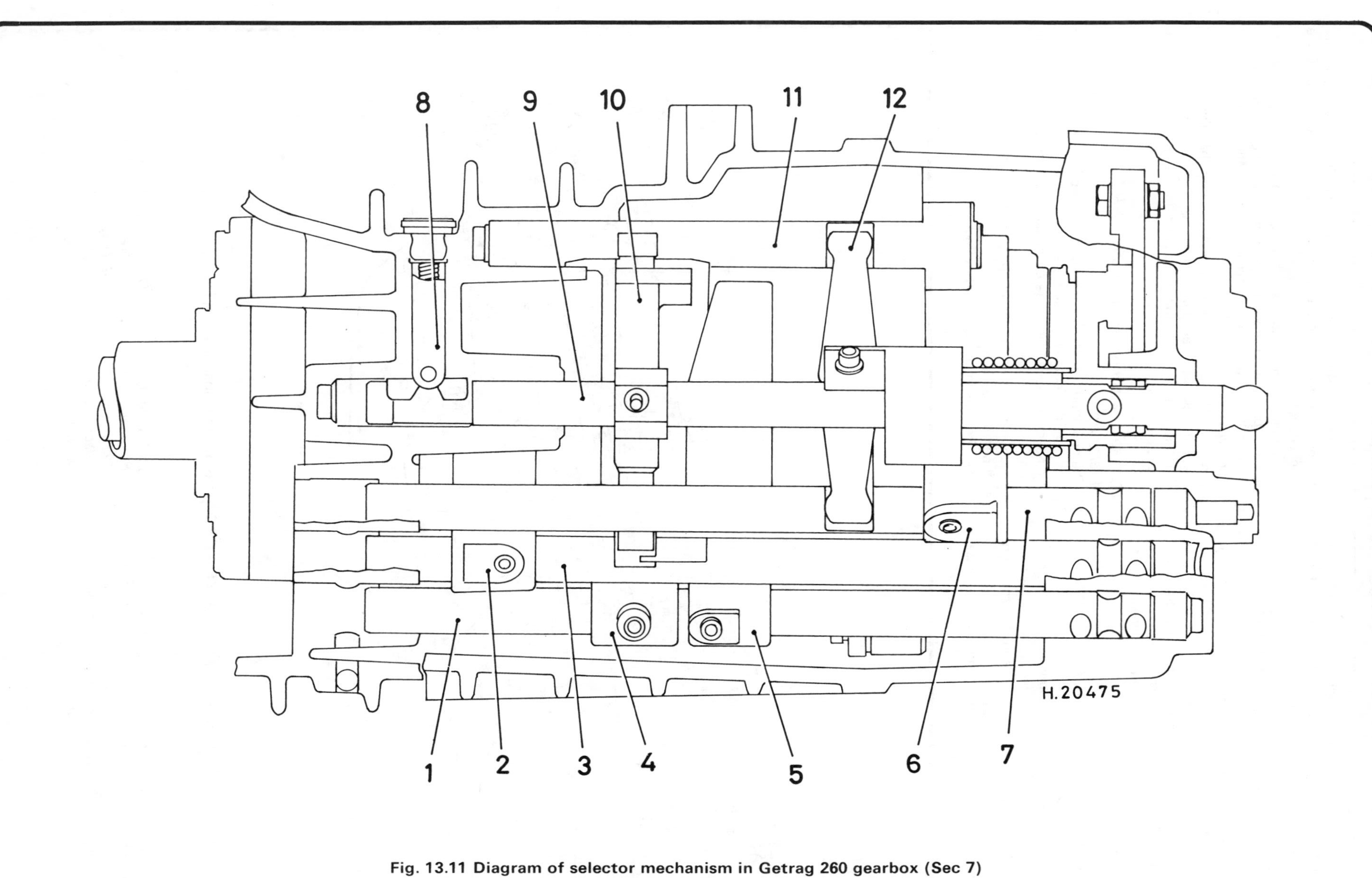

Fig. 13.11 Diagram of selector mechanism in Getrag 260 gearbox (Sec 7)

1 1st/2nd selector rod
2 3rd/4th selector fork
3 3rd/4th selector rod
4 Dog
5 1st/2nd selector fork
6 Reverse/5th selector fork
7 Reverse/5th selector rod
8 Detent (lock) pin
9 Selector shaft
10 Selector arm
11 Selector rail
12 Operating lever

8 Fit the synchro hub just halfway into the synchro sleeve, and insert and depress the balls sufficiently to enable the hub to be pressed fully into the sleeve.

Manual gearbox oil seals (all models) – renewal in situ

Output shaft

9 The procedure is similar to that described for the automatic transmission (Chapter 6, Section 16).

Selector shaft

10 Remove the output flange, engage 3rd gear and disconnect the selector rod from the shaft. Prise out the old oil seal.

11 Oil the lips of the new seal and fit it using a piece of tube. Reconnect or refit the other disturbed components.

Automatic transmission (type ZF 4 HP 22 EH) – description

12 This transmission is an electronically controlled type, using a similar control unit to that responsible for the Motronic engine management system. The engine management and transmission control systems are related.

13 Impulses corresponding with road speed are monitored by a pulse wheel and speed sensor, and signalled to the ECU, where the shift points for the transmission are determined for optimum performance and fuel economy.

14 A program control switch is provided for increased driver control.

15 A safety circuit is incorporated in the wiring arrangement so that in the event of failure of the electronics the car can still be driven in 3rd gear or reverse.

16 A downshift interlock prevents the driver from changing down into 2nd gear at high roadspeeds in the event of electronic malfunction.

17 The program control unit is located in the boot, behind the left-hand side trim panel.

Automatic transmission (type ZF 4 HP 22 EH) – removal and refitting

18 The operations are similar to those described in Chapter 6, Section 17, but note the following differences.

19 Remove the speed and reference mark sensors as described in Section 6.

20 Disconnect the wiring harness plug (bayonet fitting) at the side of the oil pan flange.

21 Refit the sensors as described in Section 6.

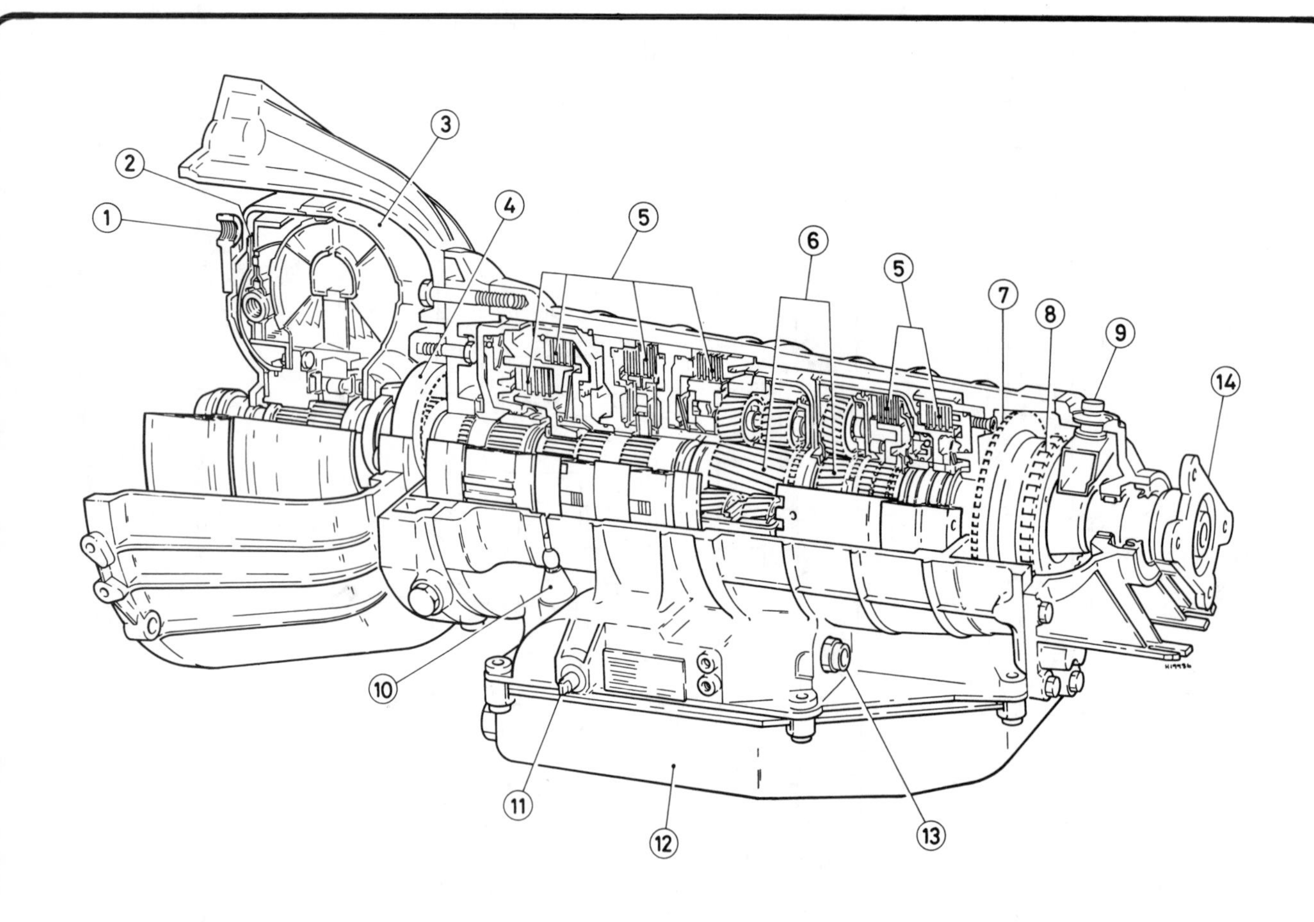

Fig. 13.12 Cutaway view of ZF 4 HP 22 automatic transmission (Sec 7)

1 Driveplate connecting lug
2 Torque converter lock-up clutch
3 Torque converter
4 Oil pump
5 Multi-plate clutches
6 Epicyclic gear set
7 Pulse gear for speed sensor (ZF 4 HP 22 EH) or centrifugal governor (ZF 4 HP 22)
8 Parking lock gear
9 Breather
10 Kickdown cable
11 Selector lever shaft
12 Oil pan
13 Connection to ECU (ZF 4 HP 22 EH)
14 Output flange

8 Roadwheels and tyres

General care and maintenance

Wheels and tyres should give no real problems in use provided that a close eye is kept on them with regard to excessive wear or damage. To this end, the following points should be noted.

Ensure that tyre pressures are checked regularly and maintained correctly. Checking should be carried out with the tyres cold and not immediately after the vehicle has been in use. If the pressures are checked with the tyres hot, an apparently high reading will be obtained owing to heat expansion. Under no circumstances should an attempt be made to reduce the pressures to the quoted cold reading in this instance, or effective underinflation will result.

Underinflation will cause overheating of the tyre owing to excessive flexing of the casing, and the tread will not sit correctly on the road surface. This will cause a consequent loss of adhesion and excessive wear, not to mention the danger of sudden tyre failure due to heat build-up.

Overinflation will cause rapid wear of the centre part of the tyre tread coupled with reduced adhesion, harsher ride, and the danger of shock damage occurring in the tyre casing.

Regularly check the tyres for damage in the form of cuts or bulges, especially in the sidewalls. Remove any nails or stones embedded in the tread before they penetrate the tyre to cause deflation. If removal of a nail *does* reveal that the tyre has been punctured, refit the nail so that its point of penetration is marked. Then immediately change the wheel and have the tyre repaired by a tyre dealer. Do *not* drive on a tyre in such a condition. In many cases a puncture can be simply repaired by the use of an inner tube of the correct size and type. If in any doubt as to the possible consequences of any damage found, consult your local tyre dealer for advice.

Periodically remove the wheels and clean any dirt or mud from the inside and outside surfaces. Examine the wheel rims for signs of rusting, corrosion or other damage. Light alloy wheels are easily damaged by 'kerbing' whilst parking, and similarly steel wheels may become dented or buckled. Renewal of the wheel is very often the only course of remedial action possible.

The balance of each wheel and tyre assembly should be maintained to avoid excessive wear, not only to the tyres but also to the steering and suspension components. Wheel imbalance is normally signified by vibration through the vehicle's bodyshell, although in many cases it is particularly noticeable through the steering wheel. Conversely, it should be noted that wear or damage in suspension or steering components may cause excessive tyre wear. Out-of-round or out-of-true tyres, damaged wheels and wheel bearing wear/maladjustment also fall into this category. Balancing will not usually cure vibration caused by such wear.

Wheel balancing may be carried out with the wheel either on or off the vehicle. If balanced on the vehicle, ensure that the wheel-to-hub relationship is marked in some way prior to subsequent wheel removal so that it may be refitted in its original position.

General tyre wear is influenced to a large degree by driving style – harsh braking and acceleration or fast cornering will all produce more rapid tyre wear. Interchanging of tyres may result in more even wear, but this should only be carried out where there is no mix of tyre types on the vehicle. However, it is worth bearing in mind that if this is completely effective, the added expense of replacing a complete set of tyres simultaneously is incurred, which may prove financially restrictive for many owners.

Front tyres may wear unevenly as a result of wheel misalignment. The front wheels should always be correctly aligned according to the settings specified by the vehicle manufacturer.

Legal restrictions apply to the mixing of tyre types on a vehicle. Basically this means that a vehicle must not have tyres of differing construction on the same axle. Although it is not recommended to mix tyre types between front axle and rear axle, the only legally permissible combination is crossply at the front and radial at the rear. When mixing radial ply tyres, textile braced radials must always go on the front axle, with steel braced radials at the rear. An obvious disadvantage of such mixing is the necessity to carry two spare tyres to avoid contravening the law in the event of a puncture.

In the UK, the Motor Vehicles Construction and Use Regulations apply to many aspects of tyre fitting and usage. It is suggested that a copy of these regulations is obtained from your local police if in doubt as to the current legal requirements with regard to tyre condition, minimum tread depth, etc.

9 Braking system

Brake, clutch and accelerator pedals

1 There have been some detail modifications to the pedal components on later RHD models. The arrangement on the driver's and the passenger's side is shown in Figs. 13.13, 13.14 and 13.15.

2 The removal operations are essentially as described in Chapters 3, 5 and 9. Adjustment dimensions are shown in Figs. 13.16 and 13.17.

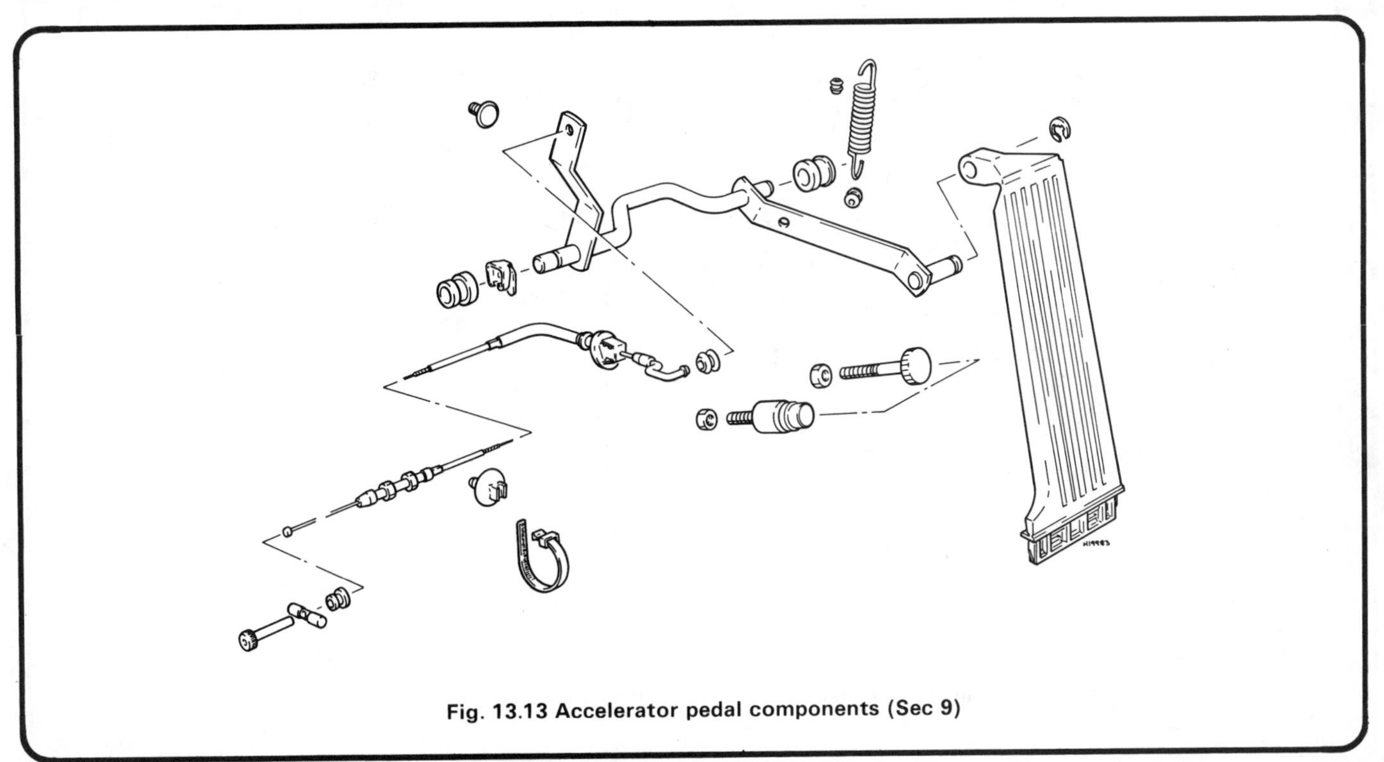

Fig. 13.13 Accelerator pedal components (Sec 9)

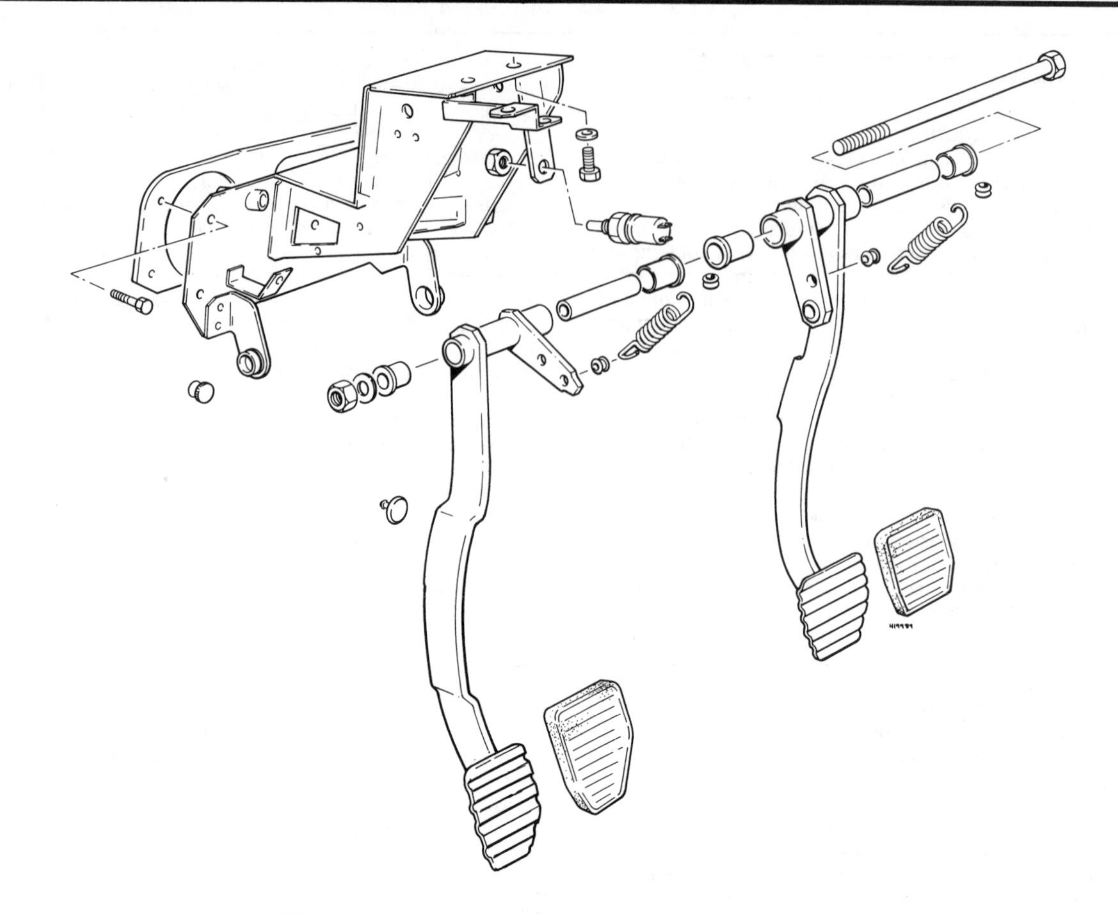

Fig. 13.14 Brake and clutch pedal components (Sec 9)

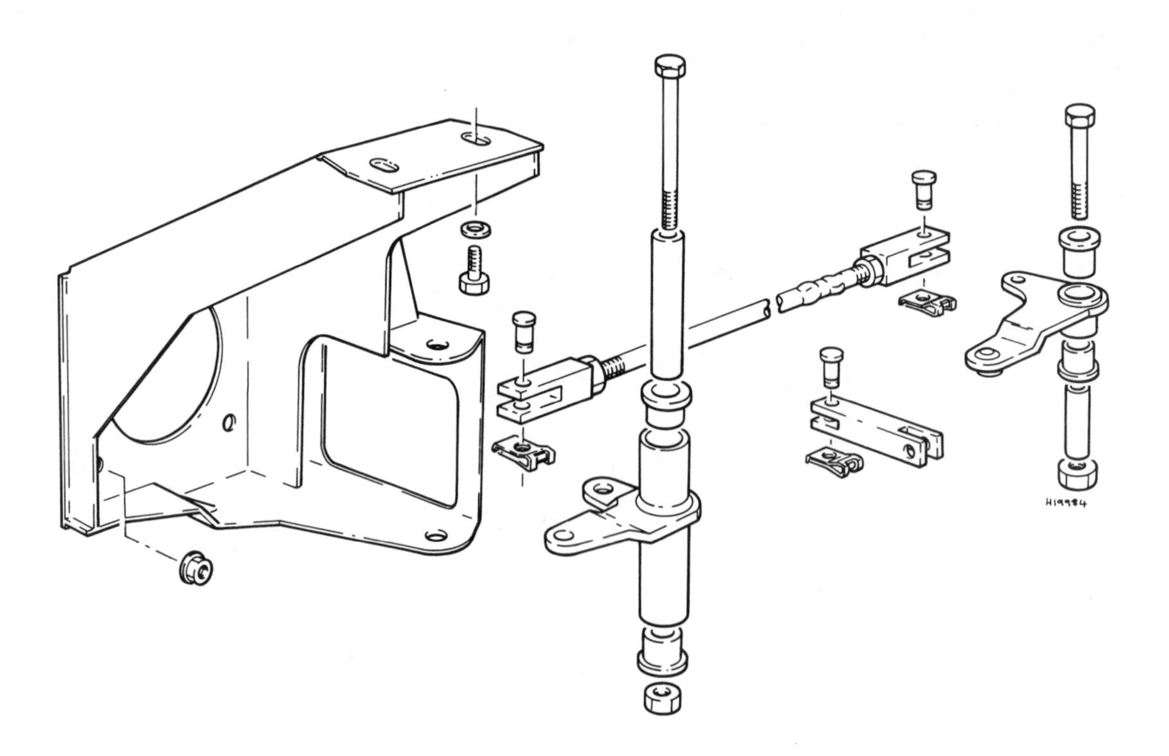

Fig. 13.15 Brake pedal cross-shaft and linkage (Sec 9)

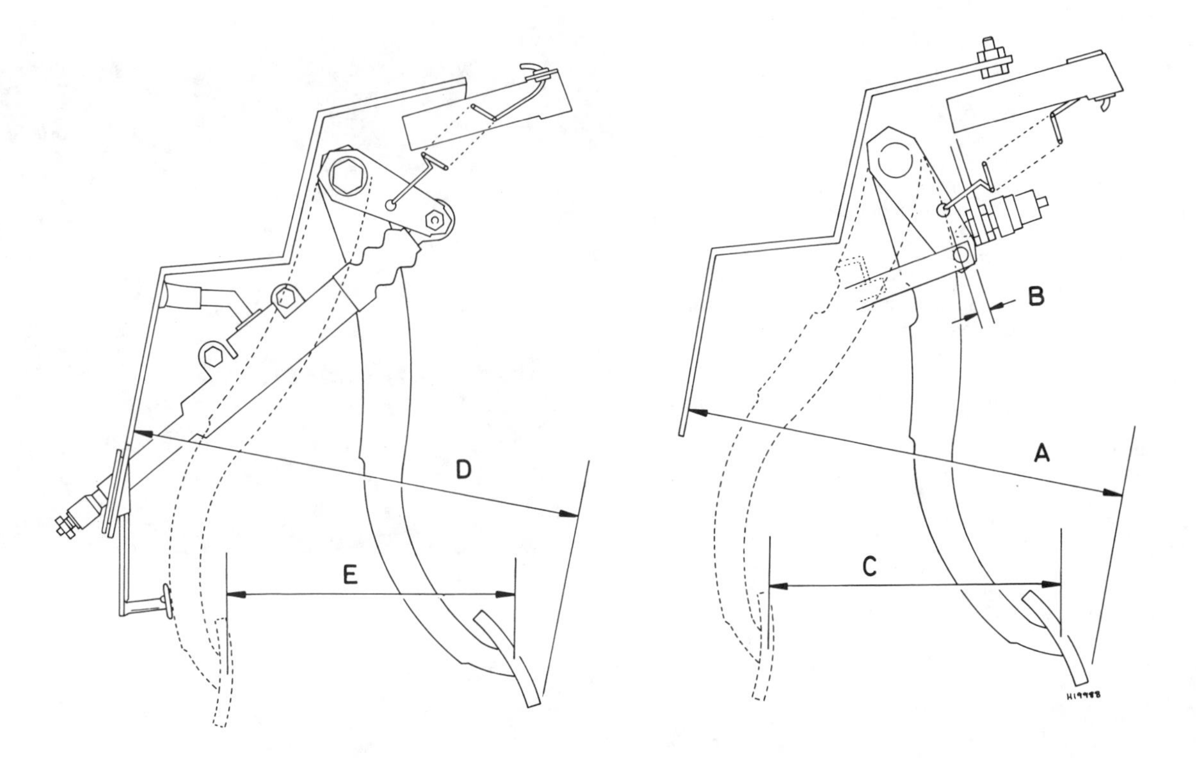

Fig. 13.16 Brake and clutch pedal adjustment dimensions (Sec 9)

A = 269 + 10 mm (10.6 + 0.4 in)
B = 5 + 1 mm (0.20 + 0.04 in)
C = 174 − 9 mm (6.9 − 0.4 in)
D = 269 + 11 mm (10.6 + 0.4 in)
E = 154 + 11 mm (6.1 + 0.4 in)

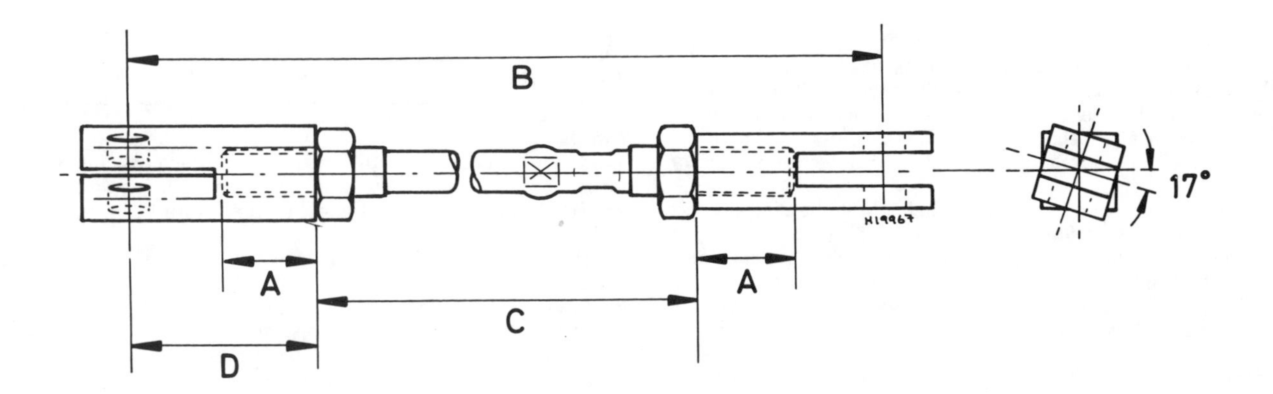

Fig. 13.17 Brake cross-shaft adjustment dimensions (Sec 9)

A = 21 ± 1 mm (0.83 ± 0.04 in)
B = 722.5 ± 1 mm (28.45 ± 0.04 in)
C = 639.5 ± 1 mm (25.18 ± 0.04 in)
D = 41.5 mm (1.63 in)

Braking system – 325i

3 The system is similar to that described for the 323i in Chapter 9, with disc brakes on all four wheels.

Master cylinder (ABS) – overhaul

4 The master cylinder used in conjunction with the anti-lock braking system (ABS) incorporates recessed piston stop pins which cannot be removed to permit overhaul. In consequence, no spare parts are available and a faulty unit must be renewed complete.

Master cylinder (later models) – overhaul

5 On later models, it may be found that the master cylinder overhaul kit does not contain piston seals alone, but complete pistons in an assembly tube. Follow any special instructions with such a kit.

Anti-lock braking system (ABS)

6 This system is fitted as standard equipment to SE and Sport models after 1986.

7 The information contained in Chapter 9 generally applies, but note the following points.

8 The control unit is located behind the glovebox on the passenger side of the facia panel (photo).

9 The hydraulic unit is located under a cover in the front left-hand corner of the engine compartment.

10 The front and rear wheel sensors are secured with socket-headed screws, requiring an Allen key to remove them (photos).

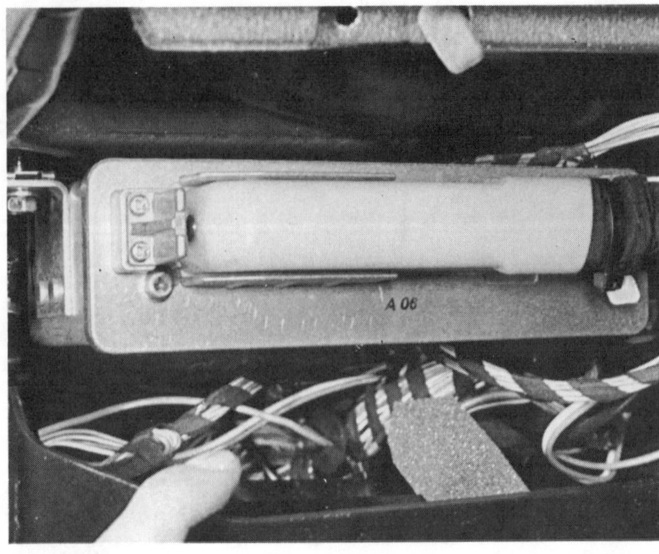

9.8 ABS control unit

9.10A ABS wheel sensor

9.10B ABS wheel sensor withdrawn

9.15 Handbrake shoe (disc/drum removed for clarity) adjuster

Handbrake (all models with rear disc brakes) – adjustment

11 Remove any rust or surface-glazing from the shoes and drum by driving a maximum of 400 yards with the handbrake lightly applied.

12 Chock the front wheels. Release the handbrake and select neutral.

13 Remove one rear wheel bolt on each side.

14 Raise and support the rear of the vehicle so that the rear wheels are free.

15 Turn one wheel to bring the bolt hole in line with the shoe adjuster (about 30° rearwards of the 12 o'clock position) (photo). Using a screwdriver through the bolt hole, turn the star wheel until the shoes lock the disc, then back it off 3 or 4 clicks. On the left-hand side, the disc will be locked by turning the star wheel upwards, on the right-hand side downwards.

16 Repeat the adjustment on the other rear wheel.

17 Check that both rear wheels can turn freely, then adjust the handbrake cables (Chapter 9, Section 29).

18 Lower the vehicle, refit the wheel bolts and tighten them to the specified torque.

Handbrake shoe linings (all models with rear disc brakes) – bedding in

19 If new linings have been fitted, bed them in after initial adjustment as follows.

20 Selecting suitable road and traffic conditions, use the handbrake alone to make five stops from approximately 30 mph.

21 Let the brakes cool down for half an hour, then repeat paragraph 20.

22 Let the brakes cool again, then repeat the adjustment procedure from paragraph 12.

10 Electrical system

Battery

1 On later models, a low-maintenance type battery is fitted. Regular inspection of the electrolyte level is still required. Topping-up should seldom, if ever, be required and then only with distilled or purified water.

2 The battery on 325i models is located behind a cover in the boot (photo).

3 The cover is secured by turn-buttons.

4 Before removing the battery, disconnect the vent tube which runs into a degassing tank under the battery mounting platform. If it is required to remove the degassing tank, be aware that it may contain acid.

Relays

5 Later models have a revised number of relays, and their locations have been changed (photos).

6 For specific details, refer to the car operating manual, but typically for 325i models, they are as given in the Specifications.

Starter motor (later models) – removal and refitting

7 Further to Chapter 10, Section 8, note the following additional points.

8 On models with L-Jetronic fuel injection, access for starter removal will be improved by removing the airflow sensor and air cleaner assembly.

9 Also on models with L-Jetronic injection, it will be necessary to drain the cooling system and disconnect the heater hoses in order to gain access to the starter motor retaining nut.
10 On 325i models, disconnect the speed and reference mark sensor wiring plugs on the left-hand side of the engine block.
11 Refill the cooling system on completion.

Headlamp bulb (1986 on) – renewal

12 Open the bonnet and remove the headlamp cover panel (photo).
13 Disconnect the wiring plug (photo).
14 Unscrew and remove the cap (photo).
15 Prise back the spring clips and withdraw the bulb (photo). Disconnect the spade connector.
16 Fit the new bulb by reversing the removal operations, but avoid fingering the bulb glass. If it is accidentally touched, wipe clean with methylated spirit.

Headlamps (1986 on) – removal and refitting

17 Open the bonnet, twist the turn-button and remove the cover panels from the rear of the headlamps.
18 Disconnect the wiring plug.
19 Working at the upper edge of the outer grille, remove the fixing clips.
20 Extract the self-tapping screws and remove the grille.
21 Remove the three headlamp mounting panel securing screws (photo) and withdraw the twin headlamp assembly.
22 Refitting is a reversal of removal, but check the beam alignment and adjust if necessary on completion.

Headlamp beam load adjuster

23 A hydraulic load adjuster device is fitted to some models to counteract the effect of variable loading of the car in relation to the headlamp beams.
24 A facia-mounted control is provided with four settings.

10.2 Battery location in boot

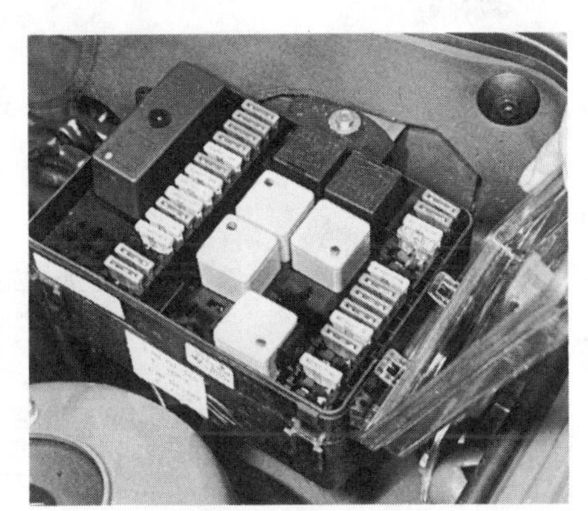
10.5A Fuse and relay block

10.5B Fuel pump and fuel injector relays

10.5C ABS hydraulic control unit with system relays

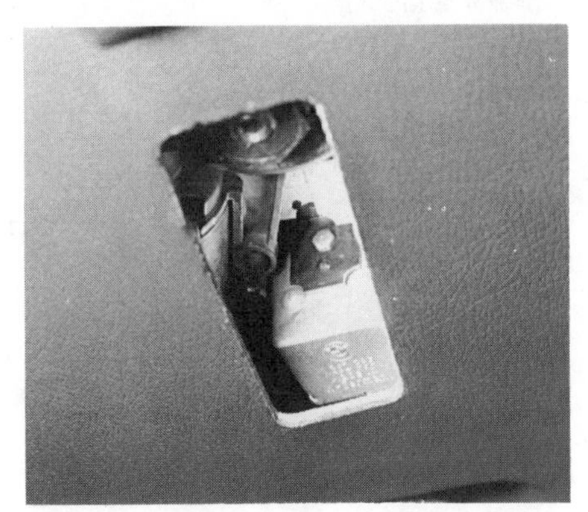
10.5D Sunroof relay

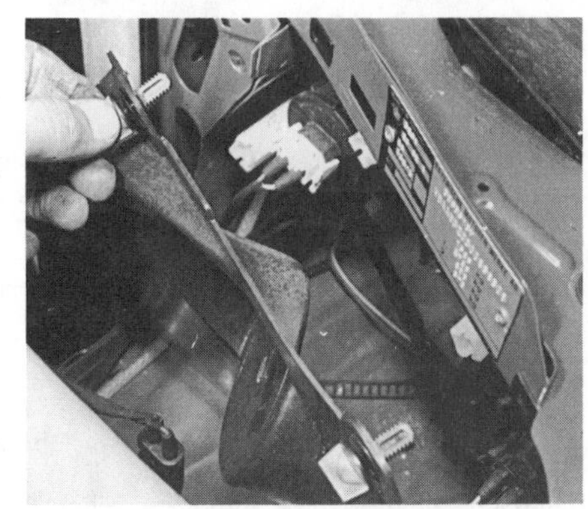
10.12 Removing headlamp rear cover panel

10.13 Headlamp wiring plug

10.14 Headlamp rear cap

10.15 Headlamp bulb removal

10.21 Headlamp mounting panel screws

10.25 Engine wiring harness multi-plug

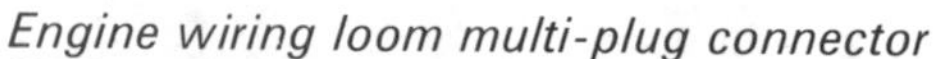

Engine wiring loom multi-plug connector

25 A multi-pin connecting plug is located on the left-hand side of the engine compartment rear bulkhead. To disconnect, release the clamp and unscrew the plug, which has a coarse thread (photo).

Door lock heating control unit

26 This is located behind the driver's door trim panel. To remove it, disconnect the wiring plug and unscrew the retaining nut.

Central door locking system (1986 on) impact switch

27 An impact lock release switch is fitted in conjunction with this system, which releases all the locks in the event of a collision.

28 The switch is located adjacent to the left-hand speaker at the side of the passenger footwell.

Electrically operated windows (Series 2 models) – further information

29 The automatic cut-out for this system is located just above the radio, and can be prised out with a small screwdriver.

30 The manual window cranking handle for emergency use is provided in the tool kit.

31 Prise out the plug from the door trim panel and remove the rubber cap then engage the handle.

Control switches (later models) – removal and refitting

Exterior mirror switch

32 Using a small screwdriver, prise the switch from the door armrest. If the wiring is to be removed, the door trim panel and mirror triangular trim panel will have to be withdrawn (photo).

33 The mirror glass heating switches on and off automatically according to temperature.

34 Refit the switch by reversing the removal operations.

EH automatic transmission program selector switch

35 Remove the rear ashtray from the centre console.

36 Unscrew the fixing nut and move the console forwards.

37 Disconnect the wiring plug from the switch.

38 Pull out the ashtray lamp.

39 Pull the knob from the program selector switch.

40 Unscrew the bezel nut and remove the switch from under the centre console.

41 Refit by reversing the removal operations.

Radio/cassette player – removal and refitting

42 Later equipment is removed by inserting two U-shaped tools into the two holes on each side of the face-plate. These tools are obtainable from accessory stores, and once inserted, act as spring retainer depressing tools and as handles to lift the radio from its housing.

43 On electronic equipment, two circular hooks are used to release and remove the control panel from the radio. The hooks are then used to depress the retaining clamps and to withdraw the equipment.

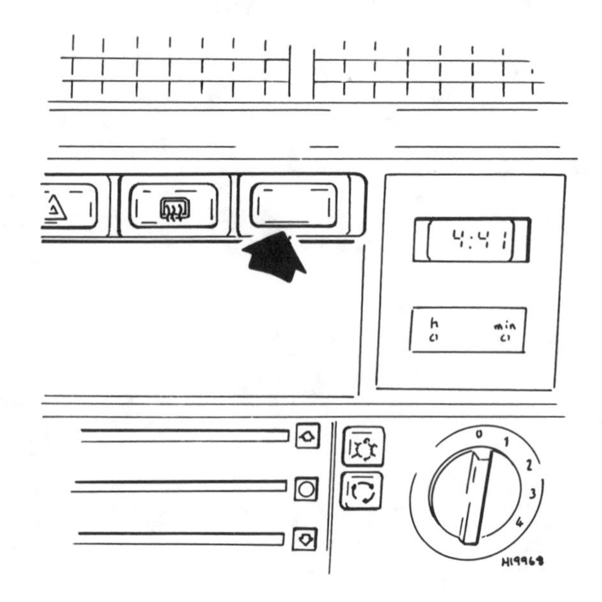

Fig. 13.18 Removing electric window cut-out (Sec 10)

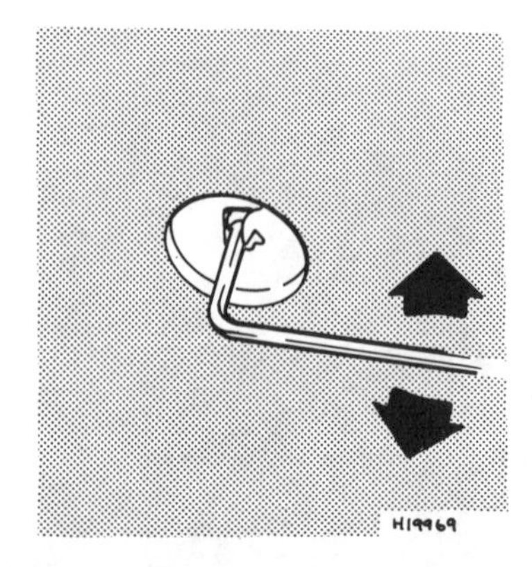

Fig. 13.19 Using electric window hand crank (Sec 10)

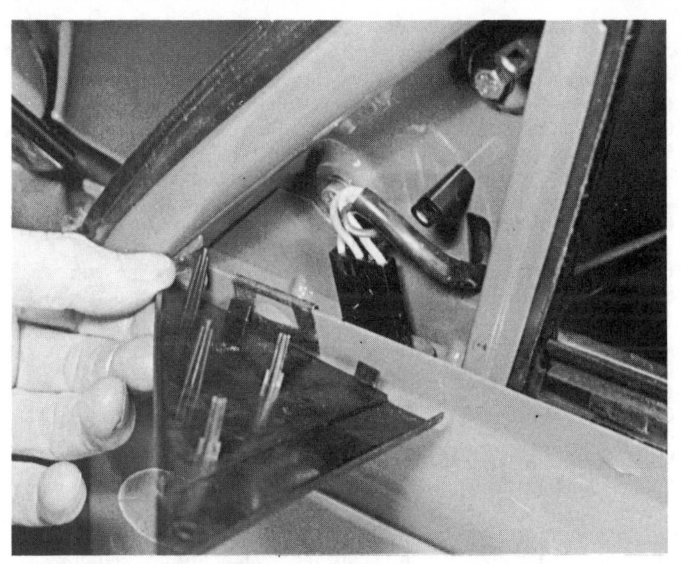

10.32 Exterior mirror trim panel removed

Electric aerial

44 This is mounted on the left-hand rear wing, access being obtained after removal of the left-hand trim panel in the boot (photo).

10.44 Electric aerial

Cruise control system components – removal and refitting

Control unit

45 Open the glovebox and disconnect the support straps by pulling out the rivets.

46 Extract the screws and remove the cover from the control unit.

47 Extract the control unit holder screws, withdraw the holder, disconnect the wiring plug and remove the control unit.

Drive motor and cable

48 Remove the facia underside trim panel from the driver's side after turning the retaining screws through 90°.

49 Pull off the drive motor wiring plug (1) (Fig. 13.20) from the auxiliary wiring harness (2).

50 Disconnect the cable (1) (Fig. 13.21) with holder (2) from the throttle valve lever.

51 Extract the screws and remove the drive motor.

52 To disconnect the cable from the motor, press down the spring retainer (3) (Fig. 13.22) and pull the cable sleeve (1) out of the drive motor.

53 Disconnect the cable from the holder.

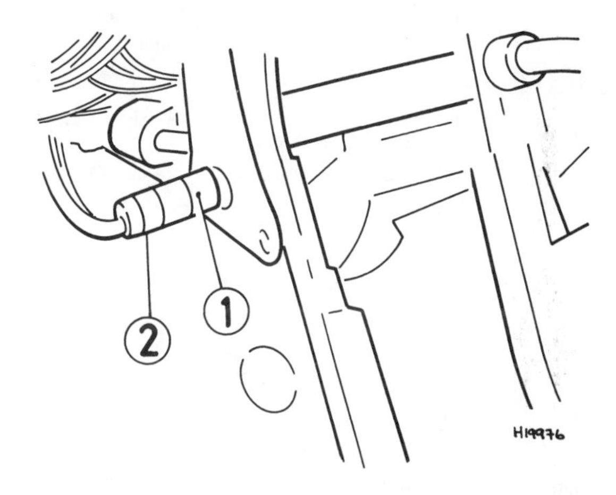

Fig. 13.20 Cruise control drive motor wiring plug (1) and auxiliary wiring harness (2) (Sec 10)

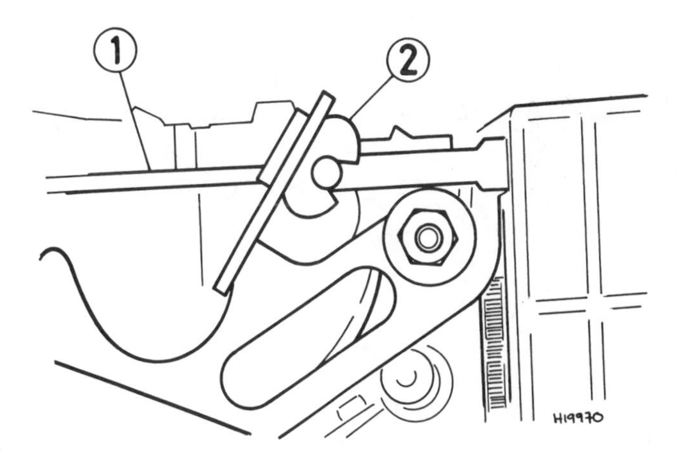

Fig. 13.21 Cruise control cable (1) and holder (2) on throttle valve lever (Sec 10)

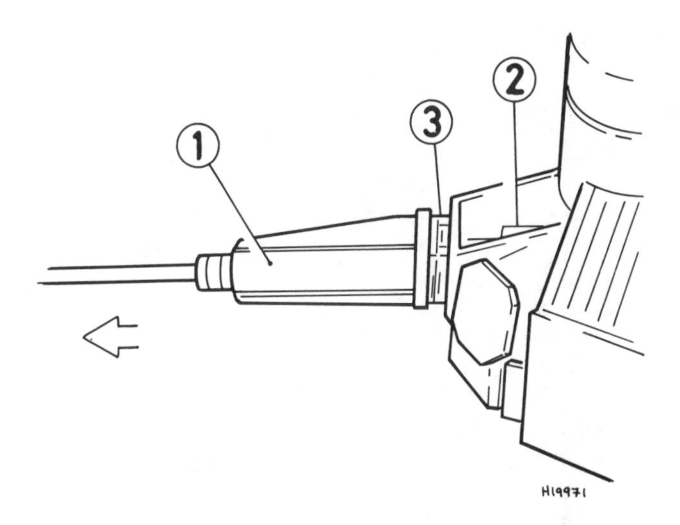

Fig. 13.22 Cruise control drive motor cable sleeve (1), drive motor (2) and spring retainer (3) (Sec 10)

54 When reassembling, check the gap A (Fig. 13.23), with the throttle valve closed and drive motor in neutral. Adjust if necessary using the knurled nut (1).

Control cable

55 Disconnect the cable with the white retainer (3) (Fig 13.24). Pull the cable from the holder (1) and clamp (2).

56 When refitting, check the gap as described in paragraph 54.

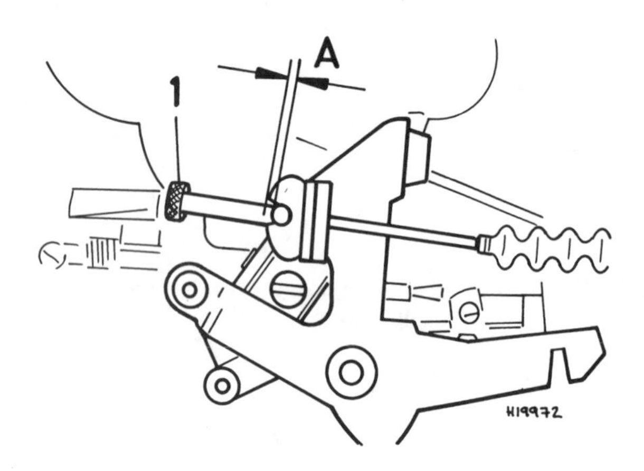

Fig. 13.23 Cruise control drive cable setting diagram (Sec 10)

A 1.0 to 1.5 mm (0.039 to 0.059 in)
1 Knurled nut

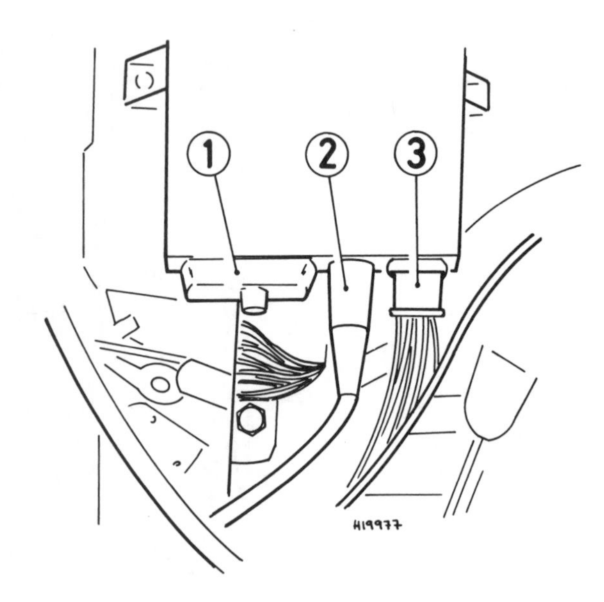

Fig. 13.25 Anti-theft alarm system control unit (Sec 10)

1 to 3 Multi-plugs

Anti-theft alarm system components – removal and refitting

57 Disconnect the battery.

Control unit

58 Remove the facia underside trim panel.

59 Disconnect the wiring plugs (1) and (3) Fig. 13.25.

60 Extract the mounting screws and remove the control unit.

Coding lock

61 Remove the door trim panel and partially peel back the waterproof sheet to expose the coding lock.

62 Prise back the clamp and disconnect the plugs from the lock.

63 Pull off the spring retainer (5) (Fig. 13.26) and remove the lock (4).

Driver's door switching unit

64 Remove the door trim panel and partially peel back the waterproof sheet.

65 Extract the screws, withdraw the switching unit and disconnect the wiring plug.

Boot switching unit

66 Peel back the floor covering and release the rear lamp cluster bulb carrier.

67 Prise up the lower edge of the rear trim panel and remove it.

68 Extract the screws which secure the switching unit, withdraw it and disconnect the wiring plug.

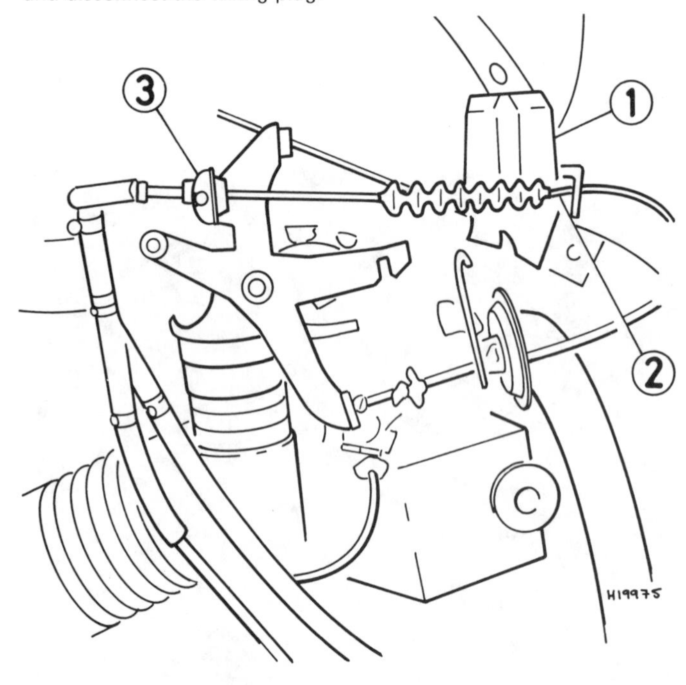

Fig. 13.24 Cruise control cable (Sec 10)

1 Holder
2 Clamp
3 Cable nipple (white)

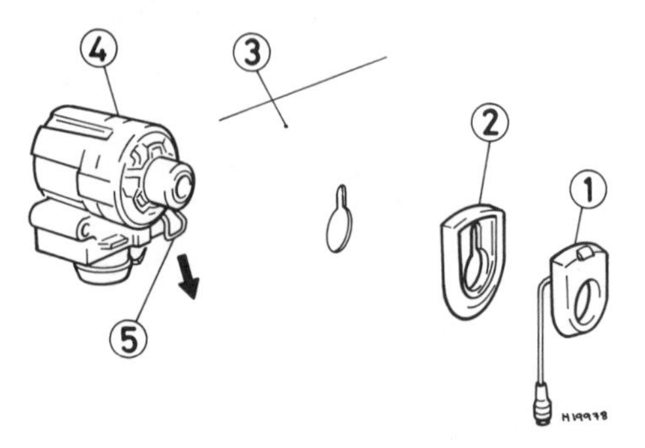

Fig. 13.26 Anti-theft alarm coding lock (Sec 10)

1 Plate
2 Liner
3 Door panel
4 Coding lock
5 Spring retainer

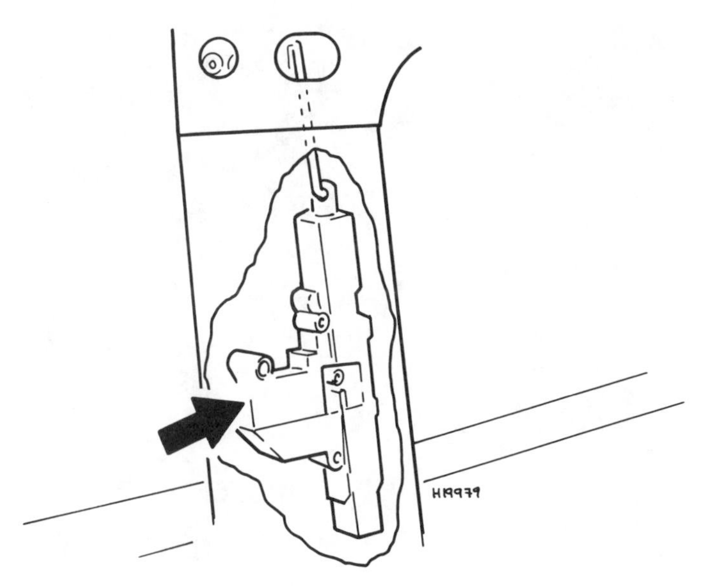

Fig. 13.27 Boot anti-theft alarm switching unit (Sec 10)

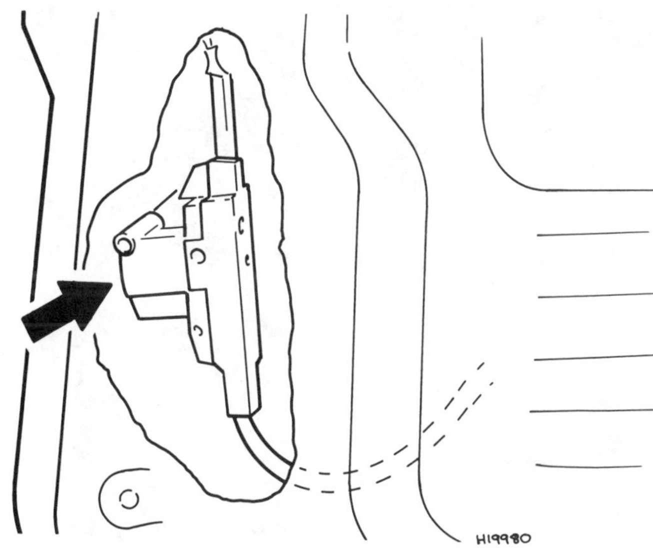

Fig. 13.28 Driver's door anti-theft alarm switching unit on two-door cars (Sec 10)

Alarm horn

69 The horn is located on the front suspension strut.

70 Disconnect the wiring plug and remove the fixing screws.

Refitting – all components

71 Refitting all components is a reversal of removal, but observe the following points.

72 When fitting the driver's door switching unit, make sure that the housing (arrowed – Fig. 13.28) faces the rear of the car on two-door models, and the front of the car on four-door models.

On-board computer components – removal and refitting

73 The computer is located above the glovebox, and the removal operations are similar to those described earlier for the cruise control system unit.

74 The relay and gong are located under the facia panel.

75 The ambient temperature sensor can be removed in the following way.

Pre-September 1985 models

76 The sensor is located in the air inlet aperture in the front spoiler. It can be removed by pressing it out with a cranked 8 mm ring spanner. Refitting is a reversal of removal.

September 1985 on models

77 Remove the front spoiler as described in Section 11 of this Supplement.

78 Disconnect the wiring plug and pull the sensor from its recess (photo). Refitting is a reversal of removal.

Rechargeable hand-lamp

79 This is located in the left-hand side of the glovebox. The lamp can remain plugged in all the time, as an integral overload cut-out prevents overcharging (photo).

10.78 Ambient temperature sensor (September 1985 on)

10.79 Rechargeable hand-lamp

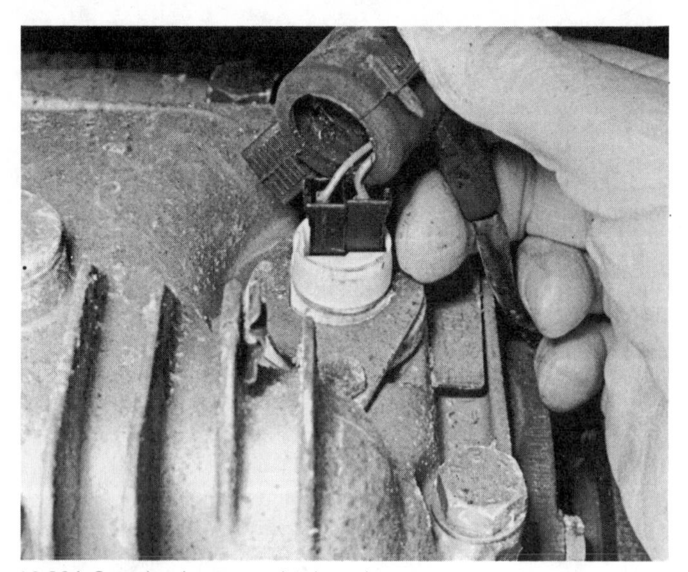

10.80A Speed pulse sensor leads and cover

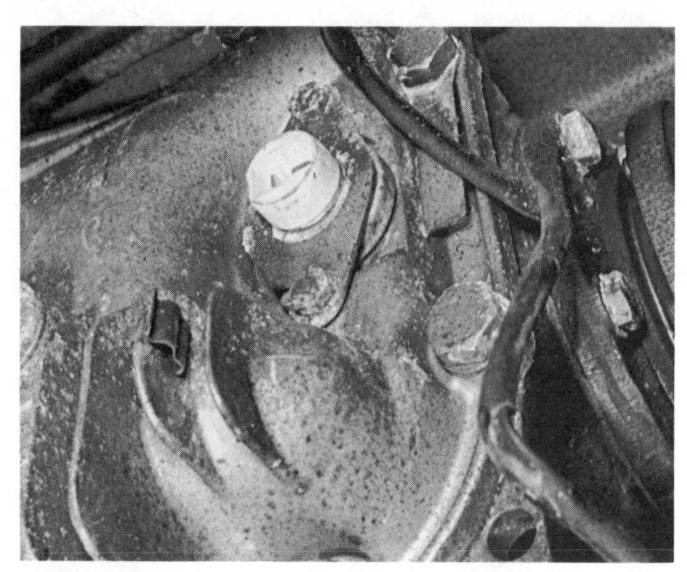

10.80B Speed pulse sensor with plug disconnected

Speed pulse sensor

80 The sensor, which is located in the rear axle, signals the speedometer and is also the source for computing the service interval mileage indicator (photos).

Check control system – general

81 The check control system monitors fluid levels and exterior light bulbs. In the event of a low fluid level or a bulb failure, the driver is warned by the flashing of the 'CHECK' light in the instrument panel, together with the illumination of the appropriate LED in the check control panel.

82 All the LEDs will light, and the 'CHECK' light will flash, when the ignition is first switched on. Depressing the brake pedal after the engine has been started should cancel all warnings if all the monitored systems are in order.

83 Removal and refitting of the check control unit and associated components is as follows.

Check control unit

84 Lift the unit out of its holder and disconnect the multi-plug from it.

85 Refit by reversing the removal operations.

Engine oil level switch

86 The switch is located on the left-hand side of the sump.

87 Disconnect the wiring plug, undo the two retaining nuts and lift the switch out of the sump. Allow the oil to drain from it before withdrawing it completely.

88 Use a new seal if necessary when refitting.

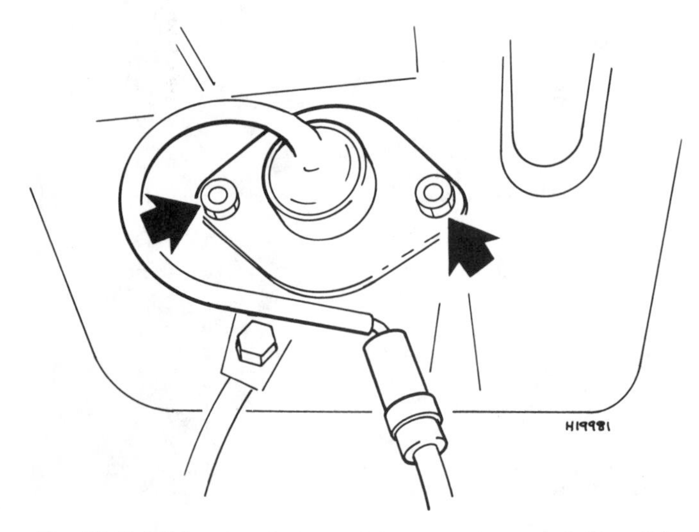

Fig. 13.29 Oil level switch retaining nuts (arrowed) (Sec 10)

Coolant level switch

89 With the engine cold, slacken the expansion tank cap to release any residual pressure in the system.

90 Disconnect the plug from the switch, undo its retaining nut and remove it from the expansion tank.

91 Refit by reversing the removal operations.

Bulb failure monitoring unit

92 Remove the trim from the left-hand side of the luggage area.

93 Remove the two securing screws, disconnect the wiring plugs and remove the bulb failure monitoring unit.

94 Refit by reversing the removal operations.

11 Bodywork and fittings

Minor body damage – repair of plastic components

1 With the use of more and more plastic body components by the vehicle manufacturers (eg bumpers, spoilers, and in some cases major body panels), rectification of more serious damage to such items has become a matter of either entrusting repair work to a specialist in this field, or renewing complete components. Repair of such damage by the DIY owner is not really feasible owing to the cost of the equipment and materials required for effecting such repairs. The basic technique involves making a groove along the line of the crack in the plastic using a rotary burr in a power drill. The damaged part is then welded back together by using a hot air gun to heat up and fuse a plastic filler rod into the groove. Any excess plastic is then removed and the area rubbed down to a smooth finish. It is important that a filler rod of the correct plastic is used, as body components can be made of a variety of different types (eg polycarbonate, ABS, polypropylene).

2 Damage of a less serious nature (abrasions, minor cracks etc) can be repaired by the DIY owner using a two-part epoxy filler repair material. Once mixed in equal proportions, this is used in similar fashion to the bodywork filler used on metal panels. The filler is usually cured in twenty minutes, ready for sanding and painting.

3 If the owner is renewing a complete component himself, or if he has repaired it with spoxy filler, he will be left with the problem of finding a suitable paint for finishing which is compatible with the type of plastic used. At one time the use of a universal paint was not possible owing to the complex range of plastics encountered in body component applications. Standard paints, generally speaking, will not bond to plastic or rubber satisfactorily. However, it is now possible to obtain a plastic body parts finishing kit which consists of a pre-primer treatment, a primer and coloured top coat. Full instructions are normally supplied with a kit, but basically the method of use is to first apply the pre-primer to the component concerned and allow it to dry for up to 30 minutes. Then the primer is applied and left to dry for about an hour before finally applying the special coloured top coat. The result is a correctly coloured component where the paint will flex with the plastic or rubber, a property that standard paint does not normally possess.

Front undershield – removal and refitting

4 The engine compartment front undershield is secured at its base by two spring clips.

5 The sides are held by special clips and nuts, with three screws under each front wing at the wing protective shield joint (photos).

6 Remove all the fixings and withdraw the undershield.

7 Refitting is a reversal of removal.

Front spoiler – removal and refitting

8 The front spoiler is secured by self-tapping screws. Extract the screws (photo), withdraw the spoiler to release it from its special side clips, and then disconnect the foglamp wiring connectors. Also disconnect the ambient temperature sensor, when applicable.

9 When refitting the spoiler, make sure that the tongues engage correctly in their slots (photo).

Front grille – removal and refitting

10 Release the bonnet and set it in the horizontal position.

11 Prise off the grille upper fixing clips (photo).

12 Extract the self-tapping screws and remove the grille (photos).

13 Refitting is a reversal of removal.

Front bumper (1985 and later models) – removal and refitting

14 Disconnect the wiring plugs from the direction indicator lamps.

15 On models built before 1986, pull out the blanking plates, or if foglamps are fitted, remove the spoiler.

16 On models built after 1986, remove the spoiler.

17 The bumper end bolts which are now exposed should be removed (photo).

11.5A Releasing undershield side clip

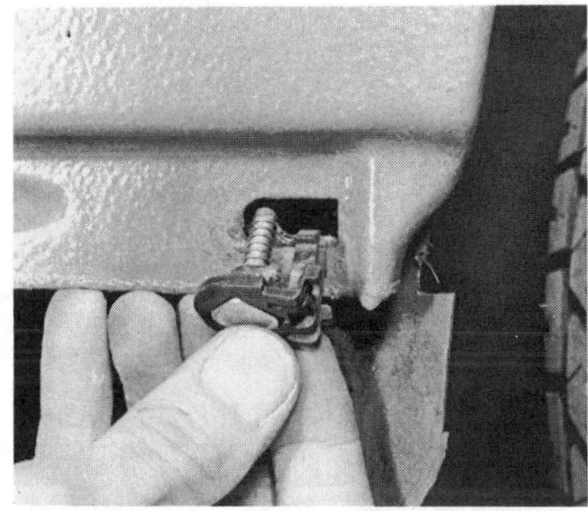

11.5B Removing side clip

11.5C Undershield screws below front wing

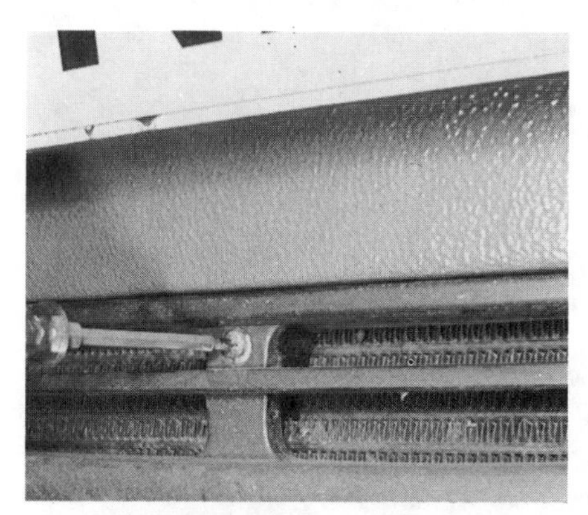

11.8 Front spoiler screw

11.9 Front spoiler locating tongues

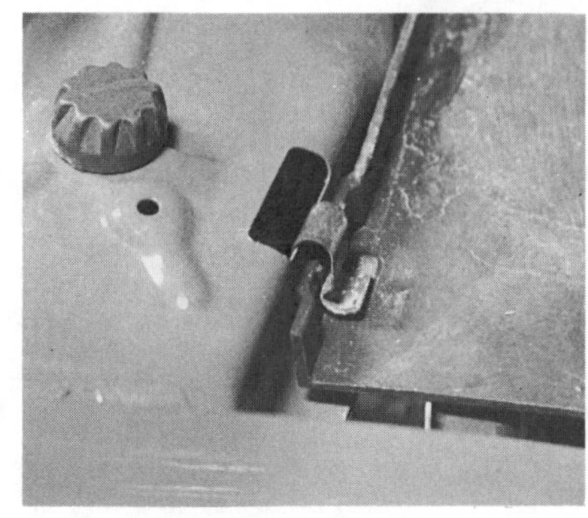

11.11 Front grille upper clip

11.12A Front grille screw

11.12B Removing front grille

11.17 Front bumper end bolt

18 Using a screwdriver, prise off the square-shaped blanking plates to expose the left-hand and right-hand bumper fixing nuts, which should be unscrewed (photos).
19 Withdraw the bumper from the car.
20 The bumper can be dismantled by removing the direction indicator lamps, compressing the clips and pulling off the rubbing strips, and then removing the section connecting screws and nuts.
21 Reassembly and refitting are reversals of dismantling and removal, but make sure that the direction indicator lamps are fitted to their correct sides – they are marked L and R.

Rear bumper (1985 and later models) – removal and refitting

22 Open the boot. When applicable, remove the battery cover for access.
23 Prise back the partly-cut blanks in the side trim panels, and unscrew the bumper end bolts now exposed (photo).
24 Working within the boot, remove the remaining bumper fixing nuts and bolts and withdraw the bumper (photo).
25 The bumper may be dismantled in the following way.
26 Lift the retaining tongue and pull off the end sections.
27 Compress the clips and pull off the rubbing strip.
28 Extract the screws and remove the side sections.
29 Reassembly and refitting are reversals of dismantling and removal.

Scuttle grille – removal and refitting

30 The scuttle (heater air intake) grilles are clipped in position and can be pulled from their locations (photo). The windscreen wiper arm must be removed if the right-hand grille is to be taken off.

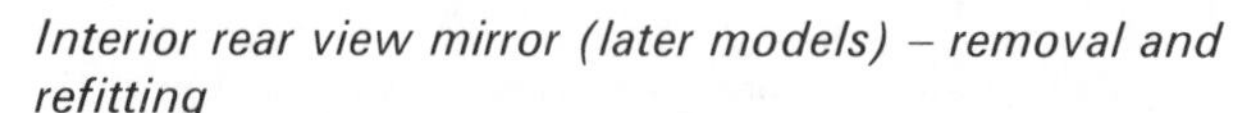

Interior rear view mirror (later models) – removal and refitting

31 When removing the mirror from Saloon models, pull the mirror stem to disengage it from the base.
32 On convertible models, twist the stem in a clockwise direction to release it.
33 When refitting the mirror, if a check control panel is fitted, prise it from its housing. Compress the spring in the base, using screwdrivers inserted from both sides. Enter the mirror stem at an angle, if necessary pushing it into engagement using the handle of a hammer or a piece of wood.

Exterior rear view mirror (later models) – glass renewal

34 To renew the glass on later type mirrors, insert a screwdriver in the slot at the base of the mirror casing and prise the retaining ring in a clockwise direction. Disconnect the wiring plug from the heated type mirror glass.
35 Fit the new glass, and secure it by turning the ring anti-clockwise.

Centre console (1986 and later models) – removal and refitting

36 When removing the centre console (see Chapter 12, Section 33) on models equipped with three-program automatic transmission, disconnect the wiring plug for the selector switch as the console is withdrawn.
37 On later models, a separate trim cover is used for the handbrake lever, and this is simply clipped into the centre console.

11.18A Releasing front bumper blanking plate

11.18B Front bumper fixing nut

11.23 Rear bumper end bolt

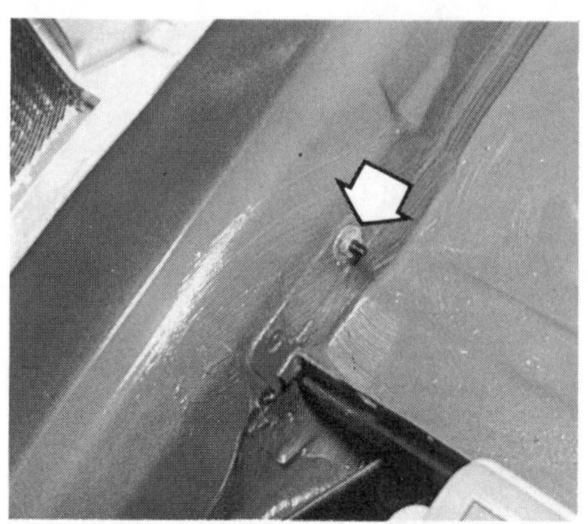

11.24 Rear bumper fixing nut (arrowed)

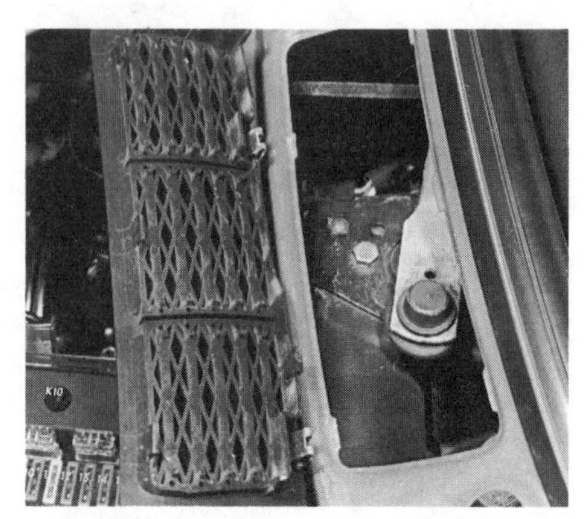

11.30 Left-hand scuttle grille removed

11.38A Console front section fixing nut

11.38B Console front fixing screw removal

11.39 Console rear section locating tongues

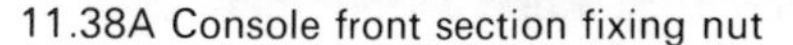

38 The gear lever gaiter is also clipped to the console, and when unclipped will expose the centre console front section fixing nut (photo). Two screws are used at the front end of the console (photo).
39 The rear section of the console is held by a nut under the ashtray and locating tongues at its forward end (photo).
40 Refitting is a reversal of removal.

Bonnet lock (later models) – removal and refitting

41 Open the bonnet.
42 If a headlamp wash/wipe system is fitted, remove the linkage and wiper arm.
43 Release the left-hand side grille clips and screws.
44 Extract the left-hand headlamp mounting plate screws. Remove the interior trim panel.
45 Unscrew the bonnet catch mounting screws, disconnect the release cable and remove the catch.
46 Refitting is a reversal of removal. Check the headlamp alignment on completion.

Boot lid lock (later models) – removal and refitting

47 Open the lid, press out the centre pins from the retaining clips and take off the rear trim panel capping.
48 Peel back the rear edge of the boot mat and remove the rear trim panel by prising it out from its lower edge.
49 Extract the fixing screws and withdraw the lock sideways.
50 If required, the lock cylinder can be removed after extracting the circlip.
51 On cars equipped with central locking, the lock incorporates a solenoid, and apart from disconnecting the wiring plug, the removal operations are similar.
52 Refitting is a reversal of removal, but adjust the striker and buffers to give light, positive closure.

Rear quarter trim panel (Convertible) – removal and refitting

53 Lift out the rear seat cushion.
54 Remove the bolts and pull the seat backrest upwards and remove it from the car.
55 Remove the side plate and seat belt cover trim.
56 Unscrew the anchor bolt and lift the seat belt away. Note the tension spring.
57 With the window fully open, extract the quarter trim panel fixing screws.
58 Pull off the weatherstrip from the door closure edge of the body, disconnect the speaker leads and remove the quarter trim panel.
59 Refitting is a reversal of removal.

Front seat belts (later models) – general

Saloon
60 The front seat belt upper anchor bolt on the body pillar may be fitted in either one of the two tapped holes provided, so that the belt will suit the size of person regularly occupying the seat.

Convertible
61 The seat belt reel may be removed after first having withdrawn the quarter trim panel as described earlier.

Rear seat belts (all models) – removal and refitting

Saloon
62 Remove the rear seat cushion and backrest.
63 Prise off the cap and unscrew the belt anchor bolt from the seat pan.
64 Unscrew the remaining anchor bolt (photo).
65 Working within the boot, unscrew the belt reel bolt.
66 Feed the belt through the parcel shelf and remove it.
67 On models built after 1986, the rear parcel shelf should be removed complete before unbolting and removing the belt reel.
Convertible
68 The anchor bolts are located at the sides of the seat pan, and the reels are accessible after removing the trim covers.
Refitting – all models
69 Refitting is a reversal of removal, but note the sequence of fitting of the anchor bolt components (Fig. 13.30).

Electric sunroof – manual operation

70 In the event of a breakdown in the electrical circuit of the sunroof, remove the blanking plate from the roof lining above the windscreen (photos).
71 Using the box spanner and the hexagon crank handle (also for electric window emergency use), release the locknut and insert the crank handle in the end of the drive spindle and open or close the roof panel as required (photos).
72 On completion, only tighten the locknut very lightly.

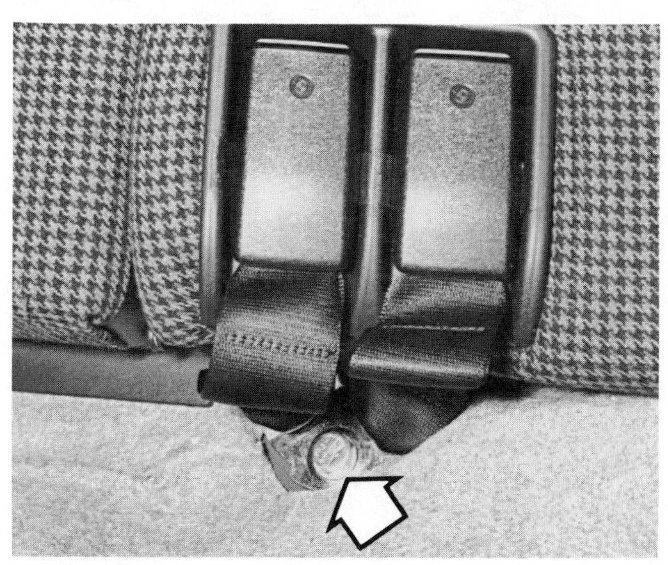
11.64 Rear seat belts – anchor bolt arrowed

11.70A Removing roof lining blanking plate

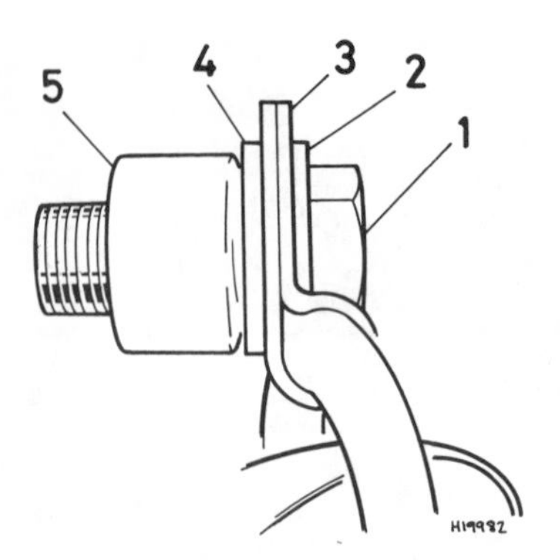

Fig. 13.30 Fitting sequence of seat belt anchor components (Sec 11)

1 *Bolt*
2 *Plastic washer (up to 1985 only)*
3 *Anchor plate*
4 *Plastic washer (up to 1985 only)*
5 *Spacer*

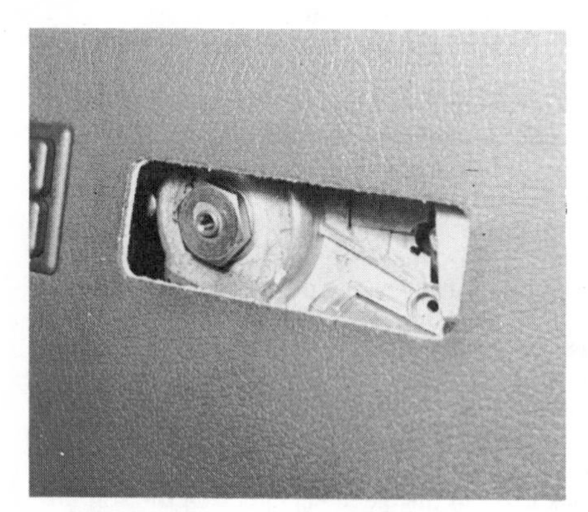
11.70B Sunroof motor drive spindle and locknut

11.71A Using box spanner to release sunroof drive spindle locknut

11.71B Using crank handle in sunroof drive spindle

Index

A

B

F

V

W

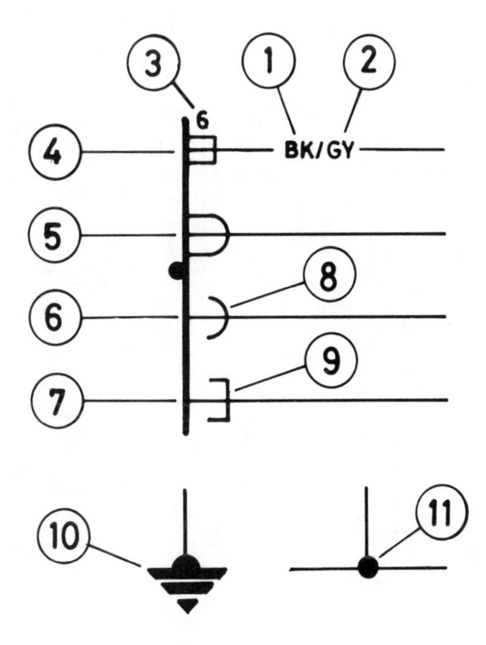

Explanation of wire identification codes

1 Primary colour
2 Secondary colour
3 Terminal designation
4 Terminal connection (galvanised wire end)
5 Screw connection (wire connector)
6 Round male plug
7 Flat male plug
8 Round female plug
9 Flat female plug
10 Earth
11 Soldered point or connection

Colour code

BK	Black
BL	Blue
BR	Brown
GR	Green
GY	Grey
O	Orange
R	Red
T	Transparent
V	Violet
W	White
Y	Yellow

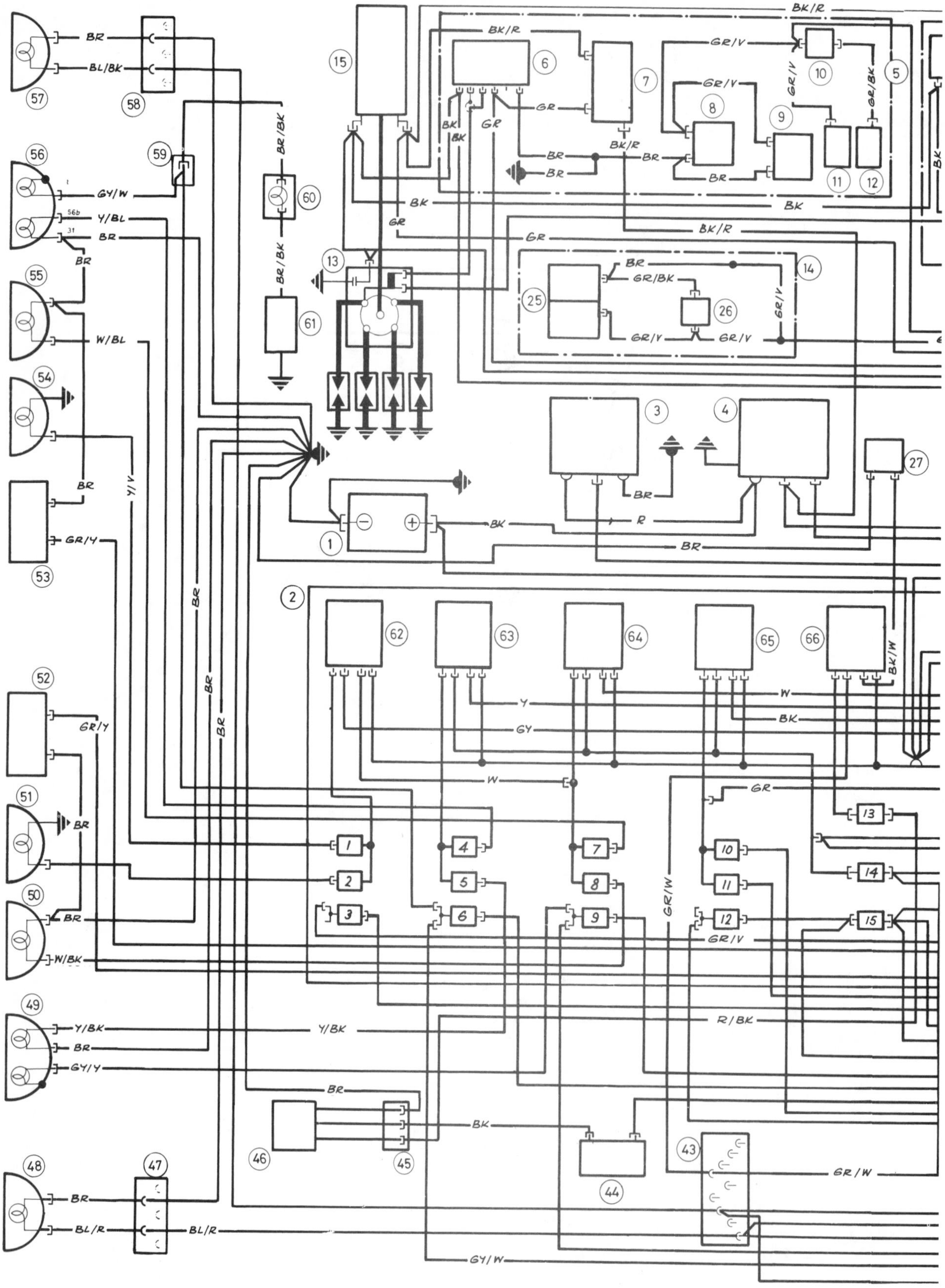

Wiring diagram for right-hand drive Series 1 320 and 323i

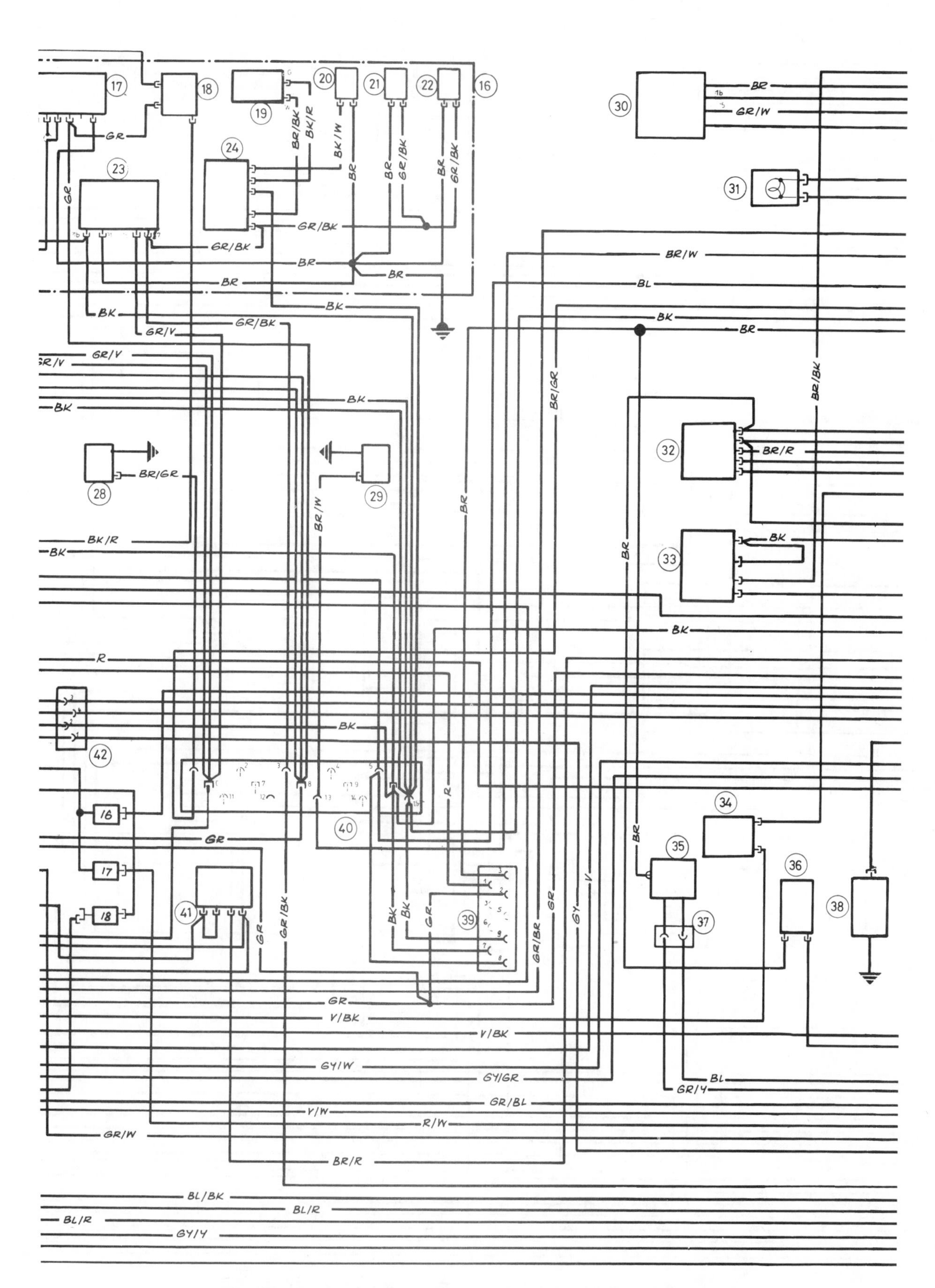

Wiring diagram for right-hand drive Series 1 320 and 323i (continued)

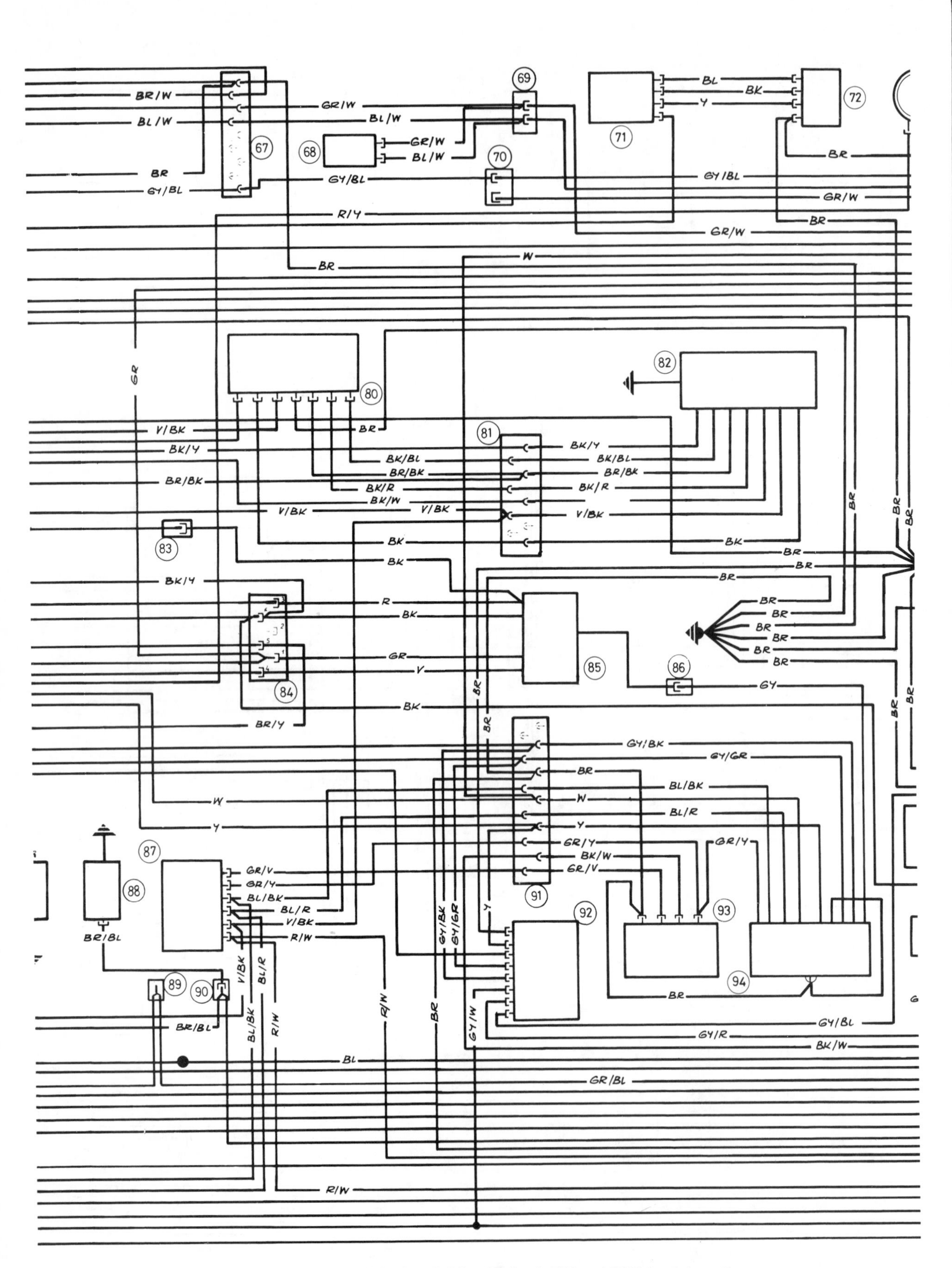

Wiring diagram for right-hand drive Series 1 320 and 323i (continued)

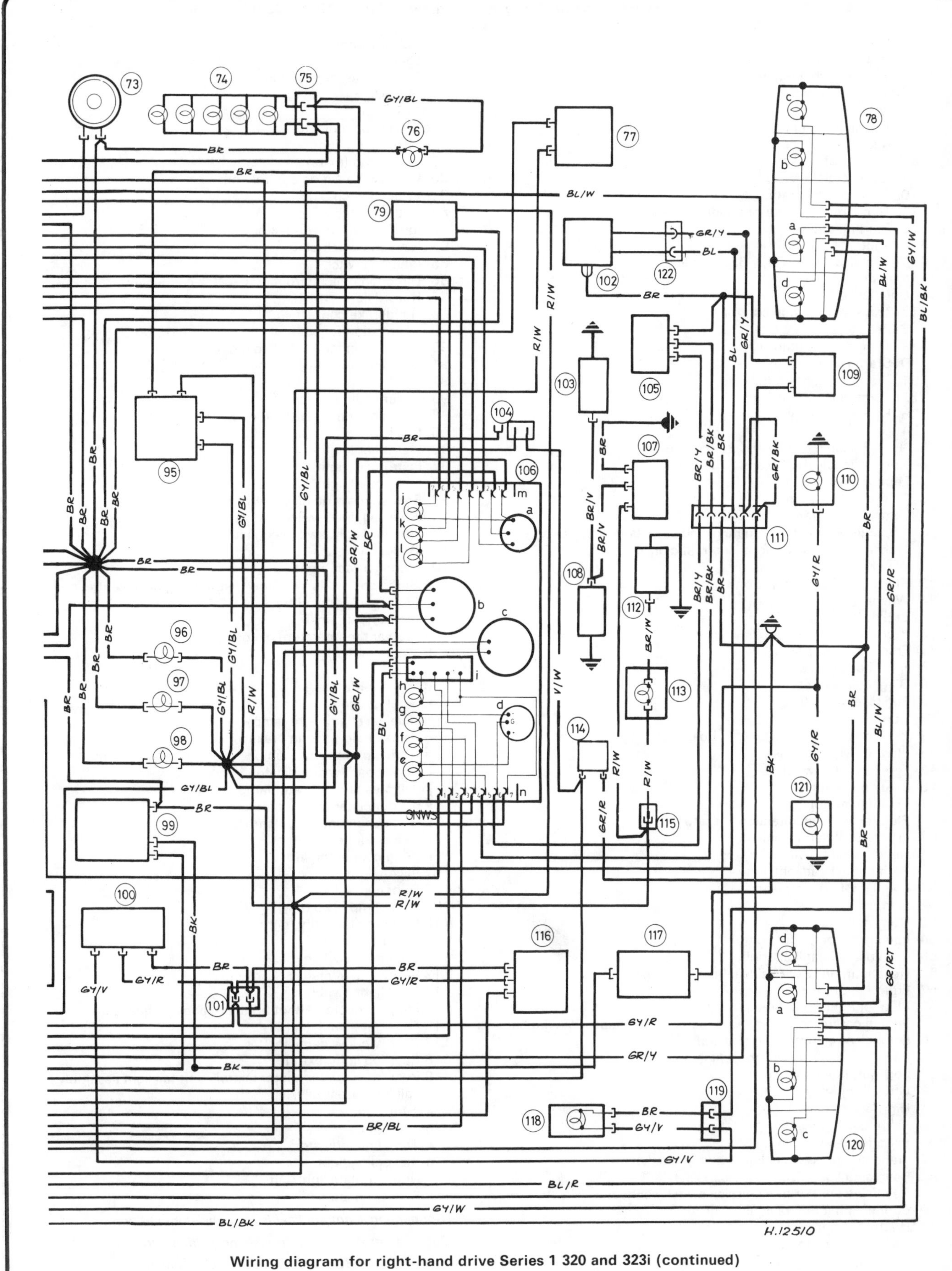

Wiring diagram for right-hand drive Series 1 320 and 323i (continued)

Key to wiring diagram for right-hand drive Series 1 320 and 323i

1 Battery
2 Central Electric Board with fuses
3 Alternator with regulator
4 Starter motor
5 Only for 320
 6 Transistor ignition control
 7 Resistors
 8 Idle cut-off valve
 9 Idle cut-off valve
 10 Coolant temperature switch
 11 Temperature motor operator for choke
 12 Starting device
13 Distributor*
14 Not applicable to 320 or 323i models
15 Ignition coil
16 Only for 323
 17 Transistor ignition control
 18 Resistors
 19 Temperature time switch
 20 Starter valve
 21 Warm-up control
 22 Throttle bypass valve
 23 Fuel pump relay
 24 Diode relay
25 Not applicable to 320 and 323i models
26 Not applicable to 320 and 323i models
27 Temperature switch
28 Oil pressure switch
29 Temperature transmitter
30 Transmission switch with range indicator (automatic only)
31 Transmission switch light (automatic only)
32 Wiper motor
33 Starter relay (automatic only)
34 Washer pump
35 Brake pad front
36 Brake fluid level control switch
37 Front brake pad plug
38 Horn button
39 Diagnosis socket
40 Engine plug
41 Horn relay
42 Plug for CEB (Central Electric Board)
43 Plug for wire harness
44 Temperature switch
45 Plug connector
46 Extra fan motor
47 Plug for left front direction indicator
48 Front left direction indicator
49 Headlight, left, with sidelight
50 High beam headlight, left
51 Fog light, front, left (extra)
52 Horn left
53 Horn right
54 Fog light, front, right (extra)
55 High beam headlight, right
56 Headlight, right, with sidelight
57 Front right direction indicator
58 Plug for right front direction indicator
59 Engine compartment light connector – right headlight wire harness
60 Engine compartment light (extra)
61 Engine compartment light switch (extra)
62 Fog light relay (extra)
63 Low beam relay
64 High beam relay
65 Power saving relay
66 Extra fan relay stage 2
67 Transmission switch plug (automatic only)
68 Reversing light switch (manual only)
69 Reversing light or transmission switch connector
70 Connection for extra equipment
71 Heater blower motor
72 Heater blower switch
73 Cigar lighter
74 Switch light
75 Switch light plug
76 Ashtray light
77 Glove box light
78 Tail light assembly, right
 a Stop light
 b Tail light
 c Direction indicator
 d Reversing light
79 Handlamp (extra)
80 Wash/wipe action control unit
81 Wiper switch plug
82 Wiper switch
83 Ignition switch connector
84 Ignition switch plug
85 Ignition switch
86 Direction indicator/dimmer switch connection
87 Hazard light switch
88 Handbrake contact
89 Connection for sunroof
90 Connection for Australian model
91 Direction indicator/dimmer switch plug
92 Light switch
93 Hazard light flasher
94 Direction indicator/dimmer switch
95 Clock
96 Instrument light
97 Instrument light
98 Instrument light
99 Rear window demister switch
100 Rear fog light switch (extra)
101 Rear fog light switch connector (extra)
102 Brake pad rear
103 Door contact, right
104 Radio connection – below instrument panel, centre, near tray
105 Fluid level transmitter
106 Instrument panel
 a Coolant temperature gauge
 b Tachometer
 c Clock
 d Speedometer
 e Fuel gauge
 f Fuel level indicator lamp
 g Brake fluid/parking brake indicator lamp
 h Direction indicator lamp
 i Brake pad wear indicator
 j Oil pressure indicator lamp
 k Battery charge indicator lamp
 l High beam indicator lamp
 m Plug connector, right
 n Plug connector, left
107 Inside light
108 Door contact left
109 Fuel pump (323 only)
110 Number plate light, right
111 Plug connector†
112 Boot lamp switch
113 Boot lamp switch
114 Stop light switch
115 Plug connector – boot front left, above wheel arch
116 Fog light switch (extra)
117 Rear window demister
118 Rear fog light (extra)
119 Rear fog light connector (extra) – left tail light assembly
120 Tail light assembly, left
 a Stop light
 b Tail light
 c Direction indicator
 d Reversing light
121 Number plate light, left
122 Plug connector

**Connection 1 not applicable for transistor ignition.*

Connections A and B for transistor ignition only

†Wire number 302 applicable to 320 model only

An explanation of the wiring codes is given on page 317

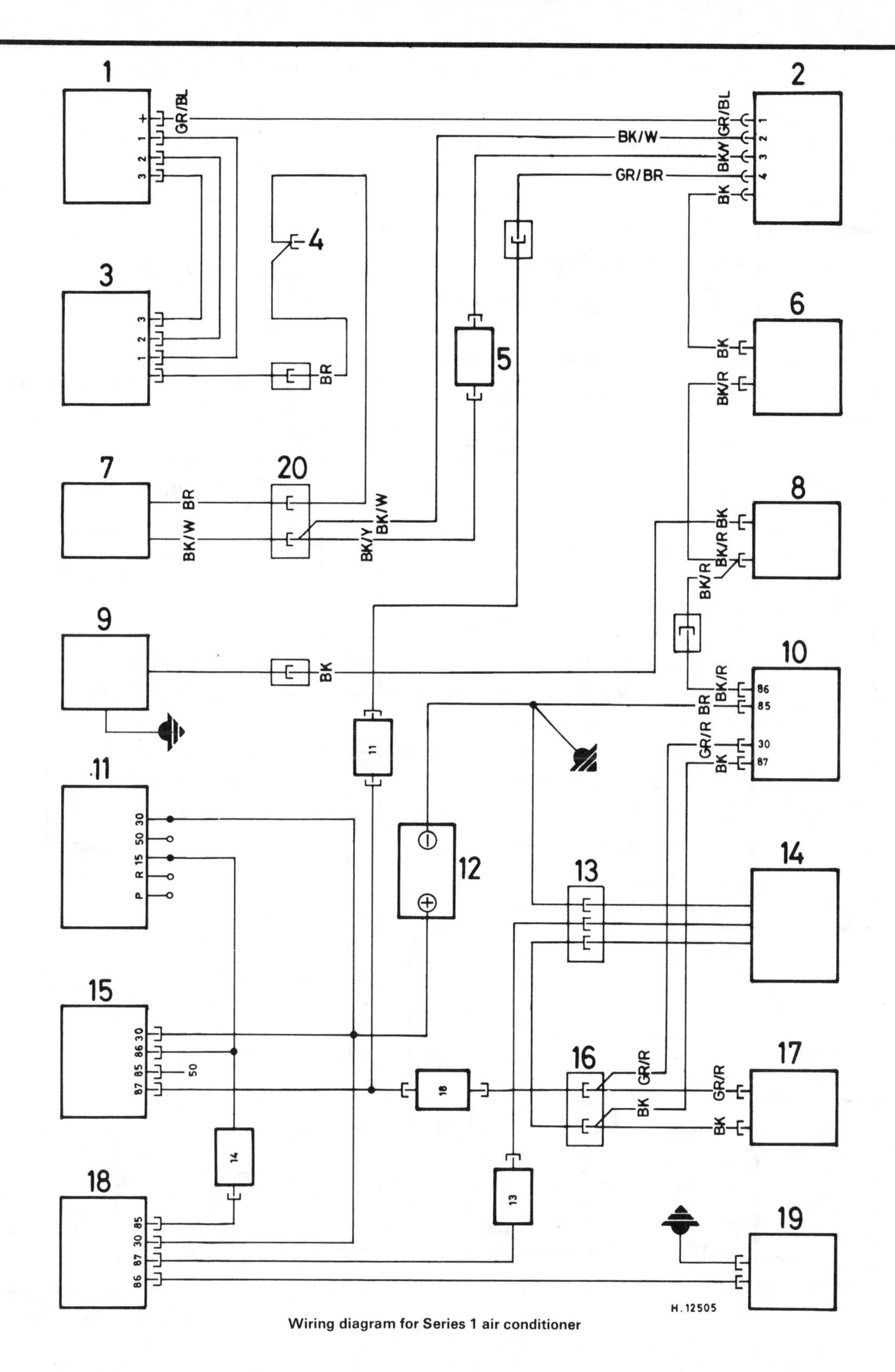

Wiring diagram for Series 1 air conditioner

1 Heater blower motor
2 A/C blower switch
3 Blower switch
4 Cigar lighter ground connector
5 Resistor
6 Temperature control switch
7 A/C blower motor
8 High pressure thermostat
9 Magnetic clutch for compressor
10 Air conditioner relay
11 Ignition switch
12 Battery
13 Plug connector
14 Extra fan motor
15 Power saving relay
16 Plug connector
17 Temperature switch 91°C
18 Extra fan relay stage 2
19 Temperature switch 99°C
20 2-pin plug connector

An explanation of the wiring codes is given on page 317

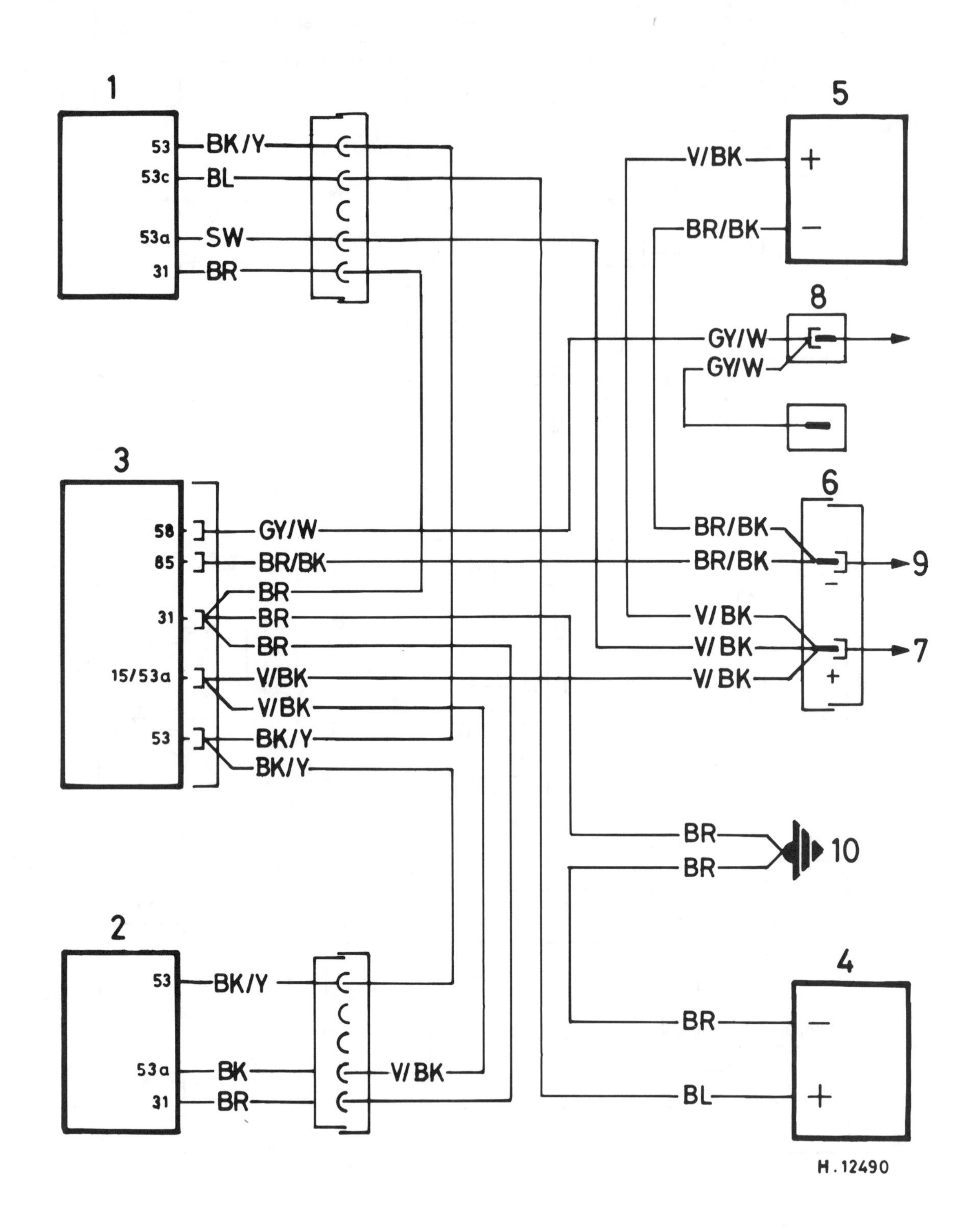

Wiring diagram for Series 1 headlight wash/wipe

1 Wiper motor, right
2 Wiper motor, left
3 Headlight cleaner sensor
4 Headlight cleaner washer pump
5 Windscreen washer pump
6 Plug connector (extra wire with washer pump wire harness)
7 To Central Electric Board fuse number 12
8 Engine compartment light connection – right headlight wire harness

An explanation of the wiring codes is given on page 317

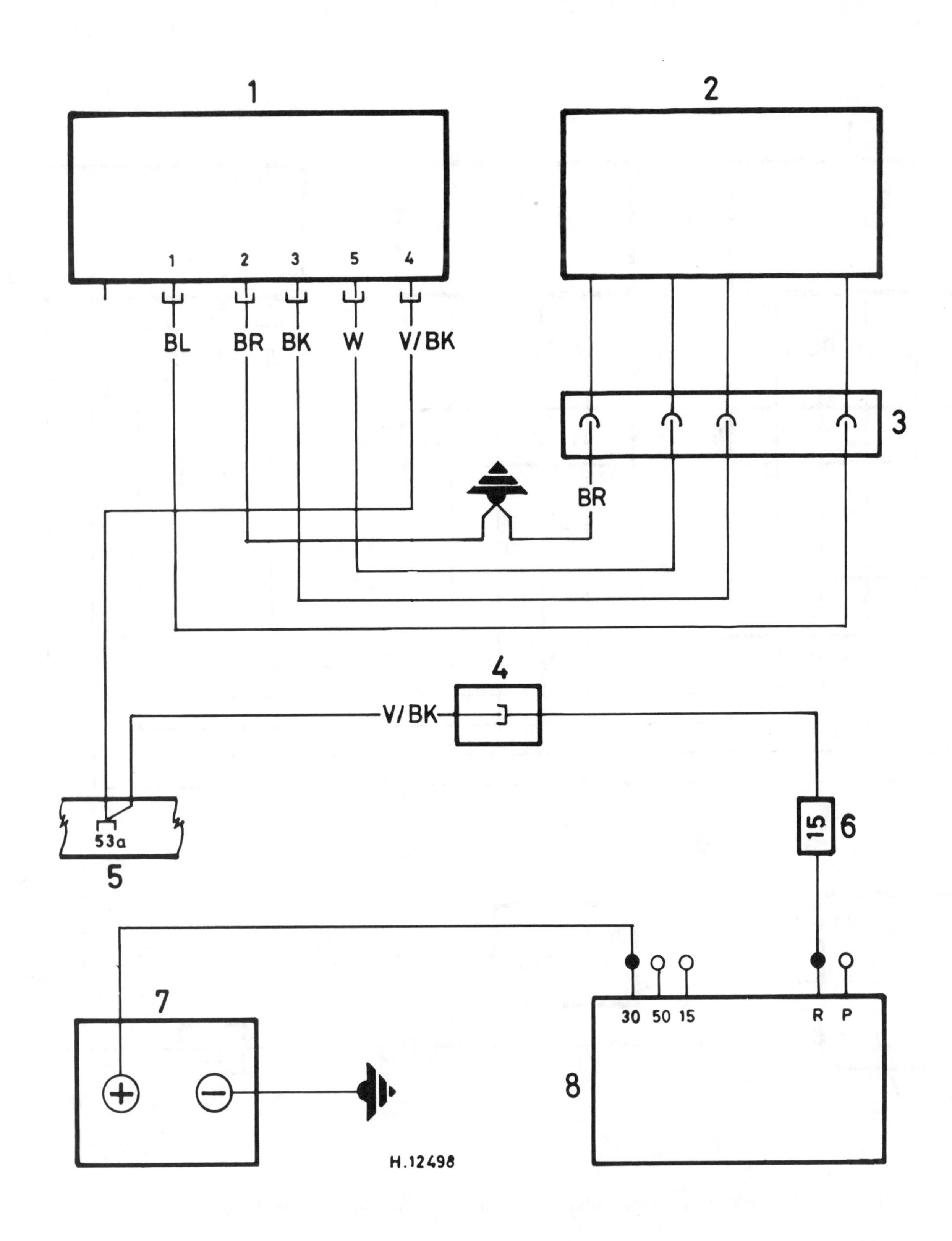

Wiring diagram for Series 1 exterior mirror, driver's door

1 Switch
2 Mirror
3 Plug connector – on inside of mirror base
4 Plug connector
5 Wash/wipe control unit
6 Central Electric Board
7 Battery
8 Ignition lock

An explanation of the wiring codes is given on page 317

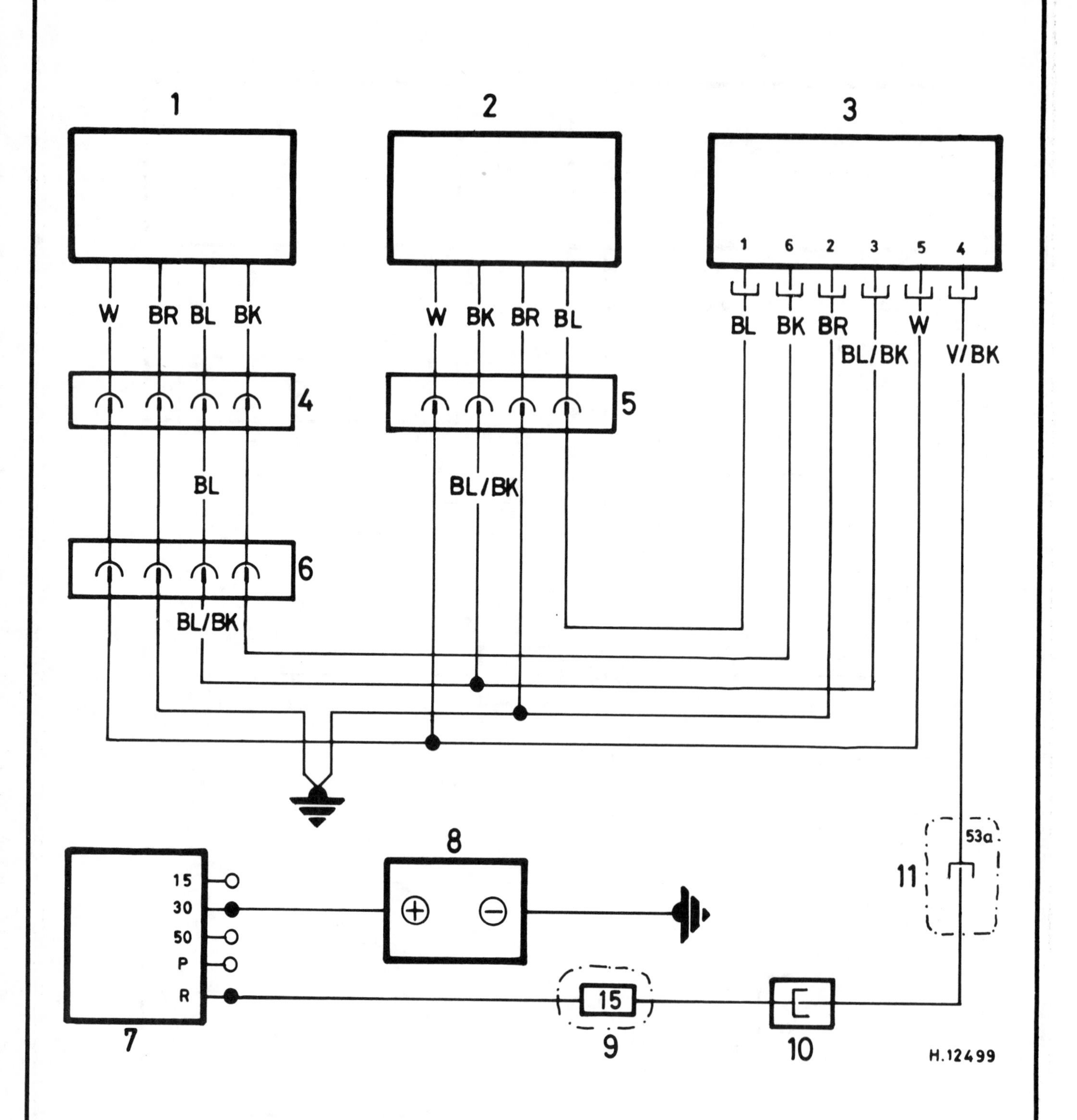

Wiring diagram for Series 1 exterior mirrors, driver and passenger doors

1 Mirror (passenger's door)
2 Mirror (driver's door)
3 Switch
4 Plug connector – on mirror base of passenger's door
5 Plug connector – on mirror base of driver's door
6 Plug connector – next to wash/wipe control unit
7 Ignition lock
8 Battery
9 Central Electric Board
10 Plug connector
11 Wash/wipe control unit

An explanation of the wiring codes is given on page 317

Key to wiring diagram on pages 329 to 334 for Series 2 320i and 323i models

1 Starter motor
2 Wiper motor
3 Washer pump
4 Fuel pump
5 Motor for electrically-operated mirror
6 Motor for electrically-operated mirror (special equipment only)
7 Heater blower motor
8 Digital clock
9 Service indicator
10 Coolant temperature gauge
11 Electronic tachometer
12 Fuel gauge
13 Fuel level transmitter
14 Economy control
15 Electronic speedometer
16 Ballast resistors for heater motor
17 Transmission switch (automatic only)
18 Reversing light switch
19 Ignition/starter switch
20 Sidelight switch
21 Rear window demister switch
22 Horn switch
23 Wiper switch
24 Hazard light switch
25 Indicator switch
26 Low beam switch
27 Sidelight switch II
28 Door contact, left
29 Door contact, right
30 Boot light switch
31 Rear fog light switch
32 Front fog light switch (323i only)
33 High beam switch
34 Rheostat switch for instrument and front fog lights
35 Switch for low beams and number plate lights
36 Glove box light switch
37 Fuse for high beam, left
38 Fuse for high beam, right
39 Fuse for turn signal indicator
40 Fuse for wash/wipe and headlight cleaner system
41 Fuse for stop lights and cruise control
42 Fuse for two-tone horns
43 Fuse for rear window demister
44 Fuse for engine electrical equipment and reversing light
45 Fuse for instruments
46 Fuse for fuel pump and fuel transfer pump
47 Fuse for radio and check control instrument
48 Fuse for low beam, left
49 Fuse for low beam, right
50 Fuse for rear fog light
51 Fuse for seat heating
52 Fuse for sunroof
53 Fuse for reversing light and mirror
54 Fuse for heater blower
55 Fuse for digital clock, interior lights, boot light and glovebox light
56 Fuse for overnight, tail and sidelights – left
57 Fuse for overnight, tail and sidelights – right
58 Fuse for hazard lights (30S/A24)
59 Fuse for door wire
60 Fuse for cigar lighter and extra heater
61 Fuse for front fog light, left (323i only)
62 Fuse for front fog light, right (323i only)
63 Battery
64 Alternator
65 Two-tone horn II
66 Two-tone horn I
67 Direction indicator, right front
68 Direction indicator, right rear
69 Direction indicator, left rear
70 Direction indicator, left front
71 Stop light, left
72 Stop light, right
73 Handbrake indicator light
74 Brake fluid indicator light
75 Oil pressure indicator light
76 Central warning light
77 Brake pad wear sensor, rear right (323i only)
78 Brake pad wear indicator
79 Brake pad wear sensor, front left
80 Fuel warning light
81 Indicator light for direction indicator, left
82 Indicator light for direction indicator, right
83 Indicator light for high beams
84 Indicator light for battery charge
85 Indicator light for front fog lights
86 Indicator light for rear fog lights
87 Horn relay (in Central Electric Board)
88 High beams relay
89 Low beams relay
90 Sunroof and seat heating relay (in Central Electric Board)

Continued overleaf

Key to wiring diagram on pages 329 to 334 for Series 2 320i and 323i models (continued)

91 Heater blower and rear window demister relay (in Central Electric Board)
92 Front fog lights relay (in Central Electric Board)
93 Rear fog lights relay (in Central Electric Board)
94 Wash/wipe action control unit (in Central Electric Board)
95 Starter lock relay (lower steering column casing) (automatic only)
96 Hazard lights relay (in steering column)
97 Bulb tester for main lights (in boot on left side)
98 Bulb tester for tail lights (in boot on left side)
99 Bulb tester for stop and number plate lights (in boot on left side)
100 Reversing light, left
101 Reversing light, right
102 Switch plate light
103 Rear window demister
104 Interior light, left
105 Interior light, right
106 Boot light
107 Handlight (chargeable)
108 Glovebox light
109 Rear fog light, left
110 Rear fog light, right
111 High beam, left
112 High beam, right
113 Low beam, left
114 Low beam, right
115 Fog light, front left (323i only)
116 Fog light, front right (323i only)
117 Tail light, left
118 Tail light, right
119 Low beam headlight, right (sidelight)
120 Low beam headlight, left (sidelight)
121 Number plate light, right
122 Number plate light, left
123 Instrument light I
124 Instrument light II
125 Cigar lighter
126 Light for heater controls I
127 Light for heater controls II
128 Stop light switch
129 Washer fluid level switch
130 Coolant level switch
131 Oil level switch
132 Driver's door mirror switch
133 Passenger's door mirror switch (special equipment only)
134 Handbrake switch
135 Brake fluid level switch
136 Oil pressure switch
137 Water valve final position switch
138 Blower switch
139 Power rail in Central Electric Board
140 19-pin plug connector for main harness to engine harness
141 26-pin connection for special equipment
142 Sunroof
143 9-pin plug connection for main harness to ignition switch
144 Plug connection for idle boost (on tunnel, automatic wire)
145 2-pin plug connection of main harness to reversing light switch
146 29-pin plug connection of main harness to instrument panel
147 Plug connection of main harness to ignition switch (151) (steering column casing)
148 8-pin plug connection (steering column casing)
149 2-pin connection for wiper motor
150 Connection for headlight cleaners
151 6-pin plug connection of main harness to wiper switch (steering column casing)
152 3-pin plug of main harness to left interior light
153 13-pin plug connector of main harness to direction indicator/dimmer switch (steering column casing)
154 3-pin plug connection of main harness to right interior light
155 6-pin plug connection of main harness to door wire
156 Plug connection of ignition/starter switch to direction indicator/headlight-dimmer switch
157 Connection for bulb tester
158 Check control
159 Instrument cluster
160 Coolant temperature sensor
161 Speed sensor
162 Plug connection for driver's door
163 Plug connection for passenger's door
164 Connection for electrically-operated exterior mirror
165 Connection for electrically-operated extra mirror (special equipment only)
166 Connection for LE-Jetronic control unit
167 13-pin plug connector of main harness to heater controls
168 Connection for air conditioner
169 7-pin connection for blower switch
170 Water valve

An explanation of the wiring codes is given on page 317

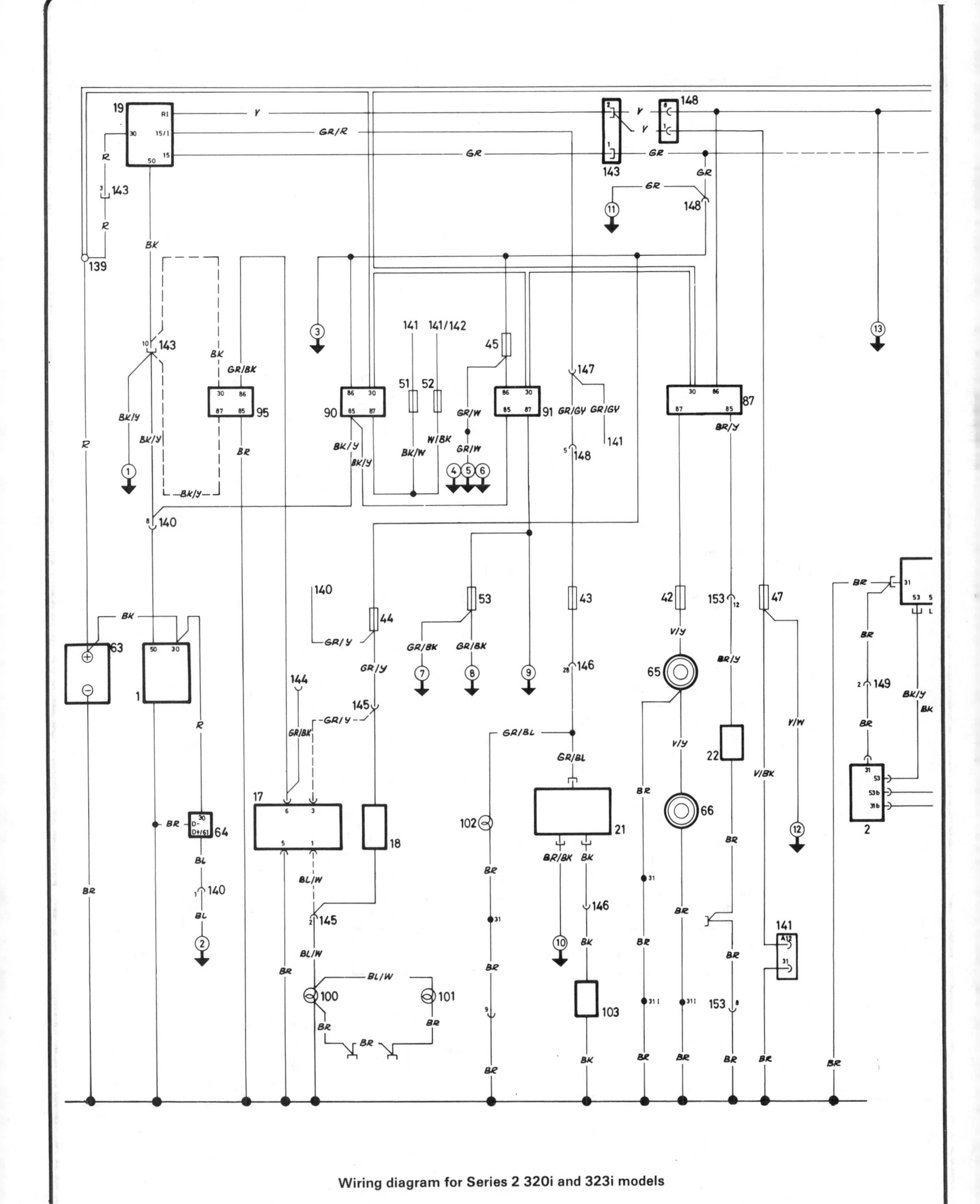

Wiring diagram for Series 2 320i and 323i models

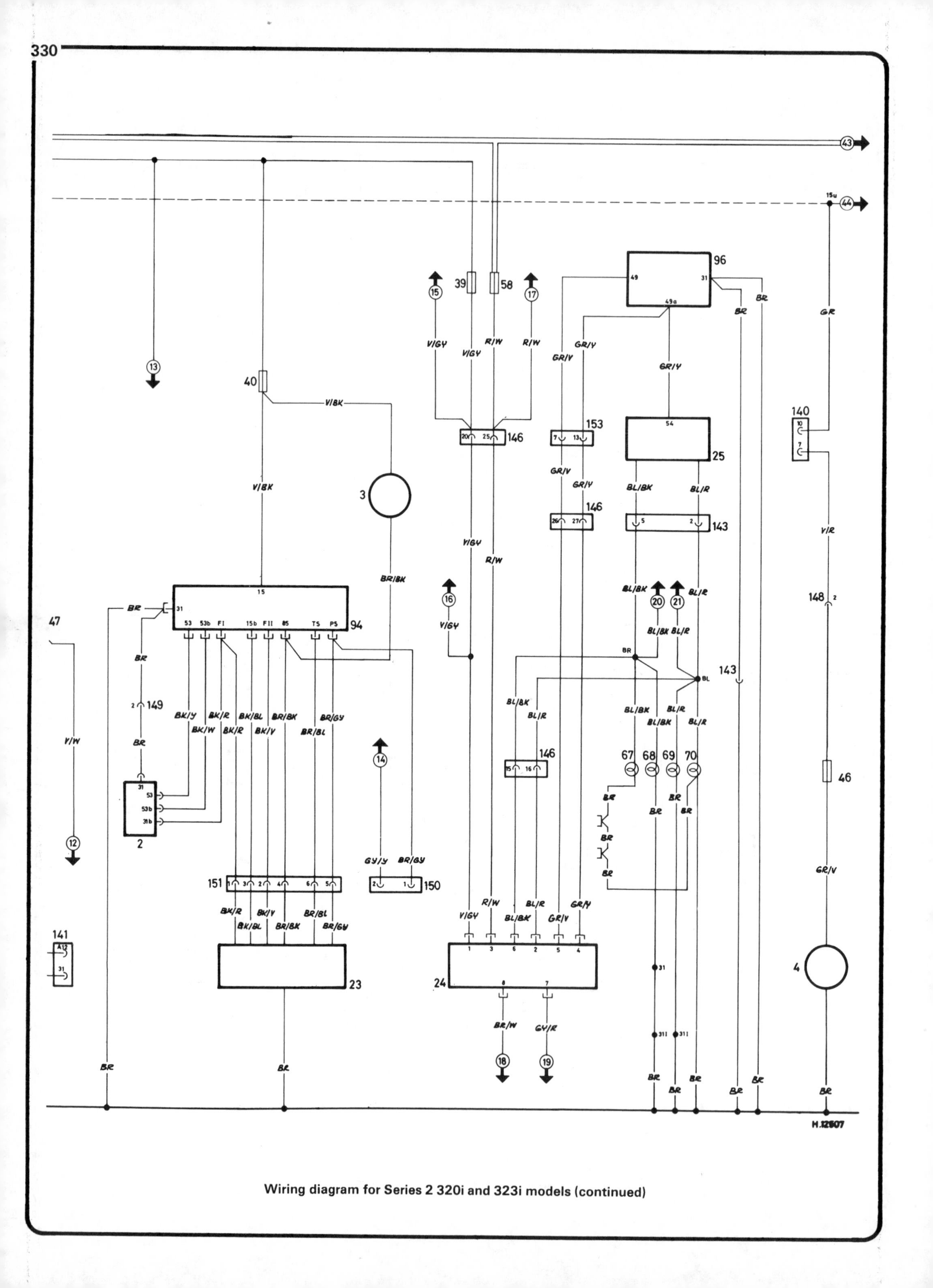

Wiring diagram for Series 2 320i and 323i models (continued)

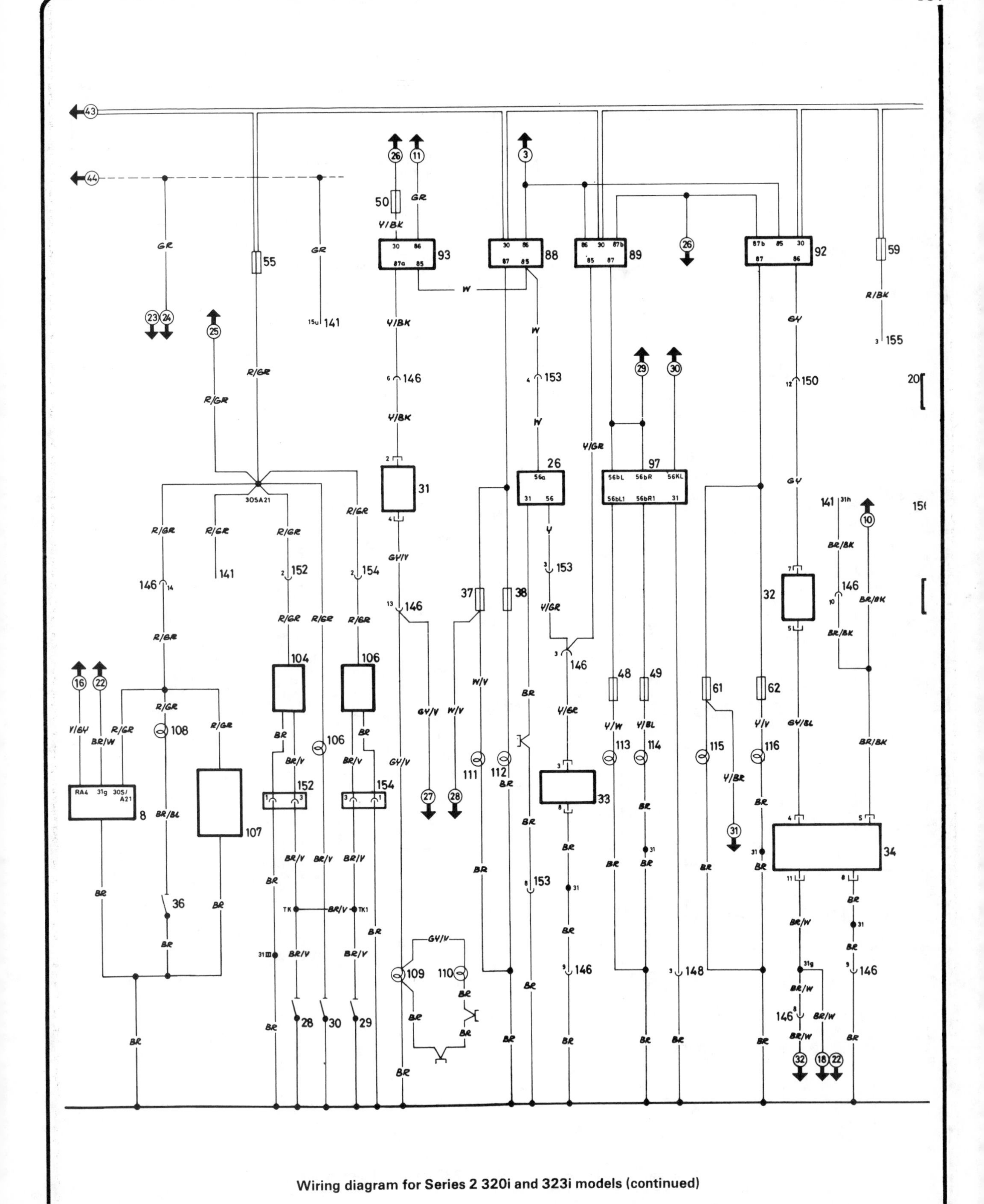

Wiring diagram for Series 2 320i and 323i models (continued)

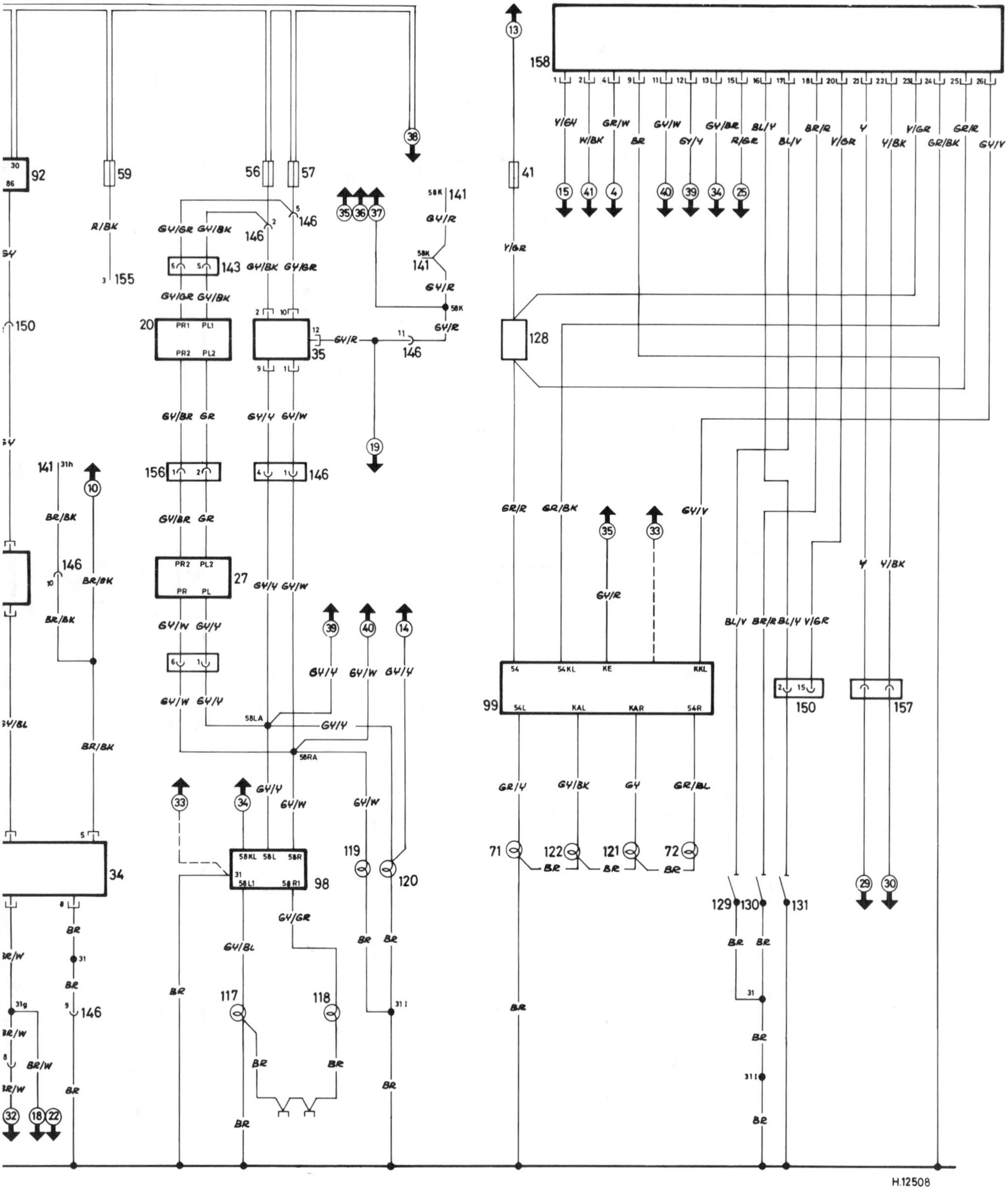

H.12508

Wiring diagram for Series 2 320i and 323i models (continued)

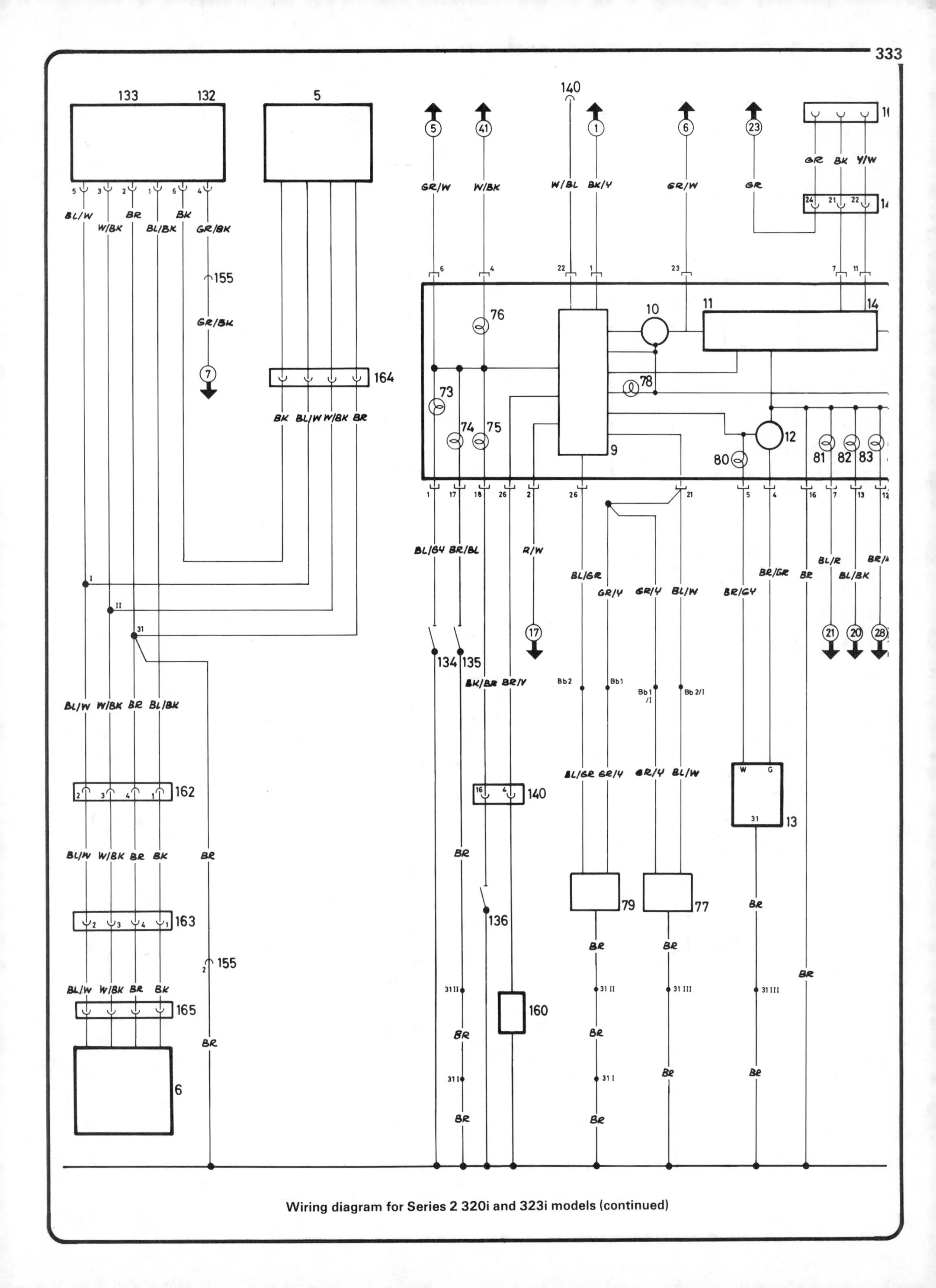

Wiring diagram for Series 2 320i and 323i models (continued)

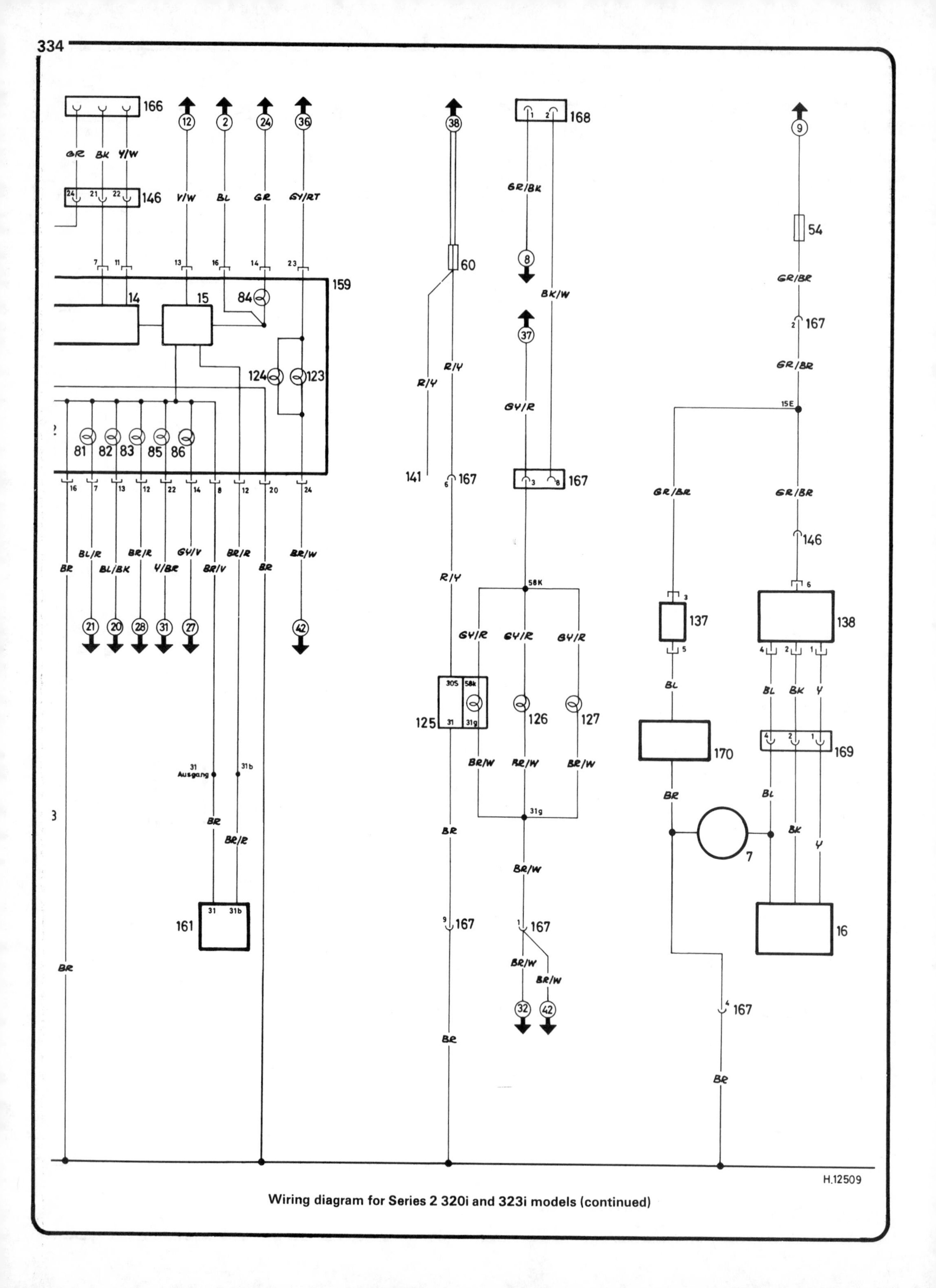

Wiring diagram for Series 2 320i and 323i models (continued)

Key to wiring diagram on pages 336 and 337 for Series 2 engine electrics and fuel injection

1 Injection control unit (in glove box)
2 Connection for injection control unit
3 Throttle switch
4 Airflow sensor
5 Fuel pump relay
6 Battery
7 Connection for 70°C temperature switch (special country version only)
8 Coolant temperature sensor
9 Injection valve
10 Cold start valve
11 Temperature time switch
12 Distributor
13 Position transmitter
14 Diagnosis connection
15 Oil pressure switch
16 Temperature transmitter
17 Oil level switch
18 Ignition coil
19 Starter motor
20 Alternator
21 Spark plugs
22 Control unit for transistor ignition (on end of heater)
23 Engine plug
24 Main wire harness
25 Service indicator
26 Oil pressure
27 Oil dynamic
28 Electric fuel pump
29 Temperature gauge
30 Oil static
31 Connection for 70°C temperature switch (for acceleration enrichment)

An explanation of the wiring codes is given on page 317

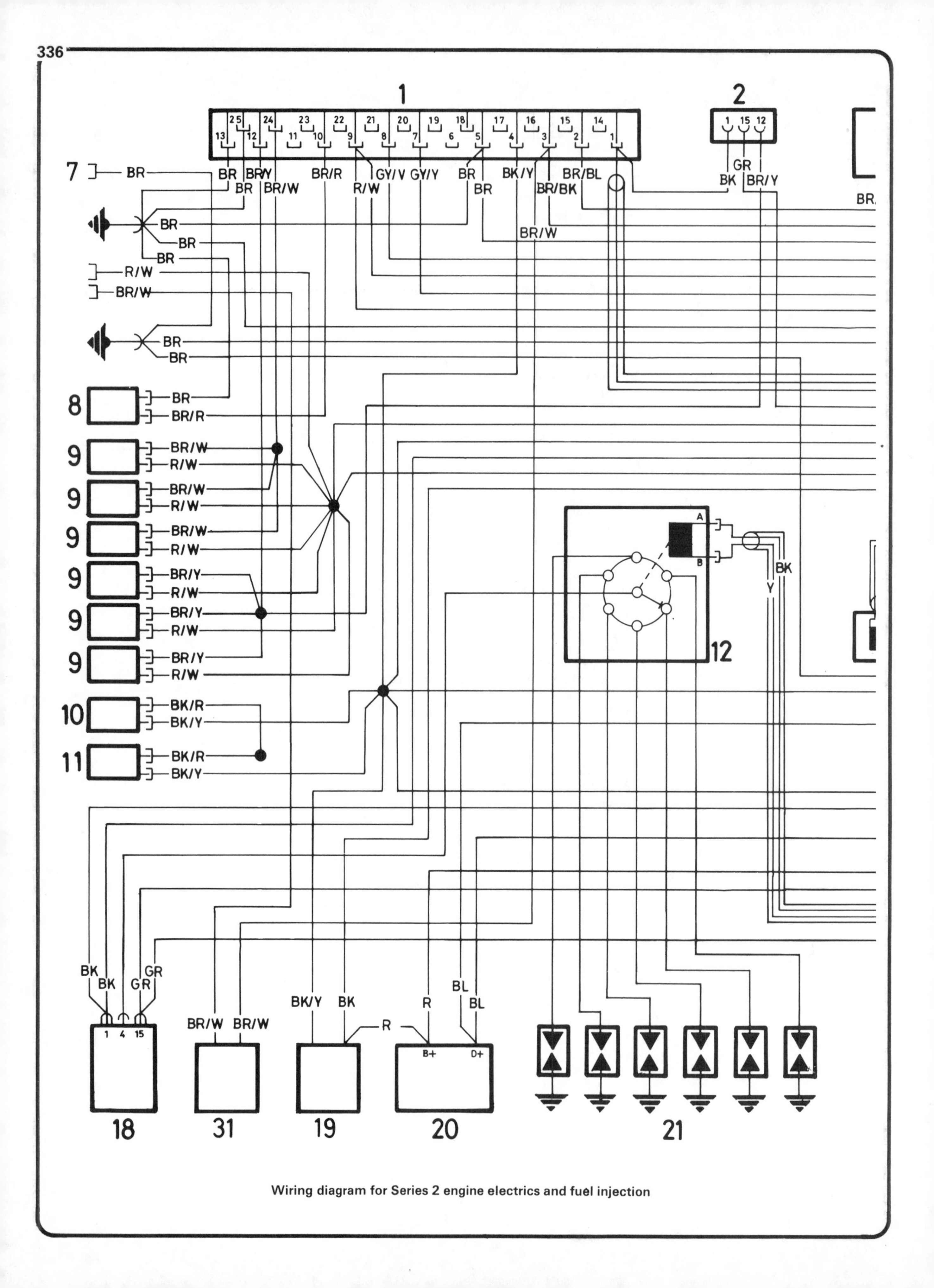

Wiring diagram for Series 2 engine electrics and fuel injection

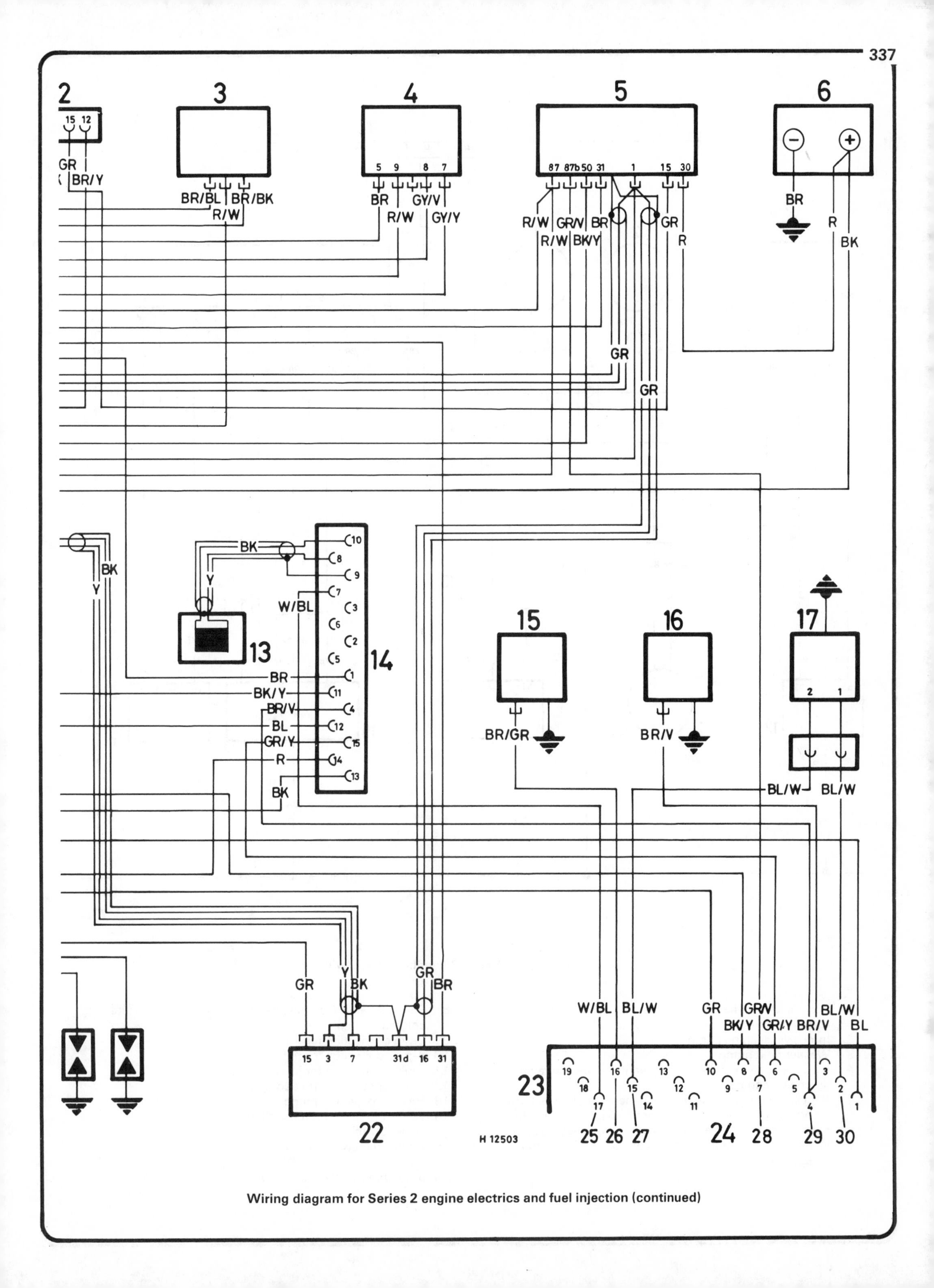

Wiring diagram for Series 2 engine electrics and fuel injection (continued)

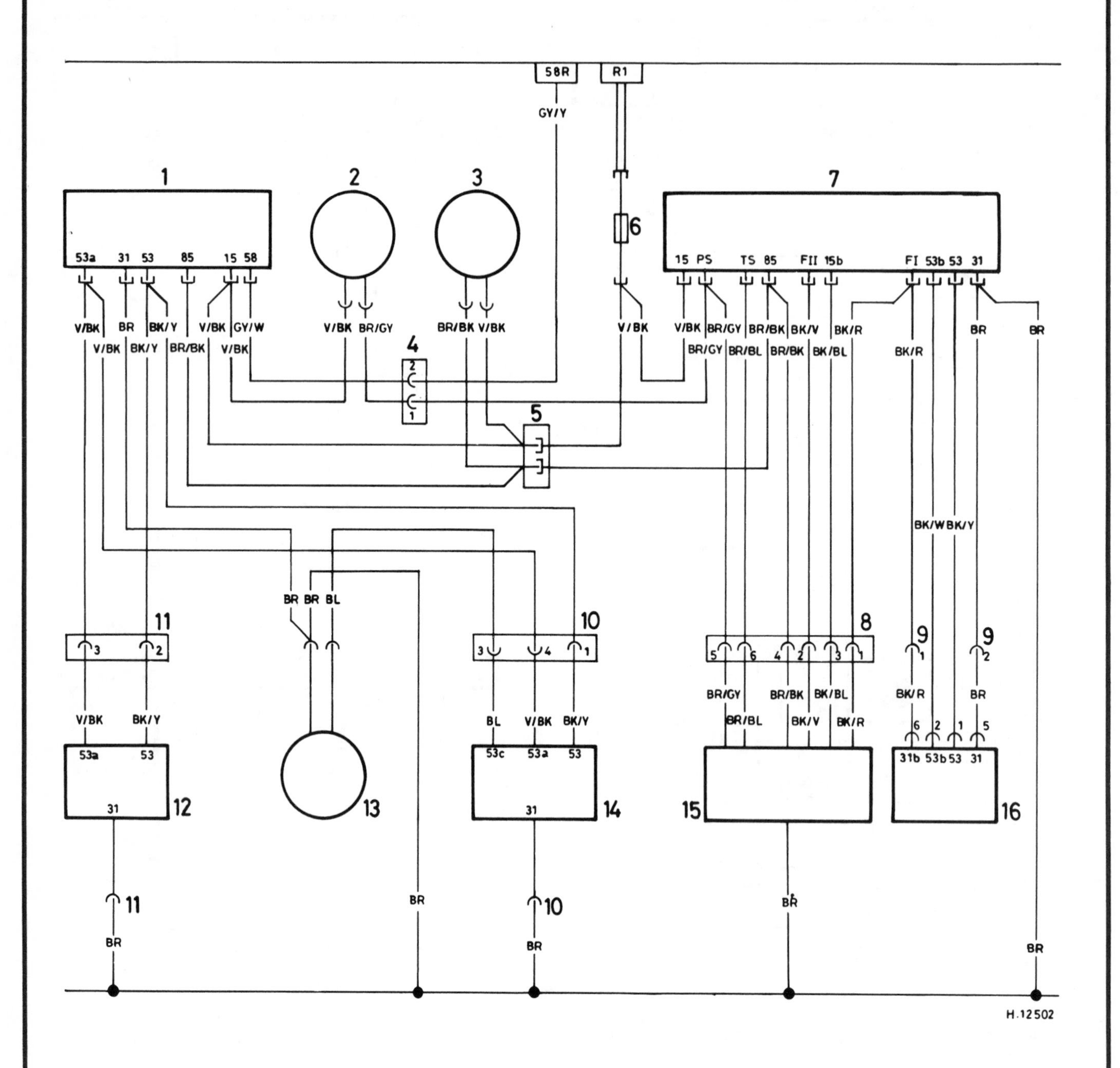

Wiring diagram for Series 2 headlight wash/wipe

1 Control unit for headlight cleaners (on tank in engine compartment)
2 Intensive cleaning pump
3 Washer fluid pump
4 Plug connection for headlight cleaners – main wire harness (in engine compartment)
5 Plug connection for headlight cleaners – main wire harness (in engine compartment) (washer fluid pump connection)
6 Fuse for headlight cleaners and intensive cleaning system
7 Wash/wipe intermittent action control unit (in Central Electric Board)
8 Plug connection of main harness for wiper switch (steering column casing)
9 2-pin connection for wiper motor
10 4-pin connection for right wiper motor
11 3-pin connection for left wiper motor
12 Wiper motor for left headlight
13 Headlight cleaner pump
14 Wiper motor for right headlight
15 Wiper switch
16 Windscreen wiper motor

An explanation of the wiring codes is given on page 317

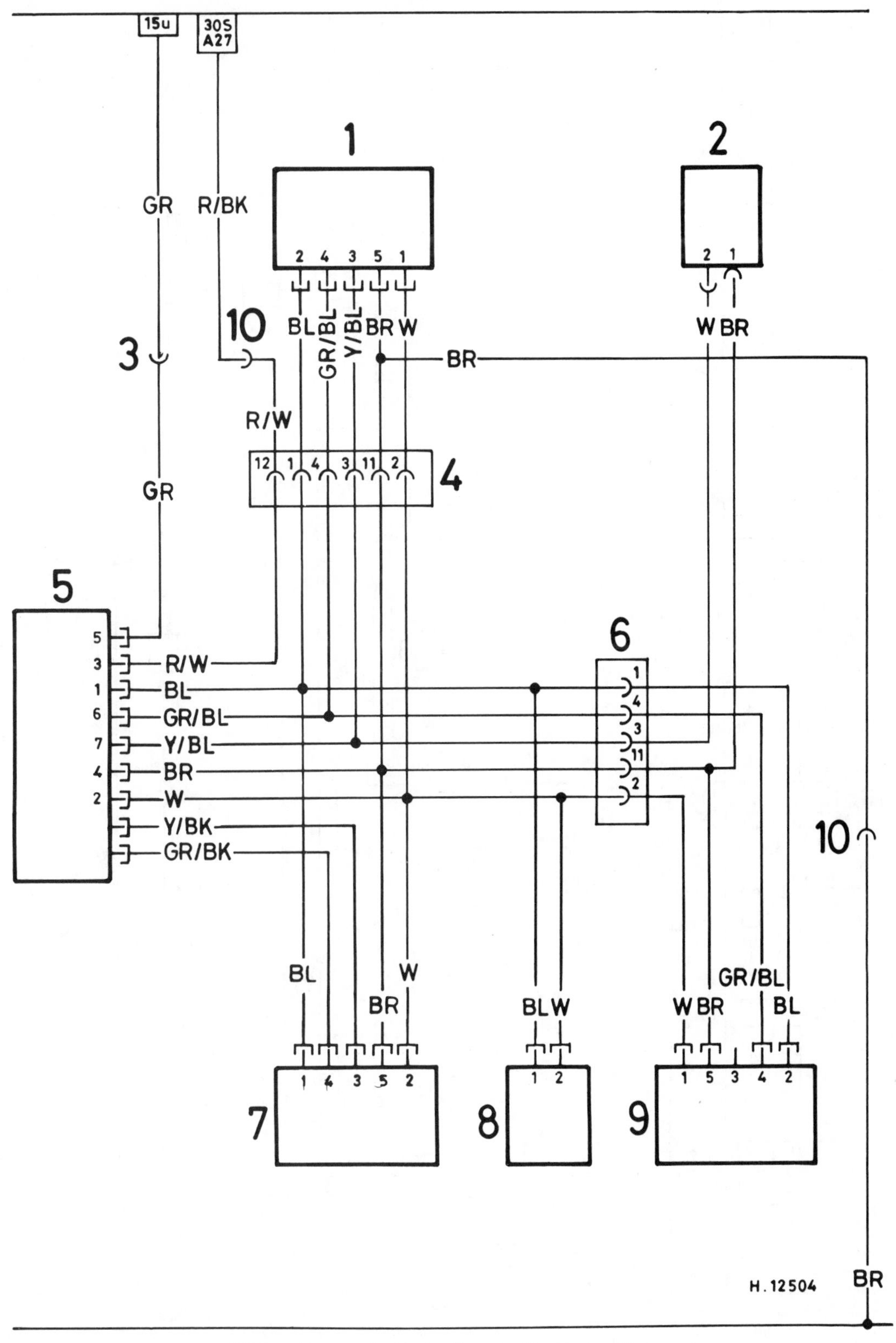

Wiring diagram for Series 2 central locking system

1 Driver's door central locking motor
2 Microswitch in passenger's door
3 Special equipment plug 15u (lower steering column casing)
4 13-pin plug connection for driver's door central locking wire
5 Central locking electronic control (in A pillar)
6 13-pin plug connection for passenger's door central locking wire
7 Boot lid central locking motor
8 Tank flap central locking motor
9 Passenger's door central locking motor
10 6-pin plug connection for driver's door main harness

An explanation of the wiring codes is given on page 317

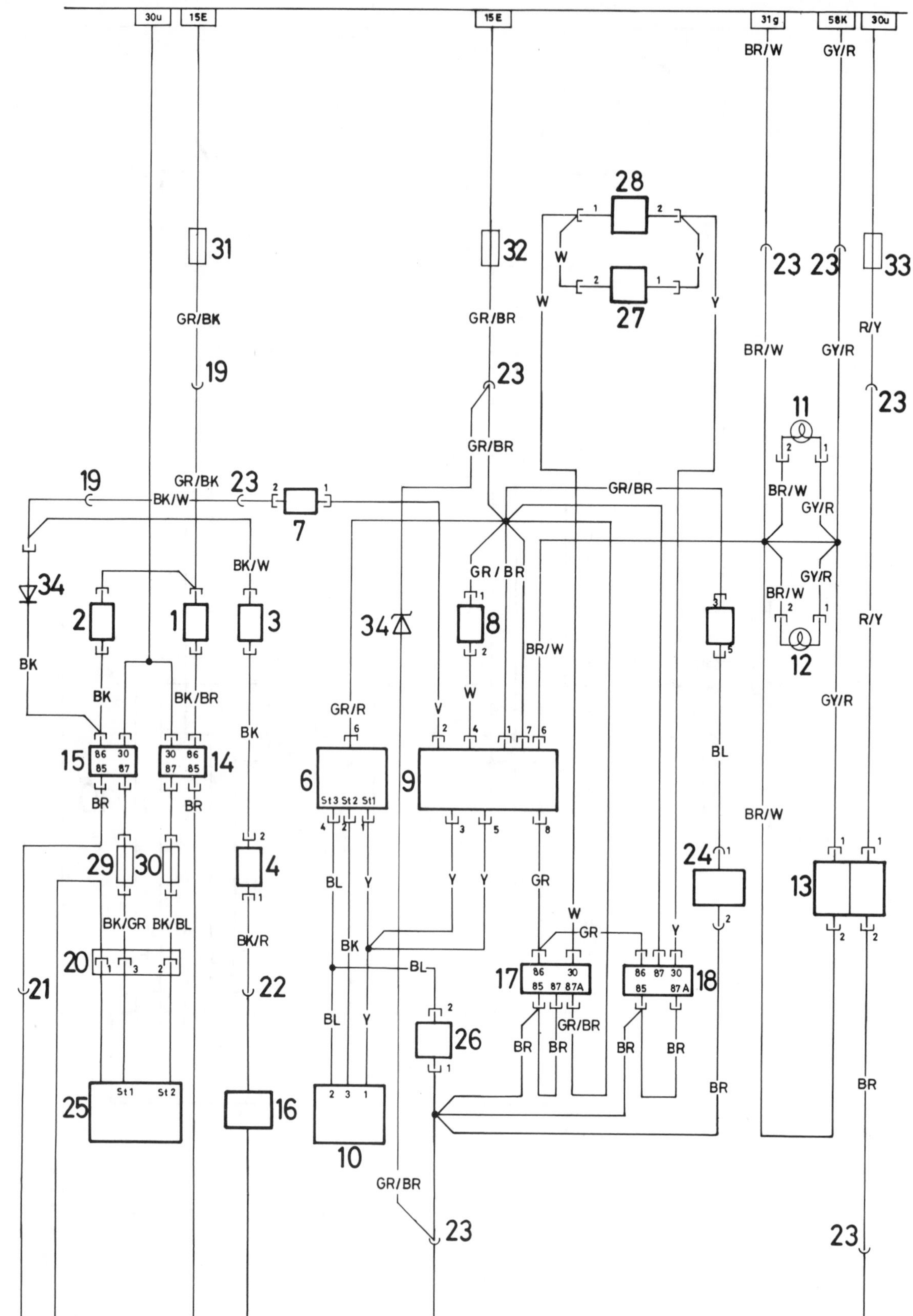

H.12506

Wiring diagram for Series 2 air conditioner

Key to wiring diagram on page 340 for Series 2 air conditioner

1 Temperature switch 99°C
2 Temperature switch 91°C
3 Low pressure pressostat switch
4 High pressure pressostat switch
5 Water valve final position switch
6 Heater blower switch
7 Evaporator thermostat
8 Air distribution final position switch
9 Bypass air switch
10 Ballast resistors for heater motor
11 Gate light 1
12 Gate light 2
13 Cigar lighter and light
14 Extra fan relay 99°C
15 Extra fan relay 91°C
16 Electromagnetic coupling for compressor
17 Fresh air/bypass air relay 1
18 Fresh air/bypass air relay 2
19 2-pin plug connection of extra fan harness to main harness
20 Connection for extra fan motor
21 8-pin plug connection
22 Connection for compressor
23 9-pin plug connection of main harness to heater/air conditioner harness
24 Water valve
25 Extra fan motor
26 Heater blower motor
27 Fresh air/bypass air blower 2 motor
28 Fresh air/bypass air blower 1 motor
29 Fuse for extra fan 91°C
30 Fuse for extra fan 99°C
31 Fuse for reversing light, door wire
32 Fuse for A/C heater blower
33 Fuse for cigar lighter
34 Diode

An explanation of the wiring codes is given on page 317

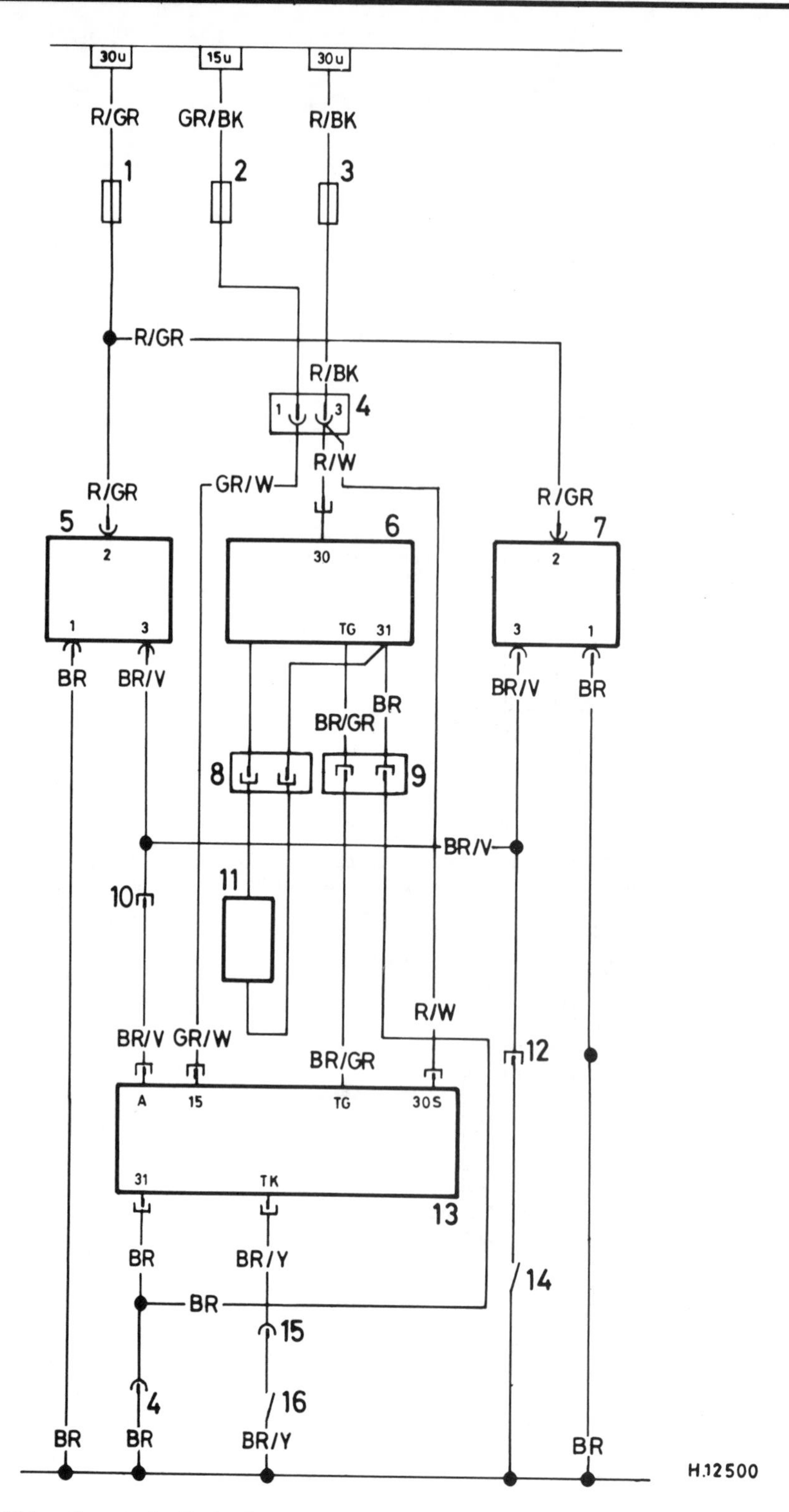

Wiring diagram for Series 2 delayed interior light and heated door lock

1 Fuse for interior lights
2 Fuse for mirror operation and heating
3 Fuse for door lock heating
4 6-pin plug connection of main harness to door wire (in A pillar)
5 Interior light, left
6 Door lock heat control unit (in A pillar)
7 Interior light, right
8 Heating ring connection
9 Door lock heating 3-pin connection
10 Plug connection of main harness for interior light delayed off-action (in A pillar)
11 Heating ring for door lock
12 Right door contact connection
13 Interior light time control unit (in A pillar)
14 Right door contact
15 Left door contact connection
16 Left door contact

An explanation of the wiring codes is given on page 317

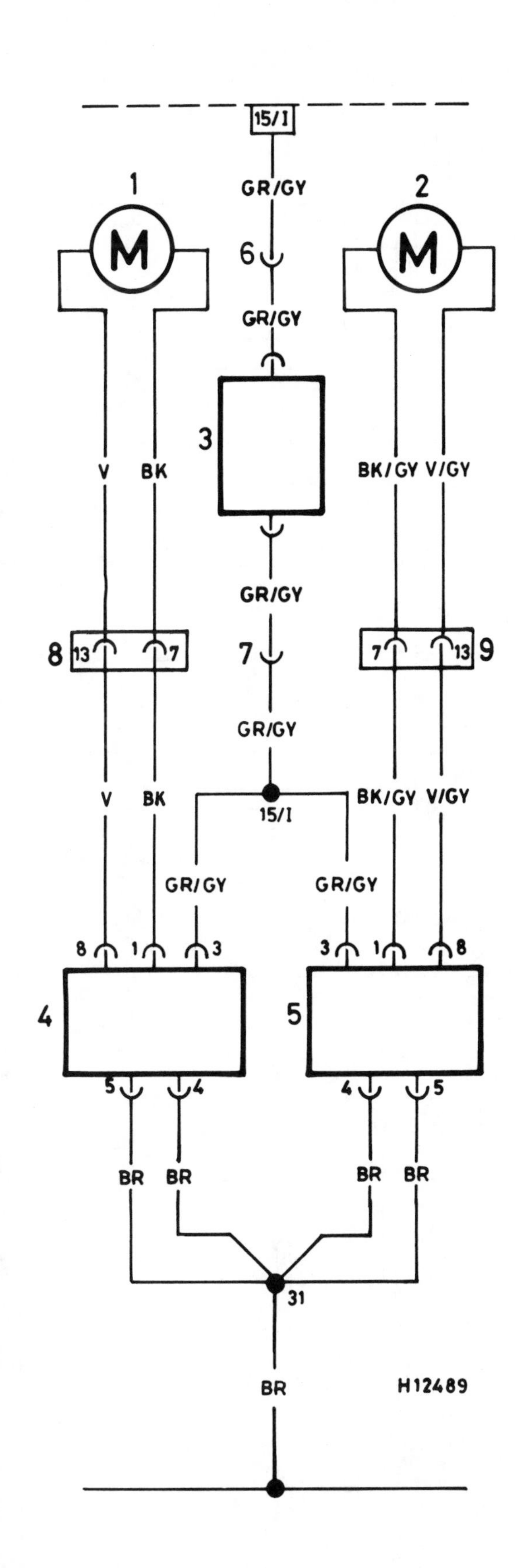

Wiring diagram for Series 2 power-operated front windows

1 Driver's door electric window motor
2 Passenger's door electric window motor
3 Electric window overload safety cutout
4 Left door electric window switch
5 Right door electric window switch
6 Special equipment plug
7 Plug connection for electric window wire overload safety cutout
8 Driver's door electric window plug connection
9 Passenger's door electric window plug connection

An explanation of the wiring codes is given on page 317

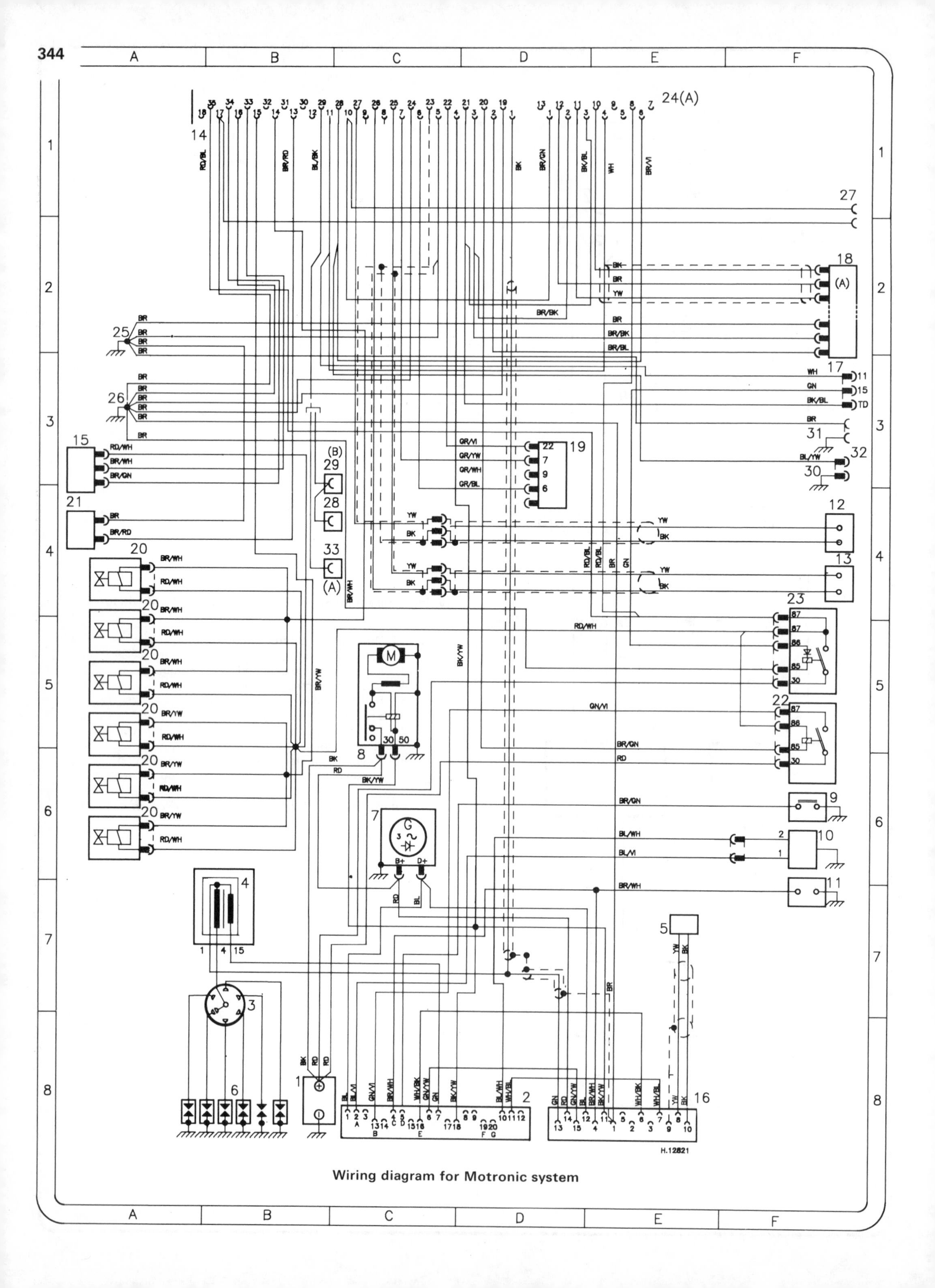

Wiring diagram for Motronic system

Key to wiring diagram on page 344 for Motronic system

No	Component	Grid location
A	Oil level	C8
B	Electric fuel pump	C8
C	Temperature gauge	C8
D	Oil pressure	C8
E	Airbag	C8
F	Oil level	D8
G	Service indicator	D8
1	Battery	B8
2	Engine plug (heater wall)	D8
3	Distributor	B7
4	Ignition coil	B7
5	Position transmitter	E7
6	Spark plugs	B8
7	Alternator	C6
8	Starter	C5
9	Oil pressure switch	F6
10	Oil level switch	F6
11	Temperature transmitter	F6
12	Speed sensor	F4
13	Reference mark sensor	F4
14	DME control unit (in glovebox)	B1
15	Idle positioner	A3
16	Diagnosis plug	E8
17	Wire harness connection (near glovebox)	F3
18	Throttle valve switch	F2
19	Airflow sensor	D3
20	Fuel injectors	A4/5/6
21	Coolant temperature sensor	A4
22	Relay 1 (relay plate)	F5
23	Relay 2 (relay plate)	F5
24	Independent electronic transmission control connection (in glovebox)	E1
25	Earth – electronics	A2
26	Earth – final stage	A3
27	Identifier plug connection – open in automatics	F1
28	A/C compressor plug	C4
29	A/C compressor clutch	C3
30	Transmission connection	F3
31	Terminal 31 connection	F3
32	Connected in cars with manual transmission	F3
33	A/C compressor connection	C4
(A)	Models with independent electronic control connections	
(B)	Models without independent electronic control connections	

For key to symbols and colour codes see page 355

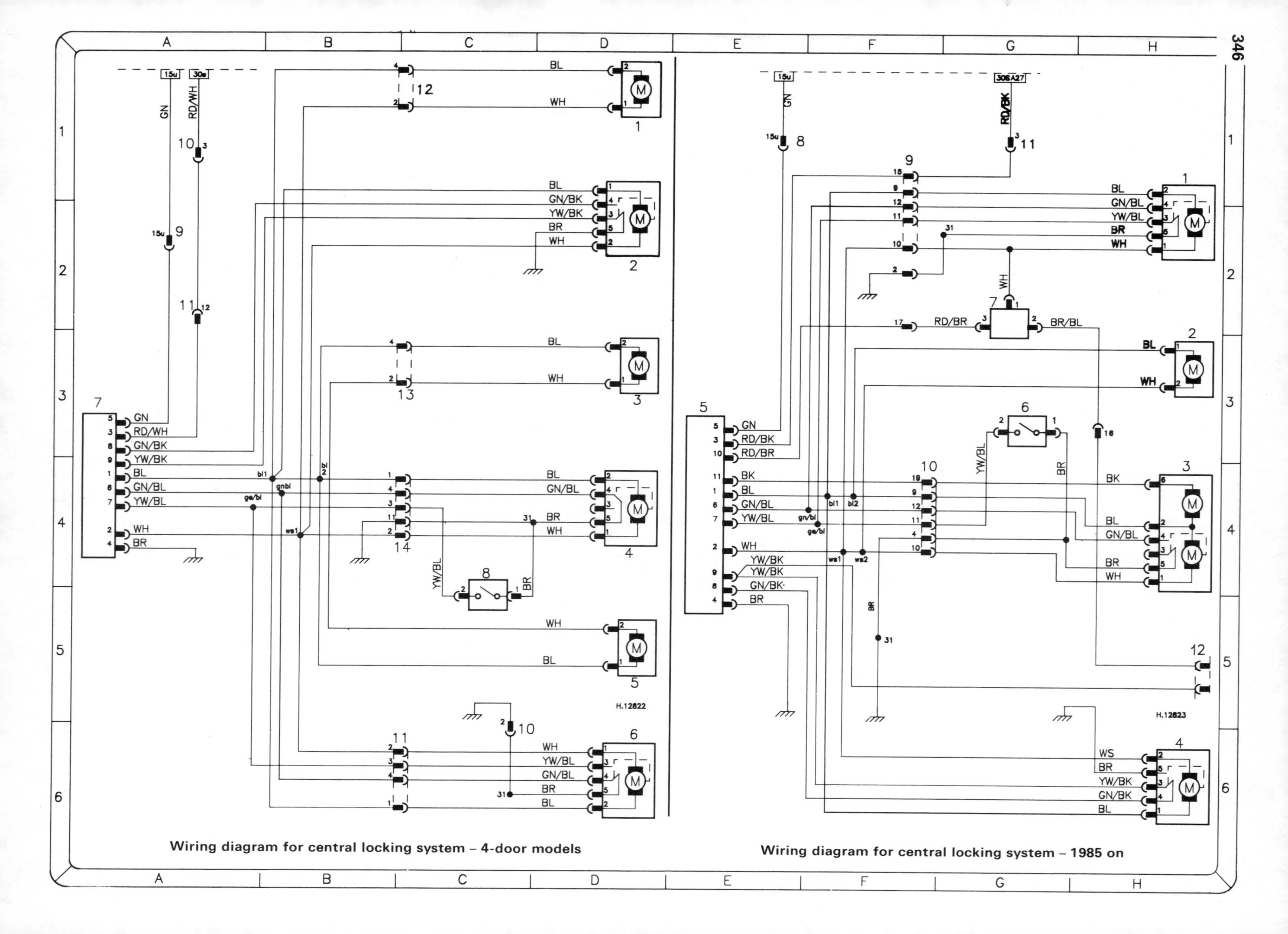

Wiring diagram for central locking system – 4-door models

Wiring diagram for central locking system – 1985 on

Key to wiring diagram on page 346 for central locking system – 4-door models

No	Component	Grid location
1	Motor – central lock of rear door, left	D1
2	Motor – central lock of boot lid	D2
3	Motor – central lock of rear door, right	D3
4	Motor – central lock of front door (passenger's)	D4
5	Motor – central lock of tank flap	D5
6	Motor – central lock of front door (driver's)	D6
7	Central lock electronic control (A pillar)	A3/4
8	Microswitch (passenger's door)	C5
9	Special equipment plug 15u (below tray on driver's side	A2
10	Plug for main wire harness – driver's door wire 6-pin (A pillar)	A1/C6
11	Plug for driver's door wire – central lock wire 13-pin	A2/C6
12	Plug for central lock wire – left rear door wire 5-pin	C1
13	Plug for central lock wire – right rear door wire 5-pin	C3
14	Plug for central lock wire – front passenger's door wire 13-pin	C4

For key to symbols and colour codes see page 355

Key to wiring diagram on page 346 for central locking system – 1985 on

No	Component	Grid location
1	Central lock motor – driver's door	H1/2
2	Central lock motor – tank flap	H3
3	Central lock motor – passenger's door	H4
4	Central lock motor – boot lid	H6
5	Central lock electronic control (in A pillar)	E4
6	Microswitch (in passenger's door)	G3
7	Microswitch in anti-theft lock cylinder	G2
8	Special equipment plug 15u (steering column casing lower section)	E1
9	Plug, central lock wire – driver's door (17 pins)	F2
10	Plug, central lock wire – passenger's door (17 pins)	F4
11	Plug, driver's door – main wire harness – 4-pins (A pillar)	G1
12	Plug, burglar alarm wire – 3 pins (left or right A pillar)	H5

For key to symbols and colour codes see page 355

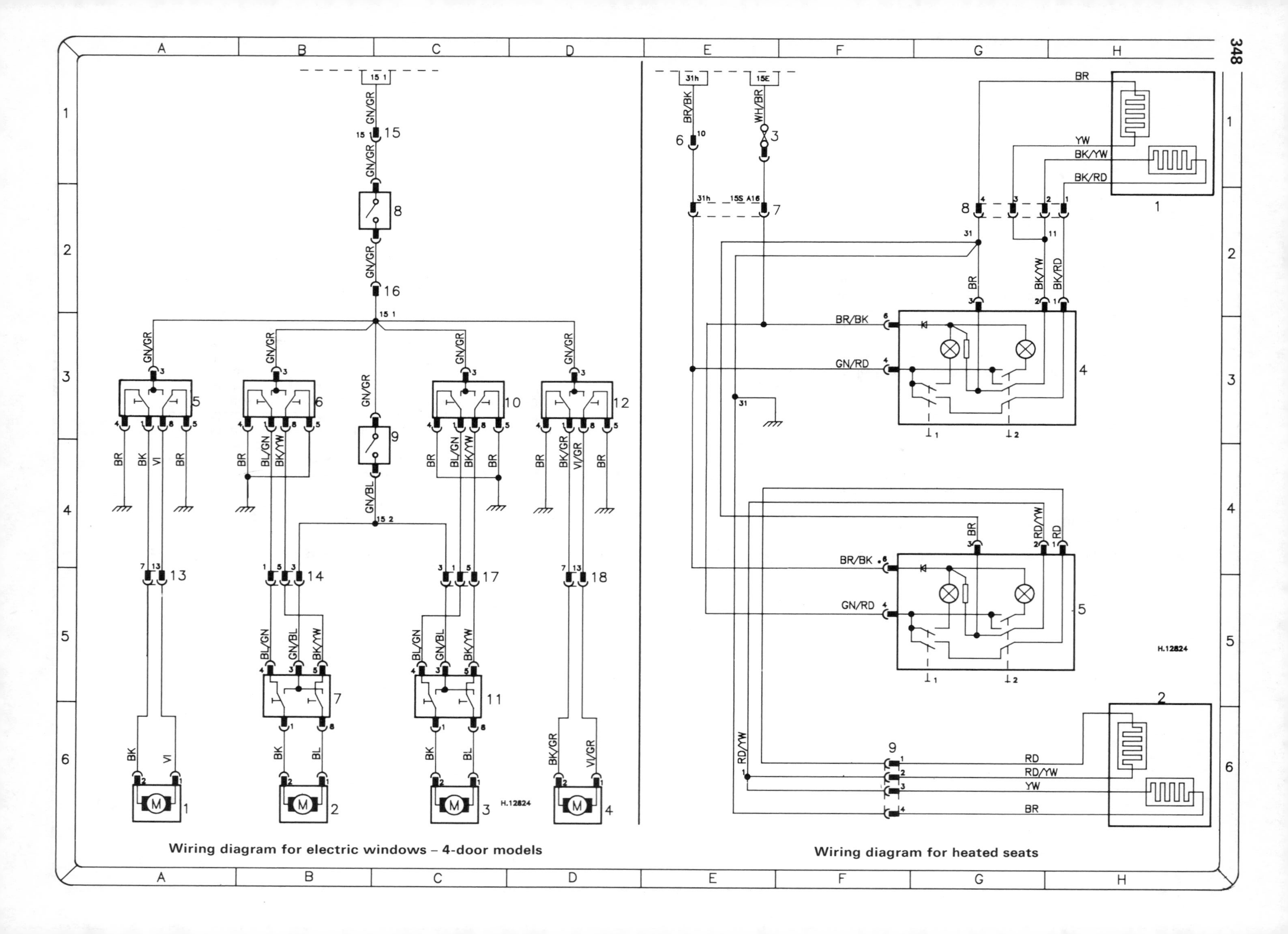

Wiring diagram for electric windows – 4-door models

Wiring diagram for heated seats

Key to wiring diagram on page 348 for electric windows – 4-door models

No	Component	Grid location
1	Electric window motor – driver's door	A6
2	Electric window motor – rear left	B6
3	Electric window motor – rear right	C6
4	Electric window motor – passenger's door	D6
5	Electric window switch – driver's door	A3
6	Electric window switch – rear left	B3
7	Electric window switch – rear left	B5
8	Excessive current switch (on tray)	C2
9	Child safety lock (on tray)	C4
10	Electric window switch – rear right	C3
11	Electric window switch – rear right	C5
12	Electric window switch – passenger's door	D3
13	Plug for electric window wire – driver's door (13-pin)	A5
14	Plug for electric window wire -- rear left door (5-pin)	B5
15	Special equipment plug 15/1 – automatic cutout wire	C1
16	Plug for electric window wire – automatic cutout wire	C2
17	Plug for electric window wire – rear right door (15-pin)	C5
18	Plug for electric window wire – passenger's door (13-pin)	D5

For key to symbols and colour codes see page 355

Key to wiring diagram on page 348 for heated seats

No	Component	Grid location
1	Seat heating – right	H1
2	Seat heating – left	H6
3	Fuse – seat heating	E3
4	Switch for seat heating – right	G3
5	Switch for seat heating – left	G5
6	Plug connection of main wire harness – wire for instrument panel (29-pin)	E1
7	Plug for special equipment	E2
8	Connection for seat heating – right	G2
9	Connection for seat heating – left	F6

For key to symbols and colour codes see page 355

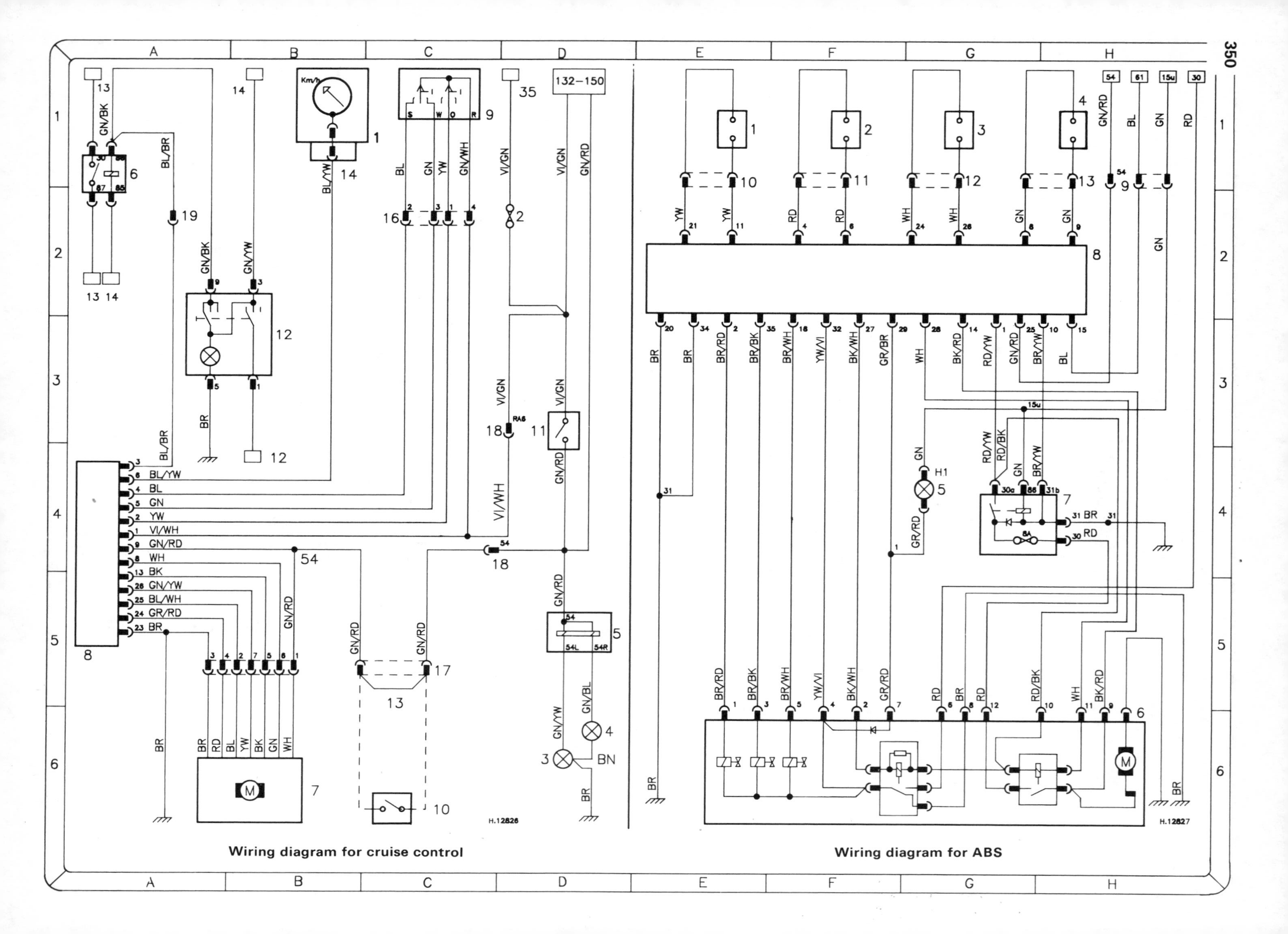
Wiring diagram for cruise control
H.12826
Wiring diagram for ABS
H.12827

Key to wiring diagram on page 350 for cruise control

No	Component	Grid location
1	Instrument cluster	B1
2	Fuse – stop-lights	D2
3	Stop-light – left	D6
4	Stop-light – right	D6
5	Bulb tester for stop-lights (only for cars with check control in boot at rear left)	D5
6	Relay – starting interlock (automatics only)	A1
7	Cruise control motor	B6
8	Cruise control electronic control (in glovebox, above injection control unit)	A4/5
9	Steering column switch	C1
10	Clutch switch	C6
11	Stop-light switch	D3
12	Transmission switch (automatics only)	B3
13	Bridge (automatic transmission)	C5
14	Plug jack on instrument cluster	B1
15	Plug for cruise control motor	B5
16	Plug for steering column switch	C2
17	Connection for clutch switch – bridge	C5
18	Plug for special equipment (below tray at front on driver's side)	D3
19	Plug for automatic wire	A2

For key to symbols and colour codes see page 355

Key to wiring diagram on page 350 for ABS

No	Component	Grid location
1	Sensor front right	E1
2	Sensor front left	F1
3	Sensor rear right	G1
4	Sensor rear left	H1
5	Lamp for ABS	G4
6	Hydraulic control unit for ABS	H6
7	Overload relay	G4
8	Electronic control unit for ABS	G2
9	Plug, wire harness for ABS special eqiupment plug	H1
10	Plug, right front sensor – ABS wire harness	E1
11	Plug, left front sensor – ABS wire harness	F1
12	Plug, right rear sensor – ABS wire harness	G1
13	Plug, left rear sensor – ABS wire harness	H1

For key to symbols and colour codes see page 355

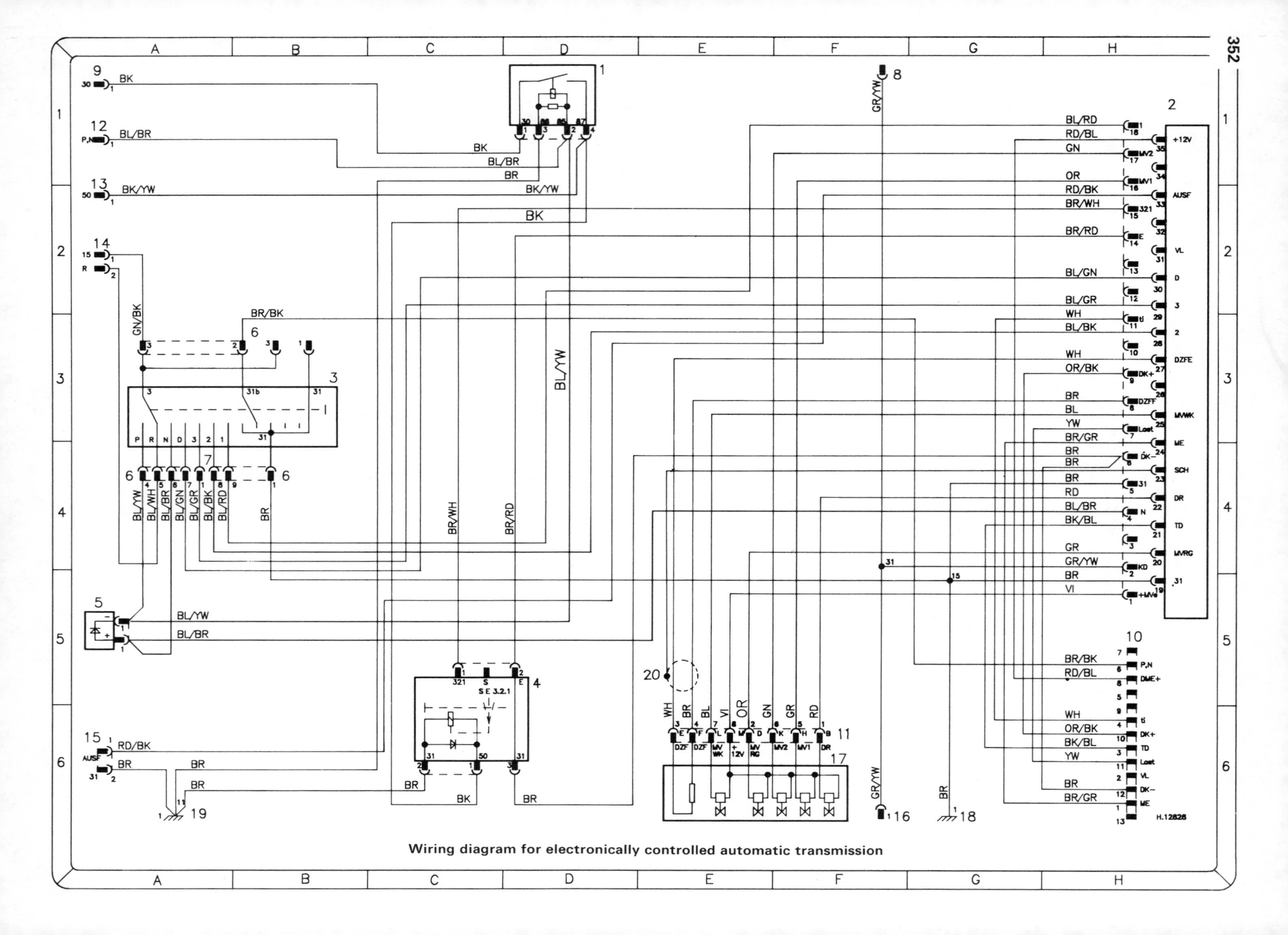

Wiring diagram for electronically controlled automatic transmission

Key to wiring diagram on page 352 for electronically controlled automatic transmission

No	Component	Grid location
1	Relay – starting interlock	D1
2	AEGS control unit (boot, left, near aerial)	H1
3	Switch – transmission	B3
4	Switch – program	C6
5	Diode	A5
6	Plug, transmission switch 9-pin	A/B4
7	Plug, transmission switch 1-pin	A4
8	Connection, for kickdown switch	F1
9	Connection, for ignition switch	A1
10	Connection, for engine wire harness	H5
11	Plug, transmission 8-pin	E6
12	Connection, for cruise control	A1
13	Connection, for wire harness terminal 50	A2
14	Connection, for main wire harness	A2
15	Connection, for failure indicator	A6
16	Connection, for kickdown switch (LHD only)	F6
17	Transmission control unit	F6
18	Battery earth	G6
19	Body earth point	A6
20	Shielding	E5

For key to symbols and colour codes see page 355

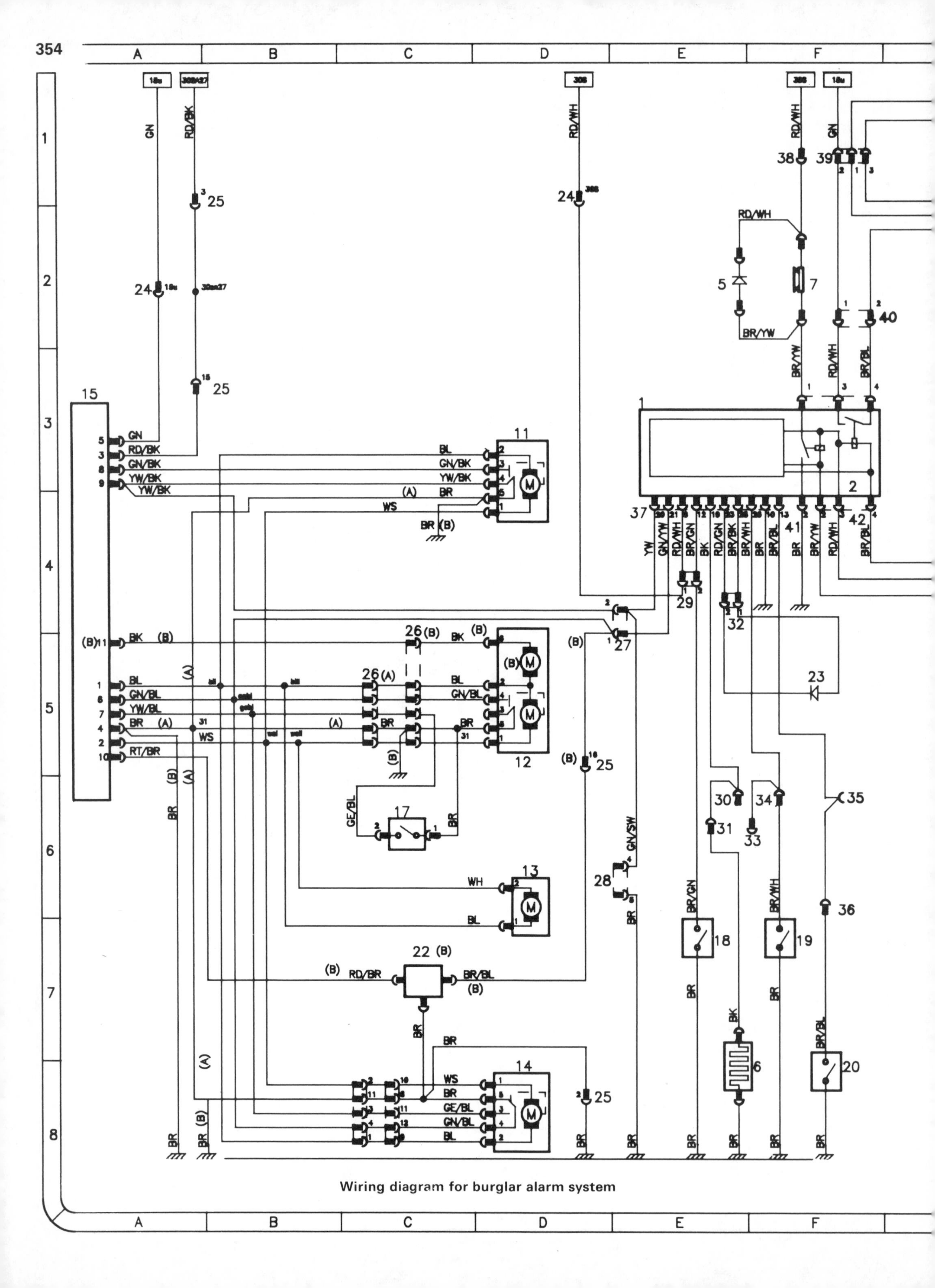

Wiring diagram for burglar alarm system

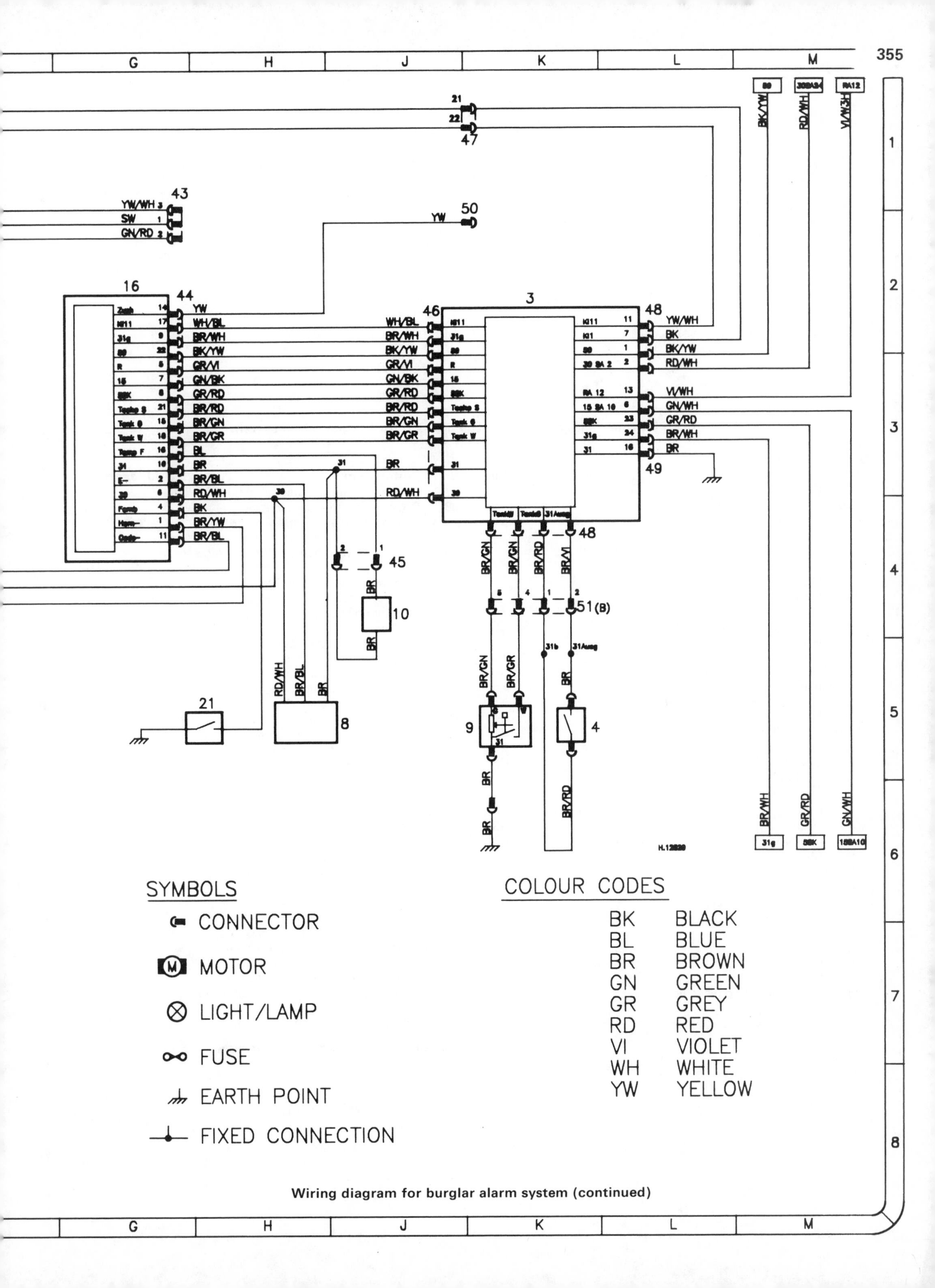

Wiring diagram for burglar alarm system (continued)

Key to wiring diagram on pages 354 and 355 for burglar alarm system

No	Component	Grid location
1	Electronic control unit for burglar alarm (instrument carrier, next to steering column)	E3
2	Relay box for burglar alarm and on-board computer (instrument carrier, next to steering column)	F3
3	Instrument cluster	K2
4	Speed transmitter	K5
5	Diode for horn (in engine compartment)	E2
6	Rear window demister	E8
7	Alarm horn (in engine compartment front left)	F2
8	Gong (lower casing left)	J5
9	Fuel level transmitter	K5
10	Temperature sensor (front left bottom in brake venting duct)	J4
11	Central lock motor – boot lid	D3
12	Central lock motor – passenger's door	D5
13	Central lock motor – tank flap	D6
14	Central lock motor – driver's door	D8
15	Central lock electronic control unit (A pillar)	A3
16	On-board computer electronic control unit (instrument carrier right)	G3
17	Microswitch – passenger's door	C6
18	Microswitch – bonnet contact	E7
19	Door contact	F7
20	Switch – boot light	F8
21	Switch – remote control	H5
22	Microswitch – burglar alarm on (in driver's door)	C7
23	Diode	F5
24	Connection, for special equipment (bottom left in footwell)	A2/D1
25	Plug – lead for driver's door	A1/A3 D5/D8
26	Plug for passenger's door lead	C5
27	Connection for central lock – driver's door	D4
28	Drive for boot lid central lock	E6
29	Plug for burglar alarm/on-board computer, (A pillar, near speaker)	E4
30	Plug, main wire harness (rear window demister)	E6
31	Plug, rear window demister	E6
32	Plug for diode	E4
33	Plug for main wire harness (behind speaker left front)	F6
34	Connection for door contact	F6
35	Plug for boot light	F6
36	Plug for boot light switch	F6
37	Connection for electronic control unit	E4
38	Connection for alarm horn	F1
39	Plug for instrument cluster wire harness (near control unit above glovebox)	F1
40	Plug of lead for on-board computer and burglar alarm (special equipment plug)	F2
41	Connection for relay box (instrument carrier left)	F4
42	Connection for relay box (instrument carrier left)	F4
43	Plug for engine wire harness (near control unit above glovebox)	G2
44	Connection for on-board computer	G2
45	Plug for temperature sensor	J4
46	Connection for instrument cluster	J2
47	Plug, main wire harness – instrument panel section (left below glovebox)	K1
48	Connection for instrument cluster	L2/4
49	Connection for instrument cluster	L3
50	Connection for parked car heater	K2
51	Plug, main wire harness – additional lead	L4
(A)	1984 models only	
(B)	1985 models only	

For key to symbols and colour codes see page 355

Key to wiring diagram on pages 360 to 365 for later Series 2 models

No	Component	Location
1	Reversing light left	3M7
2	Reversing light right	3M2
3	Switch plate light	3M5
4	Rear window demister	3K3
5	Fuse – turn signal indicator	2K2
6	Fuse – wipe/wash system, headlight cleaners, intensive cleaning system	2J2
7	Fuse – two-tone horns	1E5
8	Fuse – rear window demister	1E5
9	Fuse – engine electric equipment, reversing light	1D4
10	Fuse – instruments	1D3
11	Fuse – fuel pump, transfer pump	2A5
12	Fuse – radio, check control, instruments	1F3
13	Fuse – seat heating	1D5
14	Fuse – sunroof	1C5
15	Fuse – reversing light, mirror	1D4
16	Fuse – hazard lights (30S/A24)	2K2
17	Fuse – mirror, air conditioner (1986 on)	1D4
18	Battery	1B4/5
19	Alternator	1B6
20	Two-tone horn II	1A2
21	Two-tone horn I	1A6
22	Turn signal, right front	1A1
23	Turn signal, right rear	3M1
24	Turn signal, left rear	3M8
25	Turn signal, left front	1A7
26	Relay – two-tone horns (in central electric board)	1F4
27	relay – sunroof and seat heating (in central electric board)	1D4
28	Relay – heater blower, rear window demister (in central electric board)	1E4
29	Relay – starting interlock only for cars with automatic transmission (below glovebox)	1C3
30	Relay – hazard lights (steering column)	2L3
31	Starter motor	1B5
32	Wiper motor	2G4
33	Washer pump	2J2
34	Fuel pump	2A5
35	Transmission switch (automatic transmission)	1C6
36	Reversing light switch	1D6
37	Parking light and ignition switch	1B2
38	Ignition switch	1B2
39	Rear window demister switch	1E6
40	Horn switch	1F6
41	Wiper switch	2J6
42	Hazard light switch	2K4
43	Turn signal/dimmer switch	2M4
44	Turn signal switch	2M4
45	Power rail in central electric board	1A1
46	As item 47, but 20-pin (1986 on)	
47	Plug of main wire harness – engine wire harness (19-pin) (engine compartment)	Various
48	Connection for special equipment (26-pin) (below glovebox)	Various
49	Plug of main wire harness wire for ignition switch (9-pin) (steering column)	Various
50	Plug for idle speed boost (tunnel)	1C5
51	Plug of main wire harness wire for reversing light switch (2-pin) (tunnel)	1D6/7
52	Plug of main wire harness wire for instrument panel (29-pin) (below glovebox)	Various
53	Plug of main wire harness wire for ignition switch (151) (steering column)	1E3
54	Plug connection (8-pin)	Various
55	Connection for wiper motor (2-pin)	2H4
56	Connection for headlight cleaners (engine compartment right)	2J1
57	Plug of main wire harness wire for wiper switch (6-pin) (steering column)	2J6
58	Plug of main wire harness wire for turn signal/dimmer switch (13-pin) (steering column)	Various
59	Plug of main wire harness wire for speed transmitter (9-pin) (inside car on right side)	Various
60	Plug connection 50	1B3
61	Check control	3H1
62	Interior light left	3A5
63	Interior light right	3B5
64	Boot light	3D6
65	Handlamp (chargeable)	3C6
66	Glovebox light	3C5
67	Rear foglight left	3M6
68	Rear foglight right	3M2
69	High beam left	1A7
70	High beam right	1A1
71	Low beam left	1A6
72	Low beam right	1A2
73	Front foglamp left	1A5
74	Front foglamp right	1A3
75	Tail light left	3E6
76	Tail light right	3E6
77	Low beam headlight right (overnight light)	3E5
78	Low beam headlight left (overnight light)	3E5
79	Licence plate light right	3M4
80	Licence plate light left	3M4

Continued overleaf

Key to wiring diagram on pages 360 to 365 for later Series 2 models (continued)

No	Component	Location
81	Ashtray light rear (1986 on)	3J6
82	Fuse – high beam left	1H5
83	Fuse – high beam right	1H2
84	Fuse – stop-light, cruise control	3E2
85	Fuse – low beam left	1K6
86	Fuse – low beam right	1K2
87	Fuse – rear foglight	1K3
88	Fuse – digital clock, inside lights, boot light, glovebox light	3B2
89	Fuse – overnight, tail, parking lights left	3E1
90	Fuse – overnight, tail, parking lights right	3E1
91	Fuse – door wiring	3A2
92	Fuse – front foglamp left	1L5
93	Fuse – front foglamp right	1L2
94	Stoplight left	3M7
95	Stoplight right	3M1
96	High beam relay	1H2
97	Low beam relay	1K2
98	Front foglamp relay	1L2
99	Rear foglight relay (in central electric board)	1G4
100	Bulb tester for low beams	1K4
101	Bulb tester (in boot left side)	3F6
102	Bulb tester for tail lights (in boot on left side)	3E6
103	Bulb tester for stop and licence plate lights (in boot on left side)	3F6
104	Digital clock	3C5
105	Parking light and ignition switch	3C2
106	Parking light switch I	3D2
107	Turn signal/dimmer switch	1J5
108	Headlight dimmer switch	1J5
109	Parking light switch II	3D3
110	Door contact left	3A7
111	Door contact right	3B7
112	Boot light switch	3D7
113	Front foglamp and rear tail light switch	1L4
114	Rear foglight switch	1G5
115	Front foglamp switch	1L4
116	Light switch	3E2
117	High beam switch	1J6
118	Regulable instrument light and front fog lamp switch	1M6
119	Low beam headlight and licence plate light switch	3E2
120	Stop-light switch	3E2
121	Washing fluid level switch	3G6
122	Coolant level switch	3G6
123	Oil level switch	3G5
124	Switch, glovebox light (1986 on)	3B6
125	Power rail in central electric board	1A1
126	As item 127, but 20-pin (1986 on)	
127	Plug of main wire harness – engine wire harness (19-pin)	Various
128	Special equipment plug (26-pin)	Various
129	Plug of main wire harness wire for ignition switch (9-pin) (steering column)	Various
130	Plug of main wire harness wire for instrument panel (29-pin)	Various
131	Plug connection (8 pin)	Various
132	Plug of main wire harness wire for inside light left (3-pin) (B pillar)	3A4/6
133	Door contact – passenger's door	3A7
134	Plug of main wire harness wire for turn signal/headlight dimmer switch (13-pin)	Various
135	Plug of main wire harness wire for inside light right (3 pin) (B pillar)	Various
136	Door contact 1 – driver's door	3B7
137	Plug of main wire harness wire for door (6-pin) (B pillar)	3A3
138	Plug of wire for ignition switch wire for turn signal/headlight dimmer switch (steering column)	3D3
139	Connection for bulb tester (central electric board)	3H3
140	Connection for check control (1986 on)	3H2
141	Plug for reading lamp (1986 on)	3E3
142	Instrument cluster	2E4
143	Transmitter – coolant temp	2B7
144	Transmitter – speed	3E7
145	Instrument light I	2E4
146	Instrument light II	2E4
147	Cigar lighter	3H4
148	Heater control light I	3J4
149	Heater control light II	3J4
150	Fuse – heater blower	3K4
151	Fuse – cigar lighter, extra heater	3H3
152	Light – parking brake	2B5
153	Light – brake fluid	2B5
154	Light – oil pressure	2B5
155	Light – central warning	2B4
156	Brake pad wear sensor, rear right	2B7
157	Light – brake pad wear	2C5
158	Brake pad wear sensor, front left	2C7
159	Light – fuel warning	2D5
160	Light – turn signal left	2D5

Key to wiring diagram on pages 360 to 365 for later Series 2 models (continued)

No	Component	Location
161	Light – turn signal right	2D5
162	Light – main beam	2E5
163	Light – battery charge	2E4
164	Light – front foglamps	2E5
165	Light – rear foglights	2E5
166	Motor – electrically operated mirror	2G5
167	Motor – electrically operated additional mirror	2G7
168	Motor – heater blower	3K7
169	Service indicator	2C4
170	Coolant temperature gauge	2C4
171	Electronic tachometer	2D4
172	Fuel gauge	2D5
173	Fuel level transmitter	2D7
174	Fuel economy control	2D5
175	Electronic speedometer	2E4
176	Ballast resistors for blower motor	3K7
177	Mirror switch assembly	2F4
178	Mirror switch – driver's door	2F
179	Mirror switch – passenger's door	2F4
180	Parking brake switch	2A7
181	Brake fluid level switch	2B7
182	Oil pressure switch	2B6
183	Water valve and switch	3J5
184	Blower switch	3K5
185	As item 186, only 20-pin (1986 on)	
186	Plug of main wire harness, engine wire harness (19-pin) (engine compartment)	2B2
187	Connection for special equipment (26-pin) (behind glovebox)	3H3
188	Plug of main wire harness wire for instrument panel (29-pin) (behind glovebox)	2D2
189	Plug of main wire harness wire for door (right A pillar)	Various
190	Plug of driver's door connecting wire between driver's/passenger's door (right A pillar)	2F6
191	Plug of passenger's door connecting wire between driver's door/passenger's door (left A pillar)	2F6
192	Connection for electrically operated mirror (in driver's door)	2G5
193	Connection for electrically operated mirror (in passenger's door)	2G7
194	Connection for LE-Jetronic control unit (below glovebox)	2D2
195	Plug of main wire harness for heater controls (13-pin) (on heater)	Various
196	As item 195, only 9-pin (1986 on)	
197	Connection for air conditioner (on air conditioner)	3K3
198	Connection of wire blower switch (7-pin) (on heater or air conditioner)	3K4/6
199	Plug of main wire harness wire for speed transmitter (9-pin) (inside car on right side)	Various
200	Outlet	3B7
201	Plug connection 30S/A28 (2-pin) below glovebox)	2B6
202	Water valve	3J6
203	Wash/wipe control	2G3
204	Transfer pump (Australia only)	2A6
205	Door contact switch LH (4-door)	3A7
206	Door contact switch RH (4-door)	3B7
(A)	Models up to 1986 only	
(B)	1986 on models only	

For key to symbols and colour codes see page 355

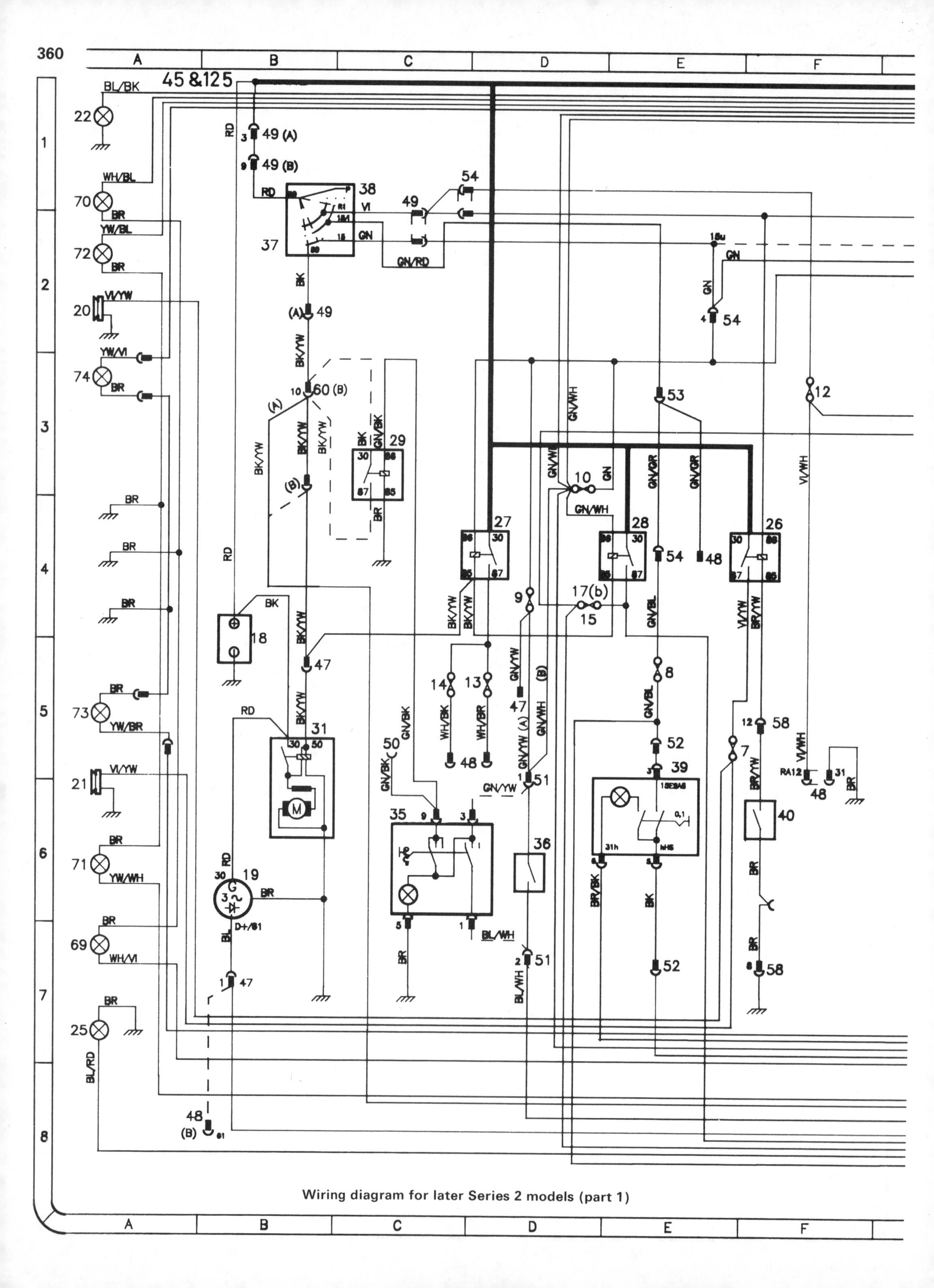

Wiring diagram for later Series 2 models (part 1)

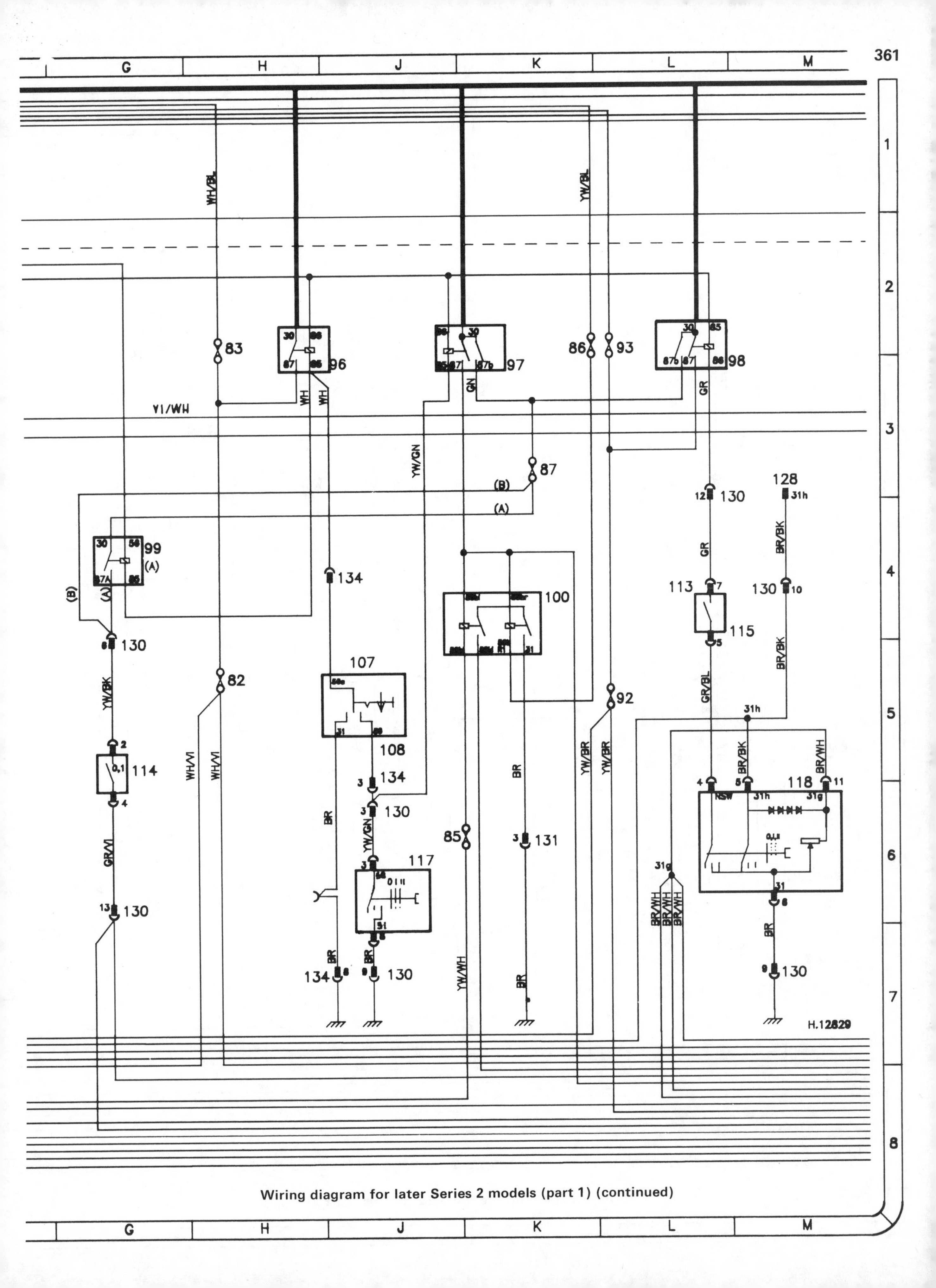

Wiring diagram for later Series 2 models (part 1) (continued)

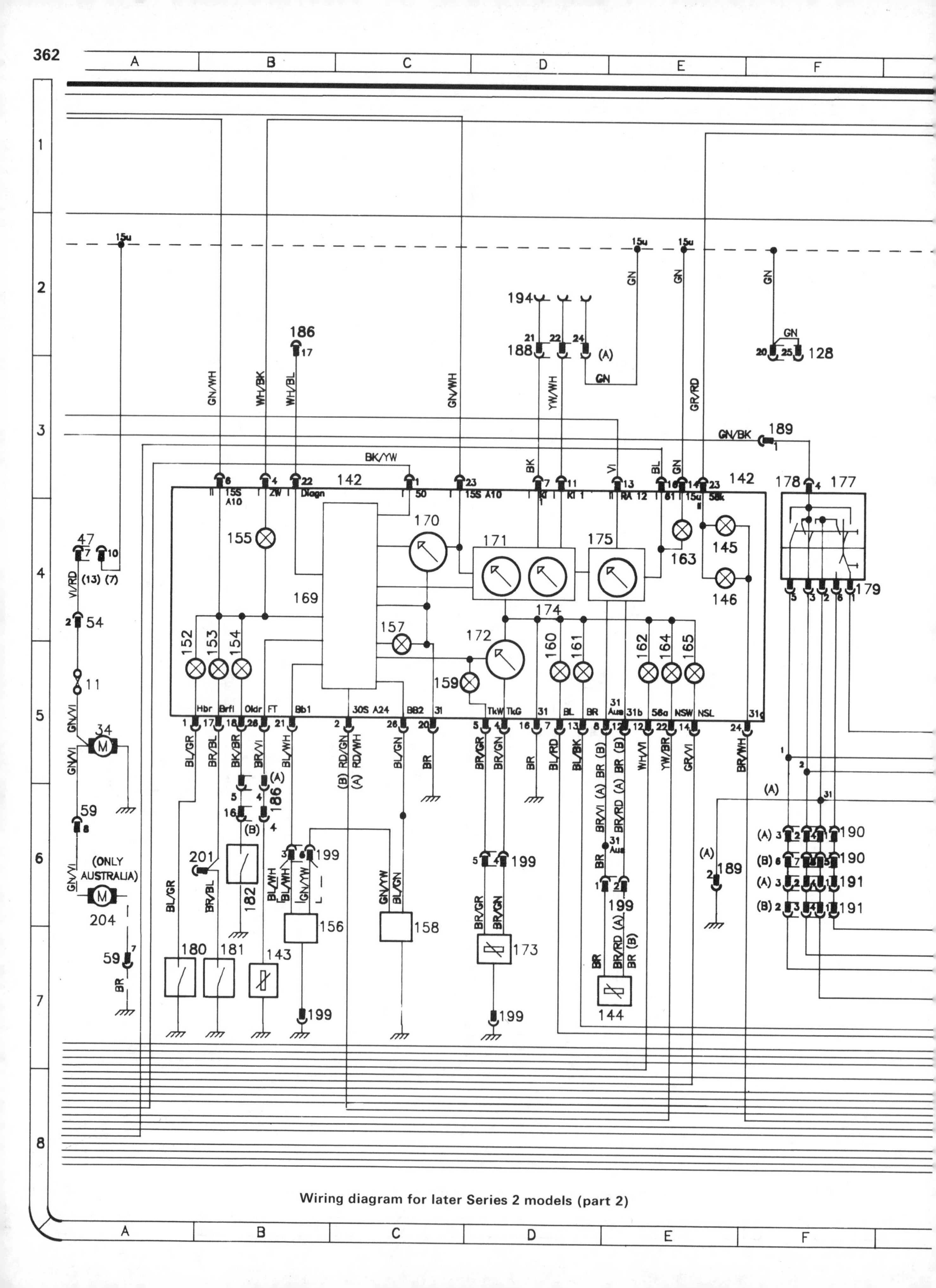

Wiring diagram for later Series 2 models (part 2)

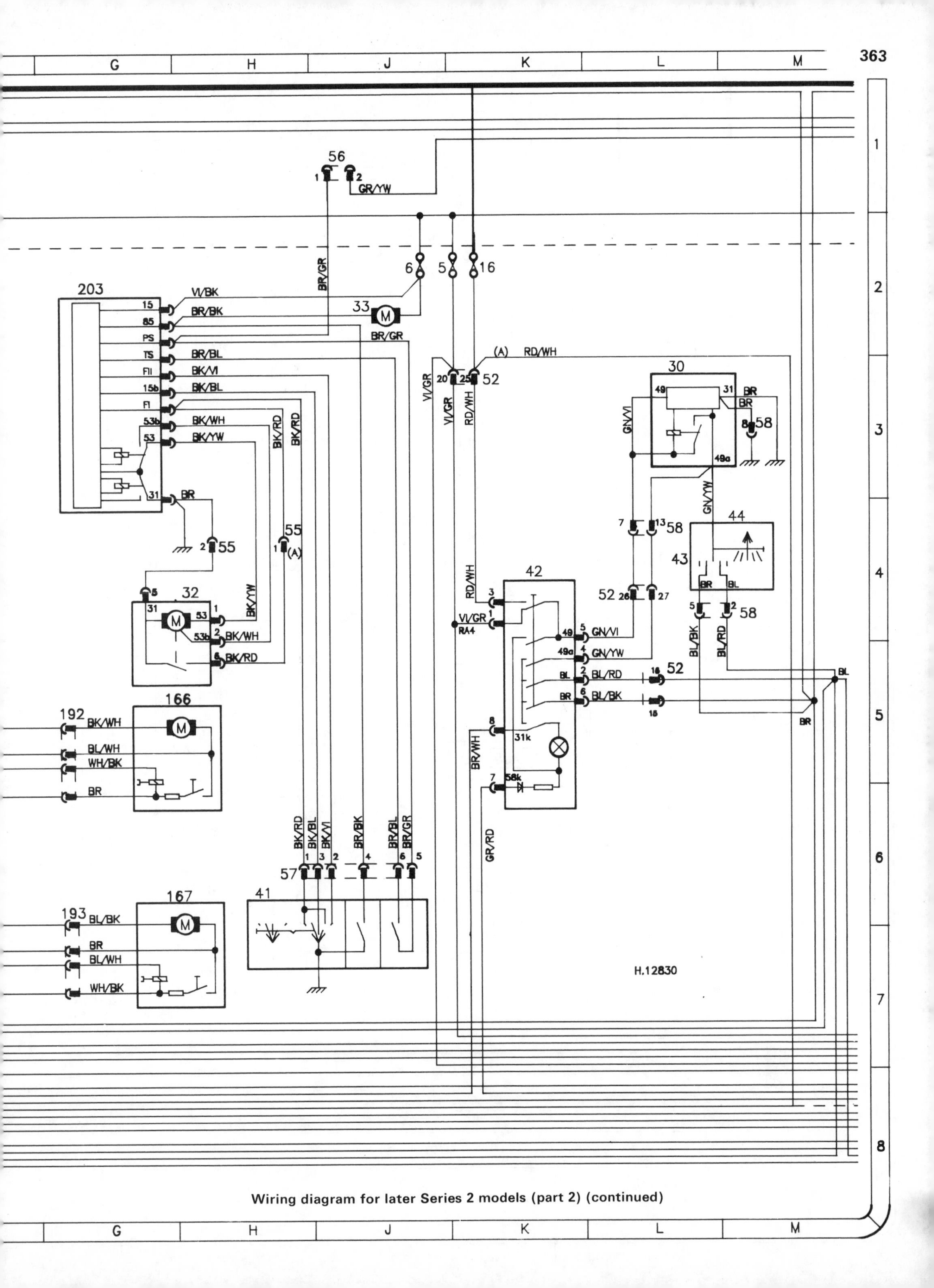

Wiring diagram for later Series 2 models (part 2) (continued)

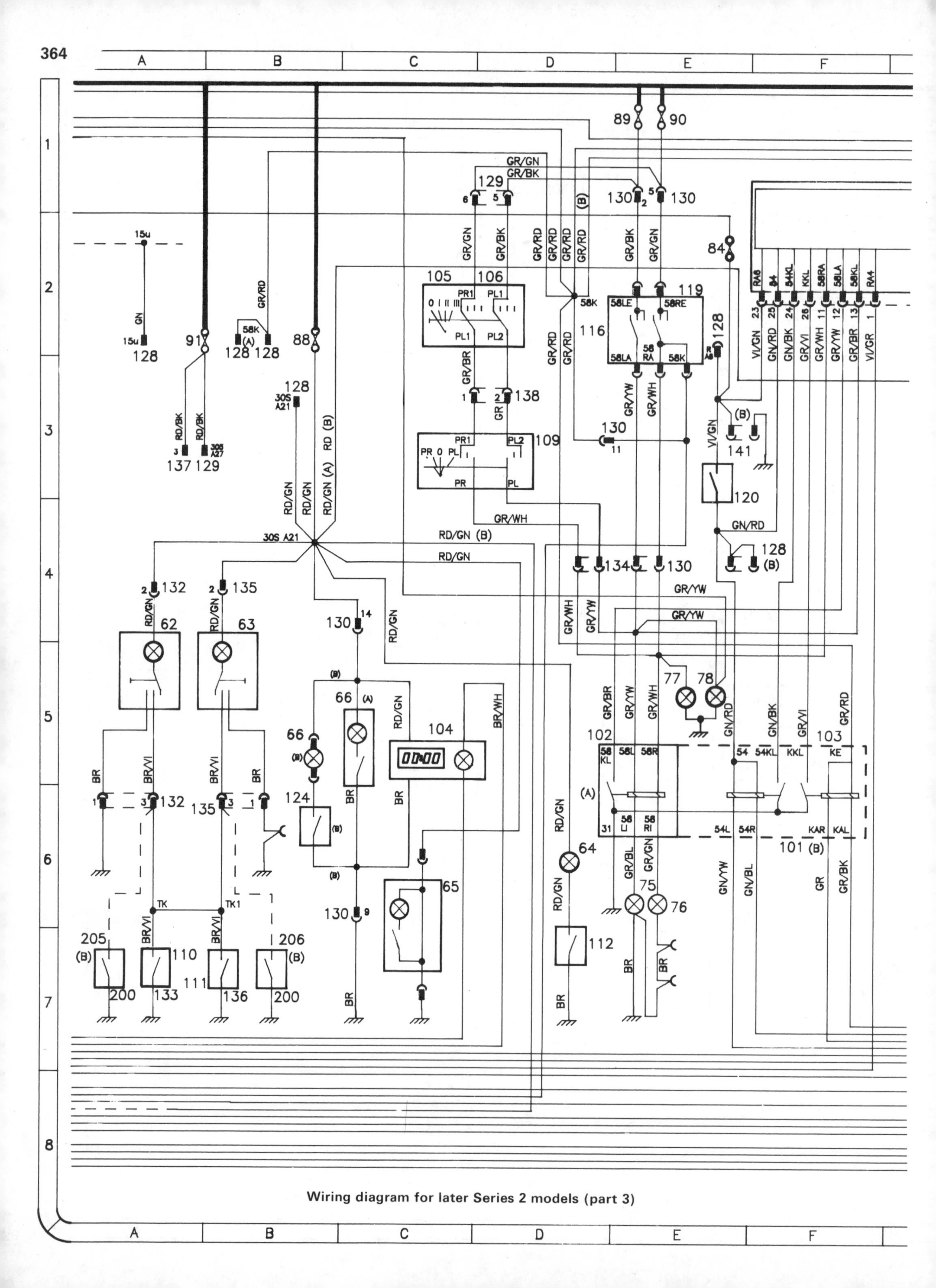

Wiring diagram for later Series 2 models (part 3)